The Oxford Handbook of Intergenerational Connections

OXFORD LIBRARY OF PSYCHOLOGY

AREA EDITORS:

Clinical Psychology
David H. Barlow

Cognitive Neuroscience
Kevin N. Ochsner and Stephen M. Kosslyn

Cognitive Psychology
Daniel Reisberg

Counseling Psychology
Elizabeth M. Altmaier and Jo-Ida C. Hansen

Developmental Psychology
Philip David Zelazo

Health Psychology
Howard S. Friedman

History of Psychology
David B. Baker

Methods and Measurement
Todd D. Little

Neuropsychology
Kenneth M. Adams

Organizational Psychology
Steve W. J. Kozlowski

Personality and Social Psychology
Kay Deaux and Mark Snyder

OXFORD LIBRARY OF PSYCHOLOGY

The Oxford Handbook of Intergenerational Connections

Edited by
Elizabeth F. Fideler

OXFORD
UNIVERSITY PRESS

Oxford University Press is a department of the University of Oxford.
It furthers the University's objective of excellence in research, scholarship,
and education by publishing worldwide. Oxford is a registered trade mark of
Oxford University Press in the UK and certain other countries.

Published in the United States of America by Oxford University Press
198 Madison Avenue, New York, NY 10016, United States of America.

© Oxford University Press 2025

All rights reserved. No part of this publication may be reproduced, stored in a retrieval system, transmitted, used for text and data mining, or used for training artificial intelligence, in any form or by any means, without the prior permission in writing of Oxford University Press, or as expressly permitted by law, by license or under terms agreed with the appropriate reprographics rights organization. Inquiries concerning reproduction outside the scope of the above should be sent to the Rights Department, Oxford University Press, at the address above.

You must not circulate this work in any other form
and you must impose this same condition on any acquirer

Library of Congress Cataloging-in-Publication Data
Names: Fideler, Elizabeth F. editor
Title: The Oxford handbook of intergenerational connections /
[edited by] Elizabeth F. Fideler.
Description: New York, NY : Oxford University Press, [2025] |
Series: Oxford library of psychology series |
Includes bibliographical references and index.
Identifiers: LCCN 2025002115 (print) | LCCN 2025002116 (ebook) |
ISBN 9780197750889 hardback | ISBN 9780197750902 epub | ISBN 9780197750919
Subjects: LCSH: Intergenerational relations | Intergenerational communication |
Older people—Social conditions | Youth—Social conditions
Classification: LCC HM726 .O94 2025 (print) | LCC HM726 (ebook) |
DDC 305.2—dc23/eng/20250411
LC record available at https://lccn.loc.gov/2025002115
LC ebook record available at https://lccn.loc.gov/2025002116

DOI: 10.1093/oxfordhb/9780197750889.001.0001

Printed by Marquis Book Printing, Canada

CONTENTS

List of Contributors ix

1. Introduction to the *Oxford Handbook of Intergenerational Connections* 1
   Elizabeth F. Fideler

Part I • Meeting Social Needs, Building Community, Reducing Age Segregation: Cross-Generational Relationships

2. Uniting Generations through Policy, Practice, and Purpose 23
   Donna M. Butts
3. Intergenerational Solutions (Not Single-Issue Solutions) to Society's Challenges 36
   Trent Stamp and *Chelsea Mason*
4. A Dose of Optimism: Data Show Americans Are Ready to Build a Multigenerational Force for Good 52
   Cal J. Halvorsen, Eunice Lin Nichols, and *Marc Freedman*
5. Child-Focused, Adult-Governed, and Elder-Led: Leveraging Generational Wisdom for a Changing America 68
   Sherreta R. Harrison and *Raymond A. Jetson*
6. Lifelong Learning, Intellectual Curiosity, and Community Building across Generations at Lasell University 82
   Joann M. Montepare and *Kimberly S. Farah*
7. CIRKEL: The Startup That Pioneered Two-Way Mentoring across Generations in the Workforce 97
   Charlotte Japp

Part II • Meeting the Need for Tutoring, Coaching, Mentoring, Housing: Older Adults Working with Younger People

8. SAGE: Building a Brighter Future by Working across Generations 117
   Stephen Higgs

9. EnCorps—STEM Professionals Serving to Inspire Students through STEM Education   130
    Kathleen Kostrzewa and *Katherine Wilcox*
10. Changing Lives through Oasis Intergenerational Tutoring   145
    Jeanne Foster, Mary Click, Stephanie McCreary, and *Paul Weiss*
11. How National Service Brings to Scale Intergenerational Programs and Initiatives: The AmeriCorps Seniors Foster Grandparent Program and The National Partnership for Student Success   162
    Atalaya Sergi, Kate Cochran, and *Dorothy Jones*
12. The Intergenerational Schools in Cleveland: Reconnection and Recovery after the Pandemic   178
    Brooke King

Part III • Community-Engaged Learning and Bridging Differences: Younger People Working with Older Adults

13. Intergenerational Diversity and Interethnic Connections: Who Will Care for Us?   195
    Fernando Torres-Gil and *Elizabeth Ambriz*
14. Viewing the Climate Crisis from Intergenerational Perspectives   203
    Ethan Bonerath, Elizabeth Bisno, Gillian Williams, Daniel George, and *Peter J. Whitehouse*
15. Applying Age-Friendly University Principles to Intergenerational Programs on College Campuses   220
    Allison Merz, Nancy Morrow-Howell, Peggy Morton, and *Ernest Gonzales*
16. Intergenerational Service-Learning Combats Social Isolation   233
    Nicole Shults, Cynthia Wilkerson, Jane Langridge, and *Barbara Bringuier*
17. Intergenerational Conversations Foster Connection in Community and College Classrooms   248
    Carrie Andreoletti and *Andrea June*

Part IV • Global Perspectives on Intergenerational Relationships

18. Generations Working Together across Scotland   265
    Lorraine George, Ruairidh Smith, and *Alison Clyde*
19. The TOY Project and Development of Intergenerational Learning Training in Europe   279
    Anne Fitzpatrick, Carmel Gallagher, Margaret Kernan, and *Giulia Cortellesi*
20. The Development of Intergenerational Initiatives in Singapore   295
    Leng Leng Thang

21. The Power of Intergenerational Relationships to Transform Education and Promote Social Cohesion in Spain's Basque Country   311
    Amaia Eiguren-Munitis, Naiara Berasategi-Sancho, Nahia Idoiaga-Mondragon, and Maitane Picaza-Gorrotxategi
22. Intergenerational Programs and Places in Japan's Super-Aging Society: What Three Good Practices Can Teach Us   326
    Masataka Kuraoka
23. Embedding Intergenerational Practice and Approaches in Northern Ireland—The Story So Far   343
    Vicki Titterington and Alan Hatton-Yeo
24. Shaping the Future of Work—Intergenerational Growing Pains and Gains in Canada's Workplaces   362
    Lisa Taylor and Emily Schmidt
25. Understanding Age-Diverse Knowledge Exchange through Social Comparison   378
    Laura Rinker, Ulrike Fasbender, and Fabiola H. Gerpott
26. Bridging Generations and Disciplines: Exploring How Interprofessional Conversations and Circle of Change Revisited Can Improve Intergenerational Practice Experience and Outcomes in Australia   392
    Xanthe Golenko, Jennifer Cartmel, Gaery Barbery, and Anneke Fitzgerald

Part V • Challenges to Generational Thinking, A Research Overview, and Recommendations for Strengthening and Sustaining the Intergenerational Movement

27. Generations and Generational Differences: A Thought Experiment   411
    Cort W. Rudolph and Hannes Zacher
28. The Sociology of Age Diversity   425
    Sasha Johfre
29. Evaluating Intergenerational Strategies to Enhance Individual and Community Development   449
    Shannon E. Jarrott
30. The Long View—Building Intergenerational Connections, Lessons Learned   468
    Nancy Henkin and Matthew S. Kaplan

Index   487

CONTRIBUTORS

Elizabeth Ambriz, PhD
   Post-doctoral scholar, University of California San Francisco
Carrie Andreoletti, PhD
   Professor, psychological science, Central Connecticut State University
Gaery Barbery, PhD
   Senior lecturer, Griffith University, Southport, Australia
Naiara Berasategi-Sancho
   Professor, Department of Didactics and School Organisation, Faculty of Education of Bilbao, University of the Basque Country
Elizabeth Bisno
   College student
Ethan Bonerath
   College student
Barbara Bringuier
   International coordinator, Les Petits Freres des Pauvres
Donna M. Butts
   Executive director, Generations United
Jennifer Cartmel, PhD
   Associate professor, Griffith University, Brisbane, Australia
Mary Click
   National intergenerational tutoring program director, The Oasis Institute
Alison Clyde
   CEO, Generations Working Together
Kate Cochran
   Managing director, NPSS

Giulia Cortellesi
   Co-director, International Child Development Initiatives, The Netherlands
Amaia Eiguren-Munitis, PhD
   Professor, Department of Didactics and School Organisation, Faculty of Education of Bilbao, University of the Basque Country
Kimberly S. Farah, PhD
   Coordinator of gerontology
Ulrike Fasbender, PhD
   Professor, business and organizational psychology, University of Hohenheim, Stuttgart, Germany
Elizabeth F. Fideler, EdD
   Member, Sloan Research Network on Aging & Work, Boston College
Anneke Fitzgerald, PhD
   Professor, health services management, Griffith University, Brisbane, Australia
Anne Fitzpatrick, PhD
   Emeritus Research Fellow, Technological University Dublin
Jeanne Foster
   Oasis tutoring, The Oasis Institute
Marc Freedman
   Co-CEO, CoGenerate
Carmel Gallagher, PhD
   Emeritus Research Fellow, Technological University Dublin

Daniel George, PhD
Professor of humanities and public health sciences, Penn State University

Lorraine George
Learning and development officer, Generations Working Together

Fabiola H. Gerpott, PhD
Professor, leadership, WHU – Otto Beisheim School of Management, Dusseldorf, Germany

Xanthe Golenko, PhD
Research fellow, Griffith University, Brisbane, Australia

Ernest Gonzales, PhD
Professor, NYU School of Social Work, director, Center for Health and Aging Innovation

Cal J. Halvorsen, PhD
Brown School of Social Work, Washington University in St. Louis

Sherreta R. Harrison
Sustainability catalyst

Alan Hatton-Yeo
D.Univ Founder of the UK Centre for Intergenerational Practice based at the Beth Johnson Foundation and Senior Fellow at Generations United

Nancy Henkin, PhD
Founder and executive director (emerita) of Temple University's Center for Intergenerational Learning, currently senior fellow, Generations United

Stephen Higgs, MS, JD
Executive director, Senior Advocates for Generational Equity in Portland

Nahia Idoiaga-Mondragon
Professor, Department of Developmental and Educational Psychology, Faculty of Education of Bilbao, University of the Basque Country

Charlotte Japp
Founder, CIRKEL

Shannon E. Jarrott, PhD
Professor, social work, The Ohio State University

Raymond A. Jetson
Chief executive catalyst

Sasha Johfre, PhD
Assistant professor of sociology, University of Washington

Dorothy Jones
Director of corporate, state, and local partnerships, NPSS

Andrea June, PhD
Coordinator of gerontology, Central Connecticut State University, an Age-Friendly University

Matthew S. Kaplan, PhD
Professor, intergenerational programs and aging, Penn State University

Margaret Kernan, PhD
Head of programmes and learning, International Child Development Initiatives, The Netherlands

Brooke King
Executive director, Intergenerational Schools

Kathleen Kostrzewa
Director, strategy, learning and impact, EnCorps

Masataka Kuraoka, EdD
Researcher, Tokyo Metropolitan Institute for Geriatrics and Gerontology

Jane Langridge
President, International Federation of Les Petits Freres des Pauvres

Chelsea Mason
Director, external relations, The Eisner Foundation

Stephanie McCreary
Chief purpose officer, The Oasis Institute

Allison Merz, LMSW
Program manager, social worker, NYU

Joann M. Montepare, PhD
Director, Fuss Center for Research on Aging & Intergenerational Studies

Nancy Morrow-Howell, PhD
Professor, social policy, Washington University of St. Louis, director, Friedman Center for Aging

Peggy Morton, DSW
Clinical associate professor, NYU School of Social Work

Eunice Lin Nichols
Co-CEO, CoGenerate

Maitane Picaza-Gorrotxategi
Professor, Department of Didactics and School Organisation, Faculty of Education of Bilbao, University of the Basque Country

Laura Rinker
Research assistant, University of Hohenheim, Stuttgart, Germany

Cort W. Rudolph, PhD
Professor of psychology, Wayne State University

Emily Schmidt
Challenge Factory

Atalaya Sergi
Director, AmeriCorps Seniors

Nicole Shults
Executive director, Little Brothers–Friends of the Elderly/Boston

Ruairidh Smith
Policy officer, Generations Working Together

Trent Stamp
CEO, The Eisner Foundation

Lisa Taylor
Founder and president, Challenge Factory, Toronto, Canada

Leng Leng Thang, PhD
Associate Professor of Japanese Studies (anthropology), National University of Singapore

Vicki Titterington
First employee who developed Linking Generations Northern Ireland (LGNI) and became Director

Fernando Torres-Gil, PhD
Professor of social welfare and public policy, UCLA

Paul Weiss, PhD
President, The Oasis Institute

Peter J. Whitehouse, MD, PhD
Professor of neurology, Case Western Reserve University

Katherine Wilcox
Executive director, EnCorps

Cynthia Wilkerson
Program director, LBFE

Gillian Williams
College student

Hannes Zacher, PhD
Professor of psychology, Leipzig University

CHAPTER
1

Introduction to the *Oxford Handbook of Intergenerational Connections*

Elizabeth F. Fideler

Abstract

The Oxford Handbook of Intergenerational Connections presents what is known about the spectrum of intergenerational initiatives in the United States and abroad. The need for connections, understanding, and respect between older adults and youth is being driven by a host of trends and challenges—including demographic shifts, workforce shortages and multigenerational teams, educational gaps and lifelong learning needs, anomie and loneliness across age-segregated groups, caregiving demands, youth and senior health and housing problems, economic insecurity, environmental losses, and rapid technological change. Drawing on advances in policy, practice, and research, the *Handbook* presents a comprehensive picture of the intergenerational movement, its successes, and its challenges.

Key Words: intergenerational connections, intergenerational relationships, demographic shifts, life span, age segregation, age inclusivity, age-friendly, bridging differences, community building, mutual benefit

Overview

The Oxford Handbook of Intergenerational Connections presents what is known about the spectrum of intergenerational initiatives in the United States and abroad—the very first to do so in reference book form. The *Handbook* addresses specifically "the purposeful and ongoing exchange of resources and learning among older and younger generations for individual and social benefits."[1] (This international definition was adopted in April 1999 by leading representatives from ten countries around the world, including the United States.) Broadly conceived, the need to develop "intentional cohesive connections and bonds between members of different generations"[2] is being driven by a host of trends and challenges—including demographic shifts, workforce shortages and multigenerational teams, educational gaps (particularly in primary grades) and lifelong learning needs, anomie and loneliness across age-segregated groups, caregiving demands, youth and senior health and housing problems, economic insecurity, environmental losses, and rapid technological change. Many of these trends and challenges, already under way, were accelerated or exacerbated by the COVID-19 pandemic.[3] Age-inclusivity, a part of some diversity, equity, and inclusion efforts today, is one important answer.

The *Handbook* contributes to the body of knowledge shared in books, reports, journal articles, fact sheets, guidebooks, symposia, and other conversations about intergenerational relationships among interest (affinity) group members.[4] Among those important sources, the *Journal of Intergenerational Relationships* stands out as the forum for sharing the latest intergenerational research, practice methods, and policy initiatives. It is the only journal focusing on the intergenerational field integrating practical, theoretical, empirical, familial, and policy perspectives. Also of note, Stanford University's magazine and website *Stanford Social Innovation Review* (or *SSRI*) claims to have put the field of intergenerational innovation on the map with a series of essays on "meeting the multigenerational moment." The series aims to answer the question "Can social innovation get us out of age-segregated spheres?" by "shining a light on some of the most promising innovations that bring older and younger people together to solve some of our most pressing problems."[5]

Following this introductory chapter with its overview of the intergenerational landscape, the *Handbook* is divided into five main sections:

- Meeting Social Needs, Building Community, Reducing Age Segregation: Cross-Generational Relationships
- Answering the Need for Tutoring, Coaching, Mentoring, Housing: Older Adults Working with Younger People
- Community-Engaged Learning and Bridging Differences: Younger People Helping Older Adults
- Global Perspectives on Intergenerational Relationships
- Challenges to Generational Thinking, A Research Overview, and Recommendations for Strengthening and Sustaining the Intergenerational Movement

These sections open with chapters from experts representing various academic fields who discuss one or more of the above-mentioned areas, why intergenerational solutions are called for, and what theoretical models and practical tools can be utilized. Once the research basis for intergenerational connections is established, the *Handbook* then offers additional chapters in each section that present a variety of well-established national, regional, and local programs and initiatives, highlighting not only *what* they do but also *why* and *how* they do it. Thus, rather than a collection of cases or a "how-to" guide, the text unpacks the underlying rationale for and the challenges of the intergenerational field. Note, too, that the *Handbook*'s authors and coauthors themselves represent the entire age spectrum (teens to elders) and kinds and levels of intergenerational experience under discussion.

Readers looking for the entire spectrum of possibilities, the purpose of and research on all types of intergenerational connections, will find that organized by category in the *Handbook*. And readers interested only in a specific type of intergenerational connection will learn the objectives for the given type of initiative, the research that underpins it, who is being served, the desired outcomes, the sponsorship/partnership that funds the work, as well as strategies and resources for and challenges to successful implementation. Each chapter that profiles a program opens with a reference chart that summarizes program strengths and limitations and other key information.

An Evolving Field

By looking across the intergenerational landscape, one can perceive an evolving field of inquiry and practice that deserves greater attention. It is a field that crosses multiple disciplines—including sociology, anthropology, organizational and social psychology, economics, gerontology, and demography—and various sectors, such as business, education, health care, housing, and the environment. While the workplace appears to be confronting the multiage phenomenon far more than other sectors,[6] an unusually wide array of nonfamilial intergenerational projects and programs has been emerging across a growing number of disciplines and settings to meet a host of social, health-related, economic, educational, environmental, and community needs. All rest on a foundation that fosters reciprocity and respect between older (ages fifty-plus) and younger (prekindergarten to age twenty-four) persons—sometimes referred to as a "barbell" or "bookends," and, to a lesser extent, the "middles" (Gen X-ers, Millennials, Gen Y-ers)—through meaningful intergenerational roles and relationships. These initiatives vary in size, scope, purpose, duration, degree of interaction between age groups, funding, partnerships, and impact/effectiveness.

According to Generations United, "Intergenerational programs intentionally unite the generations in ways that enrich participants' lives and help address vital social and community issues while building on the positive resources that young and old have to offer each other and to their communities. These programs bring people of different generations together for ongoing, mutually beneficial, planned activities, designed to achieve specified program goals and promote greater understanding and respect between generations."[7] Programs may focus on various areas, including academic achievement and enrichment; physical, cognitive, and mental health; social isolation and loneliness; cultural identity; environmental awareness and action; affordable housing; job readiness and entrepreneurship; neighborhood revitalization; structural racism and inequalities; technology access and use; caregiving; food insecurity; community change; substance use; and ageism.[8] As argued by Ai-jen Poo, cofounder of Caring Across Generations, "Co-generational innovation is going to be essential to navigating the future. There's wisdom at every age, and we can't afford not to be drawing on all of that wisdom to try new things and to test new ideas."[9]

Some examples: Literations is a reading tutoring program that addresses the literacy achievement gap one student at a time. Funded by AARP Foundation Experience Corps and AARP Massachusetts, Literations engages some two hundred volunteer literacy coaches who provide one-to-one structured reading practice to first- through fourth-grade students in nine Boston public schools, two Framingham public schools, and three Boys & Girls Clubs of Boston. Foster Grandparents and Cal State Fresno students come together to teach emotional literacy to youth ages seven to twenty in after-school programs, a charter school, and a foster care agency. CoGenerate (formerly Encore.org) collaborates with Krista Tippett's On Being Project (among others) to advance social healing and mental wellness by means of intergenerational sharing and creative works—essays, poetry, video, visual arts, audio, and more. In October 2023 CoGenerate joined forces with More Perfect, a coalition of national service and bridge-building groups that is advocating for a dramatic expansion of cogenerational national service and volunteering, including opportunities to engage one million young and five hundred thousand older Americans in national service by 2033. The coalition's plan describes national service (including AmeriCorps State and National, AmeriCorps VISTA, AmeriCorps NCCC, AmeriCorps Seniors, Conservation Corps, Peace Corps, and a variety of corps at the national and state levels) as "uniquely poised to bring generations together across divides for mutual benefit and social impact."[10]

Other programs feature cross-generational conversations (Generations Over Dinner); storytelling, music, and dance (Circle of Chairs); hospice visits (DreamCatchers); and cooking together (young people making kimchi, a sacred practice, with elders) as social healing in Los Angeles's Koreatown. SWAN 3G engages former Sesame Workshop employees in a three-generation mental wellness initiative in which they mentor high school students who, in turn, mentor preschoolers using curated Sesame Street segments that spark discussion, empathy, and joy. A program called Papa helps health plans and employers connect older adults and families with "pals" who provide companionship, assistance with everyday tasks, transportation, and more. Eldera, a global virtual village, connects young people (ages five to eighteen) with vetted older members (ages sixty and up) for weekly virtual conversations and activities. Yet another initiative, led by CoGenerate senior fellow Gara LaMarche, employs focus groups and one-on-one conversations that enable older and younger social justice activists to engage in cross-generational exchange on topics such as leadership and power/politics in social change organizations, funding challenges, trends in the workplace, and differing generational expectations and ideologies.

An increasing number of organizations are using interactive technology to foster mentorship and supportive relations between the generations. Generation Connect connects high schoolers with older adults to offer tech support, online gaming, and common-interest bonding during intergenerational programs. In return, teens receive mentorship, soft skill training, and community service hours. Similarly, DOROT has younger people teach older adults about technology and how to use it to foster deeper connections in the virtual world, bringing the generations together in a mutually beneficial partnership of elders, volunteers, and professionals.

Bridge Meadows, a nonprofit headquartered in Portland, Oregon, offers safe, affordable, multigenerational housing for families adopting children out of foster care and for adults over age fifty-five. The organization describes its goal as "creating a mutually beneficial network of support with a primary focus on helping children formerly in foster care to heal from trauma."[11] Bridge Meadows develops and sustains supportive intergenerational neighborhoods focused on empowering community members to build strong, interdependent relationships so that resources and solutions can be found within the community. It connects youth, parents, and elders through a variety of activities and therapeutic programmatic offerings facilitated by mental health specialists, such as community gatherings, weekly shared meals, support groups called "circles," and classes initiated and taught by community members.

While all intergenerational initiatives share the best of intentions, some entail only occasional or even one-time participation, while others foster ongoing, intensive engagement and investment.[12] Note that those featured in the *Handbook* are in the deep-engagement category. Moreover, to be considered something more than a diverse collection of well-intentioned efforts requires a research base, shared definitions (although even the use of generational labels is debated), goals, standards, a shared body of knowledge (evidence-based best practices, benefits, and obstacles), and the organization, leadership, resources, and training and support that are essential to a cohesive field. To that end, the *Handbook* suggests a course of action for academics, researchers, policymakers, social innovators, practitioners, and funders aiming to strengthen and sustain the intergenerational movement.

Intergenerational Connections Are Not Really New

To be sure, cross-generational exchange has existed in one form or another for a long time both within different cultures and in nature, too. One early advocate was Maggie Kuhn, founder of the Gray Panthers, who believed in age and youth in action. In another sphere entirely, as Jared Farmer's *Elderflora: A Modern History of Ancient Trees* tells us, "A living tree embodies a genetic heritage and a climatic heritage. And, as in human communities, every different age group has its part to play—not on its own but in relation to all the others."[13] Farmer says that a seedling's very survival may depend on the cooperative assistance of a big, old tree.

The intergenerational theme anchors another recent book, *The One-in-a-Million Boy*, by Monica Wood. In this novel a special rapport develops between Ona, a lonely 104-year-old woman with stories to tell and the unnamed 11-year-old-boy scout assigned to help her out with chores around the house on Saturdays. When the boy dies suddenly, his father, Quinn, a professional guitarist whose gigs have kept him on the road, decides to fulfill the requirements for his son's Boy Scout badge as a way of atoning for years of parental neglect and lending support to the boy's grieving mother, Belle. In doing so, the father not only gains insight into his unusual son and respect for Ona but also finds himself. What had begun as a simple community-outreach project in scouting becomes "a layered tale of generation-spanning connections."[14]

Traditional cross-generational learning, by which elders (often grandparents) share wisdom and perpetuate family and community values and culture with younger generations, dates back to humanity's earliest days. But because it is no longer as common for extended families to live in close proximity, more recently *non*familial or *extra*familial connections have increasingly been seen as a substitute, effectively addressing those demographic, social, and economic developments that limit contact between old and young people.[15] Thus, while familial intergenerational relationships—for example, grandparents caring for their own grandchildren—remain important, the subject of the majority of *Handbook* chapters is *non*familial intergenerational relationships.

Intergenerational connections have received a sustained though modest degree of attention from academics since the late 1960s to early 1970s when attitudinal differences rising to the level of social conflict between older and younger generations were referred to as the "generation gap." The University of Pittsburgh's Sally Newman created and served as executive director of Generations Together—the first university-based intergenerational studies program in the United States—and in 2003 was the founding editor in chief of the above-mentioned *Journal of Intergenerational Relationships*. Dr. Newman coauthored the first textbook on intergenerational issues, *Intergenerational Programs: Imperatives, Strategies, Impacts and Trends*, in 1989 and was senior author of the textbook *Intergenerational Programs: Past, Present and Future* in 1997. She was also the founder and first cochair of the International Consortium of Intergenerational Programmes (ICIP), a global networking voice for intergenerational collaboration, founded in 1999.[16]

The Stanford Center on Longevity's New Map of Life Program is focusing on the problem of age segregation (the term in use today), particularly in housing and education, and calling for a shift in our culture to reduce age-related bias and promote awareness and acceptance of the people around us. Two of the Center's five top action steps for building age awareness and acceptance are home-sharing (mixed-age living arrangements) and scaling up community programs that connect older and younger people and build reciprocity through volunteering or learning activities.[17]

Professional associations have also picked up the baton. The Gerontological Society of America's Learning, Research, and Community Engagement Interest Group and the American Society on Aging's Lifetime Education and Renewal Network (LEARN) offer webinars that examine some of the societal and demographic changes that have created the need for intergenerational programs and that feature intergenerational success stories. For example, Andrea Weaver, founder and executive director of Bridges Together, has been working in the field since 1991. Her flagship program, Bridges: Growing Older, Growing Together, has touched more than ten thousand lives across Massachusetts and Michigan. Then there are programs with even wider scope; two U.S. programs with national outreach are AmeriCorps (part of the Corporation for National and Community Service since 1993) and Generations United, founded in 1986.

Other partnerships unite intergenerational program sponsors, businesses, care facilities, and local government entities such as senior centers and schools. Janet M. Hively, an innovator and organizer, started the Buddy System and the Youth Coordinating Board out of the mayor's office in Minneapolis in 1985, "and it's gone on from there." Dr. Hively observes that attention has swung from the last twenty years' focus on how later life has changed and how that is affecting Boomers as they have aged during their second half of life. The new focus, she says, is on strengthening connections between old and young to learn from each other about what works *across the life span*. It's exemplified by the shift from Encore.org to CoGenerate, from "I" to "we."[18] (As of October 2022, CoGenerate rededicated its team to intergenerational opportunities that "combine forces for mutual benefit and social impact, co-generating solutions to society's toughest problems and co-creating a better future."[19]) Reinforcing the importance of intergenerational connections are the 2023 findings from the Harvard Adult Development Study, now in its eighty-fifth year and said to be the world's longest scientific study of happiness. By analyzing what factors contributed to longer, healthier, and happier lives, asking not only about physical health but also mental and social health, the study reported that deep relationships with family and friends and *across generations in the community* are the key to well-being.[20]

Intergenerational Connections Abroad

Intergenerational connections have been flourishing outside the United States as well. Bear in mind that categories and terminology commonly used in the United States do not apply to countries whose culture, politics, and history differ from ours; thus, the diverse models that exist in other countries should be seen as consistent with their individual social, educational, and cultural values. The Beth Johnson Foundation has been responsible for supporting and tracking much of the intergenerational activity in Great Britain, Spain, and other countries.[21] Topics include, for instance, the influence of intergenerational cooperation on relationships and performance at work, the benefits of multigenerational housing, and the use of virtual intergenerational programs to reduce social isolation and improve communication with and the educational outcomes of the younger generation.

Overlap with Age-Friendly Initiatives

Intergenerational programs are not synonymous with so-called age-friendly initiatives in communities, cities, workplaces, higher education, and health care—most of which focus exclusively on older adults, not young people. Yet some overlap can be discerned, as discussed in several chapters in the *Handbook* (3, 6, 15, 17, and 23). The World Health Organization (WHO) took the lead in 2007 by launching Age-Friendly Cities and Communities to enable older people to age actively. It aimed to meet their needs in eight domains: social participation, communication and information, civic participation and employment, housing, transportation, community support and health services, outdoor spaces and buildings, and respect and social inclusion. Technology (digital solutions) was added later.[22]

The Age-Friendly Institute (institute.agefriendly.org) coordinates efforts by its partners across the so-called Age-Friendly Ecosystem "to jumpstart the co-creation of shared strategies for program leaders, providers, and stakeholders to plan and measure collective impact across settings." The Institute's overall aim is to improve the quality of life for older adults. Among its goals are promoting positive social attitudes toward aging and older adults. diversifying living and working spaces by age, and facilitating intergenerational two-way learning. Age inclusivity, particularly in higher education, overlaps with the goal of intergenerational two-way learning and is one of the Gerontological Society of America's concerns. The term refers to older adults seeking opportunities at colleges and universities for personal development and/or to meet professional needs when pursuing extended work lives.

As broad and ambitious as the age-friendly agenda is for meeting older adults' needs, what's missing, according to some close observers, is greater attention to their strengths, or *assets*. Indeed, intergenerational programs, particularly in the early days, have been criticized for employing a *deficit* model; later programs may have begun with a singular focus on deficits and then pivoted to a strengths-based one. In any case, the vast majority soon realized the mutual benefits of intergenerational connections, a refrain heard throughout this *Handbook*. As the executive director of Generations United states in chapter 2, "Quality intergenerational programs are intentional, reciprocal, respectful, purposeful, and value people at all ages and stages of life. They are built with the understanding that all generations benefit when relationships are forged between people of different age groups."

Questions about the Use of Terms

Before proceeding with an outline of the *Handbook's* five main sections, it is important to acknowledge what the American Society on Aging calls a "vocabulary problem."[23] Society in general and even gerontologists typically speak of "seniors" and "those sixty-five-plus" as though they have the same or very similar capacities, experiences, identities, needs, and beliefs. *Handbook* authors' use of those terms is merely a convenience, not an assertion that aging is the same for all. It is also important to acknowledge voices with serious questions about the validity of the term "generations" and the use of generational categories. Rudolph and colleagues argue that "evidence for their existence is, at best, scant," and their use can lead to stereotyping and age discrimination.[24] They cite a study from the National Academies of Sciences, Engineering, and Medicine that concluded, "Categorizing workers with generational labels like 'baby boomer' or 'millennial' to define their needs and behaviors is not supported by research, and cannot adequately inform workforce management decisions." These authors acknowledge that "generations" remains "a useful *heuristic* in the process of social sensemaking" that helps give meaning to the complexities and intricacies of aging and human development in the context of changing societies."[25] Yet they attribute the wide acceptance of generational categories to a lack of knowledge about alternative theoretical explanations.

King and colleagues point out that "sweeping group differences depending on age or generation alone don't seem to be supported. . . . In fact, there is a considerable variety of preferences and values *within* any of these groups. . . . So what might really matter at work are not actual differences between generations but people's *beliefs* that these differences exist. These beliefs can get in the way of how people collaborate with their colleagues, and they have troubling implications for how people are managed and trained."[26] Duffy also finds people in different age groups more alike than different and calls out generational clichés propagated by marketing firms to sell products and services and by social media.[27]

Posing additional thorny questions, Menand's "Generation Overload" asks, for example, whether the generations differ according to the imprint of the historical events they lived through. "We tend to assume that there is a rhythm to social and cultural history that maps onto generational cohorts, such that each cohort is shaped by, or bears the imprint of, major historical events—Vietnam, 9/11, COVID. But we also think that young people develop their own culture, their own tastes and values, and that this new culture displaces the culture of the generation that preceded theirs."[28] Furthermore, deeply embedded decade thinking causes us "to imagine generational differences to be bright-line distinctions. . . . People talk as though there were a unique DNA for Gen-X."[29] Along similar lines comes the admonition to remember that "generations are clues, not a box . . . people are far more complicated than the year that they were born." They can and do change.[30]

Readers should keep that admonition in mind as they explore the chapters that follow.

The *Handbook's* Five Main Sections

Meeting Social Needs, Building Community, Reducing Age Segregation: Cross-Generational Relationships

"Uniting Generations through Policy, Practice, and Purpose," by Butts, leads off the discussion of cross-generational relationships and how they can strengthen communities and countries. Generations United is an established national network whose mission is "to improve the lives of children, youth, and older people through intergenerational collaboration, public policies, and programs for the enduring benefit of all." Generations United focuses on movement building and as such "plays a key role uniting, validating, and elevating the field." The organization convenes conferences and learning collaboratives, provides technical assistance/training, develops materials for practitioners and policymakers (e.g., toolkits, how-to guides, briefs, and reports), and strives to influence federal and state legislation by advancing intergenerational solutions that address interdependence, shared need, and family and community well-being.

The Eisner Foundation, the only U.S.-based foundation exclusively focused on intergenerational programs, sees them as a key tool for combatting a raft of society's challenges—health and wellness, education, housing, the workplace, civic engagement, and social cohesion, plus ageism and generational stereotypes—in Los Angeles County and New York City. In 2015 the foundation shifted from funding youth and older adult programs separately to funding programs that bring the two together because that was a more efficient and effective approach than trying to solve complicated problems with simple solutions. Leveraging the two groups to help each other, as Stamp and Mason maintain in "Intergenerational Solutions (Not Single-Issue Solutions) to Society's Challenges" (chapter 3), is not just nice, but necessary.

Next, "A Dose of Optimism: Data Show Americans are Ready to Build a Multigenerational Force for Good," by Halvorsen, Nichols, and Freedman, reviews the results from a nationally representative survey of 1,549 Americans ages 18 to 94 that gauges how American adults think about cogeneration, or intergenerational collaboration, to solve problems and bridge divides. Commissioned by CoGenerate (formerly Encore.org) and conducted by NORC at the University of Chicago using its AmeriSpeak® Panel, the survey finds "deep interest from people of all ages in cogeneration." The survey also uncovers respondents' attitudes toward working for a better future with people often much older or younger than themselves, the issues each generation selects as top priorities for cogenerational action, and the obstacles people see to acting on this interest. The chapter concludes with examples of cogenerational initiatives addressing specific social problems (e.g., mental health, climate change, and inequality) and a call to action.

Harrison and Jetson, coleaders of MetroMorphosis in Baton Rouge, Louisiana, are meeting social needs, building community, and reducing age segregation through cross-generational relationships. In "Child-Focused, Adult-Governed, and Elder-Led: Leveraging Generational Wisdom for a Changing America," they focus on "the intersection of age diversity and community change/movement building and its implications for community-serving organizations," reminding us that "age diversity is not a new challenge in the area of community change and movement building and must be addressed if community movements are to succeed." Moreover, they suggest that community-serving organizations address the issue of age diversity in a way that builds a more equitable workforce. The chapter reviews "a generations framework" for understanding community change before offering "an evolved model of leadership that reimagines organizational leadership as a shared responsibility between people of differing generations."

"Lifelong Learning, Intellectual Curiosity, and Community Building Across Generations at Lasell University," by Montepare and Farah, describes "age demographic shifts prompting higher education to embrace more age-inclusive approaches to teaching and learning." Lasell University (a small New England institution in Newton,

Massachusetts) offers opportunities for intergenerational exchange based on the Age-Friendly University model in collaboration with its university-based retirement community, Lasell Village. Residents of Lasell Village complete an individualized continuing education program comprising 450 hours of learning and fitness activities annually. The authors share empirical research that informs best practices and lessons learned from mounting intergenerational programs on the Lasell campus.

Cross-generational relationships are the fulcrum of a tech-enabled platform that connected professionals aged fifty-plus with younger workers for two-way mentoring and career support. The company, CIRKEL, was originally established as a New York City–based event series to foster cross-generational networking and later evolved into a tech startup offering an intergenerational community membership for monthly introductions. "CIRKEL: The Startup That Pioneered Two-Way Mentoring Across Generations in the Workforce," by Japp, presents "an overview of CIRKEL's evolution and the key challenges and opportunities that enabled the business to change how it connected older and younger professionals over the course of five years [before lack of funding forced its closure]. It also offers specific data about CIRKEL's target market and the impact intergenerational connections made on real careers."

Answering the Need for Tutoring, Coaching, Mentoring, Housing: Older Adults Working with Younger People

"SAGE: Building a Brighter Future by Working Across Generations," by Higgs, explains that Senior Advocates for Generational Equity was inspired by an ancient Greek proverb about elders planting trees whose shade they know they will never sit in. The organization's supporters believe in "generational equity—the principle that each generation should leave the world better off." They call on older adults to create opportunities in education, the environment, and the economy for younger and future generations to thrive. The work of inspiring people to give forward and training and supporting them entails listening across generations, collaborative problem solving (in partnership with young people), and building public will.

Kostrzewa and Wilcox's chapter, "EnCorps—STEM Professionals Serving to Inspire Students through STEM Education," presents "an organization of intergenerational learning that simultaneously helps aging populations and K–12 students thrive, drawing upon rich STEM industry expertise to inspire the next generation of scientists, engineers, inventors, and entrepreneurs." Since 2007 EnCorps has addressed the critical shortage of STEM (science, technology, engineering, and math) teachers by recruiting and training qualified STEM professionals to teach and tutor in underresourced middle and high school classrooms in California, Colorado, and New York. The STEM Teachers Program places experienced career-changing STEM experts as "EnCorps Fellows" into partner schools, enabling them to translate their work experience into rewarding new teaching careers.

Since its founding in 1989 in St. Louis, the Oasis Intergenerational Tutoring Program has been pairing older adult volunteers with children who need assistance with reading and literacy skills. According to "Changing Lives through Oasis Intergenerational Tutoring," by Foster, Click, McCreary, and Weiss, as of 2023 Oasis Tutoring was projected to be in 15 states, 22 cities, 84 school districts, and 441 schools across the United States. Its benefits extend beyond improved student reading scores to the caring, supportive mentoring relationships that are formed between tutors and youngsters. Evidence of the program's relevance for school staff, children, and older adults comes from both qualitative and quantitative data combined with information gleaned from interaction with the program's stakeholders.

"How National Service Brings to Scale Intergenerational Programs and Initiatives: The AmeriCorps Seniors Foster Grandparent Program and The National Partnership for Student Success," by Sergi, Cochran, and Jones, explains why AmeriCorps, the federal agency for national service and volunteerism, is an effective mechanism for scaling intergenerational programs and initiatives. The AmeriCorps Seniors Foster Grandparent Program that launched in 1965 with 21 demonstration projects by 2022 had 271 projects in 49 states, the District of Columbia, Puerto Rico, and the Virgin Islands. While scaling up, the program has consistently produced positive outcomes for both the older adults serving and the children being served. National service has also proved to be a cost-effective investment of federal dollars and an effective way to operationalize public-private partnerships to meet national needs, utilizing intergenerational program models such as the National Partnership for Student Success.

From programs reaching across the nation to one that is city-specific brings us to "The Intergenerational Schools in Cleveland: Reconnection and Recovery," by King. For more than two decades, three K–8 public charter schools in one of the nation's high-poverty urban centers have focused on literacy and relationship building through ongoing intergenerational activities, such as the Learning Partner program and the Intergenerational Visits program. The chapter describes major problems the schools faced during the pandemic and continue to face post-COVID, including health-related challenges, staffing shortages, and the switch from in-person to online classes. Each hurdle has been met and overcome with innovative thinking, dedicated leadership, and resilience.

Community-Engaged Learning and Bridging Differences: Younger People Helping Older Adults

Heading the section on community-engaged learning and bridging differences is "Intergenerational Diversity and Interethnic Connections: Who Will Care for Us?" Coauthors Torres-Gil and Ambriz begin by acknowledging the salience of intergenerational relationships and the influence of well-researched demographic trends. Yet even more important than how we promote interactions between the old and the young, they say, is "how we foster intergenerational relationships that are interethnic and interracial in a majority-minority nation." Instead of age-segregated initiatives in which older Whites interact primarily with younger Whites, they ask, "Can the paradigm be expanded to one where we pursue an intergenerational, interethnic, and interracial set of relationships?" They would move the discussion to "a broader, more nuanced, and potentially more complex and problematic space" in order to consider how we might learn from and benefit from cultures and norms of diverse groups.

Connecting generations and connecting with nature are the twinned themes of "Viewing the Climate Crisis from Intergenerational Perspectives," by Bonerath, Bisno, Williams, George, and Whitehouse. Each of the authors has initiated or joined in school- or community-based intergenerational projects aimed at "challenging assumptions, building relationships, and deepening appreciation for connections with nature." They write about online and in-person conversations in which dialogue about the global climate crisis is guided by a process of listening and sharing without judgment, potentially leading to community and cultural transformation. The word "collaboration" appears often here, applying not only to various multiage and international connections, but also to the multiage, "intergenerative" discussion and writing partnership that Dr. Whitehouse organized for the chapter.

"Applying Age-Friendly University Principles to Intergenerational Programs on College Campuses," by Merz, Morrow-Howell, Morton, and Gonzales, describes three intergenerational initiatives based on Age-Friendly University principles. The intergenerational home-sharing program sponsored by New York University's Center for Health and Aging Innovation, in partnership with the New York Foundation for Senior Citizens, reduces social isolation while increasing housing affordability for graduate students and adults aged sixty-plus. A service-learning course at NYU matches a person with early-stage Alzheimer's and related dementias with an undergraduate "buddy." And at Washington University in St. Louis, the When I'm 64 course has older adults along with incoming students exploring large social issues, such as population aging and human longevity, from interdisciplinary perspectives. Obstacles to scaling up the initiatives are discussed.

Shults, Wilkerson, Langridge, and Bringuier describe the work of the Boston chapter of Little Brothers–Friends of the Elderly (LBFE) in "Intergenerational Service-Learning Combats Social Isolation." From its start in France as Les Petits Frères des Pauvres nearly a century ago, LBFE has added chapters in ten countries and partnerships across the globe, all committed to relieving isolation and loneliness among older adults. In the United States, LBFE operates as a national network of nonprofit, volunteer-based organizations in five major cities. The Boston chapter employs a community-based program model that brings intergenerational programming into the neighborhoods and communities where older adults live, particularly non–English speakers and residents of public and affordable housing. CitySites and Digital Dividends are two LBFE initiatives that provide benefits to both older adults and college and university students: "Mattering to someone who matters to you helps to combat ageism and to build value between generations."

Andreoletti and June's chapter presents the service-learning initiative housed at Central Connecticut State University. In "Intergenerational Conversations Foster Connection in Community and College Classrooms," they discuss the objectives, outcomes, and challenges of Working Together: Intergenerational Student/Senior Exchange (WISE), which is an intergenerational service-learning component of courses in aging and gerontology, designed to bring college students together with older adults from assisted living facilities and senior centers for the purpose of building connection and increasing understanding across the generations. The experience aims to reduce ageism and increase feelings of "generativity" (contributing to the next generation) through small-group intergenerational discussions around topics of mutual interest such as relationships and technology.

Global Perspectives on Intergenerational Relationships
The chapters in this section stand out because they feature intergenerational connections in Europe, Asia, and Australia that are national in scope and in some cases are international. The section opens with "Generations Working Together across Scotland," by George, Smith, and Clyde. In partnership with the Scottish National Government, Generations Working Together (GWT) operates locally and nationally to raise awareness, share, and expand knowledge and understanding of intergenerational practice and its impact. GWT provides training, shares a resource library, organizes learning events, facilitates eighteen local and four thematic networks, and works in partnership with local/national groups and organizations to deliver innovative pilot projects and participate in academic research projects.

"The TOY Project and Development of IGL Training in Europe," by Fitzpatrick, Gallagher, Kernan and Cortellesi, describes the research and development work of a group of nongovernment organizations and higher education institutions in seven European countries with a particular focus on intergenerational interaction between young children and older adults. Aiming to create a community of practice, the Together Old and Young Project (TOY) has added to the scholarship about intergenerational practice, integrating knowledge and insights about human development and relationships to deepen understanding of intergenerational connections as they are experienced in different cultural contexts. Building on that work, TOY delivers training using research-informed practice guidelines and tools for practitioners working in early childhood education and care, community development, and social and elder care.

In "The Development of Intergenerational Initiatives in Singapore," Thang examines the landscape of state and grassroots efforts to promote intergenerational bonding in Singapore. Thang highlights policy and sociocultural characteristics that define the trajectories of development in intergenerational connections, including a focus on the family and kampong (village) creation in the community. Her chapter highlights the "intergenerational contact zone" as a conceptual tool for exploring ways to enable and expand the creation of effective, meaningful, and sustainable spaces for intergenerational encounters.

It further urges adoption of an intergenerational lens so that intergenerational connection is not merely an add-on but an integral part of policy and practice.

"The Power of Intergenerational Relationships to Transform Education and Promote Social Cohesion in Spain's Basque Country," by Munitis, Sancho, Mondragon, and Gorrotxategi, presents findings from interviews of professionals working in the intergenerational field in Basque Country (Spain) schools. The results demonstrate the power of intergenerational experiences to break down stereotypes and strengthen relationships in favor of greater social cohesion that can extend beyond the school setting to different contexts in the wider community. The Basque Country research verified the importance of cross-generational relationships and cultural interaction employing bidirectional learning to contribute to society.

Kuraoka offers insights into intergenerational practices in Japan and how they empower individuals in "Intergenerational Programs and Places in Japan's Super-Aging Society: What Three Good Practices Can Teach Us." Responding to the needs of the country's rapidly aging society as well as a decline in the number of three-generation households, Japan has many programs with different purposes and settings that bring generations together for mutual care and support outside the home. Kuraoka describes the shift from programs that rely mainly on government officials and instructors to programs independently managed by community-dwelling people. Three examples are highlighted: Shibasaki Irodori Station, a community-based intergenerational place, welcomes people of all generations; REPRINTS involves senior volunteers reading aloud at local schools, kindergartens, nursery schools, and libraries; and Kotoen fosters exchanges between nursing home residents and nursery school children.

"Embedding Intergenerational Practice and Approaches in Northern Ireland—The Story So Far," by Titterington and Hatton-Yeo, lays out the seminal role of the Beth Johnson Foundation (BJF) in the intergenerational field and how Northern Ireland is prospering as a result. The BJF took up intergenerational work twenty-five years ago to replace negative views of older people as needy and passive with asset-based thinking, seeing them as vital contributors to the well-being of others. The BJF was also concerned about a growing disconnect between generations and the absence of opportunities for young people to experience positive engagement and to be part of mutually supportive networks. One outgrowth of the BJF's intergenerational work in the United Kingdom was the Linking Generations Northern Ireland program (LGNI), launched in 2009 with a grant from The Atlantic Philanthropies. LGNI and its region-wide network address high-impact social issues within multiple sectors—community, education, local and central government, and health and social care.

Taylor and Schmidt's chapter, "Shaping the Future of Work—Intergenerational Growing Pains and Gains in Canada's Workplaces," discusses the importance of intergenerational approaches to social, workforce, and economic challenges in Canadian workplaces. It explores three case studies of current workplace programs engaging diverse age groups to present a better understanding of the benefits and barriers the programs face. Using Challenge Factory's Broken Talent Escalator® model, the authors argue for an intergenerational, systemic approach to workforce management that responds to the career needs of younger *and* older workers. In addition, they point to the lack of specifically age-aware initiatives within Canada's workspaces, even those with a strong commitment to diversity, reflecting the challenge of addressing workplace ageism.

The authors of the next chapter present a study of the multiage workforce from a different angle. For "Understanding Age-Diverse Knowledge Exchange through Social Comparison," Rinker, Fasbender, and Gerpott looked at the transfer of unique knowledge between younger and older employees and compared three theories—social comparison theory (individuals' tendency to evaluate themselves by comparing their attributes, skills, and achievements with those of others), social identity theory (formation of social identities based on group membership), and intergroup contact theory (interactions between members of diverse groups mitigating biases and encouraging constructive, collaborative relationships)—that could explain whether age-diverse knowledge exchange among employees is likely to contribute to knowledge retention—that is, ensuring the preservation of organizational memory, and/or to the creation of new knowledge through innovation and enhancing employee development.

In "Bridging Generations and Disciplines: Exploring How Interprofessional Conversations and Circle of Change Revisited Can Improve Intergenerational Practice Experience and Outcomes in Australia," Golenko, Cartmel, Barbery, and Fitzgerald show how cross-disciplinary collaboration between professionals from various industries and disciplines can give rise to a number of challenges, such as miscommunication, misunderstanding, and hierarchical barriers, that can undermine the potential benefits of intergenerational programs. The authors introduce the concepts of interprofessional conversations and circle of change revisited, discuss them in the context of intergenerational practice, and then provide case study examples of how the concepts can be applied when addressing complex issues, pursuing common goals, and enacting meaningful change.

Challenges to Generational Thinking, A Research Overview, and Recommendations for Strengthening and Sustaining the Intergenerational Movement

The first two chapters in this section question the validity of "generation" itself. Rudolph and Zacher's "Generations and Generational Differences: A Thought Experiment" considers "generation" as a suspect, socially constructed category of human development and challenges the evidence base regarding generations, their existence, and our ability to identify differences between them. They argue that studies of generations and generational differences are flawed, and they offer a thought experiment to demonstrate the impossibility of proving scientifically whether age, time period, or cohort can explain a given behavior.

Johfre's "The Sociology of Age Diversity" sees age as a multidimensional construct, not merely a chronological (generational) one, and examines how this affects outcomes of intergenerational connections. Humans are classified into social categories because they are useful, age being a central way people make sense of one another. Further, age is a "status characteristic" like gender, race, and class that helps position a person within social interactions and institutions, determining what level of respect, resources, or opportunities are due. However, age categories are not only arbitrary, but they can produce ageist barriers to intergenerational connections—segregation, stereotyping, discrimination—that affect the workplace, the economy, and society as a whole.

Jarrott weaves together the *Handbook*'s diverse threads with her chapter, "Evaluating Intergenerational Strategies to Enhance Individual and Community Development." Her overview of the development of intergenerational program evaluation keys in on the shift from a deficit-based orientation to a strength-based one. This shift resulted in intergenerational program expansion (greater diversity of participants, program content, and settings) and new challenges for evaluators—for example, sufficient resources and reliable, valid measures. Next, specific intergenerational program evaluation strategies are described and illustrated, particularly evaluation plus practice partnerships that engage all organizational stakeholders, aligning evaluation plans with program goals and available resources (e.g., time, expertise, materials, and funds), and communicating evaluation outcomes. The chapter concludes with a four-step call to action for practitioners, funders, and evaluators invested in comprehending intergenerational program processes and outcomes for different groups.

Two of the most experienced thought leaders in the intergenerational field, Henkin and Kaplan, provide a fitting and instructive conclusion to this volume with "The Long View—Building Intergenerational Connections, Lessons Learned." Drawing on interviews with other thought leaders in the United States and abroad, they review what has been accomplished in terms of programs/practice, policy, and research over the past fifty years, including an expanded view of the potential of intergenerational relationships and corresponding shifts in terminology. The chapter goes on to address barriers to growth and calls for a multifaceted, multilevel approach to "changing mindsets, integrating an intergenerational lens into systems, and creating social structures that reflect the opportunities presented by an age-diverse society." Along with recommended next steps, readers of this chapter will find provocative questions—about increasing funding support, ensuring equity, attracting new partners, and strengthening collaboration across sectors—that are essential for the long-term viability of intergenerational connections.

Notes

1. Alan Hatton-Yeo and Toshio Ohsako, eds., "Intergenerational Programmes: Public Policy and Research Implications, An International Perspective." UNESCO Institute for Education and The Beth Johnson Foundation (2000), https://unesdoc.unesco.org/ark:/48223/pf0000128018.
2. Maria Cruz-Saco and Sergei Zelenev, eds., *Intergenerational Solidarity* (New York: Palgrave Macmillan, 2010). Based on a United Nations Department of Economic and Social Affairs conference in 2007.
3. *Nature Aging*, "Strengthening Intergenerational Connections," *Nature Aging* 1 (2021): 323, https://doi.org/10.1038/s43587-021-00061-3.

4. One such network, led by Clint Wilkins and Jim McGinley, meets monthly via Zoom for presentations, sharing ideas in "fishbowl" sessions, and building community.
5. Stanford Social Innovation Review (SSIR), "Meeting the Multigenerational Moment." Published in partnership with Encore.org (now CoGenerate) and the Eisner Foundation, March 2021), https://ssir.org/meeting_the_multigenerational_moment; Marc Freedman and Trent Stamp, "Overcoming Age Segregation," *Stanford Social Innovation Review*, March 2021, https://ssir.org/articles/entry/overcoming_age_segregation.
6. Megan Gerhardt, Josephine Nachemson-Ekwall, and Brandon Fogel, *Gentelligence: The Revolutionary Approach to Leading an Intergenerational Workforce* (Lanham, MD: Rowman & Littlefield, 2021).
7. "Making the Case for Intergenerational Programs," Generations United, 2021, https://www.gu.org/resources/making-the-case-for-intergenerational-programs/.
8. Generations United 2012 Fact Sheet, www.gu.org.
9. Ai-jen Poo, influencer, labor organizer, author, quoted on CoGenerate website. September 28, 2023, Cogenerate.org.
10. Eunice Lin Nichols, "Coalition Releases a Bold Cogenerational Vision for National Service," October 19, 2023, www.Cogenerate.org.
11. Bridge Meadows, www.bridgemeadows.org.
12. For a scale of engagement, see Dr. Matthew S. Kaplan, professor of intergenerational programs and aging, Penn State University. www.aese.psu.edu.
13. Verlyn Klinkenborg, "Trees in Themselves," *New York Review* LXX, no. 5 (2023): 36–37. Review of *Elderflora: A Modern History of Ancient Trees*, by Jared Farmer (New York: Basic Books, 2022).
14. Monica Wood, *The One-in-a-Million Boy* (New York: Houghton Mifflin Harcourt, 2016).
15. Sally Newman and Alan Hatton-Yeo, "Intergenerational Learning and the Contributions of Older People," *Ageing Horizons* 8 (2008): 31–39; Oxford Institute of Ageing, https://www.ageing.ox.ac.uk.
16. Mariano Sánchez et al., "Intergenerational Programmes: Towards a Society for All Ages" (Barcelona: La Caixa Foundation, 2007), www.LaCaixa.es/ObraSocial.
17. Sasha Shen Johfre, "Report on Intergenerational Relationships," Stanford University, Center on Longevity, New Map of Life Program, August 2021, https://longevity.stanford.edu/wp-content/uploads/2021/11/Johfre_NML_IntergenerationalRelationships.pdf.
18. Joan Ditzion and Janet M. Hively, "Aging Women Transforming Cultural Myths: An Intergenerational Conversation," At the 2021 SAGE-ing International Online Summit: "Evolving Elders: Shifting from I to We," October 29–31, 2021.
19. Marc Freedman and Eunice Lin Nichols, "CoGeneration: Is America Ready to Unleash a Multigenerational Force for Good?" October 2022, https://papers.ssrn.com/sol3/papers.cfm?abstract_id=4448785. See also Marc Freedman, *How to Live Forever: The Enduring Power of Connecting the Generations* (New York: Public Affairs, 2018).
20. Marc Schulz and Robert Waldinger, *The Good Life: Lessons from the World's Longest Scientific Study of Happiness* (New York: Simon & Schuster, 2023).
21. Hatton-Yeo and Ohsako, "Intergenerational Programmes"; Alan Hatton-Yeo, "Intergenerational Solidarity: A Framework for Well-Being," *Journal of Intergenerational Relationships* 7, no. 4 (2009): 351–54, https://doi.org/10.1080/15350770903288647; Alan Hatton-Yeo and the Beth Johnson Foundation, "Looking Back, Looking Forward: Reflections on the 10th Anniversary of Beth Johnson Foundation Centre for Intergenerational Practice, United Kingdom," *Journal of Intergenerational Relationships* 9, no. 3 (2011): 318–21, https://doi.org/10.1080/15350770.2011.593444; Mariano Sánchez and Alan Hatton-Yeo, "Active Ageing and Intergenerational Solidarity in Europe: A Conceptual Reappraisal from a Critical Perspective," *Journal of Intergenerational Relationships* 10, no. 3 (2012): 276–93, https://doi.org/10.1080/15350770.2012.699819; Alan Hatton-Yeo and Mariano Sánchez, "2012 and Beyond: Toward a Socially Sustainable Intergenerational Europe," *Journal of Intergenerational Relationships* 10, no. 3 (2012): 211–13, https://doi.org/10.1080/15350770.2012.699813.
22. Joost Van Hoof and Hannah R Marston, "Age-Friendly Cities and Communities: State of the Art and Future Perspectives," *International Journal of Environmental Research and Public Health* 18, no. 4 (2021): 1644. https://doi.org/10.3390/ijerph18041644.
23. American Society on Aging, *Generations Journal*, Fall 2023. info@asaging.org.

24. Cort W. Rudolph et al., "Generations and Generational Differences: Debunking Myths in Organizational Science and Practice and Paving New Paths Forward," *Journal of Business and Psychology* 36, no. 6 (2021): 945–67, https://doi.org/10.1007/s10869-020-09715-2.
25. Rudolph et al., "Generations and Generational Differences."
26. Eden King et al., "Generational Differences at Work Are Small. Thinking They're Big Affects Our Behavior," *Harvard Business Review*, August 1, 2019, https://hbr.org/2019/08/generational-differences-at-work-are-small-thinking-theyre-big-affects-our-behavior.
27. Bobby Duffy, *The Generation Myth: Why When You're Born Matters Less Than You Think* (New York: Basic Books, 2021).
28. Louis Menand, "Generation Overload," *New Yorker*, October 18, 2021, 63–67. Biographer Walter Isaacson ponders much the same question (Do people shape history or do events shape people?) when deciding how to tell a subject's story. Walter Isaacson, "Lessons about Living with Geniuses," Leon Levy Center for Biography, CUNY Graduate Center, September 28, 2023, https://www.youtube.com/watch?v=AlBqprmhbhs.
29. Isaacson, "Lessons about Living with Geniuses."
30. Emma Goldberg, "Gen X Has Moved into the Executive Suite," *New York Times*, July 9, 2023, Business section, 3.

Bibliography

Cruz-Saco, Maria, and Sergei Zelenev, eds. *Intergenerational Solidarity*. New York: Palgrave Macmillan, 2010.

Ditzion, Joan, and Janet M. Hively. "Aging Women Transforming Cultural Myths: An Intergenerational Conversation." At the 2021 SAGE-ing International Online Summit: "Evolving Elders: Shifting from I to We" (October 29–31), 2021.

Duffy, Bobby. *The Generation Myth: Why When You're Born Matters Less Than You Think*. New York: Basic Books, 2021.

Freedman, Marc. *How to Live Forever: The Enduring Power of Connecting the Generations*. New York: PublicAffairs, 2018.

Freedman, Marc, and Eunice Lin Nichols. "CoGeneration: Is America Ready to Unleash a Multigenerational Force for Good?" October 2022. https://papers.ssrn.com/sol3/papers.cfm?abstract_id=4448785.

Freedman, Marc, and Trent Stamp. "Overcoming Age Segregation." *Stanford Social Innovation Review*. March 2021. https://ssir.org/articles/entry/overcoming_age_segregation.

Generations United. "Generations United 2012 Fact Sheet." www.gu.org.

Generations United. "Making the Case for Intergenerational Programs." 2021. https://www.gu.org/resources/making-the-case-for-intergenerational-programs/.

Gerhardt, Negan, Josephine Nachemson-Ekwall, and Brandon Fogel. *Gentelligence: The Revolutionary Approach to Leading an Intergenerational Workforce*. Lanham, MD: Rowman & Littlefield, 2021.

Goldberg, Emma. "Gen X Has Moved into the Executive Suite." *New York Times*, July 9, 2023, Business section, 3.

Hatton-Yeo, Alan. "Intergenerational Solidarity: A Framework for Well-Being." *Journal of Intergenerational Relationships* 7, no. 4 (2009): 351–54. https://doi.org/10.1080/15350770903288647.

Hatton-Yeo, Alan, and the Beth Johnson Foundation. "Looking Back, Looking Forward: Reflections on the 10th Anniversary of Beth Johnson Foundation Centre for Intergenerational Practice, United Kingdom." *Journal of Intergenerational Relationships* 9, no. 3 (2011): 318–21. https://doi.org/10.1080/15350770.2011.593444.

Hatton-Yeo, Alan, and Toshio Ohsako, eds. "Intergenerational Programmes: Public Policy and Research Implications, An International Perspective." UNESCO Institute for Education and The Beth Johnson Foundation. 2000. https://unesdoc.unesco.org/ark:/48223/pf0000128018.

Hatton-Yeo, Alan, and Mariano Sánchez. "2012 and Beyond: Toward a Socially Sustainable Intergenerational Europe." *Journal of Intergenerational Relationships* 10, no. 3 (2012): 211–13. https://doi.org/10.1080/15350770.2012.699813.

Johfre, Sasha Shen. "Report on Intergenerational Relationships." Stanford University, Center on Longevity, New Map of Life Program. August 2021. https://longevity.stanford.edu/wp-content/uploads/2021/11/Johfre_NML_IntergenerationalRelationships.pdf.

King, Eden, Lisa Finkelstein, Courtney Thomas, and Abby Corrington. "Generational Differences at Work Are Small. Thinking They're Big Affects Our Behavior." *Harvard Business Review*. August 1, 2019. https://hbr.org/2019/08/generational-differences-at-work-are-small-thinking-theyre-big-affects-our-behavior.

Klinkenborg, Verlyn. "Trees in Themselves." *New York Review* LXX, no. 5 (2023): 36–37.

Menand, Louis. "Generation Overload." *New Yorker* (October 18, 2021): 63–67.

Nature Aging. "Strengthening Intergenerational Connections." (2021). 1: 323. https://doi.org/10.1038/s43587-021-00061-3.

Newman, Sally, and Alan Hatton-Yeo. "Intergenerational Learning and the Contributions of Older People." *Ageing Horizons* 8 (2008): 31–39. https://www.ageing.ox.ac.uk.

Rudolph, Cort W., Rachel S. Rauvola, David P. Costanza, and Hannes Zacher. "Generations and Generational Differences: Debunking Myths in Organizational Science and Practice and Paving New Paths Forward." *Journal of Business and Psychology* 36, no. 6 (2021): 945–67. https://doi.org/10.1007/s10869-020-09715-2.

Sánchez, Mariano, Donna M. Butts, Alan Hatton-Yeo, Nancy A. Henkin, Shannon E. Jarrott, Matthew S. Kaplan, et al. "Intergenerational Programmes: Towards a Society for All Ages." La Caixa Foundation. December 2007. www.LaCaixa.es/ObraSocial.

Sánchez, Mariano, and Alan Hatton-Yeo. "Active Ageing and Intergenerational Solidarity in Europe: A Conceptual Reappraisal from a Critical Perspective." *Journal of Intergenerational Relationship*s 10, no. 3 (2012): 276–93. https://doi.org/10.1080/15350770.2012.699819.

Schulz, Marc, and Robert Waldinger. *The Good Life: Lessons from the World's Longest Scientific Study of Happiness*. New York: Simon & Schuster, 2023.

Stanford Social Innovation Review (SSIR). "Meeting the Multigenerational Moment." Published in partnership with Encore.org and the Eisner Foundation. (2021). https://ssir.org/meeting_the_multigenerational_moment.

Wood, Monica. *The One-in-a-Million Boy*. New York: Houghton Mifflin Harcourt, 2016.

PART I

Meeting Social Needs, Building Community, Reducing Age Segregation: Cross-Generational Relationships

PART 1

CHAPTER 2

Uniting Generations through Policy, Practice, and Purpose

Donna M. Butts

> **Abstract**
>
> This chapter explores movement building in the context of intergenerational programs and public policies designed to create a world that values people at all ages and stages of life. Essential elements in value creation and efforts to develop national and international networks are highlighted as well as the roles they play in establishing the field of high-quality intergenerational practice. Guidelines for using an intergenerational lens in developing and advocating for public policies that encourage intergenerational interdependence are outlined. Emerging trends that could benefit from intergenerational solutions are identified. These include demographic changes, social isolation and loneliness, post-traumatic pandemic shock, and environmental activism.
>
> **Key Words:** intergenerational, advocacy, coalitions, movement building, community planning

Introduction

>We formed Generations United to argue for a caring society.
>
>—*Jack Ossofsky, CEO, National Council on Aging and cofounder of Generations United, 1986*

Generations are intricately connected throughout time. Humans receive and give care across their lives. We cannot survive or thrive without each other. As the late Rosalynn Carter said, "There are only four kinds of people in the world—those who have been caregivers, those who are caregivers, those who will be caregivers, and those who will need caregivers."[1] Babies couldn't survive without care; experiencing physical and emotional trauma requires care to heal; and as individuals age they often need care along a continuum as their ability to remain independent changes. We are interdependent, yet public policies and the ways in which communities are planned and services are developed and delivered are siloed and parsed by age. This is starkly evident in family policy. It's a disservice to all generations that policies and programs that are intended to benefit babies, children, and adolescents are independent of policies and programs meant to support people as they grow older. Advocates that specialize in one population or another plant stakes in the ground and face off ready to do battle and make the case for why investments in their constituents are more critical than those for other age groups. With increasing social challenges related to poverty and other factors, the age-old social compact that ties generations together is under major stress. The social compact is based on reciprocity—giving and receiving across the life course—and the belief that societies progress because of the investments past generations have made in future generations to carry knowledge and culture forward. It recognizes that people of all generations—past, present, and future—are bound together as a means to survive and thrive. It is a bond that needs to be intentionally tended through intergenerational practices.

Establishing Generations United
Conditions were fraught with distrust in 1986 when Generations United was founded by the leading child-focused, youth, and aging organizations in the United States. Tensions were high in Washington DC as policy makers debated and framed the need for budget cuts as young versus old and kids versus canes—have-nots against have-nots, two populations with the weakest voices and greatest need for investments. David Liederman, head of the Child Welfare League of America, and Jack Ossofsky, head of the National Council on Aging, stood together at a press conference as they announced the formation of a new coalition with a united voice. Ossofsky said, "Generations United, and all of its members and friends, is in the business of cooperation and not conflict, strengthening and not destroying the positive qualities of intergenerational American life and in laying the groundwork for the politics of family, community, and generational solidarity."

The two leaders believed a country rich in resources shouldn't have to choose between its bookend generations—young and old—that hold our civil society together. Within two years, the Children's Defense Fund and AARP joined them, and over the next ten years they grew the coalition to more than a hundred members representing over sixty-five million Americans.

As a loose-knit coalition, Generations United found early success advocating for access to health care and creating a national service movement that became the Corporation for National and Community Service. It continues to advance intergenerational service opportunities for people of all ages, connecting young and old to their communities.

From 1986 to 1996 Generations United operated as a coalition of child-focused, youth, and senior organizations working together to forge a common agenda. It functioned using part-time staff and resources contributed by the founding organizations and soliciting small grants. While Generations United was successful at holding the line and preventing the "haves" from dividing and conquering the "have-nots" by providing the roundtable where groups could gather, it was clear by the 1990s that to really flourish, the organization would need to become an independent, free-standing entity.[2] The four founding organizations took the bold step of incorporating Generations United as a nonprofit organization and recruiting additional CEOs and corporate representatives. Each agreed to pay $5000 in dues each year for three years. The idea was to determine whether such an organization with the mission of supporting all ages by advancing intergenerational public policies and programs was viable and relevant. More than twenty-five years later, Generations United has grown from an annual budget of $186,000 to more than $4 million and from two and a half staff to more than twenty. The mission is more germane than ever—to improve the lives of children, youth, and older people through intergenerational collaboration, public policies, and programs for the enduring benefit of all.

Progress of National and International Organizations

Generations United has stood the test of time and flourished where many other international, national, and regional entities have floundered. In 1998, an international group of intergenerational enthusiasts founded the International Consortium on Intergenerational Programmes (ICIP) following a meeting hosted by the University of Dortmund in Dortmund, Germany. ICIP conducted its inaugural conference in Maastricht, the Netherlands, in 1999. Its members went on to cohost additional conferences in partnership with in-country host organizations in Keele, England (2002), Victoria, British Columbia (2004), Melbourne, Australia (2006), Singapore (2010), and Honolulu, Hawaii (2015).

ICIP was an attempt to build an international association like Generations United in the United States that would act as the convener and catalyst for intergenerational programs globally. It was an enormous undertaking with few resources. ICIP was incorporated in the Netherlands with a Dutch constitution. Originally, the Beth Johnson Foundation, headquartered in the United Kingdom, provided staff and some financial support (see *Handbook* chapter 23). Others on the leadership team volunteered their time and expertise. In addition to the conferences, ICIP published an electronic newsletter and hosted a website.

Founders of ICIP also supported efforts to begin countrywide networks in Japan, Spain, and the United Kingdom. It was an inaugural supporter of the *Journal of Intergenerational Relationships* in 2003. Unfortunately, the lack of resources and paid staff slowed the organization's progress, and it has become dormant.

Efforts to develop a country-wide presence continue in areas like Scotland, where Generations Working Together (see *Handbook* chapter 18) has successfully conducted conferences and spearheads Global Intergenerational Week—celebrated by fourteen countries in 2023.[3] In Japan, academics created the Japan Intergenerational Unity Association and have published a series of books focused on intergenerational practices. The Australian Institute for Intergenerational Practice tracks programs and provides training opportunities. Each has limitless potential but finite resources.

Other countries continue to explore the potential. In Canada, an anonymous donor supported an assessment of intergenerational programs in the country, hoping to identify one they could invest in that would pick up the mantle and provide the umbrella and leadership needed to grow this work across the country. After more than a year they switched gears to identify a national organization that could add this work to their portfolio and attach it to their mission saying, "We don't have a Generations United in Canada."

Why is a strong national organization essential to building an intergenerational movement? In the case of Generations United it plays a key role uniting, validating, and elevating the field. It takes a two-pronged approach supporting an intergenerational solutions lens by focusing on programs and public policies. It sets standards for intergenerational programs and annually awards "Programs of Distinction" and "Programs of Merit" designations based on rigorous criteria created by a panel of intergenerational experts. This recognition lends credibility to the programs as they raise awareness and funding for their work in their local communities.[4]

As the national convener and thought leader, Generations United provides expert commentary and is a frequent source for journalists and opinion leaders. It hosts a biennial global conference, the only one of its kind focused solely on intergenerational practices, that has fueled the movement country-wide. As one participant said, "I found my tribe." In between conferences, the organization hosts topical educational webinars that feature leaders and practitioners from across the country as expert presenters. It engages a strong cadre of intergenerational specialists and forms teams to provide technical assistance on a fee-for-service basis that results in higher-quality programming.

Generations United creates toolkits, how-to guides, and comprehensive briefs that make the case for the relevance of intergenerational practices. It is host to several learning collaboratives that generally meet quarterly to highlight programs and advancements, identify gaps and needs, and, most importantly, connect people working in like areas. These include those that focus on housing, shared sites, and diversity in programming.

Generations United collects and shares information on intergenerational programs across the United States by maintaining a program database that is accessible at gu.org. Currently, the database includes over eight hundred programs, with each state represented. It can be searched by program, keywords, or state.[5]

Generations United continues as the longest-lasting national organization focused solely on the intergenerational field.

What Are Intergenerational Programs, and Why Are They Important?

Intergenerational programs are defined as programs, policies, and practices that increase cooperation, interaction, and exchange between people of different generations, allowing them to share their talents and resources and support each other in relationships that benefit both the individuals and their community.[6]

These programs are often categorized by the direction of service. This includes young serving old, old serving young, and young and old serving together. Using these categories, however, can lead to overlooking a key element in the programs—reciprocity. Quality intergenerational programs are intentional, reciprocal, respectful, and purposeful and value people at all ages and stages of life. They are built with the understanding that all generations benefit when relationships are forged between people of different age groups.[7]

The concept of intentionally bringing generations together to serve as resources to each other and to their communities has become increasingly popular as a vehicle for addressing critical societal needs and strengthening cross-age relationships. Beginning with the Foster Grandparent and RSVP programs in the 1960s, early intergenerational programs focused primarily on dispelling age-related stereotypes, fostering cross-age understanding, reducing social isolation, and providing financial support for low-income elders.[8] Now a part of AmeriCorps Seniors (see *Handbook* chapter 11), the early national programs have evolved with the changing interests of older adults and expanding opportunities. While the original Foster Grandparents may have been content to rock babies, today's older adults are as likely to be interested in rocking the boat.[9]

Recognizing value beyond just connecting different age groups, the World Health Organization recently published a guide to intergenerational programs as part of their campaign to combat ageism. They found that intergenerational contact is one of three key elements needed to succeed in this battle, saying interventions that typically bring together older and younger people in activities that encourage cross-generational bonding and address issues that affect one or both age groups and their wider community can reduce intergroup prejudice and stereotypes. Interventions for intergenerational contact are among the most effective for reducing ageism against older people and also show promise for reducing ageism against younger people.[10]

Intergenerational Programs and Shared Sites

Another type of intergenerational programming is found in intergenerational shared sites. These are settings where children, youth, and older adults participate in services and/or programs concurrently at the same site or on the same campus. Younger and older people interact during regular planned intergenerational activities, as well as through informal encounters. Shared sites also refer to intergenerational spaces, centers, parks, campuses, and more. Research has shown that using facilities and outdoor spaces to connect generations benefits the participants, families, and communities.[11]

Using an age-integrated rather than age-segregated approach, intergenerational shared sites are designed to strengthen the web of support that is so integral to families and communities. In these facilities, people of different ages come together to learn, play, and grow. Shared sites are more than physical places; they are shared spaces that have collective meaning for participants of different ages. Their relational focus differentiates them from multigenerational sites, which are designed primarily to accommodate the needs and abilities of different age groups but not necessarily promote cross-age interaction.[12]

Research shows that intergenerational shared sites increase the health and well-being of both young and older participants, reduce social isolation, and create cost efficiencies. They are joyful places. And unsurprisingly, the concept is a popular one; when asked,

Americans are overwhelmingly in favor of shared sites. A 2018 Harris poll commissioned by Generations United and the Eisner Foundation found that nearly all Americans believe older adults and children have skills and talents to help one another and that 85 percent would prefer a shared site that fosters intergenerational connection over an age-segregated facility if they or a loved one needed care.[13]

While successful shared sites exist in countries around the world—including Japan, the United Kingdom, Canada, Australia, Spain, and Singapore (see *Handbook* chapters 22, 23, 24, 26, 21, and 20)—there are fewer than 150 of them in the United States, compared to the tens of thousands of age-segregated care facilities around the country.

Intergenerational Community Building

Reaching beyond a single site or space, interest is growing in creating and living in intergenerational communities where multiple generations are present and able to engage regularly with one another. Community members, regardless of age or generational grouping, have access to community assets and opportunity for involvement in community activities. An intergenerational community is one that not only meets the needs and interests of multiple age groups but provides space and opportunity for them to engage one another, whether through recreation, education, or community planning and exploration activities.[14]

Previously viewed as a nice thing to do, these community-based solutions are seen as a critical element in the social determinants of health. In his landmark report, "Our Epidemic of Loneliness and Isolation," the U.S. Surgeon General proposed a national strategy to advance social connection.[15] Two of the six pillars are especially germane to intergenerational community solutions.

The first pillar, Strengthen Social Infrastructure, points out that connections are influenced by physical elements in a community such as parks, libraries, and other community spaces. It calls upon communities to design environments that establish and scale community connection programs and invest in bringing people together. A new guide published by the American Planning Association provides a roadmap to do just this.[16]

The other cross-cutting strategy is to cultivate a culture of connection—connection to people and to place that is key to promoting a sense of belonging. This sense of belonging is diminishing, as pointed out in a recent national survey on belonging. The survey found that 68 percent of Americans feel a sense of nonbelonging in the nation, rising to 74 percent feeling a sense of nonbelonging in their local community.[17] A sense of belonging can be cultivated through frequent positive interactions grounded in care and concern.[18] A sense of belonging is ripe for cultivation through intergenerational programs, which often result in cross-age friendships.

Grandfamilies and Multigenerational Households

While intergenerational programing engages unrelated people of different generations, intergenerational families are growing in number and importance. A survey conducted in January 2021 by Harris Poll on behalf of Generations United found that an estimated 26 percent of all Americans are now living in a multigenerational household. The years from 2011 to 2021 saw a dramatic increase (7 percent vs. 26 percent).[19] The organization estimates that 66.7 million adults age 18 and older in the United States are living in a multigenerational household; that's more than one in four Americans. Among those living in a multigenerational household, nearly six in ten (57 percent) say they started or are continuing to live together because of the COVID-19 pandemic. About seven in ten of those currently living in multigenerational households plan to continue doing so long-term, citing benefits in areas such as caregiving and financial well-being.[20] They may have come together because of need, but they stayed together by choice.

Multigenerational households are defined as three or more generations under one roof. "Grandfamilies" (i.e., grandparents and other relatives raising children) generally are skipped-generation households made up of two generations. Grandfamilies are diverse and exist across various geographies, socioeconomic statuses, races, and ethnicities. Yet they are disproportionately Black, African American, American Indian, Alaska Native, and in some areas, Latino.

Grandfamilies are formed when events—such as parental death, mental health and substance use disorders, incarceration, deportation, divorce, or military deployment—separate children from their parents. Children in grandfamilies fare well and thrive when they and their caregivers receive appropriate supports. Compared to children in foster care with nonrelatives, children in grandfamilies have increased stability, higher levels of permanency, and more feelings of belonging and acceptance. They experience greater preservation of cultural identity and community connections, as well as better behavioral and mental health outcomes.[21]

Public Policy through an Intergenerational Lens

Using an intergenerational lens results in stronger, more impactful policies that benefit all generations. For example, the Child Abuse Protection and Treatment Act was signed into law in 1988. It took thirty-six years, until 2010, to extend similar protections to older adults through the Elder Justice Act. If they had used an intergenerational impact lens, policy makers could have addressed abuse in a more comprehensive manner much earlier.

Generations United's policy work is designed to encourage this approach by engaging advocates for children, youth, and older adults as joint partners in improving the lifetime well-being of all people and to improve the lives and well-being of children, youth, older adults, and the families that care for them through effective federal government policies. Generations United and its members recognize that older adults, people with disabilities, and children do not live in silos. They are interdependent. They live in families and communities. Policy changes that eliminate or reduce critical benefits, supports, and services of family members, caregivers, and neighbors negatively impact the children, youth, older adults, and people with disabilities that they live with, support, and care for. Likewise, smart investments in people of one generation reap benefits for those in other generations in the form of a stronger workforce and by ensuring quality of life and well-being. They will make America more competitive and help achieve fiscal sustainability. If thoughtful investments across the life span and the interdependence of generations are ignored, policy-makers risk failure in the form of wasteful spending, increased public divisiveness, and policies injurious to American families and communities.

Generations United believes it is important to address immediate challenges while laying the groundwork for long-term stability. A respectful and ongoing discussion about the changing demographics in the United States and acknowledgement of our racist history and ongoing systemic racism are vital to be effective. As the baby boomer generation ages and new immigrant and racial/ethnic minority populations grow, it is important to ensure that the most vulnerable populations—regardless of their age or background—are supported.

Generations United uses the following principles to guide its policy work and assess the intergenerational impact of legislation:

- Make lifetime well-being for all the highest priority.
- Consider the impact of every action on each generation.
- Unite rather than divide the generations for the greatest social and financial impact.
- Recognize and support each generation's ability to contribute to the well-being of their families and communities.

Corresponding to the principles, a model intergenerational law or policy would also do the following:

- Use innovative or proven approaches to improve lifetime well-being for all generations.
- Include an assessment of both short- and long-term impacts on each generation and demonstrate benefits for multiple ages.
- Actively promote innovative and proven strategies to unite two or more generations.
- Actively promote innovative and proven strategies to support and engage every generation's ability to contribute to the well-being of their families and communities.
- Promote the interdependence of the generations.
- Encourage intergenerational transfers through shared care or services.
- Be sensitive to intergenerational family structures (e.g., grandparents who are raising grandchildren).
- Promote racial equity and culturally appropriate services by proactively examining their racial and cultural implications.

Emerging Issues

Demographic changes, housing costs, failing immigration policies, an epidemic of social isolation and loneliness, and intensifying concern about the environment and global warming are only a few of the serious issues facing the United States and other countries. The issues are complex and require intergenerational solutions that understand young and old are experiencing the same problems or will experience the same problems as time goes by. The solutions are multifactoral, multisectoral, and multigenerational. Economies of scope illustrate that rather than address issues for a single age group, intentionally creating solutions for all generations is more efficient and wide-reaching, producing longer-lasting, impactful results. The sections below discuss several emerging issues.

Changing Demographics Are a Reality

The trajectory long projected in population studies cannot be stopped. In 2013, Generations United cited statistics (such as one in five US residents will be age sixty-five or older in 2043, and by 2042, more than half of the nation will be people of color) that together pointed to a growing racial generation gap. Today, more than half of Americans under the age of five are people of color, compared to fewer than one in five Americans over sixty-five.[22]

Demographic studies continued to highlight the changes. In 2020, the diversity index of the total population was 61.1 percent, meaning that there was a 61.1 percent chance that two people chosen at random were from different racial or ethnic groups. In 2010, there was a 54.9 percent chance. This indicates how much the diversity of the US population increased in just one decade.[23]

Among all age groups at the national level, the chance that two people chosen at random were from different racial or ethnic groups was highest for those under five years old, at 69.0 percent, and lowest for those eighty-five to ninety-nine years old, at 36.9 percent.[24] In the United States, the White, non-Hispanic population was the largest racial or ethnic group for every age category. Its share of the population varied from 47.0 percent for the under-five age group to 78.5 percent for those eighty-five to ninety-nine years of age.[25]

According to the Pew Research Center's 2019 estimates, the most common age for White non-Hispanics in the United States was fifty-eight years, while it was eleven years for Hispanics, twenty-seven years for Blacks, and twenty-nine years for Asians.[26] Our demographic diversity—in age and race—is our country's greatest asset. Yet we are far from realizing the potential power of all-generation solutions because we continue to age-segregate our policies, service delivery systems, community planning, and society. We disparage large segments of our population based solely on age, failing to recognize that all generations are part of the solution and have a stake in decisions made about them.

Solutions, like the one Hal, a retired minister, championed when he founded the Gaithersburg Beloved Initiative, a multifaceted intergenerational program, can be found at the community level. Hal said, "By building the relationships we are dealing with the racial divide. Amazing things have happened. We all hunger for this relationship."[27]

Posttraumatic Pandemic Shock

The COVID pandemic resulted in people isolating, with long-lasting impact on individuals, families, businesses, and community life. Two groups—young and old—were especially affected by the isolation and loneliness the pandemic caused and were slower to recover. Loneliness is often considered a problem of the elderly, but loneliness can affect people of all ages. Studies that have explored the prevalence and frequency of lonely feelings across the life course have found, contrary to popular wisdom, that loneliness is highest in young adults and then declines throughout adulthood until oldest old age, at which time it increases and can surpass the prevalence and frequency seen in young adults.[28] High loneliness levels troubling younger and older adults is a pandemic-related problem that begs for an intergenerational solution.

Opioid Epidemic

While the United States has faced substance abuse crises in the past, none has been as powerful as the current drug epidemic. It hits grandfamilies particularly hard: the children and caregivers are left behind when parents are incarcerated, in and out of treatment programs, or dead. The correlation is clear, between 2002 and 2019, grandparents reporting parents' substance use as a reason for caring for their grandchildren jumped from 21 percent to 40 percent. The states with the highest percentages of grandparents raising grandchildren are also the states with the highest opioid-prescribing rates.[29] Yet as states determine how to use their opioid settlement dollars, grandfamilies are not at the table or considered in the discussions.

Environmental Activism and Climate Change

The first Earth Day, organized more than fifty years ago, was an intergenerational activity with communities celebrating solutions that benefited generations then alive and those to come. Perhaps nothing so well illustrates the degree to which one generation cares about future generations as how much it invests in protecting the environment. Learning about and cherishing a healthy environment is taught, not passed on genetically. Elders always have been, and always should be, the keepers of this covenant and have always worked to pass on a commitment to the environment. Intergenerational environmental programs are a valuable mechanism for fulfilling this role.[30] Protecting the earth and its resources is an intergenerational undertaking. Using resources to connect generations is a better, greener use of resources. Multigenerational households have a lower environmental impact footprint. These households, including accessory dwelling units, demonstrate lower energy and water use and consumption of fewer building materials.

Climate change, one of the most pressing societal issues of our time, presents both opportunities and challenges for intergenerational relations and solidarity. In terms of challenges, climate change could lead to intergenerational tension whereby younger generations blame older generations or hold them responsible for the current state of the climate as well as for previous inaction to address the issue.[31] Ayalon and colleagues have advocated for an intergenerational approach to addressing climate change.[32] They argue that it presents a common and pressing problem that could benefit from older and younger generations working together to address it. This is an area where volunteering can intersect with intergenerational relations. Increasingly opportunities are available for older adults to engage in climate change–related volunteerism. However, little work has been done on a widespread scale to create climate change–related volunteering opportunities that include an intergenerational component.[33]

Conclusion

Early intergenerational approaches were considered nice but not necessary. While it was sweet to connect generations so that one age group benefited, it took years of practice and research to demonstrate the validity of using intergenerational solutions to address society's most pressing issues. In a world increasingly jaded and divided, efforts to shore up and strengthen connections between generations are imperative. The human capital asset of young and old can and should be engaged to strengthen communities and countries now and in the future.

Notes

1. Rosalynn Carter Institute for Caregivers, https://rosalynncarter.org/.
2. "Generations United Annual Report 1997–2000," Generations United, accessed December 2023, https://www.gu.org/app/uploads/2018/05/AnnualReport-1997-2000.pdf, 3–35.
3. "Global Intergenerational Week," Generations Working Together, accessed December 2023, https://generationsworkingtogether.org/global-intergenerational-week.
4. "Announcing the 2022 Intergenerational Program Certification Designees," Generations United, accessed December 2023, https://www.gu.org/news/announcing-the-2022-intergenerational-program-certification-designees/.
5. "Intergenerational Program Database," Generations United, accessed December 2023, https://www.gu.org/home/ig-program-database/.
6. "Intergenerational Program Certification," Generations United, accessed December 2023, https://www.gu.org/projects/program-certification/.
7. Generations United and The Eisner Foundation, "All In Together: Creating Places Where Young and Old Thrive," 2018, https://www.gu.org/app/uploads/2018/06/SignatureReport-Eisner-All-In-Together.pdf.
8. Nancy Z. Henkin and Donna M. Butts, "Intergenerational Practice in the United States: Past, Present and Future," *Quality in Ageing and Older Adults* 13, no. 4 (2012): 249–56, https://doi.org/10.1108/14717791211286913.
9. Generations United, "Intergenerational Program Database."
10. Sagal Adam and Alana Officer, "Connecting Generations: Planning and Implementing Interventions for Intergenerational Contact," World Health Organization, October 10, 2023, https://www.who.int/publications/i/item/9789240070264.
11. "Sharing Our Space: A Toolkit for Developing and Enhancing Intergenerational Shared Sites," Sharing Our Space, Generations United, http://www.sharingourspace.org/.
12. Generations United, "Sharing Our Space."
13. Generations United and The Eisner Foundation, "All In Together: Creating Places Where Young and Old Thrive," 2018, 3. https://www.gu.org/app/uploads/2018/06/SignatureReport-Eisner-All-In-Together.pdf.
14. Matthew Kaplan, Mariano Sanchez, and Jaco Hoffman, *Intergenerational Pathways to a Sustainable Society* (New York: Springer, 2017).
15. Office of the Surgeon General, "New Surgeon General Advisory Raises Alarm about Devasting Impact of Loneliness and Isolation in the United States," U.S. Department of Health and Human Services, May 3,

2023, https://www.hhs.gov/about/news/2023/05/03/new-surgeon-general-advisory-raises-alarm-about-devastating-impact-epidemic-loneliness-isolation-united-states.html.
16. Irv Katz and Matthew S. Kaplan, "Intergenerational Community Planning," *American Planning Association*, 2023. https://www.gu.org/resources/intergenerational-community-planning/.
17. Nichole Argo and Hammad Sheikh, "The Belonging Barometer: The State of Belonging in America," American Immigration Council and Over Zero, May 2023, https://www.americanimmigrationcouncil.org/research/the-belonging-barometer.
18. Theodore R. Johnson, "Why So Many Americans Feel Left Out," *Washington Post*, March 21, 2023. https://www.washingtonpost.com/opinions/2023/03/21/why-americans-feel-left-out/.
19. Generations United, "Family Matters: Multi-generational Living Is on the Rise and Here to Stay," 2021, https://www.gu.org/app/uploads/2021/04/21-MG-Family-Report-WEB.pdf.
20. Generations United, "Family Matters."
21. Generations United, "Building Resilience: Supporting Grandfamilies' Mental Health and Wellness," *2023* State of Grandfamilies Overview, November 2023, https://www.gu.org/app/uploads/2023/11/GU_2023-Grandfamilies-ExecutiveSummary-Final-Interactive.pdf, 1.
22. Generations United and The Generations Initiative, "Out of Many, One: Uniting the Changing Faces of America," 2013, https://www.gu.org/app/uploads/2018/05/SignatureReport-Out-of-Many-One.pdf, 4.
23. Megan Robe and Eric Jensen, "Exploring the Racial and Ethnic Diversity of Various Age Groups," U.S. Census Bureau, September 6, 2023, https://www.census.gov/newsroom/blogs/random-samplings/2023/09/exploring-diversity.html.
24. Robe and Jensen, "Various Age Groups."
25. Robe and Jensen, "Various Age Groups."
26. Katherine Schaeffer, "The Most Common Age among Whites in U.S. is 58—More than Double that of Racial and Ethnic Minorities," Pew Research Center, July 30, 2019, https://www.pewresearch.org/short-reads/2019/07/30/most-common-age-among-us-racial-ethnic-groups/.
27. Donna Butts and Kristin Bodiford, "Family and Intergenerational Relationships," in *Social Isolation of Older Adults: Strategies to Bolster Health and Well-Being*, ed. Lenard W. Kaye and Clifford M. Singer (New York: Springer, 2019), 197–217.
28. Louise C. Hawkley et al., "Loneliness from Young Adulthood to Old Age: Explaining Age Differences in Loneliness," *International Journal of Behavioral Development* 46, no. 1 (2020): 39–49. https://www.ncbi.nlm.nih.gov/pmc/articles/PMC8734589/.
29. Generations United, "Building Resilience," 9.
30. Sheri Y. Steinig and Donna Butts, "Generations Going Green: Intergenerational Programs Connecting Young and Old to Improve Our Environment," *Generations* 33, no. 4 (2009): 64–69.
31. Sanjooti Roy and Liat Ayalon, "Intergenerational Relations in the Climate Movement: Bridging the Gap toward a Common Goal," *International Journal of Environmental Research and Public Health* 20, no. 1 (2022): 233. https://doi.org/10.3390/ijerph20010233.
32. Roy and Ayalon, "Intergenerational Relations."
33. Liat Ayalon and Senjooti Roy, "The Perceived Contribution of Older People to Climate Change Impact, Mitigation, and Adaptation: Measurement Development and Validation," *Innovation in Aging* 7, no. 8 (2023). https://doi.org/10.1093/geroni/igad095.

Bibliography

Adam, Sagal, and Alana Officer. "Connecting Generations: Planning and Implementing Interventions for Intergenerational Contact." World Health Organization. October 10, 2023. https://www.who.int/publications/i/item/9789240070264.

Argo, Nichole, and Hammad Sheikh. "The Belonging Barometer: The State of Belonging in America." American Immigration Council and Over Zero. June 24, 2024. https://www.americanimmigrationcouncil.org/research/the-belonging-barometer.

Ayalon, Liat, and Senjooti Roy. "The Perceived Contribution of Older People to Climate Change Impact, Mitigation, and Adaptation: Measurement Development and Validation." *Innovation in Aging* 7, no. 8 (2023): igad095. https://doi.org/10.1093/geroni/igad095.

Butts, Donna M., and Kristin Bodiford. "Family and Intergenerational Relationships." In *Social Isolation of Older Adults: Strategies to Bolster Health and Well-Being*, edited by Lenard W. Kaye and Clifford M. Singer, 197–217. New York: Springer, 2019.

Generations United and The Eisner Foundation. "All In Together: Creating Places Where Young and Old Thrive." 2018. https://www.gu.org/app/uploads/2018/06/SignatureReport-Eisner-All-In-Together.pdf. https://www.gu.org/resources/all-in-together-creating-places-where-young-and-old-thrive/.

Generations United and The Generations Initiative. "Out of Many, One: Uniting the Changing Faces of America." 2013. https://www.gu.org/app/uploads/2018/05/SignatureReport-Out-of-Many-One.pdf, 4.

Generations United. "Generation United Annual Report 1997–2000." https://www.gu.org/app/uploads/2018/05/AnnualReport-1997-2000.pdf.

Generations United. "Announcing the 2022 Intergenerational Program Certification Designees." https://www.gu.org/news/announcing-the-2022-intergenerational-program-certification-designees.

Generations United. "Building Resilience: Supporting Grandfamilies' Mental Health and Wellness. 2023 State of Grandfamilies Report." November 8, 2023. https://www.gu.org/resources/building-resilience-grandfamilies-mental-health-and-wellness/.

Generations United. "Family Matters: Multi-generational Living Is on the Rise and Here to Stay," 2021. https://www.gu.org/app/uploads/2021/04/21-MG-Family-Report-WEB.pdf.

Generations United. "Intergenerational Program Certification." https://www.gu.org/projects/program-certification/.

Generations United. "Intergenerational Program Database." https://www.gu.org/home/ig-program-database/.

Generations United. "Programs of Distinction." 2023. https://www.gu.org/projects/program-certification/.

Generations United. "A Toolkit for Developing and Enhancing Intergenerational Shared Sites." Sharing Our Space. February 17, 2022. http://www.sharingourspace.org/.

Generations Working Together. "Intergenerational Week." https://generationsworkingtogether.org/global-intergenerational-week.

Hawkley, Louise C., S. Buecker, T. Kaiser, and M. Luhmann. "Loneliness from Young Adulthood to Old Age: Explaining Age Differences in Loneliness." *International Journal of Behavioral Development* 46, no. 1 (2020): 39–49. https://doi.org/10.1177/0165025420971048.

Henkin, Nancy Z., and Donna M. Butts. "Intergenerational Practice in the United States: Past, Present and Future." *Quality in Ageing and Older Adults* 13, no. 4 (2012): 249–56. https://doi.org/10.1108/14717791211286913.

Johnson, Theodore R. "Opinion | Why so Many Americans Feel Left Out." *Washington Post*, March 21, 2023. https://www.washingtonpost.com/opinions/2023/03/21/why-americans-feel-left-out/.

Kaplan, Matthew, Mariano Sanchez, and Jaco Hoffman. *Intergenerational Pathways to a Sustainable Society*. 1st ed. New York: Springer, 2017.

Katz, Irv, and Matthew S. Kaplan. "Intergenerational Community Planning." Generations United. 2023. https://www.gu.org/resources/intergenerational-community-planning/.

Office of the Assistant Secretary for Health (OASH). "New Surgeon General Advisory Raises Alarm about the Devastating Impact of the Epidemic of Loneliness and Isolation in the United States." U.S. Department of Health and Human Services. May 3, 2023. https://www.hhs.gov/about/news/2023/05/03/new-surgeon-general-advisory-raises-alarm-about-devastating-impact-epidemic-loneliness-isolation-united-states.html.

Robe, Megan, and Eric Jensen. "Exploring the Racial and Ethnic Diversity of Various Age Groups." U.S. Census Bureau. November 21, 2023. https://www.census.gov/newsroom/blogs/random-samplings/2023/09/exploring-diversity.html.

Rosalynn Carter Institute for Caregivers, https://rosalynncarter.org/.

Roy, Senjooti, and Liat Ayalon. "Intergenerational Relations in the Climate Movement: Bridging the Gap toward a Common Goal." *International Journal of Environmental Research and Public Health* 20, no. 1 (2022): 233. https://doi.org/10.3390/ijerph20010233.

Schaeffer, Katherine. "The Most Common Age among Whites in U.S. Is 58—More than Double That of Racial and Ethnic Minorities." Pew Research Center. July 30, 2019. https://www.pewresearch.org/short-reads/2019/07/30/most-common-age-among-us-racial-ethnic-groups.

Steinig, Sheri Y., and Donna M. Butts. "Generations Going Green: Intergenerational Programs Connecting Young and Old to Improve Our Environment." *Generations* 33, no. 4 (2009): 64–69.

CHAPTER 3

Intergenerational Solutions (Not Single-Issue Solutions) to Society's Challenges

Trent Stamp *and* Chelsea Mason

Abstract

This chapter explores six seemingly intractable challenges facing our society: health and wellness, education, housing, the workplace, civic engagement, and social cohesion. These challenges have not lacked for proposed or attempted solutions; however, they persist as these solutions have not taken a wider lens. The authors instead propose an intergenerational approach that engages the skills and knowledge of several generations, in joint efforts where all parties are equally valued, to solve problems while building connections and creating stronger communities. In each section, they provide concrete and replicable examples of how intergenerational solutions are working to combat these challenges while also addressing ageism and generational stereotypes.

Key Words: intergenerational solutions, social cohesion, civic engagement, ageism, generational stereotypes

Introduction

The problems that plague society are big, messy, and complicated. But one of the reasons we struggle is that we try to address complicated problems with simple solutions. Faced with child hunger, we as Americans are compassionate and focus on providing food to children; but we don't connect that work to increasing the minimum wage, even though the vast majority of food-insecure children in the United States have working parents.[1] We try to find shelters for our growing homeless population but avoid embracing foster-care reform, despite the knowledge that half of Americans experiencing homelessness spent time in the foster-care system.[2] We create initiatives to alleviate the climate crisis by promoting new forms of recycling and endless beach clean-ups, without building in advocacy for substantive policy changes that stop pollution at its source.

We face massive challenges, and expansive solutions are necessary—solutions that involve *all* of us, regardless of age, because the complicated challenges require the whole of society to contribute to those solutions.

At The Eisner Foundation, we believe that intergenerational programs are a key tool for combatting society's challenges. The Eisner Foundation supports intergenerational programs in Los Angeles County and New York City. We have operated under this mission since 2015, when we shifted from funding youth and older adult programs separately to funding programs that bring the two together. Today, we are the only U.S.-based foundation exclusively focused on intergenerational programs, though we have been happy to see other foundations add it as a focus area in recent years.

We made the switch because we saw how efficient and effective it was to engage different generations in combatting multiple challenges at once. For example, when an older adult tutors a child, not only does the child receive the needed support, but the older adult benefits from the increased well-being that comes with volunteering and engagement. And then the community as a whole benefits from more productive and supported children, older adults who are valued and involved, and greater social cohesion between two groups we were led to believe should be at odds.

As foundation executives, we recognize that some of our limitations in efficacy stem from our industry's structural challenges. Foundations can only fund initiatives that have nonprofit partners capable of enacting them. And, when it comes to measuring impact, it's far easier to focus on outputs (such as the number of bags of garbage collected from a polluted lake) than on system change (such as a law that would prohibit corporations from dumping garbage in the water supply in the first place).

Some of the reliance on simple solutions in the face of complicated issues is a by-product of how foundations are set up in the first place. They are segmented not only based on geography and mission, but also by whom they seek to serve. When foundations explain what they do, the answer is usually "We fund women's issues" or "We're focused on scholarships for at-risk kids." Seldom is the response "We look for creative and expansive ways to make the world a better place." Confining our work to silos in the name of expediency and consistency limits our efficacy. Silos are good at doing simple things. But they do nothing for the big, the messy, and the complicated.

Philanthropy is not the only culprit here. Policy leaders, corporate CEOs, so-called influencers, and even nonprofit advocates can join the lineup. Our entire society is designed to silo programs, funding, and expertise. "Stay in your lane" results in a myopic view of the challenges our society faces as well as the solutions subsequently available to us.

But it doesn't have to be this way. We know from nearly a decade of experience working intersectionally, and specifically by embracing and endorsing intergenerational solutions to society's most difficult challenges, that these approaches are more comprehensive and transformational. By looking systemically and leveraging all available resources, including the skills and talents of everyday people of all ages, we can more effectively solve the major challenges facing us today.

Challenges and Opportunities
What are the factors at play here?

1. Our society is aging, and there are associated social challenges. The number of older adults in our country is growing, and those over age sixty now outnumber those under age eighteen.[3] We, as a society, have a choice: we can either see these older adults as "finished" or we can leverage their decades of personal and professional experience to strengthen our communities and society at large. There's also an economic angle: while social isolation is estimated to cost Medicare more than $6.7 billion each year, older adults who feel connected to their communities report concrete improvements in their mental and physical health.[4] Not only do we have a moral obligation to engage older adults as full participants in society, but we have a fiscal obligation as well.
2. Young people still need our help too. Seventeen percent of U.S. children live in poverty, and millions more are just barely above the poverty line.[5] Children and youth in the U.S. are subject to a range of structural barriers to success, many of which are linked to poverty, including residential segregation, poor-quality schools, inadequate transportation, worse health outcomes, greater exposure to neighborhood crime and violence, and more adverse childhood events. Nonprofits, particularly those using community-based solutions, are working to find solutions to these challenges, but without broad societal engagement, it's hard to make systemic change.
3. Bringing older and younger people together to help each other makes sense, and they can work toward solving additional social problems together, too. Older adults are particularly well suited to working with youth. Volunteer managers regularly report that they tend to be more patient and connect with children better than younger adults. They tend to be more reliable and stay longer with an organization. And, crucially, they tend to have the time and experience to do this work effectively.[6]

Children with a caring adult in their lives, regardless of relation, perform better in school and have fewer behavioral problems—increasing their lifetime income and reducing their dependence on the social safety net and their involvement with the criminal justice system.[7] In addition, caring older adults get firsthand experience of the structural barriers facing the children with whom they work.

Younger participants have improved self-esteem and academic performance, enhanced social skills, and positive attitudes toward themselves and older adults. Older adults show improvements in their own self-esteem, cognitive function, and productivity; have greater satisfaction with life; and have improved outcomes in their mental and physical health.

Intergenerational programs break down ageism in both directions, strengthen our communities, and can also combat specific challenges in the process. A 2019 Cornell study found that educational efforts combined with intergenerational interactions significantly reduced ageist attitudes while also increasing younger participants' comfort with older people and ideas about growing old themselves—and even increased interest in careers in geriatrics and gerontology.[8] In addition to reducing ageism, intergenerational interactions also contribute to increased social cohesion, which has been shown to reduce depression and anxiety in young people and older people alike.[9]

Intergenerational programs are relatively low-cost and easily incorporated into the work of most organizations endeavoring to solve social problems, resulting in a high return on investment when done properly. In this chapter, our goal is to show six seemingly intractable challenges facing our society and provide concrete and replicable examples of how intergenerational solutions are working to combat those challenges. The areas to which we refer are health and wellness, education, housing, the workplace, civic engagement, and social cohesion.

Health and Wellness

The first area challenging our society that benefits from intergenerational interventions is health and wellness. The state of mental health in the United States is alarming, with major implications for physical health and the viability of the social safety net. The two loneliest groups of people in America are teenagers, usually girls, and seniors, often men.[10] This is a crisis that affects many aspects of our society, not to mention these two vulnerable groups who desperately need our help.

But older adults who have a sense of purpose are healthier and happier and less lonely. Older adults who are active in their communities report higher levels of well-being: 93 percent report an improvement in mood, 79 percent report lowered stress levels, 75 percent report feeling physically healthier, and 34 percent report better management of chronic conditions.[11] Intergenerational programs and shared sites give older adults the opportunity to mentor, tutor, or simply engage with younger people, and they realize concrete health benefits as a result. As a 2002 study demonstrated, intergenerational engagement and play have cognitive benefits and contribute to improved social skills and well-being.[12] With expanded opportunities for old and young to engage with and learn from each other, they increase their feelings of community connection and reap the mental and physical benefits that come with it.

A prominent example of intergenerational programming in this arena is ONEgeneration, an intergenerational shared site with both an adult day center and a child care facility on campus. While each group has independent programming, they come together throughout the day for structured activities like crafts, games, and meals. At the nearby senior center, high schoolers provide older adults with tech tutoring and become informal mentees. This creates an empowering, joyful atmosphere that transforms the older adults from recipients of care to providers of care. Meanwhile, the children and youth become more empathetic and more comfortable with older adults and those with disabilities for years to come.[13]

A different kind of intergenerational health intervention is the New York University (NYU) Langone Alzheimer's Disease & Related Dementias Family Support Buddy Program. This partnership with the NYU School of Social Work is a course and service-learning opportunity that matches a person with early-stage Alzheimer's and related dementias (the "mentor") with an undergraduate (the "buddy"). The program provides respite time for caregivers, but instead of simply putting older adults in a room until their caregivers return, the adults are in a stimulating environment with young people trained to interact with them. They are no longer passive recipients of services, but active participants. Meanwhile, students get training and experience in gerontological theory and practice, creating a pipeline to a sector desperately in need of more professionals.[14]

Intergenerational health interventions can be quite simple. "Friendly calling" programs are relatively easy to implement, and many of The Eisner Foundation's grantee partners established or dramatically scaled up such efforts during the COVID-19 pandemic. These programs generally serve older adults at risk of loneliness and social isolation, but as many of our partners found, some call recipients were younger as well. With volunteer callers ranging widely in age, sustained intergenerational connections have an impact on the mental health and well-being of volunteers and recipients alike. In fact, one study showed that recipients of friendly calls were more likely to visit a primary care provider or subspecialist, suggesting a greater motivation to care for their own health.[15]

There are many creative ways to bring old and young together in ways that have positive, long-term effects on health and wellness. Initiatives of this kind also help to change the attitudes of those in their formative years toward older adults, fostering a sense of appreciation rather than indifference or even animosity in a political and media environment that thrives on generational warfare. As a result, people of all ages can feel more connected to those of different ages and reap the mental health benefits that result.

Education
One of society's largest challenges is education, particularly our ability to provide kids with the skills they need to be prepared for an evolving economy in a fast-changing society. Despite decades of political rhetoric, our public schools remain underfunded, and learning outcomes remain low for many in underresourced areas.[16] But this is an area where we have empirical evidence that intergenerational solutions can provide access and opportunity for those being left behind. We know that older adults, often retired and underutilized, can serve as resources for student success. Tutoring and mentorship programs augment what students learn in the classroom and give students consistent interaction with a caring adult.[17]

Incorporating older adults into school programs as volunteer tutors, mentors, and aides to the teachers is the most common type of intergenerational intervention, and it's common for a reason—it's relatively easy to start and maintain, and older adults make particularly good volunteers. The children get consistent one-on-one or small-group attention from a caring adult, and the adult gains the mental and physical benefits we've already discussed.[18] Another benefit of incorporating older adults into underresourced schools is that often the older adults acquire a fresh perspective on our education system. And when more community members understand the structural challenges students, teachers, and schools face, they're better equipped to help fix them, whether in a hands-on way or by their choices at the ballot box.

An example of an intergenerational intervention creating multiple positive outcomes for all is Generation Xchange, a program that places older adults in Los Angeles public schools. The older volunteers are matched with a single teacher for a full school year and commit to being in the classroom at least fifteen hours a week. There, they assist the students with their work, do one-on-one interventions as needed, and help deal with behavioral problems. Volunteers are trained and have weekly group meetings where they discuss successes and challenges. Many of these volunteers stay with a teacher for several years and become part of the school community. And because these volunteers are recruited from the neighborhoods where the students live, they feel a deeper connection to the wider community as well.

The health implications of volunteering with Generation Xchange are impressive for the older adults. This program was started by Dr. Teresa Seeman in UCLA's gerontology department, and that affiliation enabled her to collect medical data to compare health markers before and throughout the volunteers' involvement. Dr. Seeman found significant improvements in cholesterol levels, mobility, and immune response in the older participants after only three months of volunteer work and further improvement after nine months, demonstrating that intergenerational programs can improve not only mental well-being but physical health as well.[19]

While most education-focused intergenerational programs are based on older adults working with younger students, there is a growing number of examples based in higher education and lifelong learning. Several universities have developed programs specifically for older adults that allow them to learn side by side with students of traditional college age. Some of these even include residential options. Institutions including Harvard University, Stanford University, and the University of Notre Dame have developed curricula specifically for cohorts of older adults that give them the opportunity to participate in certain undergraduate and graduate courses. Right now, many of these programs can be expensive and require participants to live close to campus, so they're not accessible to everyone. However, some programs, like that at the University of Oregon, offer adults aged sixty-five and older the opportunity to audit certain university courses at no charge,[20] and community colleges across the country have long served students of all ages, creating opportunities for age-integrated classrooms at a lower cost to older participants who bring their wisdom and experience to the table.

Another model in higher education centers on senior living communities. Some colleges and universities partner with nearby communities to facilitate two-way engagement between the student body and older residents. Some bring students interested in gerontology into the senior living centers to meaningfully engage or even work there, while others allow older residents to enroll in courses on campus. These efforts burst the age-segregated bubble that both university campuses and senior living communities tend to create and make both groups feel part of a wider community. (See *Handbook* chapter 17 for Central Connecticut State University's program.)

A prominent example of lifelong learning is Lasell Village, located on the campus of Lasell University in Newton, Massachusetts. (See *Handbook* chapter 6 for a full description of Lasell University's program.) This was the nation's first senior living community to require each resident to commit to a goal-oriented program of education. Residents commit yearly to a 450-hour minimum of learning and fitness activities, and virtually all who live there exceed this minimum requirement. Residents can attend classes alongside undergraduate students, serve as mentors to students, participate in community service and other volunteer activities, and more.[21] As a result, older and younger people, who live in settings that are usually highly age-segregated, have the opportunity to build relationships and learn from each other while enjoying the benefits to their health and well-being (as discussed in the previous section).

From improving student outcomes to increasing the mental and physical health of all involved, education-focused intergenerational programs offer unique opportunities to bring together groups of people who typically don't interact, thereby creating healthier, more connected communities.

Housing

Another challenge ripe for intergenerational solutions is housing. As housing costs skyrocket nationwide, young people and older people are particularly affected. A generation of young people faces the very real challenge of not being able to embrace the American dream of homeownership, and for those without adequate means, rising rents increase the potential for homelessness, reduce economic development, and decrease overall wealth building among low-income and historically marginalized groups. For older adults on fixed incomes, rising rents, property taxes, and the cost of upkeep can destabilize housing security as well. And yet, housing is another area where intergenerational solutions can provide some relief and expand opportunity. Intergenerational housing programs allow older adults to age in place in the community and create more affordable housing options.

One intergenerational housing solution is that of home-sharing programs like Nesterly or the Center for Health and Aging Innovation at New York University (see *Handbook* chapter 15), where older adults share parts of their homes with younger community members. Particularly in expensive cities where young people have trouble finding affordable places to live and empty nesters have extra space, it's mutually beneficial when a younger person can enjoy cheaper rent in exchange for helping around the house. As a result, older adults feel comfortable staying in their homes longer.[22] This is a common-sense arrangement in a society where more than twenty-one million adults aged sixty-five and older live alone, and almost half of them spend 30 percent or more of their income on housing—a key indicator of vulnerability to housing displacement.[23] Today, as older adults are the fastest-growing demographic in the unhoused population,[24] it is essential that we promote solutions like intergenerational living arrangements to keep older adults safely housed.

Opportunities are not limited to existing homes; creative efforts exist in development as well. These require intentional design and a commitment to ongoing community building, but there are many residential models that show great promise. One prominent example is Eisner Prize–winner Bridge Meadows, based in Oregon (see *Handbook* chapter 1.) This is a group of multigenerational housing communities offering affordable apartments to older adults as well as foster youth and their families. Their goal is to help children heal from the trauma of foster care by providing stable and affordable housing for adoptive families, therapeutic programs, and intergenerational community support. Elders are an important element in the community, serving as mentors, friends, and caregivers to the children and one another, forming a safety net of care and interdependence. There are constant opportunities for intergenerational engagement, whether in various indoor and outdoor community spaces or regular community-wide programming. Residents are expected to be active participants in those offerings. As a result, the older adults demonstrate an increased sense of community and purpose and score higher on emotional well-being and flourishing scales than their peers. Meanwhile, youth resilience increases, as they feel a strong sense of connection to their community and access healthcare at higher rates than other children in the foster care system.[25]

We're also seeing a rise in families living in multigenerational households. According to a 2021 study by Generations United, one in four Americans lives in a household with three or more generations—a 271 percent increase since 2011. Reported benefits of these arrangements include deeper relationships among family members, ease of caretaking, reduced pressure on household finances, improved physical and mental health, and increased opportunity for career advancement due to improved access to education or job training.[26]

The advantages of intergenerational housing demonstrate how a major social challenge can be addressed in a manner that has exponentially positive implications for all involved. While older and younger people get relief from increasing housing pressures, they also enjoy the benefits of long-term intergenerational interaction, making them happier and healthier, and thus increasing the community's vitality and cohesion.

The Workplace

With the rise of remote work and a new labor force that prefers a different work-life balance than their older peers do, it is clear that many business experts are interested in the implications of changes to the workplace environment. We believe that this is another arena where a commitment to intergenerational solutions can create positive outcomes for all involved, including America's businesses. There are now five generations in the workforce, and without mutual respect and understanding, they cannot effectively work together. In addition, with increasing longevity, older adults who retire in their sixties likely have decades left to give. Our society has not yet learned how to effectively leverage their wisdom and talents on a broader scale.

In many larger organizations, it's not uncommon for coworkers of multiple generations to have vastly different experiences and perspectives. How do we make sure that their interactions are meaningful and that each generation values the others' contributions? Mentorship in the workforce (traditionally an older person mentoring a younger person but also the reverse) ensures that valuable expertise gets passed along. When multiple generations are working side by side, they can and should learn from each other. Some organizations intentionally pursue multigenerational teams. A 2020 AARP survey found that 83 percent of global business leaders recognize that multigenerational workforces are key to the growth and long-term success of their companies, and 68 percent would purposefully design mixed-aged teams to leverage the advantages that both younger and older employees bring to the table.[27]

But this doesn't happen without an understanding of what each generation expects and responds to in the workplace. At the risk of over-generalizing, there are some notable trends that employers and leaders should be aware of as they build and manage their staff and, more crucially, transition leadership to the next generation. Younger workers are more likely to change jobs frequently, be interested in participatory leadership, and prioritize work-life balance. As employers nurture the next generation of leaders, they need to adapt their approach to those realities.[28]

Intergenerational efforts can also reframe beliefs about aging and retirement. When someone hits age sixty-five, why should all their knowledge and experience be lost to the organization? They can certainly work past that age if they choose, and if not, there should be other ways for their experience to continue benefitting others. After older adults retire from full-time jobs, many still have much to give. Fellowship programs, for instance, offer the opportunity for them to share their expertise with nonprofits while working reduced schedules.

An excellent example of this type of intergenerational workplace development is the Encore Fellows program, which matches retired professionals with nonprofits that can draw on their expertise. Often, people who retire still want to use their skills, but not in a full-time capacity. Fellows work about twenty hours a week and are paid a salary that is partially subsidized by the program. In many cases, fellows did not work in the nonprofit sector in their previous careers, so the learning goes both ways: nonprofits get new ideas on how to approach marketing or finance, while the fellow learns more about the sector and the focal areas of the organization. They can also mentor younger staff and find new connections in their community.

As a new generation advances in the workforce and older generations continue to work longer, we would be remiss as a society to not take full advantage of opportunities presented by a multigenerational, collaborative workforce.

Civic Engagement

Civic life has changed drastically in the past few decades as opportunities for community engagement have waned. Religious affiliation and service attendance are trending downward,[29] and participation in social and service organizations is also declining.[30] Meanwhile, serious challenges facing our society and world are growing, but so are openings for intergenerational connection and collective action. For example, climate change activism has historically been seen as a young person's endeavor, not least because the impact of climate change will be greatest on them and on future generations. Public opinion studies show that this issue is very important to young people,[31] but older people are also concerned. Some come to this work knowing their generation contributed to the crisis, while others want to ensure a healthy, stable future for young people. (See also *Handbook* chapter 14.)

The best-known example here is the work of Bill McKibben, a longtime climate activist, who founded ThirdAct in 2021 to encourage adults over age sixty to leverage their expertise, political power, and resources to advocate for climate solutions. Current campaigns include pushing banks to stop financing climate destruction, fighting voter suppression laws, and supporting grassroots, volunteer-led working groups organized by affinity or by geographic location. In 2008, while in his forties, McKibben had founded 350.org with seven college students to advocate for a clean energy future. McKibben has always worked alongside young people as a climate activist, but his more recent decision to engage older adults reflects how important it is for all ages to work together to find climate solutions.[32]

Civic connection and community building can also come from bringing together intergenerational affinity groups. Organizations like the Southeast Asian Community Alliance (SEACA) in Los Angeles have connected immigrant elders with Southeast-Asian American youth to help each other and advocate for their community's needs. This group has rallied support for affordable housing, COVID vaccination access, and voting access, among many other initiatives.

Similarly, organizations that serve and advocate for the LGBTQIA+ community are responding with intergenerational alliances to the political and physical attacks they increasingly face. In many ways, history is repeating itself, but while the experience of being discriminated against is not new to older generations within the community, it's novel to many younger queer people, especially in areas that have historically been more hospitable to queer identities. Organizations like Little Brothers/Friends of the Elderly (LBFE) in Boston are creating intergenerational mentorship programs where older people in the LGBTQIA+ community can share their experiences and perspectives with younger people who are facing levels of discrimination they did not grow up with (see *Handbook* chapter 16). Through these connections, they can learn from and reassure each other and also build collective power to push back on discriminatory attitudes and legislation.

Intergenerational collective action is already counteracting decline in the types of civic engagement that were common decades ago. This can help lay the foundation for increased social cohesion, which we will discuss in the final section of this chapter.

Social Cohesion

The final area for review is social cohesion, or sadly, the lack thereof. We don't have to look hard to see how American society is fracturing. Increased polarization and an us-versus-them mentality are making it harder for us to pull together for the good of our whole society. Increased levels of violence increase distrust. And research shows that severe polarization correlates with democratic decline.[33] The worsening state of mental health, particularly among adolescents, is also challenging our ability to create a stable foundation for future generations.[34]

Intergenerational programs help change the way our society thinks about older adults. Recall the beginning of the pandemic when the media described people over age sixty as vulnerable and frail and needing to be confined at home. This reinforced the image of older adults as "finished" instead of as people with a lifetime of experience who have much to give.

Research shows that intergenerational programs reduce ageism and the associated attitudes that contribute to generational polarization.[35] We also know that social connections make us happier. The decades-long Harvard Study of Adult Development has proven that social connection with friends and family is a significant factor in overall happiness.[36] Furthermore, volunteering and a sense of connection and purpose benefit people between the ages of forty-five and eighty the most.[37]

In addition, as mentioned earlier, it has been shown that children with a caring adult in their lives are more likely to become successful contributors to society. Unfortunately, schools and education-focused nonprofits are fighting structural challenges that disadvantage many children. We at The Eisner Foundation hear time and time again from older volunteers that engaging in public schools or in the child welfare system opens their eyes to the obstacles facing children and their families in our society and that by getting to know young people who struggle, they also become hopeful about change for the better.[38]

A relevant example is Sages & Seekers, which matches high schoolers and older adults in an eight-week program specifically designed to combat social isolation and ageism for all participants. Participants actively discuss stereotypes that the generations have about each other. One-on-one connections develop over the course of the program. Younger people learn about their sage's life story and how they're still active in their community, while the older adults learn from their seekers how they see the world and want to make it better. By the end, they've built a relationship that in many cases lasts beyond the program.

Repeated and sustained interactions are the key. In a survey of intergenerational programs, one group of researchers found that programs with weekly or biweekly sessions were far more effective than one-off or occasional interactions, as measured by a range of evaluation tools.[39] To maximize the social cohesion that results from intergenerational programs, participants must be given the opportunity to form real bonds. So much of social trust is built on mutual understanding, and intergenerational programs facilitate that understanding. Whether it's simply exposure to the perspective of someone from a different generation or experiencing systemic challenges in new ways, intergenerational programs can help us understand one another and break down barriers.

Conclusion

In closing, we share a firm belief that intergenerational solutions, when implemented with clarity, purpose, and intentionality, are a cost-effective and highly transformational tool for addressing seemingly overwhelming challenges in education, housing, the changing workplace, social movements, health and welfare, and our fraying social fabric. Intergenerational solutions aren't a miracle, but they are tried and true and worthy of wider societal expansion.

Our demographic trends aren't going to change any time soon, so we should leverage rather than bemoan them. The proportion of older adults in our society will grow every year and will require increasing levels of social and financial support, but intergenerational programs can reduce that need and improve quality of life, to the benefit of our whole society. It is also a fact that children who thrive at a young age are better equipped to be successful adults who contribute to society, with less reliance on social programs. And children are more likely to thrive with an adult in their life who cares about them, even if that adult is much older, and even if that adult is not related to them.

Leveraging these two groups to help each other is an efficient, effective way to address social challenges and strengthen our communities. Given the growing number of older adults and the pressing needs of our youth, we have an opportunity and an obligation to connect the two in meaningful ways. Doing so will not only reduce pressure on the social safety net, but make our communities more connected, happier, and healthier. It's not just nice; it's necessary.

Notes

1. William M. Rodgers, "The Impact of a $15 Minimum Wage on Hunger in America," September 1, 2016, https://tcf.org/content/report/the-impact-of-a-15-minimum-wage-on-hunger-in-america.
2. Shalita O'Neale, "Foster Care and Homelessness," Foster Focus, August 2015, https://www.fosterfocusmag.com/articles/foster-care-and-homelessness.
3. Cal J. Halvorsen, "What Does It Mean to Have a Society with More Older People than Younger Ones?" Encore.org, Boston College School of Social Work, and Center on Aging & Work at Boston College, 2019, https://cogenerate.org/wp-content/uploads/2022/12/Societywithmoreolderthanyoung.pdf.
4. AARP Public Policy Institute, "Medicare Spends More on Socially Isolated Older Adults," 2018, https://www.aarp.org/pri/topics/health/coverage-access/medicare-spends-more-on-socially-isolated-older-adults/.

5. Center on Poverty & Social Policy at Columbia University, "Absence of Monthly Child Tax Credit Leads to 3.7 Million More Children in Poverty in January 2022," February 17, 2023, https://www.povertycenter.columbia.edu/publication/monthly-poverty-january-2022.
6. The Eisner Foundation, "Experienced Helping Hands: A New Handbook," October 31, 2017, http://eisnerfoundation.org/news/experienced-helping-hands-engaging-older-volunteers/.
7. Search Institute, "Relationships First: Creating Connections That Help Young People Thrive," 2017, https://page.search-institute.org/relationships-first.
8. David Burnes et al., "Interventions to Reduce Ageism against Older Adults: A Systematic Review and Meta-Analysis," *American Journal of Public Health* 109, no. 8 (2019): e1–9, https://doi.org/10.2105%2FAJPH.2019.305123.
9. Josefien J. F. Breedvelt et al., "The Effects of Neighbourhood Social Cohesion on Preventing Depression and Anxiety among Adolescents and Young Adults: Rapid Review," *BJPsych Open* 8, no. 4 (2022): e97, https://doi.org/10.1192/bjo.2022.57.
10. U.S. Department of Health and Human Services, "Our Epidemic of Loneliness and Isolation: The U.S. Surgeon General's Advisory on the Healing Effects of Social Connection and Community," 2023, https://www.hhs.gov/sites/default/files/surgeon-general-social-connection-advisory.pdf.
11. United Health Group, "Doing Good Is Good for You," September 2017, https://www.unitedhealthgroup.com/viewer.html?file=/content/dam/UHG/PDF/2017/2017_Study-Doing-Good-is-Good-for-You.pdf.
12. Lindsay Davis, Elizabeth Larkin, and Stephen B. Graves, "Intergenerational Learning through Play," *International Journal of Early Childhood* 34 (2002): 42–49, https://doi.org/10.1007/BF03176766.
13. The Eisner Foundation and Generations United, "All In Together: Creating Places Where Young and Old Thrive," 2018, https://dl2.pushbulletusercontent.com/Moj5hxfxqtBGfGfXb2O0qeQvIeie9vmi/18-Report-AllInTogether.pdf.
14. Peggy Morton, Ernest Gonzales, and Allison Merz, "Service Learning with Alzheimer's Disease: The Development of an Intergenerational Service Learning Course," Center for Health and Aging Innovation at NYU Silver School of Social Work, March 2023, http://hdl.handle.net/2451/64386.
15. Nina L. Blachman et al., "The Impact of a Friendly Telephone Calls Program on Visits with Physicians during Pandemic," *Journal of the American Geriatrics Society* 69, no. 11 (2021): 3061–63, https://doi.org/10.1111/jgs.17403.
16. The Commonwealth Institute, "Unequal Opportunities: Fewer Resources, Worse Outcomes for Students in Schools with Concentrated Poverty," October 26, 2017, https://thecommonwealthinstitute.org/research/unequal-opportunities-fewer-resources-worse-outcomes-for-students-in-schools-with-concentrated-poverty/.
17. Julia Freeland Fisher, *Who You Know: Unlocking Innovations That Expand Students' Networks* (Hoboken, NJ: Jossey-Bass, 2018).
18. Trent Stamp, "Intergenerational Programs Can Help Out-of-School Kids," *EdSource*, July 29, 2020, https://edsource.org/2020/intergenerational-programs-can-help-out-of-school-kids/637150.
19. Teresa Seeman et al., "Intergenerational Mentoring, Eudaimonic Well-being and Gene Regulation in Older Adults: A Pilot Study," *Psychoneuroendocrinology* 111 (2020): 104468, https://doi.org/10.1016/j.psyneuen.2019.104468.
20. University of Oregon, "Continuing and Professional Education," accessed August 17, 2023, https://continue.uoregon.edu/discover/lifelong_learning.php.
21. Lasell Village, "Lifelong Learning," accessed August 17, 2023, https://lasellvillage.com/lifestyle/.
22. Noelle Marcus, "Tackling the Housing Crisis and Bridging Generational Divides through Home-Sharing," *Stanford Social Innovation Review*, March 22, 2021, https://ssir.org/articles/entry/tackling_the_housing_crisis_and_bridging_generational_divides_through_home_sharing.
23. Jon Marcus, "Nonprofit Home-Sharing Groups Match Older Adults with Younger Tenants," AARP Blog, October 25, 2019, https://www.aarp.org/home-family/friends-family/info-2019/home-sharing.html.
24. Margot Kushel, "Homelessness among Older Adults: An Emerging Crisis," American Society on Aging, 2020, https://generations.asaging.org/homelessness-older-adults-poverty-health.
25. Bridge Meadows, "2022 Bridge Meadows Impact Report," accessed August 17, 2023, https://bridgemeadows.org/wp-content/uploads/2023/03/2022-Impact-Report-Bridge-Meadows.pdf.
26. Generations United, "Family Matters: Intergenerational Living Is on the Rise and Here to Stay," 2021, https://www.gu.org/app/uploads/2021/04/21-MG-Family-Report-WEB.pdf.

27. Rebecca Perron, "Global Insights on a Multigenerational Workforce," AARP Research, August 2020, https://doi.org/10.26419/res.00399.001.
28. Frances Kunreuther, "Up Next: Generation Change and the Leadership of Nonprofit Organizations," Annie E. Casey Foundation, July 2005, http://www.aecf.org/upload/PublicationFiles/LD2928K643.pdf.
29. Public Religion Research Institute, "Religion and Congregations in a Time of Social and Political Upheaval," May 16, 2023, https://www.prri.org/research/religion-and-congregations-in-a-time-of-social-and-political-upheaval/.
30. Erin Schneider and Tim J. Marshall, "At Height of Pandemic, More Than Half of People Age 16 and Over Helped Neighbors, 23% Formally Volunteered," United States Census Bureau, January 25, 2023, https://www.census.gov/library/stories/2023/01/volunteering-and-civic-life-in-america.html.
31. Cary Funk, "Key Findings: How Americans' Attitudes about Climate Change Differ by Generation, Party, and Other Factors," May 26, 2021, https://www.pewresearch.org/short-reads/2021/05/26/key-findings-how-americans-attitudes-about-climate-change-differ-by-generation-party-and-other-factors/.
32. Third Act, "Our Work," accessed August 17, 2023, https://thirdact.org/our-work/.
33. Davis et al., "Intergenerational Learning through Play."
34. Centers for Disease Control and Prevention, "Youth Risk Behavior Survey: Data Summary and Trends Report," 2021 https://www.cdc.gov/healthyyouth/data/yrbs/pdf/YRBS_Data-Summary-Trends_Report2023_508.pdf.
35. David Burnes et al., "Interventions to Reduce Ageism against Older Adults: A Systematic Review and Meta-Analysis," *American Journal of Public Health* 109, no. 8 (2019): e1–9. https://doi.org/10.2105%2FAJPH.2019.305123.
36. Matthew Solan, "The Secret to Happiness? Here's Some Advice from the Longest-Running Study on Happiness," Harvard Health Blog, October 5, 2017, https://www.health.harvard.edu/blog/the-secret-to-happiness-heres-some-advice-from-the-longest-running-study-on-happiness-2017100512543.
37. Faiza Tabassum, John Mohan, and Peter Smith, "Association of Volunteering with Mental Well-Being: A Lifecourse Analysis of a National Population-based Longitudinal Study in the UK," *BMJ Open* 6, no. 8 (2016): e011327. http://doi.org/10.1136/bmjopen-2016-011327.
38. The Eisner Foundation, "Video Grant Spotlight: Sages & Seekers," May 20, 2021, https://eisnerfoundation.org/eisner-journal/video-grant-spotlight-sages-seekers/.
39. Teresa Martins et al., "Intergenerational Programs Review: Study Design and Characteristics of Intervention, Outcomes, and Effectiveness," *Journal of Intergenerational Relationships* 17, no. 1 (2019): 93–109. https://doi.org/10.1080/15350770.2018.1500333.

Bibliography

Blachman, Nina L., Yi Shan Lee, Mauricio Arcila-Mesa, Rosie Ferris, and Joshua Chodosh. "The Impact of a Friendly Telephone Calls Program on Visits with Physicians during Pandemic." *Journal of the American Geriatrics Society* 69, no. 11 (2021): 3061–63. https://doi.org/10.1111/jgs.17403.

Breedvelt, Josefien J. F., Henning Tiemeier, Evelyn Sharples, Sandro Galea, Claire Niedzwiedz, Iris Elliott, et al. "The Effects of Neighbourhood Social Cohesion on Preventing Depression and Anxiety among Adolescents and Young Adults: Rapid Review." *BJPsych Open* 8, no. 4 (2022): e97. https://doi.org/10.1192/bjo.2022.57.

Bridge Meadows. "2022 Bridge Meadows Impact Report." Accessed August 17, 2023. https://bridgemeadows.org/wp-content/uploads/2023/03/2022-Impact-Report-Bridge-Meadows.pdf.

Burnes, David, Christine Sheppard, Charles R. Henderson, Monica Wassel, Richenda Cope, Chantal Barber, et al. "Interventions to Reduce Ageism against Older Adults: A Systematic Review and Meta-Analysis." *American Journal of Public Health* 109, no. 8 (2019): e1–9. https://doi.org/10.2105%2FAJPH.2019.305123.

Center on Poverty & Social Policy at Columbia University. "Absence of Monthly Child Tax Credit Leads to 3.7 Million More Children in Poverty in January 2022." February 17, 2023. https://www.povertycenter.columbia.edu/publication/monthly-poverty-january-2022.

Centers for Disease Control and Prevention. "Youth Risk Behavior Survey: Data Summary and Trends Report." 2021. https://www.cdc.gov/healthyyouth/data/yrbs/pdf/YRBS_Data-Summary-Trends_Report2023_508.pdf.

Commonwealth Institute. "Unequal Opportunities: Fewer Resources, Worse Outcomes for Students in Schools with Concentrated Poverty." October 26, 2017. https://thecommonwealthinstitute.org/research/unequal-opportunities-fewer-resources-worse-outcomes-for-students-in-schools-with-concentrated-poverty/.

Davis, Lindsay, Elizabeth Larkin, and Stephen B. Graves. "Intergenerational Learning through Play." *International Journal of Early Childhood* 34 (2002): 42–49. https://doi.org/10.1007/BF03176766.

Eisner Foundation. "Experienced Helping Hands: A New Handbook." 2017. http://eisnerfoundation.org/news/experienced-helping-hands-engaging-older-volunteers/.

Eisner Foundation. "Video Grant Spotlight: Sages & Seekers." May 20, 2021. https://eisnerfoundation.org/eisner-journal/video-grant-spotlight-sages-seekers/.

Eisner Foundation and Generations United. "All In Together: Creating Places Where Young and Old Thrive." 2018. https://dl2.pushbulletusercontent.com/Moj5hxfxqtBGfGfXb2O0qeQvIeie9vmi/18-Report-AllInTogether.pdf.

Fisher, Julia Freeland. *Who You Know: Unlocking Innovations That Expand Students' Networks*. Hoboken, NJ: Jossey-Bass, 2018.

Flowers, Lynda, Ari Houser, and Claire Noel-Miller. "Medicare Spends More on Socially Isolated Older Adults." AARP. November 27, 2017. https://www.aarp.org/pri/topics/health/coverage-access/medicare-spends-more-on-socially-isolated-older-adults/.

Funk, Cary. "Key Findings: How Americans' Attitudes about Climate Change Differ by Generation, Party and Other Factors." May 26, 2021. https://www.pewresearch.org/short-reads/2021/05/26/key-findings-how-americans-attitudes-about-climate-change-differ-by-generation-party-and-other-factors/.

Generations United. "Family Matters: Intergenerational Living Is on the Rise and Here to Stay." 2021. https://www.gu.org/app/uploads/2021/04/21-MG-Family-Report-WEB.pdf.

Halvorsen, Cal J. "What Does It Mean to Have a Society with More Older People than Younger Ones?" Encore.org, Boston College School of Social Work, and Center on Aging & Work at Boston College. 2019. https://cogenerate.org/wp-content/uploads/2022/12/Societywithmoreolderthanyoung.pdf.

Kunreuther, Frances. "Up Next: Generation Change and the Leadership of Nonprofit Organizations." Annie E. Casey Foundation. July 2005. http://www.aecf.org/upload/PublicationFiles/LD2928K643.pdf.

Kushel, Margot. "Homelessness Among Older Adults: An Emerging Crisis." American Society on Aging. 2020. https://generations.asaging.org/homelessness-older-adults-poverty-health.

Lasell Village. "Lifelong Learning." Accessed August 17, 2023. https://lasellvillage.com/lifestyle/.

Marcus, Jon. "Nonprofit Home-Sharing Groups Match Older Adults with Younger Tenants." AARP Blog. October 25, 2019. https://www.aarp.org/home-family/friends-family/info-2019/home-sharing.html.

Marcus, Noelle. "Tackling the Housing Crisis and Bridging Generational Divides through Home-Sharing." *Stanford Social Innovation Review*. 22 March 22, 2021. https://ssir.org/articles/entry/tackling_the_housing_crisis_and_bridging_generational_divides_through_home_sharing.

Martins, Teresa, Luís Midão, Silvia Martínez Veiga, Lisa Dequech, Grazyna Busse, Mariola Bertram, et al. "Intergenerational Programs Review: Study Design and Characteristics of Intervention, Outcomes, and Effectiveness." *Journal of Intergenerational Relationships* 17, no. 1 (2019): 93–109. https://doi.org/10.1080/15350770.2018.1500333.

Morton, Peggy, Ernest Gonzales, and Allison Merz. "Service Learning with Alzheimer's Disease: The Development of an Intergenerational Service Learning Course." Center for Health and Aging Innovation at NYU Silver School of Social Work. March 2023. http://hdl.handle.net/2451/64386.

O'Neale, Shalita. "Foster Care and Homelessness." *Foster Focus*. August 2015. https://www.fosterfocusmag.com/articles/foster-care-and-homelessness.

Perron, Rebecca. "Global Insights on a Multigenerational Workforce." AARP Research. August 2020. https://doi.org/10.26419/res.00399.001.

Public Religion Research Institute. "Religion and Congregations in a Time of Social and Political Upheaval." May 16, 2023. https://www.prri.org/research/religion-and-congregations-in-a-time-of-social-and-political-upheaval/.

Rodgers, William M. "The Impact of a $15 Minimum Wage on Hunger in America." Century Foundation. September 1, 2016. https://tcf.org/content/report/the-impact-of-a-15-minimum-wage-on-hunger-in-america.

Schneider, Erin, and Tim J. Marshall. "At Height of Pandemic, More Than Half of People Age 16 and Over Helped Neighbors, 23% Formally Volunteered." United States Census Bureau. January 25, 2023. https://www.census.gov/library/stories/2023/01/volunteering-and-civic-life-in-america.html.

Search Institute. "Relationships First: Creating Connections That Help Young People Thrive." 2017. https://www.search-institute.org/wp-content/uploads/2017/12/2017-Relationships-First-final.pdf.

Seeman, Teresa, Sharon Stein Merkin, Deena Goldwater, and Steven W. Cole. "Intergenerational Mentoring, Eudaimonic Well-Being and Gene Regulation in Older Adults: A Pilot Study." *Psychoneuroendocrinology* 111 (2020): 104468. https://doi.org/10.1016/j.psyneuen.2019.104468.

Solan, Matthew. "The Secret to Happiness? Here's Some Advice from the Longest-Running Study on Happiness." Harvard Health Blog. October 5, 2017. https://www.health.harvard.edu/blog/the-secret-to-happiness-heres-some-advice-from-the-longest-running-study-on-happiness-2017100512543.

Stamp, Trent. "Intergenerational Programs Can Help Out-of-School Kids." *EdSource*. July 29, 2020. https://edsource.org/2020/intergenerational-programs-can-help-out-of-school-kids/637150.

Tabassum, Faiza, John Mohan, and Peter Smith. "Association of Volunteering with Mental Well-being: A Lifecourse Analysis of a National Population-Based Longitudinal Study in the UK." *BMJ Open* 6, no. 8 (2016): e011327. http://doi.org/10.1136/bmjopen-2016-011327.

Third Act. "Our Work." Accessed August 17, 2023. https://thirdact.org/our-work/.

United Health Group. "Doing Good Is Good for You." September 2017. https://www.unitedhealthgroup.com/viewer.html?file=/content/dam/UHG/PDF/2017/2017_Study-Doing-Good-is-Good-for-You.pdf.

University of Oregon. "Continuing and Professional Education." Accessed August 17, 2023. https://continue.uoregon.edu/discover/lifelong_learning.php.

U.S. Department of Health and Human Services. "Our Epidemic of Loneliness and Isolation: The U.S. Surgeon General's Advisory on the Healing Effects of Social Connection and Community." 2023. https://www.hhs.gov/sites/default/files/surgeon-general-social-connection-advisory.pdf.

CHAPTER 4

A Dose of Optimism: Data Show Americans Are Ready to Build a Multigenerational Force for Good

Cal J. Halvorsen, Eunice Lin Nichols, *and* Marc Freedman

Abstract

America today is the most age-diverse society in human history—and arguably the most age-segregated. It's no surprise that there are signs of generational tension, that ageism continues to be directed toward both old and young adults, and that social isolation and loneliness have reached epidemic proportions, with older and younger people being the two most isolated groups in society. But new data suggest that Americans are ready for a change. In this chapter, we review the results from a nationally representative survey of 1,549 Americans ages eighteen to ninety-four that gauges how American adults think about cogeneration, or intergenerational collaboration, to solve problems and bridge divides. Commissioned by CoGenerate (formerly Encore.org) and conducted by NORC at the University of Chicago using its AmeriSpeak® Panel, the survey finds deep interest from people of all ages in cogeneration. The survey also uncovers generational motivations, the issues each generation selects as top priorities for cogenerational action, and the obstacles people see to acting on this interest. The chapter concludes with examples of cogeneration in action and a call to action.

Key Words: cogeneration, fellowships, social issues, intergenerational initiatives, nationally representative survey

Introduction

There are almost equal numbers of people alive today at every age, from birth to age seventy and beyond.[1,2] With more people living longer, five-generation workplaces and three-generation households are surging.[3] The opportunity to tap the unique and complementary talents of people of all ages and build a multigenerational force for good is here.

But are we ready? Will we squander the moment—even worse, allow it to sow more societal divisions? Or will we make the most of it?

In 2022, CoGenerate (formerly known as Encore.org) commissioned a nationally representative survey to find out what Americans think about cogeneration—a strategy to bring older and younger people together to solve problems and bridge divides. We got a dose of optimism and clarity in return.

To start, the findings paint a picture of pent-up demand. This is a solution wanting to happen. A sizable segment of the younger and older populations is hungry for opportunities not only for intergenerational connection, but for cogenerational action—the chance to join forces in cocreating a better future.

Just as striking is where the strongest of that strong interest resides: in young people and people of color across the age spectrum. It's no wonder that so many young people, growing up in diverse and multigenerational environments, would come so naturally to this direction. You can almost hear the next generation calling their elders to action, delivering the message that we can't do this without you.

The survey reveals a commonsensical fit in the motivations behind this interest. Older people want to share what they have learned from life, and younger people are eager to incorporate their insights. There is a fundamental humility to these impulses, the recognition that bringing about significant change often takes years, even generations, and that no one group can accomplish this work alone.

That said, different generations articulate different priorities. Older people's top priority for cogenerational work is the environment, a finding that underscores their deep interest in the world they will leave behind. For young people, mental health tops the list. Given the pandemic's toll of loneliness and purposelessness on both older and younger people,[4] it's not hard to imagine a coalition of older and younger people working together to improve mental health. A cross-generational alliance on the environment holds great promise as well.

Younger and older people recognize the challenges ahead. It's hard to know how to get started working across generational lines when daily life is so segregated by age. We need more formal opportunities to make coming together for common purpose easier.

For all these cautions, the overarching message from this study is clear: America's growing age diversity represents an extraordinary opportunity to come together in joy, understanding, and action. Let's seize it.

Chapter Outline

This chapter outlines the methods, and then the results, of our nationally representative cogeneration survey. It continues with examples of cogenerational initiatives throughout the United States that are focused on many of the issues identified in our survey. And it concludes with thoughts on how to move this field forward.

The Cogeneration Study

In early 2022, CoGenerate (then called Encore.org) collaborated with researchers at NORC at the University of Chicago to design and field a nationally representative survey of 1,549 Americans ages 18 to 94 to gauge how American adults think about cogeneration, defined as bringing older and younger people together to solve problems and bridge divides.

NORC at the University of Chicago AmeriSpeak® Panel

Respondents were part of NORC's AmeriSpeak® probability-based panel, which was designed to be representative of the U.S. household population. To create the panel, NORC researchers randomly selected U.S. households using area probability and address-based sampling with a known, nonzero probability of selection from the NORC National Sample Frame that covers approximately 97 percent of the U.S. household population. (People with P.O. box–only addresses, some addresses not listed in the USPS Delivery Sequence File, and some newly constructed dwellings were not included in the sampling frame.) During recruitment, sampled households were contacted by U.S. mail, telephone, and face-to-face field interviewers. AmeriSpeak households could complete surveys online on computers, tablets, or smartphones or by telephone. The AmeriSpeak panel is widely used by governmental agencies, academic researchers, corporations, and members of the media.[5] The survey was fielded from March 9 through 23, 2022.

Survey Focus and Questions

We designed the survey to focus on respondents' attitudes toward, experiences with, interests in, and perceived barriers to working for a better future with people older and younger than themselves. For most questions, we focused on wide age gaps—asking respondents about working with people at least twenty-five years older or younger than themselves—to assess interest and experience in working to "improve the world around you . . . in any capacity—volunteering, getting involved in an issue you care about, or working in a paid job."

The survey focused on four key areas. First, it asked respondents about their efforts to improve the world around them in the *past twelve months* while working with people at least twenty-five years older or younger than themselves. Second, it asked respondents about their interest in improving the world around them *in the future* while working with people at least twenty-five years older or younger than themselves. Third, it asked respondents about perceived barriers to working with people of different generations to improve the world around them. And fourth, it asked respondents about specific social problems (such as mental health, climate change, and inequality) they would like to address by joining forces with people of different generations. The full survey and complete, anonymized data are available to the public.[6]

Analysis

We compiled descriptive statistics with a focus on how answers differed by generation as well as race and ethnicity. We used generational definitions from the Pew Research Center to determine our age categories in March 2022: Gen Z (ages eighteen to twenty-five), Millennial (twenty-six to forty-one), Gen X (forty-two to fifty-seven), Boomer (fifty-eight to seventy-six), and Silent Generation (seventy-seven and older).[7] Race and ethnicity were categorized as White, Black, Hispanic, and Asian. (The White, Black, and Asian groups are all non-Hispanic.

Due to sample-size limitations, we do not report results for additional groups.) All analyses were weighted to be representative of the U.S. population by age, race, ethnicity, gender, and education using benchmarks from the U.S. Current Population Survey.

Results

Finding 1: People of all ages want to work across generations to help others and improve the world around them.

Despite persistent reports of deep generational divides, we found that large majorities of younger and older adults want to work with people of other generations to solve the country's problems. More than four-fifths (80.6 percent) of survey respondents say they want to work with others twenty-five years older or younger than themselves to improve the world around them.

As shown in figure 4.1, majorities say that working together across generations will be good for individuals and the nation. Nearly all respondents agree that working across generations can help America "better solve its problems" (96.4 percent) and make us "less divided as a society" (93.7 percent). More than half of adults of all generations "strongly agree" that working together is important because it helps generations better understand each other (71.4 percent), enriches the lives of older and younger generations (67.7 percent), and produces better solutions (67.0 percent).

For many, these beliefs come from experience. Nearly half (46.7 percent) of respondents have worked for change in the past year with someone at least twenty-five years older, and 39.3 percent with someone at least twenty-five years younger. Most found the experience positive. Of those who worked with someone at least twenty-five years older, 79.9 percent rated the experience as "very positive" or "positive." Of those who worked with someone at least twenty-five years younger, 72.5 percent say their experience was "very positive" or "positive."

About half (49.2 percent) of those who have not worked across generations in the past are interested in doing so in the future.

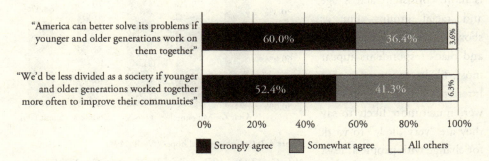

Figure 4.1 Visions of CoGenerational impact (*N* = 1,549).

Source: CoGenerate.

Finding 2: While interest is widespread, young people, and Black and Hispanic people of all ages, are especially keen to work across generations.

As shown in figure 4.2, almost three-quarters (72.0 percent) of survey respondents say they wish they had more opportunities to work across generations for change. This is especially true among the youngest respondents.

In fact, 21.4 percent of those surveyed say the opportunity to work across generations makes them "much more likely" to get involved, with the highest-level responses among young people, Black people, and Hispanic people. As shown in table 4.1, Gen Z respondents are almost twice as likely to say they are "much more likely" to be motivated by the opportunity to work across generations as are Silent Generation respondents, and Black and Hispanic respondents are almost twice as likely as White and Asian respondents to be motivated by the opportunity.

The data also show that the youngest respondents and people of color are most ready to act soon on this enthusiasm. More than half (55.0 percent) of Gen Z respondents say they are "very likely" to work for change with others at least twenty-five years older in the next few years, compared to 45.7 percent of Millennial, 38.8 percent of Gen X, and 23 percent of Boomer respondents.

Respondents of color show much more interest and intent than White respondents about working with people at least twenty-five years older. Interest in doing this work someday is more than ten percentage points higher among Black (88.0 percent) and Hispanic (89.2 percent) respondents, and more than five percentage points higher among Asian (84.0 percent) respondents, than among White (78.7 percent) respondents.

Similarly, and as shown in table 4.2, half of Black respondents, and just under half of Hispanic and Asian respondents, say they are "very likely" to work for change with people at least twenty-five years older in the next few years, compared to about a third of White respondents.

Interest in someday working for change with others at least twenty-five years younger is more consistent across age and racial groups—but as shown in table 4.2, Gen X and Black respondents appear most likely to act on that interest. Gen X respondents were much more likely to say they are "very likely" to work for change with people at least twenty-five years younger in the next few years than other

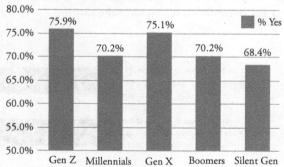

Figure 4.2 CoGenerational hopes (*N* = 1,549).

Note: Gen Z (*N* = 196), Millennial (*N* = 456), Gen X (*N* = 358), Boomer (*N* = 460), Silent Gen (*N* = 79).

Source: CoGenerate.

Table 4.1 Draw of cogenerational action, by generation and race

"Does the opportunity to work with people of different generations make you more likely or less likely to join efforts to improve the world around you?"

	Much more likely (%)	Somewhat more likely (%)	It has no impact (%)	Somewhat less likely (%)	Much less likely (%)
Gen Z	29.2	32.8	34.4	3.1	0.5
Millennials	21.5	30.7	44.1	1.8	1.8
Gen X	22.9	35.8	38.5	1.1	1.7
Boomers	17.8	34.1	43.0	3.3	1.1
Silent Gen	16.3	46.3	33.8	1.3	2.5
Asian	17.0	37.2	44.7	0.0	0.0
Black	33.9	36.6	23.1	2.7	3.8
Hispanic	32.4	30.9	32.8	1.5	1.9
White	16.6	33.6	46.0	2.4	1.0

Note: Sample sizes by generation: Gen Z (*N* = 196), Millennial (*N* = 456), Gen X (*N* = 358), Boomer (*N* = 460), Silent Gen (*N* = 79). Sample sizes by race: Asian (*N* = 93), Black (*N* = 186), Hispanic (*N* = 262), White (*N* = 969). Percentages may not add up to 100% due to "don't know" or skipped responses, as well as due to the exclusion of two race categories (another race, non-Hispanic; and two or more races, non-Hispanic) due to low sample sizes.

Source: CoGenerate.

generations, particularly Boomer and Silent Generation respondents. Further, Black respondents were much more likely to say they are "very likely" to work for change with others at least twenty-five years younger in the next few years than Asian, Hispanic, and White respondents.

Interest in someday working for change with others at least twenty-five years younger, when sorted by generation, was high: Millennial, 92.2 percent; Gen X, 95.6 percent; Boomer, 94.6 percent; Silent Generation, 94.6 percent. Interest in someday working for change with others at least twenty-five years younger by race was just as high: Asian, 98.3 percent; Black, 92.5 percent; Hispanic, 94.4 percent; White, 93.6 percent.

Finding 3: The fit is a powerful one: Young people want to learn from older people; older people want to share what they know. And vice versa.

Why do those who have worked across generations for social change value the experience—and why do they want to do more of it? Learning, sharing knowledge, and increasing appreciation for other generations are by far the most frequently cited answers. Moreover, the learning and knowledge-sharing dynamics are notably two-way.

The top reason both Gen X (64.9 percent percent) and Boomer (74.2 percent) respondents say they had a positive experience working with people at least twenty-five

Table 4.2 Likelihood of cogenerational action, by generation and race

"In the next few years, how likely are you to work with someone at least 25 years younger/older than you to improve the world around you?"

	Younger				Older			
	Very likely (%)	Somewhat likely (%)	Somewhat unlikely (%)	Very unlikely (%)	Very likely (%)	Somewhat likely (%)	Somewhat unlikely (%)	Very unlikely (%)
Gen Z	34.7	35.9	16.7	12.4%	55.0	41.9	3.1	0.0
Millennials	47.4	41.4	8.6	2.6%	45.7	46.3	5.8	1.9
Gen X	33.8	50.6	12.9	2.7%	38.8	47.3	11.6	2.4
Boomers	20.4	68.5	9.3	1.9%	23.0	47.0	21.2	8.8
Silent Gen					7.7	61.5	19.2	11.5
Asian	22.8	54.4	15.8	7.0%	45.6	42.6	11.8	0.0
Black	51.6	34.7	9.7	4.0%	50.0	38.6	9.1	2.3
Hispanic	38.5	37.3	17.8	6.5	47.4	39.5	10.5	2.1
White	35.5	46.2	11.5	6.6	34.6	50.4	10.8	4.2

Note: The "younger" question was asked of the 93.8% of respondents, and the "older" question was asked of the 82.0% of respondents, who reported interest in working with someone at least 25 years younger or older, respectively, to improve the world around them (Gen Z was excluded from the "younger" question due to their age). Percentages may not add up to 100% due to "don't know" or skipped responses, as well as due to the exclusion of two race categories (another race, non-Hispanic; and two or more races, non-Hispanic) because of low sample sizes. *Source:* CoGenerate.

years younger was, "It allowed me to share what I know." Almost three-quarters (73.0 percent) of Silent Generation respondents say, "It increased my appreciation for younger generations."

Among those who have worked for change with people at least twenty-five years older than themselves, 37.9 percent of Gen Z, 48.6 percent of Millennial, and 50.4 percent of Gen X respondents said the experience was positive because it increased their appreciation for older generations.

Looking forward, every generation includes the desire to share knowledge and to learn among the top reasons they want to work for change with older and younger people.

Those who have worked with people at least twenty-five years younger say they found it positive because it allowed them to share what they know (70.0 percent), showed them that younger and older generations can produce better solutions when they work together (53.9 percent), and taught them something they wouldn't have learned otherwise (40.9 percent).

Those who have worked with people at least twenty-five years older say they found it positive because it taught them something they wouldn't have learned otherwise (55.0 percent), showed them that younger and older generations can produce better solutions when they work together (51.4 percent), and allowed them to share what they know (44.2 percent).

Looking forward, strong percentages of older and younger people say they want to work across generations because it will increase their appreciation for people of other ages. Gen X (38.4 percent), Boomer (46.4 percent), and Silent Generation (58.5 percent) respondents say they want to work with people at least twenty-five years younger because it will increase their appreciation for younger generations. And Gen Z (46.3 percent), Millennial (44.1 percent), Gen X (46.9 percent), and Boomer respondents (54.6 percent) say they want to work with people at least twenty-five years older because it will increase their appreciation for older generations.

Finding 4: Older and younger people want to work together on some of the same issues—but there are striking differences by age and race.

Which issues are ripe for cogenerated solutions? Mental health topped the list for younger generations, while the environment came first among older ones.

As shown in table 4.3, more than half of Gen Z and Millennial respondents say they want to work across generations on mental health, which wasn't included among the top five issues cited by Boomer or Silent Generation respondents. Both the environment and climate change were included in the top five issues by Gen Z, Boomer, and Silent Generation respondents. Education was the only issue all generations included in their top five.

Some stark differences by race appeared among prioritized issues. For example, and as shown in table 4.4, Black respondents cited racial justice (62.2 percent) more than twice

Table 4.3 Top five cogenerational issue areas, by generation

Gen Z (N = 196) (%)	Millennial (N = 456) (%)	Gen X (N = 358) (%)	Boomer (N = 460) (%)	Silent Gen (N = 79) (%)
Mental health (54.4)	Mental health (50.8%)	Mental health (38.5)	Environment (41.3)	Environment (51.3)
Education (43.6)	Education (46.0%)	Education (37.2)	Education (37.6)	Healthcare/caregiving (47.5%)
Environment (40.8)	Housing/homelessness (42.1)	Housing/homelessness (34.9)	Healthcare/caregiving (36.3)	Climate change (40.5%)
Climate change (40.5)	Environment (41.9)	Healthcare/caregiving (31.0)	Housing/homelessness (36.2)	Education (38.0)
Employment (40.0)	Healthcare/caregiving (36.2)	Employment (29.6)	Climate change (32.0)	Racial justice (35.4); vets and military families (35.4)

Source: CoGenerate.

as frequently as White respondents did (24.4 percent). Healthcare/caregiving was cited by more than half of Asian respondents (52.1 percent) but only about a third of White respondents (34.7 percent). And housing/homelessness was cited by more than half (52.2 percent) of Black respondents but fewer than a quarter (21.5 percent) of Asian respondents.

Finding 5: Despite strong interest in working across generations, fully half of respondents cited a range of obstacles preventing them from acting on it.
More than 40 percent of each generation selected "nothing" when asked what prevents them from working for change across generations. But each group also cited concrete obstacles that will need to be addressed to unleash this force.

The survey was fielded in March 2022 while the United States was just recovering from its largest surge in reported COVID-19 infections.[8] Unsurprisingly, 19.2 percent of respondents cited COVID-19 as an obstacle to working across generations for change, with older generations expressing more concern. Overall, Gen Z respondents were most likely to cite non-COVID barriers to working across generations. More surprisingly, every generation selected "I can't find opportunities to work with people of other generations" as a top obstacle. And a key obstacle for all but the oldest respondents is not knowing how to get started.

The youngest and the oldest respondents cited difficulty communicating as a top-five obstacle to working across generations—but that response was more than two times stronger among Gen Z respondents than those in the Silent Generation and more than four times stronger than Gen X respondents.

Table 4.4 Top five cogenerational issue areas, by race and ethnicity

Asian ($N = 93$) (%)	Black ($N = 186$) (%)	Hispanic ($N = 262$) (%)	White ($N = 969$) (%)
Education (53.2)	Racial justice (62.2)	Mental health (42.9)	Education (39.8)
Healthcare/ caregiving (52.1)	Housing/ homelessness (52.2)	Housing/ homelessness (42.0)	Environment (39.0)
Mental health (47.3); environment (47.3)	Education (51.9)	Environment (39.1)	Mental health (38.9)
Climate change (44.7)	Mental health (47.3)	Inequality (32.2)	Healthcare/ caregiving (34.7)
Employment (43.0)	Early childhood learning/care (41.9)	Education (31.8)	Housing/ homelessness (34.6)

Note: Asian, Black, and White respondents are all non-Hispanic. Two additional categories were excluded from this table due to low sample sizes: another race, non-Hispanic ($N = 14$) and two or more races, non-Hispanic ($N = 25$). *Source:* CoGenerate.

Persistent age segregation likely plays a role in limiting people's contact with those of other generations. More than a quarter (25.8 percent) of all respondents "strongly agree" with the statement "I would like to spend more time with people of different generations who are not in my family"; another 58.7 percent said they "somewhat agree."

Some 42.6 percent of respondents said they hadn't spoken seriously in the past year with non–family members of other generations about a social, community, or political issue—and almost half (48.5 percent) of them said this was because they don't spend much time around people of other generations.

Cogeneration in Action

Age separation—younger people in school, middle generations at work, and older people marginalized, often living only with other older people—is an ingrained part of so many lives. But we see the beginnings of a new, cogenerational story, most prominently told in all avenues of popular culture.

Tony Bennett and Lady Gaga, sixty years apart in age, won Grammys for their duets. Brandi Carlisle, age forty-one, hosted the 2023 Gershwin Prize awarded to her good friend Joni Mitchell, then aged seventy-nine. Groundbreaking, award-winning television shows like *The Last of Us*, *Hacks*, *Abbott Elementary*, and *Only Murders in the Building* feature older and younger characters working together. Films like *A Man Called Otto*, *Hunt for the Wilderpeople*, *Driveways*, and *Everything Everywhere All at Once*, feature Hollywood icons crossing generational divides to find purpose, allies, and belonging. And major media stories about intergenerational friendships—"She's 86. She's 28. They love their hang time as the wallpaper queens of Los Angeles"[9] and "The Joy of May-December Friendship,"[10] just to name two—have become a reliably viral sensation.

Age diversity isn't as readily apparent in efforts to make the world a better place. CoGenerate is working to change that. In recent years, we've run an Innovation Fellowships program that has attracted more than four hundred applicants, all reaching across generations to solve problems, build bonds, and bridge divides.[11]

Many of the fellows are working to help ease mental health issues, including loneliness and social isolation, the issue Gen Z, Millennial, and Gen X respondents to the NORC research ranked at the top of their list of causes ripe for cogenerational solutions. Our fellows are bringing the two most isolated groups in society together to help both thrive.

Loneliness and Social Isolation

In 2009, Innovation fellow Elly Katz founded Sages & Seekers to connect people over age sixty with younger people, ages fifteen to twenty-four, for online and in-person conversations to develop empathy and diminish social isolation and ageism "while meeting the universal and compelling need of both young adults and elders to find meaning and purpose in their lives."[12] A study conducted by University of Southern California professor Dr. Mary Helen Immordino-Yang found that the program increased adolescents' sense of social connectedness, psychological well-being, and purpose in life. Older participants, Immordino-Yang found, showed improved memory performance and increased generativity.[13] Since its inception, Sages & Seekers has reached over six thousand teens and older adults in twenty-nine states and six countries.

Big & Mini, cofounded by Innovation fellow Aditi Merchant when she was a student at the University of Texas, takes a similar approach to easing loneliness, but its matches are entirely virtual. The organization is "our best effort at using technology to shrink the generational divide into a small crack."[14] As of this writing, the group had matched 6,124 older and younger people in all fifty U.S. states and twenty-seven countries.

Innovation fellow Nicole Kenney is the founder of Hey Auntie!, an "intergenerational ecosystem" working "to close the racial mental health gap by connecting Black women across ages and life stages" to support one another.[15] The group's name, Kenney writes, is inspired by her aunt and "by the historical and cultural legacy of the Black Auntie who can be traced back to West Africa. Aunties have served as a protective factor for our mental health for generations, and I am excited to build on that legacy for the 21st century and beyond."[16] A digital wellness platform and community, the organization curates groups of six women (half over and half under age fifty) who are matched for a series of virtual conversations. In 2021, Kenney won the $50,000 grand prize awarded by the Economy League's #WellCityChallenge in Philadelphia. Hey Auntie! is just getting started.

Education

Education is the only cause that all generations surveyed by NORC included among their top five priorities for cogenerational action. CoGenerate's Innovation fellows and grantees are leveraging the unique skills and assets of older and younger generations to support student learning and academic outcomes.

Ampact—a CoGenerate grantee working to age-integrate national service efforts—mobilizes more than five hundred age-diverse AmeriCorps members in Georgia and Minneapolis to serve as tutors, helping K–8 students build their reading and math skills and become better learners.[17] Intergenerational friendships between the older and younger tutors develop organically, since they serve at the same school and work in the same designated space for eight hours a day. They also serve the community together and have opportunities to engage with one another during professional development, training, and other activities. In a recent survey of tutors who work in multiage teams, 70 percent of respondents said serving alongside a member of a different generation increased opportunities to interact meaningfully; 48 percent said serving on an intergenerational team made them better at establishing strong relationships with the students they tutored; and 60 percent said it made them better tutors. "A cogenerational approach allows several generations to serve together and learn from one another," Georgia Reading and Math Corps executive director Dr. Shawonna Coleman said. "They leverage their different strengths while building lasting friendships. That's great for the tutors, but it has bigger ramifications, too."[18]

Innovation fellow Lewis Bernstein, a retired executive from Sesame Workshop, is engaging a similar, three-generation approach. He is the founder of SWAN 3G Mentoring, a mental-wellness initiative in which older adults (mostly older people who worked for Sesame Workshop) mentor high school students who are then empowered to mentor preschoolers. With the use of brief, carefully selected Sesame Street segments to spark discussion and joy, the program builds multigenerational relationships, empathy, and communication skills.[19]

Innovation fellow Roderick Heath—the chief executive officer and founder of Generation Uplift and assistant vice chancellor for student affairs and dean of students at Fayetteville State University in North Carolina—is helping young people, ages sixteen to twenty-five, use the power of film to capture the rich stories and history of older generations in North Carolina and to help solve community problems, from homelessness to gun violence. "I want to teach young adults how to tell stories through video and photography and to support them in solving community problems they're passionate about by connecting them with older adults who have experience in those areas."[20]

Affordable housing for college students is another educational issue attracting cogenerational solutions. As a graduate student in New York City, Innovation fellow Noelle Marcus discovered that by 2035 one in three households will be led by a person over age sixty-five. At the same time, she knew from experience that college students in many cities like New York and Boston can't find affordable housing. She put the two together and founded Nesterly, which matches homeowners who need income and a helping hand with college students who are willing to help out for reduced rent.[21] Many of these pairs—now located in Boston, Louisville (Kentucky), and Columbus (Ohio)—have become close friends, as PBS NewsHour reported in 2019. "We fell in together very well and very smoothly," Boston homeowner Brenda Atchison told the reporter about her then-housemate, graduate student Abbie Herbst. "If I feel a little bit lonely or like I want to talk to somebody," Herbst said, "I just come downstairs and sit in the kitchen."[22]

Another Innovation fellow, Carrie Buck, is also a proponent of home-sharing, noting that one in five college students in a 2022 survey reported housing insecurity.[23] For example, at Long Beach City College in Long Beach, California, campus officials designated a parking lot for students to sleep overnight in their cars.[24] At the same time, Buck—the former leader of Homeless Intervention Services of Orange County[25]—found that thousands of older homeowners had rooms to spare. Like Noelle Marcus, Buck began making mutually beneficial matches of older homeowners and college students. Today, in Orange County the HomeShare OC program is helping to solve the housing insecurity issue while reducing loneliness and creating friendships and mentorships—building relationships that allow both older and younger people to learn and grow.[26]

Examples of cogeneration in action come in many forms. Some are naturally occurring, like the volunteers who come together regularly to support local food banks or park clean-up projects. Some are institutional, like tutoring and mentoring programs (AARP Experience Corps,[27] Reading Partners,[28] Oasis Tutoring [see *Handbook* chapter 10],[29] and Big Brothers Big Sisters,[30] to name a few) that bring together older and younger volunteers, school and program staff, and young children. Many are relatively new, small, and vulnerable, as founders seek elusive funding and proof of impact.

It's our hope that the number of innovators piloting new cogenerational ideas grows by the day, that these pilots become easier to support and study, that these beacons for our multigenerational future break through and inspire a wider rethinking of the way we live, learn, serve, and work. The survey data we share here suggest that the examples of cogenerational solutions we have cited would, if they were more widely known, be overwhelmingly welcomed.

Conclusion: Seizing the Moment

It's too easy to see the divides in our nation—across age, race, culture, identity, income, and politics. It's harder to see areas of agreement, but our research with NORC at the University of Chicago reveals many.

We found powerful and widespread enthusiasm for cogeneration. People believe that working across generations will create a stronger nation, less divided and better able to solve its problems. They want to teach and learn from one another.

And yet there are notable, and in some cases surprising, differences in perspective by generation and race. These differences shed light on critical issues—mental health, climate change, and education—and on motivations and priorities. They have implications for all who advocate for change.

There are roadblocks, too.

Survey respondents cited a range of obstacles that must be addressed if we are to unleash and scale a multigenerational force for good: End the age segregation that keeps older and younger people apart and stereotypes that underestimate the old and the young. Create more opportunities to work across generations for social change and easier ways to find them. Recognize that opportunities to work together across age divides can be an enticement to serve, a selling point for any cause.

This survey uncovers the potential for cogeneration, now a largely untapped strategy for social impact and cohesion. Realizing that potential will help create an enormous multigenerational and, given the increasing diversity of our youngest generations, multicultural force for good.

It would be hard to find a more welcome message in these times.

Notes

1. This chapter expands upon the Cogeneration report, published in 2022, and is used with permission from CoGenerate. Learn more at https://cogenerate.org/research/cogeneration/. The authors thank Stefanie Weiss, Barbara Rosen, Jim Emerman, and Bruce Kelley for their efforts in designing, implementing, and communicating the results of the Cogeneration survey.
2. Sasha Shen Johfre, "Report on Intergenerational Relationships," New Map of Life Program, Stanford Center on Longevity, August 2021, https://longevity.stanford.edu/wp-content/uploads/2021/11/Johfre_NML_IntergenerationalRelationships.pdf.
3. Cal J. Halvorsen, "What Does It Mean to Have a Society with More Older People than Younger Ones?" Encore.org, Boston College School of Social Work, and Center on Aging & Work at Boston College, 2019, https://dx.doi.org/10.2139/ssrn.4405144; Jo Ann Jenkins, "How Longevity Is Shaping the Workforce of the Future," Leader to Leader 2020, no. 96 (2020): 7–12, https://doi.org/10.1002/ltl.20491; D'Vera Cohn et al., "The Demographics of Multigenerational Households," Pew Research Center, March 24, 2022, https://www.pewresearch.org/social-trends/2022/03/24/the-demographics-of-multigenerational-households/.
4. Mareike Ernst et al., "Loneliness before and during the COVID-19 Pandemic: A Systematic Review with Meta-Analysis," *American Psychologist* 77, no. 5 (2022): 660–77. https://doi.org/10.1037/amp0001005; Natasha R. Magson et al., "Risk and Protective Factors for Prospective Changes in Adolescent Mental Health during the COVID-19 Pandemic," *Journal of Youth and Adolescence* 50, no. 1 (2021): 44–57, https://doi.org/10.1007/s10964-020-01332-9.
5. NORC at the University of Chicago, "Technical Overview of the AmeriSpeak® Panel: NORC's Probability-Based Household Panel," February 8, 2022, https://amerispeak.norc.org/content/dam/amerispeak/research/pdf/AmeriSpeak%20Technical%20Overview%202019%2002%2018.pdf.
6. Cal J. Halvorsen et al., "A Nationally Representative Dataset of 1,549 Americans Aged 18 to 94 on Interest in, Experience with, and Barriers to Cogeneration, Defined as Working with Older and Younger People for Social Good," *Data in Brief* 45 (2022): 108753, https://doi.org/10.1016/j.dib.2022.108753.
7. Michael Dimock, "Defining Generations: Where Millennials End and Generation Z Begins," Pew Research Center (Blog), January 17, 2019, https://www.pewresearch.org/short-reads/2019/01/17/where-millennials-end-and-generation-z-begins/.
8. Johns Hopkins Coronavirus Resource Center, "New COVID-19 Cases Worldwide," March 16, 2023, archived at https://web.archive.org/web/20230819053650/https://coronavirus.jhu.edu/data/new-cases.
9. Deborah Netburn, "She's 86. She's 28. They Love Their Hang Time as the Wallpaper Queens of Los Angeles," *Los Angeles Times*, September 18, 2022, https://www.latimes.com/california/story/2022-09-18/reita-green-the-wallpaper-queen.
10. Catherine Pearson, "The Joy of May-December Friendship," *New York Times*, August 3, 2023, https://www.nytimes.com/2023/08/03/well/family/friendship-intergenerational-age-gap.html.
11. Cal J. Halvorsen et al, "The CoGenerate Innovation Fellowship: Supporting Leaders of Intergenerational Initiatives," *Journal of Intergenerational Relationships* 22, no. 3 (2023): 1–8, https://doi.org/10.1080/15350770.2023.2220707.
12. Sages and Seekers Incorporated, "About Us," Internet Archive, archived June 16, 2023, accessed February 13, 2025, https://web.archive.org/web/20230616134052/https://sagesandseekers.org/about/.

13. Mary Helen Immordino-Yang, "Sages and Seekers: Values-Based Life Goals in Intergenerational Conversations Increase Low-SES Adolescents' Life Purpose and Sense of Community Participation," working paper, University of Southern California, accessed September 29, 2023, https://drive.google.com/file/d/1ONanuBiY1eQUeYrgt0XDz7dxpXtPcxye/view.
14. "Big & Mini."
15. "Hey Auntie!"
16. "Our Story," Hey Auntie!, 2023, https://www.heyauntie.io/gettoknowus.
17. "Ampact."
18. Sarah McKineey Gibson, "In Georgia, These AmeriCorps Members Are Building Intergenerational Bonds," CoGenerate, May 24, 2023, https://cogenerate.org/in-georgia-these-americorps-members-are-building-intergenerational-bonds/.
19. Sarah McKinney Gibson, "This Sesame Workshop Retiree Created a 3-Gen Solution to Loneliness," CoGenerate, January 24, 2023, https://cogenerate.org/lewis-qa/.
20. Sarah McKinney Gibson, "He's on a Mission to Get the Generations Talking—Via Film," CoGenerate, January 20, 2023, https://cogenerate.org/roderick-qa/.
21. "A Better Way to Share, Nesterly, 2023, https://www.nesterly.com/.
22. Stephanie Leydon, "In Boston, a Housing Innovation That Connects the Generations," *PBS NewsHour*, July 8, 2019, https://www.pbs.org/newshour/show/in-boston-a-housing-innovation-that-connects-the-generations.
23. Sara Goldrick-Rab et al., "California Community Colleges #RealCollege Survey," Hope Center, March 2019, https://www.evc.edu/sites/default/files/2022-04/RealCollege-CCCCO-Report.pdf.
24. Jaysha Patel, "Long Beach City College Creates Program That Will Let Homeless Students Sleep in Cars on Campus," ABC7 Los Angeles, November 2, 2021, https://abc7.com/long-beach-city-college-homeless-students-parking-pilot-program-sleeping-in-cars/11191128/.
25. "HIS-OC."
26. Homeless Intervention Services of OC, "The HomeShare OC Program," 2021, Internet Archive, archived September 27, 2023, https://web.archive.org/web/20230927050058/https://his-oc.org/our-work/home-share-oc/.
27. "AARP, Experience Corps," AARP, accessed September 29, 2023, https://www.aarp.org/experience-corps/.
28. "Creating Equitable Access to Literacy Education," Reading Partners, 2023, https://readingpartners.org/.
29. "Interested in Becoming an Oasis Tutor?" Oasis Intergenerational Tutoring, 2023, https://tutoring.oasisnet.org/.
30. "Programs," Big Brothers Big Sisters of America, February 13, 2025, https://www.bbbs.org/programs/.

Bibliography

AARP. "Experience Corps." Accessed September 29, 2023. https://www.aarp.org/experience-corps/.
Ampact. "Ampact." 2023. https://www.ampact.us.
"Big & Mini." 2023. https://bigandmini.org/about.
Big Brothers Big Sisters of America. "Programs." February 13, 2025. https://www.bbbs.org/programs/.
Cohn, D'Vera, Juliana Menasce Horowitz, Rachel Minkin, Richard Fry, and Kiley Hurst. "The Demographics of Multigenerational Households." Pew Research Center. March 24, 2022. https://www.pewresearch.org/social-trends/2022/03/24/the-demographics-of-multigenerational-households/.
Dimock, Michael. "Defining Generations: Where Millennials End and Generation Z Begins." Pew Research Center Blog. January 17, 2019. https://www.pewresearch.org/short-reads/2019/01/17/where-millennials-end-and-generation-z-begins/.
Ernst, Mareike, Daniel Niederer, Antonia M. Werner, Sara J. Czaja, Christopher Mikton, Anthony D. Ong, et al. "Loneliness Before and During the COVID-19 Pandemic: A Systematic Review with Meta-Analysis." *American Psychologist* 77, no. 5 (2022): 660–77. https://doi.org/10.1037/amp0001005.
Gibson, Sarah McKinney. "He's on a Mission to Get the Generations Talking—Via Film." CoGenerate. January 20, 2023. https://cogenerate.org/roderick-qa/.
Gibson, Sarah McKinney. "In Georgia, These AmeriCorps Members Are Building Intergenerational Bonds." CoGenerate. May 24, 2023. https://cogenerate.org/in-georgia-these-americorps-members-are-building-intergenerational-bonds/.

Gibson, Sarah McKinney. "This Sesame Workshop Retiree Created a 3-Gen Solution to Loneliness." CoGenerate. January 24, 2023. https://cogenerate.org/lewis-qa/.

Goldrick-Rab, Sara, Christine Baker-Smith, Vanessa Coca, and Elizabeth Looker. "California Community Colleges #RealCollege Survey." Hope Center. March 2019. https://www.evc.edu/sites/default/files/2022-04/RealCollege-CCCCO-Report.pdf.

Halvorsen, Cal J. "What Does It Mean to Have a Society with More Older People than Younger Ones?" Encore.org, Boston College School of Social Work, and Center on Aging & Work at Boston College. 2019. https://dx.doi.org/10.2139/ssrn.4405144.

Halvorsen, Cal J., Bruce Kelley, Jim Emerman, Stefanie Weiss, David Gleicher, Jacob Stolmeier, et al. "A Nationally Representative Dataset of 1,549 Americans Aged 18 to 94 on Interest in, Experience with, and Barriers to Cogeneration, Defined as Working with Older and Younger People for Social Good." *Data in Brief* 45 (2022): 108753. https://doi.org/10.1016/j.dib.2022.108753.

Halvorsen, Cal J., Eunice Lin Nichols, and Janet Oh. "The CoGenerate Innovation Fellowship: Supporting Leaders of Intergenerational Initiatives." *Journal of Intergenerational Relationships* 22, no. 3 (2023): 1–8. https://doi.org/10.1080/15350770.2023.2220707.

Hey Auntie! "Our Story." 2023. https://www.heyauntie.io/gettoknowus.

Homeless Intervention Services of OC. "The HomeShare OC Program" (2021). Internet Archive. Archived September 27, 2023. https://web.archive.org/web/20230927050058/https://his-oc.org/our-work/home-share-oc/.

Immordino-Yang, Mary Helen. "Sages and Seekers: Values-Based Life Goals in Intergenerational Conversations Increase Low-SES Adolescents' Life Purpose and Sense of Community Participation." Working paper. University of Southern California. Accessed September 29, 2023. https://drive.google.com/file/d/1ONanuBiY1eQUeYrgt0XDz7dxpXtPcxye/view.

Jenkins, Jo Ann. "How Longevity Is Shaping the Workforce of the Future." *Leader to Leader* 2020, no. 96 (2020): 7–12. https://doi.org/10.1002/ltl.20491.

Johfre, Sasha Shen. "Report on Intergenerational Relationships." New Map of Life Program. Stanford Center on Longevity. August 2021. https://longevity.stanford.edu/wp-content/uploads/2021/11/Johfre_NML_IntergenerationalRelationships.pdf.

Johns Hopkins Coronavirus Resource Center. "New COVID-19 Cases Worldwide." March 16, 2023. Archived at https://web.archive.org/web/20230819053650/https://coronavirus.jhu.edu/data/new-cases.

Leydon, Stephanie. "In Boston, a Housing Innovation That Connects the Generations." *PBS NewsHour*. July 8, 2019. https://www.pbs.org/newshour/show/in-boston-a-housing-innovation-that-connects-the-generations.

Magson, Natasha R., Justin Y. A. Freeman, Ronald M. Rapee, Cele E. Richardson, Ella L. Oar, and Jasmine Fardouly. "Risk and Protective Factors for Prospective Changes in Adolescent Mental Health during the COVID-19 Pandemic." *Journal of Youth and Adolescence* 50, no. 1 (2021): 44–57. https://doi.org/10.1007/s10964-020-01332-9.

Nesterly. "A Better Way to Share." 2023. https://www.nesterly.com/.

Netburn, Deborah. "She's 86. She's 28. They Love Their Hang Time as the Wallpaper Queens of Los Angeles." *Los Angeles Times*. September 18, 2022. https://www.latimes.com/california/story/2022-09-18/reita-green-the-wallpaper-queen.

NORC at the University of Chicago. "Technical Overview of the AmeriSpeak® Panel: NORC's Probability-Based Household Panel." February 8, 2022. https://amerispeak.norc.org/content/dam/amerispeak/research/pdf/AmeriSpeak%20Technical%20Overview%202019%2002%2018.pdf.

Oasis Intergenerational Tutoring. "Interested in Becoming an Oasis Tutor?." Oasis. 2023. https://tutoring.oasisnet.org/.

Patel, Jaysha. "Long Beach City College Creates Program That Will Let Homeless Students Sleep in Cars on Campus." ABC7 Los Angeles. November 2, 2021. https://abc7.com/long-beach-city-college-homeless-students-parking-pilot-program-sleeping-in-cars/11191128/.

Pearson, Catherine. "The Joy of May-December Friendship." *New York Times*. August 3, 2023. https://www.nytimes.com/2023/08/03/well/family/friendship-intergenerational-age-gap.html.

Reading Partners. "Creating Equitable Access to Literacy Education." 2023. https://readingpartners.org/.

Sages and Seekers Incorporated. "About Us." Internet Archive. Archived June 16, 2023. Accessed February 13, 2025. https://web.archive.org/web/20230616134052/https://sagesandseekers.org/about/.

CHAPTER 5

Child-Focused, Adult-Governed, and Elder-Led: Leveraging Generational Wisdom for a Changing America

Sherreta R. Harrison *and* Raymond A. Jetson

Abstract

Age diversification, the graying of America and its workforce, and the continual increase of the population overall raise quite a few issues for American society. Many scholars across multiple disciplines have outlined these challenges explicitly. This chapter focuses on the intersection of age diversity and community change/movement building and its implications for community-serving organizations, and it makes two arguments. The first, a matter of framing, is that age diversity is not a new challenge in the area of community change and movement building and must be addressed if community movements are to succeed. The second, a matter of technique, is that community-serving organizations have an opportunity to address the issue of age diversity in a way that builds a more equitable workforce. The chapter reviews a generations framework for understanding community change before offering an evolved model of leadership that reimagines organizational leadership as a shared responsibility between people of differing generations.

Key Words: movements, leadership, intergenerational, community-based organizations, multi-generational workplace

MetroMorphosis	Urban Leadership Development Initiative	Intergenerational coleadership
Strengths/impact	• Provides a space for change agents to practice Sankofa • Develops leadership practices of all ages	• Leverages wisdom from multiple generations • Provides a mechanism to manage the multigenerational workforce
Limitations	• Largely structured to engage those of working age	• Requires organizational structure shifts • Adds to personnel budget and labor costs

Introduction

As society ages, new challenges emerge. That's the bad news. The good news is that as new challenges arise, new tools, technology, and resources also become available. One just needs to look at a timeline of the world's inventions to solidify the connection between societal advancement and innovation. As the years roll on, societal norms change, resulting in problems that need to be solved or issues that need to be addressed. Often, through a multidisciplinary understanding of these new problems and issues, an idea or concept emerges that solves the problem or addresses the issue. This innovation takes society into the next phase of its development, and the cycle repeats when a new challenge arises.

Of course, not all innovation is the result of completely new challenges. In many cases, innovative solutions are the result of evolving or persistent challenges that, because of new understandings, new knowledge, or new technology, have taken on new conceptualizations. Still, the new conceptualization begets an innovation, and society continues toward advancement.

The relationship between challenge and innovation is well documented—so much so that some practitioners are abandoning the language of challenge in favor of "asset-based framework" to underscore the notion that any challenge, new or newly conceptualized, can be viewed as an opportunity for innovation. The connection between challenge and innovation and the opportunities that affords is the first premise of this chapter.

The second premise is that our aging society, here referring to the fact that people are living longer and thus creating a society in which older adults outnumber youth and newborns, is not simply the contributor to new and newly conceptualized challenges, but that the aging of society is itself a challenge. Specifically, the fact that, for the first time in history, we have more people over the age of sixty-five than we do under the age of eighteen is a challenge for our healthcare,[1] education, housing,[2] and workforce systems, which means that the "graying" is, by default, also a challenge for the social service sector. It is the latter two factors on which this chapter will focus.

The world's population continues to increase, but whereas the number of young people is growing[3] in other countries, in America the older population is rapidly growing. It is estimated that by 2030, 20 percent of the country's population will be over the age of sixty-five and more than 2 percent will be eighty-five years and older.[4] The growing number of older Americans also means that our workforce is aging. The U.S. Bureau of Labor Statistics projects that by 2028, more than 25 percent of the labor force will be fifty-five years or older and nearly 10 percent will be over the age of sixty-five.

To be clear, the younger demographic isn't disappearing. Though the number of people considered young in America is declining relative to the number of Americans ages sixty-five and older, the American population is still increasing.[5] Several projections for the American population of the future show increases across age ranges[6] and forecast that American birth rates will remain largely unchanged. Therefore, not only can we expect to see more Americans, but we can also expect to see a more age-diverse America.

This age diversification, the graying of America and its workforce, and the continual increase of the population overall, raise several issues for American society. Many scholars across multiple disciplines have outlined these challenges explicitly. This chapter focuses on the intersection of age diversity and community change/movement building and its implications for community-serving organizations. For the purposes of this chapter, "community" is used in its broadest sense, referring to a group of people with a common social experience. To that end, the chapter makes two arguments.

The first is a matter of framing. Age diversity is not a new challenge, especially in the area of community change and movement building. Communities are inherently generational and as such have always had to navigate age differences. Furthermore, as communities work to achieve equity and justice, a challenge that has persisted across many years, bridging generational divides takes center stage. Generational Division is a persistent challenge, and whether real or perceived, it hinders social progression. We take the position that in order for communities to thrive, change efforts must intentionally bring generations together to solve the most pressing problems.

The second argument is one of technique. Evolving challenges are persistent challenges that, because of new understandings, new knowledge, or new technology have taken on new conceptualizations. When public will and timing align, evolving challenges become pressing challenges that demand innovative solutions. The increasing number of older Americans, their tendency to remain in the workforce longer, and the increasing visibility and vocality of younger generations have certainly made age diversity a pressing challenge for a number of sectors, particularly the social sector. Organizations and entities that serve communities have a unique opportunity to address age diversity in a way that goes beyond tried-and-true solutions and to build a more equitable workforce in the process. We offer one way to do so through a model of organizational leadership that reimagines it as a shared responsibility between people of differing generations.

The Evolving Challenge of Age Diversity in Community Movements

Community movements, or social movements, as they are more widely referred to, are the collective actions of a group of people who share a common goal for societal change. These movements begin for a variety of reasons and can take many forms, but they typically share three characteristics. Researchers generally agree that movements emerge relatively spontaneously, are loosely organized, and must be sustained over time.[7]

Age and generational differences have long been a component of social movements. Explorations into social change movements and community organizing make note of these differences, though to various degrees of significance. Sociologist Karl Mannheim believed that understanding generations was "indispensable"[8] to understanding social movements, attributing some of the disorganization of social collaboration to a tendency for generations to overlook knowledge that has come before them. He wrote, "Everyone starts out afresh from his own point of view . . . never pausing to consider the various aspects as part of a single general problem."[9] Simon Biggs also noted the discord between generations. Drawing from psychology and citing researchers who found that both younger and older people viewed the other in a negative light[10] and that younger individuals saw their older counterparts as feeble and in cognitive decline, he saw generational differences manifest in rivalries and antagonistic behaviors. Even in conceptualizations where intergenerational interaction is seen as harmonious and "protective,"[11] Biggs concluded that generational conflict is par for the course and may even be necessary for addressing pressing challenges.

Howe and Strauss[12] believed that age and generations are fundamental to understanding movements. Their fourth turning framework explains social change as a four-generation cycle (or turnings) of highs, awakenings, unravelings, and crises, with a person's involvement in social change efforts being largely influenced by the interaction of their developmental stage and the turnings.

The Four Turnings

The fourth turning refers to the notion that there are cycles of historical events that shape generations. These turnings take place every twenty years or so. The turnings as identified by Howe and Strauss are the following:

1. **High:** A period of time following crises that is marked by strong social institutions and collective action
2. **Awakening:** A period of time following a high that is marked by increasing individualism and undermining of social institutions
3. **Unraveling:** A period of time following an awakening that is marked by strong individualism and weakened, untrusted social institutions
4. **Crisis:** A period of time following an unraveling in which social institutions are destroyed and rebuilt, ushering in a renewed sense of community purpose

Developmental Stages and Generational Archetypes

The fourth turning framework depends on four life stages: childhood, adulthood, midlife, and elderhood. Generations are cohorts of people with similar behavioral patterns at each developmental stage. According to Howe and Strauss, the patterns that characterize a generation are shaped by the turnings. As a result, they identified four generational archetypes.

Generations born during a high are referred to as "prophets" who, after being coddled as children, emerge into adulthood during an awakening, and become the wise elders during a crisis. Those born during an awakening are called "nomads" and after being neglected in childhood, emerge as practical leaders during a crisis, and become tough elders during the next high. "Heroes" are born during unravelings, are reared in protected environments, and become the workers during a crisis before emerging into elderhood under attack by the next awakening. The last of the archetypes, the "artist," is born during a crisis, experiences an overprotected childhood, becomes a sensible adult during a high and an indecisive leader during a new awakening before becoming a compassionate elder during yet another unraveling. Supporters of this view place the more traditionally named

Table 5.1 Generations as archetypes

Archetype	Childhood	Adulthood	Midlife	Elderhood	Generation
Artists	Crisis	High	Awakening	Unraveling	Silent Generation (1925–1942)
Prophets	High	Awakening	Unraveling	Crises	Baby Boomer (1943–1960)
Nomads	Awakening	Unraveling	Crises	High	Generation X (1961–1981)
Heroes	Unraveling	Crisis	High	Awakening	Millennials (1982–1995)
Artists	Crisis	High	Awakening	Unraveling	Gen Z (1996–2010)
Prophets	High	Awakening	Unraveling	Crises	Gen Alpha (2010–)

Note: Generation names and the years associated with them are not uniform throughout the literature. The names and years listed here are those used by Strauss and Howe, except in the cases of Gen Z and Gen Alpha, as the two generations had not been born at the time of the publication of *The Fourth Turning*.

generations into these groups as a way of understanding their roles in social movements. Table 5.1 shows the traditionally named generations associated with each archetype.

What Manneheim, Biggs, Strauss, and Howe all seem to be saying is that age and generational differences are not new, and these differences can provide context for understanding the collective movements of a society. Of course, not all researchers agree with the distinctions between generations or even that the arbitrary groupings are helpful in explaining differences. (See *Handbook* chapters 27 and 28.) Still, a look into key movements through American history supports the notion that youth-elder collaboration contributes to the success of social change at multiple levels.

In an examination of the factors that contribute to successful movements, connection emerges as a prime factor. Nardini[13] discusses the importance of connecting people to the shared goal when establishing the movement, connecting people to one another when growing the movement, and connecting people to other groups when sustaining the movement. This is especially important given the various strategies and tactics employed by movements as well as the various demographics, ideologies, perspectives, and experiences that are represented. Because movements rely on a critical mass of people acting toward a common goal, success lies in helping those involved see more of what unites them than what divides them.

While it may be useful to understand the differences between generations, if communities are to ever solve their most pressing challenges, they must move beyond those differences and join together to leverage the wisdom and experiences of multiple generations. The fourth turning framework is particularly useful in illustrating the need to harness wisdom from multiple generations. Consider any pressing community challenge as a crisis. A prophet who spent adulthood during an awakening and unraveling (marked by increased individualism and decreased trust in institutions) may lead with a crusader mentality and become hyperfocused on restoring social collectivism. A nomad whose adulthood was fraught with weak institutions and destruction may lean toward the more practical response of resiliency over innovation. A hero, who experienced both the destruction and rebuilding of society during adulthood, may become too idealistic and focus on power. And an artist may become hyperfocused on getting everyone to conform to a process to restore order as a result of experiencing the high after the rebuilding of a crisis and awakening to the limits of social institutions. In isolation each of these archetypes may execute a strategy that does not address the issue in totality.

However, if social movements are indeed cyclical, then each generation has a unique perspective to offer during a crisis. When the fourth turning framework is overlaid with a common practice of Indigenous communities in which communities are youth-centered, adult-governed, and elder-led, the imperativeness of bridging generations for community good becomes even clearer.

In what will be referred to henceforth as the multigenerational approach to community, thriving communities are the result of interplay between members at each stage of development (adulthood and midlife are combined). In this approach, youth are highly respected and valued for their contributions to the future of the community and as such are given responsibilities to help prepare them for their roles. Adults are responsible for guiding youth and structuring the community in a way that protects them. Elders are respected for their wisdom and experience and serve to provide context and history for the community. As a result, youth are empowered, generations learn and work together, and communities are more resilient in the face of challenges or crises.

Revisiting the idea that each pressing community challenge is a crisis and marrying the fourth turning framework to the multigenerational approach, the value of connecting generations becomes evident. Too often, however, each archetype responds to isolated events based on its own experiences and challenges. Goldstone's exploration of demography and social movements noted that "activists of different generations thus formed their own persistent outlooks, identities, and modes of movement action."[14] It is these singular paradigms, identities, and ways of reacting that threaten the long-term success of community movements and the communities themselves. Mannheim believed that new generations offer a society the opportunity to examine itself and use the information to fortify the future. As such, new generations are critical to the longevity of communities. However, the longevity is not dependent on the criticality of new generations alone. As encouraged by the Ghanaian principle of Sankofa (literally translated to "go back and get it"), communities must make use of the past to chart a path forward. When the generations are separated, a community loses the opportunity to examine its history through fresh eyes. However, when the generations are combined and the challenge is placed in the proper context, not only does the bigger picture emerge but so do the values and aspirations of the community. The dual emergence of the complete challenge and the community aspiration generates solutions that don't repeat the status quo or the mistakes of the past or allow a community merely to survive its challenge. Instead, when generations join forces, communities are better able to thrive.

How Can Generations Work Together to Achieve Change?

Scholars across disciplines and popular culture have all discussed the apathetic youth or the older leader who doesn't know when to let go. Even when generational differences are met with skepticism or presented with caution, frequently, social movements are labeled with sweeping generalizations.

The work of MetroMorphosis, the Baton Rouge, Louisiana–based social enterprise where the authors of this chapter work to achieve social, economic, and racial equity, focuses on designing movements that matter enough to people so that they take ownership and grow them beyond what any one organization can do. In an effort to achieve the mission of transforming urban communities from within, the organization set out to establish a set of strategies to address the most pressing issues facing communities of color. What quickly emerged were three fundamental truths:

1. There was no shortage of community assets and resources. What was lacking was a coordinated approach to serving communities in a way that led to thriving.
2. The people most impacted by a challenge are uniquely suited to address the challenge but are often left out of conversations around solutions.
3. Collective action is aided by the presence of catalytic partnerships, or relationships between two or more people that allow them to accomplish together what neither could do alone.

These truths were consistent with notable community change models and the literature surrounding community transformation and as such became the foundation on which several MetroMorphosis strategies were built.

Activating Community Assets and Leveraging Resources

MetroMorphosis adopted an asset-based framework for its work. Trabian Shorters of BMe Community explains asset-framing as defining people by their aspirations and characteristics and not their challenges. This framing affirms the inherent value of people and communities and provides a different lens through which to view community work. Often, community-based organizations lead with the challenge—this chapter certainly did—and when that happens, communities and the people who live in them become problems to fix or people to save. This view, one that says communities are broken, ignores what Yosso[15] refers to as community cultural wealth and the different types of capital that exist in communities of color. Yosso lists six forms of capital that can be found in communities—aspirational, navigational, social, linguistic, familial, and resistant capital—each denoting an asset (such as institutions and physical structures) that marginalized communities possess. What's important about these two frameworks for understanding community assets is that they urge community-based organizations to identify assets, leverage them into resources for community change, and coordinate action toward a more vibrant community.

What was once considered the signature strategy of MetroMorphosis aimed to do just that. In 2016, MetroMorphosis launched the Urban Congress on African-American Males (UC) to "create action around the strengths and challenges of African American boys and men in Baton Rouge."[16] The UC was immediately positioned as an asset-based movement that convened men, women, and children of various demographics and organizations of various sectors to coordinate efforts to enhance the life outcomes of Black males in our city. At the height of its run, before the COVID-19 pandemic shifted its focus, the UC had mobilized more than a thousand citizens annually around seven goals, brought together more than sixty community-based organizations to plan action, identified another hundred or so community assets that aligned with the UC goals, spent more than three hundred hours listening to the experiences of Black males in Baton Rouge, and identified eighteen high schoolers to form a Youth Advisory Council. The structure of the UC relied heavily on in-person convenings, first in centralized locations and then, at the urging of Black boys and men, in spaces such as barbershops, community gyms, and churches, where they felt more comfortable. The result was a city-wide effort to shift the conditions that were keeping Black boys and men in Baton Rouge from thriving.

Through the listening sessions that took place over the UC's five years of active membership, several lessons emerged. Chief among them was the need to ground all efforts in a multigenerational approach for community change. The notion of being youth-centered, adult-governed, and elder-led was known to the organization, but it was somehow forgotten during programming. The UC was adult-governed but had not fully realized its youth-centered or elder-led components. Subsequent attempts to mitigate this by introducing a Youth Advisory Council and an Urban Elders Council had just begun to have an impact when the pandemic hit and MetroMorphosis shifted UC's efforts to the larger, nationally known My Brother's Keeper Initiative.

Despite the shift, the lesson of being intentional about bringing generations together remains a part of the organization's ethos to this day.

Equipping Citizen Leaders and Centering Lived Experience

The longest-running strategy of MetroMorphosis speaks to the value of lived experience as a credential. The Urban Leadership Development Initiative (ULDI) equips emerging leaders with the tools and knowledge to lead change in their communities. The ten-month fellowship embodies the principle of Sankofa by combining the history of Baton Rouge and the perspectives of the city's older change agents with a renowned leadership framework to inspire the next generation of innovative leadership practitioners.

ULDI brings together twenty community activists, educators, entrepreneurs, and social service advocates and workers a year. Ranging in age from eighteen to sixty, fellows meet monthly to gain perspectives on the city's evolving challenges, share their experiences and skill sets, and develop a community of people working together for a better Baton Rouge. ULDI lifts up two important ideas. The first is the idea that leadership is not a position but a practice that does not require permission and as such can be undertaken by anyone at any time. The second is that our society's most pressing challenges are not new but have evolved from previous iterations of challenges that were worked on and likely advanced by previous generations. These two tenets remind citizens of their power to enact change and the need to understand community issues holistically before acting.

As a result of this work to equip citizens and center lived experience, more than a hundred Baton Rougeans are practicing leadership for systems change in community with one another and, in many cases, with those who came before them.

Fostering Collaborative Leadership and Bridging Divides

The work of transforming inner-city neighborhoods cannot be successful with organizational isolation. MetroMorphosis believes that organizations must act in concert with other organizations and programs in ways that enhance the overall impact of their collective efforts. As such, through recent strategic learnings, the organization began to develop collective action networks. Drawing from the "science" of collaboration known as collective impact, collective action networks comprise organizations and individuals who agree to focus their efforts on a common agenda with mutually reinforcing activities and shared outcomes. By aligning efforts and, eventually, resources, organizations are able to make a greater impact on a single issue than they would by working alone. While collaboration can happen without a collective action network, the network dramatically increases the impact and the likelihood of success of shared initiatives and serves as a catalyst for the movement. Collective action networks address specific challenges, such as poverty, economic inclusion, poor educational outcomes, workforce shortages, and community revitalization, and increase the overall effectiveness of social service programs and the organizations working to address them. By prioritizing intentional cross-sector collaboration and deepening community engagement, collective action networks lead to better outcomes.

The fundamental building blocks of collective action networks are catalytic partnerships. MetroMorphosis defines catalytic partnerships as the tight, trusting relationships between approximately two or three individuals who, by virtue of their partnership and commitment to something bigger than themselves, are able to accomplish something together that likely could not have been accomplished alone. These tight and trusting relationships accelerate collective efforts and sustain the networks as they strive for change.

MetroMorphosis has cultivated a number of catalytic partnerships over its twelve-year history on its quest to transform Baton Rouge from within.

To be clear, MetroMorphosis addresses evolving challenges facing urban communities by activating community assets and leveraging resources, equipping citizen leaders and centering lived experience, and fostering collaborative leadership and bridging divides. Each of these strategies is intended to upend obstacles that have plagued communities, especially communities of color, for generations and build on innovative solutions and models for change developed over the years by social service organizations. Consistent with the definition of evolving challenges cited earlier, what was innovative in the past needs to be reconfigured in response to new circumstances.

The rest of this chapter discusses how MetroMorphosis altered its organizational structure to address the pressing challenge that age diversity presents for the workplace.

An Evolved Model of Leadership

As previously stated, age diversity in America is not just a pressing challenge for community movements, but it is also an opportunity to respond in new, equitable ways. One area that has implications for community-based organizations is the multigenerational workforce and its intersection with organizational leadership.

It has already been established that there is an increasing number of older Americans, and that increase is slated to continue until the year 2050. For various reasons, many aging citizens are remaining in the workforce longer than their counterparts from previous generations did. The National Bureau of Economic Research has noted that the number of people over the age of fifty-five doubled in twenty years, and while some are choosing to retire, many are choosing to continue working.[17] The Social Security Administration raised the retirement age from sixty-five to sixty-seven, reflecting what some are calling the graying of the workforce.

Clark and Ritter[18] identify three main tensions that organizations must manage when it comes to the aging workforce. The first is cost. Labor costs for older employers can soar, but letting older workers leave in droves threatens the loss of institutional knowledge as well as a hefty price tag when employers try to replace more experienced and knowledgeable employees. The second tension concerns productivity. Research is unclear as to whether age impacts productivity. Are older workers more productive, are younger workers more productive, or are differences in productivity individual rather than generational? The third tension, sustainability, refers to organizations either modifying working conditions to accommodate a multigenerational workforce or maintaining the status quo, which could result in the loss of workers from many generations.

These three tensions are not the only ones facing workplaces as the generations change. Issues of diversity, equity, and inclusion; work-life balance and mental well-being; employee turnover; and organizational effectiveness all require organizational leadership. It is not uncommon for leadership structures to adjust to changing dynamics in the workforce. As a matter of fact, leadership models have changed throughout the course of history as a result of shifts in society.[19] In the nineteenth century, America saw leadership practices that were focused on innate characteristics and posited that leaders were born and not made or trained. The era of The Great Man reserved leadership for the rare individual. By the 1930s, the goal was to identify the right combination of characteristics required to be an effective leader. This was known at the Trait Era and led to the development of personality tests as assessments for leadership that are still in use today.

Despite the use of psychometrics, no consistent set of leadership characteristics was identified, and the paradigm shifted to a behavioral one. During this era, leadership was seen as something that could be developed, and it was during this time that leadership styles emerged. Critics of this view of leadership says it ignores context which is consistent with criticisms of the behaviorist view of learning. The 1960s recognized the significance of the environment in leadership ability and offered a view that matched a leadership style with a situation. This eventually gave way to the complex view of leadership that emerged in 1990s and early 2000s.

The so-called New Leadership Era reflected a rapidly changing and disruptive environment and called for leadership models that focused on the interactions between those in leadership, those in followup, the situation, and the systems in which the leading occurs. This led to the development of transactional theory and a transformational theory of leadership, with each having utility based on the stage the organization is in at the time. Transformational leadership is particularly useful when an organization is undergoing change. Newer theories of leadership that have emerged since the early 2000s seem to be evolved versions of transformational leadership. Shared, inclusive, and contemporary leadership theories have emerged to address the ever-changing dynamics of a modern world.

If there were ever any "ever-changing dynamics," the age composition of our workforce is certainly one of them. Furthermore, age diversity in the workplace requires a more inclusive practice of leadership. In 2022, MetroMorphosis officially transitioned to an intergenerational coleadership model. The model was developed in 2020 when the organization considered what changes would be necessary for guiding the organization in the future. Led by its founder (who had been serving the community for more than thirty years) and staffed mostly by team members under the age of forty, the reality of the multigenerational workforce began to impact team dynamics and leader well-being. Fortunately, the organization had cultivated emerging leadership as a practice and had evolved a form of shared leadership quite organically. It seemed a no-brainer to explore options that would both improve relations between different generations on our small team and allow the founder to prioritize other interests and responsibilities.

The intergenerational coleadership model is the intentional practice of having two or more team members of different generations in senior-level leadership positions. Together, the intergenerational leadership team manages staff, oversees finances, and steers the organization according to individual skill sets and interests. The intergenerational coleadership model prioritizes three commitments. First, organizations that practice the model commit to viewing their work through an intergenerational lens. This means understanding that, regardless of what the product or end result is, it has implications for those in childhood, adulthood, midlife, and elderhood. As such, members of each developmental stage should be at minimum considered in, and hopefully consulted on, the final product or end result. Second, organizations practicing this model commit to developing and equipping individuals of all ages for leadership. This entails building leadership access points for various skill levels and allowing individuals to have "on-the-job training" in leadership roles. Lastly, organizations practicing intergenerational coleadership commit to building inclusive strategies for leadership that speak to a wide range of situations, candidates, and populations. This entails abandoning outdated views of leadership that unfairly prioritized values and practices rooted in systems of oppression.

By implementing this model, organizations are better positioned for sustainable solutions. Whether building a business or addressing critical social ills, most organizations are undertaking work that will span years, outlast a single person's tenure, and impact people at multiple stages of life. Because of this, the work cannot be adequately addressed in short, finite periods of time, in single lifetimes, or from a single perspective. Intergenerational coleadership allows organizations to leverage the wisdom of multiple generations to build sustainable models that anticipate transitions and successions, connect with audiences at different life stages, and ensure that the organization is well managed over time. In addition, intergenerational coleadership builds a partnership between two people that buffers the loneliness of leading and establishes allyship, which not only lightens the load but also encourages empathy, inclusivity, and other positive behaviors.

MetroMorphosis identified five reasons for practicing the intergenerational coleadership model. First, it provides a mechanism that evens the playing field for BIPOC, female, older, and younger workers who may be unfairly overlooked for leadership positions due to outdated practices that favor middle-aged white males or a lack of access to leadership development. Second, it mitigates loneliness and burn-out through partnership and shared responsibility. Third, intergenerational coleadership helps organizations plan for transitions, avoiding the loss of institutional knowledge. The fourth reason is that intergenerational coleadership supports movement building by leveraging the wisdom that exists across generations. And the fifth reason is that intergenerational coleadership provides an innovative way for organizations to support workers across the life span. When leadership is shared across generations, older workers aren't pushed out and younger workers don't have to wait until older workers decide to vacate roles. In a method that MetroMorphosis colead Raymond A. Jetson calls "moving over not out," older workers have the ability to make space for younger workers while sharing their knowledge, and younger workers have the benefit of easing into leadership roles with a built-in champion.

Conclusion

Age diversity, while seemingly an invention of modern society, is actually an evolving challenge for communities and the organizations that serve them. Throughout history, communities have needed to reckon with age and generational differences as they also wrestle with enacting change. Age difference, whether real or perceived, can be a source of conflict and division or be understood as an opportunity to develop innovative solutions to some of society's most pressing issues. Of course, this requires new techniques that reflect both the learnings of the past and desires for the future. One such technique, the intergenerational coleadership model, allows community-serving organizations to successfully navigate the intersection of age diversity and the multigenerational workforce. Though intergenerational coleadership has its origins in the organic practices of MetroMorphosis, a social enterprise dedicated to building a critical mass of citizens equipped to transform their communities, the model has been adopted by other organizations and, just like all innovative solutions, continues to evolve in response to new understanding, knowledge, and technology.

Notes

1. Robert Sade, "The Graying of America: Challenges and Controversies," *Journal of Law, Medicine & Ethics* 40, no. 1 (2012): 6–9, doi:10.1111/j.1748-720X.2012.00639.x.
2. Adam Nagourney, "Old and On the Street: The Graying of America's Homeless," *New York Times*, May 31, 2016, https://www.nytimes.com/2016/05/31/us/americas-aging-homeless-old-and-on-the-street.html.
3. "World Populations Prospects 2022," United Nations Populations Division, last modified September 30, 2023, https://population.un.org/wpp/Graphs/DemographicProfiles/Line/840.
4. U.S. Census Bureau, "The Next Four Decades: The Older Population in the United States: 2010–2050" (Washington, DC: U.S. Department of Commerce, 2010), https://www.census.gov/content/dam/Census/library/publications/2010/demo/p25-1138.pdf.
5. "World Populations Prospects 2022,"
6. "U.S. Population Projections: 2005-2050," Pew Research Center, last modified February 11, 2008, https://www.pewresearch.org/hispanic/2008/02/11/us-population-projections-2005-2050/; "The Demographic Outlook: 2023 to 2053," Congressional Budget Office, January 2023, https://www.cbo.gov/system/files/2023-01/58612-Demographic-Outlook.pdf.
7. "Types of Social Movements," Britannica, last modified September 30, 2023, https://www.britannica.com/topic/social-movement/Types-of-social-movements.
8. Karl Mannheim, "The Problem of Generations," in *Karl Mannheim: Essays*, ed. Paul Keeskemeti (London: Routledge, 1952), 286.
9. Mannheim, "The Problem of Generations," 287.
10. Angie Williams and Jon F. Nussbaum, *Intergenerational Communication Across the Life Span* (Mahwah, NJ: Lawrence Earlbaum, 2001).
11. Simon Biggs, "Thinking about Generations: Conceptual Positions and Policy Implications," *Journal of Social Issues* 63 (2007): 704.
12. William Strauss and Neil Howe, *The Fourth Turning: An American Prophecy* (New York: Broadway Books, 1997).
13. Gia Nardini, et al., "Together We Rise: How Social Movements Succeed," *Journal of Consumer Psychology* 31 (2020): 112–45.
14. Jack A. Goldstone, "Demography and Social Movements," in *The Oxford Handbook of Social Movements*, ed. Donatella della Porta and Mario Diani (Oxford, England: Oxford University Press, 2015), 149.

15. Tara J. Yosso, "Whose Culture Has Capital? A Critical Race Theory Discussion of Community Cultural Wealth," *Race Ethnicity and Education* 8 (2005): 69–91, https://doi.org/10.1080/1361332052000341006.
16. Danielle Thomas, "Urban CongressComprehensive Report," Urban Congress on African American Males (Baton Rouge, LA: MetroMorphosis, 2017), 1.
17. "Monthly Labor Report," US Bureau of Labor Statistics, last modified September 28, 2023, https://www.bls.gov/opub/mlr/2020/beyond-bls/what-to-do-about-our-aging-workforce-the-employers-response.htm.
18. Robert Clark and Beth Ritter, "How Are Employers Responding to an Aging Workforce," NBER Working Paper Series (Cambridge, MA: National Bureau of Economic Research, 2020).
19. Sihame Benmira and Moyosolu Agboola, "Evolution of Leadership Theory," *BMJ Leader* 5 (2021): 3–5.

Bibliography

Benmira, Sihame, and Moyosolu Agboola. "Evolution of Leadership Theory." *BMJ Leader* 5 (2021): 3–5.

Biggs, Simon. "Thinking about Generations: Conceptual Positions and Policy Implications." *Journal of Social Issues* 63 (2007): 695–711.

Britannica. "Types of Social Movements." Last modified September 30, 2023. https://www.britannica.com/topic/social-movement/Types-of-social-movements.

Clark, Robert, and Beth Ritter. "How Are Employers Responding to an Aging Workforce?" NBER Working Paper Series. Cambridge, MA: National Bureau of Economic Research, 2020.

Congressional Budget Office. "The Demographic Outlook: 2023 to 2053." Congressional Budget Office, January 2023. https://www.cbo.gov/system/files/2023-01/58612-Demographic-Outlook.pdf.

Goldstone, Jack A. "Demography and Social Movements." In *The Oxford Handbook of Social Movements*, edited by Donatella della Porta and Mario Diani, 149. Oxford, England: Oxford University Press, 2015.

Mannheim, Karl. "The Problem of Generations." In *Karl Mannheim: Essays*, edited by Paul Keeskemeti, 276–322. London: Routledge, 1952.

Monthly Labor Review. "What to Do About Our Aging Workforce—the Employers' Response." 2023. https://www.bls.gov/opub/mlr/2020/beyond-bls/what-to-do-about-our-aging-workforce-the-employers-response.htm.

Nagourney, Adam. "Old and on the Street: The Graying of America's Homeless." *New York Times*, May 31, 2016. https://www.nytimes.com/2016/05/31/us/americas-aging-homeless-old-and-on-the-street.html.

Nardini, Gia, Melissa G. Bublitz, Laura A. Peracchio, Tracy Rank-Christman, Samantha N. N. Cross. "Together We Rise: How Social Movements Succeed." *Journal of Consumer Psychology* 31 (2020): 112–45.

Pew Research Center. "U.S. Population Projections: 2005-2050." 2008. https://www.pewresearch.org/hispanic/2008/02/11/us-population-projections-2005-2050/.

Sade, Robert M. "The Graying of America: Challenges and Controversies." *Journal of Law, Medicine & Ethics* 40, no. 1 (2012): 6–9.

Strauss, William, and Neil Howe. *The Fourth Turning: An American Prophecy*. New York: Broadway Books, 1997.

Thomas, Danielle. "Urban CongressComprehensive Report." Urban Congress on African American Males, Baton Rouge, LA: MetroMorphosis, 2017.

United Nations Populations Division. "World Populations Prospects 2022." Last modified September 30, 2023. https://population.un.org/wpp/Graphs/DemographicProfiles/Line/840.

US Census Bureau. *The Next Four Decades: The Older Population in the United States: 2010–2050*. Washington, DC: U.S. Department of Commerce, 2010.

Williams, Angie, and Jon F. Nussbaum. *Intergenerational Communication across the Life Span*, Mahwah, NJ: Lawrence Earlbaum, 2001.

Yosso, Tara J. "Whose Culture Has Capital? A Critical Race Theory Discussion of Community Cultural Wealth". *Race Ethnicity and Education* 8, no. 1 (2005): 69–91.

CHAPTER 6

Lifelong Learning, Intellectual Curiosity, and Community Building across Generations at Lasell University

Joann M. Montepare *and* Kimberly S. Farah

> **Abstract**
>
> Contemporary educational ventures such as the Age-Friendly University (AFU) initiative have advocated for integrating intergenerational exchange in classroom practices to facilitate the reciprocal sharing of expertise between learners of all ages. This chapter describes age demographic shifts prompting higher education to embrace more age-inclusive approaches to teaching and learning. Opportunities for intergenerational exchange have been designed at Lasell University within the AFU model in collaboration with its university-based retirement community (UBRC) Lasell Village. Empirical research is used to inform best practices and lessons learned from mounting intergenerational programs on our campus.
>
> **Key Words:** age-friendly university, age inclusivity, age diversity, intergenerational, higher education

Talk of Ages	Designated intergenerational courses	Intergenerational course modules
Strengths/impact • Common group approach brings together older and younger learners around issues of mutual interest • Offers broad ways to engage in intergenerational exchange	**Strengths/impact** • Older and younger learners engage in educational exchange across diverse courses in the curriculum • Opportunity to exchange different perspectives that enhance the learning experience	**Strengths/impact** • A time-efficient way to bring older and younger learners together in the classroom • Faculty connect intergenerational teaching using ongoing course content
Limitations • Developing and implementing quality programming requires resources and dedicated personnel	**Limitations** • Some faculty lack the expertise to foster engagement among learners from different generations.	**Limitations** • The logistics of developing modules in advance, managing enrollment, organizing meeting spaces, and other logistics requiring attention

Shifting Age Demographics: Implications for Higher Education and Intergenerational Exchange

Historic changes in age demographics are reshaping societies and challenging higher education to respond to aging populations through new approaches to teaching, research, and community engagement.[1] As communities worldwide becoming more age-diverse than ever,[2] these transformations in social structure have wide-ranging implications for students who will envision extended longevity and enter an age-diverse professional world. Higher education can help to prepare them for their longer lives and the multigenerational workforce they will encounter through more age-inclusive curricular practices. Through such classroom experiences, institutions can also help to combat the ageism that persists in society with negative consequences for both younger and older individuals.[3]

Foreseeing these shifts, scholars in the aging field have long recognized the need for educational models to guide how institutions of higher education will adapt their programs, policies, and partnerships.[4] The Age-Friendly University (AFU) initiative represents one distinctive model reflecting the work of an interdisciplinary team convened at Dublin City University, in collaboration with Arizona State University and the University of Strathclyde, to identify the contributions higher education can make in responding to aging populations.[5] The AFU team identified ten principles institutions can use to inform age-friendly efforts, gaps, and opportunities (see box 6.1).

Box 6.1. Ten Principles for an Age-Friendly University (AFU)

1. To encourage the participation of older adults in all the **core activities** of the university, including educational and research programs.
2. To promote personal and career development in the second half of life and to support those who wish to pursue **second careers**.
3. To recognize the **range of educational needs** of older adults (from those who were early school-leavers through to those who wish to pursue master's or PhD qualifications).
4. To promote **intergenerational learning** to facilitate the reciprocal sharing of expertise between learners of all ages.
5. To widen access to **online educational opportunities** for older adults to ensure a diversity of routes to participation.
6. To ensure that the university's **research agenda** is informed by the needs of an aging society and to promote public discourse on how higher education can better respond to the varied interests and needs of older adults.
7. To increase the understanding of students of the **longevity dividend** and the increasing complexity and richness that aging brings to our society.
8. To enhance access for older adults to the university's range of **health and wellness** programs and its **arts** and **cultural activities**.
9. To engage actively with the university's own **retired community**.
10. To ensure regular **dialogue** with organizations representing the interests of the aging population.

Reproduced by permission of Age-Friendly University Global Network, www.afugn.org.

AFU principles advocate that older adults be enabled to participate in educational, career, cultural, and wellness activities at institutions. In addition to promoting lifelong learning, the principles call for increasing younger adults' understanding of the longevity dividend and the complexity and richness that aging brings to society. To this end, AFU principles advocate for bringing younger and older learners together in educational exchange to facilitate the reciprocal sharing of expertise. To date, the AFU initiative has grown to a burgeoning global network of over a hundred institutions, with momentum continuing to grow.

The value of intergenerational exchange articulated in the AFU principles can be seen on many fronts. From a practical, demographic perspective, intergenerational experiences can help younger and older individuals learn to navigate the evolving age-diverse social structure more effectively. Considering that learning is a lifelong process and goal for many people, with higher education fast becoming a destination for many generations, intergenerational classrooms can offer a way for individuals of all ages to stay engaged in learning. Moreover, considering that many communities are exploring how they can meet the interests of their age-diverse populations, their efforts would benefit from the intergenerational connections higher education can provide students who will become community members. Finally, intergenerational contact offers a way to enhance students' interest in careers in aging that are seeing growth across many professions and job sectors.

The case can also be made that intergenerational exchange has value from a personal, educational perspective.[6] Specifically, it can support learning about and between groups with diverse identities, experiences, and knowledge, as it prompts individuals to explore their own generational and social identities. It can expand awareness of social, psychological, temporal, and other correlates of life span development. Intergenerational exchange also can create opportunities for mutual collaboration, community building, and fostering of solidarity across generations, which are key to combatting ageism.[7]

Theory and research support the case for age-inclusive intergenerational practices as vehicles for disrupting ageist beliefs. In particular, Levy's Positive education about aging and contact experiences (PEACE) model asserts that providing students with facts on aging, positive models who dispel inaccurate images of older adults, and positive intergenerational experiences that are personal and cooperative, and promote equal status are central to reducing ageism and building intergenerational cohesion.[8] Supporting the PEACE model and AFU principles, studies have found that strengthening students' knowledge about aging in college-level courses and providing opportunities for intergenerational exchange are effective ways to shape positive age attitudes. These include courses with a specific aging focus,[9] specialized courses in the health professions,[10] and non-aging-focused courses across the curriculum.[11] The evidence also includes experimental studies[12] and qualitative research.[13] Intergenerational contact through service activities with older community members also offers valuable opportunities to counteract ageism.[14]

Intergenerational interaction also serves as a pathway to healthy aging. Krzeczkowska et al.[15] conducted a systematic review evaluating the impact of intergenerational engagement on cognitive, social, and health outcomes in older adults. Results identified benefits for cross-age attitudes, anxiety, generativity, and physical activity. Similarly, a review by Knight et al.[16] of intervention studies of nonfamilial intergenerational interactions found evidence for a positive impact on younger and older individuals. When the reciprocal giving of time, skill, knowledge, or self was offered in some way by each generation, positive psychosocial outcomes were observed, including more positive age attitudes, reduced stereotypic thinking, broader views of self, greater social connectedness, reduced depression, and an increase in hope for the future. Moreover, life span development research has argued that inculcating positive age attitudes at younger ages through experiences like intergenerational interaction can mitigate negative consequences at later life stages.[17]

Lasell University and Lasell Village: An Age-Friendly Partnership

Campuses and communities have a long history of educational partnerships, and new partnerships around learning and living are emerging as shifting age demographics unfold. In particular, university-based retirement communities (UBRCs) are increasing as desirable housing options for older adults.[18] In the United States, approximately one hundred UBRCs have partnerships with nearby campuses, and the aging of populations coupled with an increase in housing needs is expected to generate new ones, especially given their appeal to older adults with advanced educational backgrounds and active lifestyles.[19] However, these partnerships can differ greatly with respect to their formal policies and educational program structures.[20] For example, Lasell Village hosted by Lasell University requires a formal commitment to lifelong learning by residents.

Lasell University is a small New England institution established in Newton, Massachusetts, in 1851 that enrolls students pursuing professional majors within a liberal arts curriculum. Seeking innovative ways to serve its educational mission and engage the community in lifelong learning, the University built Lasell Village in 2000, which is home to approximately 225 residents ranging in age from 70 to 100-plus living in 13 residential buildings on campus. Lasell Village features an individualized continuing education program in which residents arrange to complete 450 hours of learning and fitness activities annually (the number of in-class credit hours completed by undergraduate students). Accommodations are made if residents are unable to fulfill their plans because of medical or related issues experienced over time.

The AFU initiative provides a guiding framework that can align institutions with UBRCs, as shown in the Lasell University–Lasell Village partnership.[21] In 2015, Lasell University joined the AFU global network, as many of the AFU principles coincided with existing practices at Lasell Village, given its focus on lifelong learning. For example, to meet their individual plans, residents participate in Village educational activities, as well as core activities of the university. Residents can take short-term classes with peers at the Village or enroll with students in semester-long courses across the curriculum. To this end, a roster of designated intergenerational courses is selected each semester. Residents enrolled in undergraduate courses do not take examinations or complete major assignments; however, they are expected to complete routine requirements and participate in daily class activities. Faculty teaching courses meet during the semester to discuss how best to support and leverage intergenerational exchange, along with classroom dynamics and related issues.

Students in other courses may engage in special projects that involve intergenerational interaction. These include interviews with residents about diverse topics such as wartime experiences, interpersonal relationships and dating, social media and privacy, family structure and work dynamics, and the personal meaning of truth, to name a few. As advocated by AFU principles, reciprocal sharing is emphasized, and instructors work with students to prepare them not simply to interview older adults, but to engage in an exchange of experiences and perspectives. Information from these exchanges is shared in final discussions or presentations of written work.

Although many of Lasell's curricular efforts match AFU principles, several challenges have called for creative thinking around designing offerings.[22] Some residents are reluctant to enroll in semester-long courses because they are involved in other activities. In addition, some instructors feel they lack the expertise or skills to mount an intergenerational course. Also, some residents are not interested in engaging in courses that focus on aging issues where there may be expected to be "the aging expert" or informant. It is also of interest to consider the potential negative consequences of such aging-focused activities. Research on age stereotyping has shown that attention to age can have a negative impact on older adults' self-perceptions and undermine performance, such as in the case of stereotype threat.[23] Thus, it may be speculated that bringing older adults' attention to their age in course activities has the potential to backfire and prompt negative internalized age attitudes. Indeed, research has shown that when older adults engage in an activity explicitly associated with age differences, they feel significantly older.[24]

Given these considerations, Montepare and Farah[25] developed an alternative format—intergenerational modules—to complement intergenerational educational efforts within a broader Talk of Ages programming model. The model and alternative format call for bringing older and younger individuals together around topics of common interest, rather than around issues that bring age or age differences into focus. The model draws on intergroup contact theory, positing that positive effects of group contact occur in situations marked by equal group status within the situation, common goals, cooperation, and the support of authority figures (such as faculty) in the setting.[26] Modules include focused activities in classes across the curriculum for one to three weekly sessions (rather than the entire semester).

Applying Evidence-Based Intergenerational Practices at Lasell

In addition to the social-psychological perspective that guided the Talk of Ages model, research by Jarrott and colleagues[27] has provided evidence-based data that speak to what factors drive successful intergenerational exchange and should be incorporated when designing activities. (See *Handbook* chapter 29.) Using a scoping review methodology, they systematically identified intergenerational practices linked to positive program outcomes from peer-reviewed reports published over two decades. These practices can be seen at work in examples of intergenerational exchange at Lasell, providing what serves as experiential confirmation of the empirical evidence.

In their review, Jarrott and colleagues[28] identified fifteen distinct intergenerational practices (see box 6.2).

Box 6.2. Evidence-Based Intergenerational Practices

Incorporate mechanisms of friendship: Participants engaged in practices that build friendship, such as self-disclosure of personal experience, background, and preferences and consistent contact with intergenerational partners.

Select or set the environment: Physical and social elements of the environment were selected or modified to support participant engagement.

Provide training to staff or participant group(s): Staff, youth, or older adults received training to facilitate the intergenerational program.

Foster empathy: Programming taught or promoted empathy for the other group, including through challenging stereotypes.

Promote intergenerational cooperation: Programming encouraged mutual support and a common goal among participants and/or between staff.

Offer meaningful roles: Broadly, roles for youth and older adults were meaningful and developmentally appropriate.

Roles emphasize decision making: Participants engaged in developmentally appropriate decision-making about programming.

Roles involve mentoring: Roles purposefully engaged youth or older person in mentoring the other.

Attend to issues of time: Programming developed with consideration of time of day, frequency, and consistency of intergenerational contact.

Structure activities for flexibility: Intergenerational program plans included potential modifications.

Authority figures endorse intergenerational contact: One or more stakeholder groups demonstrated awareness of, input on, or support for the intergenerational program.

Use technology: Technology was the focus of programming or the means by which young and old participants engaged with each other.

Facilitate to promote interaction: Facilitators used strategies that encourage interaction.

Offer something novel: Novel programming focused attention on the activity, relieving some pressure of meeting someone different.

Convey equal group status: Programming was designed to convey that each age group had something to offer and gain from the interaction.

Source: Jarrott et al. (2021).

Beneficial practices included offering meaningful roles that allow older and younger participants to use their talents and interests and conveying equal group status by communicating that each age group has something to offer and gain from the interaction. It is also important to give participants time and opportunity to share information, explore ideas, and solve problems—in short, promoting cooperation by building on common goals and encouraging mutual support. Successful programs also provided opportunities for participants to develop social connections, friendship, and empathy by talking about their backgrounds, personal experiences, interests, and challenges. Focusing on something novel in intergenerational exchange was an effective strategy because novel programming draws attention to the activity and relieves pressure from the experience that could hold some participants back. The researchers[29] also identified logistical practices that contributed to successful intergenerational program planning, such as providing training, even if simply to ensure that participants understood the learning objectives and expectations. It was also important to consider when and where the intergenerational exchange takes place and if it accommodates the needs of all participants. In addition, they found that successful programs and their creators were recognized for their efforts.

In line with the intergenerational practices identified by Jarrott and colleagues,[30] Lasell encourages courses across the curriculum that allow older and younger individuals to explore topics like social and cultural issues within courses like Wealth and Poverty, incorporate shared activities like art and service projects in courses such as Ceramics or Environmental Justice, and venture into unique and novel experiences in courses like Juvenile Delinquency and Gangs. Intergenerational exchange is also encouraged by way of the Talk of Ages Speakers Series organized around an annual common interest theme (e.g., Healthy Living and the Environment, Exploring Life through Science and Art, The Practice of Politics). When possible, speakers present work on life-span development to enhance students' understanding of the longevity dividend and the complexity of aging rather than focus on overt age comparisons. Lasell also hosts an annual Intergenerational Symposium, an Intergenerational Women's History Month Celebration, and various intergenerational events around issues such as gun violence, voting, food insecurity, and immigration. Other intergenerational efforts have included social events such as talent and musical shows. Both younger and older participants are encouraged to bring their talents, interests, and skills to these exchanges, reinforcing the recommended intergenerational practices of incorporating meaningful roles, cooperation, and equal status into intergenerational programs.

To facilitate interaction, instructors use classroom strategies such as interactive lectures, intergenerational panels, and group discussions. Modules have also been designed around book clubs, film screenings and discussions, class demonstrations, collaborative projects, and other hands-on activities. The topics have been equally diverse. The instructor in a first-year writing course used assigned readings to organize intergenerational small-group discussions around topics such as heroes, artificial intelligence, and the culture of sports. The instructor then built the information into students' essay-writing assignments. The instructor in a social psychology course brought together intergenerational learners to explore social attitudes around civil rights by way of an invited speaker in one class, a film screening in another, and small-group discussions in a final class. These modules are apt examples of drawing on novel topics and developing interactive activities where all age groups can engage and contribute.

Despite the short-term nature of many activities, the importance of logistical practices—scheduling, recruitment, and other planning details—cannot be overlooked. Instructors should take time to inform participants about the goals of the activity and their roles, reinforcing the intergenerational practice regarding training. Participating instructors are offered a small professional development stipend for their efforts and are encouraged to make note of their work in their record of professional scholarship. Faculty efforts are acknowledged in annual campus reports in line with the intergenerational practice recommending recognition for intergenerational programming.

One goal of Lasell's approach to intergenerational exchange is to use a cross-curricular lens when designing activities. For example, in a forensic science class residents worked with the instructor to craft a murder mystery scenario. The instructor then set up a mock crime scene with evidence for students to collect and analyze in the laboratory. Residents played roles as "suspects" for students to interview. After completing their investigation, students put together a "who did it" presentation for an intergenerational audience where they presented their findings and identified the "perpetrator."[31] Course evaluations revealed that students felt the intergenerational activity greatly impacted their learning, However, their attitudes toward older adults were less affected, which may be because the interactions were not specifically designed to foster the exchange of personal experiences and perspectives as Jarrott et al.[32] recommended. Moreover, the science focus of the course and requirement to master laboratory procedures may have detracted from attitude change, and additional efforts at fostering exchange may be needed to impact a noticeable change in attitudes. Instructors in other courses have noted the importance of building opportunities for younger and older individuals to socialize and develop personal connections as a foundation for positive education exchange. Opportunities for intergenerational social interaction outside of classes at campus events can be a useful way to build community connections that spill over into classroom interactions—all of which support the intergenerational practices of incorporating mechanisms of friendship.

Intergenerational efforts can also build empathy by being dementia-inclusive. As part of a Living and Learning with Dementia course, students met with older adults diagnosed with dementia who lived at Lasell Studios, the supportive living unit of Lasell Village. Students completed online training in TimeSlips, a creative, collaborative storytelling technique designed to promote social connections and engagement in older adults experiencing cognitive impairment.[33] Students facilitated weekly storytelling sessions. Evaluations of students' experiences showed that while they retained fears and concerns about dementia, they expressed a greater appreciation for preserving the dignity of individuals with dementia and the desire to be treated with patience, understanding, respect, and a sense of normalcy if they were to develop dementia at an older age.[34]

Lasell's Talk of Ages Campus Conversations project demonstrates the value of reciprocal learning via mentoring. In this module, residents were conversation partners in a writing class designed for international students. Residents and students met for several weeks and participated in interactive activities designed by the instructor to help students practice and hone their language skills. Students then prepared presentations about their home cultures for residents. All participants reported positive reactions, and the instructor found that the activity enhanced the overall classroom experience. In a related module, a psychology internship instructor developed a mock interview activity in which residents served as job recruiters. In a health sciences capstone class, residents with a background in research served as advisors for students conducting research projects. In addition to showing how mentoring can support educational goals such as skill development and career readiness, these activities illustrate how older adults can be assets in the classroom and more broadly contribute to the educational mission of higher education.

Instructors have also used technology for programming and for engaging participants. For example, they have arranged for research scholars, community leaders, film directors, and others to meet virtually with intergenerational classes to explore a variety of issues. While the Lasell setting is more conducive to in-person interaction, other AFU campuses report an increase in the demand for virtual programs.[35]

Lessons Learned and Future Directions

Three lessons can be gleaned from the experiences of intergenerational exchange on the Lasell campus. First, the pedagogical practices related to age inclusivity can be part of broader educational diversity efforts. Models such as contact theory have been used to guide educational exchange that aims to bring students together from different racial and ethnic groups.[36] Intergenerational exchange can likewise be incorporated into more encompassing curricular efforts that encourage students to explore individual differences and societal contexts that impact human behaviors, perspectives, emotional experiences, and intellectual processes. In this way, age inclusivity should be integrated into the diversity, equity, and inclusion efforts advocated by institutions.[37]

Second, it is important to track, recognize, and publicize innovative age-friendly efforts. A recent study of AFU campuses found that many students, faculty, and staff did not know about various age-friendly programs that were in place.[38] If momentum is to be created and sustained around intergenerational exchange, attention to building awareness is key. This includes communicating about the contributions of faculty that can serve as an inspiration and model to others.

Third, one cannot underestimate the importance of logistics and the need to understand how planning, incentives, support, recognition, and other factors can enrich instructors' efforts and encourage others to get involved. Instructors also have noted the need to plan for cohort-related and individual age-related differences that bring diversity to classroom activities. As one instructor observed, "An underlying concept when designing courses for adults who may vary in age, cognitive, and physical levels is to consider a variety of choices in the way information is acquired, demonstrated, and assessed. Choices built into the course give students of all ages agency and diminish the isolating effects of having to create ad hoc concessions to age-related learner variability."[39] Instructors also note differences in students' learning expectations; whereas some younger students may enroll in courses because they meet a requirement, older participants may seek out courses because they satisfy a curiosity.[40] Different motivations can lead to imbalances in engagement with course content and fellow students. Instructors further note that as more experienced learners, older adults may come prepared to challenge content and participate in discussions. Left unmanaged, such enthusiasm can occasionally result in older participants dominating the discussion, which in turn can be intimidating to younger students who may hesitate to disagree. While such dynamics are not new to classrooms, instructors in intergenerational courses may address them differently because of the unique status of the older participants. Lasell instructors find it useful to communicate with them at the onset of a course about expectations and classroom practices. Many Lasell Village residents hold undergraduate and advanced graduate degrees and have work experience and professional backgrounds that can emerge as skill differences in the classroom. One approach to these differences is to be mindful of incorporating topics or activities that draw on different levels of skill or perspectives. Another strategy is to approach skill differences as a learning opportunity. For example, students often approach presentations to an older audience with more seriousness and attention to detail than when presenting to peers.[41] These observations are consistent with assertions that bringing generations together in higher education can serve as a strategy for sharpening basic academic skills and broadening content knowledge.[42]

Looking to the future, more research into intergenerational practices is needed. While evaluations of intergenerational exchange yield strong evidence demonstrating the positive impact of activities on aging-related attitudes, less is known about the extent to which it impacts content acquisition, skill learning, and related educational outcomes. As Jarrott and colleagues[43] further note, while the intergenerational practices they identified reflect extant theory and research, robust implementation research is needed to advance evidence-based intergenerational practice. This is especially true as efforts such as the AFU initiative cultivate more intergenerational opportunities in higher education.

Notes
1. Carrie Andreoletti, Joann Montepare, and Nina Silverstein, "Higher Education and Aging: The Age-Friendly Movement," Gerontological Society of America, 2019; Joann M. Montepare, "Introduction to the Special Issue-Age-Friendly Universities (AFU): Principles, Practices, and Opportunities," *Gerontology & Geriatrics Education* 40, no. 2 (2019): 139–41; Craig A. Talmage et al., "Age Friendly Universities and

Engagement with Older Adults: Moving from Principles to Practice," *International Journal of Lifelong Education* 35, no. 5 (2016): 537–54.

2. Wan He, Daniel Goodkind, and Paul Kowal, "An Aging World: 2015 International Population Reports," 2015, https://ifa.ngo/wp-content/uploads/2016/04/An-Aging-World-2015-Census-bureau-and-WHO.pdf; U.S. Census Bureau, "65 and Older Population Grows Rapidly as Baby Boomers Age," U.S. Census Bureau, June 25, 2020, https://www.census.gov/newsroom/press-releases/2020/65-older-population-grows.html.

3. Joann M. Montepare and Lisa M. Brown, "Age-Friendly Universities (AFU): Combating and Inoculating against Ageism in a Pandemic and Beyond," *Journal of Social Issues* 78, no. 4 (2022): 1017–37; Susan Krause Whitbourne and Joann Montepare, "What's Holding Us Back? Ageism in Higher Education," in *Ageism: Stereotyping and Prejudice against Older Persons*, 2nd ed., ed. T. Nelson (Cambridge, MA: MIT Press, 2017), 263–90.

4. Sandra L. McGuire, Diane A. Klein, and Donna Couper, "Aging Education: A National Imperative," *Educational Gerontology* 31, no. 6 (2005): 443–60.

5. Christine O'Kelly, "What Is the Age-Friendly University Initiative," Dublin City University, 2015. https://www.dcu.ie/sites/default/files/inline-files/age-friendly-university-initiative.pdf.

6. Mariano Sánchez and Matthew Kaplan, "Intergenerational Learning in Higher Education: Making the Case for Multigenerational Classrooms," *Educational Gerontology* 40, no. 7 (2014): 473–85.

7. Sheri R. Levy, "Toward Reducing Ageism: PEACE (Positive Education about Aging and Contact Experiences) Model," *Gerontologist* 58, no. 2 (2016): gnw116.

8. Ashley Lytle and Sheri R. Levy, "Reducing Ageism: Education about Aging and Extended Contact with Older Adults," *Gerontologist* 59, no. 3 (2017): 580–88; Ashley Lytle and Sheri R. Levy, "Reducing Ageism toward Older Adults and Highlighting Older Adults as Contributors during the COVID-19 Pandemic," *Journal of Social Issues*, 78, no. 4 (2022): 1066–1084.

9. Shira Hantman et al., "Bringing Older Adults into the Classroom: The Sharing Community Model," *Gerontology & Geriatrics Education* 34, no. 2 (2013): 135–49; Rona J. Karasik et al., "Two Thumbs Up: Using Popular Films in Introductory Aging Courses," *Gerontology & Geriatrics Education* 35, no. 1 (2013): 86–113; Sandy K. Wurtele and LaRae Maruyama, "Changing Students' Stereotypes of Older Adults," *Teaching of Psychology* 40, no. 1 (2012): 59–61.

10. Ernest Gonzales, Nancy Morrow-Howell, and Pat Gilbert, "Changing Medical Students' Attitudes toward Older Adults," *Gerontology & Geriatrics Education* 31, no. 3 (2010): 220–34.

11. Ashley E. Ermer, Katie York, and Katharine Mauro, "Addressing Ageism Using Intergenerational Performing Arts Interventions," *Gerontology & Geriatrics Education* 42, no. 3 (2020): 308–15; Ashley Lytle, Nancy Nowacek, and Sheri R. Levy, "Instapals: Reducing Ageism by Facilitating Intergenerational Contact and Providing Aging Education," *Gerontology & Geriatrics Education* 41, no. 3 (2020): 1–12; Joann M. Montepare and Kimberly S. Farah, "Talk of Ages: Using Intergenerational Classroom Modules to Engage Older and Younger Students across the Curriculum," *Gerontology & Geriatrics Education* 39, no. 3 (2017): 385–94.

12. Takashi Yamashita et al., "Impact of Life Stories on College Students' Positive and Negative Attitudes toward Older Adults," *Gerontology & Geriatrics Education* 39, no. 3 (2017): 326–40; Lytle, "Instapals," 5.

13. Frankline Augustin and Brenda Freshman, "The Effects of Service-Learning on College Students' Attitudes toward Older Adults," *Gerontology & Geriatrics Education* 37, no. 2 (2015): 123–44; Lisa S. Wagner and Tana M. Luger, "Generation to Generation: Effects of Intergenerational Interactions on Attitudes," *Educational Gerontology* 47, no. 1 (2020): 1–12.

14. Carrie Andreoletti and Jessica L. Howard, "Bridging the Generation Gap: Intergenerational Service-Learning Benefits Young and Old," *Gerontology & Geriatrics Education* 39, no. 1 (2016): 46–60; Skye N. Leedahl et al., "Implementing an Interdisciplinary Intergenerational Program Using the Cyber Seniors® Reverse Mentoring Model within Higher Education," *Gerontology & Geriatrics Education* 40, no. 1 (2018): 71–89; Jennifer Tehan Stanley et al., "An Age-Friendly University (AFU) Assists with Technology Learning and Social Engagement among Older Adults and Individuals with Developmental Disabilities," *Gerontology & Geriatrics Education* 40, no. 2 (2019): 261–75.

15. Anna Krzeczkowska et al., "A Systematic Review of the Impacts of Intergenerational Engagement on Older Adults' Cognitive, Social, and Health Outcomes," *Ageing Research Reviews* 71 (2021): 101400.

16. Tess Knight et al., "The Act of Giving: A Systematic Review of Nonfamilial Intergenerational Interaction," *Journal of Intergenerational Relationships* 12, no. 3 (2014): 257–78.

17. Knight, "The Act of Giving," 263; Montepare and Brown, "Age-Friendly Universities (AFU)."
18. Molly Maxfield et al., "Mirabella at Arizona State University: A Case Example in Innovation at a University-Based Retirement Community," *Journal of Aging and Environment* 38, no. 3 (2023): 1–20; Talmage et al., "Age Friendly Universities," 550.
19. Carle, Andrew, "University-Based Retirement Communities: Criteria for Success," iAdvance Senior Care, September 1, 2006, https://www.iadvanceseniorcare.com/university-based-retirement-communities-criteria-for-success/; Mary Kate Nelson, "What Senior Living Residents Really Want from University Partnerships," Senior Housing News, December 7, 2017, https://seniorhousingnews.com/2017/12/07/senior-living-residents-really-want-university-partnerships/; Erin Kate Smith, Ellen K. Rozek, and Keith Diaz Moore, "Creating SPOTs for Successful Aging: Strengthening the Case for Developing University-Based Retirement Communities Using Social-Physical Place over Time Theory," *Journal of Housing for the Elderly* 28, no. 1 (2014): 21–40.
20. Su-I Hou and Xian Cao, "Promising Aging in Community Models in the U.S.: Village, Naturally Occurring Retirement Community (NORC), Cohousing, and University-Based Retirement Community (UBRC)," *Gerontology and Geriatric Medicine* 7 (2021): 233372142110154.
21. Montepare, "Introduction to the Special," 139.
22. Montepare and Farah, "Talk of Ages," 390; Joann M. Montepare and Lisa M. Brown, "Age-Friendly Universities (AFU): Combating and Inoculating against Ageism in a Pandemic and Beyond," *Journal of Social Issues* 78, no. 4 (2022): 1017–37.
23. Alison L. Chasteen, Sonia K. Kang, and Jessica D. Remedios, "Aging and Stereotype Threat: Development, Process, and Interventions," Oxford Academic, January 1, 2012, https://doi.org/10.1093/acprof:oso/9780199732449.003.0013.
24. Matthew L. Hughes, Lisa Geraci, and Ross L. De Forrest, "Aging 5 Years in 5 Minutes," *Psychological Science* 24, no. 12 (2013): 2481–88.
25. Montepare and Farah, "Talk of Ages," 390.
26. Gordon W. Allport, *The Nature of Prejudice* (Cambridge MA: Addison-Wesley, 1954); Thomas F. Pettigrew and Linda R. Tropp, "A Meta-Analytic Test of Intergroup Contact Theory," *Journal of Personality and Social Psychology* 90, no. 5 (2006): 751–83.
27. Shannon E. Jarrott et al., "Implementation of Evidence-Based Practices in Intergenerational Programming: A Scoping Review," *Research on Aging* 43, no. 7–8 (2021): 283–93.
28. Jarrott et al., "Implementation of Evidence-Based Practices," 288.
29. Jarrott et al., "Implementation of Evidence-Based Practices," 289.
30. Jarrott et al., "Implementation of Evidence-Based Practices," 291.
31. Kim Farah and Joann M. Montepare, "Unusual Suspects for Age-Friendly University (AFU) Intergenerational Classroom Exchange: A Classroom Case Study in Forensic Science," *Gerontology & Geriatrics Education* 44, no. 1 (2022): 41–50.
32. Jarrott et al., "Implementation of Evidence-Based Practices," 291.
33. T. Fritsch et al., "Impact of TimeSlips, a Creative Expression Intervention Program, on Nursing Home Residents with Dementia and Their Caregivers," *Gerontologist* 49, no. 1 (2009): 117–27.
34. Joann Montepare, "Integrating Dementia Inclusive Teaching and Learning on an Age Friendly University (AFU) Campus," poster for annual meeting of the American Psychological Association, Washington, DC, August 6, 2020.
35. Cathy McKay, "The Value of Contact: Unpacking Allport's Contact Theory to Support Inclusive Education." *Palaestra* 32, no. 1 (2018): 21–25.
36. Nancy Morrow-Howell et al., "Making the Case for Age-Diverse Universities," *Gerontologist* 60, no. 7 (2019): 1187–93.
37. Nina M. Silverstein et al., "Assessing Age Inclusivity in Higher Education: Introducing the Age-Friendly Inventory and Campus Climate Survey," *Gerontologist* 62, no. 1 (2021): e48–61.
38. Jason Dauenhauer et al., "Faculty Perceptions of Engaging Older Adults in Higher Education: The Need for Intergenerational Pedagogy," *Gerontology & Geriatrics Education* 43, no. 4 (2021): 1–22.
39. Joann Montepare and Mark Sciegaj, "College Classrooms as Intergenerational Contact Zones," in *Intergenerational Contact Zones: Place-Based Tools and Tactics for Promoting Social Inclusion and Belonging*, ed. Matthew Kaplan et al. (New York: Routledge, 2020), 137–45.
40. Montepare and Sciegaj, "College Classrooms as Intergenerational Contact Zones," 139.
41. Montepare and Farah, "Talk of Ages," 390.

42. Sánchez and Kaplan, "Intergenerational Learning in Higher Education," 480.
43. Jarrott et al., "Implementation of Evidence-Based Practices," 291.

Bibliography

Allport, Gordon W. *The Nature of Prejudice*. Cambridge, MA: Addison-Wesley, 1954.

Andreoletti, Carrie, and Jessica L. Howard. "Bridging the Generation Gap: Intergenerational Service-Learning Benefits Young and Old." *Gerontology & Geriatrics Education* 39, no. 1 (2016): 46–60. https://doi.org/10.1080/02701960.2016.1152266.

Andreoletti, Carrie, Joann Montepare, and Nina Silverstein. "Higher Education and Aging: The Age-Friendly Movement." Gerontological Society of America, 2019. https://www.geron.org/publications/what-s-hot.

Augustin, Frankline, and Brenda Freshman. "The Effects of Service-Learning on College Students' Attitudes toward Older Adults." *Gerontology & Geriatrics Education* 37, no. 2 (2015): 123–44. https://doi.org/10.1080/02701960.2015.1079705.

Breck, Bethany M., Cory B. Dennis, and Skye N. Leedahl. "Implementing Reverse Mentoring to Address Social Isolation among Older Adults." *Journal of Gerontological Social Work* 61, no. 5 (2018): 513–25. https://doi.org/10.1080/01634372.2018.1448030.

Carle, Andrew. "University-Based Retirement Communities: Criteria for Success." iAdvance Senior Care. September 1, 2006. https://www.iadvanceseniorcare.com/university-based-retirement-communities-criteria-for-success/.

Chasteen, Alison L., Sonia K. Kang, and Jessica D. Remedios. "Aging and Stereotype Threat: Development, Process, and Interventions," Oxford Academic. January 1, 2012. https://doi.org/10.1093/acprof:oso/9780199732449.003.0013.

Dauenhauer, Jason, A. Hazzan, K. Heffernan, and C. M. Milliner. "Faculty Perceptions of Engaging Older Adults in Higher Education: The Need for Intergenerational Pedagogy." *Gerontology & Geriatrics Education* 43, no. 4 (2021): 1–22. https://doi.org/10.1080/02701960.2021.1910506.

Ermer, Ashley E., Katie York, and Katharine Mauro. "Addressing Ageism Using Intergenerational Performing Arts Interventions." *Gerontology & Geriatrics Education* 42, no. 3 (2020): 308–15. https://doi.org/10.1080/02701960.2020.1737046.

Farah, Kim, and Joann M Montepare. "Unusual Suspects for Age-Friendly University (AFU) Intergenerational Classroom Exchange: A Classroom Case Study in Forensic Science." *Gerontology & Geriatrics Education* 44, no. 1 (2022): 41–50. https://doi.org/10.1080/02701960.2022.2106479.

Fritsch, T., J. Kwak, S. Grant, J. Lang, R. R. Montgomery, and A. D. Basting. "Impact of TimeSlips, a Creative Expression Intervention Program, on Nursing Home Residents with Dementia and Their Caregivers." *The Gerontologist* 49, no. 1 (February 1, 2009): 117–27. https://doi.org/10.1093/geront/gnp008.

Gonzales, Ernest, Nancy Morrow-Howell, and Pat Gilbert. "Changing Medical Students' Attitudes toward Older Adults." *Gerontology & Geriatrics Education* 31, no. 3 (August 26, 2010): 220–34. https://doi.org/10.1080/02701960.2010.503128.

Gruenewald, Tara L., E. K. Tanner, L. P. Fried, M. C. Carlson, Q. L. Xue, J. M. Parisi, et al. "The Baltimore Experience Corps Trial: Enhancing Generativity via Intergenerational Activity Engagement in Later Life." *Journals of Gerontology Series B: Psychological Sciences and Social Sciences* 71, no. 4 (2015): 661–70. https://doi.org/10.1093/geronb/gbv005.

Hantman, Shira, M. B. Oz, C. Gutman, and W. Criden. "Bringing Older Adults into the Classroom: The Sharing Community Model." *Gerontology & Geriatrics Education* 34, no. 2 (2013): 135–49. https://doi.org/10.1080/02701960.2012.679372.

He, Wan, Daniel Goodkind, and Paul Kowal. "An Aging World: 2015 International Population Reports," 2015. https://ifa.ngo/wp-content/uploads/2016/04/An-Aging-World-2015-Census-bureau-and-WHO.pdf.

Hou, Su-I and Xian Cao. "Promising Aging in Community Models in the U.S.: Village, Naturally Occurring Retirement Community (NORC), Cohousing, and University-Based Retirement Community (UBRC)." *Gerontology and Geriatric Medicine* 7 (2021): 233372142110154. https://doi.org/10.1177/23337214211015451.

Hughes, Matthew L., Lisa Geraci, and Ross L. De Forrest. "Aging 5 Years in 5 Minutes." *Psychological Science* 24, no. 12 (2013): 2481–88. https://doi.org/10.1177/0956797613494853.

Jarrott, Shannon E., R. M. Scrivano, C. Park, and A. N. Mendoza. "Implementation of Evidence-Based Practices in Intergenerational Programming: A Scoping Review." *Research on Aging* 43, no. 7–8 (2021): 283–93. https://doi.org/10.1177/0164027521996191.

June, Andrea, and Carrie Andreoletti. "Using an Age-Friendly University Lens to Explore Community Member Engagement during the Pandemic." *Gerontology & Geriatrics Education* 44, no. 1 (2021): 27–40. https://doi.org/10.1080/02701960.2021.2005039.

Karasik, Rona J., R. Hamon, J. Writz, and A. Moddu Reddy. "Two Thumbs Up: Using Popular Films in Introductory Aging Courses." *Gerontology & Geriatrics Education* 35, no. 1 (2013): 86–113. https://doi.org/10.1080/02701960.2012.749253.

Knight, Tess, H. Skouteris, M. Townsend, and M. Hooley. "The Act of Giving: A Systematic Review of Nonfamilial Intergenerational Interaction." *Journal of Intergenerational Relationships* 12, no. 3 (2014): 257–78. https://doi.org/10.1080/15350770.2014.929913.

Krzeczkowska, Anna, D. M. Spalding, W. J. McGeown, A. J. Go, M. C. Carlso, and L. A. B. Nicholls. "A Systematic Review of the Impacts of Intergenerational Engagement on Older Adults' Cognitive, Social, and Health Outcomes." *Ageing Research Reviews* 71 (2021): 101400. https://doi.org/10.1016/j.arr.2021.101400.

Leedahl, Skye N., M. S. Brasher, E. Estus, B. M. Breck, C. B. Dennis, and S. C. Clark. "Implementing an Interdisciplinary Intergenerational Program Using the Cyber Seniors® Reverse Mentoring Model within Higher Education." *Gerontology & Geriatrics Education* 40, no. 1 (2018): 71–89. https://doi.org/10.1080/02701960.2018.1428574.

Levy, Sheri R. "Toward Reducing Ageism: PEACE (Positive Education about Aging and Contact Experiences) Model." *The Gerontologist* 58, no. 2 (2016): gnw116. https://doi.org/10.1093/geront/gnw116.

Lytle, Ashley, and Sheri R. Levy. "Reducing Ageism: Education about Aging and Extended Contact with Older Adults." *Gerontologist* 59, no. 3 (2017): 580–88. https://doi.org/10.1093/geront/gnx177.

Lytle, Ashley, and Sheri R. Levy. "Reducing Ageism toward Older Adults and Highlighting Older Adults as Contributors during the COVID-19 Pandemic." *Journal of Social Issues* 78, no. 4 (2022): 1066–1084. https://doi.org/10.1111/josi.12545.

Lytle, Ashley, Nancy Nowacek, and Sheri R. Levy. "Instapals: Reducing Ageism by Facilitating Intergenerational Contact and Providing Aging Education." *Gerontology & Geriatrics Education* 41, no. 3 (2020): 1–12. https://doi.org/10.1080/02701960.2020.1737047.

Maxfield, Molly, L. Beagley, A. Peckham, M. A. Guest, H. L. Giasson, D. R. Byrd, et al. "Mirabella at Arizona State University: A Case Example in Innovation at a University-Based Retirement Community." *Journal of Aging and Environment* 38, no. 3 (2023): 1–20. https://doi.org/10.1080/26892618.2022.2158512.

McGuire, Sandra L., Diane A. Klein, and Donna Couper. "Aging Education: A National Imperative." *Educational Gerontology* 31, no. 6 (2005): 443–60. https://doi.org/10.1080/03601270590928170.

McKay, Cathy. "The Value of Contact: Unpacking Allport's Contact Theory to Support Inclusive Education." *Palaestra* 32, no. 1 (2018): 21–25.

Montepare, Joann M. "Introduction to the Special Issue-Age-Friendly Universities (AFU): Principles, Practices, and Opportunities." *Gerontology & Geriatrics Education* 40, no. 2 (2019): 139–41. https://doi.org/10.1080/02701960.2019.1591848.

Montepare, Joann, M. "Integrating Dementia Inclusive Teaching and Learning on an Age Friendly University (AFU) Campus." Poster presented at the annual meeting of the American Psychological Association, Washington, DC, August 6, 2020.

Montepare, Joann M., and Lisa M. Brown. "Age-Friendly Universities (AFU): Combating and Inoculating against Ageism in a Pandemic and Beyond." *Journal of Social Issues* 78, no. 4 (2022): 1017–37. https://doi.org/10.1111/josi.12541.

Montepare, Joann M., and Kimberly S. Farah. "Talk of Ages: Using Intergenerational Classroom Modules to Engage Older and Younger Students across the Curriculum." *Gerontology & Geriatrics Education* 39, no. 3 (2017): 385–94. https://doi.org/10.1080/02701960.2016.1269006.

Montepare, Joann, and Mark Sciegaj. "College Classrooms as Intergenerational Contact Zones." In *Intergenerational Contact Zones: Place-Based Tools and Tactics for Promoting Social Inclusion and Belonging*, edited by Matthew Kaplan, L. L. Thang, M. Sanzhez, and A. J. Hoffman, 137–45. New York: Routledge, 2020.

Morrow-Howell, Nancy, E. F. Lawlor, E. S. Macias, E. Swinford, and J. Brandt. "Making the Case for Age-Diverse Universities." *Gerontologist* 60, no. 7 (2019): 1187–93. https://doi.org/10.1093/geront/gnz181.

Nelson, Mary Kate. "What Senior Living Residents Really Want from University Partnerships." Senior Housing News. December 7, 2017. https://seniorhousingnews.com/2017/12/07/senior-living-residents-really-want-university-partnerships/.

O'Kelly, Christine. "What Is the Age-Friendly University Initiative." Dublin City University. 2015. https://www.dcu.ie/sites/default/files/inline-files/age-friendly-university-initiative.pdf.

Pettigrew, Thomas F., and Linda R. Tropp. "A Meta-Analytic Test of Intergroup Contact Theory." *Journal of Personality and Social Psychology* 90, no. 5 (2006): 751–83. https://doi.org/10.1037/0022-3514.90.5.751.

Sánchez, Mariano, and Matthew Kaplan. "Intergenerational Learning in Higher Education: Making the Case for Multigenerational Classrooms." *Educational Gerontology* 40, no. 7 (2014): 473–85. https://doi.org/10.1080/03601277.2013.844039.

Silverstein, Nina M., S. K. Whitbourne, L. M. Bowen, J. M. Montepare, T. Jansen, C. Beaulieu, et al. "Assessing Age Inclusivity in Higher Education: Introducing the Age-Friendly Inventory and Campus Climate Survey." *Gerontologist* 62, no. 1 (2021): e48–61. https://doi.org/10.1093/geront/gnab090.

Smith, Erin Kate, Ellen K. Rozek, and Keith Diaz Moore. "Creating SPOTs for Successful Aging: Strengthening the Case for Developing University-Based Retirement Communities Using Social-Physical Place over Time Theory." *Journal of Housing for the Elderly* 28, no. 1 (2014): 21–40. https://doi.org/10.1080/02763893.2013.858091.

Stanley, Jennifer Tehan, L. B. Morrison, B. A. Webster, J. R. Turner, and C. J. Richards. "An Age-Friendly University (AFU) Assists with Technology Learning and Social Engagement among Older Adults and Individuals with Developmental Disabilities." *Gerontology & Geriatrics Education* 40, no. 2 (2019): 261–75. https://doi.org/10.1080/02701960.2019.1572009.

Talmage, Craig A., Rob Mark, Maria Slowey, and Richard C. Knopf. "Age Friendly Universities and Engagement with Older Adults: Moving from Principles to Practice." *International Journal of Lifelong Education* 35, no. 5 (2016): 537–54. https://doi.org/10.1080/02601370.2016.1224040.

U.S. Census Bureau. "65 and Older Population Grows Rapidly as Baby Boomers Age." U.S. Census Bureau. June 25, 2020. https://www.census.gov/newsroom/press-releases/2020/65-older-population-grows.html.

Wagner, Lisa S., and Tana M. Luger. "Generation to Generation: Effects of Intergenerational Interactions on Attitudes." *Educational Gerontology* 47, no. 1 (2020): 1–12. https://doi.org/10.1080/03601277.2020.1847392.

Whitbourne, Susan Krause, and Joann Montepare. "What's Holding Us Back? Ageism in Higher Education." In *Ageism: Stereotyping and Prejudice against Older Persons*, 2nd ed., edited by T. Nelson, 263–90. Cambridge, MA: MIT Press, 2017.

Wurtele, Sandy K., and LaRae Maruyama. "Changing Students' Stereotypes of Older Adults." *Teaching of Psychology* 40, no. 1 (2012): 59–61. https://doi.org/10.1177/0098628312465867.

Yamashita, Takashi, S. J. Hahn, J. M. Kinney, and L. W. Poon. "Impact of Life Stories on College Students' Positive and Negative Attitudes toward Older Adults." *Gerontology & Geriatrics Education* 39, no. 3 (2017): 326–40. https://doi.org/10.1080/02701960.2017.1311884.

CHAPTER 7

CIRKEL: The Startup That Pioneered Two-Way Mentoring across Generations in the Workforce

Charlotte Japp

Abstract

CIRKEL was a first-of-its-kind tech-enabled platform that connected professionals aged fifty-plus with younger workers for two-way mentoring and career support. The company was originally established as a New York City–based event series to foster cross-generational networking and later evolved into a tech startup offering an intergenerational community membership for monthly introductions. This chapter presents an overview of CIRKEL's evolution and the key challenges and opportunities that enabled the business to change how it connected older and younger professionals over the course of five years. It also offers specific data about CIRKEL's target market and the impact intergenerational connections made on real careers. Lastly, the chapter presents an example of an intergenerational program that services its community using a for-profit business model, offering marketing and business insights to other programs that hinge on a revenue model.

Key Words: mentoring, career transitions, career support, intergenerational, startup, future of work, career longevity, five-generation workforce, networking

CIRKEL

Strengths/impact
- Appealing brand and positioning that resonated with five generations of participants
- Significant press (*Wall Street Journal, New York Times, Forbes, Washington Post*)
- Revenue-driven through paid memberships and commercial partnerships
- Highly engaged community with members who participated for years at a time
- Members' progress in their careers (new jobs, cross-generational hiring, member-to-member collaboration on projects, and general shifts in how members perceived and appreciated other generations.

Limitations
- Lack of funding
- Postpandemic slowdown in the public's desire for virtual communities
- A product that members were unaccustomed to using or paying for (i.e., a new category)
- Inconsistency in match quality and lack of guarantee for a membership's outcome

CIRKEL's Origin Story and Finding a "Why"

CIRKEL was founded in 2018 by Charlotte Japp when she was twenty-eight years old. She was five years into a marketing career working at VICE Media, a self-proclaimed "youth media" company known for its bold verité-style documentaries and news journalism. VICE made a point of publicizing the young ages of its workforce, and former employees remember jokes about trap doors appearing as soon as VICE employees aged beyond their twenties.

For most VICE employees, the lack of age diversity reinforced a feeling of being part of a special club whose members all spoke the same language and cited commonly understood cultural references. In a *Fast Company* article from 2014,[1] Ciel Hunter, one of the thirty-something company leaders who had advanced up the ranks at VICE, was interviewed: "One might also expect what Hunter called the VICE career trajectory to include being kicked out the back door once you hit thirty. But a surprising number of senior employees have been with the company for more than five years and, more importantly, have come up through the ranks across disciplines. Grooming leaders from within the company—people who have done everything from shoot video to answer phones—helps fortify a company culture against the disruptive influence of rapid growth."

For Charlotte Japp, the lack of age diversity started to feel more and more palpable as the company experienced growing pains. With new investment and expanding teams, there was little thought put toward employees' professional development. Most of the VICE workforce had never worked at another company and were missing key skills in leadership training. Charlotte found herself unsure of how to have hard conversations at work or ask for help learning a particular skill. Unlike her colleagues, however, Charlotte had a secret weapon: her parents.

After graduating from Georgetown University, Charlotte moved back home to live with her parents in New York for the first four years of her career. While Charlotte was initially embarrassed about the decision, the cogenerational housing situation ended up becoming a productive and meaningful part of her career transition, as well as that of her parents.

Charlotte's parents, Michael and Christina Japp, were originally from England and Germany, respectively, but met in Paris and started a family there. In 1992 when Michael was offered a competitive job opportunity to work at an advertising firm in New York, the family moved to the United States. Michael's time at the firm did not last more than a couple of years and, when the firm lost a client, he was laid off at the age of fifty. Despite the countless awards under his belt, Michael was a middle-aged creative director in a new country, where his professional network was limited.

Christina Japp had three children before starting her career in the art auction business. She began as an intern at Sotheby's, the esteemed auction house. She worked her way up over the course of fifteen years until she was a Senior Vice President in Sotheby's 20th Century Design Department. She was let go during the financial crisis in 2008. Noticing that she was in the company of several colleagues over age forty, she inquired with the HR department to see the ages of each person affected in the layoff but decided not to pursue the issue further.

Both Michael and Christina had to make key career transitions when their initial careers ended. In both cases, they ended up starting their own businesses and becoming entrepreneurs. During the four years when Charlotte lived with her parents, all three of them were experiencing pivotal career transitions. Charlotte was beginning her first job, and Michael and Christina were transitioning into their second careers. Charlotte and her parents were on opposite ends of their careers, but their respective skills and experiences turned out to be remarkably complementary.

Charlotte's work during the dawn of social media apps like Facebook, YouTube, Instagram, and Twitter meant that she could help her parents navigate through a new age of technology, especially when it came to promoting their fledgling businesses. In turn, they shared their decades of work experience with Charlotte, who struggled with such basic workplace challenges as disagreeing about a project idea with a coworker or negotiating a raise with her boss. While Charlotte's VICE colleagues were scratching their heads figuring out how to find a mentor in an all-millennial office, Charlotte was having daily conversations about her work projects and career plans with two experienced professionals who happened to be genetically related to her. And, of course, she was giving her own version of that guidance right back to them.

CIRKEL's origin story is important, because it created a model for intergenerational connections in a professional context that was very different from existing archetypes. This was neither a top-down transfer of wisdom from older to younger nor a sterile corporate program structured around specific job functions. The model demonstrated that mentoring can and should be a two-way street and that there are ways to design the experience so that it feels aspirational, blending personal growth with career development.

The CIRKEL Model (and Evolution)

The format for CIRKEL evolved over time as both current events and team capabilities evolved. CIRKEL launched as an intergenerational networking event series on June 8, 2018 at the Bowery Poetry Club in New York City. Given the founder's background in digital media, she organized a presentation by a successful media mogul from the baby boomer generation, Diane di Costanzo. Diane tracked her four decades in publishing, from her start at a fashion magazine to working at a paperback book publisher, to ending up in digital media and brand partnerships at Meredith Group. The presentation was accompanied by colorful slides complete with personal photos from milestones and lessons learned along the way.

The audience was made up of approximately fifty guests, ranging in age from early twenties to early seventies. After the presentation, they participated in a networking game called "The CIRKEL Game." The game randomly assembled small groups of four attendees from different generations who were each given a color-coded quarter of a circle that matched three other quarters throughout the room. Once each group formed, they were given prompts to spark conversation, for example, "What's one misconception about your generation that you want to correct? How is it a misconception?" and "What's a challenge you're currently having in your career?" These prompts were designed to generate some vulnerability quickly and invite the others in the group to offer ideas or insights from their various backgrounds. With a cash bar in the mix, it was an energetic beginning to what would later become hundreds of events.

In one notable example, CIRKEL hosted an event at the designer Prabal Gurung's boutique in Manhattan's West Village[2] that featured a panel of fashion powerhouses from three generations: Gen Z (Lindsay Peoples Wagner, editor-in-chief at "The Cut" within *New York Magazine*), Millennial (Michelle Lee, former editor-in-chief of *Allure*), and Silent Generation (Bethann Hardison, former supermodel and talent agent). The true testament to CIRKEL's power in creating relevance around intergenerational dialogue was demonstrated when Anna Wintour, the Vogue icon herself, walked into the room.

CIRKEL's event programming picked up momentum and even piqued the interest of Marci Alboher, an executive at CoGenerate (formerly known as Encore.org) who wrote a piece in *The New York Times* called "The New 50s: Far from Retirement"[3] and included CIRKEL as an example of how working adults can leverage new tools and communities to address midlife's evolution.

In later CIRKEL events, attendees began offering feedback for ways to improve the experience. Many midlife workers felt sheepish about introducing themselves to younger attendees without a warm introduction. They needed personalized connections earlier on in the run-of-show, essentially looking for ways to be introduced to other attendees upon arrival. For the CIRKEL organizers, making curated introductions onsite seemed like too heavy a lift, but it sparked an idea for a version of CIRKEL that could be rooted in asynchronous curated introductions that could be facilitated without an event.

By mid-2019, Charlotte had brought on a cofounder, Jun Yung, who specialized in finance, operations, and business strategies. Together they devised a new version of CIRKEL that had bigger potential for scale and impact. It was a membership community where professionals were invited to join for a fee of $49 per month. Launched for professionals in the New York City area, members received a new match on the first of each month, free access to CIRKEL events, and if they met their match at CIRKEL's preferred restaurant, they could enjoy a free coffee or cocktail by showing their membership card. The team launched the application process in September 2019.

The new membership model revolutionized traditional mentorship programs in three ways. First, it invited people to participate in a two-way exchange of career support. It was crucial to make this style of mentorship very clear in order to attract members who understood the CIRKEL ethos: *everyone has something to learn and something to teach.* In some cases, prospective members reacted defensively upon learning that the fee structure had members of all ages paying the same membership fee. Those applicants—typically on the older side of the spectrum—would argue that their career experience was invaluable and that they were doing charitable work in offering to share it with a younger person. Those applicants were denied membership. Remaining true to the ethos of two-way exchange ensured that everyone in the community shared a core value, which increased the likelihood of good conduct in the matches.

Second, CIRKEL's model of new matches each month was a sharp departure from the "soulmate" mentorship model, where traditional programs assemble one match and encourage participants to extract all lessons out of this single individual. In keeping with the sentiment of the original events, CIRKEL's membership model offered professionals access to a more age-diverse professional network. As the saying goes, "If you're the smartest person in the room, you're in the wrong room." CIRKEL put curious people of any age in contact with numerous older and younger members who could offer different perspectives and insights based on their unique set of experiences.

Like companies that have a board of advisors, CIRKEL sought to build that same network of advisors for its members. Through monthly introductions, members got regular access to a new curated introduction. Some of these connections turned into lifelong friendships, others into business partnerships, and others into new LinkedIn connections that can be contacted as needed. With a personal board of advisors, CIRKEL members have an expansive, multigenerational network of people to reach out to—each with unique expertise.

Note that with five generations in the workforce, twenty different intergenerational combinations could be made (as per the CIRKEL game). A Gen Z member, for example, could have an equal chance of being matched with a Millennial, Gen X, Boomer, or Silent Generation member. Sometimes pairings that were less extreme in age difference—separated by only nine years or so—were even more impactful. It all depended on the individuals and their professional goals.

Lastly, the CIRKEL experience was rooted in its unique member onboarding process. Applicants filled out a few preliminary questions on the website and completed checkout. The form gathered information on their age, work experience, skills they have mastered, skills they want to learn, and how they would describe their superpower. From there, a CIRKEL team member reached out for a one-on-one interview. In the interview, the team member explained how CIRKEL membership worked and reiterated the values of two-way knowledge exchange to ensure that each member would both give and receive support. Then the CIRKEL team member asked questions about the applicant's professional background and current career transition. What did they want to get out of the CIRKEL experience? What key motivations inspired them to work in their current career? Which learnings did they want to share with other generations? After the interview, the CIRKEL team member wrote a short bio that summarized all the attributes of the incoming member. The goal was to tell their story in a way that highlighted their life and work experience so all members would be represented on an even playing field, regardless of their age.

Not only did the onboarding process help in ensuring that members enjoyed their experience and made quality connections, but the "high-touch" nature of the experience led to $717 lifetime value per customer and overall retention of members. In fact, the average length of a membership with CIRKEL was fifteen months. At peak membership, the cohort was growing at a rate of 16 percent each month. Monthly churn of members leaving was only 6 percent.

Common Challenges with Intergenerational Programs and How to Avoid Them

There are many ways to organize an intergenerational program, and for that reason it can be difficult to pinpoint a universal recipe for success. To begin, there are several pain points that would inspire someone to connect generations, and defining success can vary depending on the goal of the program. The solutions will differ greatly between, for example, a goal of combatting loneliness among individuals over age seventy aging in place and onboarding retirees as nannies to fill the child care gap. All intergenerational programs need to figure out a few key challenges: program design, attracting participants, financial support, delivering results, and scaling impact.

Program Design

Intergenerational programs must first organize their unique structure and format. Who are the target participants (defined for both older and younger groups)? Why are they joining the program? What are they looking to get out of the experience? How are people brought together to achieve their respective goals? Each intergenerational program has the challenge of being a two-sided marketplace, with each side being one age group. So organizers are building an experience for two target groups at once. This is often the part that creates the most friction, because an offering that appeals to one age group might not attract the other.

The principles of design thinking say to focus on the end users and be empathic to understand what they want out of the program. From there, test your solution and gather feedback from participants to make changes. According to the Interaction Design Foundation, design thinking can be defined as follows: "Design thinking is a non-linear, iterative process that teams use to understand users, challenge assumptions, redefine problems, and create innovative solutions to prototype and test. Involving five phases—Empathize, Define, Ideate, Prototype and Test—it is most useful to tackle problems that are ill-defined or unknown."[4]

CIRKEL's founding team decided to focus on matching generations of professionals who were engaged in either full-time or part-time work. The structure was moved from group connections in the event environment to one-on-one introductions that allowed each participant to get a more thorough level of mentorship. Participants had at least a few years of career experience under their belts (thus, no recent graduates) to ensure that there were valuable skills that could be transferred to in both directions. See tables 7.1, 7.2 and 7.3.

Attracting Participants

Intergenerational programs only work if both sides of the equation are equally drawn to the concept, and as such, many programs struggle to attract participants. For example, to organize a high school volunteer program at senior living communities, it might be

Table 7.1 Industries in which CIRKEL members work, shown by generation

Members' industry experience (3/23/21)

Industry	Overall (%)	Silent Gen and Baby Boomers (%)	Gen X (%)	Millennial and Gen Z (%)
Media and advertising	17	19	24	13
Science or technology	11	12	9	12
Nonprofit	7	4	7	9
Entertainment and music	7	7	9	6
Fine arts or performing arts	7	8	4	7
Finance or accounting	6	4	2	9
Writing or publishing	5	5	9	4
Community building	5	4	7	4
Education	4	8	4	1
Retail and ecommerce	4	5	4	3
Other	4	4	4	4
Health (medicine and wellness)	4	1	7	4
Fashion and beauty	4	3	2	5
Hospitality or food and beverage	4	1	4	5
Politics or government organization	4	3	2	4
Management consulting	3	3	0	4
Real estate and city planning	2	4	0	1
Manufacturing and sourcing	2	3	0	1
Law	1	1	2	1
Professional services	1	1	0	1
Total	100	100	100	100

Source: CIRKEL, 2021.

Table 7.2 General sectors in which CIRKEL members work, shown by generation

Members' industry experience (3/23/21)

Industry Type	Overall (%)	Silent Gen and Baby Boomers (%)	Gen X (%)	Millennial and Gen Z (%)
Creative	43	43	52	40
Social Impact	23	20	26	24
Finance and Law	13	13	4	16
Tech	11	12	9	12
Other	9	12	9	8
	100	100	100	100

Source: CIRKEL, 2021.

Table 7.3 Members' goals for participation, shown by generation

CIRKEL member goals (6/30/21)

Primary goal (%)	Overall (%)	Silent Gen and Baby Boomer (%)	Gen X (%)	Millennial and Gen Z (%)
Continual learning	26	38	25	20
Grow professional network	17	10	16	21
Career transition	13	8	9	16
Start or grow a business	12	8	16	13
Explore new opportunities	9	10	9	9
Get hired	6	6	9	5
Develop sales leads	6	2	9	6
Get life advice for personal growth	6	2	6	8
Make new friends	6	15	0	3
Total	100	100	100	100

Source: CIRKEL, 2021.

easier to attract older adults than it would be to attract teenagers to spend time with residents. Senior residents benefit from socializing with energetic young people who bring a breath of fresh air to the community, and despite data proving that intergenerational connections are beneficial for younger people too, teenagers might prefer to spend their after-school time with friends. In this example, it's incredibly important to think about the program's positioning, which will likely be different for each of the groups. From the program description, to where it is promoted, to visual components, positioning will have a major impact on who opts in.

CIRKEL participants were asked to pay for their membership, much like they would for a gym membership or a social club. In this way, CIRKEL would feel like an aspirational community full of impressive, inspiring individuals who brought valuable insights to the group. For younger professionals, positioning focused on career development. Newsletters and social media content explored topics like the value of experienced professionals as mentors and why a person should be mentored by someone outside their office where there is a safe space to be vulnerable. For older workers, the positioning focused on working later in life and maintaining relevance even as industries evolve over time. For each group, there was a secondary message of generosity and that mentorship works in *both* directions. The tagline resonating with both groups was "Long live your career," and all promotional materials were designed to look like a sexy consumer product rather than a local volunteer program.

Financial Support

Intergenerational work often finds itself in the "feel good" category and can be easily lumped in with charity work. As such, leaders need to be strategic in how they assemble resources that allow programming to continue consistently. Many intergenerational programs pursue the nonprofit route and are able to work with foundations that value the benefits of connecting generations for the sake of fighting loneliness and promoting mental health. There are also several government agencies and local aging offices that look to partner with intergenerational programs to provide services.

CIRKEL was registered as a Delaware C corporation, meaning a for-profit business that funded itself from revenue (membership fees). The pricing model's strategy was to incentivize participants to fully engage and have some "skin in the game." If participants paid to be in the community, they would be more likely to honor the process and schedule meetups with their matches. In fact, from 2019 to 2021, 90 percent of matched participants actually met each month.[5] The nominal fee kept participants actively engaged, which in turn produced a better CIRKEL experience for everyone.

In 2021, the CIRKEL founders went out to raise venture capital, an entirely new process to figure out. It was not difficult to translate the value of the CIRKEL experience to investors. However, the challenge was in proving quantifiable outcomes for each member. For this reason, CIRKEL did not succeed in raising outside capital and continued to support itself through the membership fees.

Several intergenerational organizations in the for-profit space have faced similar challenges in building a sustainable financial model. In one example, a tech platform that connects older adults with children for reading stories and homework help never monetizes its community on principle. The founder has received investments from angel investors, but without a sustainable model for ongoing financial support, such an organization will not be able to fund its basic operations. Keeping a financial model in mind while building the program may help founders avoid pitfalls and guarantee longevity for the program.

Delivering Results

Whether it's convincing someone to participate in an intergenerational program or closing an investment from a venture capital fund, program outcomes need to be clear and quantifiable. In the CIRKEL example, connecting older and younger professionals resulted in many positive outcomes. At first, postmatch survey results seemed amazing: nearly three-quarters of participants immediately scheduled a second meeting or planned to stay in touch, and more than two-thirds reported both members being equally helpful to each other. Members over fifty reported getting the following from the experience: ideas/inspiration and insights into different career paths. Members ages twenty to fifty reported getting the following from the experience: fun and receiving professional advice and life advice.[6]

However, as CIRKEL leadership spoke with potential investors and accelerator programs, it became clear that having a myriad of possible outcomes is actually not a good thing, even if the various outcomes are all positive. When making any kind of proposition, the problem and its solution need to be crystal clear. Most CIRKEL members join the community for a similar but loosely defined reason: wanting to improve their career prospects by learning from older/younger professionals. The challenge is that improving career prospects can look different for different people: from getting a job to simply learning something new about an industry. The less defined or quantifiable an organization's results are, the more difficult it is to prove linear success and close a pitch.

In order to tighten the offering, goals should be SMART: specific, measurable, achievable, relevant, and time-bound. If a participant joins an intergenerational program, what are they guaranteed to get out of it? Are there metrics to prove these goals are consistently delivered, or is there a system tracking whether the metrics improve over time? Investors and donors alike will want to know that their dollars are guaranteed to make an impact, and it's up to organizers to prove that their organization's formula works.

Scaling Impact

Intergenerational work is inherently personal. At the root of connections are individuals with various life experiences, vulnerabilities, needs, and degrees of open-mindedness. Matching people can have all kinds of outcomes—sometimes surprising. A pair that seems like a match made in heaven can sour if one person arrives late to the meeting or a sensitive topic arises before real trust has been established. In the "two-sided market" of connecting generations, humans are essentially the "product." Unlike selling a typical product manufactured in a factory, however, humans are difficult to regulate, and therefore the quality of matches can be inconsistent. For these reasons, it makes complete sense to match "by hand" with a human going person by person and making pairs based on gut feeling.

This manual approach is often successful. Humans are relatively talented in discerning which people will fit well together and which ones will repel like oil and water. There is also a "white glove" quality to this approach that makes participants feel considered. But what happens when this approach is so successful that many more participants decide to join? Curating ten matches feels very different than making one hundred, not to mention one thousand or more.

Consequently, program leaders must learn how to scale their operations through technology. In CIRKEL's case, the organizers needed to translate their manual process of matching members into an algorithm. Members had joined the community with a set of areas where they needed support and a set of areas where they were capable of offering support. A pattern emerged in which certain types of members tended to have successful meetings with a member who had particular areas of support or need. CIRKEL's leadership translated these qualifiers into "need states" and "give states." For example, a member who joined the community looking to learn a very specific skill was given the "apprentice" need state. A member joining who was looking to pass along particular skills was given the "teacher" give state. The apprentice and the teacher were deemed a strong match and thereby ranked highly in the algorithm's code. Each member who joined was given one need state and one give state based on their onboarding information. With this algorithm, the CIRKEL team replaced a monthly matching process that once took a team a few hours into one that took an individual a few minutes.

Not only is scale an important factor to consider when planning for a successful intergenerational program that will grow and require more resources to administer, but it's also important information for prospective investors or benefactors. Backers want to know that the program has a system in place to prosper and grow.

Proving the World Needs Intergenerational Programs

Sometimes the things that seem most obviously "good" are the most difficult to quantify. In the case of intergenerational connections, this is certainly true. Think tanks like the Milken Institute's Center for The Future of Aging, university centers like The Stanford Center on Longevity, and national nonprofit organizations like CoGenerate (see *Handbook* chapter 4) all carry out regular research and conduct surveys to prove the need for their programming and demonstrate success.

Throughout the life of CIRKEL, research has been instrumental in validating the reason for building an intergenerational program that caters to the five generations in the workforce. At CIRKEL's inception in 2018, New York City lacked programs focused on addressing the needs of older workers through mentoring. Instead, programs were designed solely around the needs of young professionals. Older workers, especially the growing group of aged-out workers, were left without resources beyond expensive career coaches.

In 2020–2021, CIRKEL collaborated with the National Institute on Ageing at Newcastle University (NICA) in the United Kingdom. The two teams were both weathering the coronavirus pandemic and witnessing how remote work and accelerated

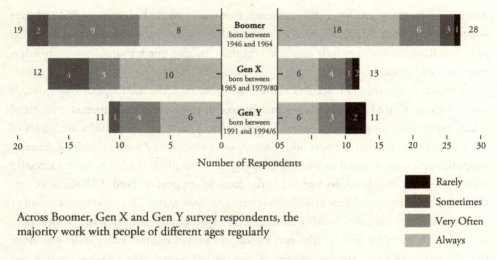

Across Boomer, Gen X and Gen Y survey respondents, the majority work with people of different ages regularly

Figure 7.1 Extent to which survey respondents work with people of different ages and generations.
Source: CIRKEL and NICA.

retirements were taking a toll on all generations in the workforce. Given the pandemic's unique impact on workers, the two teams felt it was an important moment to understand the status of aging and work. Thus began an extensive research project to quantify and qualify generational sentiments around the multigenerational workforce. See figure 7.1.

The process was divided into four key stages: design research, surveying, workshop, and summarizing. The findings were presented at the 2021 Generations United Conference.[7]

The key findings and insights were the following ($n = 107$):

- Career focus and motivations were shared across the generations, and these provide opportunities to connect people around purpose, experience, and learning.
- "Finding purpose in my work" received the second highest number of votes by Gen Y survey respondents (after "Supporting myself and my family"), highlighting the interest in purposeful work among younger survey respondents.
- For survey respondents aged sixty-five and over and approaching retirement age, the majority were focused on either their current role or future roles, rather than moving into retirement.
- Some intergenerational working relationships and workforce topics may require additional support, training, and empathy to build understanding of individual needs and emotions and to challenge stereotypes and assumptions.

- Just under one quarter of Gen Y respondents (twenty-two in all) managed someone older than themselves (the highest category for this group), highlighting intergenerational work responsibilities for these respondents (see figure 7.1).
- "Digital skills and literacy" and a "willingness to change" generated more age-specific comments and perceptions in the workshop than discussions about education and learning and caregiving. Comments included a reference to "digital immigrants" for those who had not grown up with the internet and assumptions about older adults: "There is an element of resistance . . . people who have been there and seen it all and are entrenched in their own views."
- Age bias experienced by both younger and older survey respondents in both formal and social situations acted as a barrier to intergenerational relationships and collaboration. Around half of total survey respondents had personally experienced age bias at work (54 respondents out of 107 total). Experiencing age bias in "social situations" at work received the second highest number of votes, after "recruitment." Gen Y respondents experienced age bias more often in social situations than in other work situations, raising questions about how much we know about age bias experienced by younger people.
- Learning does not have to happen in a classroom or seminar. Survey respondents pointed to continual learning, learning from peers, and being able to access training and development as factors that helped them to keep their skills and experience relevant in current/recent roles.
- Seventeen respondents found it difficult to keep skills and experience relevant. Factors included limited support for training and development in their organizations and, especially for digital skills, not knowing which skills to develop and how to do so. One participant commented, "Especially at my age, it's about continuing to learn, and being able to take what I already know and have learned and share that with other people. I think that's critical to make one have a sense of purpose or feel relevancy, which is a big word for me right now."

According to NICA and CIRKEL, "Designing age-blind company policies and employee support masks the 'real-world' lived experiences of both younger and older workers, in both formal and social situations at work. This risks overlooking ageism in the workplace. Instead, committing to recognize ageism in the workplace alongside other forms of demographic diversity and discrimination—and focusing on connecting people around purpose, experience, and learning—will help companies to understand and challenge barriers to intergenerational working, as well as foster more inclusive and supportive workplaces."[8]

The CIRKEL/NICA partnership recommends the following:

- **Invest in informal and inclusive collaboration:** Promote intergenerational friendship and conversations for collaboration and learning. Build inclusive and collaborative relationships across the workforce to harness experience and skill sharing.
- **Use a *life-course* rather than *life-stage* approach:** Consider dynamic life paths and transitions in employee support, training, and development to reflect career motivations and priorities rather than assumed life-stages.
- **Provide incentives that matter and connect:** Motivate your employees with incentives that really matter to them and help connect individuals across the organizations around purpose, impact, and learning.
- **Support flexible careers:** Facilitate career breaks and continual learning through policies and financial support to harness skills and experience across the life-course.
- **Encourage learning by doing:** Develop a better understanding of the opportunities, impacts, and value of intergenerational relationships at work by "learning by doing" and through mentoring schemes.

CIRKEL conducted another study in January 2023 that focused on exploring the rise of self-employment among workers of all ages, but particularly older workers. Seventy-six participants responded to an online survey and shared their most up-to-date work status. This survey revealed how older workers experience professional challenges when they work alone and siloed from other generations (see figures 7.2, 7.3, and 7.4).

To get deeper into the specifics of self-employment, the survey asked respondents for their top three goals for 2023. Tied for first place were "increasing my personal income/

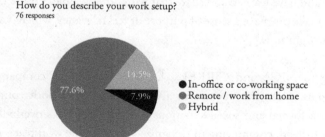

Figure 7.2 Work location.

Source: CIRKEL. Self-employment in 2023. Survey conducted January 2023 (unpublished).

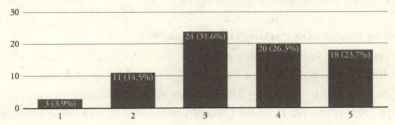

Figure 7.3 Level of satisfaction with current career.

Source: CIRKEL. Self-employment in 2023. Survey conducted January 2023 (unpublished).

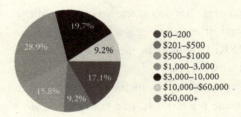

Figure 7.4 Anticipated expenditures on professional development.

Source: CIRKEL. Self-employment in 2023. Survey conducted January 2023 (unpublished).

salary" and "growing my network for personal and professional advancement," which each received thirty-eight votes. Second was "increasing business revenue," and third was "gain clarity and focus." These results indicated that older entrepreneurs are experiencing significant challenges that are foundational to their businesses: from struggling to focus a business to growing revenue and personal income. In comparison to challenges employees in the CIRKEL/NICA study experienced, self-employed workers only eat what they kill, rendering these aforementioned challenges existential.

When the survey asked entrepreneurs which professional development tools and approaches they had previously tried, the results ran the gamut. Networking communities were most common, both online and offline, followed by hiring a coach. When asked which tactics the participants planned to use in 2023, they responded with "in-person networking communities" as the top selection, followed by "career coaching" and a tie for third place between "online networking communities" and "mentors."

Despite the lack of intergenerational tools in the entrepreneurs' toolkits, postsurvey interviews commonly cited intergenerational networking and mentoring as a key focus for professional development. Putting together the desire for intergenerational connections with the rest of the survey responses, it can be deduced that self-employed workers in the second or third stage of their careers are seeking community as part of their career growth, especially among professionals of different generations.

Expanding Impact via Partnerships

As with any business venture, there is always the question of scale. Once a business model is established, how does one expand its reach to grow revenue, or in the case of nonprofits, impact? As a for-profit enterprise, CIRKEL approached scale through various methods of marketing, from paid advertising on LinkedIn and Facebook to promoting the membership at conferences and any public speaking opportunity offered to the founder.

It is important to note that 15 percent of applicants who applied to join the CIRKEL community came through CoGenerate's newsletter and digital communications. Charlotte Japp, CIRKEL's founder, participated in CoGenerate's Innovation Fellowship program in 2020 and through this involvement was able to get CoGenerate's support in promoting CIRKEL to that organization's extensive online audience. CoGenerate is focused on amplifying the efforts of entrepreneurs and organizers who bring generations together, and promoting CIRKEL's initiatives meshed neatly with that effort, creating a win for both CIRKEL and CoGenerate.

Another 10 percent of applicants found CIRKEL through newspaper or magazine articles mentioning the platform. In one example, *Millie Magazine*, a women's finance magazine that was packaged with *Real Simple*, featured an interview with Charlotte Japp. As a result, thirty-two readers applied to join CIRKEL within the following weeks. Publicity is not easy to replicate, but when done well, it has proven to be effective in telling CIRKEL's story to audiences looking for intergenerational networking resources.

Lastly, partnerships can have a commercial nature, benefiting both parties in a monetary sense. In CIRKEL's case, this took shape in 2021 through a partnership with T-Mobile, which was promoting a new mobile phone plan called "Magenta Unlimited 55," where adults aged fifty-five and older could get a steep discount on two lines. T-Mobile was willing to pay CIRKEL a sizeable fee to collaborate on a series of events that would engage with CIRKEL's community, which aligned perfectly with T-Mobile's target audience.

The result was a media partnership in which T-Mobile paid CIRKEL to host events with older adults in the audience. CIRKEL produced two virtual events that explored topics that were top of mind for older professionals: digital nomadism and the rise of older influencers. Hundreds of attendees came to each event, outpacing T-Mobile's prior event attendance. The event speakers shared useful insights and resonated with the discerning audience of older professionals in a genuine way. The partnership grew CIRKEL's annual revenue, allowing the team to function more efficiently and extend the operating runway longer without taking outside investment.

Commercial partnerships hinge on two partners working together to approach mutual goals and, when done well, can be hugely successful for both parties involved. As mentioned, commercial partnerships allow organizations like CIRKEL to operate without taking outside capital and retaining full ownership. The key in media partnerships is to build up a sizable niche audience that is highly engaged and likely to trust the partners and content that the company puts in front of them. If the content does not feel relevant or the commercial aspect of the partnership takes precedence over the authenticity of the experience, partnerships can risk turning an audience against the brand. In other words, partnerships run the risk of being perceived as "selling out." In the T-Mobile case, CIRKEL's audience enjoyed the content so much that their interest in the T-Mobile brand increased authentically after seeing the brand partner with a community they trusted.

Conclusion

In September 2023, CIRKEL leadership matched the last cohort of CIRKEL matches. It was exactly four years since the first cohort was organized. Ahead of this last match, cofounders Charlotte Japp and Jun Yung sent a letter to the membership explaining that CIRKEL was closing down:

> Between the lack of funding opportunities for this kind of social enterprise and the post-pandemic slowdown of virtual communities, it's been difficult to give the CIRKEL community the love, time, and resources it needs to thrive.
>
> It's been an honor to get to know each of you, and we're grateful for all the trust you've put into this process (even when we founders were tinkering and figuring things out). If more people expressed an ounce of the generosity and kindness you've all given to each other, the world would be a better place.[9]

CIRKEL set out to support a more multigenerational approach to work, especially in a world where life spans are lengthening. As a tool to equip professionals of all ages, CIRKEL sought to build bridges between generations and offer two-way support along the longer work span. In the five years of CIRKEL's existence, including over a thousand intergenerational introductions, the community successfully impacted hundreds of professional lives. The company changed people's perceptions of working with collaborators in other age groups. Moreover, CIRKEL members put their new connections in action as several members collaborated on work projects, hired each other for roles, and built meaningful mentorships and friendships. The world CIRKEL was born into, before and during the pandemic, is not the same one it concluded in. For the organization, this meant that its offering may not have been as relevant or in-demand after the coronavirus peak. However, this reality does not undermine CIRKEL's impact during its lifetime. And despite the initial expectation that an intergenerational program would only appeal to older adults, younger members expressed gratitude for the experience. In a heartfelt response to the closure letter, Alexa Fleet and her brother Brooks (both Millennials) listed their favorite memories from their CIRKEL memberships. Here are some of their highlights:

1. [Brooks] matched with someone in his new country and later visited [his CIRKEL match], Alessandro, at the monastery [where he lived]. Brooks moved to Rome in February 2020 knowing nobody, and their friendship continues.
2. [Alexa and Brooks] connected with older adults and got to reflect on career-plans and life courses together.
3. [Both valued] the light that CIRKEL was in the pandemic.

Notes

1. There is a time and a place for everything. True to Alexa and Brooks's last item on the list, CIRKEL was a light for members aged twenty-one to seventy-five during the pandemic. At a time when isolation was pervasive, CIRKEL's virtual intergenerational program offered connection and purpose. The pandemic also proved to be a time of career uncertainty. For some, this meant furloughs and layoffs, and for others, who were luckier, it meant remote work in quarantine—often working longer hours than usual and balancing child care and other factors at home while doing so. For members in either camp (as well as those who were no longer working full-time), the CIRKEL community was a safe space to ask questions about work and life. Members could share their career anxieties with people who had relevant experience, insights, and wisdom to offer. While CIRKEL did not last forever, it was no less of a success.

    Finally, to bring things full circle, Charlotte Japp recently met with several of her VICE Media colleagues at a reunion hosted in October 2023. In each conversation, her colleagues admitted to watching the CIRKEL journey over the years and being affected by its message of workplace age inclusion. Despite the Millennial-only office described in part one of this chapter, each former VICE colleague shared a personal story of how they changed their own approaches to work after hearing about CIRKEL. Some people changed the hiring practice in their current role to proactively include older applicants. Others made an effort to mentor their parents going through career transitions, from job hunting to learning new skills to staying up to date in their industry. There is more work to be done in creating a more age-inclusive professional world, but progress has been made.

    Jeff Beer, "Take a Look Inside the Headquarters of Vice," Fast Company, September 3, 2014, https://www.fastcompany.com/3034207/take-a-look-inside-the-headquarters-of-vice
2. :Online Event Registration for CIRKEL fashion: an intergenerational conversation featuring fashion leaders who are modeling a more inclusive industry. Moderated by Prabal Gurung," January 10, 2019, https://www.eventbrite.com/e/cirkel-fashion-tickets-53368474544?aff=oddtdtcreator
3. Marci Alboher, "The New 50s: Far From Retirement." *New York Times*, December 4, 2018, https://www.nytimes.com/2018/12/04/business/retirement/50s-far-from-retirement.html
4. "What is Design Thinking?" Interaction Design Foundation – IxDF, accessed November 20, 2023, https://www.interaction-design.org/literature/topics/design-thinking.
5. Data taken from monthly CIRKEL members' surveys administered between September 2019 and February 2021.
6. Data taken from monthly member surveys administered between May 2020 and February 2021.
7. NICA and CIRKEL. "Moving from Multigenerational to Intergenerational Workforce: Connecting Purpose, Experience and Learning for Inclusive and Improved Collaboration," presented at Generations United's 21st Global Intergenerational Conference, June 15–17, 2021. https://www.gu.org/.
8. Ibid.
9. Excerpt from letter written by Charlotte Japp and Jun Yung to the CIRKEL community. Unpublished. August 28, 2023.

PART II

Meeting the Need for Tutoring, Coaching, Mentoring, Housing: Older Adults Working with Younger People

CHAPTER 8

SAGE: Building a Brighter Future by Working across Generations

Stephen Higgs

> **Abstract**
> A wise Greek proverb says, "A society grows great when its elders plant trees whose shade they know they shall never sit in." SAGE is a nonprofit organization that works to elevate this proverb and the role that older adults play to create opportunity for younger and future generations to thrive. The organization's supporters believe in generational equity—the principle that each generation should leave the world better off. This chapter describes SAGE's vision, mission, and goals and its efforts to inspire people over age fifty to give forward by working across generations to build a brighter future. Readers will learn about the origin of SAGE, unexpected benefits that have come from its focus on younger and future generations, and some lessons learned in its evolution into a more intergenerational organization.
>
> **Key Words:** future, generational equity, multigenerational, intergenerational, mentoring, tutoring, coaching, education, environment, economy

SAGE

Strengths/impact
- Leadership training
- Raising awareness about major challenges in education, the environment, and the economy
- Inspiration for older adults and for younger adults
- Listening across generations
- Innovative, collaborative problem solving
- Practices that advance equitable outcomes
- Building public will to advocate for the future

Limitations
- Siloing of generations
- Serious and long-term social challenges
- Additional time commitments

Introduction

> Society is a partnership of the dead, the living and the unborn.[1]
> —Edmund Burke

Over ten years ago, SAGE's founder, Ward Greene, woke up late for an important meeting. He rushed to get dressed and leave the house. When he walked into the large meeting room, he saw hundreds of older adults waiting anxiously for him to take urgent action to help the future. Suddenly, he woke up, realizing the meeting was all just a dream, a particularly vivid one for Greene, who seldom remembers his dreams. But this dream was so real, and the name of the group hosting the meeting was so real. It was SAGE: Senior Advocates for Generational Equity.

That morning, Ward shared his dream with his wife. Coincidentally, she had just read a Greek proverb in a magazine: "A society grows great when its elders plant trees whose shade they know they shall never sit in."[2] Together, they felt inspired by the dream and the proverb. After speaking with friends and listening to their concerns for the future, they realized that many older adults dwell on the challenges facing future generations and a sense that they, as elders, have a key role to play in planting trees of opportunity for succeeding generations. One of Greene's friends, after hearing about his dream, asked him, "Ward, what are you going to *do* about it?" They took action and formed SAGE as a nonprofit to inspire older adults to focus more attention and take action on those challenges. Today, the organization sparks the imagination and commitment of people over age fifty who believe in generational equity: the concept that each generation has the responsibility to give forward and improve the quality of life for the next.

This chapter describes how SAGE has embraced an intergenerational approach to its work, as well as the expected and unexpected outcomes of this approach. The first section describes SAGE's mission, goals, and focus on the future. The second section highlights four lessons from its work across generations: lean into relationships, listen better to younger voices, cocreate programs, and look for win-wins. The final section identifies four benefits for future generations that flow from this intergenerational approach: inspiration for older adults, inspiration for younger adults, innovative problem solving, and building public will to advocate for the future.

SAGE's Mission, Goals, and Focus on the Future

In June 2012, SAGE hosted its first event when eight older adults came together to share what they were grateful for, their concerns for the future, and how they could make a difference. Over the years, this gathering became known as a SAGE social, where guests could connect informally and share experiences and views. After hosting dozens of these events, mostly with older adults, SAGE identified three focus areas where it could play a role in creating opportunity for the future: strengthening education, restoring our environment, and promoting economic security.

Today, SAGE continues to raise awareness about major challenges in education, the environment, and the economy. The organization does so through small-group events and a large annual speaking event known as the Visiting SAGE. In its work, SAGE is particularly alert to long-term generational equity concerns that can impact society for decades. There are trade-offs that underlie these concerns. For example, there can be a tug of war between generations—where a swifter response to a problem like climate change can result in near-term costs, but a slower response can result in higher long-term costs. There can also be time bombs between generations—where a practice or policy like incurring debt to pay today's bills does not significantly threaten people today but presents significant challenges for the future.

In addition to raising awareness about generational equity concerns, SAGE connects people to resources and opportunities for getting involved in their local communities and promotes direct service roles with over thirty nonprofit partners. Further, SAGE trains and assists people who want to engage in social causes and the work of nonprofit organizations. As one measure of progress, each year SAGE seeks to inspire, train, and support more than a thousand people who give forward in their communities.

Why does the organization focus on older adults? Because in these times, many older adults have much to give. In the United States, over ten thousand people turn sixty-five every day[3] and by 2030, 20 percent of the population will be over age sixty-five.[4] Many older adults are beneficiaries of the longevity revolution—the lengthening of lifetimes in a brief period of history. As a result, today's older adults have more opportunities to give forward than any previous generation.

Working across Generations

The Greek proverb centered the role elders play in planting trees of opportunity. While retaining its focus on the future, SAGE also expanded its mission in its second year to focus on the needs of younger generations. SAGE did so because Generations X, Millennial, Z, and Alpha also face serious challenges, and an investment in younger people is also an investment in the future. Plus, generational equity concerns are tough problems that have persisted for decades and require action over time. For this reason, a society can only grow great when *everyone* plants trees for the future.

Once SAGE started to engage younger people in its work, the organization became more mindful of practices intended to connect generations. For example, SAGE started to celebrate newborns through the SAGE Babies Club, hosted children's choirs at events, and began to set up an empty chair at workshops symbolically reserved for the voice of future generations.

Today, SAGE continues these practices and offers more substantive intergenerational programs.[5] To illustrate, SAGE has trained seventy-four legacy fellows in its nine-month leadership program to help volunteers launch high-impact community benefit projects of their own design. SAGE has helped fellows establish a public park, create a giving foundation, establish a mentoring program, and more. While the program was conceived as a fellowship for older adults, it quickly evolved into SAGE's first intergenerational initiative. Nearly half of the fellows are under age fifty, and all fellows have experienced the magic—in the form of inspiration, fun, new thinking, and support—that comes from working across generations.

Through this and other experiences, SAGE has gained several insights for more effective intergenerational work. Here are four lessons learned: act out of the relationships we form, listen more deeply to younger voices, grow by cocreating programs, and, look for win-wins to help people of different ages within the same program.

Act through the Relationships We Form

The first word in SAGE's mission is to "inspire" people to give forward. Over the years, the organization's leaders have read, studied, and deliberated on how one goes about inspiring, motivating, or bringing about the practice of giving forward through volunteerism and advocacy. One important insight from intergenerational work is that people of all ages are inspired to act by the relationships they form with each other.

As Dr. George Vaillant stated in *Aging Well*, "*Inspiration* . . . is a metaphor for how we take other people inside. Through our lungs, through our guts, and through our hearts."[6] In other words, we cocreate this world through our relationships and, in doing so, we inspire one another to take care of others and to give forward for the future, too. Three principles to guide our work across generations have emerged from the SAGE Legacy Fellowship and other intergenerational efforts:

- Each generation can improve the quality of life for the next.
- People in each generation need each other, and together we are stronger.
- Everyone can give forward so that future generations can thrive.

Listen Better to Younger People

One of SAGE's first events was a meeting with a group of younger students where the speaker talked about challenges facing them in the future and what everyone could do to help. Too much presentation, too little listening. At the meeting's close, the host, who had worked with students for years, suggested holding another meeting but the next time, to *listen* to what younger people say and get their thoughts on how SAGE could help.

In other words, before offering a solution, it is most important to understand the views and experiences of the people you are trying to help. Listening to understand is a well-known truism,[7] and as Marc Freedman shared in *How to Live Forever*, better listening (before advice giving) is what younger people appreciate the most: "Young people want mentors who show up—and who, for the most part, shut up. They want mentors who are focused on listening much more than talking. Research on what young people are looking for in relationships with adults bears this out. At the top of the list is listening, followed by providing useful, concrete help. At the bottom: imparting advice."[8]

Deeper listening is also consistent with a key value or need in cross-generational collaboration, which is to acknowledge and address generational power dynamics so people can show up as equal participants.[9] On a related note, one major recommendation for groups seeking to cultivate a culture of collaboration across generations is to legitimize youth voices. As Dairanys Grullon-Virgil and Sydelle Barreto note in their report "Beyond Passing the Torch," "We live in an adult-centric society that too often portrays young people as not being sufficiently civically engaged. Organizations in the civic field need to champion young people—proactively through program design, feedback mechanisms, and action—as legitimate actors within civil society."[10]

While not always easy given the frenetic pace of nonprofit work, SAGE strives to incorporate better listening into program development. For example, after the initial presentation with students, SAGE formed a Young Leaders Advisory Board (LAB) to serve as a multigenerational bridge advancing solutions to our shared future. Over the years, SAGE's LAB has engaged young leaders in their teens, twenties, and thirties to identify and prioritize challenges and to confront them through multigenerational action. The LAB has developed its own programs for SAGE, and its leaders have also served on SAGE committees and in strategic planning. The LAB also provides an avenue for younger people to develop skills, experiences, and networks through community service, and some LAB leaders have joined SAGE's board, which has strengthened the organization's leadership.

In addition to the LAB, SAGE has nurtured better listening across generations through workshops on how to volunteer across generations, mentor across generations, and promote giving across generations and has moderated intergenerational focus groups on issues such as tackling student debt. Program offerings are stronger when organizations prioritize deeper listening from the people the programs are intended to help.

Cocreate Intergenerational Programs with Younger People

These intergenerational conversations were well received, but a missing piece remained: younger people were not as actively involved in next steps. Beyond conversations there was no real partnership across generations.

One major reason for engaging younger voices in program development is that younger people offer new ways of learning and doing. As an example, one of the LAB's first decisions was to adopt an equity lens to guide their work. At the time, SAGE did not have an equity lens. Inspired by the LAB, SAGE's board later adopted an equity lens and additional practices to advance equitable outcomes. Thanks to the LAB, the broader organization better understood the realities of diverse groups of people based on race, gender, economic position, education, and more and developed practices to tackle inequities today so that they do not carry forward tomorrow.

Cocreating programs offers opportunities for people to learn and act together. Research shows that nearly eight out of ten adults want to spend more time with people outside their age group.[11] Because we act out of the relationships we form, SAGE has built more breathing room into its process for developing programs so the people involved can get to know each other and build rapport and trust. For example, last year SAGE offered two events that focused on generations working together to address climate change. The first was developed internally, and the second was developed with a youth-led high school group. While planning the second event took more time, through the process, planners got to know each other, built relationships, and produced better ideas, such as inviting guests to develop their own climate solutions.

More recently, SAGE worked with the LAB to develop a new program called Service Across Generations. As envisioned, three to four times a year, people of different generations will connect and engage in a hands-on service project, such as a beach cleanup or helping build a home for a family in need. Each event will offer opportunities for people of different generations to socialize and serve together. This creative program emerged because of conversations between younger and older adults where advisors from multiple generations emphasized the need to move beyond talk and to act together.

As another example, SAGE has worked with middle school students as emcees and exhibitors at climate solutions fairs. These experiences are meaningful and fun for students when their peers speak on the mic and host their own exhibits about climate solutions. Because these fairs are cocreated with younger people, the events take on more meaning. Younger and older adults are thinking globally, acting locally, and doing so intergenerationally.

Look for Win-Win Programs That Can Help People of All Ages

SAGE has also begun to develop win-win programs to help people from different generations forge bonds. For example, SAGE sponsors online and in-person mentoring for English-language learners in a middle school. Today, millions of children would benefit from the care and support of a mentor, and millions of older adults experience isolation and feel the lack of purpose and meaning. Through this program, SAGE nurtures supportive relationships that help children to gain a better start in life and elders to retain a sense of purpose and fulfillment through deeper connection with schools. The program's first goal is to help English-language learners become proficient readers and, at the same time, SAGE also seeks to improve mentors' quality of life, recognizing that one of the most significant pathways to the well-being and happiness of older adults is nurturing of and engagement with the young.[12] As one mentor put it, "This program has been a wonderful experience for me. My student is so happy to see me and so willing to continue learning."

Remarkable benefits come from intergenerational programs that are built on geographic proximity.[13] Colocation of a school or youth-serving organization with a senior center or housing for older adults can enhance opportunities for people to volunteer across generations.[14] SAGE has also followed the lead of other groups offering online programs that support intergenerational connections, even for people who do not live nearby.[15]

Benefits for Future Generations

There is excellent research that demonstrates the value of working across generations for people living today.[16] There are at least four reasons why this is important for the future as well—intergenerational work inspires older adults to give forward, intergenerational work inspires younger people to act, it can result in creative problem solving, and it can build public will to advocate for the future.

Inspiration for Older Adults to Give Forward

By working with younger people, older adults develop a personal bond that can motivate them to give forward in ways they might not otherwise consider. This impulse, known as generativity,[17] "involves the demonstration of a clear capacity to unselfishly guide the next generation," and it means "community building."[18] By creating connections between older and younger people, intergenerational work taps the natural desire of older adults to build a legacy.

To illustrate, SAGE offers one-to-one coaching for older adults to help them identify a meaningful pathway to give forward. While there are millions of possibilities, one-to-one coaching helps people reflect on what is most important to them and where they might make a meaningful difference. It is wonderful to experience the glow on someone's face when they learn about a local mentoring, tutoring, or coaching opportunity where they can help a young person learn to read, improve in school, or get involved in sports, music, or the arts. Older adults appreciate the energy, creativity, and idealism of youth, and it is these qualities that inspire older adults to engage in community service.

As another example, SAGE legacy fellow Roberta Schwarz helped to raise millions of dollars to preserve a twenty-acre grove of white oak savanna, but she did not do it alone. Schwarz succeeded in part because she brought thousands of kids, teenagers, and adults of all ages together for numerous habitat-restoration projects and, in doing so, helped people across generations develop a shared relationship with the land that they sought to protect. It is inspirational to work side-by-side with people of all generations who are working to build a brighter future.

Unfortunately, research shows that two-thirds of adults do not feel motivated by a clear sense of purpose to pursue goals that are personally meaningful and contribute to the greater good.[19] Hence, there is real value in creating programs that are intentionally intergenerational because they can help people who are not already engaged in community service to get started. There are also significant health and longevity benefits for older adult volunteers who help others, particularly those who make a deeper commitment to their cause.[20] The act of giving forward can also enrich one's friendships and sense of belonging.[21] In other words, when one is immersed in service, the experience can provide multiple benefits.

Inspiration for Younger People to Give Forward

Working across generations inspires younger people to give forward too. Most of the social causes SAGE tackles have been the focus of nonprofits for decades because they are tough problems. When younger people join in, they inherit significant histories filled with successes, setbacks, and lessons learned. They also get the benefit of meaningful relationships with adults in their communities who care about social causes and gain experience through civic engagement and leadership positions.[22]

Over the years, SAGE has facilitated several intergenerational conversations on climate change because this issue is often viewed as a quintessential generational equity concern whereby actions today will impact many generations to come. Many young people experience significant stress about this challenge, as do older adults. A few years ago, SAGE facilitated an intergenerational forum on climate choices using a discussion guide from the National Issues Forum. During the forum, one young participant expressed heartfelt gratitude for being in community with older adults who care about the issue. Cross-generational work can strengthen commitment to the cause. As Grullon-Virgil and Barreto note, these opportunities can "spark authentic relationships and organic network building, which in turn can create genuine excitement for working together toward a common cause."[23]

When younger people commit to service, they are more apt to continue over the years. The cofounder of the national Encore Network, Doug Dickson, points out that "people who volunteer the most in terms of years worked and hours committed are the least likely to leave."[24] Hence, the sooner individuals engage in community service, the more likely they will stay. By working with older adults who are planting trees for the future, younger people also learn to plant their own trees, too. Plus, younger people who engage in meaningful relationships with adults are more likely to improve in academic outcomes, display less risky behaviors, be more independent, and experience less depression.[25] These positive outcomes for young people are important building blocks for a brighter future.

Creative Problem Solving

Working across generations also creates conditions for creative problem solving. Current and future generations face enormous challenges, and there is a need to invest in current solutions and to conceive of new ones, too. Great promises and synergies arise from intergenerational teamwork, connecting the ideas and experiences of younger people with those of older people.

As Jon Katzenbach and Douglas Smith write in *The Wisdom of Teams*, "Teams outperform individuals acting alone or in larger organizational groupings, especially when performance requires multiple skills, judgments, and experiences."[26] Research also shows that organizations with inclusive, multigenerational teams outperform all others.[27] Writing about the innovations that stem from people working across generations, Freedman describes *inventors* who dream up radical new ideas, *integrators* who bring existing institutions, like senior centers and preschools, together, and *infiltrators* who inject older or younger people into settings where they might not have been found before.[28] With the myriad problems facing communities, the inventors, integrators, and infiltrators offer new or better solutions.

Build Public Will to Advocate for the Future

Working across generations can also elevate the human spirit and stimulate public will to advocate more intentionally for needs and opportunities on the horizon. Future generations will face serious challenges, and people living today can make a positive difference. To inform its work, SAGE regularly references the words of Terry Tempest Williams, "the eyes of the future are looking back at us and they are praying for us to see beyond our own time."[29] The reason why SAGE offers a chair for the future at workshops is to remind attendees (young, midlife, and old) of our link in the human chain and our moral responsibility to create opportunity in years to come.

Thinking about the future is not always easy, particularly when people experience serious and daily stress. This challenge is made more difficult by real and perceived generational differences that pit people against one another. In their report, "Beyond Passing the Torch," Grullon-Virgil and Barreto reflect on interviews with multiple groups about their growing concern regarding siloing of generations, both ideologically and physically. They note that this siloing "in civic leadership spaces must be addressed with time, intentionality, and vulnerability."[30] On a related point, Ruby Belle Booth writes in the report "Intergenerational Civic Learning," that when we are "distracted by generational conflict, we miss the opportunity to leverage intergenerational interactions for civic repair."[31] Belle spotlights the benefits to the future when we work across generations today: "Working together across generational lines helps individuals develop mutual respect, communication skills, collaboration, and power sharing. It also has been shown to increase generativity—a feeling of responsibility toward the well-being of future generations—and a sense of community while decreasing generational stereotypes that drive societies apart."[32] Along these lines, writer David Brooks has said, "Healthy moral ecologies don't just happen. They have to be seeded and tended."[33] When people work across generations, they contribute to our shared culture and amplify the spirit of generativity that is at the heart of SAGE's mission.

There is a second society-wide benefit to working across generations: promoting better mental health for people living today, which will help the future, too. In the United States, mental health is declining according to multiple metrics, and suicide rates have risen by about 30 percent since 2000.[34] U.S. Surgeon General Murthy writes, "At any moment, about one out of every two Americans is experiencing measurable levels of loneliness. This includes introverts and extroverts, rich and poor, and younger and older Americans."[35] Murthy also points to good news: "Helping people is one of the most powerful antidotes to loneliness."[36]

Over 90 percent of Americans believe intergenerational activities can help reduce loneliness across all ages.[37] Every age group benefits from these types of programs.[38] According to Grantmakers in Aging, intergenerational programs are known as "effective vehicles for reducing social isolation and depression, enhancing physical and mental well-being, and increasing self-esteem/self-confidence of older adults as well as addressing critical community concerns."[39] Grantmakers continues, "Mobilizing multiple generations to support each other and collectively address community concerns helps build social capital, address historic community divisions, and support individuals across the life course."[40]

What are the implications of these findings for the future? Simply put, when someone is healthy enough to start planning for their own future,[41] they can also plant trees for people they will never meet and children who are not yet born, so that a society can indeed grow great. That is the essence of the Greek proverb.

Conclusion

Recall that Ward Greene started SAGE after dreaming that he woke up late for its first meeting. That meeting involved many older adults, but there were probably younger people in the room too. Today, SAGE retains its focus on the wisdom of the Greek proverb because there is a leadership role for older adults to plant trees of opportunity for the future. At the same time, it has also embraced the idea that these trees, in their many forms, grow deeper roots and taller trunks, and bear more fruit, when they are planted in partnership with younger people.

Intergenerational practices strengthen the social compact across generations and over time.[42] Further, there is a need to view serious and long-term social challenges through an intergenerational lens.[43] By working across generations, people can experience a connection to the past, present, and future. Putting out a symbolic chair at a workshop invites the future to the event, allowing people of all generations to see their lives as part of a larger, deeper human story with thousands of generations who have come before and thousands to come after. By involving younger people in this work, organizations create the conditions for the work to continue for generations to come.

Notes

1. "Edmund Burke Quotes," Goodreads, accessed June 6, 2025, https://www.goodreads.com/quotes/1004069-society-is-a-partnership-of-the-dead-the-living-and.
2. "Anonymous Greek Proverb," Goodreads, accessed June 6, 2025, https://www.goodreads.com/quotes/666987-society-grows-great-when-old-men-plant-trees-whose-shade. SAGE has modified this proverb and is not aware of the origin. The spirit of this proverb is reflected in different traditions and embodies the ethic of generativity discussed in this chapter.
3. "Aging," U.S. Department of Health and Human Services, accessed June 6, 2025, https://www.hhs.gov/aging/index.html.

4. Danielle Arigoni, "Preparing for an Aging Population," AARP, accessed June 6, 2025, https://www.aarp.org/livable-communities/about/info-2018/aarp-livable-communities-preparing-for-an-aging-nation.html.
5. For a helpful definition of intergenerational programs and practices, see "Making the Case for Intergenerational Programs," Generations United, 2021, 2, https://www.gu.org/resources/making-the-case-for-intergenerational-programs/: "Intergenerational programs intentionally unite the generations in ways that enrich participants' lives and help address vital social and community issues while building on the positive resources that young and old have to offer each other and to their communities. These programs bring people of different generations together for ongoing, mutually beneficial, planned activities, designed to achieve specified program goals, and promote greater understanding and respect between generations. Reciprocity, sustainability, intentionality, training, support, and viewing younger and older people as assets are hallmarks of successful programs."
6. George E. Vaillant, *Aging Well*, (Little, Brown & Company, 2002), 139.
7. Steven R. Covey, *The 7 Habits of Highly Effective People*, (New York: Simon & Schuster, 1989). (Describing habit number five as "Seek first to understand, then to be understood.")
8. Marc Freedman, *How to Live Forever* (New York: PublicAffairs, 2018), 137.
9. Dairanys Grullon-Virgil and Sydelle Barreto, "Beyond Passing the Torch: Recommendations on Leveraging Age Diversity to Build a Stronger Democracy Now," Generation Citizen, CoGenerate, Millennial Action Project, 2023, 12, https://cogenerate.org/wp-content/uploads/2023/02/Beyond-Passing-The-Torch.pdf.
10. Grullon-Virgil and Sydelle Barreto, "Beyond Passing the Torch," 23.
11. "Fact Sheet: Intergenerational Programs Benefit Everyone," Generations United, 2021, 3, https://www.gu.org/resources/fact-sheet-intergenerational-programs-benefit-everyone/
12. Freedman, *How to Live Forever*, 9. Freedman summarizes the benefits of connecting across generations and notes, "There is significant evidence from evolutionary anthropology and developmental psychology that old and young are built for each other. The old, as they move into the latter phases of life, are driven by a deep desire to be needed by and to nurture the next generation; the young have a need to be nurtured. It's a fit that goes back to the beginning of human history."
13. As one example, Bridge Meadows uses the power of community to help children heal from the trauma of foster care. The program includes high-quality affordable housing, therapeutic programs, and intergenerational community support. Elders live in the community, serving as mentors, friends, and caregivers to the children and each other, forming a safety net of care and interdependence. Learn more at https://bridgemeadows.org/.
14. Doug Dickson, "Older Workers as Volunteers," in *The Rowman & Littlefield Handbook on Aging and Work*, ed. Elizabeth F. Fideler (Lanham, MD: Rowman & Littlefield, 2022), 449.
15. SAGE and other partners offer online mentoring and tutoring programs that have achieved very positive outcomes for younger and older people. An example of online programming that has created opportunities for meaningful connections across generations is The Long Distance Grandparent, offering meaningful advice and plans to manage the challenge of geographic distance with loved ones. Learn more at https://thelongdistancegrandparent.com/.
16. For an excellent summary of the benefits for different age groups from working across generations (babies to elders), see "Making the Case for Intergenerational Programs," Generations United, 2021, https://www.gu.org/resources/making-the-case-for-intergenerational-programs/.
17. Freedman, *How to Live Forever*, 10–11. Freedman notes, "We have an impulse toward meaningful relationships that grow as we realize fewer days are ahead than behind. We have a deeply rooted instinct to connect in ways that flow down the generational chain. And we have a set of skills—patience, persistence, and emotional regulation, among others—that, study upon study shows, blossom with age."
18. Vaillant, *Aging Well*, 47.
19. Freedman, *How to Live Forever*, 17. Freedman summarizes a 2018 Stanford University Graduate School of Education study that found two-thirds of older adults in the United States are without purpose beyond their self in their lives, purpose meaning "they identify, prioritize, adopt, and actively pursue goals that are both personally meaningful and contribute to the greater good."
20. Dickson, "Older Workers as Volunteers," 445.
21. Dickson, "Older Workers as Volunteers," 451. Dickson notes, "Many older adults report feeling alienated from friends who don't share their interest in volunteering and relieved upon finding a community of people who do. That community not only reinforces the urge to give back but also provides a supportive environment for sharing opportunities and deepening commitment."

22. "Fact Sheet," Generations United, 2, https://www.gu.org/resources/fact-sheet-intergenerational-programs-benefit-everyone/.
23. Grullon-Virgil and Barreto, "Beyond Passing the Torch," 15.
24. Dickson, "Older Workers as Volunteers," 451.
25. Grullon-Virgil and Barreto, "Beyond Passing the Torch," 5.
26. Jon R. Katzenbach and Douglas K. Smith, *The Wisdom of Teams* (New York: McKinsey & Company, 1993), 9.
27. Dickson, "Older Workers as Volunteers," 450.
28. Freedman, *How to Live Forever*, 85.
29. "Terry Tempest Williams Quotes," Goodreads, https://www.goodreads.com/quotes/640120-the-eyes-of-the-future-are-looking-back-at-us.
30. Grullon-Virgil and Barreto, "Beyond Passing the Torch," 15.
31. Ruby Belle Booth, "Intergenerational Civic Learning," Brennan Center for Justice, 2021, 3, https://www.brennancenter.org/our-work/research-reports/intergenerational-civic-learning.
32. Booth, "Intergenerational Civic Learning," 4.
33. David Brooks, "How America Got Mean," *The Atlantic*, August 14, 2023, 76, https://www.theatlantic.com/magazine/archive/2023/09/us-culture-moral-education-formation/674765/.
34. Jamie Ducharme, "America Has Reached Peak Therapy. Why is Our Mental Health Getting Worse?" *Time Magazine*, August 28, 2023, 2.
35. Vivek H. Murthy, "Surgeon General: We Have Become a Lonely Nation. It's Time to Fix That," *New York Times*, April 30, 2023, https://www.nytimes.com/2023/04/30/opinion/loneliness-epidemic-america.html.
36. Murthy, "Surgeon General."
37. Generations United, "Fact Sheet," 2.
38. Ibid, 3.
39. Nancy Henkin and Emily Patrick, "Intergenerational Strategies," Grantmakers in Aging, accessed June 6, 2025, https://www.giaging.org/issues/intergenerational-strategies/.
40. Ibid.
41. Ducharme, "America Has Reached Peak Therapy." This article emphasizes the importance of assessing whether someone's mental health is improving. A key question is whether they are able to start planning for their future.
42. Henkin and Patrick, "Intergenerational Strategies." The authors describe the goal of intergenerational practices as "strengthening the social compact—the implicit obligations we have to each other over time."
43. Generations United, "Fact Sheet," 1, https://www.gu.org/resources/fact-sheet-intergenerational-programs-benefit-everyone/. This source cites fifteen different social needs that warrant an intergenerational lens: academic achievement and enrichment; physical, cognitive, and mental health; social isolation and loneliness; cultural identity; environmental awareness and action; affordable housing; job readiness and entrepreneurship; neighborhood revitalization; addressing structural racism and inequalities; technology access and use; caregiving; food insecurity; community change; substance use; ageism.

Bibliography

Arigoni, Danielle. "Preparing for an Aging Population." AARP. Accessed June 6, 2025. https://www.aarp.org/livable-communities/about/info-2018/aarp-livable-communities-preparing-for-an-aging-nation.html.

Booth, Ruby Belle. "Intergenerational Civic Learning." Brennan Center for Justice. 2021. https://www.brennancenter.org/our-work/research-reports/intergenerational-civic-learning.

Brooks, David. "How America Got Mean." *The Atlantic*. August 14, 2023. https://www.theatlantic.com/magazine/archive/2023/09/us-culture-moral-education-formation/674765/.

Covey, Steven R. *The 7 Habits of Highly Effective People*. New York: Simon & Schuster, 1989.

Ducharme, Jamie. "America Has Reached Peak Therapy. Why Is Our Mental Health Getting Worse?" *Time Magazine*, August 28, 2023.

Dickson, Doug. "Older Workers as Volunteers." In *The Rowman & Littlefield Handbook on Aging and Work*, edited by Elizabeth F. Fideler, 441–455. Lanham, MD: Rowman & Littlefield, 2022.

Freedman, Marc. *How to Live Forever*. New York: PublicAffairs, 2018.

Generations United. "Fact Sheet: Intergenerational Programs Benefit Everyone." 2021. https://www.gu.org/resources/fact-sheet-intergenerational-programs-benefit-everyone/.

Generations United. "Making the Case for Intergenerational Programs." 2021. https://www.gu.org/resources/making-the-case-for-intergenerational-programs/

Grullon-Virgil, Dairanys, and Sydelle Barreto. "Beyond Passing the Torch: Recommendations on Leveraging Age Diversity to Build a Stronger Democracy Now." Generation Citizen, CoGenerate, Millennial Action Project, 2023. https://cogenerate.org/wp-content/uploads/2023/02/Beyond-Passing-The-Torch.pdf.

Goodreads. Edmund Burke Quotes. Accessed June 6, 2025. https://www.goodreads.com/quotes/1004069-society-is-a-partnership-of-the-dead-the-living-and.

Goodreads. "Anonymous Greek Proverb." Accessed June 6, 2025. https://www.goodreads.com/quotes/666987-society-grows-great-when-old-men-plant-trees-whose-shade.

Goodreads. "Terry Tempest Williams Quotes." Accessed June 6, 2025. https://www.goodreads.com/quotes/640120-the-eyes-of-the-future-are-looking-back-at-us.

Henkin, Nancy, and Emily Patrick. "Intergenerational Strategies." Grantmakers in Aging. Accessed June 6, 2025. https://www.giaging.org/issues/intergenerational-strategies/.

Katzenbach, Jon R., and Douglas K. Smith. *The Wisdom of Teams*. McKinsey & Company, 1993.

Murthy, Vivek H. "Surgeon General: We Have Become a Lonely Nation. It's Time to Fix That." *New York Times*, April 30, 2023. https://www.nytimes.com/2023/04/30/opinion/loneliness-epidemic-america.html.

US Department of Health and Human Services. "Aging." Accessed June 6, 2025. https://www.hhs.gov/aging/index.html.

Vaillant, George E. *Aging Well*. Little, Brown & Company, 2002.

CHAPTER 9

EnCorps—STEM Professionals Serving to Inspire Students through STEM Education

Kathleen Kostrzewa *and* Katherine Wilcox

> **Abstract**
>
> This chapter highlights EnCorps, an organization of intergenerational learning that simultaneously helps aging populations and K–12 students thrive, drawing upon rich STEM (science, technology, engineering, and math) industry expertise to inspire the next generation of scientists, engineers, inventors, and entrepreneurs. The reader will learn about EnCorps's approach to addressing the critical shortage of STEM teachers by recruiting and training qualified STEM professionals to teach and tutor in our nation's most underresourced classrooms. Since 2007, EnCorps has recognized that enabling those over fifty years of age to translate their work experience into rewarding new teaching careers is a solution for all generations.
>
> **Key Words:** EnCorps, intergenerational, STEM, teach, tutor

---

EnCorps STEM Teachers Program® and EnCorps STEMx Tutors Program

Strengths/impact
- **Using refined rubrics**, experienced STEM professionals are matched with students to bring out student's full potential.
- Student and STEM professional enter the program with a **growth mindset**, ready to learn.
- **Commitment**: Students, tutors, guest teachers, and school partners commit to fully participate.
- **Professional staff:** EnCorps staff focus on individual STEM professionals, not on generational groups.
- **Operational agility:** Intergenerational groups require flexible and adaptable processes, allowing educators to choose how they prefer to work.
- **Social supports:** Participants are supported by program staff when solving problems such as changes in scheduling, matches that aren't working, and unforeseen issues that may arise.
- **Impact measurement and management:** Quantitative and nonstatistical data are used to document impact and to communicate to all stakeholders.

Limitations
- School-defined schedules can create time constraints for individuals still working and unable to volunteer at specific times.
- Educators do not receive compensation for participation in programs, which can make it more difficult to recruit individuals into programs.

The Urgent Need to Innovate

According to the 2018 literacy performance assessments conducted by the Program for International Student Assessment, American students ranked thirty-first in math and tenth in science compared to their global peers. In 2022, the National Assessment of Educational Progress reported that only 27 percent of eighth-grade students nationwide are proficient in math, while 14 percent of Latinx and 9 percent of Black/African American students meet eighth-grade math standards. Low student achievement in these subject areas is caused, in part, by insufficient numbers of qualified STEM (science, technology, engineering, and math) teachers. Students across the nation, especially those experiencing poverty and attending high-needs public schools, deserve our very best ingenuity and out-of-the-box thinking in this new era of education sector uncertainty.

EnCorps is poised to take up the mantle through the EnCorps STEM Teachers Program®, whose innovative approach addresses the critical shortage of STEM teachers by recruiting and training qualified STEM professionals (an untapped resource) to teach in our nation's most underresourced classrooms. Student academic needs and the context of their lived experiences are the driving forces behind EnCorps's work.

EnCorps's Mission

EnCorps advocates for STEM educational equity. Anchored in our belief that traditionally underrepresented students belong in STEM, we prepare STEM role models to educate and inspire students who lack access to a high-quality science, technology, engineering, and math education. We see a future where students from underresourced schools have the education and confidence to choose a STEM career so they can thrive in an increasingly complex and diverse world.

The EnCorps STEM Teachers Program recruits, selects, and supports STEM professionals and experts from STEM fields as an innovative, long-term solution to the STEM teacher shortage and to counter the alarming lack of math and science proficiency of middle and high school students nationwide.

The EnCorps STEMx Tutors Program matches middle school students currently underperforming in math with volunteer STEM professionals, subject-matter experts, and STEM college majors to increase math skills and confidence prior to students entering high school. With an unwavering resolve to do what is best for traditionally left-behind students, EnCorps works diligently to make our nation's distressed public school classrooms more representative and engaging by bringing a pipeline of educators with increased racial, gender, and higher education attainment diversity to education's doorstep.

We are dedicated to creating a thriving society of generations working together for the benefit of all.

The EnCorps Community

Key Beneficiaries—Students

Students who are impacted by an EnCorps educator are the key beneficiaries—they come first. Serving over 250 high-needs middle and high schools in California, Colorado, and New York, the STEM Teachers Program places experienced career-changing STEM experts as EnCorps fellows into partner schools to guest teach alongside a host teacher for a semester. Through this experience, the students are exposed to real-life stories and learn about exciting new careers while the EnCorps fellows spend time in the classroom, which helps them make an informed decision as they explore becoming a STEM teacher.

During the start of the COVID pandemic, EnCorps recognized that students were struggling with virtual math learning. To address this problem, in November 2020 EnCorps launched the STEMx Tutors Program with two of their partner schools. The tutoring program matches middle school students who are underperforming in math with current and retired STEM professionals. The tutor is online while students take part in virtual tutoring on the school site to receive supervision and technical support from school staff. Since 2020, EnCorps has expanded this program to additional partner schools.

EnCorps Educators—STEM Professionals

The vital links in STEM education are highly qualified educators who can deliver high-quality math and science curriculum and instruction to students. However, it is difficult for states to attract STEM experts to teaching when they can opt for better-paying jobs in the private sector. EnCorps addresses this problem by recruiting STEM professionals who are either retired or are career-changers and provides them with resources and access to educational opportunities in underresourced communities. These mature individuals bring a reality of life to the classroom by drawing on their lived experience.

EnCorps's framework is based on the transformative pedagogy of Martin Haberman's *Star Teachers: The Ideology and Best Practice of Effective Teachers of Diverse Children and Youth in Poverty*.[1] Recruiting the right individuals, and training and supporting them, will ensure success with students and educators. The right individual leads students to become lifelong learners guided by what they continue to learn. EnCorps developed and continues to use a set of rubrics, based on the Haberman model[2] to assess STEM professionals before they are invited to join the EnCorps STEM Teachers Program or EnCorps STEMx Tutors Program.

Only a candidate with the following competencies is invited to join EnCorps:

Leadership and influence
- Creates and executes organized plans that successfully meet goals
- Has the ability to motivate, inspire, or influence others
- Communicates effectively and can convey information in ways that others understand

Mission fit with EnCorps
- Desires to expand STEM achievement, access, and literacy opportunities to high-need schools and communities
- Views themselves as a potential solution to problems in public education

Achievement in STEM fields
- Demonstrates a record of high academic and professional achievement
- Transfers real-life professional knowledge and experience to academic settings
- Exhibits a high level of competency and knowledge in STEM fields

Resilience/grit
- Works to overcome challenges
- Believes goals can be accomplished despite obstacles
- Understands the difficulty inherent in being an effective educator

Personal responsibility
- Accepts responsibility for student learning
- Takes ownership in situations; does not blame external factors or barriers
- Believes that all students can succeed

Growth mindset/lifelong learning orientation
- Reflects on their own strengths, challenges, and areas for improvement
- Is humble about developing new knowledge and a new skill set
- Has the willingness to learn from feedback and mistakes in order to improve

Cultural awareness and sensitivity
- Is committed to equity and social justice
- Holds an asset-based perspective on minority or underrepresented demographic groups
- Is aware of how their own demography (race, ethnicity, social class, gender, etc.) influences their world view

Educators come from all generations; ages range from eighteen to eighty-four, with the average age being forty-six years old. See figure 9.1 for additional demographic information.

Since 2007, EnCorps has recruited 1,700 STEM educators and impacted 282,500 students in underserved communities in California, Denver, Colorado, and New York City. The five-year EnCorps teacher retention rate is 80 percent, well over the national average of 50 percent. Additional data showing the impact of the STEM Teachers Program and the STEMx Tutors Program can be seen in figure 9.2.

▶ **Years of STEM Industry Experience**

- EnCorps Educators: 15

▶ **Highest Level of Education of EnCorps Educators**

- 64% Masters or PhD
- 36% Bachelor's Degree

▶ **Ethnicity / Race of EnCorps Educators**

- 49% White / Caucasian
- 25% Asian
- 9% Latinx
- 7% Black / African American
- 5% Other
- 4% Multi-Racial
- 1% Native American or Pacific Highlander

▶ **Gender Identity of EnCorps Educators**

- 55% Male
- 42% Female
- 3% Other / Undeclared

Figure 9.1 EnCorps educators: additional demographics.

Source: EnCorps STEM Teachers Program® and STEMx Tutors Program © 2023 EnCorps, Inc.

Students Share Feedback on EnCorps Fellows Guest Teaching.

81% Said EnCorps Fellow made them more aware of STEM career opportunities.

97% Reported that EnCorps Fellow answered questions in a helpful way.

91% Stated that EnCorps Fellow made them aware of relevance of STEM.

Students in the STEMx Tutors Program:

84% Reported feeling more confident when taking a math test

97% Believed they improved in math because of their EnCorps STEMx Tutor

84% Increased their math proficiency

Figure 9.2 EnCorps program impact.

Source: EnCorps STEM Teachers Program® and STEMx Tutors Program © 2023 EnCorps, Inc.

The EnCorps Staff and Board of Directors

Similar to the recruitment of the STEM professionals, EnCorps selects staff members based on a set of core and leadership competencies. As with the educators, the top qualification for staff is a commitment to the mission of the organization as a whole and alignment with organizational values. Leaders are sought who create and support regular opportunities for individuals of all backgrounds to contribute their knowledge, skills, and perspectives in a variety of ways, none more apparent than the team's commitment to their justice, equity, diversity, and inclusion work.

EnCorps's team comprises a set of diverse people dedicated to providing quality STEM education to all students. It is truly intergenerational, with team members spanning Generation Z to Baby Boomers. All generations bring their own areas of specialization to the discussion, with Generation Z and Millennials contributing their knowledge of current inclusion topics, while Generation X and Baby Boomers bring maturity and years of working experience. EnCorps's former executive director joined the EnCorps STEM Teachers Program to bring her industry experience into the classroom before being tapped to lead the organization. In addition, two current directors came into EnCorps on an EnCore fellowship, now part of CoGenerate, an organization that focuses on what the growing older population can do in collaboration with younger generations to solve our nation's most pressing problems. Two directors have served as STEMx tutors since the program's inception. All of these experienced individuals were attracted to the EnCorps mission of STEM educational equity.

Two members of EnCorps's board have had a significant impact on the Encore, now CoGenerate (referenced above), movement. Current board chair Sherry Lansing, formerly chairman of Paramount Pictures, founded EnCorps in 2007. Ms. Lansing, once a math teacher, founded EnCorps with the idea of recruiting career-changing, retiring STEM professionals and assisting them to become teachers. Marc Friedman, co-CEO and founder of CoGenerate, is one of the nation's leading experts regarding our multigenerational future. He served on the EnCorps board of directors from 2017 to 2022 and was instrumental in expanding the organization's reach.

An Organization of Intergenerational Learning

EnCorps is an organization of intergenerational learning that simultaneously helps aging populations and K–12 students thrive, drawing upon rich industry expertise to inspire the next generation of scientists, engineers, inventors, and entrepreneurs. Traditionally, the education system approaches teacher recruitment and training from the university undergraduate perspective, neglecting those advanced in age and career stage. EnCorps leverages a nontraditional teacher pipeline because we are committed to the core belief that solutions uniting multiple generations are the key to access, equity, and human progress. Since 2007, we have been working diligently to place experienced STEM experts into the public schools, enabling older populations to leverage their work experience to embark on exciting new careers benefitting subsequent generations. At a transition point in their lives, at an average age of forty-six years, qualified STEM professionals join EnCorps to experience the benefits of exploring an encore career, working with students in a low-risk, high-reward way. EnCorps STEM Teachers Program fellows and STEMx tutors are given exceptional opportunities to meaningfully engage and participate in their communities, to continue learning and expanding existing skill sets, and to impart critical knowledge acquired from hands-on work in STEM industries.

The aging population contains highly skilled professionals primed to build the future pipeline into the workforce—students. EnCorps demonstrates that all students can excel in the classroom and prepare for college, career, and community success when they have access to quality mentors, tutors, and teachers who connect learning to workplace relevance and provide real-world insight.

Bringing Generations Together to Teach and Learn

Normative public school hiring practices place young, recently credentialed graduates with little experience and with a standard across-the-board curriculum into educational environments that are the most difficult to negotiate and for which they are generally ill equipped: urban, rural, and suburban pockets of students in poverty. EnCorps's work disrupts the traditional unproductive relationship between and among students and teachers. As John Maynard Keynes, the well-known British mathematician turned economist, observed in an oft-quoted quip about our resistance to change, "The difficulty lies not in the new ideas but in escaping from the old ones."[3]

EnCorps recognizes that one size does not fit all. There is no single best way to teach, tutor, or mentor. Every student will need something different, challenging educators to find ways to reach each student uniquely. "Whenever students are directly involved in a real-life experience, it is likely that good teaching is going on."[4] Knowledge is free. Whenever students are being helped to see major concepts, big ideas, and general principles, and are not merely memorizing isolated facts, good teaching is going on.[5] The value of teaching and mentoring lies in the person who is able to deliver that knowledge. "How" is just as important as "what." We must help students cultivate effective habits of mind and intellectual skills so that they are able to generate their own questions, find their own answers, and develop an intrinsic love of learning.

Teaching and learning are very human pursuits. The relationship between student and educator is the centerpiece of the learning process. Because of this dynamic, the more educators know about themselves, the more they can understand their students and the more effective the teaching and learning will be.

As stated previously, recruiting the right individuals, and training and supporting them, will ensure success with students and educators. Upon selection into EnCorps and participation in orientation and training, each fellow will impact an average of sixty students through mentoring and guest teaching before continuing their transition to teaching. Host teachers provide in-classroom support while EnCorps staff coach and mentor educators as they participate in 120 hours of EnCorps professional development programs via Google classroom and access our library of online resources with titles such as "The Power of Positive Student Relationships"[6] and "The Science of Hope: The First Emotion You Ever Learn."[7] Separately, EnCorps conducts in-person professional development events and coordinates regional social gatherings to foster community among fellows and tutors.

Tutors participate in orientation and online training before being matched with a student for whom they provide an average of forty hours per year of online tutoring. Tutors also participate in Google classroom and in-person and virtual professional development. Professional development is not math or science subject matter focused. Instead, EnCorps prioritizes the development and delivery of a timely, culturally relevant curriculum that is focused on student and educator growth, learning, and well-being.

EnCorps Profiles and Stories of Impact—Educating from Experience

Not only do EnCorps educators have a passion for STEM, but they bring with them high levels of STEM education and years of professional experience in a STEM career. All EnCorps fellows and tutors have a bachelor's degree, with 64 percent also having achieved an advanced degree. The average time spent in the STEM industry for all EnCorps Educators is fifteen years, with many tutors having thirty, forty, and even fifty years of experience.

To illustrate the intergenerational relationships, this section features two EnCorps STEM teachers and an EnCorps STEMx tutor. They all come from different generations but have one thing in common—a passion for educating and inspiring young students.

Ashley—Goodbye Laboratory, Hello Classroom (Millennial)

Ashley, a Millennial STEM professional with a doctorate in biology, knew fairly early in her research career that she wanted to be a teacher. She joined EnCorps in 2014, completed the STEM Teachers Program and started teaching high school biology two years later. She forsook the comfort of the laboratory and her six-figure salary to teach in a high school where the majority of the students live in poverty, are learning English, or face other challenges. Ashley changed careers for the same reason most STEM professionals come to EnCorps: they want to *find value in their work*, they like the *social interaction of working with young people*, and, most importantly, they want to *impact a young person's life*.

In her first year of teaching, Ashley was named Los Angeles Unified School District "Rookie of the Year," and the following year she was a finalist for the 2017 Educator of the Year by the California League of High Schools. Here is what the high school principal had to say about Ashley: "She is a huge blessing. Her energy, her knowledge, her willingness to work with students, especially those who are more of a challenge . . . She's the reason kids are here."

Ashley is now in her tenth year as an EnCorps educator and is continuing to give back to EnCorps by hosting a new EnCorps fellow through guest teaching and inspiring the fellow to become the next EnCorps STEM educator.

Bill—From Engineer to EnCorps STEM Educator (Silent Generation)

Bill, born in 1945, is a member of the Silent Generation. After spending fifty years as a construction and engineering project manager, Bill came to EnCorps in 2017 as an

EnCorps fellow. He received his teaching certificate, taught engineering for one year and then, due to the COVID pandemic, switched to the EnCorps STEMx Tutors Program, which provided him the ability to work part-time while still pursuing his passion.

Bill has been tutoring middle school students in math since October 2021 and has logged a total of 139 tutoring hours. In 2022–2023, he logged the most tutoring time of anyone for that school year—a whopping ninety-three hours. Recognizing Bill's dedication, EnCorps submitted him for AARP's Andrus Award for Community Service. Here are just a few of the reasons he was nominated. "Bill is so amazing in how he connects with students, often leaning into his fun-loving nature, and his students really respond to it! One of the students he worked with consistently this year showed great improvement by the end of the year. In addition to tutoring hours he also attends many of our professional development sessions, which shows a growth mindset, as he is still finding new ways to expand his skills and knowledge."

Charles—From EnCorps STEM Teacher to EnCorps Board Member (Baby Boomer)

Charles, a Lockheed Martin aerospace engineer for thirty-four years, retired in 2014 and assumed he would spend retirement indulging his love of golf and volunteering to mentor youth. Instead, he found EnCorps and decided to get his teaching degree in math and science so he could teach at an underresourced school in Los Angeles. Charles grew up in the South Bronx and was inspired by an eighth-grade teacher who was a pilot. He has said that the satisfaction he gets from watching his students become engaged in aerospace equals the satisfaction of working on amazing aircraft. When asked why he made this move at this age, Charles simply answered, "This is basically a passion."

It is clear from the following testimonials that Charles has inspired an interest in engineering and aerospace in his students: "Having our teacher come from an aerospace background is amazing. He incorporates the aerospace workspace into the class, he always tells us about the times he did stuff related to what we are working on." And "I never really knew what was out there, in terms of the field. He tells us about how he got there and I can see myself doing that a few years from now."

After retiring from teaching Charles went on to join the EnCorps board of directors. He continues to tell his story and inspire STEM professionals to share their STEM industry experience and impact student learning. In Charles's words, "At the end of the day, what's going to be your legacy? What have you impacted? As I share my experience, students realize 'I too can do that'. They will be better individuals because I am here."

Intergenerational Challenges

Both the STEM Teachers Program and the STEMx Tutors Program call upon five current workforce generations to participate, bringing with them years of life and work experiences (see figure 9.3).

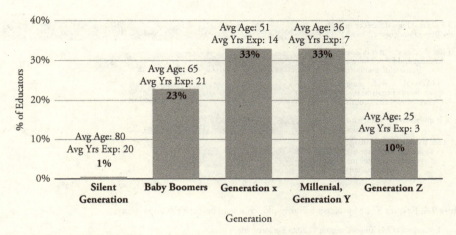

Figure 9.3 Percent of educators all-time by generation (for those reporting birthdate).
Source: EnCorps STEMx Tutors Program © 2023 EnCorps, Inc.

To best understand the EnCorps journey working with multiple generations, this chapter will turn its focus to the STEMx Tutors Program, the program with the widest age differences, the most direct working experience with the educators, and the most learning from an intergenerational point of view supported by data.

Tutor Coordinators Dispel Generational Stereotypes

EnCorps employs tutor coordinators who are responsible for onboarding tutors, matching them successfully with students, training them, and providing guidance throughout the school year. The close relationship between the tutors and coordinators has resulted in a better understanding of the contributions each generation makes to the EnCorps STEMx Tutors Program.

When the program first started, EnCorps staff were likely to hold some of the typical generational stereotypes, such as "Older tutors are more serious and disciplined, demanding a rigorous tutoring process and needing extensive support to handle the technology, while younger tutors relate better to the students, are more fun-loving, and need much less support with technology." However, with three-plus years of collected data, working across several generations, the STEMx tutor coordinators have discovered that they can attribute key challenges and opportunities not to specific ages or generations of the tutors but, rather, to the situations and working styles of each individual. This was surprising to all until, upon further exploration, they concluded that EnCorps's recruitment and onboarding processes tend to contribute to more commonality across generations than differences.

These are the top reasons that typical stereotypes are not evident across the generations in EnCorps:

- **Alignment to mission:** All tutors enter the program with clear alignment to the EnCorps mission. Tutors do not receive pay for their work; they volunteer their time. EnCorps

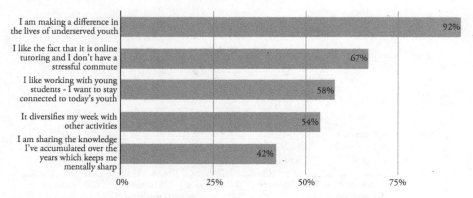

Figure 9.4 Reasons STEM professionals fifty-plus choose to become EnCorps tutors.
Source: EnCorps STEMx Tutors Program © 2023 EnCorps, Inc.

believes this may make recruitment more challenging; however, once volunteers are offered a position, they participate in orientation and training and are anxious to start. In a recent survey of tutors fifty-plus years of age, 92 percent report the reason they are STEMx tutors is that they are "making a difference in the lives of underserved youth" (see figure 9.4).

- **Experienced and ready to learn:** The tutors are experienced STEM professionals with an average of fifteen years of work experience. Most worked in a constantly changing discipline and had to become very adept at learning and dealing with challenges, solving issues, and managing work outcomes. They come to tutoring with a growth mindset and a willingness to learn and accept feedback from the tutor coordinators and, most importantly, to learn from their students. Here is a testimonial from one of the tutors:

    I always wanted to tutor math, but most programs are not flexible with timing and location. This program allows flexibility, so that is great. I also wanted to do something with students because I wish someone had been more open and encouraging with me at that age. I like the program's focus on being open and sharing, and the emotional aspects of learning. It's so important. I think the program has impacted me more than my student! I love interacting with her; it forces me to focus on someone else's learning and be flexible, and encourage her, be creative with her on how to solve problems, how they relate to her life, and feel a sense of teamwork with her. As a side note, for me, as a person with no kids, it's just a delight to work with her twice a week and have some time with the younger generation. I was lucky to get to tutor my student!

- **Flexible matching process:** EnCorps has developed a well-constructed process to match and support the three key stakeholders of the tutor program—the student, the tutor, and the school staff—to ensure student and tutor success. They have a highly qualified and professional team that manages the process to achieve maximum impact from the tutoring hours spent. Each student-tutor match is handled by a tutor coordinator who monitors the match by working with both the tutor and the school coordinator. After every tutoring session, the tutor must submit feedback that includes a summary of what topics were covered and a "tutor testimonial," which describes anything the tutor wants to relate to the school coordinator and the math teacher. If there are signs that the match is weak in the short term or long term, the tutor coordinator will match the student with a different tutor. (Sometimes another match is done simply based on schedule changes.)

Some tutors have been matched with the same student since the start of the program. Many of these relationships have grown into mentor relationships. Several matches are now in their third or fourth year and have logged between one hundred to over two hundred hours of tutoring. One tutor started tutoring her student in sixth grade and continues this year while her student is a freshman in high school. Some former students who started as sixth or seventh graders who left the program are reaching out to their former tutors to ask for help with their high school coursework.

- **EnCorps staff focus on the individual tutor:** Most importantly, EnCorps has built a program that is run by tutor coordinators who are very professional, and when asked if they witnessed typical generational stereotypes, both positive and negative, they surprised us with their answer: "For every example of an older (fifty-plus) tutor we thought about examples with our younger tutors as well. Our older tutors bring a wealth of life and STEM experience, but that's not to say that those under fifty haven't also. An immediate example that feels stereotypical is technology, but it is not necessarily true, it is the willingness to learn. We end up supporting tutors of all ages with technology/EnCorps systems."

EnCorps takes time to develop these STEM professionals into excellent math tutors by providing professional development courses, tutor community hours, and individual one-on-one coaching if that is needed. Flexibility is a key factor to each tutor's success, as everyone enters the program with different schedules and working styles. The key to a successful program is for the EnCorps staff to understand the individual tutor rather than making a judgment based on their age or any other stereotypes.

Ultimate Goal of All Tutors—Student Success

As noted previously, the main reason the STEM professional volunteers to tutor is to impact a student's life. EnCorps measures impact by collecting various student data such as change in math proficiency, math confidence, perseverance, critical thinking, and STEM career awareness. During the 2022–2023 academic year, 84 percent of students in the EnCorps STEMx Tutors Program increased their math diagnostic scores; the average increase was twenty-two points. EnCorps also collects nonstatistical data by directly surveying all program stakeholders, including students, parents, tutors, and school partners. This provides a comprehensive view of all program constituents' attitudes to ensure that the program is producing the desired impact.

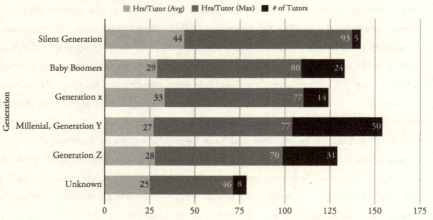

Figure 9.5 STEMx Tutor Program 2022–2023 tutoring statistics.

Source: EnCorps STEMx Tutors Program © 2023 EnCorps, Inc.

As EnCorps focused on impacting more students, program directors started to analyze various demographics of the tutors, such as STEM area of expertise, STEM education, years of STEM experience, and years of life experience, and they found that the STEM professional who is semiretired or retired has tutored the most hours and over the longest period of time. EnCorps attribute more tutoring hours not to the age of the tutor but, rather, to the fact that the older generations have more flexible schedules and more time to devote to volunteer work. Figure 9.5 shows that in the 2022–2023 school year, tutors with the greatest average tutoring hours were from the Silent Generation.

Here are some additional interesting facts:

- The oldest EnCorps Tutor is seventy-seven years old and tutored the most hours last year.
- The tutor with the most hours tutoring all-time is seventy-three years old.
- Both of these tutors have just signed up for their fourth year of tutoring.

Promising Practices and Opportunities for the Future

EnCorps remains the only organization that has successfully recruited highly qualified and passionate STEM individuals to serve in low-income communities for fifteen years. The selection process, along with curated training and ongoing professional development and support, ensures that committed and well-prepared educators nurture student academic success, the development of a STEM identity, and a sense of belonging. Our recruitment, selection, support, and placement processes are documented[8] and can be adopted by others.

Speaking about how intergenerational relationships can transform our future, Susan Curnan, Brandeis professor and executive director of the Center for Youth and Communities, has said, "The key is pairing great potential with great experience." EnCorps Educators' wisdom from life experience, emotional intelligence, generativity and the drive to "give back," align with the skills and abilities that enhance young people's ability to thrive.[9]

As our educators impact the lives of students, they too are growing and learning. The impact is mutually beneficial. When entering the STEMx Tutors Program, participants commit to tutor two hours per week for a minimum of one semester per academic year. More than 50 percent of the tutors return from year to year. EnCorps attributes this return rate to the tutors' understanding of the two-way impact. One educator expressed it this way, saying, "Tutoring helped me realize just how much a one-to-one relationship where I'm nurturing learning feeds me." Others have commented about the impact in this way: "I wanted to make a difference in a young person's life." And "I am so grateful for the relationship that I built with my student."

Given the growing number of long-term relationships of students and tutors transitioning into students and mentors, EnCorps is looking to develop the EnCorps STEM Mentors Program, which will support secondary students as they think about entering college, technical schools, or the workforce. EnCorps will provide one-on-one mentoring for students to align identified aptitudes and certifications with academic and career opportunities and continue support with a professional network tailored to students' education and career goals.

Notes
1. Martin Haberman, *Star Teachers: The Ideology and Best Practice of Effective Teachers of Diverse Children and Youth in Poverty* (Houston, TX: Haberman Educational Foundation, 2005), 47–58.
2. Kwirz Admin, "The Haberman Model," November 8, 2017, https://habermanfoundation.org/the-haberman-model/.
3. John Maynard Keynes, *The General Theory of Employment, Interest, and Money* (New York: Palgrave Macmillan, 2018).
4. Haberman, "Star Teachers," 56.
5. Haberman, "Star Teachers," 55.
6. EnCorps STEM Teachers Program, *The Power of Positive Student Relationships* (EnCorps, 2020).
7. EnCorps STEM Teachers Program, *The Science of Hope: The First Emotion You Ever Learn* (EnCorps, 2023).
8. EnCorps., *The EnCorps STEM Teachers Program® Playbook* (EnCorps, 2023).
9. Amy Yotopoulos, "Hidden in Plain Sight: How Intergenerational Relationships Can Transform Our Future," Stanford Center on Longevity, June 2016, https://longevity.stanford.edu/wp-content/uploads/2017/06/Intergenerational-Relationships.pdf.

Bibliography
Admin, Kwirz. "The Haberman Model." November 8, 2017. https://habermanfoundation.org/the-haberman-model/.

EnCorps. *The EnCorps STEM Teachers Program® Playbook*. EnCorps, 2023.
EnCorps STEM Teachers Program. *The Power of Positive Student Relationships*. EnCorps, 2020.
EnCorps STEM Teachers Program. *The Science of Hope: The First Emotion You Ever Learn*. EnCorps, 2023.
Haberman, Martin. *Star Teachers: The Ideology and Best Practice of Effective Teachers of Diverse Children and Youth in Poverty*. Houston, TX: Haberman Educational Foundation, 2005, 47–58.
Keynes, John Maynard. *The General Theory of Employment, Interest, and Money*. New York: Palgrave Macmillan, 2018.
Yotopoulos, Amy. "Hidden in Plain Sight: How Intergenerational Relationships Can Transform Our Future." Stanford Center on Longevity. June 2016. https://longevity.stanford.edu/wp-content/uploads/2017/06/Intergenerational-Relationships.pdf.

CHAPTER 10

Changing Lives through Oasis Intergenerational Tutoring

Jeanne Foster, Mary Click, Stephanie McCreary, *and* Paul Weiss

Abstract

This chapter explores the success of the Oasis Intergenerational Tutoring Program over a span of thirty-five years. Established in 1989 as a community engagement opportunity, the tutoring program has grown to be the primary volunteer program of the Oasis Institute. Older adult volunteers are paired with children who benefit from assistance with reading and literacy. The caring, supportive relationships that the Oasis tutors form with the students offer a mentoring component as the children regularly interact with an adult role model. How the program continues to be relevant for school staff, children, and older adults is highlighted through both qualitative and quantitative data combined with information gleaned from interaction with the program's stakeholders. Challenges to implementation and continued expansion of the Oasis Tutoring Program are also delved into.

Key Words: Oasis, literacy tutors, volunteers, intergenerational, mentors

Oasis Intergenerational Tutoring
Strengths/impact   • Longevity   • Number of tutors and children participating   • Ongoing growth/expansion
Limitations   • Funding for research   • Overall funding for the tutoring program   • Obtaining needed statistics from participating school districts

Introduction

Established in 1989, Oasis Intergenerational Tutoring trains older adult volunteers across the country to connect with school-age children who struggle with reading and literacy and could benefit from a one-on-one mentoring relationship with a caring adult. Children selected by their teachers to participate in Oasis Tutoring are usually those most likely to "fall through the cracks" because they are not yet reading at grade level but do not qualify for special services. The program is appreciated by principals, teachers, children, and older adults alike, leading educators to welcome Oasis tutors year after year. While improvement of reading scores is important, the long-term mentoring relationships developed between the students and their tutors are also a powerful incentive. A review of study data, as well as qualitative data reported by stakeholders, reveals the benefits and importance of these relationships. A summary of the founding of Oasis and establishment of Oasis Intergenerational Tutoring sets the stage for today's program and its success and challenges.

Founding of Oasis

In 1978, Marylen Mann, educator, curriculum development specialist, and recognized community activist, was invited by Father Lucius Cervantes, Commissioner of the Mayor's Office on Aging, to tour senior centers in St. Louis. After she and her friend, Margie May, spent a day with Cervantes in church basements visiting with older adults playing bingo, making crafts, or sitting idly by, Mann told Cervantes, "We can do better than this for older adults." From that day forward, Mann has worked tirelessly to establish the organization known today as The Oasis Institute.

By 1982, Oasis, with a two-year demonstration grant, had launched a lifelong-learning curriculum at its first location in St. Louis. Additional locations in Baltimore, Cleveland, and Los Angeles opened soon after. By 1988, in partnership with the May Department Stores Company Foundation, Oasis had expanded to eighty-five locations serving three thousand older adults.

Recognizing the need for additional opportunities for older adults, many of whom had raised families, held jobs, and engaged in other productive activities, Mann worked with experts at local St. Louis universities to develop a reading and language curriculum. The program would provide well-trained, reliable volunteers to work with children weekly to help them practice reading and gain a love of learning. Superintendents welcomed the program; Oasis Intergenerational Tutoring was under way.

The Oasis Intergenerational Tutoring Program

From the beginning, Oasis Intergenerational Tutoring had five primary goals: (1) promote motivation, success, and enjoyment of reading; (2) help develop language, build vocabulary, and expand background knowledge; (3) increase confidence and self-esteem in children; (4) provide purposeful volunteer opportunities for older adults; and (5) strengthen the ties between generations.

To accomplish these goals, Oasis partners with school districts,[1] where a tutoring facilitator, chosen by the district, helps recruit, train, and oversee tutors. In addition, the facilitators organize tutor support/enrichment meetings and work with school staff and Oasis building liaisons, who match tutors with students recommended by teachers for the program.

Oasis tutors are known for their flexibility, patience, compassion, enthusiasm, humor, and perseverance. Once tutors have joined the program, they are expected to attend training to learn the Oasis approach, commit to meeting with their students once a week throughout the school year, attend tutor meetings offered by the district tutoring facilitator, and notify the building liaison should problems arise. Above all, the most important qualification to be an Oasis tutor is a strong desire to help a child with reading.

Depending on the school district, training may be in-person or partially online. Trainers may be district facilitators, Oasis staff, or independent professionals. Oasis tutors learn how to choose and read books effectively, talk with children to draw out thoughts and ideas, help children write down their stories and read their stories aloud, develop learning activities using the children's stories, and build success through review activities. In recent years, the mentoring component of Oasis Tutoring has been requested more and more frequently by school district personnel. To meet that need, Oasis worked with the National Mentoring Resource Center to develop a mentoring module that has been added to the training.

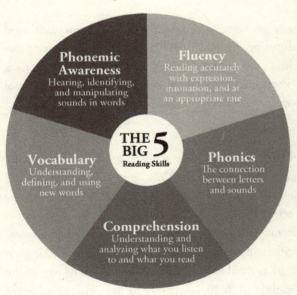

The foundation of Oasis Tutoring is a six-part session plan, covered thoroughly in training. Oasis provides partnering school districts with a library of books and session plans that address what are known as the "Big 5" literacy skills: phonemic awareness, phonics, oral reading fluency, vocabulary, and reading comprehension strategies (see figure 10.1).[2]

Figure 10.1 The "Big 5" reading skills emphasize reading aloud, word recognition, listening, vocabulary expansion, pronunciation, writing, and understanding content.

Source: Timothy Shanahan, The National Reading Panel Report: Practical Advice for Teachers, 2004. Graphic by The Oasis Institute, Oasis Intergenerational Tutoring Program, 2023.

In addition to the initial training, Oasis provides tutors with a kit containing items that they use regularly when working with their students. Each tutor receives a canvas bag with a copy of the Oasis Tutor's Handbook, a copy of "My Journal" for their students to record the stories they create, an "All About Me" booklet for them to complete, and a booklet titled "Words I'm Learning" and "Words I Know," where the children note their progress. Tutors have access to "Tutor Power," a resource for session plans located on the Oasis website. The regularly scheduled meetings held by the school district facilitators provide ongoing support and supplementary training. In some programs, tutors also receive books to give their students for their home libraries and may be offered additional opportunities to attend enrichment sessions facilitated by education professionals both in-person and online. The national Oasis Tutoring office sponsors virtual summer literacy celebrations open to tutors across the nation.

Oasis Tutoring Research

Since its inception, research in various forms has been an important component of Oasis Intergenerational Tutoring. Research has delved into different aspects of the program and assisted the tutoring staff in making improvements and modifications to the program. These changes keep the program vital and relevant for today's school districts. Research, both qualitative and quantitative, examines students' academic achievement as well as the social/emotional effects of this intergenerational program on the students and the older adult tutors.

Qualitative Survey Data

Early on, Oasis staff recognized the importance of stakeholder input for the continued growth and improvement of Oasis Tutoring. Every spring, Oasis tutors, participating elementary school principals, and teachers are asked to complete an online survey regarding their experience and their students' experience with the tutoring program during the school year. The data reveal consistent responses to similar questions posed over several years.[3]

PRINCIPALS

When asked if Oasis tutors are a valuable addition to their schools, principals consistently responded with 99 percent to 100 percent agreement. In 2021, at the end of the first full school year of the COVID-19 pandemic when tutors were not able to meet with their students in person, the percentage dropped to 92 percent agreement. By 2022, when tutors could again tutor in-person, the percentage rose to 99 percent once more. Principals were also asked if they planned to participate in the program in the upcoming school year. Again, the responses were consistent: 97 percent to 100 percent intended to be part of the program. The percentage dropped slightly in 2020, likely due to the unique challenges created by the COVID-19 pandemic. The percentage rose again to 99 percent in 2023.

In 2023, administrators were asked if they thought that the focus of the Oasis six-part session plan based on state learning standards for vocabulary, comprehension, phonemic awareness, phonics, speaking, listening, and writing helped achieve their districts' goals for student outcomes. The response was unanimous, with 100 percent in agreement.[4]

TEACHERS

Prior to the pandemic, teachers were asked about students' academics as well as other questions pertaining to their students' school experience. Their responses were consistent over several years. When asked if the tutored students' academic performance improved, agreement ranged between 88 percent and 93 percent.[5] Regarding students' attitude toward language arts, between 91 percent and 96 percent of teachers felt their students improved. Between 85 percent and 90 percent agreed that their tutored students' participation in classroom discussions and activities was positive. Since many students referred for tutoring lack confidence and self-esteem, teachers were asked if improvement also occurred in those areas, with 88 percent to 96 percent concurring. Over 60 percent felt that students' attendance improved, with several noting that their students were always present on their tutoring day.[6]

TUTORS
Recently, Oasis volunteers were asked if they felt tutoring added a purposeful element to their lives. From 2019 to 2023, 96 percent to 100 percent agreed with the statement. It was during the pandemic that the percentage dropped to 96 percent as the tutoring program model changed to reflect tutors' lack of access to schools for in-person sessions. It rose again to 99 percent as tutors returned to the traditional in-person model in 2022.

Until 2021, between 96 percent and 99 percent of respondents planned to return as tutors in the upcoming school year. Reasons cited for not returning included declining health, the health of a spouse or partner, no longer driving, relocating to be closer to family, and wishing to try another volunteer opportunity. When asked about changes in their students, 99 percent to 100 percent of tutors noted a generally positive overall change in their students or a more positive attitude toward school. However, in 2021 and 2022, the percentage dropped to 40 percent and 60 percent, respectively, while the program was only offered virtually or as a Postal Pal (pen pal). In 2019 and 2020, tutors were asked if they noticed a change in their students' confidence and self-esteem, with 99 percent responding positively. The question was not asked in pandemic years 2021 and 2022 since the tutors did not meet with their students in person. In 2023, 74 percent noted a positive change.[7]

Survey Data Influence Program Development
While the survey results indicate that Oasis Tutoring serves the needs of older adults, children, and school staff, there are always opportunities for enhancement or modifications. When combined with in-person discussions and participant comments, the findings are used for program improvement to ensure Oasis Tutoring's relevance for today's school and older adult experiences. Changes, such as the addition of online tutor training and the mentoring component, were initiated after the possibility was broached by various stakeholders. Principals and building liaisons recognized the students' need for social/emotional support, which led staff to strengthen the mentoring portion of the training by including modules on social-emotional learning and the Science of Reading research.[8] School administrators and tutors appreciate that Oasis aligns program components with the strategic direction of partnering school districts.

Today's volunteers are more computer savvy and willing to participate in asynchronous training, leading to the development of some web-based training modules. The Oasis Tutoring online training module was originally developed to condense the in-person training experience for those volunteers who were still working but whose employers offered the option for volunteer service during the work day. After completing the online module, the volunteers' in-person training was shortened from two (approximately six-hour) days to one. The online training is also widely used by school district facilitators, Oasis staff, and consultants as a means to prepare volunteers for in-person training by providing background knowledge prior to attending the first session.

Quantitative Data on Benefits to Older Adults—"The Effects of Volunteerism on Older Adults"

In 2020, Oasis Tutoring was awarded a grant from the RRF Foundation for Aging to conduct a study of the effects of volunteering on older adults' health (physical, emotional, and cognitive) and social engagement. Specifically, the funding was designated to study the effects of tutoring on social isolation and health outcomes and how those effects vary by subgroups, the effects of tutoring on additional civic engagement, and the attributes of the Oasis program that contribute to high retention rates of volunteers. Oasis partnered with researchers Peter C. Sun and Nancy Morrow-Howell from Brown School, Washington University in St. Louis, to undertake the study.

The original plan was to survey tutors in four cities offering Oasis Intergenerational Tutoring: St. Louis, Albuquerque, Indianapolis, and Pittsburgh. However, due to the COVID-19 pandemic, the tutoring program was forced to pivot to a different model during the 2020–2021 school year. Since tutors were unable to meet with students in person, two other options were offered to tutors who still wished to volunteer: either virtual tutoring or as Postal Pals (pen pals). Consequently, the first full year of the study (2021–2022) only evaluated tutors' reactions after implementing these two models.

PANDEMIC NECESSITATES CHANGE, 2020–2021

Due to the pandemic, the first year of the study was limited to tutors in the St. Louis area since in-person tutoring was paused. The original two-year research grant encompassing a survey in the summer of 2020, a pretest in the fall of 2020, and a posttest and focus group in the spring of 2021 was expanded into a three-year project, which offered an extra year to study the impact of virtual volunteerism on the older adult population. It also offered an opportunity to take a critical look at the effects of online tutoring compared to in-person engagement, which helps inform best practices and contributes to research regarding virtual volunteering.

Most St. Louis respondents (73.5 percent) indicated a preference for in-person tutoring, but when asked if they would participate in a virtual tutoring program, 60.6 percent responded that they were "somewhat likely" or "very likely" to participate.[9] While not a replacement for in-person tutoring, respondents saw virtual tutoring as beneficial. It would allow tutoring from home while still having a one-on-one relationship with a student. Respondents also felt that ongoing virtual tutoring would improve the students' performance at school.[10]

Tutors' concerns included difficulty in establishing a personal connection with their students and doing a hands-on activity when using an online platform. They also mentioned that they had not yet been trained to tutor remotely and worried about keeping the children engaged in the tutoring session.[11] This limited study of tutors in the St. Louis region concluded that "a successful transition would be contingent on training volunteers on both the technological and pedagogical aspects of virtual tutoring."[12] It is seen as a promising alternative for those who wish to volunteer but have mobility or distance concerns.[13]

PANDEMIC PIVOT: VIRTUAL TUTORS AND POSTAL PALS

In the summer of 2020, Oasis staff sent a recruitment letter to 104 tutors who were participating as Postal Pals (pen pals), virtual tutors, or both. Of those, eighty-seven respondents filled out consent forms to participate in the study, and eventually, sixty-one completed both the pre- and posttest surveys. The final sample included thirty-nine pen pals and twenty-two virtual tutors.[14] Four pen pals and seven virtual tutors participated in two separate ninety-minute online focus groups following the posttest.[15] Pen pals spent approximately 2.3 hours per month volunteering, while virtual tutors spent approximately 7.0 hours.[16]

Volunteers' responses to posttest questions showed agreement or strong agreement (42.9 percent) that they increased social activities, used time productively (37.5 percent), contributed to the well-being of children (89.3 percent), and felt better about themselves (84.2 percent). Most volunteers felt their overall health was about the same as at the beginning of the school year. However, 17.9 percent saw improvement to their physical health, 22.8 percent to their cognitive health, and 25.0 percent to their emotional health because of their volunteer activity.[17] More virtual tutors (75.0 percent) than pen pals (18.9 percent) thought that connecting with their students through these options presented challenges. Both groups (73.9 percent) reported that engaging with their students remotely was less effective than in-person, and 74.0 percent indicated that forming relationships remotely was more difficult.[18]

The pen pal focus groups stated that the opportunity to forge a meaningful relationship with a child was still rewarding and provided "a buffer against the social isolation caused by the pandemic and lockdowns—a psychological 'boost' that 'added something' to their lives."[19] In the virtual tutoring focus groups, a recurrent theme of "something on my calendar" captures the tutors' feeling of ambivalence about the program. They did appreciate the extensive collection of digital books available for them to access for their sessions. Because they perceived virtual tutoring as transitional, they were uncertain of the benefits, with some stating that "virtual volunteering was better than nothing."[20] They were eager to return to in-person tutoring.

Several ideas presented themselves as future possibilities. While volunteers strongly preferred in-person tutoring, the virtual and pen pal options could open possibilities for those who wish to volunteer but are unable to do so at a school. Many were hesitant to attempt new technology and suggested additional training. They also thought opportunities to engage remotely with other volunteers to share ideas, stories, and challenges, much like the in-person tutor support meetings, would enhance the virtual experience.[21]

FOUR-CITY STUDY, 2021–2023

In the 2021–2022 and 2022–2023 school years, most volunteers were welcomed back to the schools for in-person tutoring. In 2021, for the originally planned RRF Foundation for Aging study, "The Effects of Volunteerism on Older Adults," a survey sample was drawn from four locations (St. Louis, Albuquerque, Indianapolis, and Pittsburgh) for a quasi-experimental study, which aimed to understand the effect of Oasis Tutoring on the health of participants.

There were 264 Oasis tutors who completed all surveys in 2021, 2022, and 2023. They were compared with a nationally representative sample of 264 older adults, drawn from the University of Michigan Health and Retirement Study (HRS).[22] The HRS group was matched with the Oasis tutors for characteristics such as education, income, and marital status in 2021.[23] The volunteers selected from the HRS group were not high-intensity volunteers (volunteering more than two hundred hours in the previous twelve months) for comparison with high-commitment Oasis tutors. Age, gender, race, and ethnicity were all taken into consideration. Oasis tutors had a slightly lower number of functional limitations than the HRS comparison group and slightly lower, but marginally significant, depression scores. Oasis tutors and the comparison group did not show a significant difference on the self-rated health scores.[24]

Overall, when compared to the nationally representative sample of older adults over this two-year period, Oasis tutors saw significant decreases in functional limitations and a trend toward decreasing depressive symptoms.[25] Preliminary results indicate that Oasis tutors experience positive benefits when volunteering in the schools. Improvements in at least two areas of physical, emotional, and/or cognitive health were reported by 13.6 percent of all tutors. Physical health improved for 10.2 percent, cognitive health improved for 15.2 percent, and 23.5 percent reported improvement in emotional health[26] (see figure 10.2).

In addition, tutors also "agreed" or "strongly agreed" that because of their involvement with Oasis, they increased their social activities, used their time more productively, contributed to the well-being of children, and felt better about themselves[27] (see figure 10.3).

In 2022, 78.8 percent of Oasis tutors agreed that their students benefited in at least one area: attitude toward learning (60.2 percent), reading or writing abilities (68.6

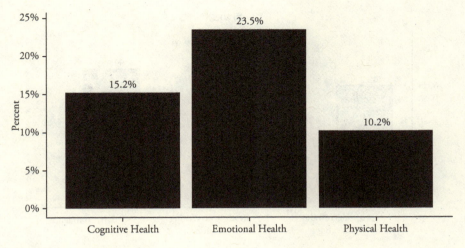

Figure 10.2 Reported Health benefits to tutors.

Source: Peter C. Sun, Nancy Morrow-Howell, Mary Click, and Kendra Minch. "Health Outcomes of the Oasis Intergenerational Tutoring Program: Preliminary Two-Year Survey Findings," 2023.

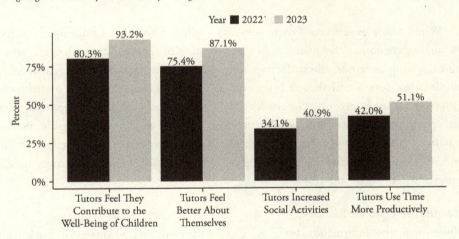

Figure 10.3 Feel They Contribute to the Well-Being of Children.

Source: Peter C. Sun, Nancy Morrow-Howell, Mary Click, and Kendra Minch. "Health Outcomes of the Oasis Intergenerational Tutoring Program: Preliminary Two-Year Survey Findings," 2023.

percent), or self-confidence (69.3 percent). Results from 2023 showed similar, and more positive, agreement that students benefited in at least one area: attitude toward learning (73.9 percent), reading or writing abilities (79.9 percent), or self-confidence (84.8 percent)[28] (see figure 10.4).

As a result of tutoring in elementary schools, tutors also gained a deeper understanding of teachers' jobs, the needs of children, and educational issues and policies. The likelihood of tutors voting in favor of public support for schools and school programs increased by 50.4 percent—a positive benefit for participating school districts.[29]

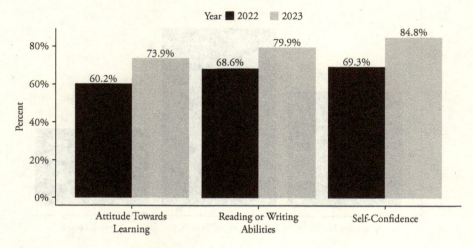

Figure 10.4 Tutor reported benefits to students.

Source: Peter C. Sun, Nancy Morrow-Howell, Mary Click, and Kendra Minch. "Health Outcomes of the Oasis Intergenerational Tutoring Program: Preliminary Two-Year Survey Findings," 2023.

When tutors were asked if there were any negative effects from tutoring, 91 percent said there were none. A few mentioned transportation or accessibility challenges, competing caregiving demands, dissatisfaction with the program (lack of training, scheduling/coordination issues, and shorter instructional time with their students), or frustration with student/home environment challenges.[30] Close to half of the tutors reported at least one unexpected benefit. Those benefits included personal benefits (socialization, personal growth, or increased appreciation of the school system), generativity and a chance to help student learning and growth, networking opportunities, and finding a pathway to other forms of social engagement.[31]

Quantitative Data for Reading

While qualitative information from the Oasis surveys proved adequate for participating school districts to continue with the Oasis Intergenerational Tutoring Program, new districts sometimes ask for quantitative data demonstrating that students who have Oasis tutors improve their reading scores. In addition, as a not-for-profit organization, Oasis Tutoring relies on the financial support of numerous foundations, corporations, and other organizations who more and more frequently request quantitative reading data. Large-scale studies of this type are very expensive and, while funders desire the data, finding an organization willing to underwrite such research is an ongoing concern. In 2013, Oasis Tutoring determined that it was critical to dedicate some general funds to a study that would provide supporting data.

OASIS INTERGENERATIONAL TUTORING STUDY, 2013–2014

Oasis formed a partnership with Maryville University's education department to conduct a study of Oasis Tutoring in seven school districts in the St. Louis region. The study included 42 elementary schools, 374 students[32] in grades one through three, 150 tutors, 140 teachers, 42 building liaisons, 7 district coordinators, and 14 literacy assessment specialists.[33] At the time of the study, two models were being used: the traditional model, where children were tutored once a week, and the "high impact," model where students met with their tutor twice a week.[34] A pretest and posttest control group design that included both models and a comparison group was implemented. Of the 374 students who completed the pretest, 331 completed the posttest, with 169 children tutored once a week, 27 children tutored twice a week, and 135 children who were not tutored but were given packets of information that parents could use at home. The literacy assessment specialists administered three identical reading assessments and a reading attitude survey in the fall of 2013 and again in the spring of 2014. Building liaisons, tutors, and teachers all completed surveys in April 2014. To provide a deeper understanding of the survey results, the chief investigator, Daniel J. Rocchio, and school district liaisons conducted two focus groups in May 2014.[35]

The reading assessment scores for the two tutored groups indicated that each group made an average instructional level reading gain of seven months during the seven-month study. This level of reading gain would be expected of average readers but is better than expected for a group of struggling readers. The struggling Oasis readers in third grade made a better-than-expected reading gain of one year during the seven-month study. The tutored children in one of the districts made a greater reading gain than the control group on one of the assessments, the graded word list. There were no significant differences among the scores of the tutored and control groups for the other six districts.[36]

A closer look at the instructional reading level gain scores of two districts and an analysis of the gains for tutored third-graders in the study indicated that Oasis Tutoring may be more effective for lower-level readers (e.g., those three to four months below grade level) than for readers near grade level. The FRL (i.e., free and reduced lunch percentage, an indication of poverty level) was 42 percent for the single district that showed reading gains for tutored children greater than the control group. In combination, these analyses suggest that Oasis Tutoring may be more effective for poverty-level children who are reading three to four months below grade level.[37]

The reading attitude and the reading confidence scores of the tutored and untutored children were very high at the beginning of the study; thus, there was little room for growth by any of the three groups at the end of the study. Results from the reading attitude postassessment indicated that the children were very pleased with the reading help provided by the Oasis tutors (i.e., average = 10.6 out of a possible 12 points). Survey results from the Oasis building liaisons, teachers, and tutors involved in the study indicated that all three groups agreed (i.e., 90 percent of each group) that the Oasis Tutoring Program improved the reading ability of the children. The key reason given for the program's success was that the one-on-one relationship with a caring adult develops the child's confidence and reading motivation. Consequently, the child improves in reading engagement and reading achievement. Additionally, feedback from the two focus group meetings indicated that working with the same children for two years tends to produce greater reading growth than a single year of tutoring.[38]

Moving Forward

Tutor Participation

Oasis Tutoring has a high percentage of tutors who return the following year (since 2003, an average of 84 percent have returned for at least one more year). In the fall of 2019, more than four thousand older adults were volunteering as Oasis tutors; many had served as tutors for multiple years. In the spring of 2020 when schools suddenly closed, they, like most people, faced the abrupt end of their volunteer commitments, which they had taken very seriously. The relationships they had spent months, in some cases years, building, ended without opportunities for closure. In the following school year, a number of tutors took advantage of the modified program and participated as Postal Pals or as virtual tutors. As previously noted in the research conducted about the pandemic pivot, these opportunities were not as fulfilling as the traditional tutoring model.[39] By the time tutors were welcomed back into the schools in the fall of 2022, the number of in-person tutors had declined drastically to two thousand. Only a few still volunteered as Postal Pals or virtual tutors. However, with early interest in tutor training, Oasis staff expect the number of Oasis tutors to increase in the coming years.

There were many reasons for this drop in the number of volunteers. The older adults who make up the Oasis Tutoring community are drawn from the population most affected by COVID-19. During the three years of the pandemic, in some instances, new health issues for themselves or their partners had arisen, some had died, others sought different volunteer opportunities because school campuses were closed to volunteers, and others simply got out of the habit of volunteering. Consequently, a primary focus for Oasis Intergenerational Tutoring became recruitment, both to add new volunteers and to bring former tutors back into the program.

Tutor Recruitment

Efforts to rebuild the program are ongoing. The best volunteer recruiters are the tutors themselves because they can testify to the benefits they personally experience by helping a child who struggles with reading and literacy skills. The Oasis Tutoring tagline best describes the experience: "One child. One tutor. One school year. Two lives forever changed." In addition to inviting their friends and family to join the program, tutors have invited Oasis staff to make tutor recruitment presentations for their residential communities, churches, clubs, and civic organizations.

In participating school districts, tutors are recruited through messages on outdoor signs, notes to parents, school newsletters, websites, and other avenues. Oasis staff reach out to retired teacher associations, as many former teachers enjoy being back in a school setting and working one-on-one with a student, which they were seldom able to do when responsible for an entire classroom. Churches, civic organizations, fraternities and sororities, and community and senior centers are also leading options for tutor recruitment.

Additional Outreach

Oasis Tutoring has traditionally served children in grades K–3. In response to recommendations from school personnel and tutors, Oasis staff are considering expansion into upper elementary and middle school grades. In the Maryville Partnership study, it was noted that children who had an Oasis tutor for more than one year made greater progress in reading. In addition, with more emphasis on the mentoring component of tutoring, an extended period to develop the student-tutor relationship would be beneficial. In some schools, tutoring already continues past third grade, and efforts are being made to expand that opportunity to additional schools.

With the current emphasis on STEAM (science, technology, engineering, arts, math), there is growing interest in tutoring students who need help with math. Frequently, potential male tutors ask if math tutoring is an option. Since most Oasis tutors are female, this could provide additional opportunities to encourage men to participate. Math tutoring is in the very early stages of development and seems promising.

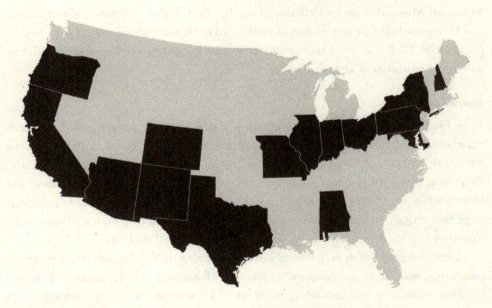

Figure 10.5 Map of Oasis tutoring locations.
Source: The Oasis Institute, 2023.

Plans for Expansion

In the fall of 2023, Oasis Tutoring was projected to be in 15 states, 22 cities, 84 school districts, and 441 schools across the United States (see figure 10.5).

As school districts enter the postpandemic "new normal," many are seeking new ways to support their students who have experienced setbacks, academically, socially, and emotionally. Oasis Tutoring is able to fill that void with reading and literacy support combined with mentoring. Efforts are under way to bring additional school districts into the Oasis Tutoring Program; one new district joined in 2023. The eight cities with Oasis education centers (Albuquerque, Los Angeles, Rochester, St. Louis, San Antonio, San Diego, Syracuse, and Washington, DC) all have tutoring program coordinators who work at the local level to recruit additional districts. Introductions made by tutors to school district administrators and by school district administrators to other administrators are fruitful. In addition, The Oasis Institute's overall strategy is to expand not only Oasis Tutoring but all Oasis programming—lifelong learning, health, and technology education—to additional locations in the Midwest.

In 2014, Oasis Tutoring received a grant from AmeriCorps Seniors Retired and Senior Volunteer Program, which, as part of the Corporation for National and Community Service, funds programs that engage older adult volunteers ages fifty-five and over in service activities throughout the country. (See *Handbook* chapter 11.) This grant provided for expansion and additional support of Oasis Tutoring in school districts in both the City of St. Louis and St. Louis County. Since then, the ongoing partnership with AmeriCorps Seniors has enabled more midwestern growth with grants to expand Oasis Tutoring into additional Missouri counties (Jefferson, Franklin, St. Charles, Audrain, Callaway, Linn, and Livingston). The program also was established in Illinois with an AmeriCorps Seniors grant for St. Clair County. Oasis continues to seek additional funding opportunities by partnering with AmeriCorps Seniors.

Summary

Since Oasis Intergenerational Tutoring was founded in 1989, the program has experienced continued growth and remains an important resource for school districts across the nation. As school staff seek additional ways to provide needed support for children who are at risk, they turn to Oasis tutors who are trained to help children with reading and literacy while providing a positive role model. The caring, supportive, mentoring relationships that tutors develop with their students are highly valued by school staff who rarely have time to provide needed one-on-one interactions with all students.

Oasis Tutoring builds on previous success by staying true to the core of the program: promoting motivation, success, and enjoyment of reading; helping develop language, building vocabulary, and expanding background knowledge; increasing confidence and self-esteem in children; providing purposeful volunteer opportunities for older adults;

and strengthening the ties between generations. The Oasis six-part plan, which is the foundation for every tutoring session, still aligns today with the reading and literacy goals of school districts across the nation. An example is the "Big 5" literacy skills: phonemic awareness, phonics, fluency, vocabulary, and comprehension.[40] Because Oasis tutors are trained to implement a specific process that supports reading achievement, there is no need for teachers to prepare lessons for the tutors to use.

Oasis Tutoring staff use data and school staff input to ensure that the program continues to meet the needs of the school districts. One area that has been highly impacted by stakeholder input is the mentoring component. By listening to principals, teachers, and tutors, it became obvious that the close, caring relationship between the tutors and their students is highly valued and fills a critical need in the schools. Consequently, Oasis staff acknowledged the need for strengthening this aspect of tutor training. They sought technical support from the National Mentoring Resource Center, and an in-depth module on mentoring was added to the tutor training in 2020. Oasis Tutoring has been awarded the National Mentoring Resource Center's stamp of approval as a program that utilizes the best practices in mentoring.

Similar to other volunteer programs, Oasis Tutoring experienced a severe drop in the number of tutors during the COVID-19 pandemic. By the time the tutors were able to return to the schools in the fall of 2021, the number of tutors had dropped by half. This significant reduction in the number of volunteers made tutor recruitment an important focus. Efforts to rebuild include adding new districts; several have expressed interest, and thirteen had joined the program as of 2023. Oasis has also received funding through AmeriCorps Seniors, resulting in twelve additional sites where Oasis Tutoring is offered as a rewarding volunteer experience.

Nonetheless, Oasis Tutoring faces several ongoing challenges. As with most not-for-profit organizations, obtaining funding to support the program is critical. Oasis advancement staff at the national level, as well as the eight Oasis centers, constantly explore grant possibilities and apply for funding to sustain the program. Few funders will support the program nationally, so most grants are specific to different localities, which creates inequities in how the program is implemented.

As part of the grant application process, many funders request data on student reading scores. However, few are willing to fund a national, comprehensive, in-depth study that would provide the data. This type of study is prohibitively expensive, and consequently, there are no results of this type to share with funders. Although Oasis staff request reading scores from participating school districts, this has proven to be problematic: some districts are unwilling or unable to provide the information, creating a dilemma. While those districts acknowledge and appreciate Oasis tutors for the support they provide their students, and agree that improved reading scores are helpful, they place greater emphasis on the close, caring, mentoring relationships that are developed through the program.

Oasis continues to address all these issues with the overarching goal of providing an Oasis tutor for every child who needs one, everywhere. One tutor. One student. One school year. Two lives forever changed.

Notes

1. While direct partnerships with school districts are the most successful, in a limited number of locations the partnership may be with another organization.
2. Timothy Shanahan, "The National Reading Panel Report: Practical Advice for Teachers." Learning Point Associates, 2004, 34. https://files.eric.ed.gov/fulltext/ED489535.pdf.
3. Oasis Institute, "Tutoring Survey Data," 2023.
4. Oasis Institute, "Tutoring Survey Data,"
5. Oasis Institute, "Tutoring Survey Data,"
6. Oasis Institute, "Tutoring Survey Data,"
7. Oasis Institute, "Tutoring Survey Data,"
8. Reading Rockets, "Introduction to the Science of Reading" (Arlington, VA: WETC, 2023), https://www.readingrockets.org/classroom/evidence-based-instruction/science-reading.
9. Peter C. Sun, et al., *Older Adults Attitudes Toward Virtual Volunteering During the COVID-19 Pandemic* (Thousand Oaks, CA: Sage Publications, 2021), 955.
10. Sun et al., *Older Adults Attitudes*, 955.
11. Sun et al., *Older Adults Attitudes*, 955.
12. Sun et al., *Older Adults Attitudes*, 956.
13. Sun et al., *Older Adults Attitudes*, 956.
14. Peter C. Sun et al., "Pandemic Pivots for Older Volunteers: Online Tutoring and Pen Pal Programs," *Journal of Gerontological Social Work* 66, no. 4 (2023): 548–66, 551.
15. Sun et al., "Pandemic Pivots," 552.
16. Sun et al., "Pandemic Pivots," 554–55.
17. Sun et al., "Pandemic Pivots," 555.
18. Sun et al., "Pandemic Pivots," 555.
19. Sun et al., "Pandemic Pivots," 557.
20. Sun et al., "Pandemic Pivots," 559–60.
21. Sun et al., "Pandemic Pivots," 561.
22. Peter C. Sun et al., "Health Outcomes of the Oasis Intergenerational Tutoring Program: Preliminary Two-Year Survey Findings," Brown School, Washington University in St. Louis, 2023, 9.
23. Sun et al., "Health Outcomes," 10.
24. Sun et al., "Health Outcomes," 10–13.
25. Sun et al., "Health Outcomes," 13.
26. Sun et al., "Health Outcomes," 16.
27. Sun et al., "Health Outcomes," 17.
28. Sun et al., "Health Outcomes," 18.
29. Sun et al., "Health Outcomes," 19.
30. Sun et al., "Health Outcomes," 20.
31. Sun et al., "Health Outcomes," 21.
32. Daniel J. Rocchio and Sam Hausfather, "The 2013-2014 Maryville University Study of the Oasis Intergenerational Tutoring Program in Seven St. Louis Area School Districts Final Report" (Maryville University, 2014), 3.
33. Daniel J. Rocchio and Sam Hausfather, "A Summary of the 2013-2014 Maryville University Study of the Oasis Intergenerational Tutoring Program in Seven St. Louis Area School Districts" (Maryville University, 2014), 1.
34. The "high impact" model was implemented for several years in a few districts but is not currently in use.
35. Rocchio and Hausfather, "A Summary," 1.

36. Rocchio and Hausfather, "A Summary," 2.
37. Rocchio and Hausfather, "A Summary," 2.
38. Rocchio and Hausfather, "A Summary," 2.
39. Sun et al., "Pandemic Pivots," 12.
40. Shanahan, "National Reading Panel Report," 34.

Bibliography

Oasis Institute. "Tutoring Survey Data." St. Louis, MO, 2023.

Reading Rockets. "Introduction to the Science of Reading." Arlington, VA: WETC, 2023. https://www.readingrockets.org/classroom/evidence-based-instruction/science-reading.

Rocchio, Daniel J., and Sam Hausfather. "A Summary of the 2013-2014 Maryville University Study of the Oasis Intergenerational Tutoring Program in Seven St. Louis Area School Districts." Maryville University, 2013–2014.

Rocchio, Daniel J., and Sam Hausfather. "The 2013-2014 Maryville University Study of the Oasis Intergenerational Tutoring Program in Seven St. Louis Area School Districts Final Report." Maryville University, 2013–2014.

Shanahan, Timothy. "The National Reading Panel Report: Practical Advice for Teachers." Naperville, IL: Learning Point Associates, 2004.

Sun, Peter C., Nancy Morrow-Howell, Mary Click, and Kendra Minch. "Health Outcomes of the Oasis Intergenerational Tutoring Program: Preliminary Two-Year Survey Findings." Brown School, Washington University in St. Louis, 2021–2023.

Sun, Peter C., Nancy Morrow-Howell, Alexander Helbach, and Elizabeth Pawloski. "Older Adults Attitudes toward Virtual Volunteering during the COVID-19 Pandemic." *Journal of Applied Gerontology* 40, no. 9 (2021): 953–57. https://doi.org/10.1177/07334648211006978.

Sun, Peter C., Nancy Morrow-Howell, and Elizabeth Pawloski. "Pandemic Pivots for Older Volunteers: Online Tutoring and Pen Pal Programs." *Journal of Gerontological Social Work* 66, no. 4 (2023): 548–66. https://doi.org/10.1080/01634372.2022.2128134.

CHAPTER 11

How National Service Brings to Scale Intergenerational Programs and Initiatives: The AmeriCorps Seniors Foster Grandparent Program and The National Partnership for Student Success

Atalaya Sergi, Kate Cochran, *and* Dorothy Jones

Abstract

This chapter discusses how AmeriCorps, the federal agency for national service and volunteerism, has demonstrated that national service is an effective mechanism for scaling intergenerational programs and initiatives. The AmeriCorps Seniors Foster Grandparent Program launched in 1965 with twenty-one demonstration projects. In fiscal year 2022 there were 271 projects in 49 states, the District of Columbia, Puerto Rico, and the Virgin Islands. While scaling over time, the Foster Grandparent Program has maintained the signature dual impact of intergenerational programs, producing positive outcomes for both the older adults serving and the children being served. It has also proved to be a cost-effective investment of federal dollars with a positive return on investment. In addition, national service is an effective way to operationalize public-private partnerships to meet national needs, utilizing intergenerational program models. The National Partnership for Student Success is a contemporary example.

Key Words: AmeriCorps Seniors, AmeriCorps, National Partnership for Student Success, intergenerational programs, Foster Grandparent Program

AmeriCorps Seniors	NPSS
Strengths/impact • A focus on direct-service. • Volunteer training is included so tutoring/mentoring experience is not necessary, • Public-private partnership with federal funding and nonfederal funding (10 percent match) braided to support programs.	**Strengths/impact** • Public-private partnership that includes the U.S. Department of Education and AmeriCorps, with the Johns Hopkins University Everyone Graduates Center as the nonprofit partner housing the NPSS Support Hub.

AmeriCorps Seniors	NPSS
Strengths/impact • Funding is available to a wide variety of organizations including, nonprofits, state and local government, faith-based, tribal nations, and tribal serving organizations. • National reach with over 270 grantees across 49 states, the District of Columbia, Puerto Rico and the Virgin Islands, serving children and youth in over 8,000 local sites. • Grantees are supported with training and technical assistance by agency staff from AmeriCorps Seniors and the Regional Operations team. • AmeriCorps Seniors implements ongoing research on program benefits to older person and children and youth and for continuous improvement.	**Strengths/impact** • National effort with over 160 supporting organizations informing the work, participating in working groups, and supporting the creation of free resources. • Strong collaboration with six national organizations (Accelerate, the National Student Support Accelerator, City Year, Communities in Schools, the National College Attainment Network, and MENTOR) that are leaders and experts in their support areas, providing nocost technical assistance to nonprofits, districts, institutions of higher education, and state or local government agencies.
Limitations • Grantees can only use funding for older adult programming, even in intergenerational projects. • Grantees must be able to manage federal grant compliance successfully.	**Limitations** • Does not provide direct services. • Does not provide funding.

Intergenerational programs have a long history in national service and a long list of benefits. We can expand and deepen those benefits as our society becomes the most age-diverse in our nation's history. We know from the 2020 Census data analysis that for the first time about a quarter of the population is represented in each age range. Sasha Johfre's analysis for CoGenerate shows that "the population distribution is now a rectangle, with almost equal numbers of people of every age from birth to 70 and beyond. One in four people (25 percent) is under 20 years old, and similarly, about one in four people (23 percent) is over 60."[1] This age diversity and distribution offers us an excellent opportunity to maximize the benefits of intergenerational programs across our nation and in every community. National Service can be the catalyst for scaling effective programs nationwide and highlighting promising initiatives.

When multiple generations are involved in a volunteer or service experience, there can be remarkable outcomes for all stakeholders. Intergenerational volunteerism and service provide spaces for knowledge exchange, the preservation of cultural heritage, the reduction of social isolation, and the breaking down of stereotypes and myths.

Our Nation Has Invested in Intergenerational Programs through Volunteerism and National Service for Generations.

National service and volunteerism have long been known to foster a civically engaged mindset—habits and qualities in individuals that demonstrate their connection to community and civic engagement. As individuals engage in volunteerism and service, they build a deeper understanding of the community and others in that community. The perceived barriers that make us different become valued and commonalities are discovered. We learn that we can contribute to the common good and that our skills, talents, and presence are needed.

AmeriCorps is the federal agency for national service and volunteerism. Annually, the agency engages over 100,000 AmeriCorps members and AmeriCorps Seniors volunteers in service and volunteerism. There are four primary programs in the agency: AmeriCorps Seniors, AmeriCorps State and National, AmeriCorps VISTA, and AmeriCorps NCCC (National Civilian Community Corps). The mission of the agency is to improve lives, strengthen communities, and foster civic engagement through service and volunteering. AmeriCorps came into existence in 1993, when Congress enacted the National and Community Service Act, creating the Corporation for National and Community Service (known as AmeriCorps since 2020). President Clinton signed the legislation soon after, and the Corporation for National and Community Service was launched the following year in 1994.

AmeriCorps engages Americans in service to address ongoing areas of need and to respond to national priorities as they arise. The six ongoing areas of need are disaster services, economic opportunity, education, environmental stewardship, healthy futures, and veterans and military families. Recent national priorities that AmeriCorps has responded to across its programs include the opioid crisis, pandemic recovery, public health, food insecurity, disaster mitigation and response, and workforce development.

Though AmeriCorps was created in 1993, there were national service programs in existence before the Corporation for National and Community Service was conceived and launched. AmeriCorps Seniors (formerly known as Senior Corps) and AmeriCorps VISTA (formerly known simply as Volunteers in Service to America) were created in the 1960s as part of the War on Poverty. When AmeriCorps was formed (at that time the Corporation for National and Community Service), Senior Corps and VISTA joined the new agency. Intergenerational programs have been a part of AmeriCorps programs since its inception and have remained an integral part of its DNA. AmeriCorps Seniors is its oldest and longest-running program with an intentionally designed intergenerational area of focus.

The Creation of an Intentionally Designed Intergenerational Program for National Service

Tracing the history of AmeriCorps Seniors back to its beginning leads to its oldest program, the Foster Grandparent Program, in 1965. However, even before that, the idea of engaging older adults in service started with the 1960 White House Conference on Aging. That conference highlighted the benefit of older adults staying actively engaged in the community and putting community service, or volunteerism, forward as a way to achieve that goal. At the same time, the nation was coming to terms with the needs of exceptional children in institutionalized educational and care settings. The confluence of these two ideas led a small group of visionary thinkers to propose, in 1964, an intergenerational program that benefited both older adults and children. That program became known as the Foster Grandparent Program. It focused on engaging older adults with low incomes as volunteers in educational and child care settings, bringing social-emotional and educational support to children in need of a caring adult's attention. The volunteers' presence and support also helped the staff in those institutions to provide the highest-quality services possible. Until the Corporation for National and Community Service, AmeriCorps, was launched, the Foster Grandparent Program and subsequent AmeriCorps Seniors Programs such as RSVP (formerly known as the Retired Senior Volunteer Program) and the Senior Companion Program were administered by the Administration on Aging.

In a report from Bernard E. Nash,[2] one of the original designers of the Foster Grandparent Program, we learn a lot about the early years. On August 28, 1965, the Foster Grandparent Program was launched nationally to connect people over the age of sixty-five who had income limitations with opportunities to provide love and attention to children in institutional group settings. This program would also provide the older adult volunteers with a sense of purpose, an opportunity to share their life experiences, and, just as importantly, help augment their poverty-level incomes. The program launched with twenty-one demonstration projects that paired adults over the age of sixty-five with children up to five years of age in educational and care settings in their community. For example, volunteers, known as foster grandparents, served twenty hours a week in institutions for children with intellectual disabilities. The organizations that received the program grants recruited, trained, and placed local community members. The grants covered the volunteer stipend, a medical exam for each volunteer, transportation costs, and the salary of the project director.

See It in Action: Fran has been showing up to serve children in southern Maine for twenty-one years. Imagine the numerous children she has tutored and mentored over those years, the number of teachers she has supported, and the many parents she has had the opportunity to encourage. Grammy Fran, as she is affectionately known, has served her children through good times and bad. Amidst the 2020 pandemic, she even served virtually. She refused to let her kindergarten students go without her help and presence during this frightening time, and she refused to let her teachers go without the vital support she has always provided them. Serving through the AmeriCorps Seniors Foster Grandparent Program has become her life's purpose; it is a part of the fabric of her life. Without this AmeriCorps Seniors program, who knows if Fran would have ever found her way to the schools and if the children would have ever found such a loving, caring, and dedicated tutor and mentor.

See It in Action: Kevin has served for six years with elementary students in Central Minnesota. The students call him Grandpa Kevin, and he loves each of them and their teachers as if they were his own. Kevin is happy to be a resource for the children he supports. He is assigned to first grade and supports children across those classrooms during the four days a week that he volunteers. In addition to being a trusted adult for the children to talk with about their joys and challenges, he also helps them with reading, math, and science. Teachers call on him to work one-on-one with children who are struggling to grasp a concept or those who need support completing their homework. Kevin takes great joy in being available for the children and being there to support teachers in getting children to their goals. He noted that children seem to thrive with one-on-one support. Kevin vividly remembers a child whom he helped with academic skills and confidence. The family had moved to the community from Minneapolis, and the child had a hard time adjusting, and he could barely recite the alphabet. Together, Kevin and the child worked an hour a day on reading, and by the time winter approached, the now-confident student had increased his reading ability and was proud of his accomplishments. Kevin came to the Foster Grandparent Program after losing his wife and retiring. He felt adrift and while sitting in a doctor's waiting room, he saw an ad for the program. It piqued his interest because he wanted to be useful and was tired of playing golf and fishing. Kevin had once been a substitute teacher and felt he had something to offer. He has found his purpose as a Foster Grandparent, and the children at his elementary school have a dedicated tutor and mentor.

The Scaling of the Foster Grandparent Program

In the same report from Bernard E. Nash we learn that by 1968, the number of programs had increased to sixty-eight. The Foster Grandparent Program was also increasing its reach; those programs spanned forty states and Puerto Rico. There were four thousand foster grandparents serving twenty-thousand children a year. The program had also experienced some programmatic changes. The maximum age of participating children had been increased to sixteen, and the settings in which older adults were serving had expanded to include juvenile justice facilities, mental health clinics, and hospitals. The program also saw a change in volunteer characteristics, as volunteers were becoming more diverse in age and race. In 1968, $10 million was appropriated for the Foster Grandparent Program, and these funds were made available to organizations to run the localized programs. It was also noted that interest continued to grow, and some states were funding their programs or seeking other funds to support program expansion.

Even now many of the foundational elements of the Foster Grandparent Program remain integral to this intentionally designed intergenerational program model. Just as there were changes reported in 1968, the program has continued to evolve today. The current iteration of the Foster Grandparent Program[3] remains focused on intergenerational relationships. The service activities continue to be centered on tutoring and mentoring; however, program grantees now include all the previous settings and public school classrooms, summer programs, after-school programs, and initiatives that support teen parents. The population served has also expanded to children who have fallen behind academically whether or not they have significant intellectual challenges. The age limit for children served is now eighteen years, and they may keep their foster grandparent beyond that age if they started with a grandparent before turning eighteen. The hourly stipend, which is meant to offset the cost of volunteering for older adults with incomes below 200 percent of poverty, has increased to $4 per service hour. It continues to lag behind the federal minimum wage intent, but in fiscal year (FY) 2023, the stipend saw its largest increase in the program's history, moving from $3.15 in FY 2022 to $4 in FY 2023.

The decision that allowed for a substantial national expansion was a deliberate change in the funding structure, a shift to a public-private partnership model. The current regulations that govern the Foster Grandparent Program, Title 45-Public Welfare,[4] require grantees to provide a minimum 10 percent nonfederal match to their federally granted funds. This match can be in-kind or cash. This has allowed for the program's overall appropriated funds to stretch further and support the scaling of the program. In FY 2022, AmeriCorps Seniors granted $107 million in congressional appropriations and grantees added $20 million in nonfederal funds to this public-private partnership. The reach and impact of the Foster Grandparent Program have grown. In FY 2022 there were 271 Foster Grandparent Programs across the nation, collectively engaging over fifteen thousand older adult volunteers. Not only has the number of volunteers increased, but in FY 2022 the program served ninety-five thousand children across forty-nine states, the District of Columbia, Puerto Rico, and the Virgin Islands.

Positive Return on Investment

Not only has the program's funding model allowed for scaling, but it has also supported a positive return on investment. In 2021 AmeriCorps engaged researchers to analyze the return on investment of two AmeriCorps Seniors programs; the Foster Grandparent Program was one of those programs. The analysis concluded that for every dollar the federal government invests, the Foster Grandparent Program returns $3.45. This return on investment may be even higher, as researchers note that the calculation is based on only the number of hours served multiplied by the market rate for the mentoring and tutoring services volunteers provide. The rate did not include the potential long-term benefits, such as long-term academic success, that children may receive.[5]

At scale, the Foster Grandparent Program continues to demonstrate the dual impact that the designers originally intended. The investment and the scaling amplify the tangible benefits across our nation, and we see across states, communities, and different cultures the positive program outcomes for both the children being served and the volunteers serving.

See It in Action: One of the longest-standing Foster Grandparent Programs is the Navajo Nation Foster Grandparent Program. This program is administered by the Navajo Area Agency on Aging and has been in existence since 1965.[6] The ninety-three elders that participate serve in Head Start, public, private, grant, and Bureau of Indian Affairs schools. They tutor and mentor children, helping them improve academically, while also passing on the cultural traditions and language of their nation. The engagement of the elders keeps them active and healthy and ensures that their culture continues for generations through the children and youth they support. Think about what could be lost from our collective culture if not for these intergenerational interactions. The slogan of the Navajo Nation's Foster Grandparent program is "Share Today, Shape Tomorrow."

Dual Impact and Positive Outcomes

As the original designers of the Foster Grandparent Program understood back in 1965 and as we continue to see today, there has always been a need for children to have access to extra support for their successful academic and social-emotional development. Recognizing the impact of the pandemic on the educational system nationally, President Biden took time to talk about these needs in his 2022 State of the Nation address.[8] He challenged states to use some of their American Rescue Plan Act funding not only to staff schools but also to extend learning by an additional four months, utilizing 250,000 new tutors and mentors to help students succeed. Research finds that tutoring programs consistently improve learning outcomes for children and are a powerful tool for schools.[9] This is consistent with what we see in outcomes for children who are partnered with tutors and mentors through the Foster Grandparent Program.

The most recent program reports, which are from FY 2021, reveal benefits to the children and youth served by AmeriCorps Seniors volunteers. For instance, in one Foster Grandparent Program outcome group, 54,156 individuals were recipients of AmeriCorps Seniors–supported services related to education, which includes students enrolled in grades K–12, out-of-school youth, preschool-age children, and individuals pursuing postsecondary education. Of these individuals, 21,689 students improved academic performance and/or skills in literacy and math, 13,232 students and children improved their academic engagement and/or social-emotional skills, and 11,266 children demonstrated gains in school readiness.

Loneliness and social isolation can impact older adults' health and well-being. In May 2023, the Department of Health and Human Services released an advisory and report from the United States Surgeon General, Dr. Vivek Murthy, sharing his concerns about loneliness and isolation and labeling it as a public health epidemic.[10] Dr. Murthy said,

> Our epidemic of loneliness and isolation has been an underappreciated public health crisis that has harmed individual and societal health. Our relationships are a source of healing and well-being hiding in plain sight—one that can help us live healthier, more fulfilled, and more productive lives. . . . Given the significant health consequences of loneliness and isolation, we must prioritize building social connection the same way we have prioritized other critical

public health issues such as tobacco, obesity, and substance use disorders. Together, we can build a country that's healthier, more resilient, less lonely, and more connected.

The negative health outcomes of social isolation for older adults include an increased risk of heart disease, stroke, and developing dementia. Older adults are more susceptible to loneliness and social isolation with the death of children, life partners, and friends. Health issues and mobility challenges contribute to the problem, as does retirement when older adults lose previously familiar social circles. The AmeriCorps Seniors Foster Grandparent Program provides a protective factor for older adults. As evident in the volunteer stories throughout this chapter and in the program structure itself, older adults find community with the children they serve, the teachers and staff they support, and even with other volunteers they meet in training and recognition events, which are a part of the program model.

These benefits to the older adult volunteers have been captured in an AmeriCorps Seniors research project entitled "Longitudinal Study of Foster Grandparent and Senior Companion Programs: Service Delivery Implications and Health Benefits to the Volunteers."[11] This study was done under the former name of AmeriCorps Seniors, Senior Corps, and included volunteers from both the Foster Grandparent Program and the Senior Companion Program. The study was launched in 2015 and collected data from more than 1,200 first-time foster grandparent and senior companion volunteers at three points in time over two years, the first being before they started the program. The areas the researchers studied were the volunteers' social, demographic, and economic backgrounds, their motivations for volunteering, their experience as a volunteer with the program, and the health and wellness outcomes. In the study, the foster grandparent and senior companion volunteer populations reported generally the same characteristics. The most notable differences were found in employment status. More senior companion volunteers reported their employment status as disabled and more foster grandparents reported working.

The study found that, overall, volunteers rated their health significantly higher than nonvolunteering older adults in similar circumstances. Further, 32 percent of volunteers who reported good health at the beginning of the study reported improved health two years later. Meanwhile, 55 percent of volunteers who reported good health at the start continued to report good health after two years. Volunteers who reported more than five symptoms of depression at the beginning of the study reported feeling less depressed two years later. Finally, 88 percent who started out describing their lives as having a lack of companionship felt less isolated at the end of the study.

See It in Action: Elnora has been serving as a foster grandparent volunteer for eleven years in Tennessee. This service gives her purpose and great joy. In 1994 Grandma Elnora lost her only child, a son, to gun violence. At the time, she was relatively young and didn't think a lot about her future. However, when she retired, she began to think about all it meant to lose her only child.

One of the major things she realized she had lost was the promise of grandchildren. She reflected on never hearing a child call her grandma, never feeling those little arms around her neck, or holding a small hand in hers. But she credits the Foster Grandparent Program with giving her a purpose and something she never thought she would have. In 2012, Grandma Elnora started serving in the preschool classroom of her local school. She was excited to be both useful and to expand a young person's thinking. What she received over the years that she had not expected was about two hundred grandchildren. She realized that it is love that creates the bond of grandparent to grandchild. Everywhere that she goes in her community children run up to her and call her grandma. Without the Foster Grandparent Program, Elnora might never have found what she thought was forever lost, and the children she serves would have missed out on the academic support she gives and the love and safety they find in her presence.

AmeriCorps' Scaling Ability and National Initiatives

The Foster Grandparent Program is a salient example of the power of AmeriCorps to use national service to scale an effective volunteer program over generations while holding true to its intention and integrity. That has been demonstrated through the AmeriCorps Seniors portfolio of programs, as RSVP and the Senior Companion program followed similar trajectories throughout their development. But AmeriCorps has also been able to use its national service programs to bring other intergenerational national initiatives to scale. This is vitally important when those initiatives are responding to an immediate issue of national concern. The National Partnership for Student Success is a contemporary example.

The National Partnership for Student Success

The National Partnership for Student Success (NPSS) is a public-private partnership between the U.S. Department of Education, AmeriCorps, and the Johns Hopkins University Everyone Graduates Center. This three-year initiative launched in July of 2022 with a call to action from the Biden-Harris administration, asking for an additional 250,000 caring individuals to serve as tutors, mentors, student success coaches, wraparound/integrated student support coordinators, and/or postsecondary transition coaches in schools and in after-school programs across the country to help support the loss of learning that happened because of the COVID-19 pandemic. These five student support categories have been shown to make a significant impact on the academic achievement and emotional and mental well-being of our children.

The Johns Hopkins University Everyone Graduates Center houses the NPSS Support Hub staff dedicated to advancing this work. The NPSS Support Hub manages several efforts, including coordinating six technical assistance lead organizations: the National Student Support Accelerator and Accelerate (for tutoring), MENTOR (for mentoring), City Year (for student success coaching), Communities in Schools (for wraparound/

integrated student support coordination), and the National College Attainment Network (for postsecondary transition coaching). The three aforementioned partners meet regularly to align strategy and support services to share resources, discuss and address obstacles and challenges, and coordinate efforts.

The NPSS Support Hub has a network of over 150 supporting champions, made of education and youth-serving organizations across the country. NPSS supporting champions are aligned leaders from nonprofit organizations; schools; districts; service providers; corporations; foundations; federal, state, and local agencies; state service commissions; and constituent organizations that represent public schools and public school staff to inform the design, implementation, and learnings of the NPSS.

As part of the strategy to reach the goal of placing an additional 250,000 caring individuals in schools and in after-school programs, the NPSS identified several large groups of volunteers and full-time and part-time staff members who can fill roles, such as college students, high school students serving as near-peer mentors, older adults and retirees, corporate volunteers, and adults working with and for large national youth-serving organizations. Efforts to engage these individuals include

- expanding access to free training available through technical assistance partners via the NPSS website;
- launching several learning communities among organizations with challenges and barriers related to the implementation of high-quality programs,
- recruiting and retaining staff and volunteers, and
- forming and maintaining strong partnerships across schools and districts.

While progress has been made toward pandemic recovery, many in our communities (including youth, educators, schools, and providers, among others) need more help to truly recover and to address long-standing inequities in our educational system. Not only has the pandemic set young people back academically, but it has also had acute consequences for mental health for youth across the country, older adults, and many others in our communities.

In the fall of 2021, the American Academy of Pediatrics, American Academy of Child and Adolescent Psychiatry, and Children's Hospital Association declared a national emergency in child and adolescent mental health. Among their recommendations was a focus on school connectedness—the belief held by students that adults and peers in school care about their learning and them as individuals, which is an important protective factor in mental health. Further, the science of learning and development demonstrates that positive relationships, safety, and belonging are essential to academic growth.[12] According to a 2022 Centers for Disease Control and Prevention (CDC) study, 47 percent of youth did not feel school connectedness during the pandemic.[13]

As mentioned above, a surgeon general advisory released in May 2023 called attention to the public health crisis of loneliness, isolation, and lack of connection in our country. "The physical health consequences of poor or insufficient connection include a 29 percent increased risk of heart disease, a 32 percent increased risk of stroke, and a 50 percent increased risk of developing dementia for older adults. Additionally, lacking social connection increases risk of premature death by more than 60 percent."[14] Furthermore, according to the CDC, "Loneliness and social isolation in older adults are serious public health risks affecting a significant number of people in the United States and putting them at risk for dementia and other serious medical conditions."[15] Other recent studies concur:

- Social isolation significantly increases a person's risk of premature death from all causes, a risk that may rival those of smoking, obesity, and physical inactivity.
- Social isolation was associated with about a 50 percent increased risk of dementia.
- Poor social relationships (characterized by social isolation or loneliness) were associated with a 29 percent increased risk of heart disease and a 32 percent increased risk of stroke.
- Loneliness was associated with higher rates of depression, anxiety, and suicide.
- Loneliness among heart failure patients was associated with nearly four times increased risk of death, 68 percent increased risk of hospitalization, and 57 percent increased risk of emergency department visits.[16]

This is particularly challenging for older Americans and youth; more than one in five adults and more than one in three young adults live with a mental illness in the United States. The good news is that volunteering has been shown to greatly improve physical and mental health. "AmeriCorps Seniors volunteers experience decreased anxiety, depression, and loneliness [as a result of their participation, compared with peers who do not volunteer]. Eighty-four percent of volunteers report stable or improving health after one year of service."[17]

One recent study, "Volunteering, Self-Perceptions of Aging, and Mental Health in Later Life," published by the National Library of Medicine found that "volunteering for 100 or more hours per year reduced older adults' depressive symptoms indirectly via changing their self-perceptions of aging." This level of commitment to volunteering was associated with more positive and fewer negative self-perceptions of aging, typically leading to older adults living longer and healthier lives.[18] Volunteering can provide a sense of purpose, belonging, and a greater contribution to local communities, all important pieces of self-perception.

So, understandably, one of the ways that the CDC helps combat the effects of loneliness on older adults is by funding programs that help those with dementia remain active, independent, and involved in their community as long as possible. And a great way for older adults to stay involved in their community is to volunteer with and stay connected through local schools and school-based programs.

Older adults and retirees can be particularly well suited to serve in roles as tutors, mentors, and postsecondary advisors because they often come from the communities being served and can help create stronger school/community connections. AmeriCorps volunteers in the Foster Grandparents program (described above) volunteer for an average of six years,[19] strengthening bonds and ties. Moreover, according to AmeriCorps' Volunteering and Civic Life in America research, which examines national rates of organizational volunteering, many older adults offer informal assistance, like helping neighbors with favors, doing child care, running errands, and other ways of supporting their community outside formal volunteerism: 57.2 percent of adults over age fifty-five provided this type of help to their neighbors, compared to 47.1 percent of younger adults (ages sixteen to fifty-four).[20]

As Eileen MacDougall, Experience Corps tutor with the AARP Foundation, noted during the NPSS first anniversary celebration, "They have their teachers, they have the principal, and then they have us, and we fill this very interesting role. We know we could use more volunteers because there are a lot of kids that are eager to join us."

See It in Action: AARP Foundation Experience Corps

AARP Foundation Experience Corps is a volunteer program that pairs people over fifty years of age with students to serve as tutors and help them achieve third-grade reading proficiency, which experts say is the single greatest predictor of future success. AARP Foundation Experience Corps programs are provided at numerous locations across the country.

AARP Foundation Experience Corps provides extensive training, peer networks, and ongoing evaluation, employing a structured, evidence-based model that improves the overall reading ability of students. This program focuses on building their fluency, accuracy, and comprehension skills, helping students succeed, older adults thrive, and communities grow stronger.

See It in Action: Oasis Tutoring

Oasis Tutoring, an AmeriCorps Seniors grantee, is a volunteer program that pairs older adults with K–3 students to deliver mentoring and tutoring in literacy, providing one-on-one support and attention for the duration of the school year. (See Handbook chapter 10.) Their Intergenerational Tutoring program has consistently improved reading levels, academic performance, and children's attitudes when it comes to learning.

Oasis Tutoring staff train tutors to use a curriculum designed by educators, and materials are provided for tutoring sessions so that the burden doesn't fall on the teacher. Tutors work with the same child each week for a year, fostering strong relationships.

See It in Action: Senior Adults for Greater Education (S.A.G.E.)

S.A.G.E. is a volunteer program that pairs people fifty-five years of age and over with students in their local school districts, typically via regularly scheduled, weekly support in classrooms but also via various episodic volunteer opportunities for those not ready to make a weekly commitment. They've seen the benefits of these partnerships across many stakeholders, including students, teachers, seniors, and the community.

S.A.G.E support staff make sure that volunteers are recruited, interviewed, trained, and then connected with the opportunities where they will be most successful. Volunteers have regular check-ins throughout the year to make sure that the match is working for both the volunteer and the teacher. Additionally, a manual is customized for each school and provided to volunteers so that expectations and responsibilities are clear and well-known ahead of the engagement.

Through focus groups and one-on-one conversations with nonprofits working in the space, the NPSS Support Hub identified a need and desire for organizations that place older adults or retirees in youth-serving roles to have a dedicated space to convene and share learnings and resources. To help fill this gap, NPSS created the Engaging Older Adults in Student Success Learning Community, which provides space and place for nonprofit organizations, schools, and state/local government entities engaging older adults in pre-K–12 student support roles to collaborate on meeting challenges and sharing best practices and lessons learned with peers around the country.

Throughout the initiative, the NPSS strives to support the field in recruitment and retention of older adults as volunteers, bringing more older adults into student support roles, making training of older adults in these roles more accessible to organizations, and creating stronger connections between students, older adults, and schools across the country.

Closing Reflections

Intergenerational volunteerism acts as a bridge to connect multiple generations. These connections and interactions foster understanding, empathy, and shared experiences. They provide a space for personal growth, cultural preservation, social equity, and the dissolution of stereotypes that lead to discrimination and exclusion.

We have focused on the connection between older adults and children in educational settings, but in both the Foster Grandparent Program and the National Partnership for Student Success initiative, older adults are also building strong, enduring relationships with teachers, principals, and other school staff. Children benefit from these positive interactions through the supported development of their academic and social-emotional skills. Older adults find purpose and help dismiss the myths of ageism. Staff working in these settings gain assistance from trained and child-focused individuals who regularly bring lived experience, skills, and passion to their service and volunteerism. Everyone involved benefits, and when these programs can be scaled, they make a societal impact.

The nation's investment in AmeriCorps and AmeriCorps Seniors has time and again shown a positive return on investment. AmeriCorps has demonstrated its ability to grow to scale both programs and initiatives focused on intergenerational connections. Support for AmeriCorps, AmeriCorps Seniors, and national service results in impactful, evidence-based programs that engage the generations for the common good.

Notes

1. Sasha Johfre, "In a World Experiencing Unprecedented Age Diversity, How Should We Think about Age?" CoGenerate, February 3, 2022, https://cogenerate.org/in-a-world-experiencing-unprecedented-age-diversity-how-should-we-think-about-age/.
2. Bernard E. Nash, "Foster Grandparents in Child-Care Settings," *Public Welfare* 26 (1968): 272–80.
3. "Make Giving Back Your Second Act," AmeriCorps, accessed November 13, 2023, https://americorps.gov/serve/americorps-seniors.
4. "Title 45/Subtitle B/ChapterXXV/Part 2552.92," Code of Federal Registry, accessed November 13, 2023, https://www.ecfr.gov/current/title-45/subtitle-B/chapter-XXV/part-2552.
5. Dominic Modicamore et al., "Return on Investment Study: AmeriCorps Seniors Foster Grandparent Program and Senior Companion Program," ICF, Inc., 2020, ES–5.
6. "Navajo Department of Health, Division of Aging and Long Term Care Support, Foster Grandparent Program (FGP)," Navajo Nation Council, accessed November 13, 2023, https://www.navajonationcouncil.org/wp-content/uploads/2022/01/FGP_Presentation_Navajo_Elder_Awareness_Day_-NN_Winter_Session_25JAN2022.pdf.
7. "Foster Grandparent Program," Division of Aging and Long Term Care Support, accessed November 13, 2023, https://daltcs.navajo-nsn.gov/Services/Foster-Grandparent-Program.
8. "Fact Sheet: Biden-Harris Administration Launches National Effort to Support Student Success," White House, accessed November 13, 2023, https://www.whitehouse.gov/briefing-room/statements-releases/2022/07/05/fact-sheet-biden-harris-administration-launches-national-effort-to-support-student-success/.
9. Andre Nickow et al., "The Impressive Effects of Tutoring on PreK-12 Learning: A Systemic Review and Meta-Analysis of the Experimental Evidence," National Bureau of Economic Research, July 2020, 2.
10. "New Surgeon General Advisory Raises Alarm about the Devasting Impact of the Epidemic of Loneliness and Isolation in the United States," U.S. Department of Health and Human Services, accessed November 13, 2023, https://www.hhs.gov/about/news/2023/05/03/new-surgeon-general-advisory-raises-alarm-about-devastating-impact-epidemic-loneliness-isolation-united-states.html.
11. Annie Georges et al., "Longitudinal Study of Foster Grandparent and Senior Companion Programs: Service Delivery Implications and Health Benefits to the Volunteers" (North Bethesda, MD: JBS International, Inc., 2018), vi–vii.
12. "Relationships," National Center on Safe Supportive Learning Environments (NCSSLE), accessed November 13, 2023, https://safesupportivelearning.ed.gov/topic-research/engagement/relationships.
13. "New CDC Data Illuminate Youth Mental Health Threats during the COVID-19 Pandemic." Centers for Disease Control and Prevention, March 31, 2022, https://www.cdc.gov/media/releases/2022/p0331-youth-mental-health-covid-19.html#:~:text=However%2C%20fewer%20than%20half%20(47,of%20Adolescent%20and%20School%20Health.
14. Office of the Assistant Secretary for Health (OASH), "New Surgeon General Advisory Raises Alarm about the Devastating Impact of the Epidemic of Loneliness and Isolation in the United States," U.S. Department of Health and Human Services, May 3, 2023, https://www.hhs.gov/about/news/2023/05/03/new-surgeon-general-advisory-raises-alarm-about-devastating-impact-epidemic-loneliness-isolation-united-states.html.
15. "Loneliness and Social Isolation Linked to Serious Health Conditions," Centers for Disease Control and Prevention, April 29, 2021, https://www.cdc.gov/aging/publications/features/lonely-older-adults.html.
16. National Academies of Sciences, *Social Isolation and Loneliness in Older Adults: Opportunities for the Health Care System. Opportunities for the Health Care System* (Washington, DC: National Academies Press, 2020), https://nap.nationalacademies.org/catalog/25663/social-isolation-and-loneliness-in-older-adults-opportunities-for-the-health-care-system.

17. AmeriCorps. "AmeriCorps Seniors," accessed November 13, 2023, https://americorps.gov/serve/americorps-seniors.
18. Huo, Meng et al., "Volunteering, Self-perceptions of Aging, and Mental Health in Later Life," *Gerontologist* 61, no. 7 (2021): 1131–40, https://pubmed.ncbi.nlm.nih.gov/33103726/.
19. "Longitudinal Study of Foster Grandparent and Senior Companion Programs," Corporation for National and Community Service, accessed November 13, 2023, https://americorps.gov/sites/default/files/evidenceexchange/Longitudinal_Study_of_Foster_Grandparent_and_Senior_Companion_Programs_FINAL_508_1.pdf.
20. "Demographics," AmeriCorps, accessed November 13, 2023, https://americorps.gov/about/our-impact/volunteering-civic-life/demographics.

Bibliography

AmeriCorps. "Demographics." Accessed November 13, 2023 https://americorps.gov/about/our-impact/volunteering-civic-life/demographics.

AmeriCorps. "Make Giving Back Your Second Act." Accessed November 13, 2023. https://americorps.gov/serve/americorps-seniors.

Centers for Disease Control and Prevention. "Loneliness and Social Isolation Linked to Serious Health Conditions." Centers for Disease Control and Prevention. April 29, 2021. https://www.cdc.gov/aging/publications/features/lonely-older-adults.html.

Centers for Disease Control and Prevention. "New CDC Data Illuminate Youth Mental Health Threats during the COVID-19 Pandemic." Centers for Disease Control and Prevention. March 31, 2022. https://www.cdc.gov/media/releases/2022/p0331-youth-mental-health-covid19.html#:~:text=However%2C%20fewer%20than%20half%20(47,of%20Adolescent%20and%20School%20Health.

Code of Federal Registry. "Title 45/Subtitle B/ChapterXXV/Part 2552.92." Accessed November 13, 2023. https://www.ecfr.gov/current/title-45/subtitle-B/chapter-XXV/part-2552.

Corporation for National and Community Service. "Longitudinal Study of Foster Grandparent and Senior Companion Programs." Accessed November 13, 2023. https://americorps.gov/sites/default/files/evidenceexchange/Longitudinal_Study_of_Foster_Grandparent_and_Senior_Companion_Programs_FINAL_508_1.pdf.

Division of Aging and Long Term Care Support. "Foster Grandparent Program." Accessed November 13, 2023. https://daltcs.navajo-nsn.gov/Services/Foster-Grandparent-Program.

Georges, A., W. Fung, J. Smith, J. Liang, C. Sum, and S. Gabbard. *Longitudinal Study of Foster Grandparent and Senior Companion Programs: Service Delivery Implications and Health Benefits to the Volunteers*. North Bethesda, MD: JBS International, 2018, vi–vii.

Huo, M., L. Miller, K. Kim, and S. Liu. "Volunteering, Self-perceptions of Aging, and Mental Health in Later Life." *Gerontologist* 61, no. 7 (2021): 1131–40. https://pubmed.ncbi.nlm.nih.gov/33103726/

Johfre, Sasha. "In a World Experiencing Unprecedented Age Diversity, How Should We Think About Age?" CoGenerate. February 3, 2022. https://cogenerate.org/in-a-world-experiencing-unprecedented-age-diversity-how-should-we-think-about-age/

Modicamore, D., A. Naugler, B. Casey, B. Miller, C. Munaretto, and J. Pershing. "Return on Investment Study: AmeriCorps Seniors Foster Grandparent Program and Senior Companion Program." ICF, Inc., 2020, ES–5.

Nash, Bernard E. "Foster Grandparents in Child-Care Settings." *Public Welfare* 26 (1968): 272–80.

National Academies of Sciences. *Social Isolation and Loneliness in Older Adults: Opportunities for the Health Care System. Opportunities for the Health Care System*. Washington, DC: National Academies Press, 2020. https://nap.nationalacademies.org/catalog/25663/social-isolation-and-loneliness-in-older-adults-opportunities-for-the-health-care-system.

National Center on Safe Supportive Learning Environments (NCSSLE). "Relationships." Accessed November 13, 2023. https://safesupportivelearning.ed.gov/topic-research/engagement/relationships.

Navajo Nation Council. "Navajo Department of Health, Division of Aging and Long Term Care Support, Foster Grandparent Program (FGP)." Accessed November 13, 2023. https://www.navajonationcouncil.org/wp-content/uploads/2022/01/FGP_Presentation_Navajo_Elder_Awareness-Day_-NN_Winter_Session_25JAN2022.pdf.

Nickow, Andre, Philip Oreopoulos, and Vincent Quan. "The Impressive Effects of Tutoring on PreK-12 Learning: A Systemic Review and Meta-Analysis of the Experimental Evidence." National Bureau of Economic Research. July 2020. 2.

Office of the Assistant Secretary for Health (OASH). "New Surgeon General Advisory Raises Alarm about the Devastating Impact of the Epidemic of Loneliness and Isolation in the United States." U.S. Department of Health and Human Services. May 3, 2023. https://www.hhs.gov/about/news/2023/05/03/new-surgeon-general-advisory-raises-alarm-about-devastating-impact-epidemic-loneliness-isolation-united-states.html.

White House. "Fact Sheet: Biden-Harris Administration Launches National Effort to Support Student Success." Accessed November 13, 2023. https://www.whitehouse.gov/briefing-room/statements-releases/2022/07/05/fact-sheet-biden-harris-administration-launches-national-effort-to-support-student-success/.

CHAPTER 12

The Intergenerational Schools in Cleveland: Reconnection and Recovery after the Pandemic

Brooke King

> **Abstract**
>
> This chapter discusses the Intergenerational Schools in Cleveland, Ohio, three high-performing K–8 public charter schools. The schools have gained recognition for their intergenerational programs, such as the Learning Partner program and Intergenerational Visits program, which focus on literacy and relationship building. Despite the many increasing challenges they have faced, especially during and post-COVID, the schools continue to grow and improve, with a focus on deepening community engagement and investing in dynamic intergenerational programming. These programs have immense social-emotional benefits for both students and intergenerational partners, as well as academic benefits for the children. During the pandemic the programs came to a halt and the schools needed to think creatively and adapt in order to continue connecting students with intergenerational partners. The post-COVID journey has been challenging in many ways, but these inner-city schools remain committed to the premise that intergenerational relationships are a valuable part of learning and growing as compassionate human beings.
>
> **Key Words:** intergenerational, program, school, student, learning

Learning partners	Intergenerational visits	Intergenerational project-based learning
Strengths/impact • Relationship building • Development of social emotional and interpersonal skills • Literacy and math focus	**Strengths/impact** • Relationship building • Interpersonal skills • Development of social emotional and interpersonal skills • Outreach to residents	**Strengths/impact** • Relationship building • Creative project content aligned with learning standards • Networking and career mentoring • Synergies of all learners
Limitations • Unstable staffing • Diversity and representation with volunteers	**Limitations** • Unstable staffing • Expense of bussing • Lack of a partner champion • Lack of resident participation or enthusiasm	**Limitations** • Finding the right volunteers and community partners • Inexperienced teachers • Resources • Schedules

The Idea

The Intergenerational Schools are a group of three high-performing K–8 public charter schools in Cleveland, Ohio. The original Intergenerational School was founded in 2000 by Drs. Catherine and Peter Whitehouse with Dr. Stephanie FallCreek (who at the time was the executive director of the Fairhill Center for Aging, where the school was housed until 2014).[1] Dr. Catherine Whitehouse, now retired, was a child psychologist turned educator, who in her former role worked with students identified as having special education needs. Her work led her to the conclusion that many students were labeled as learning disabled when in actuality the problem was a "teaching disability" in a flawed system of education. She saw each child as an individual and nuanced learner on a developmental path and rejected the factory-based industrialized model of grade-based schooling. She taught in both public and private schools before opening her own public school soon after Ohio passed a charter school law in 1998. Her husband, Peter Whitehouse, M.D., Ph.D., professor of neurology (and coauthor of chapter 14 in this volume), is a gerontologist working in the field of healthy aging and brain health.[2] Many of the patients in his practice were experiencing mild to moderate dementia, and he was focused on improving their cognition, memory, and quality of life.

Peter and Catherine saw parallels in their students and patients in terms of how they learn. They concluded that the learning process does not differ between someone who is five or eighty-five years old and that these two groups of lifelong learners could benefit greatly from learning together, both with and from each other, in a safe and welcoming environment. Thus, the original intergenerational school and the two that followed operate today under these foundational tenets: (1) learning is a lifelong developmental process, and (2) we learn best through relationships.

Success and Growth as an Educational Innovation

The Intergenerational Schools have gained local, state, and national attention as an educational innovation with multiage classrooms and intergenerational programs, although the concept of intergenerational learning itself is actually as old as time.[3,4] The innovation lies in marshalling basic and natural human experiences that connect people of all ages to learn together and breaking down barriers between children and their peers and children and the community that exist in one of today's most separated and societal structures: public education.

Early intergenerational volunteers were often patients referred by Dr. Whitehouse or seniors looking for new ways to engage and stay mentally and physically active. Families came through word of mouth (the school had no advertising budget). They were often attracted by the safe school environment, and only after their child was enrolled for a while would they fully realize the value of the multigenerational school community. As one school grew and eventually was replicated across town, Intergenerational School students were consistently outperforming their peers on state test scores, especially in reading, despite Cleveland's rank among the top five of our country's most impoverished cities.

The schools have two flagship intergenerational programs—the Learning Partner program (formerly the Reading Mentor program), where adults come into the schools, and the Intergenerational Visits program, where classes of students make monthly outreach visits to area elder care facilities for colearning activities. Both programs have always been heavily centered on literacy and fostering a love of reading. Other project-based intergenerational learning grew out of individual interests that aligned with curricular and learning standards. Multigenerational groups studied local ecosystems, researched the Holocaust together, coauthored a book about local environmental activism, put on a theatrical production of *Peter Pan*, held various social justice book clubs, and so on.

Some important lessons learned over the years include implementing structure in staffing and partnerships and ensuring flexibility in program design. Intergenerational programming in a school can thrive with consistent staffing but will stumble if responsibilities are added to the long and ever-growing list of teacher duties. Because classroom teachers are part of the stakeholder team that makes a program successful, they must, ideally at the time of hire, be educated on, and in full alignment with, the overall philosophy and positive benefits of these programs for their students. This may be a challenge for some educators who prefer a more traditional approach. Teachers hired at the Intergenerational Schools receive very clear written information on this aspect of the job. It does require a certain comfort level with volunteer visitors in the classroom and with responsibility for ongoing visits and for student preparation and reflection time before and after.

Clarity is equally important for the volunteer learning partners and with the organizational partners. The initial outreach, recruitment, and relationship building required for the volunteers and organizational partners should be managed by a single staff person. These relationships require regular ongoing communication and detailed focus on logistics (reserving buses for transportation, arranging schedules and communicating schedule changes such as snow days, preparing supplies and materials, etc.). Before COVID-19 hit, each of our schools, which have 250 or fewer students by design, had a full-time staff member responsible for intergenerational programs and student recruitment and enrollment, combined.

Successful program design, however, requires a high level of collaboration, flexibility, and adaptability. Being less prescriptive in this area has led to more creative and organic ideas about colearning. Teachers must be brought into the planning and reflecting processes needed for growing and developing individual activities into vibrant programmatic experiences. Teachers know their students best, and they understand the learning standards that should be incorporated into the intergenerational activities.

Learning partners, who can be high school or college students, adult family members, and community members, are allowed to bring their own ideas, interests, and experiences into the programming. When adults share hobbies like photography, fishing, gardening, and knitting, these new skills are then combined with expanded community service projects or student-run exhibits. The best results occur when all stakeholders are part of the design decisions based on their mutual interest in learning more about an issue or topic and contributing something to their community. A basic framework may include the following: the activity addresses one or more specific learning standards or skills, all participants have an assignment and contribute meaningfully, and the final product enhances the future of the learning community. The details are filled in by the participants and are often adjusted and adapted during the process.

For example, a graduate student interested in local ecology offered to help set up a STEM (science, technology, engineering, and math) project for students. Near West Intergenerational School already had relationships with the Ohio City Farm, a local urban farm run by Refugee Response (now called Re:Source Cleveland), a local nonprofit serving Cleveland's growing refugee population, as well as the residents at a nearby senior living home.[5] The Intergenerational Program coordinator worked with the graduate student, the school's science teacher, and community partners to implement a multidisciplinary intergenerational program where students and senior residents collected and studied zebra mussels (an invasive species on the shores of Lake Erie), used them to make their own fertilizer, and conducted experiments growing and analyzing vegetables grown at the farm and at the senior center. What they learned, along with their intergenerational partners, helped benefit the senior center's garden, as well as the work of the Ohio City Farm. Programs like these are not prescribed and assigned to a class; rather, they grow from synergies created by the various lifelong learners involved and develop a life of their own. Having clear staffing structures, frameworks, and project champions in place (the capacity of intergenerational staff, teachers with clear learning expectations, community partners, senior center program directors who enthusiastically lead, etc.) creates an environment from which more creative and robust programming can emerge. These features are hard to replicate and should be built upon in future iterations with new and different stakeholders so that each experience is organic, unique, and innovative for that group of lifelong learners, as opposed to being prescribed.

Whether there is a direct cause-effect relationship between these types of intergenerational programs and students' academic standardized test scores is unclear; but the overall school experience, of which these programs are an integral part, clearly results in student growth and development as contributing, compassionate members of society. With regard to benefits for elder volunteers, studies[6] have found statistically significant differences in cognitive retention and quality of life among the group who regularly participated in The Intergenerational School's programs. What is evident is that this holistic approach to building a school community based on relationships and shared learning has clear social emotional benefits for all participants, regardless of age.[7]

Challenges and Silver Linings during the Pandemic

As COVID-19 began to spread in the winter of 2020, The Intergenerational Schools temporarily canceled all in-school Learning Partner and Intergenerational Visits programming to protect the seniors who were most vulnerable to severe illness from the disease. Unbeknownst to school leaders, this proactive and precautionary measure would end up lasting for a full year and a half. The pandemic and related aftermath brought insurmountable challenges to all schools, especially those serving economically disadvantaged, minority students and families.[8] Preexisting equity issues were now magnified as families navigated work schedules and child care (or unemployment) and home connectivity. Our schools responded quickly, equipping students with Chromebooks and providing hotspots including paid monthly internet service for any family in need. Within about two weeks every child was connected, new software was up and running, and the educational model was redesigned for a new era of online teaching and learning. Every staff member, whether an educator or not, was assigned to a group of families for regular check-ins by phone and, if needed, help in connecting them to area resources. Several nonteaching roles in the organization were reconceptualized for remote living and learning, with redeployed staff responding to different needs. Instead of one intergenerational program/enrollment coordinator at each school, these individuals specialized, so one held the intergenerational programming role for all three schools, one focused solely on student enrollment and recruitment, and one focused on digital community outreach. In-person contact was no longer possible, but community connection remained imperative.

In fall 2020, the schools received $125,000 from the OCER fund (Ohio Collaborative for Educating Remotely), a competitive grant "to address immediate and effective work that addresses inequitable circumstances related to delivering quality education remotely during the COVID-19 crisis."[9] The schools sought to implement a focused approach to K–3 literacy, which would supply all K–3 students with home libraries curated to their reading levels and create a virtual Learning Partner program for sharing books together online. Putting real books in the hands of students was a priority while they were isolated at home during the shutdown.

This was also after the summer of George Floyd's murder, and massive protests against racial injustice swept all over the world. Although the schools had invested in diversity training for staff before this, it was time to closely reexamine all facets of the organization's educational operation and embrace equitable, antiracist, inclusive practices across every area of programming, including intergenerational programs.

It had always been clear that, just like the majority White staff, the majority of learning partners serving in the schools were White, middle to upper class, and residing in well-off suburbs of Cleveland, while the majority of students were Black, receiving social assistance, and living in one of the poorest cities in the United States.[10] Just like the home library books were carefully curated for reading levels and main character representation of the students, this new program had learning partners undergoing both training on K–3 literacy and cultural competence training for the first time, as part of their onboarding. Almost all learning partners embraced this new part of their training as true lifelong learners. Very few were opposed, denied they could benefit, or flat-out refused. Those that did ended up parting ways with the organization, which was likely in the best interest of the students.

Training included basics on how reading is taught at these ages, how to operate the Zoom software in our virtual classrooms, as well as identifying one's own biases and bridging the inherent cultural divides in these relationships with an asset-based mindset as opposed to a deficit mindset. Learning partners were more prepared than ever before to celebrate the students and their backgrounds and make connections between the main characters in the stories and themselves.

Although The Intergenerational Schools were some of the first to reopen in late February of 2021, it was under vastly different circumstances than before COVID. Only about half of the families decided to bring their children back into the buildings, while the other half opted to continue online learning for a variety of reasons, including having relatives in the home at higher risk for serious illness. Students who came back in person learned behind masks and desk shields and at least six feet away from each other, while air purification machines whirred in the background (these machines are still a part of everyday classroom life today). Teachers taught the in-person students and the online students concurrently in elaborately planned hybrid lessons involving some whole-class Zoom sessions and then small-group and independent work. It was exhausting for all involved, especially teachers. Although some learning partners wanted to come to school, a medical advisor at MetroHealth Medical Center advised against any outside visitors in order to keep the "pods" as fixed as possible, in the interest of tracking and reporting cases. The only intergenerational programming occurring during this time was the virtual Learning Partners/OCER book-sharing project.

By the end of the 2020–2021 school year, 16,185 books were delivered to 440 students' homes, igniting excitement about reading and discussing their books with eighty-six learning partners, including family members who participated. The Intergenerational Schools had decreases in overall state test scores across the board, like most schools. However, during this time period, students in this program at all three Intergenerational Schools outscored their peers at other public schools in Cleveland on the state tests, showing that strategies like this assisted in lessening learning loss for these students.[11]

Learning partners reported satisfaction with the experience, even though there were occasional technical difficulties. "As much as I practiced on Zoom, I forgot exactly what I was supposed to do, but the kids talked me through it. I told them, 'We really are learning partners, aren't we?'" The program brought learning partners, some who did not even live in the same state, together with students and their families for mutual benefit at a time of unprecedented isolation. In some surprising ways, the pandemic deepened connections within and across the classrooms, families, and learning partners. One of the teachers said she learned more about her students, their families, and her assigned learning partners than when school was in-person, although she would still prefer in-person learning over teaching remotely.

Even in a global pandemic, the fundamental tenets of The Intergenerational Schools hold true: (1) learning is a lifelong developmental process (for all of us as we navigate unprecedented times); and (2) We learn best through relationships. Staying grounded in these ideals helped the schools adapt and innovate for the benefit of students and adults. The hope is that the schools can take the best of this experience as they continue to recover from the pandemic. Out of necessity, technology enabled caring volunteers to participate from anywhere and connect to students in a deeper way than during their typical previous school time. And bias and equity training can and will be carried into future programming for more authentic and equitable relationships between volunteers and students.

Reopening: Disillusionment and Rebuilding with a Focus on Equity

The post-COVID era has been in some ways even more challenging within the world of public education. Our mission has remained an anchor through a new set of trials that do not seem to be subsiding any time soon. Recommitting to the roots of the pedagogy, including the commitment to seeing older adults as valuable assets in the larger learning community, is critically important to the sustainability of this unique educational model.

The fall of 2021 was full of hope and excitement to be back together in the school buildings for in-person learning, only to quickly turn to exhaustion and constant adaptation to increased needs. Under the law it was no longer an option for Cleveland's charter schools to provide online classes unless they opened and managed a separate legal entity to do so. The schools suffered enrollment losses largely because many families were just not ready to come back to brick-and-mortar buildings.

As the staff grappled with rapidly changing (and sometimes conflicting) health and safety guidance, leadership soon realized that beyond the ever-changing physical health precautions and quarantines, student, staff, and family mental health challenges and student behavior challenges were far more intense and frequent than before.[12] Aside from many students being out for extended periods due to infection or exposure quarantines, the school communities were stressed and just surviving as opposed to thriving. Young students were not prepared socially and emotionally for a school environment. Almost all students were showing signs of dysregulation, and some frequently struggled to manage their frustration and anger. Many of the oldest students, after experiencing prolonged uncertainty and being exposed to more social media than ever, lacked the ability to concentrate and interact positively with peers and staff. Crisis management became the consistent issue at hand, at a time when Cleveland was experiencing a shortage of mental health support resources and school staff were neither trained nor equipped to deal with the types of traumatic incidents unfolding before them. The current national teacher and staff shortage also began to manifest at this time, first as a lack of substitutes and special education teachers, forcing teachers to forgo planning and break times to fill in.[13] This created an environment where most everyone was struggling in some significant way. Still, one very important, positive outcome was that all three schools took every necessary precaution and had zero in-school transmissions of COVID-19, based on contact tracing protocols.

The structure and capacity within our intergenerational programs deteriorated, and the intergenerational programming coordinator position became vacant. Filling that role was very difficult; luckily, a classroom teacher was interested, and she worked some additional hours in the evenings and on weekends to try to revive some of the prior community partner relationships and reconnect with volunteers to prepare for what was to be a relaunch of in-person intergenerational programs during the following (2022–2023) school year.

Unfortunately, some of the residual impacts of the pandemic came in delayed waves, and the national teacher shortage hit hardest during the summer of 2022. Not only did teachers leave the profession altogether, but with more openings available at higher-paying district schools, charter schools, like the Intergenerational Schools, lost many qualified teachers, including the one who had planned to move into the intergenerational program coordinator role. The schools were hit hard by this shift in the workforce, and unbelievably, this same scenario happened a second time when another teacher was hired into the role and, after a strong start, resigned in November because she was recruited to her suburban home district for more pay. The role remained vacant for the next seven months, with administrators and teachers doing the best they could to hold things together, at least for the Learning Partner program and for a significantly reduced number of senior center visits.

The schools' intergenerational strategy shifted to concentrating on students' own families and extended families, as well as local neighborhoods. The idea was that programming should radiate from these existing assets in students' lives as a strong school culture and community was being rebuilt. So much of what was implemented that year occurred through a focus on family engagement and inviting the parents, aunts, uncles, grandparents, cousins, and neighbors of our students, into the schools. Recognizing, emphasizing, and celebrating the strength of the inherent intergenerational relationships that already exist within our students' networks is an important part of the current strategy to recruit volunteers that look more like our students.

A local nonprofit, Art Resistance through Change (ART-C), had students of all ages thinking about their own identities and communities and expressing themselves through visual art.[14] Older students (Refining and Applying, grades 5 through 8) each chose a social justice issue or historical event that was meaningful to them and wrote creative essays. They did research, contacted elected representatives, and connected with organizations that support various causes. They then created amazing art pieces to be exhibited publicly at the Akron Art Museum, where their families and friends were invited to a special grand opening event, and several of the students were invited to speak about their experience (see figure 12.1). This produced invitations for interviews on two local podcasts highlighting their young activist voices in action. After ART-C, the students were given the choice to sell their art and donate the proceeds to the nonprofit organization working toward their cause. This might not be thought of as a traditional intergenerational activity, yet the students made many real-life connections to adults in the outside community during the project. This helped develop valuable interpersonal skills while educating the adults on the importance of their young and insightful perspectives, bridging the gap between generations.

Similarly, during Black History Month, two programs brought in family and community in meaningful ways. The Black History Expo was the culmination of family research projects that concluded with students and family members hosting stations that highlighted Black excellence by serving traditional African, Caribbean, and American foods. They dressed up as and presented the lives of people like Opal Lee, the grandmother of Juneteenth, and Garret Morgan, an inventor from Cleveland, and highlighted the achievements of Black mathematicians, scientists, engineers, and astronauts that have been part of NASA. The event was family-led and had people of all ages learning from each other. Also, during the month, the school hosted an African-American Read-In, where community and family members were invited to read to classes of all ages. Whether it was a picture book featuring a Black protagonist, or one of Martin Luther King Jr.'s speeches, students and staff engaged in rich intergenerational discussions with their guests and created stronger ties to their community.

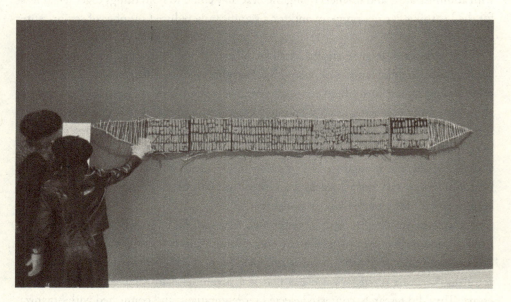

Figure 12.1 A family views another student's artistic depiction and piece of writing about a slave ship, at the Akron Art Museum.

Source: Intergenerational Schools

The schools' continued relationship with the founder, Dr. Peter Whitehouse, led to an opportunity that connected students not only with Case Western Reserve University on the other side of the city but to Joe Brewer, an international thought leader on bioregionalism from Columbia. Through collaboration with Dr. Whitehouse, the schools cohosted an interactive dialogue on campus centered on environmental regeneration through a bioregional lens.[15] Dr. Brewer spent time with students in their classroom, and then they were bussed to the university to participate in a forum where prominent local experts like Dr. Whitehouse, Dr. David Orr, and David Beach, among others, spoke. Students then reflected through their writing on what their greatest environmental concerns were, their estimation of the current generation's response, and how their own generation can act locally. The event was educational and thought-provoking, especially by opening their eyes to a college campus (including a very popular visit to the food court), which none of the students had experienced previously. Students and families saw tremendous value in this type of exposure to real-world issues and experts and were equally glad to visit a university campus, an environment in which they could imagine themselves studying in the future.

Deepening Roots and Continuing to Grow

The last few years have been extremely difficult in public education. Nevertheless, all three schools were designated Ohio Community Schools of Quality in 2022 based on their prior year's state test scores (both achievement and growth), and fortunately, the recognition came with some additional funding that is guaranteed for three years.[16] This presents the challenge of retaining the funding beyond the initial three years and the opportunity to invest in the educational model for continued improvement and excellence.

In addition to several teacher training and coaching supports, given the new reality of needing to "grow your own" as the candidate pool becomes smaller and less experienced, the schools invested in adding a new higher-level position, director of intergenerational programming and lifelong learning. This new hire is a licensed educator and administrator who can create and train others in dynamic project-based intergenerational learning. (The programming coordinator position responsible for managing volunteer relationships and logistics became intergenerational community coordinator. Both positions were newly staffed in July 2023.) The new director will not only bring more standards-aligned lessons and project-based learning experiences to the students, but he will incorporate them into the intergenerational programming while helping inexperienced teachers learn to plan and facilitate this type of nontraditional teaching and learning.

With this added capacity, shared by the three schools, ongoing teacher training covers what intergenerational programming should look, feel, and sound like for new teachers. Both the director and coordinator attend most of the senior center visits along with the classroom teacher, after planning and preparing the intergenerational activities and helping teachers to prepare their students. Class visits are scheduled about once a month throughout the school year, a goal that has not been reached since before COVID. At the time of this writing, over sixty class visits had occurred before winter break. Those community partnerships continue to grow stronger, and the hope is for some organic and creative programming to stem from the regular relationship building and side-by-side learning activities.

About twenty volunteer learning partners have been welcomed back and "retrained" at a back-to-school event. Learning partner recruitment continues, beginning with family connections and then expanding to the broader community and ideally beyond (for those interested in remote volunteer experiences). The goal is to have at least two consistent in-person learning partners for every classroom, which would be about seventy in total, which was achieved pre-COVID. A Math Learning Partner program, piloted during the pandemic in a couple of classes, will be expanded and may help attract adults who are interested in coming to play math games designed to meet learning standards, instead of reading with students.

New experiences continue to emerge. A recent scheduling problem has led to a creative and inspiring solution. Unfortunately, when one of the community partners pulled out of the Intergenerational Visits program, some applying stage (seventh- and eighth-grade) students' visits were canceled. Instead of trying to find a new partner at short notice, the director of intergenerational programming, the community coordinator, and teachers decided that smaller groups of these older students would start accompanying the younger classes on their visits, as facilitators between the younger students and residents. These applying stage "chaperones" have a responsibility to keep the conversation going and help facilitate the learning games or activities as the leaders of their small groups. These visits will also count toward their community service goals for eighth-grade graduation and add to their high school applications. This added intergenerational layer has so far proved to enrich the experience for all participants. Now, almost every applying stage class of students is electing to accompany younger classes in this way, to help build their leadership and interpersonal skills and forge intergenerational connections.

At the time of this writing in the fall of 2023, bright spots are emerging more often and with more students each week. The schools are still navigating their way through the challenges presented by less experienced staff and the lingering issues of serving a population hit hardest by the pandemic. There remain a lot of mental health and behavioral issues that are difficult and test both our new and experienced staff. But more and more often people can see the glimmers of hope that intergenerational programming can bring to a learning community. A developing stage (third and fourth grades) teacher recently reported that her class is really struggling with interpersonal issues and problem solving and that students often resort to mean and hurtful behavior toward each other. However, during their intergenerational visits this year (three so far), something clicks, and every student behaves kindly, not only toward the residents but also toward each other. This is the magic of these experiences; they bring out the best in everyone involved.

One new teacher wanted a couple of her most challenging and often dysregulated students to be kept back from a visit, "just in case" they have an outburst. She was reassured by school leaders that the director of intergenerational programming and the community coordinator would be there to assist in the event of any problematic behaviors. She was shocked to observe those students so enthralled with playing the "get to know you" games with the residents that they not only participated and enjoyed themselves during the entire visit but showed empathy and compassion toward others. Staff often talked about it later to remind the students of their innate ability to connect and be role models during that wonderful experience. There was also a refining stage (fifth and sixth grades) student who had experienced a lot of trauma in the last couple of months with the passing of her father, several moves, and so on. Her teacher reported that she hadn't seen her smile and laugh like she was able to with her two new "best friends" at their nursing home visit. When it was time to go, she didn't want to leave. The good news is, she will be back every month this year.

At a time when social-emotional learning is as (if not more) important than academics, the intergenerational programs at The Intergenerational Schools are once again gaining traction, with a genuine asset-based focus on identity and relationships and on diversity, equity, and inclusion. With increased organizational capacity and understanding, the partnerships will continue to strengthen and the schools will continue to recruit volunteers with a passion for their own lifelong learning as well as for giving back to the younger generations. The schools now, more than ever, are emphasizing the universal concept of lifelong learning for all staff, with the introduction of more progressive ways of training and adult learning. In 2023 professional development includes a coaching model for real-time adult learning, as well as additional asynchronous resources in a growing learning library for teachers. The organization's recent experiences will carry forward into stronger, more equitable intergenerational programming and lifelong learning for students, staff, and all who become part of the growing community. And, as the past twenty-three years have shown, the organization has an unwavering commitment to the two founding tenets about learning and relationships. Those guiding principles have remained The Intergenerational Schools' beacon through the most challenging of times, and they continue to show the way forward. The future of The Intergenerational Schools looks bright.

Notes

1. Fairhill Partners, https://fairhillpartners.org/.
2. Peter J. Whitehouse and Daniel R. George, *The Myth of Alzheimer's: What You Aren't Being Told about Today's Most Dreaded Diagnosis* (New York: St. Martin's Press, 2008); Daniel R. George and Peter J. Whitehouse, *American Dementia: Brain Health in an Unhealthy Society*. (Baltimore: JHU Press, 2021).
3. "Recognition," Intergenerational Schools, https://igschools.org/recognition/.
4. Rich Exner, "Decade after Being Declared Nation's Poorest Big City, 1-in-3 Clevelanders Remain in Poverty," cleveland.com, September 18, 2014, https://www.cleveland.com/datacentral/2014/09/decade_after_being_declared_na.html. See also the Intergenerational School's Report Cards for 2003–2014,

for example, "Intergenerational School, The 2013-2014 Report Card," https://reportcardstorage.education.ohio.gov/archives-2014/2014-133215.pdf.
5. Ohiocityfarm, https://www.ohiocityfarm.com/; "Pathway for Newcomers," Re:Source Cleveland, https://www.resourcecleveland.org/?fbclid=IwAR3-89ArT3DZNJbBEkl7YgK_66TFATQS7OKD2V-b8lrhRQ5fvyKWSjYrZ7o.
6. Whitehouse and George, *The Myth of Alzheimer's*; George and Whitehouse, *American Dementia*; Daniel R. George and Mendel E. Singer, "Intergenerational Volunteering and Quality of Life for Persons with Mild to Moderate Dementia: Results from a 5-Month Intervention Study in the United States." *American Journal of Geriatric Psychiatry* 19, no. 4 (2011): 392–96. https://doi.org/10.1097/jgp.0b013e3181f17f20.
7. "Generations United Making the Case Fact Sheet: Intergenerational Programs Benefit Everyone," Generations United, https://www.gu.org/app/uploads/2021/03/2021-MakingTheCase-FactSheet-WEB.pdf.
8. Sarah Mervosh, "The Pandemic Hurt These Students the Most." *New York Times*, September 7, 2021, https://www.nytimes.com/2021/07/28/us/covid-schools-at-home-learning-study.html.
9. "Philanthropy Ohio and Ohio Department of Education Announce Grants from The Collaborative Fund for Educating Remotely and Transforming Schools," Philanthropy Ohio, August 12, 2022, https://www.philanthropyohio.org/news/philanthropy-ohio-and-ohio-department-education-announce-grants-collaborative-fund-educating.
10. Zachary Smith, "Poverty Rate Dips in Cleveland but Remains among the Nation's Highest: 2021 Census Estimates." cleveland.com, September 20, 2022, https://www.cleveland.com/data/2022/09/poverty-rate-dips-in-cleveland-but-remains-among-the-nations-highest-2021-census-estimates.html.
11. "Intergenerational School, The 2021-2022 Report Card," Intergenerational School, https://reportcardstorage.education.ohio.gov/archives-2022/2022-133215.pdf?sv=2020-08-04&ss=b&srt=sco&sp=rlx&se=2031-07-28T05:10:18Z&st=2021-07-27T21:10:18Z&spr=https&sig=nPOvW%2Br2caitHi%2F8WhYwU7xqalHo0dFrudeJq%2B%2Bmyuo%3D; "Near West Intergenerational School 2021-2022 Report Card," Intergenerational School, https://reportcardstorage.education.ohio.gov/archives-2022/2022-012030.pdf?sv=2020-08-04&ss=b&srt=sco&sp=rlx&se=2031-07-28T05:10:18Z&st=2021-07-27T21:10:18Z&spr=https&sig=nPOvW%2Br2caitHi%2F8WhYwU7xqalHo0dFrudeJq%2B%2Bmyuo%3D; "Lakeshore Intergenerational School 2021-2022 Report Card," Intergenerational School, https://reportcardstorage.education.ohio.gov/archives-2022/2022-014913.pdf?sv=2020-08-04&ss=b&srt=sco&sp=rlx&se=2031-07-28T05:10:18Z&st=2021-07-27T21:10:18Z&spr=https&sig=nPOvW%2Br2caitHi%2F8WhYwU7xqalHo0dFrudeJq%2B%2Bmyuo%3D.
12. Julian Shen-Berro, "Student Behavior Remains Concerning amid COVID's Impact, Educators Say," Chalkbeat, November 9, 2023, https://www.chalkbeat.org/2023/3/7/23628032/student-behavior-covid-school-classroom-survey/.
13. "The Pandemic Has Exacerbated a Long-Standing National Shortage of Teachers," Economic Policy Institute, https://www.epi.org/publication/shortage-of-teachers/.
14. "Art For Resistance through Change Event at Akron Art Museum," Akron Art Museum, https://akronartmuseum.org/media/events/art-resistance-through-change-pop-up/.
15. "Regenerating Bioregions: Co-Designing Our Future Together," Eventbrite, https://www.eventbrite.ca/e/regenerating-bioregions-co-designing-our-future-together-tickets-523171218197.
16. "Quality Community School Support Fund," Ohio Department of Education," https://education.ohio.gov/Topics/Community-Schools/quality-community-school-support-fund.

Bibliography

Akron Art Museum. "Art For Resistance through Change Event at Akron Art Museum." June 13, 2025. https://akronartmuseum.org/media/events/art-resistance-through-change-pop-up/.

Economic Policy Institute. "The Pandemic Has Exacerbated a Long-Standing National Shortage of Teachers." https://www.epi.org/publication/shortage-of-teachers/.

Eventbrite. "Regenerating Bioregions: Co-Designing Our Future Together." https://www.eventbrite.ca/e/regenerating-bioregions-co-designing-our-future-together-tickets-523171218197.

Exner, Rich. "Decade after Being Declared Nation's Poorest Big City, 1-in-3 Clevelanders Remain in Poverty." cleveland.com. September 18, 2014. https://www.cleveland.com/datacentral/2014/09/decade_after_being_declared_na.html.

Generations United. "Generations United Making the Case Fact Sheet: Intergenerational Programs Benefit Everyone." https://www.gu.org/app/uploads/2021/03/2021-MakingTheCase-FactSheet-WEB.pdf.

George, Daniel R., and Mendel E. Singer. "Intergenerational Volunteering and Quality of Life for Persons with Mild to Moderate Dementia: Results from a 5-Month Intervention Study in the United States." *American Journal of Geriatric Psychiatry* 19, no. 4 (2011): 392–96. https://doi.org/10.1097/jgp.0b013e3181f17f20.

George, Daniel R., and Peter J. Whitehouse. *American Dementia: Brain Health in an Unhealthy Society*. Baltimore: JHU Press, 2021.

Intergenerational School. "Intergenerational School, The: 2013-2014 Report Card." https://reportcardstorage.education.ohio.gov/archives-2014/2014-133215.pdf.

Intergenerational School. "Intergenerational School, The: 2021-2022 Report Card," https://reportcardstorage.education.ohio.gov/archives-2022/2022-133215.pdf?sv=2020-08-04&ss=b&srt=sco&sp=rlx&se=2031-07-28T05:10:18Z&st=2021-07-27T21:10:18Z&spr=https&sig=nPOvW%2Br2caitHi%2F8WhYwU7xqalHo0dFrudeJq%2B%2Bmyuo%3D.

Intergenerational School. "Lakeshore Intergenerational School 2021-2022 Report Card." https://reportcardstorage.education.ohio.gov/archives-2022/2022-014913.pdf?sv=2020-08-04&ss=b&srt=sco&sp=rlx&se=2031-07-28T05:10:18Z&st=2021-07-27T21:10:18Z&spr=https&sig=nPOvW%2Br2caitHi%2F8WhYwU7xqalHo0dFrudeJq%2B%2Bmyuo%3D.

Intergenerational School. "Near West Intergenerational School 2021-2022 Report Card." https://reportcardstorage.education.ohio.gov/archives-2022/2022-012030.pdf?sv=2020-08-04&ss=b&srt=sco&sp=rlx&se=2031-07-28T05:10:18Z&st=2021-07-27T21:10:18Z&spr=https&sig=nPOvW%2Br2caitHi%2F8WhYwU7xqalHo0dFrudeJq%2B%2Bmyuo%3D.

Intergenerational Schools. "Recognition." https://igschools.org/recognition/.

Mervosh, Sarah. "The Pandemic Hurt These Students the Most." *New York Times*, September 7, 2021. https://www.nytimes.com/2021/07/28/us/covid-schools-at-home-learning-study.html.

Philanthropy Ohio. "Philanthropy Ohio and Ohio Department of Education Announce Grants from the Collaborative Fund for Educating Remotely and Transforming Schools." August 12, 2022. https://www.philanthropyohio.org/news/philanthropy-ohio-and-ohio-department-education-announce-grants-collaborative-fund-educating.

Ohio Department of Education. "Quality Community School Support Fund." https://education.ohio.gov/Topics/Community-Schools/quality-community-school-support-fund.

Re:Source Cleveland. "Pathway for Newcomers." https://www.resourcecleveland.org/?fbclid=IwAR3-89ArT3DZNJbBEkl7YgK_66TFATQS7OKD2V-b8lrhRQ5fvyKWSjYrZ7o.

Shen-Berro, Julian. "Student Behavior Remains Concerning amid COVID's Impact, Educators Say." Chalkbeat. November 9, 2023. https://www.chalkbeat.org/2023/3/7/23628032/student-behavior-covid-school-classroom-survey/.

Smith, Zachary. "Poverty Rate Dips in Cleveland but Remains among the Nation's Highest: 2021 Census Estimates." cleveland.com. September 20, 2022. https://www.cleveland.com/data/2022/09/poverty-rate-dips-in-cleveland-but-remains-among-the-nations-highest-2021-census-estimates.html.

Whitehouse, Peter J., and Daniel R. George. *The Myth of Alzheimer's: What You Aren't Being Told about Today's Most Dreaded Diagnosis*. New York: St. Martin's Press, 2008.

… PART III

Community-Engaged Learning and Bridging Differences: Younger People Working with Older Adults

CHAPTER 13

Intergenerational Diversity and Interethnic Connections: Who Will Care for Us?

Fernando Torres-Gil *and* Elizabeth Ambriz

> **Abstract**
>
> This chapter seeks to expand the narrative and the meaning of intergenerational relationships and to move the discussion to a broader, more nuanced, and potentially more complex and problematic space. It speaks directly to the demographic trends that will heighten the importance of these types of relationships—importance that is increasingly related to diversity given the fact that the growing ethnic, racial, and immigrant groups are largely composed of young persons, while the older populations, at least for the foreseeable future, are largely composed of White non-Hispanics. The real issue may become not how we promote interactions between the old and the young but how we foster intergenerational relationships that are interethnic and interracial in a majority-minority nation. Can the paradigm be expanded to one where we pursue an intergenerational, interethnic, and interracial set of relationships—one where a diverse society benefits from a diverse set of generational relationships?
>
> **Key Words:** intergenerational, interethnic, interracial, majority-minority nation, age-segregated

Introduction

The relationships between generations are no doubt important, but they take on added significance as the life span increases. And as longevity and multigenerational households become more common, how and in what ways can we enable integration among various age groups? This question is a salient issue for society and civic welfare. Much of the literature on this topic extolls the benefits of older persons interacting with young persons, grandparents caring for grandchildren, and age-integrated programs such as elders working with children.

This chapter seeks to expand the narrative and the meaning of intergenerational relationships and to move the discussion to a broader, more nuanced, and potentially more complex and problematic space. The title of this chapter speaks to a more robust perspective in promoting the value of intergenerational activities, relationships, and initiatives. It presents a broader context to the age-segregated features of U.S. society and public policy.

It speaks directly to the demographic trends that will heighten the importance of these types of relationships—importance that is increasingly related to diversity, given the fact that the growing ethnic, racial, and immigrant groups are largely composed of young persons, while the older populations, at least for the foreseeable future, are largely composed of White non-Hispanics. The real issue may become not how we promote interactions between the old and the young but how we foster intergenerational relationships that are interethnic and interracial in a majority-minority nation.

Reframing this narrative might hinge on a basic existential question: Who will care for us? If we can move beyond the goal of intergenerational relationships giving a sense of purpose and improving physical and mental health, we can then discuss the broader social ramifications of intercultural connections and self-interest, such as a young, diverse population becoming crucial to the welfare of an older White generation. Do we seek ethnic and racial segregation with intergenerational relationships, where it remains White elders interacting with young White people? Or can we expand the paradigm to one where we pursue an intergenerational, interethnic, and interracial set of relationships—one where a diverse society benefits from a diverse set of generational relationships?

The Present Narrative

The literature is replete with the benefits of, and the need for, generations to come together. Discussions of intergenerational relationships focus mainly on intergenerational tensions, ageism, age segregation, loneliness, and social isolation among elders, as well as relationships between parents and children. With few exceptions, however, the extant literature does not consider intergenerational relationships with interracial/interethnic groups.[1] This gap in the literature creates a narrative that intergenerational relationships are the domain of a homogenous population and/or are not relevant to the growing diversity of this nation. Yet we suggest that ethnic, immigrant, and minority groups can benefit from generational interactions as well as provide lessons on how to maintain such relationships.

The nature of our U.S. society over the last 100 years, which has made the United States perhaps one of the world's most age-segregated cultures, is the catalyst for concerns about age segregation. How and why U.S. society appears to value individualism and age-segregated social activities is debatable, but examining public policy provides clues. The decades following the Great Depression of the 1930s saw a politics of aging whereby older persons advocated for the elderly to promote public benefits based on age categories.[2] Thus, over the years came Social Security, Medicare, Medicaid, and the Older Americans Act. These benefits are heavily weighted toward reaching an older age (e.g., sixty-two years for early Social Security benefits, sixty years to participate in senior centers, and sixty-five years to obtain Medicare benefits). A host of advocacy and civil rights achievements (e.g., allowing those as young as age fifty to join AARP and age forty for protections under the Age Discrimination in Employment Act) drew on this "ageist" approach. Over the decades, White House conferences on aging were predicated on bringing senior citizens to Washington, DC, to continue promoting age-based programs and benefits. And other sectors of society (e.g., TV, movies, the arts, social media) fostered moving away from age-integrated relationships. However this all occurred, we have in this country a culture of age groups coalescing with like age groups and fostering a norm of generational segregation. And it's useful to note that during the period of a politics of aging, which has been occurring since the 1930s, the United States was a largely homogenous—heavily non-Hispanic White—society.

The Demographic Trends Reshaping the Narrative

Two books in this new century alerted us to the coming changes: Taylor's *The Next America* and Frey's *Diversity Explosion*.[3] These seminal publications laid out in graphic detail the demographic trends that will change the face of America by 2060 and the impact of ethnicity and immigration in remaking America. Taylor and Frey postulated that by 2060, the decline of the non-Hispanic White population and the dramatic increase in the AAPI (Asian American/Pacific Islander) and Hispanic populations would make the United States a majority-minority society for the first time in its history. Taylor's research focused on implications for various cohorts. For example, with the passing of the Greatest Generation, Baby Boomers, who are mostly White, became the largest generation. But with the advent of Generation X, followed by Millennials, the population moved toward greater ethnic diversity and more racial groups, all now seen vividly in Generation Z (those who are between ten and twenty-six years of age in 2023)—the first majority-minority cohort. Frey drew on this research to expand the implications that AAPIs and Latinos would have not just the greatest impact numerically, but that their culture, traditions, and immigration experience would have major social, linguistic, and cultural influences on American society and that these influences could reinvigorate traditional American values.

The reality of these demographic trends has been further amplified with the release of the 2020 current population reports, titled "Demographic Turning Points for the United States: Population Projections for 2020-2060,"[4] which raised key trends and milestones that will reshape the United States's demographic profile—changes that will impact and influence how we view diverse relationships and, most importantly, how the current paradigm of intergenerational relationships will need to incorporate this new diversity.

It helps to be reminded that this country is aging and that the sixty-five-and-older population will double between 2016 and 2060. Yet what is most telling is that the non-Hispanic White population is projected to shrink over the coming decades, from 199 million in 2020 to 179 million in 2060. Two profound trends will amplify this new America: the nation's foreign-born population will increase from 44 million in 2016 to 69 million in 2060 (from 14 to 17 percent of the total population), and the United States will see growing racial and ethnic pluralism. By 2020, in fact, we saw that fewer than half of children born were projected to be non-Hispanic White; and by 2028, the foreign-born share of the U.S. population is projected to be higher than at any time since 1850. Combine these trends with the continued decline of life expectancy among non-Hispanic Whites, a decline in the number of children in this population, and the larger number of children among foreign-born and minority groups, and we have a new equation for planning and promoting intergenerational relationships in an age-segregated society.

But what might this mean for diverse groups? Are they falling victim to age segregation, or might they exhibit age integration related to their cultures and norms? If the latter occurs, how do we benefit from and maintain them? And are present initiatives involving intergenerational activities inadvertently perpetuating age-race segregation, with older Whites interacting primarily with younger Whites?

The Nexus of Diversity and Intergenerational Relationships

The fact that the extant literature on intergenerational relationships seems to focus mainly on White elders interacting with younger White persons can be positive, of course; and the various strategies, initiatives, and activities to unite younger and older adults in this homogenous fashion is a good step forward. But what happens when that largely older White cohort of Baby Boomers gives way to a Gen Z cohort that is now mostly composed of Latino, AAPI, Native American, Black, immigrant, and refugee clusters? What does it mean that Gen Z has a minority of young White children, with the remainder belonging to a diverse set of groups? In their influential treatise "The Politics of a Majority-Minority Nation," Torres-Gil and Angel argue that U.S. society, both civically and politically, must give way to a new set of cultural, ethnic, and racial norms that take into account the dramatic growth of these groups by not only ethnicity, race, and immigration status but also by their reshaping of U.S. social norms.[5] And with this new diversity, we may see the revitalization of age-integrated and intergenerational relationships.

More recent studies show that first-generation Latinos and AAPIs are more likely to have grandparents, parents, and children interacting with each other and living in the same household. For example, Xie et al. found that Latinx mothers perceived a substantive level of grandparental support for a child's physical activity.[6] He and Jia, in "Exploring Multigenerational Co-Residence in the United States," found that immigrants, as well as Asians and African Americans, tend to live in multigenerational coresidential units, although this is influenced by household income (with those having lower incomes being more likely to live in such households).[7] Examining the influx of Central Americans, Fuller-Thomson and Minkler found that one in twenty were caregiving grandparents.[8] And among Chinese immigrant families, Sun and Mulvaney found that grandparent support and collectivism predicted decreased parenting stress.[9]

What these incipient studies of the new diversity and intergenerational relations appear to show is that, first, diverse communities are still more likely to have intergenerational households, and second, this situation provides positive benefits. Whether further studies will demonstrate continued intergenerational supports remains to be seen, but given current patterns for diverse and immigrant groups, efforts to promote age-integrated initiatives must begin to include diversity. Looking to the future, even in the second and third generations, acculturation and assimilation do not fully obviate the tendency by AAPIs, Latinos, and African Americans to continue to seek out and support intergenerational connections. Evidence shows that among Latino and AAPI groups there is a tendency by later cohorts of immigrants to continue providing support for their immigrant families, even if they no longer are in the same household.[10] If this is the case, then how can we cross boundaries so that we can continue to support indigenous and cultural intergenerational norms? And perhaps more telling, how can we foster greater connections between older Whites and younger, diverse populations?

These two themes are the central contributions the coauthors of this chapter present for broadening the current discourse of the intergenerational narratives: that it is no longer enough to extoll the virtues of reversing this country's generational segregation, and it must now expand to include multicultural and diverse voices.

The Benefits of Interethnic and Interracial Voices

There is a robust set of reasons why diversity can broaden and benefit age-integrated approaches. This includes the current recognition of the many social benefits of old and young coming together. But it must also include cultural, policy, and political self-interests in moving toward interethnic and interracial approaches across the generations.

First, various ethnic and immigrant groups come to this country with the "old-fashioned" values of caring for their elders and taking intergenerational households as a given. Of course, this mindset is partly influenced by the exigency of relying on one another as they struggle to survive and prosper in this country. Over time, the second generation of offspring tend to get assimilated and become "Americanized" with age-segregated lifestyles. The Latino paradox amply demonstrates that Mexicans, Cubans, and Central Americans who face tremendous adversity immigrating to the United States actually maintain healthier outcomes, both physical and mental.[11] They fare better on most measures than native-born Americans, largely because they maintain the values of extended families, resiliency, and commitment to one another, regardless of age. And they are more likely to have intergenerational households, with elders caring for children while parents seek livelihoods. Sadly, this positive paradox diminishes over time, but it is not fully lost. Even second- and third-generation Latinos are more likely to provide care coordination and engage in intergenerational connections, even if they live apart.[12] The COVID pandemic highlighted this phenomenon along with a profound dilemma. During the pandemic, Latinos faced the highest rates of COVID infections and mortality precisely because they were more likely to share households and interact with one another, whether visiting their elders or having the grandparents care for the grandchildren. As earlier studies showed, much of this was due to the low-income status that forced old and young to live in tight quarters because they could not afford larger homes. This in itself raises another conundrum for intergenerational experts: What role can they play in mitigating the housing, built infrastructure, transportation, and socioeconomic disparities that diverse communities face? This is a much larger theme for others to pursue, but it is worth noting.

For now, we can assume that diverse communities, especially Latino, AAPI, and African American households, are striving to maintain intergenerational connections. So how can we learn from and foster them in the face of acculturation and assimilation? How might we reverse the process of becoming Americanized (e.g., with fast food, gun violence, individualism, and ageism)? As importantly, and perhaps over time, let's make the following a priority: crossing cohort, generational, ethnic, and racial boundaries to have a fully robust commitment to intergenerational relationships that are based on the true diversity of the next America.

Crossing Ethnic and Racial Boundaries

The premise that generational segregation is injurious to the civic culture is laudatory; and the promotion of the idea that age integration, especially with longevity, can lead to more elders seeking a sense of purpose and fulfillment by interacting with young persons is commendable. But is this solely about older Whites interacting with younger Whites? We run the risk of a more insidious ramification with an ageist society—in terms of not just age-segregated lifestyles but also a geographic dispersion that reinforces a homogenous approach to age segregation.

Today we see a great migration—a movement by more affluent retirees to retirement locales that reinforce age and homogeneity. The mainstream press is replete with "the 10 best places to retire" and age-friendly communities. But upon closer inspection, this migration appears as affluent, largely White retirees fleeing to affluent, largely White retirement locales. Whether the new retiree destinations are the Carolinas, Idaho, Sedona, Arizona, or anywhere that caters to economic émigrés, this is largely about those with retirement security taking advantage of lower-cost, racially homogenous desirable locations. California is infamous for retirees cashing in on their home equity to leave the increasingly diverse metropolitan areas of San Francisco and Los Angeles to move to Nevada, Arizona, and Texas and seek like-minded communities based on age and race. If this becomes the norm, then how will it impact a broader goal of an intergenerational society that is based on the new diversity? How and when can we encourage older Whites to be willing to interact with young Blacks, Latinos, Asians, immigrants, and refugees? This, then, is the central challenge. If we truly want to promote intergenerational relationships, we must also commit to providing diverse relationships where today's largely older White cohort interacts with a largely diverse younger cohort. We may not be able to dissuade affluent White retirees in San Francisco and Los Angeles from fleeing to Idaho, Montana, or another place with like-minded, homogenous groups, but perhaps we can enlist their support for public policies that engender housing, health, transportation, and other initiatives that enable a majority-minority nation to lessen its racial and economic disparities. And for those older Whites who elect to stay in increasingly diverse locales, we can expand the current discourse on the benefits of intergenerational programs to one that looks at innovative approaches to age-race-ethnic-immigrant-intergenerational integration. This, then, is the central premise of this piece, and we'd like to add one more reason to strive for these goals: the self-interest of who will take care of whom.

The Final Rationale: Self-Interest and Who Will Care for Us

In a society where the largely older and White population will be dependent on the industriousness and productivity of a majority non-White younger society, the highlighting self-interest is a powerful tool for a new awakening. Simply put, the continued fiscal solvency of entitlement programs—especially Social Security, Medicare and Medicaid—will depend on the labor of young immigrant, minority, and refugee groups. The need to expand the long-term care workforce to care for older persons will depend on the continued willingness and influx of young immigrants, refugees, and largely minority females. The future national security of this nation will depend on a military mostly composed of diverse men and women. These existential realities reinforce the mantra of "who will care for us." The future of the United States and the laudable goal of shifting this society from its history of age segregation must now account for a new America—one where a diverse young population will want to care for older persons and will benefit from age-race-ethnic intergenerational solidarity.

Notes

1. K. Fingerman et al., "The Baby Boomers Intergenerational Relationships," *Gerontologist* 52, no. 2 (2012): 199–209; A. Lytle and M. Apriceno, "Understanding Intergenerational Tension during the COVID-19 Pandemic: The Role of Ambivalent Ageism," *Journal of Intergenerational Relationships* 21, no. 4 (2023): 461–76; A. Steward and K. McDevitt, "Otherwise We Would Be Like an Island: A Phenomenological Understanding of Intergenerational Engagement Aimed at Reducing Social Isolation," *Journal of Intergenerational Relationships* 21, no. 2 (2023): 215–33.
2. R. H. Binstock, "A New Era in the Politics of Aging: How Will the Old-Age Interest Groups Respond?" *Generations: Journal of the American Society on Aging*, 19, no. 3 (1995): 68–74; F. Torres-Gil, *The New Aging: Politics and Change in America* (Westport, CT: Auburn House, 1992).
3. P. Taylor and Pew Research Center, *The Next America* (New York: Public Affairs, 2014); W. N. Frey, *Diversity Explosion: How New Racial Demographics Are Remaking America* (Washington, DC: Brookings Institution, 2015).
4. J. Vespa et al., "Demographic Turning Points for the United States: Population Projections for 2020 to 2060," U.S. Department of Commerce, U.S. Census Bureau, February, 2020, https://www.census.gov/library/publications/2020/demo/p25-1144.html.
5. F. Torres-Gil and J. Angel, *The Politics of a Majority-Minority Nation: Aging, Diversity and Immigration* (New York: Springer, 2019).
6. H. Xie et al., "Latinx Mothers' Perception of Grandparents' Involvement in Children's Physical Activity," *Journal of Intergenerational Relationships* 20, no. 4 (2021): 424–41.
7. W. He and S. Jia, "Exploring Multigenerational Co-Residence in the United States," *International Journal of Housing Markets and Analysis* (2022).
8. E. Fuller-Thomson and M. Minkler, "Central American Grandparents Raising Grandchildren," *Hispanic Journal of Behavioral Sciences* 29, no. 1 (2007): 5–18.

9. K. Sun and M. K. Mulvaney, "Intergenerational Support in Chinese Immigrant Families: The Influences of Grandparent Support, Cultural Value, and Orientations in Parenting Stress," *Journal of Intergenerational Relationships* 21, no. 1 (2023): 40–61.
10. J. Angel et al., "Institutional Context of Family Eldercare in Mexico and the United States," *Journal of Cross-Cultural Gerontology* 31, no. 3 (2016): 327–36; K. S. Markides et al., "Sources of Helping and Intergenerational Solidarity: A Three Generation Study of Mexican-Americans," *Journal of Gerontology: Social Sciences* 41 (1986): 506–11.
11. Markides et al., "Sources of Helping."
12. F. Riosmena et al., "Explaining the Immigrant Health Advantage: Self-Selection and Protection in Health-Related Factors among Five Major National-Origin Immigrant Groups in the United States," *Demography* 54, no. 1 (2017): 175–200.

Bibliography

Angel, J., Ronald J. Angel, Mariana López-Ortega, Luis Miguel Gutiérrez Robledo, and Robert B. Wallace. "Institutional Context of Family Eldercare in Mexico and the United States." *Journal of Cross-Cultural Gerontology* 31, no. 3 (2016): 327–36.

Binstock, R. H. "A New Era in the Politics of Aging: How Will the Old-Age Interest Groups Respond?" *Generations: Journal of the American Society on Aging* 19, no. 3 (1995): 68–74.

Fingerman, K., Karl A. Pillemer, Merril Silverstein, and J. Jill Suitor. "The Baby Boomers Intergenerational Relationships." *Gerontologist* 52, no. 2 (2012): 199–209.

Frey, W. N. *Diversity Explosion: How New Racial Demographics are Remaking America*. Washington, DC: The Brookings Institution, 2015.

Fuller-Thomson, E., and M. Minkler. "Central American Grandparents Raising Grandchildren." *Hispanic Journal of Behavioral Sciences* 29, no. 1 (2007): 5–18.

He, W., and S. Jia. "Exploring Multigenerational Co-Residence in the United States." *International Journal of Housing Markets and Analysis* 17, no. 2 (2022): 517–538.

Lytle, A., and M. Apriceno. "Understanding Intergenerational Tension during the Covid-19 Pandemic: The Role of Ambivalent Ageism." *Journal of Intergenerational Relationships* 21, no. 4 (2023): 461–72.

Markides, K. S., J. S. Boldt, and L. Ray. "Sources of Helping and Intergenerational Solidarity: A Three Generation Study of Mexican-Americans." *Journal of Gerontology: Social Sciences* 41 (1986): 506–11.

Riosmena, F., R. Kuhn, and W. C. Jochem. "Explaining the Immigrant Health Advantage: Self-Selection and Protection in Health-Related Factors among Five Major National-Origin Immigrant Groups in the United States." *Demography* 54, no. 1 (2017): 175–200.

Steward, A., and K. McDevitt. "Otherwise We Would Be Like an Island: A Phenomenological Understanding of Intergenerational Engagement Aimed at Reducing Social Isolation." *Journal of Intergenerational Relationships* 21, no. 2 (2023): 215–33.

Sun, K., and M. K. Mulvaney. "Intergenerational Support in Chinese Immigrant Families: The Influences of Grandparent Support, Cultural Value, and Orientations in Parenting Stress." *Journal of Intergenerational Relationships* 21, no. 1 (2023): 40–61.

Taylor, P., and Pew Research Center. *The Next America*. New York: PublicAffairs, 2014.

Torres-Gil, F. *The New Aging: Politics and Change in America*. Westport, CT: Auburn House, 1992.

Torres-Gil, F., and J. Angel. *The Politics of a Majority-Minority Nation: Aging, Diversity and Immigration*. New York: Springer, 2019.

Vespa, J., L. Medila, and D. M. Armstrong. "Demographic Turning Points for the United States: Population Projections for 2020 to 2060." United States Department of Commerce, U.S. Census Bureau. February 2020, https://www.census.gov/library/publications/2020/demo/p25-1144.html.

Xie, H., A. Besnilian, and D. Boyns. "Latinx Mothers' Perception of Grandparents' Involvement in Children's Physical Activity." *Journal of Intergenerational Relationships* 20, no. 4 (2021): 424–41.

CHAPTER 14

Viewing the Climate Crisis from Intergenerational Perspectives

Ethan Bonerath, Elizabeth Bisno, Gillian Williams, Daniel George, *and* Peter J. Whitehouse

Abstract

The climate crisis is an existential threat to all living creatures. The Great Acceleration in human population starting in the middle of the last century marks the beginning of a new geological epoch—the so-called Anthropocene—defined by the global impact of humans, especially the Baby Boom generation. Addressing these challenges will require long-term thinking and a commitment to future generations of humans and other living creatures. This chapter blends stories and data about effective intergenerational programs in which the authors have participated to share current best practices and design elements essential for future efforts to connect the generations in the climate conversation. The steps in this process led to the challenging of assumptions, building of relationships, and a deepening appreciation for connections with nature. These lessons focused on the importance of *process* in creating open, honest, and fruitful intergenerational conversations that can lead to community and cultural transformation.

Key Words: intergenerational, climate crisis, elderhood, intergenerativity, gardens, farming, transdisciplinary, Bohm-inspired dialogue

Global Leadership Project to Foster Intergenerational Connections	Intergenerational Dialogues in the Climate Dialogue Group	Awareness @ Work	Hospital-based Farmers Market & Community Garden	Intergenerational Schools
Strengths/impact • Provides enriching learning opportunities • Develops new concepts about climate crisis • Deepens connections to the environment and others • Promotes action for concrete change	**Strengths/impact** • Cultivates respect between generations • Includes people living in severely affected regions • Encourages honesty and finding shared meaning (Bohm priorities) • Includes brainstorming for intergenerational collaboration	**Strengths/impact** • Fosters intergenerational conversations • Creates conditions that allow worldviews to shift • Encourages looking at unexamined assumptions • Promotes an inclusive and comfortable environment • Adapts to both virtual and in-person settings	**Strengths/impact** • Promotes intergenerational nature of teaching hospitals • Brings all ages together concerning food production, healthy eating • Regionalizing food production can lower carbon footprint • Markets, gardens provide a platform to educate customers about climate change • Deepens the bond local citizens feel to the land and broader environment	**Strengths/impact** • Encourages creative thought and innovation • Builds relationships in community • Develops generalist, big-picture thinking • Creates confidence in participants
Limitations • Limited interest due to comfort and busy lives • Difficulty motivating organizations • Disconnect from nature reducing willingness for action	**Limitations** • Fewer youth than elders • Need to ensure participants are Bohm dialogue experts	**Limitations** • Required reading about challenging Bohm-inspired dialogue • Difficulty attracting younger people (poor outreach)	**Limitations** • Solutions rooted at the local level, not explicitly engaged with broader systems of power/influence. • Building community bonds in a social landscape where so many feel alienated • Requires sustained educational efforts for linking food production practices and environmental stewardship	**Limitations** • Bureaucratic status quo • Financial sustainability • Political polarization

Introduction

The climate crisis is an existential threat to all living creatures. The Great Acceleration in human population starting in the middle of the last century marks the beginning of a new geological epoch, the so-called Anthropocene, defined by the global impact of humans, especially the so-called Baby Boom generation. Planetary boundaries demarcating the ability to support life are being exceeded as temperatures and ocean waters rise in association with "weather weirding" (i.e., dramatic changes in meteorological patterns). The ecological crisis, which includes other environmental factors beyond climate change, like pollution, is also associated with social injustice, deterioration in human health, and threats to democratic governance.[1]

These intensifying, wicked problems require fundamental transformations in individuals and societies, especially concerning our relationships in nature. They will require long-term thinking and a commitment to future generations of humans and other living creatures. Older people hold more manifest social and economic power than younger individuals. Hence, multiage, intergenerational conversations are critical to developing the trust and solidarity needed to design fair and equitable approaches to addressing our complex poly-problems.

What do we know about intergenerational issues surrounding the climate crisis? In the 2021 Ontario Student Drug Use and Health Survey conducted on students from grade 7 to grade 12 by the Centre for Addiction and Mental Health, 50 percent of students stated that they were depressed about the future because of climate change.[2] A survey of 13,749 U.S. adults (900 of whom were Gen Z) by the Pew Research Center in April 2021 revealed that 37 percent of U.S. adults from Gen Z and 29 percent from the Baby Boom generation say that addressing climate change is their top personal concern.[3] In general, youth who have less political power and more at stake in the future express greater concern about climate. People at both ends of the age spectrum—frail and vulnerable children, youth, and older people—share common mental health problems such as loneliness, risk for suicide, and substance abuse.[4] Young adults face the decision of whether to bring children into the world. The term "solastalgia" was coined to express a sense of alienation from our home planet experienced by people of all ages.[5]

This chapter blends stories and data about effective intergenerational programs in which the authors have participated to share current best practices and design elements essential for future efforts to connect the generations. Limitations and challenges are also outlined in the introductory table and explicated in the text.

The process of writing this chapter modeled the kind of conversations and organizational activities that we believe are essential to creating this more sustainable future. Each author will share their program and contribution to it in a separate section, followed by a general discussion about lessons learned across all the projects. We have preserved the characteristics of the individual voices and included autobiographical elements when essential to the program descriptions and conclusions drawn. By happenstance, the order of presentations is by age of author, not because of chronology but because of the nature of the individual projects and how they tie together. We met through our common interest in intergenerational conversations about climate, in different locations—classrooms, Zoom rooms, homes, and conference rooms. As the reader will see, this writing collaboration, initially organized by Peter Whitehouse, led to increasing interactions among the authors and their respective projects. Hence, this chapter itself can be seen as a project celebrating intergenerational connections.

The chapter is organized into several sections following this introduction. Ethan Bonerath, a first-year college student at McMaster University, describes his high school project to foster intergenerational conversations focusing on his recent work on regenerative farming in the context of bioregional development. Elizabeth Bisno, another college student, outlines her work in the Climate Dialogue Group, focusing on a project called Equatorial Voices. Gillian Williams, a recent university graduate, continues our discussion of deep dialogue in the context of her work on climate in the Awareness @ Work group. Dr. Daniel George, a Millennial and professor in humanities and public health, shares a story of engaging community by involving his medical school, a farmers' market, and a community garden. Finally, Dr. Peter Whitehouse, a Baby Boomer transdisciplinary professor, describes the creation of three public intergenerational schools and their network of international collaborations.

Common to all the projects is conversation (live and by Zoom). Two projects specifically used Bohn-inspired dialogue, a communicative process to deepen conversation, challenge assumptions, and broaden thinking. Although there are differences in the details, all the conversations were built around practicing listening, seeking the common threads in conversation, challenging assumptions, exploring differences, and inclusive participation. All conversations were international and interdisciplinary, as well as intergenerational and occasionally interspecies! In three of the stories the participation of family members added to the intergenerational flavor.

The writing process involved regular Zoom meetings among the authors but also sessions with each of the dialogue groups that are the foci of the sections below. The process varied depending on the group and its historical practices, but all involved ten to fifteen people of different ages discussing the nature and value of intergenerational connections sparked by questions that were chosen by the authors to reflect the background and interests of each group. All sessions involved a check-in focusing on the participant's recent activities, which served to build relationships. Each session was composed of a core of regular participants to which others involved in our writing project across the different groups were invited to join.

Global Leadership Project to Foster Intergenerational Connections

In 2021, Ethan Bonerath began a high school capstone project to foster intergenerational conversations—inspired by his multigenerational home—about societies' most complex current challenges. The Global Leadership Program at Pickering College, his high school, aims to inspire students to apply inquiry-based critical thinking within a global context, taking theory to action in creative and innovative ways.

Ethan started participating in various intergenerational events to hone his skills in communication and interaction with diverse age groups. The environment and climate crisis kept emerging as the central complex issue for participants in the discussions. His engagement developed further via collaborative efforts with diverse groups possessing expertise in intergenerational dialogue and environmental discourse. An example was his dialogue with Dr. Peter Whitehouse as part of the Pass It On Network's four-part series titled "Reweaving the Web of Life, Feeling Entangled Roots." Pass It On Network is an international group fostering elder rights, and they are struggling, as many activist groups of older people are, to engage with youth.

Their dialogue centered on the importance of intergenerational connections and the art of balancing dialectical perspectives in deeper conversations. They discussed the imperative to seek proactively to become conscientious ancestors for future generations and to maintain an awareness of what we would like to see emerge in the future. The dialogue enriched Ethan's thinking and perspectives and advanced his project further than anticipated. Questions about youths' greatest concerns were raised. Based on responses to those questions and from his experience in other dialogues, Ethan focused his project on intergenerational engagements toward climate crisis action.

These initial conversations led to insights that showed how intergenerational connections can foster compassion and creativity, serve as a catalyst for change, act as a driving force for transformation, and positively impact individual mental health and well-being. Motivated by this understanding, Ethan hosted an intergenerational climate event at his high school, featuring presentations by an environmentalist and an indigenous elder. More than forty students and twenty community members were present for the discussions on the application of indigenous and scientific learning systems to ecological restoration within bioregions (human communities in ecological systems).

Ethan's Global Leadership Project led to an environmental regeneration effort at his high school's farm, integrating intergenerational dialogue and collaboration. The farm became a Greater Toronto Bioregional Learning Center site due to these endeavors. Berry bushes were planted by multiple generations during the summer, an activity that brought together environmentally aware individuals from various age groups, potentially setting the stage for impactful changes. In fact, the farm directors established ties with experts in regenerative agriculture, paving the way for the farm to become a beacon of regenerative practices for both students and the community.

The project has faced several challenges, however. Engaging individuals in intergenerational and environmental events is difficult, despite outreach efforts, posters, and social media. People are reluctant to participate due to complacency—a perception that the problems are not personal—and competing priorities. They tend not to act until societal challenges become crises. They are often disconnected from nature and therefore not concerned with protecting ecosystems.

Ethan noticed that his peers spent less time in nature than earlier cohorts. This disconnect, particularly prevalent in urban areas, negatively impacts both environmental initiatives and individual mental well-being. Ethan and others observed that most school systems no longer focus on the complete education of a person but on more utilitarian approaches—namely, becoming productive within an industrialized, highly marketized society. However, there is cause for optimism: institutions like Pickering College strive to nurture well-rounded students, and many other schools are introducing gardens and environmental clubs.

Climate Dialogue Group, a Bohm-inspired Dialogue Process

Starting in 2022, Elizabeth Bisno began working with the Climate Dialogue Group (CDG), which operates online to connect its members from across the globe, including the United Kingdom, United States, Uganda, Kenya, India, Canada, the Congo, and Tanzania. Their website serves as the hub for thirty-four members, including approximately fifteen regulars who meet weekly over Zoom. Their mission is: "to be a catalyst in bringing together those voices and constituencies, challenged with climate change and social injustice, who wish to be heard and to hear each other, in finding emergent perspectives and solutions through Bohm-inspired Dialogue. To sow the seeds of this work through the teaching and modeling of Bohm-inspired Dialogue, such that communities take ownership of this practice in developing collaborative leadership in sustainable climate and social justice initiatives."

What gives the group a unique niche in the communication space is the framework of Bohm dialogue, a specific type of in-depth conversation developed by theoretical physicist and activist David Bohm.[6] When Bohm witnessed more and more conflicts in the world in the middle of the last century, he designed a conversation process that can be used for proprioception—namely, to identify the thought patterns that cause human problems and conflicts. He developed a conceptual framework for the conversation. First, Bohm dialogue establishes a "container," a safe space of respect so that each person feels comfortable finding their voice and speaking from the heart. This can elicit valuable unedited truths, as participants often find themselves uttering things they wouldn't have said in any other setting. This is partly achieved through another step, which is suspension of judgments and preconceptions. Once they're deep into the dialogue, participants focus on *process* rather than *outcome* and embrace the shared meaning that emerges along the way. Dialogue is not led or "facilitated"; rather, it's a process that invites participants to share as they feel called. Since participants are encouraged to express views that differ from others', the dialogue reaches levels deeper than those reached in most conventional meetings, in which people tend to default to agreement for the sake of coming to conclusions so that they can get things done.

In bringing together numerous people who are experiencing severe climate change effects, CDG creates a space for listening to one another and offers them Bohm dialogue as a tool to share past experiences, cultivate shared meaning, and inspire ideas for environmental solutions and action. One recent focus has been on the equatorial regions of the planet. In its annual Climate Change Vulnerability Index, U.K.-based risk analysis firm Maplecroft lists the top thirty-two countries at "extreme risk" from climate change. The top ten are all tropical countries.[7] Thanks to CDG member David Albert, the group was introduced to hundreds of people in equatorial countries, most of them under thirty years old. All were connected to David Albert through his efforts on behalf of human rights, health, clean water, and other issues in those regions. CDG had been intending to become more intergenerational since starting as a small, primarily older group composed mostly of graduate school professors. The search for younger participants prompted Elizabeth's involvement in the group.

Soon after CDG began collaborating with the people from equatorial regions, three of them (one each from India, Kenya, and Uganda) formed the Equatorial Voices Network (EVN) and became CDG's official EVN coordinators. They are part of the CDG core team, participate in the weekly meetings, and are the liaisons between the main group and other equatorial members who are not on the core team (but some of whom have given deeply informative climate-focused presentations via the CDG platform). The EVN coordinator from Uganda once expressed that even though he favors concrete action, he believes in the power of Bohm-inspired dialogue to cultivate respect, identify the nature of problems, and suggest a variety of ways to address challenges.

Awareness@Work: a Bohm-Inspired Dialogue Focused on Organizational Issues

As a college student in 2020, Gillian Williams began participating in Awareness@Work, a dynamic Bohm-inspired dialoguing group that convenes weekly via Zoom. It was originally an exploration focused on bringing Bohm-inspired dialogue into workplaces. The intent was to fostering meaningful dialogue within workplaces, an initiative seen as essential owing to the significant amount of time people invest in work. Currently, most dialogues sponsored by Awareness@Work are held online and bring together individuals with diverse perspectives and experiences. The group embraces the richness of these virtual dialogues, which allows them to build connections and exchange insights across physical boundaries. Awareness@Work's mission is to create a space where individuals can engage in open, authentic, and nonjudgmental conversations to explore deep and complex ideas. They aim to foster deep listening, mutual respect, and collective inquiry through a Bohmian-inspired dialogic process. The hope is that through this process, one can transcend individual perspectives and arrive at new insights and shared meaning.

Awareness@Work inquiry spans three continents and involves individuals currently ranging in age from twenty-two to eighty-one. Having a diverse group of participants, which Zoom supports, is an essential part of Bohm-inspired dialogue because Bohm believed that participants should represent a microcosm of a diverse society. Historically, Bohm-inspired dialogue has attracted an older demographic, as Bohm noted in the 1990s.[8] However, younger generations need to be involved in dialogues because they offer new perspectives and the potential for deep conversations that lead to change and hopefully to a better future. Unfortunately, the way many people are socialized causes younger people to hesitate about speaking their minds when in the presence of elders. Yet through repeatedly participating in dialogues, reservations and feelings of anxiety do dissipate.

In these dialoguing sessions, participants strive to follow some of the essential characteristics of Bohm's dialogic process as the group interprets it. Usually, when they meet, there is no agenda. This is based on the belief that what is meant to arise in conversation will emerge without a set structure. The lack of an agenda aids the listening process because participants cannot form preconceived talking points before the dialogue begins. This approach encourages participants to step back from automatic thinking and reflect on the silences that materialize in dialogue. Having longer silences slows things down and creates the conditions to deepen the conversation. By intensively listening to one another without obligation to share information, but engaging if/when they feel moved, participants often generate new insights.

Bohm-inspired dialogue is directly relevant to the climate crisis. By creating conditions that might (1) allow one's worldview to shift, (2) disrupt automatic and often fragmented thought patterns, and (3) foster intergenerational communication, one can begin to address the root causes of problems and create space for something new to occur. The group hopes for movement to more conscious, coherent, and grounded perspectives that lead to a more sustainable and harmonious collective future. It is through these dialogues that one actively cultivates positive change within oneself and society, leading everyone toward meaningful solutions to the climate crisis and other pressing issues of today.

Although Bohm-inspired dialogue offers a multitude of benefits, some challenges still arise. One is that people usually need to be prepared to engage in the process before participating because it is different from typical modes of conversation. A second challenge is that for various reasons, including time constraints, anxiety, and lack of internet access, participants may be unwilling to spend their free time in dialogue with people they do not know. Lastly, due to the potentially transformative nature of Bohm-inspired dialogue, those who are invested in the status quo and benefit from it may resist participating.

In addition to effectively dismantling various interpersonal and intrapersonal challenges, Bohm-inspired dialogue has several inherent strengths. First, it can adapt to both virtual and in-person settings, providing flexibility and accessibility. Second, the relaxed nature of the dialogic process allows participants to contribute as much or as little as they wish, promoting an inclusive and comfortable environment. Lastly, Bohm-inspired dialogue is experiencing a resurgence in popularity, offering individuals the opportunity to engage in a wide range of these conversations that can easily accommodate their schedules.

Hospital-Based Farmers Market and Community Garden

Starting a decade ago, Daniel George, a medical anthropologist and professor of humanities and public health sciences, led the development of intergenerational programs to engage his medical school in local community experiences and programs related to environmental health. While other sectors (e.g., agriculture, transportation, military, etc.) are often identified as disproportionately impacting the environment, the healthcare sector is annually responsible for over 4 percent of global CO_2 emissions (10 percent in industrialized nations) while generating 5.2 billion tons of waste. Given this major environmental footprint, healthcare organizations are well positioned to make major impacts in local, regional, and planetary health.[9]

Institutional change across health systems has, however, been elusive. Medical schools, with their disproportionate focus on biomedical training, have historically been less oriented to environmental- or systems-level issues. While that is beginning to change due to emergent threats to human health from climate change as well as a growing focus on health systems science as a pillar in medical school curricula, it remains difficult to get broad institutional traction in these areas. Daniel's collaborative work has sought to use a college of medicine and the resources of a broader medical center as an organizational platform to begin building better structures, processes, and systems responsive to climate change. It draws on the inherent intergenerational nature of a medical school nested within a broader healthcare system to engender institutional adaptations.[10]

Specifically, the efforts have concentrated on building organizations that help local communities develop greater resilience to climate change and other contemporary threats (e.g., supply chain disruption, economic recession, and natural disasters). Daniel worked with intergenerational leadership teams of Millennials and Boomers to initiate a farmers' market and community garden on the hospital campus of Penn State College of Medicine. Both sites, which were planned by college employees and implemented by hospital administration, have served as shared sites that bring people of all ages together around the act of food production and healthy eating.

The market, which launched in 2010, was envisioned as an intervention to not only improve the hospital's commitment to preventive health in the region but also to benefit the climate. Specifically, by regionalizing food production, farmers' markets contribute to lowering the carbon footprint of food. Consumers support the proximate economy by giving their dollars directly to producers and by supporting farmers who are ethical stewards of local land (e.g., who are committed to organic farming, soil health, humane treatment of animals, etc.). Running weekly from May through November, the market has also offered free tables for community groups, including local environmental advocacy organizations. These groups help educate customers about climate change–related issues and focus efforts on fostering educational programming for children. Overall, the goal of this community outreach programming is to diffuse climate change as a hot-button culture war issue and find creative inroads to connect with customers/hospital patrons in rural Pennsylvania around the benefits of better environmental stewardship.

A 2-acre, 234-plot community garden followed in 2014, also the result of an intergenerational leadership team from the College of Medicine working with hospital administration. While the establishment of the garden was undertaken in response to the hospital's inaugural community health needs assessment, which documented high rates of chronic disease and loneliness in central Pennsylvania,[11] its emphasis on localizing food production also aimed to reduce reliance on global corporate supply chains and lower the carbon footprint of foods.

Specific programs implemented through the garden in partnership with the hospital have enabled clinicians to refer high-risk, food-insecure patients to the garden. In 2018, a Prescription Produce initiative enabled clinicians to "prescribe" young (Millennial) adult cancer survivors a garden plot and to pair them with older (Boomer, GenX) local master gardeners to learn how to cultivate and prepare healthy foods over a growing season. Subsequent initiatives have used this intergenerational model to engage patients at risk for cardiovascular disease. Both programs have shown preliminary benefits for patients,[12] as have Prescription Produce programs staged at the farmers' market.[13] Ultimately, the goal of these programs is to empower participants to source their food locally and feel capable of being at least partially self-sustaining as producers. Overall, it is hoped that the garden and its programs will help deepen the bond local citizens feel to the land and broader environment.[14]

Indeed, the garden, which has attracted gardeners young and old (offering raised beds for elders), has served as a catalyst for other environment-oriented programs. For instance, in 2016, a medical student developed a composting partnership with hospital food services that diverted 220 pounds of organic food waste from the cafeteria to the garden compost pit each week.[15] In 2017, hospital employees established five beehive colonies in proximity to the garden and advocated for the institution to replace mowed turf grass with native plants and wildflowers. At present, the hospital is exploring converting ten acres of additional land into an organic farm.

Intergenerational Learning: from Elementary Schools in Cleveland to International Programs

Peter Whitehouse is a geriatric neurologist, cognitive neuroscientist, and environmental bioethicist who cofounded three public intergenerational schools with his wife Catherine, a developmental psychologist. Prior to this intergenerational project, he had a long career as a researcher and clinician in the health field, particularly involving brain and mental health aspects of aging.[16] He employed a life-course perspective, working in public health and the arts to encourage long-range thinking of children as future elders. In this context, he became gravely concerned about the consequences of the climate crisis and other environmental degradations for the future of human beings, particularly vulnerable children, the elderly, and other living creatures.

In 2000 the first intergenerational school was founded in Cleveland, Ohio, based on a developmental, experiential, and relationship-based model of learning.[17] (Also see *Handbook* chapter 12.) It was chartered by the state of Ohio as an elementary community public school. Peter Whitehouse felt that older individuals needed places in their community to feel valuable and to enjoy the company of children. Catherine Whitehouse believed that children benefited from having older adults in their lives in a school context to boost both skills and confidence. Many of the younger students came from families under considerable social and economic stress, including single-parent and grandparent-based households. Children were not assigned to standard grade levels based on chronological age; they were placed in clusters based on developmental stage. Other key features included small classrooms and a culture of respect. Informal, comfortable spaces were created where adults and children could interact outside the classroom in pairs or small groups. The signature program was originally called Reading Mentoring, signaling the importance of literacy.

Many of the children were from disadvantaged neighborhoods and exhibited delayed skills upon entry to kindergarten. The children developed long-term relationships with volunteers who met regularly with specific groups of younger children, mostly one-on-one. Older adults came from the community, but the learning experiences also included regular visits to residents in long-term care facilities. Eventually the signature program was renamed Learning Partners, as the mentoring relationships extended beyond reading to math and other subjects. The "partner" terminology also signaled that both the adults and the children learn from the relationship. Gardening and attention to the natural world through field trips became central to the program.

Despite being a small, relatively underfunded school, it maintained support for the arts, music, and physical education throughout its now over twenty-year history. Eventually, two other schools were founded in other parts of Cleveland to compose a network of intergenerational schools. Partnerships with other learning organizations, including Case Western Reserve University, led to opportunities for older students to experience field placements in the school and conduct school-based research.[18]

From its early days, the intergenerational school achieved high academic outcomes as measured by state tests and the matriculation of students into quality post–elementary school programs. Currently, it is the highest-performing nonprofit charter school network in the state of Ohio. It has received many local, national, and international awards during its two decades of operation.

Another successful aspect of the program was to involve older adults with cognitive challenges in the school. People with mild to moderate dementia came to the school to participate in the relationship-based learning programs. Some required support for their short-term memory problems, but for many whose long-term memories were still intact, the opportunity to share stories from their past provided meaning. Students visited other adults with dementia in long-term care facilities. Award-winning research by one of this chapter's coauthors, Daniel George, with his mentor Peter Whitehouse, demonstrated the value of volunteering in the intergenerational school for people with dementia using a mixed methods analysis focusing on quality-of-life outcomes.

In 2014, the school won the Eisner Prize for lifelong achievements in intergenerational programming. This led to the creation of Intergenerational Schools International and expanded long-standing collaborations with other intergenerational learning programs in other countries, including Japan, Canada, the United Kingdom, and Spain.[19] After five years, this nonprofit organization was transformed into a digital platform called InterHub based in the Presencing Institute, founded by Otto Scharmer, who developed the Theory U learning model at MIT.[20] InterHub was part of a project called GAIA (Global Activation of Intention and Action). This international effort was designed to transform civilization based on rethinking and revaluing underlying concepts in modernity, including colonization and indigenization. As a part of this larger project, InterHub focused on imagining futures that were transdisciplinary and intergenerative—the latter concept referring to the emergently generative dynamics that can emerge from connecting different domains of individual and social creativity. These connections can be made between disciplines, professions, nations, faiths, etc., not just generations. It is a future oriented concept that implies going "between to go beyond."[21]

The transdisciplinarity work was based primarily in higher education institutions, including Case Western Reserve University. Transdisciplinarity calls not only for collaboration among disciplines ("inter" meaning between) but also for exploring the boundaries between the disciplines in order to create new forward-looking scholarship and action ("trans" meaning beyond).[22] Transdisciplinarity specifically challenges universities to address the complex, so-called wicked problems evident in society, such as the climate crisis and associated social injustices and income inequities. These "poly-crises" do not present themselves to universities labeled as a problem to be solved by specific disciplines, but rather, emerge through potentially transformative collaborative forms of scholarship that embrace uncertainty and mystery.

Some of the programs associated with these transdisciplinary efforts involved students from the intergenerational schools, undergraduates, and elders from the community. One such effort was a course called "Wising Up: Designing a Course for the Future." The process of developing wisdom was examined from a variety of perspectives, ranging from neuroscience to spirituality. The focus was not on individual wisdom but on creating collective wisdom.[23]

In 2023, the intergenerational school organized a community design process focusing on the concept of regenerating bioregions with several other community organizations, including Case Western Reserve University. One of this chapter's authors, Gillian, joined Peter and others on the planning team for the conference. This effort was part of the Great

Lakes Basin and other international efforts to develop the ability to think of our communities not just in terms of their human element but also in terms of ecological features like watersheds. Scaling up such activities may be critical if we are to adapt as the climate crisis intensifies.[24]

Peter's latest collaborative project with the intergenerational schools and several universities, including Oxford and the University of Toronto, involves exploring the transition from elderhood to ancestorhood. *Elderhood* is both a state of mind and an identified role in society, achieved by those who celebrate and practice lifelong, community-based wisdom-seeking.[25] *Ancestorhood* is the next stage beyond elderhood, yet we often forget the power of our deceased relative's stories to influence the still living. But death can be viewed as a social as well as a biological phenomenon. A deeper reconsideration of elderhood and beyond should embrace our own mortality. Considering death itself as an essential part of life creates genuine hope that dying is part of our legacies as participants in an ongoing cycle of life, not only as individuals, but as a species.[26]

The strengths of these intergenerational learning programs lie in their ability to marshal creative thought across a variety of domains of life. They involve developing new curricula and organizational forms. They answer the need for generalized approaches rather than specialization. They foster relationship building in social and natural communities. Big picture thinking is welcome, at the level of transforming civilization. They specifically signal a commitment to the future of all living creatures.

The weaknesses or challenges of these approaches are due primarily to the conservative nature of educational organizations. Ironically, learning institutions do not innovate and change easily. Financial support and career advancement are often based on existing hierarchical structures (for instance, grade levels and disciplines). Moreover, politics, which rightfully influences the content and processes of teaching, is polarized and dysfunctional. As a result, schools and universities are hard-pressed to maintain their influence in the world, while having to change if they are to meet the needs of the future.

Conclusions

During the process of writing this chapter over several months, we experienced the hottest summer on record with some of the most violent floods and out-of-control forest fires. We became even further convinced that the climate crisis is accelerating. Many of us took action, but we also came to deeply appreciate the opportunity to take time to talk, learn, and reflect together. Exploring intergenerative themes while building our online and in-person communities and celebrating our deep connections to nature allowed us to challenge assumptions, build relationships, and explore possibilities for our individual and collective futures. We endeavored collectively and creatively to engage younger people in our discourse, create space for silence and reflection, share power across the generations, and see learning as a matter of not just intellect and thought but also passions and compassion. Acting was never far from our minds and hearts. In table 14.1, we summarize the

Table 14.1 Lessons learned and actions proposed

Lessons learned	Actions proposed
Learning and mentoring can and should be bidirectional	Structure interactions to allow space for shared exploration and relationship-building conversation, including small groups (two to six people)
Recognize that specific generational identification varies and is controversial	Avoid generational labels unless self-applied and allow openness about the concept of a generation
Promote thinking about time span and different conceptions of time	Plan conversations or watch for emergent themes about exploring the deeper past and future ("seven or more generations")
Maintain a spirit and practice of openness (neutrality)	Create or join community groups open to people of different ages and backgrounds
Be aware that technology can disconnect people from nature	Create conversation spaces in nature-rich settings like gardens; consider using nature-inspired rituals to open and close meetings
Celebrate existing relationships between people of different ages to demonstrate possibilities	Share stories online and in-person of past intergenerational successes; allow for individual check-ins and check-outs
Appreciate the value of silence but also encourage people less likely to speak (sometimes shy youth)	Dedicate part of the introduction to emphasizing that youth voices are valued, and encourage youth to start speaking early in the dialogue
Express gratitude for other peoples' comments and helpfulness	Create space in dialogue for such recognition

Source: Bonerath, Bisno, Williams, George, and Whitehouse

lessons learned across all or most of the projects in which we participated individually and collectively, and make some suggestions for actions built on these learnings.

For the most part, our lessons learned and proposed actions are about process, not about content. Some actions are for people who design future intergenerational dialogues, while others are action steps for people who are looking to enliven the intergenerational connections in their work and personal lives. At the heart of our reflections is the need to create new intergenerative stories of multiage collaboration and social commitment. The core unifying values of community stories include the diversity of listeners and tellers in the space/time in which they are created and shared, but stories change with context and needs of the place and time. Experiencing and understanding more deeply the patterns of meaning in the fabric of the modern world will allow us to "decolonize" our minds from the often-simplified view of human beings that modernity offers—for example, as rational economic agents. Deeper dialogue, as we experienced in our projects, designed to open up spaces where individual hearts and minds can expand and converge, will be critical as we rediscover the vital importance of youth and elders and their relationships to each other. Intergenerational relationships in past eras, when we lived in smaller multiage communities, were generally much stronger than those we find today. We need to renew this strength and expand from *intergenerational* to *intergenerative*; indeed, the futures of people currently living, and of people and other living creatures yet to be born, depend on it.

Acknowledgments

We deeply appreciate the leadership of all the organizations with which we worked and the participants in our many conversations who generously shared their time, stories, and insights. We offer a special thanks to those who read and commented on earlier drafts of this chapter. Thanks also to our families for their encouragement. Our love and gratitude know no bounds.

Notes

1. IPCC, *Climate Change 2014: Synthesis Report. Contribution of Working Groups I, II and III to the Fifth Assessment Report of the Intergovernmental Panel on Climate Change*, ed. Core Writing Team, R. K. Pachauri, and L.A. Meyer (IPCC, Geneva, Switzerland, 2014), 151; Peter Whitehouse et al., "Emergent Cosmic Return: The Field of Possibilities for Aging in a Proposed New Geological Epoch," in *Aging Studies and Ecocriticism*, ed. Nassim Balestrini (Lanham, MD: Lexington Books, 2023), 201–24.
2. CAMH, *The Well-Being of Ontario Students: Findings from the 2021 Ontario Student Drug Use and Health Survey* (Toronto: CAMH, 2021).
3. Cary Funk, *Key Findings: How Americans' Attitudes about Climate Change Differ by Generation, Party and Other Factors* (Washington, DC: Pew Research Center, 2021).
4. Emily Brignone, Daniel George, and Jennifer Kraschnewski, "Trends in the Diagnosis of Disease of Despair in the United States, 2009–2018: A Retrospective Cohort Study," *BMJ Open* 10 (2020): 1–11.
5. Whitehouse, *Emergent Cosmic Return*, 201–24.
6. David Bohm, *On Dialogue*, 2nd ed. (London: Routledge, 2004).
7. Richard Martin, "Climate Change: Why the Tropical Poor Will Suffer Most," *MIT Technology Review* (2015).
8. Bohm, *On Dialogue*, 6–48.
9. Daniel George et al., "Examining Feasibility of Mentoring Families at a Farmers' Market and Community Garden," *American Journal of Health Education* 47, no. 2 (2016): 94–98; Susan Veldheer and Daniel George, "Strategies to Help Healthcare Organizations Execute Their Food System Leadership Responsibilities," *AMA Journal of Ethics* 24, no. 10 (2022): E994–1003.
10. Susan Veldheer et al., "Growing Healthy Hearts: Gardening Program Feasibility in a Hospital-Based Community Garden," *Journal of Nutrition Education and Behavior* 52, no. 10 (2020): 958–63.
11. Daniel George and Amy Ethridge, "Hospital-Based Community Gardens as a Strategic Partner in Addressing Community Health Needs," *American Journal of Public Health* 113, no. 9 (2023): 939–42.
12. Renate Winkels et al., "Opportunities for Growth: A Community Gardening Pilot Intervention Pairing Adolescent and Young Adult Cancer Survivors with Master Gardeners," *Journal of Adolescent and Young Adult Oncology* 9, no. 1 (2020): 115–19; Veldheer, "Growing Healthy Hearts," 958–63.
13. George, "Examining Feasibility," 94–98.
14. Winkels, "Opportunities for Growth," 115–19.
15. Adri Galvan, Ryan Hanson, and Daniel George, "Repurposing Waste Streams: Lessons on Integrating Hospital Food Waste into a Community Garden," *Journal of Community Health* 43, no. 5 (2018): 944–46.
16. Peter Whitehouse, "Fifty Years of Dementia: A Transdisciplinary and Intergenerative Lifelong Learning Adventure in the Field," *Journal of Alzheimer's Disease* 83, no. 2 (2021): 487–90.
17. Peter Whitehouse et al., "Intergenerational Community Schools: A New Practice for a New Time," *Educational Gerontology* 26 (2000): 761–70.
18. Daniel George and Peter Whitehouse, "Intergenerational Volunteering and Quality of Life for Persons with Mild-to-Moderate Dementia: Results from a 5-month Intervention Study in the United States," *Journal of the American Geriatrics Society* 58, no. 3 (2010): 526–27.

19. Terry Hokenstad and Peter Whitehouse, "International Attention for The Intergenerational School," *Intercom International Federation on Ageing Special Issue* 12, no 3 (2005): 16.
20. Otto Scharmer, *The Essentials of Theory U: Core Principles and Applications* (Oakland, CA: Berrett-Koehler, 2018).
21. Peter Whitehouse, "Learning among Generations: From Intergenerational to Intergenerative," *Generations Journal* 41, no. 3 (2017): 68–71.
22. Whitehouse, *Emergent Cosmic Return*, 201–24.
23. Nicholas Brennecke et al., "Wising Up: Designing a Course for the Future: A Report on a New Transdisciplinary and Intergenerational Course," *Journal of Intergenerational Relationships* 18, no. 4 (2020): 465–69.
24. Whitehouse, *Emergent Cosmic Return*, 201–24.
25. Peter Whitehouse, "The Courage to Speak: Ethics and Elderhood," *Aging Today* (2016).
26. Whitehouse, *Emergent Cosmic Return*, 201–24.

Bibliography

Bohm, David. *On Dialogue*. 2nd ed. London: Routledge, 2004.

Brennecke, Nicholas, Farah Almhana, Peter Pesch, and Peter Whitehouse. "Wising Up: Designing a Course for the Future: A Report on a New Transdisciplinary and Intergenerational Course." *Journal of Intergenerational Relationships* 18, no. 4 (2020): 465–69.

Brignone, Emily, Daniel R. George, and Jennifer L. Kraschnewski. "Trends in the Diagnosis of Diseases of Despair in the United States, 2009–2018: A Retrospective Cohort Study." *BMJ Open* 10 (2020): e037679. https://doi.org/10.1136/bmjopen-2020-037679.

CAMH. *The Well-Being of Ontario Students: Findings from the 2021 Ontario Student Drug Use and Health Survey*. CAMH, Toronto (2021).

Funk, Cary. "Key Findings: How Americans' Attitudes about Climate Change Differ by Generation, Party and Other Factors." Washington, DC: Pew Research Center (2021). https://www.pewresearch.org/short-reads/2021/05/26/key-findings-how-americans-attitudes-about-climate-change-differ-by-generation-party-and-other-factors/.

Galvan, Adri, Ryan Hanson, and Daniel R. George. "Repurposing Waste Streams: Lessons on Integrating Hospital Food Waste into a Community Garden." *Journal of Community Health* 43, no. 5 (2018): 944–46.

George, Daniel R., and Amy E. Ethridge. "Hospital-Based Community Gardens as a Strategic Partner in Addressing Community Health Needs." *American Journal of Public Health* 113, no. 9 (2023): 939–42.

George, Daniel R., Jennifer L. Kraschnewski, and Liza S. Rovnia. "Public Health Potential of Farmers' Markets on Medical Center Campuses: A Case Study from Penn State Hershey Medical Center." *American Journal of Public Health* 101, no. 12 (2011): 2226–36.

George, Daniel, Monica Manglani, Kaitlin Minnehan, Alexander Chacon, Alexandra Gundersen, Cheryl Dellasega, et al.. "Examining Feasibility of Mentoring Families at a Farmers' Market and Community Garden." *American Journal of Health Education* 47, no. 2 (2016): 94–98.

George, Daniel R., and Peter Whitehouse. "Intergenerational Volunteering and Quality of Life for Persons with Mild-to-Moderate Dementia: Results from a 5-month Intervention Study in the United States." *Journal of the American Geriatrics Society* 58, no. 3 (2010): 526–27.

George, Daniel R., Catherine Whitehouse, and Peter Whitehouse. "A Model of Intergenerativity: How the Intergenerational School is Bringing the Generations Together to Foster Collective Wisdom and Community Health." *Journal of Intergenerational Relationships* 9, no. 4 (2011): 16.

Hokenstad, Terry, and Peter Whitehouse. "International Attention for The Intergenerational School." *Intercom International Federation on Ageing Special Issue* 12, no 3 (2005): 16.

IPCC. *Climate Change 2014: Synthesis Report. Contribution of Working Groups I, II and III to the Fifth Assessment Report of the Intergovernmental Panel on Climate Change*, edited by Core Writing Team, R. K. Pachauri, and L. A. Meyer. IPCC, Geneva, 2014.

Martin, Richard. "Climate Change: Why the Tropical Poor Will Suffer Most." *MIT Technology Review* (2015).

Scharmer, Otto. *The Essentials of Theory U: Core Principles and Applications*. Oakland, CA: Berrett-Koehler, 2018.

Veldheer, Susan, and Daniel R. George. "Strategies to Help Healthcare Organizations Execute Their Food System Leadership Responsibilities." *AMA Journal of Ethics* 24, no. 10 (2022): E994–1003.

Veldheer, Susan, Maxfield Whitehead-Zimmers, Candace Bordner, Olivia Weinstein, Hena Choi, Kira Spreenberg-Bronsoms, et al. "Growing Healthy Hearts: Gardening Program Feasibility in a Hospital-Based Community Garden." *Journal of Nutrition Education and Behavior* 52, no. 10 (2020): 958–63.

Whitehouse, Peter. "Taking Brain Health to a Deeper and Broader Level." *Neurological Institute Journal* 3, no. 1 (2010): 17–22.

Whitehouse, Peter. "The Courage to Speak: Ethics and Elderhood." *Aging Today* (2016).

Whitehouse, Peter J. "Learning among Generations: From Intergenerational to Intergenerative." *Generations Journal* 41, no. 3 (2017): 68–71.

Whitehouse, Peter. "Fifty Years of Dementia: A Transdisciplinary and Intergenerative Lifelong Learning Adventure in the Field." *Journal of Alzheimer's Disease* 83, no. 2 (2021): 487–90.

Whitehouse, Peter. "Emergent Cosmic Return: The Field of Possibilities for Aging in a Proposed New Geological Epoch." In *Aging Studies and Ecocriticism: Interdisciplinary Encounters*, edited by Nassim W. Balestrini, 201–24. Lanham, MD: Lexington Books, 2023.

Whitehouse, Peter, Eve Bendezu, Stephanie Fallcreek, and Catherine Whitehouse. "Intergenerational Community Schools: A New Practice for a New Time." *Educational Gerontology* 26 (2000): 761–70.

Winkels, Renate, Rick Artip, Maegan Tupinio, Susan Veldheer, Smitha C. Dandekar, and Daniel R. George. "Opportunities for Growth: A Community Gardening Pilot Intervention Pairing Adolescent and Young Adult Cancer Survivors with Master Gardeners." *Journal of Adolescent and Young Adult Oncology* 9, no. 1 (2020): 115–19.

CHAPTER 15

Applying Age-Friendly University Principles to Intergenerational Programs on College Campuses

Allison Merz, Nancy Morrow-Howell, Peggy Morton, *and* Ernest Gonzales

Abstract

Universities are positioned to be robust facilitators of intergenerational connections and educational opportunities. A set of principles by the Age-Friendly University Network serve as a useful framework for conceptualizing, implementing, evaluating, and scaling programs in university settings. This chapter reviews three examples of intergenerational programs on college campuses that exemplify age-friendly university principles. These include two distinct course models that bring students and older adults into consistent, meaningful contact with one another and an intergenerational home sharing program that reduces social isolation while increasing housing affordability. Student and participant statements of impact are included. Future planning for policy and advocacy working groups intended to address policy barriers that currently limit this impactful programming is discussed.

Key Words: intergenerational programming, age friendly universities, diversity, equity, and inclusion

When I'm 64 Course	Intergenerational Home Sharing	Service-Learning Course
Strengths/Impact Informed by AFU principles 1, 4, 7, and 10 Promotes student awareness of issues related to aging Provides academic and discussion space for intergenerational contact between undergraduate students and older adults in the community	**Strengths/Impact** Informed by AFU principles 1, 4, 7, 8, 9, and 10 Increases housing and education affordability for older adults and graduate students Reduces social isolation and loneliness through intergenerational living Reduces ageist beliefs across generations	**Strengths/Impact** Informed by AFU principles 1, 4, 7, 8, and 10 Boosts student understanding of the trajectory of Alzheimer's Disease and Related Dementias Builds reciprocally rewarding intergenerational relationships between students and mentors

When I'm 64 Course	Intergenerational Home Sharing	Service-Learning Course
Limitations Greater participation options available to older adults with high mobility and transportation access, but more options are needed for those with access needs Course is better at increasing objective knowledge about aging rather than shifting attitudes about aging	**Limitations** Policy barriers make home sharing not feasible for some older adults on public benefits Limited by paper-based application process that slows down matching	**Limitations** Maximum course enrollment caps limit availability Older adult mentors need to be in a particular window of their disease trajectory to be able to participate

Age-Friendly University Network

Across the globe, older adults and college students remain largely siloed. In recent years, multiple generations have increasingly united over shared challenges and opportunities related to economic security, social isolation, and healthy aging.[1] Although limited in number and scope, universities have proven to be a successful setting to foster diverse intergenerational collaboration and engagement on shared challenges.[2] The Age-Friendly University (AFU) Global Network is comprised of institutions of higher education around the world that are committed to becoming age-diverse and age-inclusive. (See for example *Handbook* chapters 6 and 17.)

Launched by Irish Prime Minister An Taoiseach and Professor Brian MacCraith at Dublin City University in 2012, the AFU network of global partners operates around a core set of ten principles to identify the distinctive contributions institutions of higher education can make in responding to the interests and needs of an aging population.[3] Arizona State University is now the lead organization of this network, connecting over fifty-one institutions in a learning collaborative.[4] The principles provide a framework for universities on how to address ageism and increase age-inclusivity through policy and practice.[5] Several of these principles invite intergenerational solutions to these issues and relate directly to existing intergenerational initiatives on college campuses (see box 15.1).

This chapter profiles three initiatives at the authors' universities that incorporate intergenerational approaches consistent with the above principles.

An Intergenerational Course: When I'm 64

When I'm 64 is a three-credit course offered to freshmen at Washington University in St. Louis. Washington University is a research-oriented, private university with about 8,000 undergraduate and 8,000 graduate students. When I'm 64 is part of an initiative called Beyond Boundaries, a program offered to incoming students who chose to explore large, social issues and interdisciplinary perspectives before committing to a major. Population aging and human longevity have been Beyond Boundaries topics from the beginning of

> **Box 15.1: Age-Friendly University (AFU) Principles that Invite Schools to Incorporate Intergenerational Approaches**
>
> Principle 1: To encourage the participation of older adults in all the core activities of the university, including educational and research programs.
> Principle 4: To promote intergenerational learning to facilitate the reciprocal sharing of expertise between learners of all ages.
> Principle 7: To increase the understanding of students of the longevity dividend and the increasing complexity and richness that aging brings to our society.
> Principle 8: To enhance access for older adults to the university's range of health and wellness programs and its arts and cultural activities.
> Principle 9: To engage actively with the university's own retired community.
> Principle 10: To ensure regular dialogue with organizations representing the interests of the aging population.
>
> Source: Reproduced by permission of Age-Friendly University Global Network, www.afugn.org.

the program. Now in its eighth year, the course has gained a positive reputation and has been fully enrolled each semester.

The premise of the course is that 18-year old students have a good chance to live into the eighth, ninth, and tenth decade of life and would be well served to understand the full implications of longevity.[6] Instructors explain that our social institutions, physical environments, and expectations about the life course were constructed when human life was nowhere near as long. They urge students to 'transform' these social and physical environments to ensure well-being for *their* long lives. Two perspectives are emphasized: the personal and the professional. How does this extension of human life relate to them personally (how might they plan differently) and professionally (how might their careers, as educators, business people, medical professionals, etc. be influenced by these demographic shifts)? The weekly topics are framed to emphasize the personal: Your World, Your Body, Your Health, Your Mind, Your Family, Your Community, Your Transportation, Your Career, Your Society. Students do weekly reflections on each topic, and they are instructed to write about the personal and professional implications of the information from class.

There is a weekly lecture with the full group as well as weekly discussion sessions where students are divided into smaller groups. On average, there have been seventy freshmen in the class every fall semester over the years. Three faculty from three different disciplines (social work, psychology, and occupational therapy) share the instructor role. These professors identify as gerontologists and co-design the curriculum of the course, including topics, readings, and exercises. Weekly discussion groups are taught by graduate students from the same three disciplines, plus public health and biomedicine. In an effort to expose undergraduates to various concepts associated with the field of gerontology, discussion leaders present their work and interests during a weekly lecture time; and guest speakers are invited from other disciplines that aren't represented on the teaching team. For example, several architects have come to work with students on designing an intergenerational space.

A signature feature of the course is inclusion of older adults as students. For the past six years, the faculty have formally sought volunteers from the community, orientated them to the class, and facilitated their participation through on-going communications and parking vouchers. The older adults receive the readings and all class materials but are not expected to do any of the assignments. They are typically drawn from two organizations: STL Village and Osher Life Long Learning Institute. The goal is ten to fifteen older students, and that level of participation has been achieved each year. Indeed, many of the older students take the course several times, participating in all aspects of the class—responding to questions and joining in group exercises.

Initially, the faculty only invited the older students to participate in the weekly lecture portion of the course. They did not ask them to attend the weekly small group sessions, thinking that it was too much to impose a second trip to campus where parking is difficult. But the older students wanted to be involved; so a more recent development is the inclusion of the older students in the weekly small group discussions. The graduate student instructors are pleased when the older students enrich their weekly discussions.

Among the assignments for the course, the younger students must complete an interview with an older person, based on a set of questions provided by the instructors. They can identify any older person for this hour-long interview, but many undergraduates choose to interview the older students in the class. Interview questions include significant life course events, major challenges, sources of strength/resilience, and big life lessons. Most of the older students agree to be interviewed, and in fact, most do more than one. Both the young and older students find the interviews very meaningful.

Using the university's assessment instruments, course ratings are consistently high, and feedback solicited informally has highlighted how important the students find the intergenerational component. Younger students report how much the older students enrich their experience and challenge the stereotypes of older people that they held. Older students report that the experience was transformative for them—being back in a college class, sitting among freshman students, participating in discussions, and sharing their experience. Instructors consistently heard from older students how the undergraduates debunked the stereotypes that they held toward younger generations. They also said that their faith in people and their hopes for the future were positively affected.

Two formal evaluations of the outcomes of the class have been completed. The aims of the first study were to document the effects of the semester-long course on students' knowledge of aging, attitudes toward older adults, and anxiety about their own aging, as well as to gain their thoughts about the effects of the experience on their choice of future undergraduate coursework, extracurricular activities, graduate education, and career.[7] The sample included seventy-eight freshman students, thirty-four of whom were enrolled in

When I'm 64. The controls were identified from a randomly-generated list of first-year students who were not enrolled in this course. Data were collected at the beginning and end of the semester using standardized measurements.

Students in the class had significantly more knowledge about aging and more positive explicit attitudes toward older adults at the end of the semester compared to students in the comparison group. However, neither group showed change in implicit attitudes toward older adults nor in anxiety about aging. There was no clear pattern of responses among students in the course as to the extent to which their future educational and career decisions would be affected. The course faculty concluded that their intergenerational and educational intervention was effective in increasing objective knowledge and attitudes about aging and older adults, but implicit attitudes and anxiety about aging appeared to be more difficult to influence.[8]

The second study sought to elucidate longer-term outcomes for the course.[9] In this study, students in the When I'm 64 course and students not enrolled in the course completed assessments before and after the course and once a year until they graduated. In total, 314 students who took the course and 353 not in the course contributed data. At all data collection periods, students rated the relevance of aging-related issues to their personal and professional lives on a scale from 0 (not at all relevant) to 5 (very relevant). Other outcomes of interest included whether they took subsequent aging-related courses, engaged in aging-related research, partook in extracurricular activities with older adults, and had summer plans involving older adults. Although personal and professional relevance increased significantly from baseline to the end of the course, subsequent observations suggested that relevance of aging-related issues returned to baseline over time. Throughout their college years, students in the course reported more engagement in aging-related courses, research, and extracurricular activities; but there was no difference between the groups on involvement with older adults over the summer. In sum, there were some long-term effects of the course; but the influence on personal and career trajectories after college has yet to be assessed.

Intergenerational Home Sharing

New York University's Center for Health and Aging Innovation (CHAI) launched an intergenerational home share program in 2018 to promote housing and economic security among graduate students and adults aged 60+. CHAI is located within NYU's Silver School of Social Work, which provides a robust and engaging environment for the education of professional social workers, offering BS, MSW, DSW, and PhD degrees. CHAI's intergenerational home share program is supported by the Eisner Foundation which identifies, advocates for, and invests in high-quality and innovative programs that unite multiple generations for the enrichment of communities.[10] (See *Handbook* chapter 3.)

Interest in intergenerational home sharing has gained the attention of the public, policymakers, and researchers because of the potential for facilitating mutual aid between generations, reducing social isolation, and fostering cross-generational cohesion. Of more than 195,000 surveyed college students, 14% of respondents reported experiencing homelessness and 48% experienced some form of housing insecurity in 2019.[11] The student housing crisis disproportionately impacts students from low-income families and students of color, perpetuating inequities in education and career growth.[12] Concurrently, housing affordability is not a single-generation issue. Nationally, more than 15 million older adults age 65+ (30%) have incomes below 200% of the federal poverty level.[13]

While the home share program temporarily suspended activity during the height of the COVID-19 pandemic to prioritize the health and safety of its participants, the program regained momentum in 2022. Through social media, in-person community events, and a feature in NYU's alumni newsletter, we reached approximately 2,000 older adults in 2022 with information about the program.[14] The program naturally draws the attention and interest of NYU graduate students in need of housing, and over the past year we reached 250 of them with minimal advertising.

NYU's intergenerational home sharing program, in partnership with the New York Foundation for Senior Citizens (NYFSC), places graduate students ("guests") in need of housing with adults age 60+ ("hosts") who have spare rooms to share. Guests and hosts undergo a detailed screening and matching process to ensure that the matches being made are socially, economically, and culturally sustainable for participants. Participants must each pass a background check, provide references, and provide proof of housing (host) or income (guest). The NYFSC then conducts 1:1 interviews with prospective participants to assess their roommate and lifestyle preferences. Next, the NYFSC hosts an introductory meeting between both parties to let them form a preliminary connection before agreeing to home share on a month-by-month basis.

On average in 2022, students contributed $1,037 each month to household expenses, more than 60% below New York City's average monthly cost for a studio apartment at $3,475.[15] Affordable, safe, and clean housing is important to health, irrespective of age, and is a proximal and primary objective of intergenerational home sharing. However, this unique kind of affordable housing initiative offers benefits that go beyond economic impact alone. The NYU Intergenerational Home Share Program has a core value of intergenerational cohesion—bringing together different generations to foster relationships and create understanding. Our program aims to promote the affordability of higher education, build equity among an increasingly diverse population, and facilitate social connections between older adults and generations of NYU students. We believe that forging relationships across generations opens us all to greater well-being, ranging from improved health outcomes to meaningful social bonds.

Ensuring those social bonds is at the heart of the intergenerational home share program. Becoming a home share host through CHAI not only contributes to social good by relieving students of housing insecurity, it offers New Yorkers and NYU alums age 60 + the chance to mentor a current NYU graduate student. Our cohort of hosts have opportunities to connect with one another via outings to museums, lunches, and theater events designed to foster a sense of community and increase access to the university's range of public activities.

Intergenerational home sharing shows great promise to promote intergenerational cohesion through the bi-directional decrease of age stigma. Hosts and students in the program report greater levels of acceptance of different generation members after participating. In a recent interview, one of our current hosts expressed a strong sense of "mutual respect and care" in her relationship with her guest, an NYU student completing her MFA in creative writing. A second host says that sharing her home with a younger person has increased her willingness to participate in other intergenerational programming and to continue home sharing with graduate students in the future.

While the benefits of intergenerational home sharing are compelling, there remain significant structural and cultural barriers to wider implementation. There are several public policy barriers limiting home sharing between generations and only a few facilitators. Current barriers include city and state-level taxation policies, municipal housing policies, limited program scalability options, and a relative lack of how-to manuals and toolkits for individuals or organizations to develop and grow programs.[16]

CHAI has produced research briefs and advocated at Senate hearings to demonstrate how re-categorizing income from home sharing as nontaxable income can contribute to affordable housing.[17] Additionally, CHAI is connecting a working group of older adults currently blocked from participating in home sharing because they receive a public benefit with students who are likewise passionate about the advantages of intergenerational living. This multi-generational policy and advocacy working group will present the vital aspects of intergenerational programming and home sharing to policymakers in New York and in Washington, D.C.

Service Learning on Alzheimer's Disease and Sharing the Lived Experience

In 2019 the NYU Langone Alzheimer's Disease and Related Dementias Family Support Program Buddy Program partnered with the NYU Silver School of Social Work to create a service-learning course. Service Learning (SL) pedagogy combines credit-bearing academic study with community service and reflection. The NYU Service Learning: Alzheimer's Disease (Buddy) course matches a person with early stage Alzheimer's and related dementias (the "mentor") with an undergraduate (the "buddy").

This course has been offered to undergraduates through NYU's Silver School of Social Work since 2019. The course provides an opportunity for students to spend weekly time with adults in the early stage of Alzheimer's and related dementias. The Buddy course was co-founded by Dr. Peggy Morton, Ann Burgunder, and Thea Micoli. This program is modeled on the Buddy Program founded by Dr. Darby Morhardt at the Northwestern Feinberg School of Medicine's Mezulum Center for Cognitive Neurology and Alzheimer's

Disease.[18] The Buddy course combines didactic course learning with weekly two-hour visits throughout the semester.

Since its inception, Buddy has consistently achieved maximum course enrollment (ten to fifteen students) over nine semesters and drawn maximum NYU waitlists. Ninety-four student buddies and ninety-four older adult mentors have completed the course. The high enrollments, interest, and waitlists for this course demonstrate the demand for this type of intergenerational service-learning course. A variety of majors across NYU are represented: pre-med, STEM, psychology, social work, economics, computer and data science, global public health, business, communication and speech disorders.

Student enrollment in this course has grown increasingly diverse, with most enrolled students identifying as Asian and South Asian. Many international students are drawn to this course because of the unique learning opportunity it presents and is likely due to cultural factors (e.g., coming from a society with higher levels of intergenerational solidarity, filial piety, and living in multigenerational households). Almost every semester, students visiting from the NYU Abu Dhabi campus and the NYU Shanghai campus have enrolled in the course.

Service Learning features the development of a dynamic, reciprocal relationship that leads to a greater understanding of various life experiences.[19] The Buddy course is unique in its benefits for students, older adults, family members, and caregivers. There are primary impacts to the paired buddy and mentor dyad as they find shared value in a relationship that fosters balanced reciprocity. Students gain direct experience with a person in the early stages of neurocognitive decline, an experience that challenges any preconceived ideas they may have had, especially stigma associated with cognitive impairment.[20] It is clear students' motivations are to gain a deeper, and more humane, perspective on the dynamic interactions between cognitive health and family caregiving. Many students are pre-med and STEM focused, while some bring additional disciplinary perspectives to the subject matter, such as social work, psychology, or economics.

Students report being inspired to find solutions to improve cognitive health and functioning. The course also disrupts misconceptions of older adults, particularly those with Alzheimer's Disease and related dementias, especially around capacities and abilities associated with aging and/or disease, as well as their attitudes and approaches to life. This finding resonates with other intergenerational programs that disrupt stereotypical attitudes about older adults and aging[21].[22] Mentors benefit from the companionship of the program and the weekly engagement with a person outside of their family/care team. Caregivers/family members receive respite because of the buddy. Altogether, since 2019 students have provided over 2,000 respite hours to families. The win-win-win experience of benefits is possible because of the service-learning course.

A secondary impact of the course is its influence on the professional and career trajectories of the student participants. Students of the course frequently report that taking this course encourages them to do gerontological and intergenerational work, thus impacting many more people in their professional careers. The following quotes highlight the experiences of Buddy course students:[23]

"I used to believe that losing one's memory is equivalent to losing one's life. 'Nick' approaches the situation quite differently. Nick's outlook on life—his 'seeing the glass as half full' attitude—has helped me connect and empathize with him even more profoundly." —Bachelor's Degree Student (2022)

"He didn't fit the archetypal, fallen-genius patient I was used to seeing in popular culture . . . These movies, popular and critically acclaimed as they are, are not representative of the typical patient." —Bachelor's Degree Student (2021)

"I became inspired by my experience to continue work in the field." —Bachelor's Degree Student (2021)

The following quotes highlight the experiences of mentors and caregivers:

"I remain hugely grateful for the program . . . it's a huge comfort and help to me." —Mentor and Caregiver (2019)

"'Beatrice' is truly a wonderful young person and 'Nora' really enjoys her visits. She has such a gentle but affirming manner. What a gift you have given us. Today I did ask her if she might help us in writing his memoirs." —Mentor and Caregiver (2021)

"We really like 'Sam'! He is respectful and calm, just what 'Gerry' needs. I especially appreciated his concern for Gerry, helping him up and making sure he was okay." —Mentor and Caregiver (2022)

Expanding AFU Principles in Action

Universities are especially well situated to make significant intergenerational impact. As these three programs demonstrate, there are numerous ways of taking the Age-Friendly University principles beyond age-segregated applications and using them to scale intergenerational programming and solutions. The AFU global network is constantly growing and innovating. Those interested in building more age-friendly institutions of higher education can follow the steps to join the AFU network of global partners outlined by the Gerontological Society of America.

Conclusion

Washington University's When I'm 64 course, CHAI's Intergenerational Home Share Program, and NYU's Buddy Program are each informed by AFU principles that encourage universities to expand the intentional development of intergenerationally-oriented services and communities. These programs uniquely increase access for older adults to university resources, engage with the university's alumni and retired network for program recruitment, and increase opportunities for intergenerational educational experiences. Each of these programs vitally contributes to intergenerational learning opportunities through a combination of coursework and lived experiences. Emerging policy and advocacy work developed by intergenerational working groups ensures regular dialogue with neighboring organizations that represent the interests of the aging population and advance intergenerational work.

These programs raise awareness of health and longevity, particularly social structures that constrain or optimize health, and bring generations together to address major challenges facing society: ageism, housing, cognitive health. Students across these programs report a greater understanding of, and connection with, another generation. Some of the younger students state that their career choices will be informed by the experience. From a psychosocial perspective, these programs help emerging adults accomplish important cognitive, social, and emotional development.[24] Older generations report improved levels of self-concept, greater self-esteem, and renewed confidence in their ability to give back to society—thereby offering some evidence that they too are accomplishing important milestones in later life.[25] In conclusion, population aging demands that we re-envision social structures to optimize health for everyone. We hope these programs, and others discussed in this *Handbook*, inspire readers to become involved in making the necessary structural changes.

Notes

1. Ernest Gonzales, et al., "A Survey of Diversity of Intergenerational Programming: Generations United and NYU." The Center for Health and Aging Innovation Issue Brief. (2022). http://hdl.handle.net/2451/64383.
2. Ernest Gonzales, "Universities as Age-Friendly Partners–NYU Intergenerational Housing Program." (2022): AARP's Equity by Design–Principles in Action Spotlight Series.
3. Gerontological Society of America, "Age Inclusivity in Higher Education," accessed November 20, 2023, https://www.geron.org/Resources/Age-Inclusivity-in-Higher-Education#:~:text=The%20Age%2DFriendly%20University%20.
4. Stephanie Firestone and Julia Glassman, "Universities as Age-Friendly Partners." AARP Principles in Action, (October 2022). https://www.aarpinternational.org/file%20library/build%20equity/aarp-universitypartnerships-casestudy-final.pdf.
5. Joann M. Montepare, "Introduction to the Special Issue—Age-Friendly Universities (AFU): Principles, Practices, and Opportunities." *Gerontology and Geriatrics Education*, 40 (2), (2019): 139–141.
6. Anne Case and Angus Deaton, "Life Expectancy in Adulthood Is Falling for Those without a BA Degree, but as Educational Gaps Have Widened, Racial Gaps Have Narrowed." *Proceedings of the National Academy of Sciences of the United States of America* 118, no. 11 (January 1, 2021). doi:10.1073/PNAS.2024777118.
7. Caroline Merz, et al., "When I'm 64: Effects of an Interdisciplinary Gerontology Course on First-Year Undergraduates' Perceptions of Aging." *Gerontology and Geriatrics Education*, 39, no. 1 (January 1, 2018): 35–45. https://search-ebscohost-com.proxy.library.nyu.edu/login.aspx?direct=true&db=gnh&AN=EP128502283&site = eds-live.
8. Ibid., 35–45.

9. Matthew Picchiello, et al., "Longitudinal Impact of an Interdisciplinary Course on Aging for First-Year Students." *Innovation in Aging*, 4, Supplement 1 (2020): 444. https://doi.org/10.1093/geroni/igaa057.1437.
10. The Eisner Foundation, "Our Focus," accessed November 27, 2023, https://eisnerfoundation.org/our-focus/.
11. Natlie Butler and Francis Torres, "Housing Insecurity and Homelessness among College Students," Bipartisan Policy Center. last modified August 15, 2023, https://bipartisanpolicy.org/blog/housing-insecurity-and-homelessness-among-college-students/.
12. Homeless Intervention Services of OC. accessed November 27, 2023, https://his-oc.org/.
13. Allison Merz, Rachel Kruchten, and Ernest Gonzales, "Who's Excluded? Public Housing Policy Barriers as a Block to Home Share Affordability Initiatives," The Center for Health and Aging Innovation, December 2022, http://hdl.handle.net/2451/64018.
14. Allison Merz, Perry Minella, and Ernest Gonzales, "Recruiting Diverse Older Adults for Intergenerational Home Sharing: Methods and Lessons Learned," The Center for Health and Aging Innovation, (February 2023). https://archive.nyu.edu/bitstream/2451/64384/4/Recruitment%20Brief%20of%20Diverse%20Older%20Adults_022423.pdf.
15. "Average Rent in New York, NY," renthop. accessed November 27, 2023, https://www.renthop.com/average-rent-in/new-york-ny#:~:text=Current%20Versus%20Historical%20NYC%20Rents&text=The%20median%20price%20of%20all,unchanged%20over%20the%20last%20year.
16. Ernest Gonzales, et al., "Intergenerational Home Sharing and Public Benefits: Barriers and Potential Solutions," The Center on Health and Aging Innovation, (March 2021). https://www.nyuchai.org/_files/ugd/ed7fa4_e5e132e4cf0349d1aff9fe587c750ae6.pdf?index=true.
17. Allison Merz, Rachel Kruchten, and Ernest Gonzales, "A Booming Online Presence: Examining Older Adult Online Activity for Intergenerational Program Recruitment," The Center for Health and Aging Innovation, (November 2022). https://archive.nyu.edu/bitstream/2451/64018/3/Issue%20Brief%20Policy_Home%20Share.pdf.
18. Darby Morhardt, "Reducing Stigma of Aging and Dementia through Experiential Learning," in *Older Women: Current and Future Challenges of Professionals with an Aging Population*, (2016): 253–69. https://doi.org/10.2174/9781681083490116010016.
19. Sue Ellen Henry and M. Lynn Breyfogle, "Toward a New Framework of 'Server' and 'Served': De(and Re)Constructing Reciprocity in Service-Learning Pedagogy," *International Journal of Teaching and Learning in Higher Education*, 17, no. 2 (2013): 27–35.
20. Peggy Morton and Dina Rosenfeld, "Review of Reconceptualizing Service-Learning during the COVID-19 Pandemic: Reflections and Recommendations." in *Shared Trauma, Shared Resilience during a Pandemic*, edited by Carol Tosone, (New York: Springer, 2021): 331–39.
21. Sadie E. Rubin, et al., "Challenging Gerontophobia and Ageism through a Collaborative Intergenerational Art Program," *Journal of Intergenerational Relationships*, 13, no. 3 (2015): 241–54, https://doi.org/10.1080/15350770.2015.1058213.
22. Ernest Gonzales, Nancy Morrow-Howell, and Pat Gilbert. "Changing Medical Students' Attitudes Toward Older Adults." *Gerontology and Geriatrics Education*, 31, no. 3 (July 1, 2010): 220–34. https://search-ebscohost-com.proxy.library.nyu.edu/login.aspx?direct=true&db=gnh&AN=EP52975916&site=eds-live.
23. Names have been changed to protect the identity of student, family, and mentor participants. This Service Learning course demonstrates how students' lives and professional careers are influenced by knowledge of and opportunities for improved care and cognitive health. Families overwhelmingly express gratitude for student/Buddy involvement. For more information or to get involved, contact Dr. Peggy Morton (peggy.morton@nyu.edu).
24. J. J. Arnett, "Emerging Adulthood: A Theory of Development from the Late Teens through the Twenties." *American Psychologist*, (January 1, 2000). https://search-ebscohost-com.proxy.library.nyu.edu/login.aspx?direct=true&db=edsbl&AN=RN078871957&site=eds-live.
25. Charles L. Slater, "Generativity Versus Stagnation: An Elaboration of Erikson's Adult Stage of Human Development." *Journal of Adult Development*, 10, no. 1 (January 2003): 53. doi:10.1023/A:1020790820868.

Bibliography

Arnett, J. J. "Emerging Adulthood: A Theory of Development from the Late Teens through the Twenties." *American Psychologist* (January 1, 2000). https://search-ebscohost-com.proxy.library.nyu.edu/login.aspx?direct=true&db=edsbl&AN=RN078871957&site=eds-live.

Butler, Natalie and Francis Torres. "Housing Insecurity and Homelessness among College Students." Bipartisan Policy Center. Last modified August 15, 2023, https://bipartisanpolicy.org/blog/housing-insecurity-and-homelessness-among-college-students/.

Case, Anne and Angus Deaton. "Life Expectancy in Adulthood Is Falling for Those without a BA Degree, but as Educational Gaps Have Widened, Racial Gaps Have Narrowed." *Proceedings of the National Academy of Sciences of the United States of America* 118, no. 11 (January 1, 2021). doi:10.1073/PNAS.2024777118.

Morhardt, Darby. "Reducing Stigma of Aging and Dementia through Experiential Learning." In *Older Women: Current and Future Challenges of Professionals with an Aging Population*, (2016): 253–69. https://doi.org/10.2174/9781681083490116010016.

The Eisner Foundation. "Our Focus." Accessed November 27, 2023. https://eisnerfoundation.org/our-focus/.

Firestone, Stephanie, and Julia Glassman. "Universities as Age-Friendly Partners." AARP Principles in Action (October 2022). https://www.aarpinternational.org/file%20library/build%20equity/aarp-universitypartnerships-casestudy-final.pdf.

Gerontological Society of America. "Age Inclusivity in Higher Education." Accessed November 20, 2023, https://www.geron.org/Resources/Age-Inclusivity-in-Higher-Education#:~:text=The%20Age%2DFriendly%20University%20.

Gonzales, Ernest. "Universities as Age-Friendly Partners–NYU Intergenerational Housing Program." AARP's Equity by Design–Principles in Action Spotlight Series. (2022).

Gonzales, Ernest, Rachel Kruchten, Emily Patrick, and Sheri Steinig. "A Survey of Diversity of Intergenerational Programming: Generations United and NYU." The Center for Health and Aging Innovation Issue Brief. (2022): http://hdl.handle.net/2451/64383.

Gonzales, Ernest, N. Levy, C. Whetung, and R. Kruchten. "Intergenerational Home Sharing and Public Benefits: Barriers and Potential Solutions." The Center on Health and Aging Innovation. (March 2021). https://www.nyuchai.org/_files/ugd/ed7fa4_e5e132e4cf0349d1aff9fe587c750ae6.pdf?index=true.

Gonzales, Ernest, Nancy Morrow-Howell, and Pat Gilbert. "Changing Medical Students' Attitudes toward Older Adults." *Gerontology and Geriatrics Education* 31, no. 3 (July 1, 2010): 220–34. https://search-ebscohost com.proxy.library.nyu.edu/login.aspx?direct=true&db=gnh&AN=EP52975916&site=eds-live.

Henry, Sue Ellen and M. Lynn Breyfogle. "Toward a New Framework of 'Server' and 'Served': De(and Re)Constructing Reciprocity in Service-Learning Pedagogy," *International Journal of Teaching and Learning in Higher Education* 17, no. 2 (2013): 27–35.

Homeless Intervention Services of OC. Accessed November 27, 2023. https://his-oc.org/.

Merz, Allison, Rachel Kruchten, and Ernest Gonzales. "A Booming Online Presence: Examining Older Adult Online Activity for Intergenerational Program Recruitment," The Center for Health and Aging Innovation (November 2022). https://archive.nyu.edu/bitstream/2451/64018/3/Issue%20Brief%20Policy_Home%20Share.pdf.

Merz, Allison, Rachel Kruchten, and Ernest Gonzales. "Who's Excluded? Public Housing Policy Barriers as a Block to Home Share Affordability Initiatives," The Center for Health and Aging Innovation (December 2022). http://hdl.handle.net/2451/64018.

Merz, Allison, Perry Minella, and Ernest Gonzales. "Recruiting Diverse Older Adults for Intergenerational Home Sharing: Methods and Lessons Learned." The Center for Health and Aging Innovation (February 2023). https://archive.nyu.edu/bitstream/2451/64384/4/Recruitment%20Brief%20of%20Diverse%20Older%20Adults_022423.pdf.

Merz, Caroline, Susan Stark, Nancy Morrow-Howell, and Brian Carpenter. "When I'm 64: Effects of an Interdisciplinary Gerontology Course on First-Year Undergraduates' Perceptions of Aging." *Gerontology and Geriatrics Education*, 39, no. 1 (January 1, 2018): 35–45. https://search-ebscohost-com.proxy.library.nyu.edu/login.aspx?direct=true&db=gnh&AN=EP128502283&site=eds-live.

Montepare, Joann M. "Introduction to the Special Issue—Age-Friendly Universities (AFU): Principles, Practices, and Opportunities." *Gerontology and Geriatrics Education*, 40 (2), 2019: 139–141.

Morton, Peggy and Dina Rosenfeld. "Review of Reconceptualizing Service-Learning during the COVID-19 Pandemic: Reflections and Recommendations." In *Shared Trauma, Shared Resilience during a Pandemic*, edited by Carol Tosone. New York: Springer, 2021: 331–39.

Picchiello, Matthew, Nancy Morrow-Howell, Susan Stark, and Brian Carpenter. "Longitudinal Impact of an Interdisciplinary Course on Aging for First-Year Students." *Innovation in Aging*, 4, Supplement 1 (December 16, 2020). https://www.ncbi.nlm.nih.gov/pmc/articles/PMC7741805/.

Renthop. "Average Rent in New York, NY." Accessed November 27, 2023, https://www.renthop.com/average-rent-in/new-york-ny#:~:text=Current%20Versus%20Historical%20NYC%20Rents&text=The%20median%20price%20of%20all,unchanged%20over%20the%20last%20year.

Rubin, Sadie E., Tracey L. Gendron, Cortney A. Wren, Kelechi C. Ogbonna, Ernest G. Gonzales, and Emily P. Peron. "Challenging Gerontophobia and Ageism through a Collaborative Intergenerational Art Program." *Journal of Intergenerational Relationships*, 13, no. 3 (2015): 241–54, https://doi.org/10.1080/15350770.2015.1058213.

Slater, Charles L. "Generativity Versus Stagnation: An Elaboration of Erikson's Adult Stage of Human Development." *Journal of Adult Development*, 10, no. 1 (January 2003): 53. doi:10.1023/A:1020790820868.

CHAPTER 16

Intergenerational Service-Learning Combats Social Isolation

Nicole Shults, Cynthia Wilkerson, Jane Langridge, *and* Barbara Bringuier

Abstract

This chapter discusses the work of Little Brothers–Friends of the Elderly (LBFE Boston) in preventing and relieving isolation and loneliness through intergenerational programs. By pairing two self-reported lonely generations, the organization has found that both age groups experience an increase in feelings of belonging, community engagement, and a decrease in feelings of loneliness. This chapter describes a program design based on equity that brings older and younger people together in relationships as a successful intervention for social isolation. Further consideration is given to providing multilingual and multicultural groups in urban, public, and affordable housing.

Key Words: social isolation, community engagement, loneliness, intergenerational friendship, equity

LBFE Boston Intergenerational Service-Learning Initiatives

CitySites	Digital Dividends
Strengths/impact • Utilizes college/university resources • Creates strong community presence • Eliminates need for older adults to find transportation • International students expand linguistic and cultural capacity of organization • Reduces feelings of loneliness • Creates a social safety net • Prevents isolation and loneliness	**Strengths/Impact** • Provides tech access and literacy to connect older adults virtually • Intergenerational model provides a platform for different ages to interact • Demonstrated increase in comfort/ability to use technology • Facilitates access to other services (like Affordable Connectivity) • Reduces feelings of loneliness

CitySites	Digital Dividends
Limitations • Transportation for students may be difficult to access • Recruiting participants takes time and trust • More difficult to set up in rural areas without local colleges and universities • Not all colleges have service-learning or community engagement infrastructure	**Limitations** • Transportation for students may be difficult • Program can be expensive (if devices and connectivity are provided) • Different learning levels can be difficult to teach • More difficult to set up in rural areas without local colleges and universities

Needs Statement

Modern culture and technology have given humans the tools to connect and communicate in more ways than ever before. In addition to old-fashioned in-person visits, we have the post office, television, phone calls, texting, video chat, social media, and countless apps that create connections. But despite the tools at our disposal, we live in a lonely world. In fact, reports from The Cigna Group[1] show that 58 percent of adults in the United States are lonely. A deeper look reveals that loneliness and isolation affect some more than others. Young people have higher reported rates of loneliness: 79 percent of young adults aged eighteen to twenty-four and 41 percent of adults over the age of sixty-six report feeling lonely. Furthermore, people with lower incomes are more likely to feel lonely: 63 percent of adults with incomes less than $50,000/year and 72 percent of adults who receive health benefits through Medicaid are lonely. People in minority racial groups are also reporting higher levels of loneliness: 75 percent of Hispanic and 68 percent of Black Americans are lonely. Loneliness is not only a mental health issue, but it is a detriment to physical health as well—a fact that has public health agencies across the globe worried. According to a 2023 report from the U.S. Surgeon General,[2]

- lonely individuals have a 26 percent and 29 percent increased risk for premature death and heart disease, respectively,
- lonely individuals have a 32 percent and 50 percent increased risk of stroke and dementia, respectively, and
- only 16 percent of Americans feel attached to their local community.

These data present a strong case for intergenerational programs as an intervention to prevent and relieve social isolation and loneliness. There is additional urgency to create intergenerational opportunities with a strong focus on racial and economic diversity. Resources must be directed to building strong communities of belonging. Supportive programming budgets at public and affordable housing communities vary greatly and often provide urgent services, such as benefit assistance, medical care coordination, and nutritional services.

LBFE Boston seeks to expand the range of activities and opportunities available to older adults living in these buildings by mobilizing community assets like schools, universities, mutual aid, and civic groups. A collaborative effort allows resident service coordinators to expand resources in the buildings they manage to better mirror the opportunities for engagement, education, and creativity in market-rate senior housing communities. In LBFE Boston's case, they utilize the great number of local colleges and universities to provide social, tech, and creative opportunities via intergenerational programs. Bringing together the young and the old for social programming addresses loneliness and isolation for two high-risk age groups and is a cost-effective, efficient, and mutually beneficial solution.

Another positive effect of intergenerational programming is its ability to address ageism—"one of the last socially acceptable prejudices."[3] Research has shown that across the age span there is an implicit and explicit bias against older adults,[4] often resulting in negative effects on health, well-being, and quality of life. These effects are seen in the workplace, healthcare system, and even older adults' opinions about themselves and their own capabilities. In American culture, messages are clear from childhood that aging is bad, reinforcing stereotypes that older people are slow, have poor memory, can't keep up, and are incapable. The messages are internalized as we age. Preconceptions about aging lead to negative feelings and higher levels of stress, which is linked to higher prevalence of disease. In fact, negative feelings about aging are directly linked to a higher prevalence of all eight of the most expensive health conditions among Americans.[5] In reality, many people have positive experiences as they age; they have time and energy for hobbies, they benefit from wisdom that comes with life experience, and they are more settled into their lives and personhood.

Intergenerational programs are a positive solution to addressing ageism, dispelling stereotypes, and creating more positive associations with aging. For example, an older CitySites program participant shared the following: "You feel that youth, not all but some, think that we older people are not worth it. That we can't do things. Because a lot of youth think like that. I think young people who spend time with us have learned and understood that we do know, that we can. We are not dying yet and we have high self-esteem. Whatever comes our way we can take on, we never say no, are always positive and always can." A younger CitySites participant noted, "I met a 95 year old . . . she likes to dance a lot and she likes to party a lot. So I'm like . . . that sounds so fun! Growing up doesn't sound that bad. Because as you grow older, it's like you're a teenager again . . . so I guess it made me . . . look forward to getting older."

A Global Perspective

When it comes to an aging population, the United States is not alone. Prior to 1820, the global life expectancy was on average twenty-five years,[6] and then quite suddenly things changed—a lot.

An increase in longevity began in Europe in the 1800s, and in the 1900s, the average human lifespan nearly doubled, going from 45 to over 85 years in a 150-year time frame. While there are many factors that influenced this, the key factors include clean water, improved hygiene, the advent of vaccines and antibiotics, and improved treatments for diseases such as heart disease and cancer.

Many still believe that an aging population and its accompanying challenges such as isolation and loneliness are just an issue in Europe and North America, but according to the World Population Aging 2017 Report, this is simply not the case. That year, the elder population (60 years and over) was 962 million around the globe, more than twice as high as in 1980 when the number was 382 million. According to UN demographic projections, by 2050, the count will increase to 2.1 billion.[7] The oldest of old people, those over a hundred, although smaller in total numbers, are the group growing the most quicky—or they were before the pandemic, when they died not just because of their increased risk but also because policies focused on children and younger adults, even though older people were at higher risk. Here, we have another example of "socially acceptable ageism." Old age often gets blamed for problems that are actually the product of policies that don't value or prioritize old people.

The UN Population Division's demographic projections also show that by 2050, 35 percent of Europe's population will be made up of the elderly, followed by North America (28 percent), Latin America and the Caribbean (25 percent), Asia (24 percent), Oceania (23 percent) and Africa (9 percent).

The World Health Organization has found that the growing numbers of older people adds to the global crisis of social isolation: in some countries up to one in three older people are lonely.[8] WHO data from 2000–2019 suggest that the young and the old are the loneliest. This signifies the importance of intergenerational programs and is a reason why Little Brothers–Friends of the Elderly continues to develop and grow such programs.

The Case for IG Programs

The U.S. Census Bureau revealed that in 2020 older adults over age sixty-five made up nearly 17 percent of the population, and the rate at which our country is aging is increasing steadily.[9] The time has come for a cultural shift in the United States that values the abilities and contributions of older adults in our society as a whole and in local communities. Individuals need to be exposed to more positive associations with aging to view their own longevity in an optimistic light and add more good years to their lives. Younger members of the workforce should have positive, supportive interactions with older adults during their formative years. The need for intergenerational programs has never been higher, and the world is starting to see that. However, long before intergenerational programs entered the common vernacular, organizations across the globe were doing just that—bringing the young and old together in fellowship and community. One such organization is Little Brothers–Friends of the Elderly.

Organization History

The COVID-19 pandemic brought loneliness and isolation to the forefront of conversation in 2020 and beyond. Governments and public health agencies began to research its effects as a public health issue. But long before "social isolation" became part of the public zeitgeist, the nonprofit organization Little Brothers–Friends of the Elderly (LBFE) was addressing loneliness among older adults. Its founder, Armand Marquiset, born outside of Paris in 1900, famously said, "The greatest poverty is the poverty of love." And while the language may seem a little flowery in today's context, the significance is as relevant as ever. We now know that without social connections, humans have a greater risk of memory loss, poor health outcomes, and early death.

In honor of his grandmother, Madame de Laumont, Marquiset dedicated his life to service and founded several organizations to support the poor and underprivileged, including Les Petits Frères des Pauvres (PFP) in France (known as Little Brothers–Friends of the Elderly in the United States). Like most charities, PFP began with a grassroots effort. Noticing the needs of older adults suddenly living alone in post-WWII Paris, Marquiset began visiting, bringing food, and celebrating holidays with older adults. His philanthropy caught on with his friends, who joined the work and started to refer to themselves as the "little brothers of the elderly." Slowly, more young people were attracted to the mission, and chapters began to form across Europe and North America. Today, LBFE has chapters in ten countries and partnerships across the globe, all based on the notion that "living is more than a roof over our heads and food on the table. In addition to offering material and physical support, we believe that living requires the presence of people who care about us and about whom we care. Living requires the little touches that bring joy, like flowers, music and shared laughter."

In the United States, LBFE is a national network of nonprofit volunteer-based organizations committed to relieving isolation and loneliness among older adults. It gives people of goodwill the opportunity to join the elderly in friendship and celebration of life. There are currently chapters in Chicago, Houghton, MI, Boston, Cincinnati, OH, and San Francisco. Each U.S. chapter is an independent entity, bound by the same mission but carried out in a variety of ways unique to the community it serves. Intergenerational programs have been especially successful in the Boston chapter.

LBFE Boston opened its doors in 1979 delivering holidays meals to older adults who would be home alone on Christmas Day. As the organization became established in the community, it continued to host regular luncheons and holiday dinners as well as holiday meal deliveries on Easter, Thanksgiving, and Christmas. It soon introduced a Friendly Visiting program matching volunteers with older adults who were without social support, as well as a small emergency food pantry and medical escort program.

Under new leadership, in 2015 the organization performed a comprehensive community needs assessment and program evaluation. At the same time, UMass Boston had just published the Aging in Boston Report,[10] and the city of Boston began the process of becoming an age-friendly city, later publishing the Age-Friendly Boston Action Plan 2017.[11] The latter focused on a survey of older residents in the areas of housing, transportation, outdoor spaces and buildings, community support and health services, civic engagement and employment, social participation, respect and social inclusion, and communication and information. From these reports, LBFE Boston learned important lessons:

1. Diversity among older adults in Boston changed immensely from 1979 to 2015. Boston became a minority-majority city, and 19 percent of older adults were linguistically isolated, meaning they spoke little to no English. LBFE Boston needed to focus on creating programming and services in more languages.
2. Many low-income older adults living alone in Boston lived in public/affordable housing buildings. LBFE Boston needed to increase outreach efforts in these communities.
3. Older adults wanted more social programs in their own neighborhoods. LBFE Boston needed to move programming from its central office into the community.
4. Older adults wanted more diversity of programs. LBFE Boston's current programs were replicated by several other organizations. It needed to provide a different type of program to appeal to new participants.
5. Ageism is a concern for older adults in Boston. LBFE Boston needed to address the root causes of ageism and create intergenerational spaces.

With these insights, LBFE Boston embarked on a major journey of transformation. The intergenerational CitySites program was piloted in 2015 and fully implemented by 2017. This new community-based program model became the flagship intergenerational program and the basis for its future expansion.

Boston Program Overview

Based on the demographic and diversity information gathered from the Aging in Boston report and the Age Friendly Boston Action Plan, LBFE Boston sought to create a community-based program model that brought intergenerational programming into the neighborhoods and communities where older adults lived. Further, LBFE Boston prioritized those who historically have less access to social programming—non-English speakers and older adults living in public and affordable housing communities in hard-to-reach neighborhoods.

LBFE Boston's community needs assessment revealed a largely untapped resource: colleges and universities. For a small organization, the largest constraints on program transformation were human and capital resources. Universities could provide students seeking community experiences, access to graduate assistants seeking research opportunities, networking opportunities with community partners, and a potential staff pipeline. There is also a large number of international students and language learners available to provide programs in the preferred languages of participants. (In spring 2023 LBFE Boston programs were offered in eight different languages). An added benefit to community engagement programs working with colleges and universities is the link between course credit and community service, ensuring regular student participation in programs.

Once identified, LBFE Boston staff began creating partnerships with the public housing authority, affordable housing management companies, and resident task forces. The decision to host programs in the common spaces of public/affordable housing buildings was an important one. The Age-Friendly surveys revealed that transportation was a major challenge for older adults living in Boston. This is especially true for low-income and minority populations who live in transportation deserts that have fewer public transportation options, often requiring several connections and long commute times that would deter older adults from attending programs. Bringing the programs to the spaces where older adults live removed financial and accessibility barriers. Further, public/affordable housing communities often lack funding to provide social engagement opportunities to their residents. The CitySites program allows resident service coordinators to bring in programming at no cost to build community, engage residents with their young neighbors, and share their interests and talents.

Strong community partnerships are key elements to the intergenerational program model. Without the support of building partners and university staff, the model fails. It is important that partnerships be made on an organizational rather than individual level so that in the inevitable case of staff turnover, programs can continue without disruption. A strong partnership is not dependent on a single champion but is baked into the culture and operations of each collaborator. LBFE Boston has discovered that with higher-education partnerships it is beneficial to start by contacting service-learning programs, community engagement offices, or specific experiential learning programs. This leads to longer-term sustainability year after year, as the partnership is not tied to a specific professor, one-time grant funding, or a student project.

With all the pieces in place, the CitySites program became replicable, effective, and sustainable. Small groups of college-aged students host weekly social activities in public/affordable senior housing communities. One student is assigned the role of "team lead" and prepares the activities, takes attendance, administers evaluation surveys, and manages the group. The same students and older participants meet at the same time and place every week for an entire semester and build relationships over the course of several months. Often students return to programs after the semester ends to maintain the friendships they built throughout their college careers. There are several instances of students and older adults remaining friends for years even after students graduate and move away from Boston. The specific activities vary from site to site depending on the talents, interests, and recommendations from the older and younger participants. All participants decide together what their particular CitySites program will look like, such as conversation circles, arts and crafts, board games, language learning, service projects, music, and tech cafes. For example, students from an advanced Mandarin course were paired with a building in Chinatown where most of the residents spoke Chinese. This group used their time together to practice speaking with each other in Chinese and English to broaden their language skills. One older adult said that after living in the United States for decades he couldn't believe that young Americans wanted to learn *his* language and what an honor it was to share his culture. At another site, participants discovered that many among them were musicians. The following week they brought their instruments down, shared the music they were interested in, and even played together. The activities matter less than the intended outcomes: reduced loneliness and isolation, reduced generational gap between younger and older participants, improved social functioning of older participants, improved quality of life for older participants, and reduced age-related stigma. The activities serve as a platform to bring older and younger people together in a low-stress, low-pressure environment. Figure 16.1 shows LBFE Boston's intergenerational program logic model and the importance of bringing an entire community together to reach the desired outcomes.

As previously mentioned, the COVID-19 pandemic led to increased levels of loneliness and isolation.[12] The world turned to the internet to maintain social contact with family and friends; however, according to the Pew Research Center, 75 percent of people over age sixty-five and only 44 percent of people over the age of eighty use the internet.[13] The same study also found that technology adoption, while increasing among older adults, is tied to educational attainment and household income. Only 46 percent of older adults with annual incomes lower than $30,000 go online, and only 27 percent of low-income older adults have high-speed internet at home. During the height of the pandemic, LBFE Boston provided tablets to many program participants and moved all its programs online. But despite best efforts, trends in attendance revealed that non–native English speakers and older adults living in public housing were falling behind. This presented a new challenge to creating intergenerational friendships.

In response to the "digital divide" during the pandemic, LBFE Boston launched Digital Dividends in 2021. To fully address digital literacy, three elements are essential: access to a device, access to internet connectivity, and the knowledge and skills to use the internet.[14] The new Digital Dividends program follows the intergenerational CitySites model to address all three barriers to digital literacy. It is hosted in public senior housing buildings across the City of Boston and relies heavily on the support and collaboration of community partners, including the Boston Housing Authority, local Aging Service Access Points who provide the resident service coordination to those buildings, service-learning university partners, and public and private foundations. LBFE provides laptops to all older adults who register for a Digital Dividends program free of charge (generally twelve to fifteen older adults in

Figure 16.1 LBFE Boston logic model.

Source: LBFE Boston, 2022

each class). The laptop is theirs to keep. LBFE also provides each participant with a prepaid, unlimited hotspot for internet connectivity for the duration of the class. After the class, LBFE helps older adults register for the Affordable Connectivity Program through the Federal Communications Commission for a longer-term, affordable solution.

The final key element of Digital Dividends is instruction. Young adults are digital natives and are uniquely qualified to help older adults learn. Small groups of three to five students host weekly Digital Dividends programs in the common areas of senior public housing buildings. Instruction is a mix of classroom, independent, and one-on-one learning. Generally, a topic (chosen by the program participants) is discussed in the larger group, and then older adults have exercises to practice that new skill. Topics include computer basics, using email, social media, YouTube, Spotify, online shopping, fraud, and video conferencing. In addition to tech training, Digital Dividends provides opportunities for older and younger adults to meet and form relationships. In one class, students helped older adults use Spotify to listen to music. One student was surprised to learn that the older adult she was helping listened to Beyoncé, her favorite artist. The pair bonded over their musical tastes, listened to songs together, and created a shared playlist to introduce each other to new music. One refrain that is heard repeatedly at LBFE Boston's intergenerational program is "I really didn't think I'd have much in common with someone much older/younger than me, but I do!"

LBFE Boston has implemented a continuous feedback loop between staff and program participants and is constantly seeking ways to evolve and improve. One of the most important elements of intergenerational programming is to view the relationship through an equity lens. In any successful relationship, each party gives *and* receives. It is important to avoid adopting a "savior" role. To create this culture of equity, LBFE Boston refers to "older and younger participants" or "students and older adults" and avoids using the words volunteer, recipient, beneficiary, or client. On the first day of each new program session, older and younger participants develop a code of conduct and group agreements to set shared expectations. All participants are asked to complete feedback surveys and have similar outcome goals. The effects of loneliness and isolation are the same for humans of all ages, and both younger and older generations are affected. A strong intergenerational program addresses the needs of all participants equally.

Evaluation

To create a culture of learning and improvement, LBFE Boston included a formal monitoring and evaluation plan in its program design. Taking advantage of the resources provided by local colleges and universities, LBFE Boston partners with the Public Evaluation Lab at Northeastern University (NU-PEL) to develop an overall evaluation plan and strategy. With NU-PEL's support, LBFE Boston surveys program participants, conducts focus groups, and holds one-on-one interviews to measure participant satisfaction and to refine and measure longer-term program outcomes.

The mission of LBFE is to relieve loneliness and isolation; the primary desired outcome for programs is for all participants, regardless of age, to report lower levels of loneliness and more social connection. Surveys also measure whether participation in weekly intergenerational activities increases participants' overall sense of connection to their neighbors and to their community at large. More specifically, older participants are asked about their willingness to ask for, or provide help to, their neighbors. This is to evaluate whether the peer-to-peer aspect of LBFE Boston's programs helps to create social safety nets for older adults where they live. Surveys also measure how much participants' feelings about aging and people of different ages change as a result of their participation in weekly intergenerational events.

LBFE measures similar metrics for younger participants to see if intergenerational engagement increases their sense of connection and affects their views on aging and on people of different ages. For younger adults, surveys also attempt to ascertain if they feel any more likely to consider working with older adults in the future, either personally or professionally. At least one former LBFE Boston student participant has changed their career trajectory from political science to working with older adults as an activities coordinator at a nursing home on Long Island.

Tracking program participants' responses to these questions allows the organization to gauge whether short-term goals for programs are being met—that is, improved tech comfort and literacy, digital engagement, social connection, and engagement with the larger community—and to refine intermediate and long-term goals for programs.

Our most recent data analyses of older program participant surveys (Fall 2021 and Spring 2022) found that LBFE "definitely" influenced maintaining social connectedness. Among survey respondents

- a majority felt a "medium" or "somewhat" level of connection with neighbors,
- a majority was "very willing" to help/offer help to their neighbors, and
- a majority felt "not lonely" or a "neutral" level of loneliness.

Mixed-method analyses of Fall 2021 and Spring 2022 participant data found

- improved quality of life,
- increased social engagement/connectedness, and
- decreased feelings of loneliness

Additionally, CitySites data indicate the following:

- Participants report a general trend of "happiness" about aging and intergenerational relationships.

- LBFE has been successful and helpful despite the pandemic.
- A majority of participants have been attending for more than a year, showing long-lasting participation in the program.

International Intergenerational Programs

Beyond combatting isolation of the elderly, intergenerational activities organized by LBFE allow different generations to meet and develop social links. In France, Petits Frères des Pauvres (PFP) recently completed a study, "Isolement des personnes âgées et liens entre générations," with CSA-Research about the links between generations. Respondents were over sixty and between eighteen and thirty years of age. The main findings of the study are that the following:

- Most intergenerational relations are in families and at the workplace.
- Friends are generally from the same generation. So, when people get older, they may become isolated when they and their friends lose mobility.
- Older and young people have the desire to meet, but it is not easy. Young people note a lack of opportunities to meet older adults, and elders believe that it is due to their different lifestyles.
- Older adults think that younger generations are not interested in them and admit they sometimes don't understand the world of the youngest.

For LBFE Boston, as well as all the organizations that make up the International Federation of PFP, mixing generations encourages young and old to get to know each other and build true friendships. Mattering to someone who matters to you helps to combat ageism and to build value between generations.

Activities proposed around the world by LBFE are similar and have the same objectives. In Ireland, Friends of the Elderly implemented a "friendly calls" program that consists of having fifteen- to sixteen-year-olds call older adults on a weekly basis. In France, PFP implemented different programs giving opportunities to the young to be volunteers. In all the regions of France, PFP established IT workshops so the older adults can learn new technologies thanks to help from younger generations. Evaluation of these programs showed that for older adults, the most valuable aspect of the program is the opportunity and time to converse with young people. For the young people, the most valuable aspect of the program is the opportunity to share their knowledge but also to realize the difficulties older adults have using new technologies and the necessity to adapt their behaviors to older adults. For more than twenty years, PFP has been providing opportunities for young people ages of eighteen to twenty-five to do their "Service Civique" (full-time year of volunteering) with the elderly. Thanks to this opportunity and its associated activities (visits, workshops, etc.) young people discover not only the challenges that come with aging but also the richness of older adults. True friendships are often forged.

PFP also has an intergenerational vacation program enabling older people to enjoy a holiday despite their isolation and financial circumstances. The vacation program is also a way to involve young people for fifteen days during the summer. As with any friends, vacations are often the best way to get to know each other better and deepen a relationship. And in Hamburg, Germany, Freunde alter Menchen offers a Generation Nachbarschaft program whose aim is to create and strengthen intergenerational neighborhood networks, making them more welcoming to older adults in both the long and short term. In sum, members of the International Federation of PFP are committed to providing opportunities for generations to meet and to building a society where all ages have a place and can make valuable contributions.

According to the PFP study, the relationship between generations is vital to 63 percent of those age sixty and older and to 50 percent of eighteen- to thirty-year-olds. PFP participants rated activities that allow generations to meet as follows:

Activity	For 60+ (%)	For 18–30-year-olds (%)
Encourage volunteering at all ages	90	84
Raise young people's awareness of the importance of intergenerational relations	90	83
Propose initiatives that enable children and the elderly to meet in schools, daycare, or retirement homes	89	83
Create the conditions to ensure that all generations are welcome in places for socializing	87	81
Develop vacation resorts that make it easier to welcome grandparents, parents, and grandchildren	81	84
Offer collective housing with common areas to facilitate exchanges between generations	79	82
Enable elderly people to earn extra income by looking after children	66	72
Share a home with a young/elderly person	63	68

Conclusion

Recent attention to the harmful effects of loneliness and isolation has brought much-needed urgency to addressing the issue.[15] However, despite the greater availability of research on social isolation, there is still a very limited data set on tested and evaluated interventions. LBFE Boston's CitySites and Digital Dividends evaluation efforts, along with the evaluation of programs across other PFP chapters in Europe and North America, have revealed promising results that intergenerational programs are a viable, sustainable, and replicable intervention to prevent and relieve isolation and loneliness among older and younger adults. These results are largely attributable to LBFE Boston's community-informed programming model that solicits continuous feedback from program participants.

While the demographic, political, economic, and cultural landscape of Boston is, like all cities and towns, unique, LBFE Boston's community-based intergenerational program model could be adapted for use in any community. A targeted needs assessment that focuses on local resources and available assets will open doors to partnerships and collaboration that bring generations together through the platform of friendship.

Notes

1. Cigna Group, *The Loneliness Epidemic Persists: A Post-Pandemic Look at the State of Loneliness among U.S. Adults* (Bloomfield, CT: Cigna, 2021), https://newsroom.thecignagroup.com/loneliness-epidemic-persists-post-pandemic-look.
2. Vivek Murthy, "Our Epidemic of Loneliness and Isolation: The U.S. Surgeon General's Advisory on the Healing Effects of Social Connection and Community," Office of the Surgeon General, 2023, https://www.hhs.gov/sites/default/files/surgeon-general-social-connection-advisory.pdf.
3. Kristen Weir, "Ageism Is One of the Last Socially Acceptable Prejudices. Psychologists Are Working to Change That," *American Psychological Association Monitor on Psychology* 54, no. 2 (2023): 36.
4. William J. Chopik and Hannah L Giasson, "Age Differences in Explicit and Implicit Age Attitudes across the Life Span," *Gerontologist* 57, no. 2 (2017): S169–77, https://doi.org/https://doi.org/10.1093/geront/gnx058.
5. Becca R. Levy et al. "Ageism Amplifies Cost and Prevalence of Health Conditions," *Gerontologist* 60, no. 1 (2018): 174–81, https://doi.org/10.1093/geront/gny131.
6. Max Roser et al., "Life Expectancy," OurWorldInData.org, 2013, 'https://ourworldindata.org/life-expectancy.
7. "World Population Ageing 2017," United Nations, Department of Economic and Social Affairs, Population Division, https://www.un.org/en/development/desa/population/publications/pdf/ageing/WPA2017_Report.pdf
8. "Social Isolation and Loneliness among Older Adults," United Nations Department of Economic and Social Affairs, 2021, https://www.who.int/teams/social-determinants-of-health/demographic-change-and-healthy-ageing/social-isolation-and-loneliness.
9. Zoe Caplan, "U.S. Older Population Grew From 2010 to 2020 at Fastest Rate Since 1880 to 1890," U.S. Dept of Commerce, 2023, https://www.census.gov/library/stories/2023/05/2020-census-united-states-older-population-grew.html.
10. Jan Mutchler et al., "Aging in Boston: Preparing Today for a Growing Tomorrow," Gerontology Institute Publications, 2014, https://scholarworks.umb.edu/gerontologyinstitute_pubs/98/.
11. Jan Mutchler et al., "Age Friendly Boston Action Plan," 2017, https://www.boston.gov/sites/default/files/embed/f/full_report_0.pdf.
12. Mareike Ernst et al., "Loneliness Before and During the Covid-19 Pandemic: A Systematic Review with Meta-Analysis," *American Psychologist* 77, no. 5 (2022): 660–77. https://doi.org/10.1037/amp0001005.
13. Monica Anderson and Andrew Perrin, "Tech Adoption Climbs among Older Adults," Pew Research Center, Internet, Science & Tech, May 30, 2020, https://www.pewresearch.org/internet/2017/05/17/tech-adoption-climbs-among-older-adults/.
14. John Horrigan and Erin York Cornwell, "Exposing the Hidden Connectivity Crisis for Older Adults: Aging Connected," 2020, https://agingconnected.org/wp-content/uploads/2021/02/Aging-Connected_Exposing-the-Hidden-Connectivity-Crisis-for-Older-Adults.pdf.
15. Murthy, "Our Epidemic of Loneliness."

Bibliography

Anderson, Monica, and Andrew Perrin. "Tech Adoption Climbs among Older Adults." Pew Research Center: Internet, Science & Tech. May 30, 2020. https://www.pewresearch.org/internet/2017/05/17/tech-adoption-climbs-among-older-adults/.

Caplan, Zoe. "U.S. Older Population Grew from 2010 to 2020 at Fastest Rate Since 1880 to 1890." U.S. Dept of Commerce. 2023. https://www.census.gov/library/stories/2023/05/2020-census-united-states-older-population-grew.html.

Chopik, William J., and Hannah L Giasson. "Age Differences in Explicit and Implicit Age Attitudes across the Life Span." *Gerontologist* 57, no. 2 (2017): S169–77. https://doi.org/https://doi.org/10.1093/geront/gnx058

Cigna Group. *The Loneliness Epidemic Persists: A Post-Pandemic Look at the State of Loneliness among U.S. Adults*. Bloomfield, CT: Cigna, 2021. https://newsroom.thecignagroup.com/loneliness-epidemic-persists-post-pandemic-look.

Ernst, Mareike, Daniel Niederer, Antonia M. Werner, Sara J. Czaja, Christopher Mikton, Anthony D. Ong, et al. "Loneliness Before and During the Covid-19 Pandemic: A Systematic Review with Meta-Analysis." *American Psychologist* 77, no. 5 (2022): 660–77. https://doi.org/10.1037/amp0001005.

Horrigan, John, and Erin York Cornwell. "Exposing the Hidden Connectivity Crisis for Older Adults: Aging Connected." 2020. https://agingconnected.org/wp-content/uploads/2021/02/Aging-Connected_Exposing-the-Hidden-Connectivity-Crisis-for-Older-Adults.pdf.

Levy, Becca R., Martin D. Slade, E-Shien Chang, Sneha Kannoth, Shi-Yi Wang, et al. "Ageism Amplifies Cost and Prevalence of Health Conditions." *Gerontologist* 60, no. 1 (2018): 174–81. https://doi.org/10.1093/geront/gny131.

Mutchler, Jan, Caitlin Coyle, and Hayley Gleason. "Age-Friendly Boston Action Plan." 2017. https://www.boston.gov/sites/default/files/embed/f/full_report_0.pdf.

Mutchler, Jan E., Bernard A. Steinman, Caitlin Coyle, Hayley Gleason, Jiyoung Lyu, Ceara Somerville, et al. "Aging in Boston: Preparing Today for a Growing Tomorrow." Gerontology Institute Publications. 2014. https://scholarworks.umb.edu/gerontologyinstitute_pubs/98/.

Murthy, Vivek. "Our Epidemic of Loneliness and Isolation: The U.S. Surgeon General's Advisory on the Healing Effects of Social Connection and Community." Office of the Surgeon General, 2023. https://www.hhs.gov/sites/default/files/surgeon-general-social-connection-advisory.pdf.

Roser, Max, Esteban Ortiz-Ospina, and Hannah Ritchie. "Life Expectancy." 2013. OurWorldInData.org. https://ourworldindata.org/life-expectancy.

United Nations, Department of Economic and Social Affairs, Population Division. "World Population Ageing 2017." 2017. https://www.un.org/en/development/desa/population/publications/pdf/ageing/WPA2017_Report.pdf.

Weir, Kristen. "Ageism Is One of the Last Socially Acceptable Prejudices. Psychologists Are Working to Change That." *American Psychological Association Monitor on Psychology* 54, no. 2 (2023): 36.

World Health Organization. "Social Isolation and Loneliness among Older Adults." United Nations Department of Economic and Social Affairs. 2021. https://www.who.int/teams/social-determinants-of-health/demographic-change-and-healthy-ageing/social-isolation-and-loneliness.

CHAPTER 17

Intergenerational Conversations Foster Connection in Community and College Classrooms

Carrie Andreoletti *and* Andrea June

Abstract

The purpose of this chapter is to discuss the objectives, outcomes, and challenges of an intergenerational program called WISE, which is an acronym for Working Together: Intergenerational Student/Senior Exchange. The WISE program is a brief intergenerational service-learning program designed to bring together college students and older adults for the purpose of building connection and increasing understanding across the generations. The goals of the program are to reduce ageism and increase feelings of generativity through small-group intergenerational discussions around topics of mutual interest such as relationships and technology. This chapter discusses the development of the program as well as program outcomes, challenges, and suggestions for addressing challenges and sustaining the program for years to come. In sharing the successes and challenges of the WISE program, the hope is that others will be inspired to use WISE as a model for fostering intergenerational connection in their communities.

Key Words: ageism, college students, generativity, intergenerational programs, service learning, older adults

Working Together: Intergenerational Student/Senior Exchange (WISE)
Strengths/impact
• Low-cost, brief, simple
• Integrated into course curriculum
• Flexible and easy to modify
• Enjoyable and fun
• Positive feedback from participants
• Reduces age stereotypes
• Increases feelings of generativity
Limitations
• Evidence-informed rather than evidence-based
• Dependent on community contact for older adult participants
• Lack of resources (e.g., dedicated space on campus to accommodate intergenerational groups)

Overview

The potential benefits of intergenerational connection and collaboration are well documented in the literature. As addressed in this volume, there are myriad reasons for bringing different generations together. In the field of gerontology and geriatrics education, a primary focus of many intergenerational programs is to reduce negative stereotypes about aging and encourage students to pursue careers working with older adults.[1] The purpose of this chapter is to discuss the objectives, outcomes, and challenges of one such program, called WISE, which is an acronym for Working Together: Intergenerational Student/Senior Exchange. The WISE program was originally conceived as a brief intergenerational service-learning program to bring together college students and older adults residing in an assisted living community for the purpose of building connection and increasing understanding across the generations.[2] In this chapter we will discuss the development of the program, how it has changed over the years, and where we would like to see it go in the future. In sharing the successes and challenges of WISE, we hope to inspire others to implement similar programs.

Developing the WISE Pilot

The WISE program was developed and implemented by the first author in collaboration with a former activity director at a local assisted living community in 2012. The pilot program was conceived as an optional service-learning experience for students taking an adult development and aging class at Central Connecticut State University. It was designed to meet the community need for low-cost, intellectually stimulating activities for residents of the assisted living community while also allowing students to gain experience interacting with older adults. Consistent with Andrew Furco's definition of service-learning,[3] we sought to give equal emphasis to both the service and learning components of the experience as well as to ensure that all participants were benefitting from the experience. We also sought to bring the younger and older participants together as equal partners with the expectation that they each had something to offer the other. Because ageism—prejudice and discrimination based on age—affects both younger and older adults, one goal of the program was to challenge age stereotypes across the life span. While we hoped to challenge negative old-age stereotypes often held by college students,[4] we also wanted to challenge negative stereotypes of young people often held by older people.[5] Another goal of the program was to foster feelings of generativity (i.e., contributing to the next generation) and well-being in the older adults through social engagement with the college students.

During the first iteration of WISE, a small group of students and older adults got together five times over the course of the semester and discussed topics ranging from relationships to technology. All but one session took place at the assisted living community over lunch and lasted about two hours. One session took place on campus, where the students watched a public showing of the 1939 movie *Goodbye, Mr. Chips* and participated in a conversation afterward. Although the program was not formerly assessed, feedback from student reaction papers and a satisfaction survey given to the older adult participants was very positive.[6] This experience encouraged us to continue offering the program, but we made some important changes with the goals of increasing student participation and making the program sustainable over time.

The biggest barrier to student participation in the WISE pilot program was that it took place outside class time. Service-learning, which typically requires twenty to thirty hours outside the classroom,[7] is a barrier for many regional public university students with full course loads in addition to work and family obligations.[8] Even ten hours outside class time proved to be too much for most of our students, who said they would like to participate but were not able to with their full schedules and other responsibilities. Thus, we adopted a brief service-learning model for the WISE program consisting of just three sessions per semester, with all sessions taking place during the seventy-five-minute class time. We also had to stop including food or lunch, as it was cost-prohibitive when scaling up the program.

The WISE Model

We have been running the WISE program at least once during most semesters over the last ten years. While the program looks a little different each semester, it follows the same general format. We aim for at least three meetings, although occasionally we can only manage two. The first meeting always consists of an ice-breaker exercise we call "speed greeting."[9] The class is divided into small groups consisting of three to five students and one to three older adults, depending on the number of participants. Each group is given a bag or list of questions ranging from simple (e.g., What is your favorite holiday?) to more personal (e.g., What do you know about your ancestors?). Halfway through the session, we ask the students to rotate tables, and we run the activity again with a new set of questions. The purpose of this is to give participants the opportunity to talk with a more diverse group of people.

While groups get attached to one another, mixing them up is also helpful in the rare cases where a group may be having difficulty connecting. We recommend starting with general questions and moving to the more personal questions in the second half. However, the questions are just a guide, as some groups spontaneously generate their own questions. The goal of this first session is to break the ice; so as long as the groups are talking, the specifics are less important. We find that students are often nervous before the first session, so the goal is to help everyone to feel comfortable and keep things light to set the stage for future sessions.

Subsequent WISE sessions vary depending on the specific course, the instructor (the second author began integrating WISE into her classes in spring 2015), and the semester. However, they typically revolve around a theme such as love and relationships, family, technology, finances, or the environment. Sometimes we ask participants for input in determining discussion themes and sometimes themes are chosen by the instructor.

Regardless of the topic, participants are divided into small intergenerational groups, just as in the first session. The instructor provides an overview of the topic for the day and provides a list of questions to facilitate conversation. Students change groups halfway through, and the instructor generally facilitates a full group discussion at the halfway point just before students rotate and again at the end of the session. This allows groups to share what they learned from one another as well as what they found most interesting or surprising about their discussions.

Initially, WISE was only integrated into courses about aging. However, over the years, we have experimented with integrating WISE into other courses, such as positive psychology and an interdisciplinary honors course focused on understanding life span development through the lenses of psychological science and contemporary literature. In these cases, after the initial ice-breaker session, participants were assigned readings or watched videos and had small-group discussions related to the course content. This model was inspired by the Talk of Ages program at Lasell University (see *Handbook* chapter 6), which offers one- to two-week modules to older learners that are integrated into full-semester courses across a wide range of disciplines.[10] We have also experimented with having groups work together on problem-solving tasks (e.g., escape or survival scenarios) or creative activities (e.g., collaborative art and poetry). We generally try to stay away from topics explicitly related to aging, as we find that participants learn about aging indirectly through their interactions. However, in aging courses, we have found intergenerational discussions on ageism to be popular and have found some excellent resources for facilitating such conversations.[11]

As much as possible, we like to vary the location of sessions between the campus and the community to allow the participants to experience each other's "home turfs." Students often have misconceptions about assisted living communities and senior centers (the most recent community partner), so visiting these locations helps them to gain a better understanding of their function. In turn, we have found that older adults enjoy visiting campus and spending time in the classroom. Several are alums or parents of alums and enjoy seeing how the university has changed over time. Off-campus sessions can be challenging for students, who may have back-to-back classes or lack transportation. However, with planning and some flexibility around start and end times, most students are able to attend at least one session off campus. Facilitating carpooling can also help create deeper connections among students, who often benefit from this additional social engagement. The closer the community partner is to the campus, the better.

Although our community partners provide transportation for older adults coming to campus, other challenges arise, such as finding easily accessible rooms on campus that are big enough to accommodate guests. Acoustics are not always ideal, and when you have five or six small groups engaged in conversation at once it can be difficult to hear one another. Fortunately, participants are understanding of these challenges, and they do not tend to hinder the overall experience. If institutions created dedicated spaces on campus for intergenerational learning and collaboration designed for all ages and abilities, it would be easier for faculty to integrate intergenerational components into their classes.

Virtual WISE

Although the WISE program was designed as an in-person experience, during the COVID-19 pandemic we were able to pivot to a virtual format. And although we did not formally assess the virtual program, student reflections and informal feedback from older participants were similar across formats. For example, after in-person sessions, students often reported that they were surprised by how "with it" the older adults are. Likewise, after one virtual session, students made similar comments and were impressed with the older participants' ability to use Zoom without difficulty. Similarly, regardless of format, older adults are often impressed and surprised by how hardworking and engaged our students are. These examples provide some evidence that negative stereotypes about both younger and older adults are being challenged. Although we prefer meeting in person, some research has demonstrated the benefits of virtual intergenerational connection.[12] The pandemic forced us all to consider how technology can be used as a tool for fostering intergenerational connection and has created new opportunities for doing so.

WISE Conversations in the LGBTQ+ Community

Building upon the success of the WISE program in partnership with our local senior center as well as the pivot to virtual programming during the pandemic, we collaborated with several community partners to pilot a virtual intergenerational conversation for the LGBTQ+ community and allies.[13] We partnered with our on-campus LGBT Center and the LGBT Moveable Senior Center,[14] an initiative among several senior centers in Connecticut to provide a welcoming pathway for the LGBTQ+ senior community to local senior center programs and resources. We also partnered with the Triangle Community Center,[15] which provides programming and resources for the LGBTQ+ community in a neighboring county that was looking to expand programming for their young adults. Although not linked to a specific course, we modeled it after the WISE program and scheduled three virtual conversations: the first as an ice-breaker and subsequent session on topics decided by the participants. Conversation centered around life as an LGBTQ+ person in different eras and on preparing for life as an older LGBTQ+ person.

Again, although we were not able to assess the program formally, feedback was positive and resulted in the planning of an intergenerational virtual rainbow happy hour to be held in subsequent months. While we consider the pilot program a success, the number of participants was smaller than anticipated; the number varied from twelve to eighteen for the first two sessions to fewer than ten for the third session. Participants ranged in age from early twenties to late seventies, and although students from two local universities were invited and expressed interest, few participated. This is consistent with our first

WISE experience (conducted outside class time) and reinforces our belief that integrating intergenerational programming into a course increases participation.

In contrast to our previous WISE experience, there was less need for ice-breakers because participants were eager to discuss shared LGBTQ+ issues right away. Furthermore, we found it advantageous to have a member of the LGBTQ+ community serve as the facilitator. Although research is needed to assess the potential benefits and best practices for fostering intergenerational connection in the LGBTQ+ community, this pilot program shows promise for creating more campus LGBTQ+ center–community partnerships and fostering connection through conversation.

WISE Pros and Cons

Since its inception, WISE has not changed significantly. Although the participants change, the basic format remains the same because it is simple, adaptable, and requires minimal preparation from semester to semester. With just a little bit of structure, facilitating intergenerational conversations in the classroom is not difficult and easily engages the participants. According to the American Association of Colleges and Universities, experiential learning is a high-impact practice that has been shown to enhance students' engagement and learning in the classroom.[16] However, increased teaching loads and expectations for service and research leave many faculty overwhelmed, resulting in limited resources and bandwidth for incorporating high-impact practices into their courses.[17] Although the WISE program requires time and effort regarding logistics and coordination with our community partners each semester, it remains manageable. The positive intergenerational energy that the program creates within the classroom makes it truly worthwhile. Although sometimes we think we should be doing something bigger and better, we do not let perfect become the enemy of good.

We can report several important outcomes resulting from the development and implementation of the WISE program. First, research assessing the benefits of the program has revealed important outcomes for both younger and older participants. Specifically, Andreoletti and Howard[18] found that participation in WISE reduced negative attitudes and stereotypes about older adults held by younger adults as measured by the Fraboni Scale of Ageism[19] using a pretest-posttest design. Qualitative data suggested that participation in the program also had a positive impact on older adults' views of younger people, and both younger and older adults realized they had more in common than they originally thought. In another study, we found that older adults who participated in the WISE program reported increased feelings of generativity as measured by the Loyola Generativity Scale[20] using a pretest-posttest design.[21] Thus, these results support our original aims: to challenge age stereotypes, increase feelings of generativity, and foster intergenerational connection. Coexisting with these encouraging results are several important limitations, which are commonly found in the research literature assessing intergenerational programs and service-learning.[22] These will be discussed in more detail below when addressing program challenges.

Aside from the research and outcomes related to the original goals of our program, another important outcome that has emerged is that WISE has helped us to engage with the local community and form longstanding relationships with community partners. These community partnerships have led to internships and other opportunities (e.g., research, jobs) for our students as well as opportunities for us to become more engaged in our local aging network. It has also resulted in good publicity for our university and helped us to get more older community members involved with our campus.

WISE and the Age-Friendly University Initiative

Furthermore, our experience with the WISE program led us to embrace the Age-Friendly University (AFU) initiative[23] and become an early member of the AFU global network.[24] The AFU initiative was inspired by the age-friendly cities and communities initiative of the World Health Organization (WHO)[25] and provides a framework for institutions of higher education to think about how they can better meet the needs of older adults and engage them in all aspects of the university. In 2012, Dublin City University convened an interdisciplinary working group that developed ten AFU principles to serve as a guide for colleges and universities to become more age-inclusive and to better educate students about the benefits of aging.

The AFU principles have been endorsed by the Gerontological Society of America (GSA) and the Academy for Gerontology in Higher Education, the educational unit of the GSA. The GSA's Age Inclusivity in Higher Education Workgroup has expanded on the AFU principles by offering the Age-Inclusivity Domains of Higher Education (AIDHE) model based on research that developed a theoretical framework for assessing age inclusivity at institutions of higher education.[26] The AIDHE model suggests that age-inclusive practices be considered within seven institutional domains: teaching, student affairs, community outreach, personnel, physical environment, research, and services and resources.[27] The AFU principle most relevant to our work is "to promote intergenerational learning to facilitate the reciprocal sharing of expertise between learners of all ages,"[28] and this falls within the community outreach domain of the AIDHE model. Viewing WISE through an AFU lens and considering where it fits within the AIDHE model has helped us to think about how WISE can be used to foster intergenerational connection more broadly, moving beyond intergenerational service-learning in aging classes. This is helping us to think about our goals for the program moving forward, which we will discuss in more detail below.

Challenges: Resources, Logistics, and Research

Overall, the WISE program has met our need for a simple and sustainable intergenerational service-learning experience that enhances student understanding and fosters community connections that benefit older adults and our community partners. However, there is always room for improvement, and there are many challenges to this type of work to be aware of, primarily resources, logistics, and research. We consider resources in terms of time and money. Logistics refers to scheduling, physical space, and transportation. Finally, research assessing the benefits of intergenerational programs can be difficult to conduct for a variety of reasons, and the published literature in this area has many limitations. Each will be discussed in turn.

Both time and money are often in short supply but are essential resources for developing and sustaining any intergenerational program, even a simple one like WISE. As previously mentioned, students and faculty can face barriers to creating or participating in intergenerational service-learning programs or experiences. Many students who have work and family responsibilities in addition to classes cannot participate in nonpaid internships or other service-learning or volunteer activities. As for faculty, although most universities value high-impact practices such as service-learning, they provide limited (if any) support for developing community partnerships. It takes time to develop relationships with community partners and create successful programs, and as we know too well, time is a limited resource.

Money is another resource challenge and one of the reasons we keep the WISE program budget-friendly. Although small internal or external community grants may provide funding for food or transportation, this is difficult to secure for the long term. Thus, we can no longer offer refreshments at our WISE sessions. It is fortunate that our community partners can transport older participants to campus, for we do not have vans or buses to take students to off-campus sessions. Understaffed and/or underfunded community organizations cannot participate in programs like WISE if they are unable to recruit participants or provide transportation. This results in a tendency to work only with community partners with adequate resources rather than in communities where the need may be greatest.

Aside from time and resources, handling logistics can be extremely frustrating. Although some aspects become more manageable over time, scheduling with community partners, recruiting enough older participants, reserving an appropriate physical space, and securing transportation are always challenging. Experience has taught us that our model works well once we get everyone in the room. The challenge is getting everyone in the room! If meeting off campus, we worry about whether our students will show up on time or show up at all. When meeting on campus, we are never quite sure how many older adults will attend. We depend on our community partners to help us achieve the shared WISE goals.

One reason we transitioned from working with a local assisted living community to a senior center was because our original collaborator at the assisted living community retired. The new staff person supported the WISE program but had a different skill set that proved less compatible with our needs. After running the program with the new person a few times, we decided to work with a new community partner closer to our campus.

Furthermore, after years of working with the residents of the assisted living community, we noticed a decline in the cognitive functioning of many of the residents who participated; that started to change the nature of the WISE program as we had originally envisioned it. This is not to say that service-learning experiences should exclude individuals with cognitive impairment. It is important to remember that nothing stays the same. When there is staff turnover, which is inevitable, it is often necessary to develop new relationships and get buy-in from all stakeholders. (Rona Karasik discusses many of these challenges and offers suggestions for handling them in her chapter on the unwritten challenges of service-learning.[29])

Yet another challenge is conducting research to assess the benefits of an intergenerational program like WISE. Although we began to assess the benefits of the initiative early on, we have not formally assessed the program to make it *evidence-based*. The outcomes, challenges, and limitations of this research are discussed in detail in a paper that describes the development of WISE and offers suggestions for improving data collection.[30] While it is fairly easy to assess outcomes for students using online surveys, we find that assessing outcomes for older adults is better done individually and in person, which takes time. Sometimes just keeping the program running from semester to semester is challenging enough. Asking older adults to participate in the program is a lot easier than asking them to also participate in a research study.

Research demonstrating the benefits of intergenerational service-learning is essential for ensuring support for such programs, yet much of the existing research on the benefits of intergenerational programs is limited in size and scope. Sample sizes tend to be small, rarely include a control group, often lack baseline measures, and only assess short-term benefits. The majority of studies assessing intergenerational programs that involve college students and older adults focus on attitude changes about aging in the younger participants while neglecting the impact on the older adults.[31] There is a need for better research on the benefits of intergenerational programs for all stakeholders as well as on how program implementation impacts outcomes. In a review of the research on intergenerational service-learning, Paul Roodin and colleagues argue for consistency in the use of valid and reliable assessment tools and research methods to make it easier to make comparisons across programs.[32] In addition to assessing older adults, they also argue for assessing the impact of intergenerational programs on all stakeholders, including faculty and community partners.

Another limitation in current research is that it rarely considers the specific features of intergenerational programs that contribute to positive outcomes, making it difficult to determine best practices. Shannon Jarrott and colleagues published a review of evidenced-based intergenerational program practices and were able to identify fifteen evidence-based practices (e.g., convey equal group status, facilitate to promote interaction) that had a positive impact on program outcomes.[33] (See *Handbook* chapter 29.) Although more research is needed to validate the relationships between evidence-based practices and program outcomes, routine adoption of those practices would contribute to the replicability of intergenerational programs and help advance the research in this area. While there are no easy solutions to the challenges that come with assessing intergenerational programs, we are encouraged by recent efforts to document evidenced-based practices and recommend that others adopt these practices moving forward.

Extending the Model

We now take a broader view of age inclusivity through the Age-Friendly University (AFU) lens and offer suggestions for how intergenerational connection might be expanded across the curriculum and campus community using the WISE program as a model. One way to do this is to integrate brief intergenerational service-learning experiences like WISE into a wider array of classes. As mentioned above, our efforts to integrate WISE into courses outside the field of aging and gerontology have been limited. Faculty need support and access to older adults interested in participating, but our current community partner cannot make arrangements for WISE in more than one class per semester. Therefore, in semesters when we each have an aging-related course, only one of us integrates the WISE program. To deal with this challenge, we have experimented with alternative ways to foster intergenerational conversation in the classroom. For the past two years, for example, the first author has been hosting a Death Café in her Introduction to Gerontology class, where older members of the campus community (faculty, staff, and students) are invited to participate in class conversations about death following the Death Café guidelines.[34] To date, these discussions have been very popular.

One way to improve participant recruitment would be to create a mechanism whereby older adult community members could sign up to be notified about opportunities for intergenerational learning and collaboration on campus. While this might be easy for a campus with a Center on Aging, no such center exists on our campus. However, recent conversations with the Office of Community Engagement and Social Research have been promising, and we envision creating a structure that would allow us to build a network of older community members interested in engaging with our students in a variety of ways. If large enough, such a network would help us recruit older adults to participate in our classes as needed and enable them to engage with our students as their interests and schedules allow.

Finding allies and partners within one's institution who can offer resources and collaborate on shared goals can be helpful. For example, we have partnered with our Office of Professional Education, which offers the Scholars for Life! speaker series for older adults in the community. During the pandemic, the program pivoted to a virtual speaker series, and participation grew nearly fivefold. A brief online survey that we administered to explore scholars' interest in some of the AFU principles revealed that 35 percent would be interested in participating in intergenerational activities with students and 53 percent were interested in opportunities to study/travel abroad with faculty and students.[35] As such, this might be a good group to recruit from when we have a formal structure in place for those interested in intergenerational opportunities.

Our collaboration with the Office of Professional Education has also led to collaborations with AARP, a well-resourced organization that is eager to work with colleges and universities within our state. In addition to advocating for policies that support older Americans, AARP offers many free educational programs to fight fraud, create livable communities, and disrupt aging.[36] Our Office of Professional Education has cohosted several events with AARP encouraging students to learn and volunteer alongside AARP members and volunteers. (These collaborations are discussed in more detail in "Coalition Building to Create an Age-Friendly University (AFU)."[37]) AARP volunteers have presented to our classes about the AARP Fraud Watch Network and have helped our students conduct walkability audits of our campus, along with creating opportunities for intergenerational conversation and connection.

We view intergenerational conversation as more than just fostering connection in communities and classrooms. While it has the power to reduce ageism and foster feelings of generativity, we must also consider its potential for offering comfort, validation, and opportunities for collaboration in an increasingly divided world. Many organizations have begun to see the value in facilitating intergenerational collaboration to address complex social problems. For example, Encore.org has rebranded as CoGenerate.org[38] to refocus their efforts to address social problems in collaboration with younger generations. (See *Handbook* chapter 4.) Another example is the Gray Panthers, whose mission is to combat ageism and achieve social justice through intergenerational collaboration and activism.[39] As communities and workplaces become increasingly diverse, intergenerational programs like WISE offer an opportunity for students to develop soft skills for career readiness, skills valued by employers but often thought to be lacking due to our increasing reliance on technology and remote schooling and work since the COVID-19 pandemic.[40]

As we review the development of the WISE program and how it has evolved over the last ten years, we see great potential in continuing and expanding the model in the years to come. Despite the challenges discussed in this chapter, it remains a manageable program that has demonstrated positive outcomes for all participants, including the faculty. Although we acknowledge that additional research is needed to robustly assess outcomes and determine which features of the program contribute to the most positive outcomes, we are committed to sustaining WISE and allowing it to evolve consistently with emerging research on best practices. We believe the program serves as a model for other organizations by demonstrating the power of simple conversations to foster intergenerational connections. Even small efforts can have a big impact over time, and so we encourage readers to get started and not let perfect be the enemy of good.

Notes

1. Frankline Augustin and Brenda Freshman, "The Effects of Service-Learning on College Students' Attitudes toward Older Adults," *Gerontology & Geriatrics Education* 37, no. 2 (2016): 123–44, https://doi.org/10.1080/02701960.2015.1079705; Ashley Lytle et al., "Instapals: Reducing Ageism by Facilitating Intergenerational Contact and Providing Aging Education," *Gerontology & Geriatrics Education* 41, no. 3 (2020): 308–19, https://doi.org/10.1080/02701960.2020.1737047.
2. Carrie Andreoletti and Jessica L. Howard, "Bridging the Generation Gap: Intergenerational Service-Learning Benefits Young and Old," *Gerontology & Geriatrics Education* 39, no. 1 (2018): 46–60, https://doi.org/10.1080/02701960.2016.1152266.
3. Andrew Furco, "Service-Learning: A Balanced Approach to Experiential Education," in *Expanding Boundaries: Service and Learning*, ed. B. Taylor (Washington, DC: Corporation for National Service, 1996), 2–6.
4. Mary E. Kite et al., "Attitudes toward Younger and Older Adults: An Updated Meta-Analytic Review," *Journal of Social Issues* 61, no. 2 (2005): 241–66, https://doi.org/10.1111/j.1540-4560.2005.00404.x.
5. D. H. Matheson et al., "Older Adults' Multiple Stereotypes of Young Adults," *International Journal of Aging & Human Development* 51, no. 4 (2000): 245–57, https://doi.org/10.2190/LL3H-VKE8-QAT1-7M9M.
6. Andreoletti and Howard, "Bridging the Generation Gap."
7. Maureen Tam, "Intergenerational Service Learning between the Old and Young: What, Why and How," *Educational Gerontology* 40, no. 6 (2014): 401–13, https://doi.org/10.1080/03601277.2013.822201.
8. Harriet L. Cohen et al., "Intergenerational Service-Learning: An Innovative Teaching Strategy to Infuse Gerontology Content into Foundation Courses," *Journal of Gerontological Social Work* 48, no. 1–2 (2006): 161–78, https://doi.org/10.1300/J083v48n01_11; Rona J. Karasik, "Breaking the Time Barrier: Helping Students 'Find the Time' to Do Intergenerational Service-Learning," *Gerontology & Geriatrics Education* 25, no. 3 (2005): 49–63, https://doi.org/10.1300/J021v25n03_04.
9. Carrie Andreoletti and Joann M. Montepare, "Activity 9.1: Intergenerational Speed Greeting Activity," in *A Hands-on Approach to Teaching about Aging: 32 Activities for the Classroom and Beyond*, ed. Hallie Baker, Tina M. Kruger, and Rona J. Karasik (New York: Springer, 2018), 270–74.
10. Joann M. Montepare and Kimberly S. Farah, "Talk of Ages: Using Intergenerational Classroom Modules to Engage Older and Younger Students across the Curriculum," *Gerontology & Geriatrics Education* 39, no. 3 (2018): 385–94, https://doi.org/10.1080/02701960.2016.1269006.
11. "On the Same pAGE Intergenerational Conversations," *Changing the Narrative* (blog), accessed November 5, 2023, https://changingthenarrativeco.org/intergenerational-conversations/.
12. Kylie Beausoleil et al., "'I Loved Interacting with This Younger Generation': Exploring the Impact of a Virtual Service-Learning Program on Social Connectedness among Older Adults during the COVID-19 Pandemic," *Gerontology & Geriatrics Education* 45, no. 1 (2022): 67–85, https://doi.org/10.1080/02701960.2022.2132241.
13. Carrie Andreoletti et al., "Reducing Ageism in the LQBTQ+ Community through Intergenerational Connection," *Innovation in Aging* 6, Supplement 1 (2022): 10–11, https://doi.org/10.1093/geroni/igac059.036.
14. "LGBTQ+ Moveable Senior Center," CT Healthy Living Collective, accessed November 5, 2023, https://cthealthyliving.org/explore-programs/lgbtq-moveable-senior-center/.
15. "Triangle Community Center: Home," Triangle Community Center, November 6, 2023, https://ctpridecenter.org/.
16. "High-Impact Practices," AAC&U, September 19, 2023, https://www.aacu.org/trending-topics/high-impact.
17. Allison White, "Understanding the University and Faculty Investment in Implementing High-Impact Educational Practices," *Journal of the Scholarship of Teaching and Learning* 18, no. 2 (2018): 118–35.
18. Andreoletti and Howard, "Bridging the Generation Gap."
19. Maryann Fraboni et al., "The Fraboni Scale of Ageism (FSA): An Attempt at a More Precise Measure of Ageism," *Canadian Journal on Aging* 9, no. 1 (1990): 56–66, https://doi.org/10.1017/S0714980800016093.
20. Dan P. McAdams and Ed de St. Aubin, "A Theory of Generativity and Its Assessment through Self-Report, Behavioral Acts, and Narrative Themes in Autobiography," *Journal of Personality and Social Psychology* 62, no. 6 (1992): 1003–15, https://doi.org/10.1037/0022-3514.62.6.1003.

21. Andrea June and Carrie Andreoletti, "Participation in Intergenerational Service-Learning Benefits Older Adults: A Brief Report," *Gerontology & Geriatrics Education* 41, no. 2 (2020): 169–74, https://doi.org/10.1080/02701960.2018.1457529.
22. Paul Roodin et al., "Intergenerational Service-Learning: A Review of Recent Literature and Directions for the Future," *Gerontology & Geriatrics Education* 34, no. 1 (2013): 3–25, https://doi.org/10.1080/02701960.2012.755624.
23. "Age-Friendly University Global Network," Age-Friendly University Global Network, accessed November 5, 2023, https://www.afugn.org.
24. Carrie Andreoletti and Andrea June, "Coalition Building to Create an Age-Friendly University (AFU)," *Gerontology & Geriatrics Education* 40, no. 2 (2019): 142–52, https://doi.org/10.1080/02701960.2019.1572008.
25. "The Global Network for Age-Friendly Cities and Communities," World Health Organization, accessed November 5, 2023, https://www.who.int/publications-detail-redirect/WHO-FWC-ALC-18.4.
26. Nina M. Silverstein et al., "Assessing Age Inclusivity in Higher Education: Introducing the Age-Friendly Inventory and Campus Climate Survey," *Gerontologist* 62, no. 1 (2022): e48–61, https://doi.org/10.1093/geront/gnab090.
27. Joann M. Montepare et al., "Age Inclusivity Domains of Higher Education (AIDHE): A Guiding Panoramic Model," *Advancing Age Inclusivity in Higher Education Newsletter*, no. 16 (Fall 2023): 1–3..
28. "Age-Friendly University Principles," Age-Friendly University Global Network, accessed November 5, 2023, https://www.afugn.org/age-friendly-university-principles.
29. Rona J. Karasik, "15: Whispers and Sighs: The Unwritten Challenges of Service-Learning," *To Improve the Academy* 23, no. 1 (2004): 236–53, https://doi.org/10.1002/j.2334-4822.2004.tb00437.x.
30. Andreoletti and Howard, "Bridging the Generation Gap."
31. Kathy Lee et al., "Documented Outcomes for Older Adults in Intergenerational Programming: A Scoping Review," *Journal of Intergenerational Relationships* 18 (2019): 1–26, https://doi.org/10.1080/15350770.2019.1673276.
32. Roodin et al., "Intergenerational Service-Learning."
33. Shannon E. Jarrott et al., "Implementation of Evidence-Based Practices in Intergenerational Programming: A Scoping Review," *Research on Aging* 43, no. 7–8 (2021): 283–93, https://doi.org/10.1177/0164027521996191.
34. "Holding Your Own Death Cafe," Death Café, accessed November 5, 2023, https://deathcafe.com/how/.
35. Andrea June and Carrie Andreoletti, "Using an Age-Friendly University Lens to Explore Community Member Engagement during the Pandemic," *Gerontology & Geriatrics Education* 44, no. 1 (2023): 27–40, https://doi.org/10.1080/02701960.2021.2005039.
36. "AARP® Official Site: Join & Explore the Benefits," AARP, accessed November 5, 2023, https://www.aarp.org/.
37. Andreoletti and June, "Coalition Building."
38. "About," CoGenerate, accessed November 5, 2023, https://cogenerate.org/about/.
39. "Home," Gray Panthers NYC, accessed November 5, 2023, https://www.graypanthersnyc.org.
40. Caroline Castrillon, "Why Soft Skills Are More in Demand Than Ever," *Forbes*, accessed November 5, 2023, https://www.forbes.com/sites/carolinecastrillon/2022/09/18/why-soft-skills-are-more-in-demand-than-ever/.

Bibliography

AAC&U. "High-Impact Practices." September 19, 2023. https://www.aacu.org/trending-topics/high-impact.
AARP. "AARP® Official Site: Join & Explore the Benefits." Accessed November 5, 2023. https://www.aarp.org/.
Age-Friendly University Global Network. "Age-Friendly University Global Network." Accessed November 5, 2023. https://www.afugn.org.
Age-Friendly University Global Network. "Age-Friendly University Principles." Accessed November 5, 2023. https://www.afugn.org/age-friendly-university-principles.
Andreoletti, Carrie, Christina Barmon, Andrea June, and Michael Bartone. "Reducing Ageism in the LGBTQ+ Community through Intergenerational Connection." *Innovation in Aging* 6, Supplement 1 (2022): 10–11. https://doi.org/10.1093/geroni/igac059.036.

Andreoletti, Carrie, and Jessica L. Howard. "Bridging the Generation Gap: Intergenerational Service-Learning Benefits Young and Old." *Gerontology & Geriatrics Education* 39, no. 1 (2018): 46–60. https://doi.org/10.1080/02701960.2016.1152266.

Andreoletti, Carrie, and Andrea June. "Coalition Building to Create an Age-Friendly University (AFU)." *Gerontology & Geriatrics Education* 40, no. 2 (2019): 142–52. https://doi.org/10.1080/02701960.2019.1572008.

Andreoletti, Carrie, and Joann M. Montepare. "Activity 9.1: Intergenerational Speed Greeting Activity." In *A Hands-on Approach to Teaching about Aging: 32 Activities for the Classroom and Beyond*, edited by Hallie Baker, Tina M. Kruger, and Rona J. Karasik, 270–74. New York: Springer, 2018.

Augustin, Frankline, and Brenda Freshman. "The Effects of Service-Learning on College Students' Attitudes toward Older Adults." *Gerontology & Geriatrics Education* 37, no. 2 (2016): 123–44. https://doi.org/10.1080/02701960.2015.1079705.

Beausoleil, Kylie, Jason Garbarino, and Laura Foran Lewis. "'I Loved Interacting with This Younger Generation': Exploring the Impact of a Virtual Service-Learning Program on Social Connectedness among Older Adults during the COVID-19 Pandemic." *Gerontology & Geriatrics Education* 45, no. 1 (2022): 67–85. https://doi.org/10.1080/02701960.2022.2132241.

Castrillon, Caroline. "Why Soft Skills Are More In Demand Than Ever." *Forbes*. Accessed November 5, 2023. https://www.forbes.com/sites/carolinecastrillon/2022/09/18/why-soft-skills-are-more-in-demand-than-ever/.

Changing the Narrative. "On the Same pAGE Intergenerational Conversations." Accessed November 5, 2023. https://changingthenarrativeco.org/intergenerational-conversations/.

CoGenerate. "About." Accessed November 5, 2023. https://cogenerate.org/about/.

Cohen, Harriet L., Bonnie Hatchett, and Darlene Eastridge. "Intergenerational Service-Learning: An Innovative Teaching Strategy to Infuse Gerontology Content into Foundation Courses." *Journal of Gerontological Social Work* 48, no. 1–2 (2006): 161–78. https://doi.org/10.1300/J083v48n01_11.

CT Healthy Living Collective. "LGBTQ+ Moveable Senior Center." Accessed November 5, 2023. https://cthealthyliving.org/explore-programs/lgbtq-moveable-senior-center/.

Death Care. "Holding Your Own Death Cafe." Accessed November 5, 2023. https://deathcafe.com/how/.

Fraboni, Maryann, Robert Saltstone, and Susan Hughes. "The Fraboni Scale of Ageism (FSA): An Attempt at a More Precise Measure of Ageism." *Canadian Journal on Aging* 9, no. 1 (1990): 56–66. https://doi.org/10.1017/S0714980800016093.

Furco, Andrew. "Service-Learning: A Balanced Approach to Experiential Education." In *Expanding Boundaries: Service and Learning*, edited by B. Taylor, 2–6. Washington, DC: Corporation for National Service, 1996.

Gray Panthers NYC. "Home." Accessed November 5, 2023. https://www.graypanthersnyc.org.

Jarrott, Shannon E., Rachel M. Scrivano, Cherrie Park, and Angela N. Mendoza. "Implementation of Evidence-Based Practices in Intergenerational Programming: A Scoping Review." *Research on Aging* 43, no. 7–8 (2021): 283–93. https://doi.org/10.1177/0164027521996191.

June, Andrea, and Carrie Andreoletti. "Participation in Intergenerational Service-Learning Benefits Older Adults: A Brief Report." *Gerontology & Geriatrics Education* 41, no. 2 (2020): 169–74. https://doi.org/10.1080/02701960.2018.1457529.

June, Andrea, and Carrie Andreoletti. "Using an Age-Friendly University Lens to Explore Community Member Engagement during the Pandemic." *Gerontology & Geriatrics Education* 44, no. 1 (2023): 27–40. https://doi.org/10.1080/02701960.2021.2005039.

Karasik, Rona J. "15: Whispers and Sighs: The Unwritten Challenges of Service-Learning." *To Improve the Academy* 23, no. 1 (2004): 236–53. https://doi.org/10.1002/j.2334-4822.2004.tb00437.x.

Karasik, Rona J. "Breaking the Time Barrier: Helping Students 'Find the Time' to Do Intergenerational Service-Learning." *Gerontology & Geriatrics Education* 25, no. 3 (2005): 49–63. https://doi.org/10.1300/J021v25n03_04.

Kite, Mary E., Gary D. Stockdale, Bernard E. Whitley Jr., and Blair T. Johnson. "Attitudes toward Younger and Older Adults: An Updated Meta-Analytic Review." *Journal of Social Issues* 61, no. 2 (2005): 241–66. https://doi.org/10.1111/j.1540-4560.2005.00404.x.

Lee, Kathy, Shannon Jarrott, and Lisa Juckett. "Documented Outcomes for Older Adults in Intergenerational Programming: A Scoping Review." *Journal of Intergenerational Relationships* 18 (2019): 1–26. https://doi.org/10.1080/15350770.2019.1673276.

Lytle, Ashley, Nancy Nowacek, and Sheri R. Levy. "Instapals: Reducing Ageism by Facilitating Intergenerational Contact and Providing Aging Education." *Gerontology & Geriatrics Education* 41, no. 3 (2020): 308–19. https://doi.org/10.1080/02701960.2020.1737047.

Matheson, D. H., C. L. Collins, and V. S. Kuehne. "Older Adults' Multiple Stereotypes of Young Adults." *International Journal of Aging & Human Development* 51, no. 4 (2000): 245–57. https://doi.org/10.2190/LL3H-VKE8-QAT1-7M9M.

McAdams, Dan P., and Ed de St. Aubin. "A Theory of Generativity and Its Assessment through Self-Report, Behavioral Acts, and Narrative Themes in Autobiography." *Journal of Personality and Social Psychology* 62, no. 6 (1992): 1003–15. https://doi.org/10.1037/0022-3514.62.6.1003.

Montepare, Joann M., and Kimberly S. Farah. "Talk of Ages: Using Intergenerational Classroom Modules to Engage Older and Younger Students across the Curriculum." *Gerontology & Geriatrics Education* 39, no. 3 (2018): 385–94. https://doi.org/10.1080/02701960.2016.1269006.

Montepare, Joann M., Nina M. Silverstein, Susan Krauss Whitbourne, and Lauren M. Bowen. "Age Inclusivity Domains of Higher Education (AIDHE): A Guiding Panoramic Model." *Advancing Age Inclusivity in Higher Education Newsletter*, no. 16 (Fall 2023): 1–3.

Roodin, Paul, Laura Hess Brown, and Dorothy Shedlock. "Intergenerational Service-Learning: A Review of Recent Literature and Directions for the Future." *Gerontology & Geriatrics Education* 34, no. 1 (2013): 3–25 https://doi.org/10.1080/02701960.2012.755624.

Silverstein, Nina M., Susan K. Whitbourne, Lauren M. Bowen, Joann M. Montepare, Taylor Jansen, Celeste Beaulieu, et al. "Assessing Age Inclusivity in Higher Education: Introducing the Age-Friendly Inventory and Campus Climate Survey." *Gerontologist* 62, no. 1 (2022): e48–61. https://doi.org/10.1093/geront/gnab090.

Tam, Maureen. "Intergenerational Service Learning between the Old and Young: What, Why and How." *Educational Gerontology* 40, no. 6 (June 2014): 401–13. https://doi.org/10.1080/03601277.2013.822201.

Triangle Community Center. "Triangle Community Center: Home," November 6, 2023. https://ctpridecenter.org/.

White, Allison. "Understanding the University and Faculty Investment in Implementing High-Impact Educational Practices." *Journal of the Scholarship of Teaching and Learning* 18, no. 2 (2018): 118–35.

World Health Organization. "The Global Network for Age-Friendly Cities and Communities." Accessed November 5, 2023. https://www.who.int/publications-detail-redirect/WHO-FWC-ALC-18.4.

PART IV

Global Perspectives on Intergenerational Relationships

CHAPTER 18

Generations Working Together across Scotland

Lorraine George, Ruairidh Smith, *and* Alison Clyde

Abstract

This chapter discusses why intergenerational work is so prevalent in Scotland and explores the part played by Generations Working Together. It considers what is needed to support the development of intergenerational work and the common challenges that may be faced. It argues that relationships (on a variety of levels) are essential, not only within intergenerational work itself but also for successful development and partnership working. Applying a relational lens beyond that of the participants, to the individuals and organizations that GWT work with, ensures that relationships stay at the heart of all that GWT does. Working relationships that are sincere and mutually beneficial with shared purpose support sustainable improvement and bring great rewards.

Key Words: intergenerational, Scotland, relationships, challenges, sustainable

Generations Working Together (GWT)	Global Intergenerational Week	GWT International Certificate in Intergenerational Learning
Strengths/impact • Intergeneration knowledge allows staff and volunteers are committed and passionate about intergenerational work. • GWT networks raise awareness, increase knowledge and confidence, and focus on improving quality through sharing best practice. • GWT handbooks/toolkits support planning and development of intergenerational work. • GWT global relationships enable development of grass roots practice, as well as embedding policy at local and national level. • Partnerships at all levels support the growth of intergenerational work, including systemic change.	**Strengths/impact** • Increased connections raised awareness. • Builds increased skills and knowledge at grassroots level. • Reduces social isolation/loneliness in the community. • Showcases and shares intergenerational programs. • Increases access to shared resources, ideas, and practice	**Strengths/impact** • The course is open to all students, Scottish and international (accessibility). • Resource library highlights new research and good practice. • Tutors signpost students to relevant research, individualized learning. • Networking opportunities support the exchange of intergenerational information between countries. • Offers accredited learning hours.

Generations Working Together (GWT)	Global Intergenerational Week	GWT International Certificate in Intergenerational Learning
Limitations • Capacity restricts development opportunities. • Education and adult social care still recovering post-COVID (engagement). • Misconception of intergenerational work restricts implementation. • Insufficient funding restricts GWT's ability to support intergenerational development.	**Limitations** • Funding is needed to further develop project work at grassroots level. • Promotion within individual countries varies.	**Limitations** • Funding is limited to further develop the platform. • Marketing and targeting are challenging, particularly in academia.

Scotland: An Intergenerational Nation

There are two extraordinary things about intergenerational work in Scotland. The first is the great number of intergenerational grassroots projects taking place, and the second is the support from the national government. The most common questions Generations Working Together (GWT) gets asked are why and how this happens. Why is there so much intergenerational working taking place in Scotland, as opposed to anywhere else, and how has GWT built successful partnerships with the national government?

There are many answers to these questions of course, one being the simple existence and development of the Scottish Centre for Intergenerational Practice, which became GWT, partly funded by the Scottish government since its inception in 2007. The Centre was developed as part of a Scottish government consultation to explore issues facing society in meeting the challenges of an ageing population. In 2015, GWT became a Scottish Charity to allow for a wider variety of work, support, and projects to be delivered. The charity's vision is to live in a Scotland where different generations are more connected and where everyone has opportunities to build relationships that help to create a more inclusive society.

As a membership and capacity-building organization, GWT operates locally and nationally raising awareness, sharing, and expanding knowledge and understanding of intergenerational practice and their impact. GWT provides training, shares a resource library, organizes learning events, facilitates eighteen local and four thematic networks, and works in partnership with local/national groups and organizations to deliver innovative pilot projects and participate in academic research projects.

Having a central organization engaging effectively on a variety of strategic levels, raising awareness of intergenerational work and its benefits, ensures that the important messages are consistently heard. GWT strongly believes that the importance of intergenerational work lies with grassroots development of initiatives supported at a management/partnership level.

Intergenerational practitioners are often working in overwhelmed sectors (particularly early years, education, and adult social care) that are still struggling to recover post-COVID, in terms of staff, recruitment, and capacity. Despite the challenges, staff and/or volunteers work hard to embed intergenerational work into their daily routines because they can see for themselves the social-impact benefits for participants. This impact then ripples out into the wider community; it doesn't remain siloed within the activity session. The young people interacting with older adults at their youth club recognize and speak to their older friends when they see them at the shops, and the young children making friends with adults in residential care then pester their families to take them to visit their friends during school holidays. These are the outcomes that motivate people to continue developing intergenerational programs, despite the ever-present challenges of staff, resources, and funding. GWT firmly believes that just as relationships are essential to the development of meaningful intergenerational work, relationships are also key to their growth and the successful development of intergenerational work in Scotland. Building relationships with others is a priority for the organization.

Belief in the wide-ranging benefits of intergenerational work and its role in reconnecting communities led GWT in 2020 to launch a call to make Scotland an intergenerational nation, publishing a detailed corporate plan outlining the key priorities and objectives necessary to achieve this end. The corporate plan starts from the strongly held belief that intergenerational learning initiatives and projects make a positive contribution to Scotland, its people, and its communities. GWT seeks to create a "policy and practice" environment in order to maximize the impact of intergenerational activities across the country. Developed through extensive dialogue with members, researchers, practitioners, and academics, the corporate plan[1] presents five strategic aims to develop intergenerational practice in Scotland in the 2020–2025 period:

1. To enable Scotland to become an intergenerational nation
2. To influence national and local policy in favor of intergenerational practice
3. To promote, support, and increase innovation in intergenerational practice
4. To increase participation in intergenerational practice
5. To ensure sound governance

By weaving intergenerational principles into governance, policy-making, and public engagement, and building relationships with key organizations, GWT is laying the necessary groundwork for intergenerational practice to thrive across Scotland.

Strategic aim 1 represents the fundamental purpose of GWT: to build an intergenerational nation. The other four aims can be seen to feed into this. The corporate plan presents a multifaceted plan encompassing publications, training, communications, policy influencing, and events, designed to steer GWT's efforts in achieving their end goal. Through a relational lens, this section will explore, in detail, what has allowed GWT to be so successful up until now and how the organization plans to continue to grow and work toward building an intergenerational Scotland.

GWT has sought to expand its reach by appointing a full-time training officer, offering online training to ensure equitable access across Scotland. The International Certificate of Intergenerational Practice allows learners from across the world to dig deep into intergenerational fundamentals, build their network, and receive support from expert practitioners and academics from across the globe, while one-day in-person training opportunities enable the multiplication of intergenerational knowledge across communities and workplaces in Scotland. Customized training programs tailored to the specific needs of partnerships and organizations have been developed, fostering a deeper understanding of intergenerational practice within a variety of contexts. Ensuring accessibility and national coverage is paramount to GWT, and therefore, training opportunities can be found across the country, with online options for those unable to attend physically.

A key focus for GWT, and what makes Scotland somewhat unique, is its determination to actively shape national and local policy to support and advance intergenerational practice. The organization focuses on external engagement, relations, policy groups, and forums to achieve this end. Externally, GWT strengthens partnerships with organizations and networks spanning various sectors, establishing the collaborative alliances that are essential for effectively promoting intergenerational practice. It maintains working relationships with key Scottish government departments, ensuring that intergenerational practice remains a priority on the government's agenda. By actively engaging with national and local policy makers, GWT positions itself as an "expert" in intergenerational practice, sharing insights and good practices learned from academics and practitioners worldwide to inform intergenerational policy development. A key narrative that GWT aims to challenge is the idea that intergenerational connections are simply "nice" ad hoc exchanges or interactions. Instead, it is important to establish greater criticality—that intergenerational learning must be recognized as a valuable, ongoing practice, underpinned by a wealth of research and positive findings. This philosophy underpins the vast work that GWT does in its efforts to influence policy in a local and national context.

GWT actively contributes expertise to key policy and practice forums, including the national implementation group for "A Connected Scotland: Recovering Our Connections 2023–2026," where intergenerational practice is cited as an essential means of challenging social isolation and loneliness and reconnecting communities post-COVID. The strategy states, "Intergenerational dialogue has a vital role in ensuring that different generations talk to each other in order to tackle the shared challenges of exclusion and isolation."[2] GWT also contributes to other notable working groups such as the Older People's Strategic Action Forum, Scottish Older People's Assembly, and several other groups relating to volunteering, ageing, and community engagement. Contributions to cross-party groups on older people, age and ageing, and children and young people; one-to-one meetings with councilors, Members of the Scottish Parliament (MSPs) and ministers; and network events ensure that intergenerational principles are considered as much as possible by key decision-makers. Adopting a nonpartisan approach is necessary in the building and maintaining of professional and strategic relationships. Comprehensive responses to a variety of relevant consultations have drawn on findings from a growing body of empirical studies, arguing the need for improved intergenerational practice within health, social care and sport, dementia strategy, human rights law, and more, emphasizing its holistic and critical value across a range of social policy domains. Impactful communication with local and national government requires a comprehensive and up-to-date knowledge of intergenerational research; thus, remaining well informed on relevant developments across a range of policy areas, from health and social care, to education to housing to urban and rural development, is imperative.

A series of Scottish parliamentary member's debates hosted in consecutive years demonstrates a political urgency regarding intergenerational development in Scotland. In April 2023, nine MSPs from four political parties and the minister for equalities, migration, and refugees recognized the need for more and greater high-quality intergenerational opportunities across the country. Crucially, MSPs stressed the need for more and better funding in local government, with Scottish Labour's Carol Mochan proclaiming, "I do believe we can [achieve an intergenerational Scotland] if we look at it with some urgency . . . we need to fund local government to allow intergenerational practice to happen." A key focus for GWT looking forward is to develop stronger partnerships with local authorities and councils to further develop support at a local level and build toward a Scotland where intergenerational practice is not only valued as an essential practice but is also deeply embedded in policy-making and societal frameworks.

In order to ensure that the goals outlined in the corporate plan are still relevant and appropriate in a postpandemic climate in which the delivery of many intergenerational projects had to change, new research was conducted in 2023. GWT consulted with their members and asked them to consider what an ideal intergenerational Scotland might look like in ten years. They were then asked to consider what actions would be required to arrive at that point. The research was conducted at three focus group events across the country (Glasgow, Huntly, and Perth) and engaged the views of twenty-eight people from a diverse range of interests. The results reinforce several of the corporate plan's proposals while also introducing new areas of focus. The insights derived from the workshops provide an updated compass to guide GWT's strategic goals in building an intergenerational Scotland. The members' collective vision reinforces the need for a multifaceted approach, including societal shifts and attitudinal transformations.

A consistent theme within the recent findings is a renewed focus on utilizing new technologies to create greater online interaction between generations. The past few years have forced practitioners to get creative in their attempts to unite generations, as lockdowns and enforced social restrictions put an abrupt end to face-to-face work. We've seen some fantastic projects, such as ROAR do Digital, whereby schoolchildren teach older adults how to use technologies, from staying safe online to using online banking and connecting with friends. Not only does a project like this support direct relationship building between generations, but it also results in the development of new skills, including online connectivity, which can be a powerful antidote to social isolation and loneliness. It's therefore important that GWT places greater emphasis on digital connectivity than initially outlined in the corporate plan, and this has been an ongoing focus. New attitudes toward technology and the shift to online working will allow GWT to reach more people in different places, allowing for more communication, connection, and consultation with our members—whose views are essential to the development of GWT and intergenerational practice more widely.

The workshop participants' emphasis on education, respect, transparency, motivation, and openness provides GWT with a clear framework to support groups in cultivating meaningful relationships and initiatives. It's also essential that GWT continues to showcase the real-world impact of intergenerational initiatives to policy-makers. Inviting policy-makers to witness these practices in action reinforces the importance of intergenerational approaches, potentially leading to policy changes that support the development of an intergenerational Scotland. This opportunity for "live learning" should not be underestimated as a strategy for raising awareness of intergenerational work and its benefits. People need only observe the interactions for themselves to understand why intergenerational learning is so important. Live learning can be crucial in establishing a shift in attitude from viewing intergenerational practice as simply "nice" to "essential." Extensive work has been done this year with regard to this, with several MSPs visiting projects of the recipients of the annual GWT Excellence Award program, an initiative that recognizes and rewards projects that exhibit a high standard of intergenerational practice. MSPs have consistently commended the work highly and pledged their support for the ongoing development of intergenerational work across the country.

Incorporating these workshop findings into GWT's strategic planning and considering them in tandem with the corporate plan's strategic aims can help to steer efforts toward building an intergenerational Scotland. GWT's role as a center of excellence for the growth of intergenerational practice across Scotland contributes significantly to the materialization of a society where intergenerational connections thrive, age stereotypes dissipate, and mutual respect flourishes among all age groups.

Global Intergenerational Week

While the primary goal of Generations Working Together (GWT) is to work toward developing an intergenerational Scotland, the organization has also set its sights on establishing a global network of like-minded and passionate intergenerational partners, developing mutually beneficial, reciprocal relationships with them. Global Intergenerational Week is an annual awareness week that seeks to engage countries around the world in one united conversation about intergenerational practice, exploring its value, successes, principles of best practice, and complexities. The campaign was first established as an exclusively United Kingdom–wide campaign by the St Monica Trust in 2020. In 2021, GWT took over as the campaign hosts, forming an executive team comprising leads from Linking Generations Northern Ireland, Bridging the Generations (Wales), and the Cares Family (The Beth Johnson Foundation took leadership for England in 2022). The campaign continues to grow steadily, with a total of fourteen countries taking part in 2023. Through regular all-country meetings, strategic planning, and thematic coordination, the campaign delivers a coordinated week of events, from local projects to stimulating webinars and workshops to political debates and more.

In 2023, country leads from Australia, Canada, England, Hungary, Ireland, Israel, Mexico, Northern Ireland, Scotland, Singapore, Spain, Sweden, the United States, and Wales, considered intergenerational ideas in the context of six diverse daily themes. Themes such as "Let's combat loneliness and social isolation" (day 3) and "Let's break down age barriers" (day 5) allowed countries to deliberate on and showcase the impact of intergenerational practice in challenging a range of social problems. For example, the campaign's Irish leads at DCU Age-Friendly University hosted their "Beyond the Number: Exploring Age-Related Bias in Finance and Insurance" session in collaboration with the Irish Senior Citizens Parliament. The Mexican and Welsh campaign partners (CorimAZ and Bridging the Generations, respectively) also came together, collaborating on the development of a series of videos designed to break down and debunk age-based stereotypes. Other themes included "Let's build intergenerational partnerships" (day 2), where the importance of intersectional approaches to intergenerational practice was explored, and "Let's celebrate intergenerational communities and spaces" (day 4), where countries could showcase unique and progressive approaches to intergenerational shared spaces. For example, GWT hosted a stimulating session titled "How can we apply an intergenerational approach to the workplace?" in which guest speaker Megan Gerhardt introduced us to key ideas from her recently coauthored book, *Gentelligence* and explored the social and productive value of building an intergenerational workforce.[3] The campaign opening and closing ceremonies also allowed country leads to come together to share their plans and summarize their work to a worldwide audience of over eighty participants.

Across the week, over 1,295 local projects hosted events globally in a range of exciting and creative ways. A combined social media reach of 539,772 impressions marked a 16 percent increase over the previous year's campaign. Global Intergenerational Week's reputation as a well-established and impactful campaign carries with it credibility that ensures that key stakeholders and decision-makers take notice. This was reflected in the aforementioned parliamentary debate held in Scotland in which nine MSPs from four political parties testified to the value of intergenerational practice across a broad range of social policy domains. More than twenty council buildings across Northern Ireland, Wales, and Scotland were lit up in pink to celebrate the week, demonstrating United Kingdom–wide support from local government to raise awareness of intergenerational practice. We are confident that the "building light-up" initiative will grow across the globe for the 2024 campaign.

The benefits of intergenerational practice are well established, as evidenced by several studies and projects. It's therefore not enough anymore to brand intergenerational connections as simply "nice" or "heartwarming" interactions. Rather, it is vitally important that intergenerational work be established as a socially, culturally, and economically essential practice. It ought to be a major consideration in upstream health policy, a regular practice within social care, an established component of educational curriculum, and an accepted consideration in urban planning and development. Intergenerational work can and should be used as a targeted approach applied to local and national priorities such as school readiness, the disadvantage gap, social action, social prescribing, and community disconnect and tension. Global Intergenerational Week creates an opportunity to refine this understanding, drawing on important findings from across the globe. The variety of themes explored across the week help to shed light on the wide relevance and applicability of intergenerational practice, across a range of policy areas—from education to urban/rural development to health and social care.

The relational element of the campaign also creates a unique opportunity for shared learning based on different perspectives and provokes consideration of how different cultural nuances can impact the way intergenerational projects might be delivered in different cultural contexts. For example, in Mexico (and in wider South American contexts), respect for elders, or *respeto*, places older people at the heart of decision-making in families, due to perceived wisdom. Nordic cultures often emphasize the need for greater political deliberation and participation of younger groups.[4] Asian cultures (though not exhaustively or exclusively), place great importance on the value of family, and households often have three and sometimes four generations cohabiting. While it is of course interesting to learn about different cultural values, these learnings also help to inform intergenerational practice in local contexts. In an ever-globalized world, in which different cultures and norms regularly intersect, it allows us to rethink the way in which projects are delivered locally. Scotland is a richly diverse and progressive nation, and therefore, understanding and incorporating ideas and cultural nuances from other countries into local projects ensures that greater inclusivity is achieved. Global Intergenerational Week is therefore not just an awareness-raising campaign; it's a unique learning experience, and one crucial to the development of intergenerational best practice in local contexts. Global Intergenerational Week is incredibly powerful and enables intergenerational practitioners from around the world, regardless of the level or scale that they work at, to build relationships and unite in a shared conversation.

The Value of Relationships

Relationships are central to the success of grassroots intergenerational work in Scotland, not just for the participants and the supporting staff, but also in the partnerships that are built at the program delivery, strategic, and research levels. In an emerging field, information about intergenerational work grows with every program that takes place and with every written evaluation, case study, and academic project report that is shared. As awareness of the benefits of intergenerational work increases so does the demand for information. It is important to recognize the significant role of grassroots practitioners in this evolution, highlighting the need for good practice and ongoing learning.

There is no doubt that the support GWT offers its members through its geographical networks is instrumental in the success and growth of intergenerational work in Scotland. The eighteen local networks, along with four thematic networks and an international network are designed to create opportunities for individuals, groups, and organizations from all sectors to increase knowledge and understanding in the field of intergenerational practice. Each network (except for the international network) meets two to four times each year (some face-to-face meetings and some online), providing opportunities for people to share their expertise and knowledge, form new partnerships, improve their practice, and access training and resources. Network meetings are designed not only to support existing intergenerational practitioners from all levels and sectors (private/public and nongovernment organizations) but also to welcome and support those new to intergenerational work and link them to potential community partners, which can often be challenging, particularly in a rural area. Attendees come from a wide range of professional fields, ranging from education, health, adult social care, local government, and libraries to architecture, the arts, and faith groups. Online meetings enable those who do not live on the mainland or who would have to travel some distance to build relationships with other practitioners. This is invaluable in enabling intergenerational work to be developed in the islands or very rural areas. Relationships are an essential part of the network, linking new practitioners to "buddies" who will support their understanding of intergenerational work as well as signpost them to training and information. The networks are a great example of not reinventing the wheel, as new members are able to access information that has been tried and tested. Intergenerational programs can be planned and developed more quickly when people can follow a "top tips" approach and avoid potential delays, frustrations, and pitfalls.

GWT networks also provide a direct communication pathway between GWT, its staff, and the wider intergenerational community in Scotland, enabling GWT to cascade information quickly and efficiently. This may be information about funding, online intergenerational events, new research, or training opportunities. The networks also provide a means of consulting directly with GWT members, gauging their opinion, asking questions, or testing ideas at the practice level. Universities and research students regularly contact GWT to source interested partners when developing funding bids, which in turn provides an opportunity for grassroots organizations in Scotland to be directly involved in ground-breaking research.

Networks also provide volunteer opportunities for members to either support local intergenerational programs or to become GWT network coordinators as their knowledge of intergenerational work deepens. Ongoing training and practical hands-on delivery experience builds people's knowledge and confidence, which in turn raises awareness as the number of intergenerational programs increases.

Collaborating on a regular basis with colleagues from other countries provides opportunities not only to share strengths and challenges but also to reflect, learn from others, and gain insight. Being part of a network of like-minded colleagues who sustain, inspire, and motivate each other has empowered GWT to be bold and aspirational. While intergenerational work across countries may share certain core principles, the delivery of intergenerational programs across diverse professional fields has meant that even developing a universal understanding of the language used within intergenerational work is problematic. Without a shared language, how can there be a universal understanding of intergenerational practice, particularly at the point of delivery?

GWT is increasingly convinced of the value of naming the language and terminology needed to describe and measure quality within intergenerational practice and is very aware of the need for this to happen at all levels, particularly the grassroots practice level. In 2022, GWT changed the criteria for their annual Excellence Awards, linking them directly to the nine intergenerational standards.[5] As a result of proactively asking applicants to reflect upon and identify standards of excellence within their programs, GWT saw a huge increase in the quality of applications. Grassroots practitioners rose to the challenge. This highlighted the need and demand for some sort of quality standard that could be used to reflect and measure the impact and value of intergenerational work. Encouraged and supported by an advisory panel of international colleagues, GWT is currently involved in writing and developing a set of quality indicators in partnership with Linking Generations (Northern Ireland) and Apples & Honey Nightingale (England) in a two-and-a-half-year National Lottery–funded pilot project called Creating Intergenerational Communities. This would not have been possible without support from our colleagues.

An ongoing challenge for an emerging field of new practice lies in the relationship between academic research and intergenerational practice, and it can often be complex. Those developing intergenerational programs often rely on research data and use it as a "go-to" in order to gather evidence-based information that substantiates a piece of work or a funding bid. Research can also help the intergenerational community to prioritize its work. For example, a recent mapping tool developed by Exeter University[6] revealed that the majority of intergenerational research focuses on evaluating early years programs; there is very little of anything else. However, it should also be acknowledged that academic research can also be a barrier to understanding intergenerational work at a deeper level because of unfamiliar terminology and "high" academic language. It can be hard for grassroots practitioners to translate written research and visualize how it would look on the ground. Consequently, research is often not fully utilized, and opportunities for further testing and implementing the learning are being lost. While GWT celebrates and shares relevant research with its members through its resource library and research network, its value is often underappreciated, which is disappointing. Moving forward to make research more relevant to practitioners, perhaps academic funding bid writers should work closely with practitioners at the planning stage so that they can fully understand how their research would translate at the delivery level. In order to draw attention to intergenerational research and its potential impact at the grassroots level, GWT has based the development of quality indicators (previously discussed) upon current research[7] and aims to illustrate the mutually beneficial relationship that could exist between the two fields.

GWT is a catalyst organization offering training and support to staff and volunteers from other organizations, who then have the skills, knowledge, and confidence to plan and deliver intergenerational projects and activities. The relationships that GWT has with other organizations are instrumental in helping to build an intergenerational Scotland, and GWT regularly collaborates with others. A good example of this is the partnership with Play Scotland in producing a new toolkit to aid practitioners in developing intergenerational relationships through the rich golden strands of play and storytelling. The toolkit supports intergenerational development, builds confidence in practitioners, and inspires best practice. Partnership work is generally mutually beneficial. For example, Education Scotland has been involved in writing curriculum links for GWT's primary school module. GWT hopes that the module will be used by teachers to prepare children for engaging with older adults and that every child in Scotland will experience and take part in an intergenerational program in their community. With support from Education Scotland, teachers will see how intergenerational work fits within the curriculum, not as an add-on to their work, but simply as a different way to deliver the curriculum.

GWT recognizes the need to find the hook to encourage more local authorities to develop intergenerational work, because when this works well, it has the potential to impact positively upon the whole community. A good example of this is Fife Local Authority, whose leaders, after attending GWT network meetings and coming to understand the benefits of an intergenerational approach, invested in intergenerational training for staff and then made the decision to fund and build the first intergenerational shared site in Scotland at Methil. The shared site consists of a new thirty-six-bed residential care home and a thirty-nine-place nursery for two- to four-year-olds, with thirty-five extra care and specific-needs bungalows for older people set around a "village green." The site also houses a café that is open to the community. Intergenerational work has much in common with local authorities' targets and priorities, particularly the ongoing challenge of reducing loneliness and isolation and reconnecting communities. Building relationships with other organizations and working effectively with them enables GWT to provide feedback to strategic groups and become involved in wider conversations in Scotland, such as ageing well, building age-friendly communities, developing intergenerational workplaces that capitalize on generational knowledge, and challenging ageism on behalf of both the old and the young.

Increasing people's knowledge of and confidence in developing intergenerational work has been a key factor in the increase of grassroots programs in Scotland. GWT's training program has been proven to increase confidence, skills, knowledge, and leadership and has been a positive way for people and organizations to network, signpost, and access good-practice resources and case studies.

It is essential that intergenerational training is offered at a variety of knowledge levels to ensure that it is not only meaningful and relevant at the practitioner level but also supports community program planning and delivery and informs policy-makers and leaders, as well as providing an international overview of intergenerational work and the fields in which it can be applied. To ensure that training remains relevant and responsive to practitioners' needs, an evaluation was recently carried out to determine the impact of the training. The evaluation concluded that GWT intergenerational training courses offer substantial benefits that empower participants to engage effectively in intergenerational practice. These benefits foster personal and professional growth and impact intergenerational connections. For GWT, the most important part of this evaluation is participants' recommendations about the type of training they need now, enabling GWT to plan and develop training accordingly.

Despite the remarkable growth in intergenerational work in Scotland, it's important to acknowledge ongoing challenges in further developing intergenerational work. One of the key challenges is that it is often driven and delivered by one person within an organization, and if that person leaves, the intergenerational work then often stops. Not only is this frustrating and time consuming, but it also has a negative impact on the different generations of people who have become friends. GWT is proactively trying to prevent this from happening by increasing the number of people wanting to lead intergenerational programs. For example, providing intergenerational experiences for young children through the primary school module should grow a number of intergenerational champions who will want to engage and volunteer in intergenerational work. GWT plans to promote this by developing a secondary-school module for young people that supports them in developing intergenerational programs in their own community. A handbook for older adults, encouraging them to volunteer and lead intergenerational programs, is also being developed. The handbook will paint a picture of the roles available to older adults within these programs, so that regardless of confidence level, skill, or ability, there will be a meaningful place for them that will make them feel valued and appreciated.

Challenging misconceptions around intergenerational work—that is, that it just involves early-years children and adults in residential care and that it is nice rather than essential—is a large part of GWT's daily work. Added to the list of misconceptions is the belief that intergenerational work can only happen if it is funded. Trying to source funding is time-consuming and often unproductive. When programs are funded, they are often time-bound, and the negative implication of this should be recognized. What happens when a program comes to an end? Is there an exit plan in place to continue the friendships that are forged? If the aim of a program is to reduce isolation and loneliness, one cannot ignore the irony when at the end of the program, participants may feel even more alone because connections have been severed. It is far better that time is spent building strong partnerships with others in the community so that resources (skills, venues, transport) can be shared to develop a *sustainable* program around the existing delivery of services or activities, rather than an add-on that requires additional resources and is hard to maintain. Effective relationships between community groups and organizations can lead to sustainable intergenerational work and reduced reliance on funding. Intergenerational programs initiated and developed by the community increase buy-in and ownership, which in turn strengthen the legacy of what takes place. It therefore makes sense to focus the development of intergenerational programs within the community, led by practitioners who already have or can build the necessary relationships. Empowering communities and shared ownership help to promote positive attitudes and tackle the very things that need to be changed, such as ageism, stereotypes, and social isolation, as well as linking with local and national outcomes.

GWT gives individuals and organizations the opportunity to build an infrastructure of strong connectedness across and between generations and communities. Intergenerational work directly helps organizations to look at health and well-being in local communities and links with social prescribing. It focuses on creating intergenerational housing, places, and spaces within the built environment and highlights the importance of connectedness between generations tackling isolation and loneliness.

GWT is determined to continue the success of intergenerational work in Scotland and champion the importance of grassroots practitioners in developing community-based programs, testing research, and defining quality and good practice. There is so much more to do, such as developing buddy programs, and establishing centers of excellence where people can access "live" learning and have an opportunity to observe and discuss good practice with like-minded colleagues. Relationships remain the key to whether this happens. For relationships to be effective, we need to continue to invest our time in developing them, taking time to talk and listen, reflect, and learn. Dr. Mariano Sánchez once commented that "interactions require a moment, relationships require a process."[8] GWT remains convinced that Scotland will become an intergenerational nation, however much there is to do.

Notes

1. "GWT Corporate Plan 2020-2025. Towards an Intergenerationally Connected Scotland," Generations Working Together, accessed September 29, 2023, https://generationsworkingtogether.org/resources/gwt-corporate-plan-2020-25.
2. "Recovering Our Connections 2023-2026," Scottish Government, accessed September 5, 2023, https://www.gov.scot/publications/recovering-connections-2023-2026/documents/.
3. Gerhardt et al., *Gentelligence: The Revolutionary Approach to Leading an Intergenerational Workforce* (Rowman & Littlefield, 2021).

4. de la Porte et al., "Introduction: Studying Successful Public Policy in the Nordic Countries," (2022), 1–24, https://doi.org/10.1093/oso/9780192856296.003.0001.; Johanna Einarsdottir and John. A. Wagner, *Nordic Childhoods and Early Education: Philosophy, Research, Policy and Practice in Denmark, Finland, Iceland, Norway, and Sweden* (IAP, 2006); Patricia Loncle et al., *Youth Participation in Europe: Beyond Discourses, Practices and Realities* (Bristol University Press, 2012).
5. Mariano Sánchez et al., "9 Quality Standards in Intergenerational Work: The Intergenerational Certificate in Intergenerational Learning's Nine Quality Standards in Intergenerational Work," Generations United, accessed September 5, 2023, https://www.gu.org/resources/9-standards-in-intergenerational-work/.
6. Generations Working Together, "New Tools for Measuring Impact of Intergenerational Work," accessed September 29, 2023, https://generationsworkingtogether.org/news/new-tools-for-measuring-impact-of-intergenerational-work-24-08-2023.
7. Sánchez et al., "Intergenerational Programs and Intergenerational Contact Zones: Aligning Notions of 'Good Quality,'" in *Intergenerational Contact Zones*," ed. Matthew Kaplan et al. (Routledge, 2020): 274–85.
8. Dr. Mariano Sánchez, Macrosad Chair in Intergenerational Studies, University of Granada, personal communication with authors, September 2021.

Bibliography

Campbell, F., R. Whear, M. Rogers, A. Sutton, E. Robinson-Carter, J. Barlow, et al. "Non-familial Intergenerational Interventions and Their Impact on Social and Mental Well-being of Both Younger and Older People: A Mapping Review and Evidence and Gap Map." *Campbell Systematic Reviews* 19, no. 1 (2023): e1306. https://doi.org/10.1002/cl2.1306.

de la Porte, Caroline, Guðný Björk Eydal, Jaakko Kauko, Daniel Nohrstedt, Paul 't Hart, and Bent Sofus Tranøy. "Introduction: Studying Successful Public Policy in the Nordic Countries." (2022): 1–24. https://doi.org/10.1093/oso/9780192856296.003.0001.

Einarsdottir, Johanna, and John A. Wagner. *Nordic Childhoods and Early Education: Philosophy, Research, Policy and Practice in Denmark, Finland, Iceland, Norway, and Sweden*. IAP, 2006.

Generations Working Together. "GWT Corporate Plan 2020-2025. Towards an Intergenerationally Connected Scotland." Accessed September 29, 2023. https://generationsworkingtogether.org/resources/gwt-corporate-plan-2020-25.

Generations Working Together. "New Tools for Measuring Impact of Intergenerational Work." Accessed September 29, 2023. https://generationsworkingtogether.org/news/new-tools-for-measuring-impact-of-intergenerational-work-24-08-2023.

Gerhardt, Megan, Josephine Nachemson-Ekwall, and Brandon Fogel. *Gentelligence: The Revolutionary Approach to Leading an Intergenerational Workforce*. Rowman & Littlefield, 2021.

Loncle, Patricia, Morena Cuconato, Virginie Muniglia, and Andreas Walther. *Youth Participation in Europe: Beyond Discourses, Practices and Realities*. Bristol University Press, 2012. https://doi.org/10.2307/j.ctt9qgr4k.

Sánchez, Mariano, Alison Clyde, and Sandra Brown. "9 Quality Standards in Intergenerational Work: The Intergenerational Certificate in Intergenerational Learning's Nine Quality Standards in Intergenerational Work." Generations United. Accessed September 5, 2023. https://www.gu.org/resources/9-standards-in-intergenerational-work/.

Sánchez, Mariano, María Pilar Díaz, Andrés Rodríguez, and Rosa Bonachela. "Intergenerational Programs and Intergenerational Contact Zones: Aligning Notions of 'Good Quality.'" In *Intergenerational Contact Zones*, edited by Matthew Kaplan, Leng Leng Thang, Mariano Sánchez, and Jaco Hoffman, 274–85. Routledge, 2020.

Scottish Government. "Recovering Our Connections 2023-2026." Accessed September 5, 2023. https://www.gov.scot/publications/recovering-connections-2023-2026/documents/.

CHAPTER 19

The TOY Project and Development of Intergenerational Learning Training in Europe

Anne Fitzpatrick, Carmel Gallagher, Margaret Kernan, *and* Giulia Cortellesi

Abstract

This chapter traces the development of the international TOY online learning course, "Together Old and Young: An Intergenerational Approach," from its concept and design phase through to its pilot delivery as a blended learning course and in many iterations as a massive online open course. A central theme in the chapter is the importance of values and attitudes in the work of intergenerational learning practitioners and the contribution of the TOY course to developing intergenerational learning and cultural awareness through the attention given to experiential learning and reflection. The chapter also critically examines the opportunities and challenges online learning offers adult learners in diverse cultural contexts.

Key Words: TOY course, intergenerational learning, experiential learning, values, online learning

Together Old and Young: An Intergenerational Approach
Strengths/impact   • Awareness of and expertise in intergenerational learning   • Development of good-quality, sustainable intergenerational practice   • Diverse backgrounds of learners from over forty countries.   • Accessible and free   • Higher-than-average completion rates
Limitations   • Difficult to sustain financially   • Dependent on volunteer model

Introduction

Human beings have a natural inclination to act together, to create together, to play together and to learn together.

—*Jerome Bruner, The Culture of Education, 1996*

There is a universality in the social relations between generations, even when inflected by cultural nuance, that is expressed in the connections between young children and the older adults in their lives, whether they be grandparents, neighbors, or seniors volunteering in community-based intergenerational learning programs.[1]

In 2012 a group of nongovernment organizations and higher-education institutions in seven countries in Europe began research and development work about intergenerational learning, with a particular focus on young children and older adults—the Together Old and Young (TOY) project. Partner organizations in TOY shared a yearning for more space and time for young children and older adults to be together, learn with and from each other, and derive meaning and joy from each other's company. This is encapsulated in Jerome Bruner's social view of learning in the epigraph above.

The research and development work at the core of the TOY project demonstrated that along with an eagerness to create opportunities for young and old to be together, there was a need to broaden and deepen the scholarship about intergenerational practice, particularly focusing on young children and older adults. This required integrating knowledge and insights about human development and relationships to deepen our understanding of intergenerational relations as they are experienced in different cultural contexts. An equally important and related task was to develop and deliver training about intergenerational learning using research-informed practice guidelines and tools for practitioners working in early childhood education and care (ECEC), community development, and social and elder care.[2] A further aim was to create a community of practice in intergenerational learning.

Developing Intergenerational Practice through the TOY Course

The TOY program is firmly rooted in the idea that values are central to developing intergenerational learning practice and must be the foundation of any training and development program. Fitzpatrick has suggested that intergenerational learning has much to offer in considering essentially philosophical questions about what we as a society want for the young and old.[3] As Bronfenbrenner insisted, a sustainable society relies on citizens who "have learned the sensitivities, motivations and the skills involved in assisting and caring for other human beings."[4]

This chapter traces the development of the TOY training course, "Together Old and Young: An Intergenerational Approach," a four-module online course about intergenerational learning involving young children and older adults, from its concept and design phase through to its pilot delivery as a blended learning course and in many iterations since as a massive online open course, or MOOC. It highlights the centrality of values and attitudes in intergenerational practice and the importance of experiential learning in developing reflective, culturally attuned, and socially aware intergenerational practitioners. Strategies that are particularly effective in supporting the development of intergenerational practitioners are identified and discussed. These include flexible learning modalities, reflective learning, and communities of practice.

Primary and secondary sources informing the chapter include the TOY Course Handbook, reflections of learners who have participated in the course, the TOY website (www.toyproject.net), which functions as a transnational platform about intergenerational learning providing access to publications, the TOY blog series, and research conducted by Anne Fitzpatrick (one of the chapter authors) about intergenerational learning as a pedagogical strategy in ECEC services.

Overview of the TOY Course Design

Between 2012 and 2014, TOY partner organizations[5] researched the benefits of intergenerational learning for young children, older adults, and their communities and developed a framework for intergenerational learning through a project funded by the European Commission's Grundtvig-Lifelong Learning Programme. Findings from this project identified a strong need to build the skills and competencies of practitioners who want to develop quality intergenerational learning practice. The learners involved in this first phase of the TOY project contributed to the development of a community of practice as they sought more opportunities to engage in cross-national exchanges enabling them to learn about good practices in different contexts and to be able to transfer this knowledge into their own practices.

Building on the findings of the first phase of the TOY project, a second project, TOY-PLUS (Together Old and Young: Practitioners Learning and Upscaling Skills) was initiated in 2016. The aim of TOY-PLUS was to develop an online training course to support the professional development of ECEC practitioners, social care practitioners, and community development workers in the field of intergenerational learning. This project was funded by the European Commission's Erasmus+ Programme–Adult Education (KA2) and coordinated as in the previous phase by International Child Development Initiatives (the Netherlands) in partnership with seven European organizations.[6]

When TOY-PLUS started, there had been a number of initiatives to promote professional development opportunities regarding intergenerational learning within Europe. However, there were no courses with a special focus on intergenerational learning practice involving young children and older adults, even though intergenerational learning is a natural fit for ECEC, given that working with families and community is central to ECEC pedagogy.[7] Creating an online course had the advantage of reaching participants from different countries, different areas of work, and diverse cultures and backgrounds. Online learning also created opportunities for practitioners to engage remotely in cross-country learning exchanges and share knowledge and reflections about intergenerational learning. Such a course could reach working professionals as well as students and volunteers, ultimately creating an international community of practice on intergenerational learning between young children and older adults. In its conceptualization phase, potential learners in the TOY course were envisaged to be

- ECEC practitioners,
- primary school teachers (working with four- to ten-year-olds),
- social care practitioners working with older adults,
- community development workers (i.e., practitioners and volunteers working in community groups, such as those linked to community social and cultural centers, sports clubs, or scouting or religious institutions),
- practitioners and volunteers working in libraries and museums,
- educational specialists in nonformal learning, and
- those in leadership, policy, and/or advocacy positions in any of the above areas.

Although the course was intended for learners in Europe, it had the ambition to reach a global audience, in part due to its online delivery mode. Other important considerations regarding the design and delivery of the TOY course are described below.

The first step in developing the TOY course was to identify learning outcomes, the formulation of which was informed by Bloom's Taxonomy of Learning (revised) and included both cognitive and affective domains.[8] The basic level of the course was put on European Qualifications Framework level 5.[9] The identified learning outcomes were as follows:

1. Know the importance and relevance of intergenerational learning in today's changing society.
2. Value the contribution of intergenerational learning to building generationally and socially inclusive communities.
3. Know what a quality intergenerational learning initiative looks like and be able to apply monitoring and evaluation approaches to assess quality in intergenerational learning activities.
4. Develop a vision, goals, and strategies for intergenerational learning in their setting and sector.
5. Understand the importance of sustainability, the factors that hinder or support intergenerational learning work, and how it can be embedded in policy and practice.[10]

The next step in development was to build the course modules and units and digitize the content for the learning platform on the website of Hellenic Open University, the technical partners in TOY-PLUS. The TOY course developers incorporated a broad range of flexible modalities and activities in each module: videos, interviews, short and longer readings, illustrated PowerPoint lectures with voice-over, reflection questions, and summary info-graphics and quizzes at the end of each module. The expected study effort per weekly module was estimated to be six hours. Engagement with fellow learners and tutors was encouraged and facilitated via discussion forums, where learners could introduce themselves and share their views, experiences, and reflections on particular aspects of intergenerational learning.

Two options were considered for the delivery of the TOY course:

- Option 1: A blended learning approach combining a four-module online MOOC with two face-to-face workshops
- Option 2: A fully online four-module MOOC

Option 1, the blended learning approach that combines online and in-person learning, was piloted and evaluated in April to June 2018. A total of eighty-two learners from Ireland, Italy, Northern Ireland, Spain, and Slovenia who worked in ECEC, social and health care services, community development, adult education, and local government participated in the MOOC and in two three-hour face-to-face workshops in their own country. Twenty-seven of those learners traveled to a week-long international workshop that took place in Dublin in May 2018. The local and cross-national in-person workshops deepened learning and provided opportunities to reflect with peers on values and attitudes that contribute to effective intergenerational practice and the development of communities of practice. Lessons learned from the pilot phase were considered in the final version of the course, which was made publicly available in October 2018.

Effective Online Learning for Adult Learners.

When the TOY online course was in its conceptualization phase in 2016 and 2017, online learning with blended learning was one of the main global trends shaping adult and higher education.[11] So-called massive open online courses (or MOOCs) were becoming an integral part of the learning process, especially in higher education.[12] The reasons for this significant expansion included the ubiquity of digital technologies, an increasingly diverse learner population, and the need for more flexible learning environments—all of which go hand in hand with lifelong learning,[13] a key value in intergenerational learning.

The flexible learning modalities inherent in online learning—in particular, self-pacing that allows learners to decide when and where they study—are very attractive to adult learners, the target audience for the TOY course, who have time constraints and competing responsibilities. Another advantage is that online learning is accessible and accommodating to diverse learners. As an effective pedagogical strategy, online discussion forums also gave participants for whom English is not the first language more time to refine their contributions.[14] (From the outset, a large proportion of the learners in the TOY course were ECEC practitioners based in Ireland. Reasons for this included the efforts of TOY partners in Ireland—North and South—to embed intergenerational learning in undergraduate and postgraduate courses in early childhood education and social sciences and the fact that the TOY course is in English and therefore easily accessible to learners in Ireland.)

However, a disadvantage of online learning is that course participants can feel disconnected from their peer learners and tutor group. High drop-out rates and low completion rates are a characteristic of online courses. A study of 221 MOOCs assessed completion rates to be between 1 percent and 52 percent with a median value of just 12 percent.[15] Thus, while adult learners are best served by the flexibility of online training programs, they may also be vulnerable to the hazards that flexibility inherently possesses. One of these concerns is being less confident in their "technology savviness or being able to navigate a learning platform."[16]

Given concerns about poor engagement and high drop-out rates, the TOY course development team paid attention to including elements proven in other MOOCs and blended learning courses to enhance positive learner experience and course retention. Such factors include engaging course content, interaction with the instructor/tutors and with other learners, and the availability of support for assisting in specific problems. Furthermore, for the pilot version of the TOY course, a decision was made to develop a curriculum that could be delivered through a blended learning approach, combining online and in-person learning and offering students the best of both learning worlds.

In summary, the TOY course modeled the following five principles of effective and meaningful blended learning.[17]

Creation of a (global) learning community	Participants are encouraged and supported to view themselves as pioneers and innovators in their sector. Peer learning is central, and each learner is a valuable resource to the group of learners and tutors. This face-to-face and online communication forms the basis of a strong community of practice.
Promotion of learning partnerships	A partnership approach to learning and teaching underpins the course with learners and tutors learning together. Partnership is mirrored in the TOY approach to intergenerational learning whereby young children and older people are cocreators of knowledge, and curriculum is viewed as emergent.
Active learning	The TOY course is based on active learning: there is time for thinking, doing, and reflecting on real settings and real practice and problems. Developing opportunities for intergenerational learning involving young children and older adults is encouraged throughout the course.
Diversity and cultural context	Social inclusion and respect for diversity are important aims in intergenerational learning. The TOY course draws on examples from a wide range of cultural and social contexts and settings and encourages reflection on values and attitudes.
Creating change	The development of the TOY course involved action research, and it built capacity for innovation and change.

Five Years of TOY Online

Since its public launch in 2018, the TOY course has been offered once or twice a year as a stand-alone four-module online MOOC that learners can complete at their own pace over a period of five to six weeks. Tutors are online and available through discussion forums and private messaging at every iteration. The eventual decision to deliver the course only in its online form was due to time, travel, and budgetary challenges for practitioners, students, and TOY tutors with respect to attending face-to-face workshops. The online delivery mode resulted in increased availability, allowing more participants from a wider range of countries to join the course and learn about intergenerational learning practice. Notably, soon after its public launch, the TOY course started attracting learners from continents other than Europe and became global, with participation from more than forty countries. At the same time, without face-to-face interaction it reduced opportunities for deepening learning and creating local or country-based communities of practice.

Since the launch, 1,903 learners have registered for the course: 1,051 started and 418 successfully completed it. Successful completion of all units in all modules and having at least 80 percent success in the quizzes deems a participant eligible to upgrade and receive a TOY Certificate of Achievement. Notably, the average completion rate is 40 percent, much higher than the retention rate of other MOOCs. A number of factors account for this. Between 2018 and 2022, the TOY course has been continuously updated to include new perspectives and experiences from intergenerational learning research and practice. While children and older adults were not directly involved in the TOY course, their active participation in planning and reviewing intergenerational activities is emphasized throughout the course. New content was added in relation to intergenerational learning and technologies, cultural diversity, social inclusion, and quality and sustainability in intergenerational learning. In revising the course, evaluation of participants' experience was central in identifying gaps both in the content and in the learning experience. Improvements were also made to the registration process, access to the discussion forum, and navigation between modules.

During the COVID-19 pandemic (2020–2022), the TOY course ran twice, in spring and autumn 2020. These were the most critical periods of lockdown, when all educational and social services were closed and opportunities for socialization and contact in general were very limited, even more so between young children and older adults. In this period, the course was revised to include content that could support practitioners regarding their immediate response during COVID and included examples of intergenerational learning initiatives featuring alternative ways to facilitate interactions that did not involve physical contact. In this period, the discussion forums served as an important exchange platform where learners could express their concerns, thus creating an online global support network and emergent community of practice.

The Importance of Experiential Learning and Reflection in Intergenerational Learning Practice

As noted earlier in the chapter, the TOY course was developed to facilitate experiential learning and reflection. A central focus of the course was on the values underpinning intergenerational practice and how these are actualized in different countries as well as in diverse social and cultural contexts. Key questions were designed for each module to elicit deliberation and responses in discussion forums. These responses and reflections were very useful for the tutors who were supporting the online learners. The forum discussions clearly helped learners develop cultural and intergenerational awareness and sensitivities. The course also sensitized participants to social exclusion and social inclusion. The forums facilitated a type of dialogue giving learners the opportunity to broaden their thinking and understanding of the diverse cultural and social scenarios where intergenerational learning could enhance the lives of children, older adults, and families.

For example, learners were asked to consider social and demographic changes observed in their work or community setting. Learners reflected on the key role of grandparents in children's lives. Their nurturing presence and role as guardians of culture and history were highlighted, as the following quotes illustrate:

I remember when I was a child I used to go to my grandparents who provided a font of activities for me: sewing, bicycling, telling stories about war, reading a journal, and (I treasure this memory), they used to teach me a lot of things about ancient music with a record player. These activities in their simplicity were for me more important than TV or plays because for me my grandparents were "chests of knowledge". Today I observe that this important role is lost and it's passed to technological devices that have deleted this fundamental social relationship.

Grandparents are a very important memory, the seed of life. They can tell us about the past and give us a more clear and true vision of our roots. Especially in times like these, where the frenzy and rhythms that society requires of us are ultra-fast, grandparents can give back to children the dynamics of slowness.

The values that can be lost by lack of relationships between young and old was a concern reflected in the discussion forums of many participants:

Overall, as a society this [children who do not have relationships with older generations] does have an impact on the values surrounding young children. Valuable storytelling and sharing can be lost, caring and empathy which should be very highly valued in society take a back seat to profitability and the work mentality. We live in a society where the lowest paid workers are nurses, front line staff, early years educators, and yet we have one of the most instrumental roles to play in society.

Practitioners also reflected on the special importance of intergenerational learning for isolated older people:

In my workplace we have a number of much older people without regular visits from family, sometimes this is because they have outlived their spouses and don't have children or grandchildren, or if they have, their family have moved further away or abroad to find employment.

In contrast, this next learner described herself as a "working granny," and she saw her situation with her own grandchildren as "timetabled." She hopes "to develop ways to provide a new family experience within my workplace that everyone can feel part of."

Learners reflected on the visibility of children and older people in their communities, and this elicited concern about the relative passivity, powerlessness, and participation of each age group. Wondering what life would be like if we did not have older adults and children, one learner noted,

We would miss our roots and wings . . . the roots that lead us to know what is our history . . . the wings that push us to have goals. Unfortunately, today both older adults and children are seen as passive subjects, as spectators, and not as protagonists of important pieces of life.

Reflecting on the visibility of children and older adults, one learner thought neither was visible, but the course has made her think. While she sees older people and children in shops, out walking, and riding their bikes, she concluded, "I am not sure that they see each other."

Another participant saw how both groups had become more visible to each other through an intergenerational learning initiative in her ECEC service:

It is a very mixed-age community. We have lots of grandparents collecting their children from the Montessori school on a daily basis, and when we walk to the local nursing home, we pass through the church grounds where we are often stopped by the older people for a chat as they are going into Mass.

Societal values came to particular prominence in forum discussions when courses were delivered in the aftermath of restrictions of movement imposed by COVID-19:

I do feel with all its challenges Covid has made us all stop and think of how we can stay connected more to the older generation (with grandparents and older neighbours, etc.) and has made us all think about that, so hopefully we will see more of a shift towards staying connected and longer-term values of empathy, caring, community belonging will surface. This is why I am excited about this course, learning more and trying to see where intergenerational community could come together to enrich our everyday lives.

Course participants identified the importance of what could be termed "the glue of intergenerational connectedness." Older adults were seen to offer solid reference points and continuity with the past, as well as contributing wisdom, patience, knowledge of traditions and values, and tenderness. Without the presence of children, course participants suggested there would be

> *a lack of spontaneity, innocence, cheerfulness, joy of life and inexhaustible energy. All are fundamental in our society, and a society without them is unthinkable and harmful.*

The positive course participant feedback highlights the values of learning from the experiences of others and the importance of reflecting on values and developing new perspectives. In this regard, a key strength of the TOY course was the diversity of learners, in both a geographic and interdisciplinary sense. The course provided a space to meet "the other" virtually, thereby making it possible for learners to step into the shoes of another age group, ethnic group, or social group. Looking at others in a new way—for example, elders, children, migrants, people with disabilities, and so on—made it more likely that any intergenerational learning interventions would be attuned to the values of all generations and social groups. This perspective was illuminated by one learner:

> *What could be more important than empathy (learning how to put yourself in another person's shoes)? This is how we gain a better understanding of ourselves and others, building our lives on mutual respect, happiness, and harmony.*

The learning experiences of the TOY participants resonate with Moss's views of the key characteristics of the ECEC practitioner: open-ended; open-minded, and open-hearted.[18] Furthermore, they reflect a key standard of intergenerational practice: intergenerational practitioners are reflective, ethical, and caring professionals, with vision and passion to facilitate intergenerational encounters.[19]

Implementing Intergenerational Learning in ECEC Practice—Lessons from Research

Following development of the TOY course, one of the TOY tutors carried out further research on intergenerational learning in ECEC services in Ireland with practitioners who had completed the TOY course. The aim of the research was to investigate the concept and potential of intergenerational learning as a pedagogical strategy in Irish ECEC services. It involved exploring the perspectives of educators (five), children (seventy), and their parents (forty-three) using qualitative methodologies. While the focus of the study was on educators' views of intergenerational learning as a pedagogical strategy in Irish ECE services, the views of children and parents contributed to a multilayered understanding of intergenerational learning and young children. A high level of enthusiasm for intergenerational learning was recorded among children using drawing and talking methodologies. Particularly valued by children were their friendships with older adults, their sense of belonging in the community, and the fun they experienced through intergenerational learning experiences. Overwhelmingly positive feedback from parents about their children's participation in intergenerational learning cited benefits including valuable learning experiences for children, nurturing relationships with older adults, and opportunities for their children to contribute positively to the lives of others. (The full study can be accessed at https://arrow.tudublin.ie/appadoc/106/). The findings from this research highlighted the pivotal role of educators and their values in initiating and implementing successful intergenerational learning. This key finding validated the methodology adopted by the TOY course, which placed the exploration of values as crucial in preparing practitioners for intergenerational learning practice.

In the Irish study, implementing intergenerational learning as a pedagogical strategy was found to reflect a particular set of values deeply held by educators about children and their learning and the role of children and older adults in communities. Critical starting points for educators implementing intergenerational learning were a strong belief in the importance of nurturing relationships for children's development and well-being, their right to live as fully fledged members of communities, and the value of intergenerational learning as a vehicle to enhance children's visibility and their participation as citizens. They said,

To be happy, that is one of the most important things [for children attending the ECEC service].
(Educator)
Nobody ever thinks of offering young children a role in the community. (Educator)

Children's contribution of their time, energy, empathy, and ideas contributed greatly to the lives of the older adults with whom they interacted, reflecting their potential as contributors and beneficiaries of social capital through intergenerational learning. Furthermore, practitioners implementing intergenerational learning had in common a strong belief in the foundational role that positive socio-emotional development played in the holistic development and well-being of children.[20]

Educators acknowledged the wide-ranging benefits of the nurturing relationships that developed between young children and older adults through intergenerational practice. Placing their trust in intergenerational learning as a relational pedagogy, educators emphasized how essential these relationships are for children feeling loved and happy, having a positive sense of identity, a link to their cultural heritage, and importantly, for facilitating the development of strong executive functions (skills to manage everyday life). Educators demonstrated their belief in the significant value that older adults who are not trained or acknowledged as teachers can bring to children's learning and development.[21] Furthermore, educators in the Irish study reflected a very broad understanding of who teachers and learners are, valuing both children and older adults in these roles. Importantly, educators implementing intergenerational learning held wide-ranging understandings of curriculum and the learning environment. They looked to the opportunities offered by the curriculum of ordinary life as they moved beyond the walls of the ECEC service, seeking out the benefits of the risk-rich environments of community spaces, including those where older adults live or spend time:

This time last year I would not have thought of a crèche visiting a day centre or a nursing home . . . why would you do such a thing . . . and now I'm asking, "why would you not do such a thing?"
(Educator)

Educators' ability to use creatively what was available in everyday life was particularly evident during COVID when they made use of drawings, postcards, letters, social media, and outdoor environments to maintain relationships between young children and older adults (see TOY blog posts for further examples: www.toyproject.net/blog/). Thus, educators in this study espoused the strengths of the "golden triangle" of community-based ECEC services, which draw together informal, nonformal, and formal approaches to learning.[22]

A further important finding of the study was educators' belief that intergenerational learning supported not only children but also parents and communities. In introducing intergenerational learning, educators were responding to parental concerns that many children did not have experience of or contact with older adults because grandparents were living at a distance or deceased:

We found it hugely beneficial as our children lost a set of grandparents in the space of five months.
(Parent)

Parents also expressed positive views of the opportunities created by intergenerational learning for their children to contribute to the lives of others:

It was wonderful to see how happy the older people were to see the younger children coming.
(Parent)

Intergenerational learning also addressed parents' concerns that their children were not out and about during the day because they were spending increasing amounts of time in age-segregated services. As well as serving children and parents, educators saw valuable possibilities for intergenerational learning to open up ECEC services metaphorically and physically to serve as places of encounter in the community. In doing so, educators believed that intergenerational practice was responding to social challenges, including ageism, social isolation, and family breakdown, as well as operationalizing a societal goal of lifelong and life-wide learning.[23]

Educator Orientation and Intergenerational Learning

Educator orientation (the pedagogical beliefs and values held by the educator) played a key role in the successful implementation of intergenerational learning in the Irish study. Educators' ability and commitment to weaving together their professional and socio-cultural knowledge while reflecting on their personal experience in what could be termed practical wisdom[24] was crucial to successful intergenerational learning.[25] Practical wisdom was demonstrated in educators' focus on children's happiness, the value of children "learning by observing and pitching in" in communities, and the wide-ranging benefits of this approach for families and communities.[26] This practical wisdom informed their rationale for embarking on intergenerational practice, the aims of which can be summarized as follows:[27]

- The positive opportunities offered by intergenerational learning for socio-emotional development, particularly for children who do not have a relationship with older adults
- The unique role of older adults as "social grandparents" in enhancing the learning and well-being of children
- The desire of children to play valuable social roles (a desire for their children that was also expressed by many parents) and a belief in children's capacity to create social capital
- The potential of ECEC services to respond to social challenges, including ageism, social inclusion, loneliness, and family breakdown, by being reimagined as places of encounter for individuals of all ages
- The less hurried pace offered by intergenerational learning, which created opportunities reflecting recently emerging research on the benefits for children of slow pedagogy
- The empowering nature of the intergenerational learning experiences for educators, both personally and professionally

When implementing intergenerational learning, educators in the study saw themselves as brokers of innovative strategies that responded to the changing needs of children, families, and communities.[28] In doing so, they demonstrated a willingness to consider diverse pedagogical strategies going beyond what was safe to discover what might be possible in a process of experimentation, while working within the curricular and regulatory frameworks of their services. Moreover, participants in the study demonstrated essential characteristics of early childhood educators to be open-ended (avoiding closure), open-minded (welcoming the unexpected), and open-hearted (valuing difference).[29] Courage, energy, passion, and a willingness to take risks were characteristics of educators implementing intergenerational learning, highlighting their confidence in their own beliefs and values.

The results of the Irish study strongly confirmed the philosophy and methodology underpinning the approach adopted by the TOY course, which supported learners who reflect on their practice and are courageous by going beyond that to consider what might be possible. This emphasis on rethinking values and attitudes in relation to children, older adults, learning, participation in communities, and social inclusion was foundational in preparing and supporting learners for sustainable intergenerational learning.

Conclusion

A strength of the TOY course has been its focus on values and attitudes as a foundation for the development of intergenerational practice. Successful intergenerational learning requires that practitioners have an opportunity to reexamine their own values and attitudes and those in relation to the people they serve. Crucially, research associated with TOY found that intergenerational practitioners in ECEC services took a holistic view of the family, community, and cultural context of their service users.[30] Feedback from participants in the TOY course demonstrates that they appreciated the benefits of intergenerational practice not only for their own service users but also for families and communities. Since participating in the TOY course, many learners have been inspired to apply their new knowledge and experience to establishing IG programs and initiatives in their communities. Some have taken the opportunity to document and share this work via the international TOY blog series, strengthening the TOY website as a platform for learning and exchange. Another strength of the course is its accessibility. At the time of writing, the TOY course has been delivered in seven iterations at minimal cost to learners, thanks to the largely volunteer time of the tutors. However, this model of delivery is not financially sustainable in the long term.

Working intergenerationally requires innovative thinking and positive risk. Until intergenerational learning becomes mainstreamed in curricula or policy and practice frameworks, intergenerational learning will remain in individual services and be associated with "intergenerational learning champions" and dependent on the unpaid work of volunteers. To promote the development of sustainable intergenerational learning, professional training and development (preservice and in-service) in the ECEC, elder care, and community sectors is required. The TOY course and related resources are valuable learning tools that serve not only as a knowledge bank but as a networking forum and fledgling community of practice.

Acknowledgments

The authors acknowledge the support of Emily Oxenaar in preparation of the endnotes and bibliography.

Notes

1. Margaret Kernan and Giulia Cortellesi, "Foreword," in *Intergenerational Bonds: The Contributions of Older Adults to Young Children's Lives, Educating the Young Child Series*, ed. Mary Renck Jalongo and Patricia A. Crawford (Cham, Switzerland: Springer Nature, 2022), v–vi.
2. Margaret Kernan and Giulia Cortellesi, "Introduction to the TOY Approach to Intergenerational Learning," in *Intergenerational Learning in Practice: Together Old and Young*, ed. Margaret Kernan and Giulia Cortellesi (Abingdon, UK: Routledge, 2020), 1–20.

3. Anne Fitzpatrick, "Towards a Pedagogy of Intergenerational Learning," in *Intergenerational Learning in Practice*, ed. Margaret Kernan and Guilia Cortellesi (Abingdon, UK: Routledge, 2020), 40–59.
4. Fitzpatrick, "Toward a Pedagogy," 52.
5. International Child Development Initiatives (ICDI), the Netherlands (coordinator); Comenius, Poland; Dublin Institute of Technology; Education Research Institute, Slovenia; Municipality of Lleida, Spain; Lunaria, Italy; Retesalute, Italy; University Aveiro, Portugal; University of Lleida, Spain.
6. The Beth Johnson Foundation (UK) and Linking Generations Northern Ireland, Technological University of Dublin (formerly Dublin Institute of Technology) (Ireland), Educational Research Institute (Slovenia), Azienda Speciale Retesalute (Italy), Hellenic Open University (Greece), and Municipality of Lleida (Spain).
7. Anne Fitzpatrick, "Intergenerational Learning: An Exploratory Study of the Concept, Role and Potential of Intergenerational Learning (IGL) as a Pedagogical Strategy in Irish Early Childhood Education (ECE) Services" (PhD diss., Technological University Dublin), 2021.
8. Lorin W. Anderson and David R. Krathwohl, *A Taxonomy for Learning, Teaching and Assessing*, abridged edition (Boston, MA: Allyn and Bacon, 2001).
9. The European Qualifications Framework is an eight-level learning outcome framework for all types of qualifications that serves as a translation tool between different national qualification frameworks (https://europa.eu/europass/en/europass-tools/european-qualifications-framework).
10. TOYPLUS Consortium, *Together Old and Young—An Intergenerational Approach: A Handbook for Tutors and Course Developers* (Leiden, the Netherlands: TOYPLUS Project, 2018), http://www.toyproject.net/publication/latest-publications/toy-handbook-tutors-course-developers/.
11. OECD, "What Does Innovation in Pedagogy Look Like?" *Teaching in Focus*, no. 21 (2018): 2–6, https://doi.org/10.1787/cca19081-en.
12. Gila Kurtz et al., "Impact of an Instructor's Personalized Email Intervention on Completion Rates in a Massive Open Online Course (MOOC)," *Electronic Journal of e-Learning* 20, no. 3 (2018): 325–35.
13. Dolores R. Serrano et al., "Technology-Enhanced Learning in Higher Education: How to Enhance Student Engagement through Blended Learning," *European Journal of Education* 54, no. 2 (2019): 273–86.
14. Serrano et al., "Technology-Enhanced Learning."
15. Katy Jordan, cited in Kurtz et al., "Impact of an Instructor's Personalized Email.".
16. Rebecca L. Jobe et al., "The First Year: Bridging Content and Experience for Online Adult Learners," *Journal of Continuing Higher Education* 66 (2018): 115–121.
17. TOY-PLUS Consortium, *Together Old and Young*.
18. Peter Moss, "There Are Alternatives! Markets and Democratic Experimentalism in Early Childhood Education and Care," Working Papers in Early Childhood Development, No. 53 (The Hague: Bernard van Leer Foundation, 2009), viii.
19. Clyde A. Sánchez and S. Brown, "Nine Standards in Intergenerational Work. International Diploma in Intergenerational Learning," University of Granada and Generations Working Together, https://www.gu.org/app/uploads/2021/03/S%C3%A1nchezClydeBrown-9-IDILs-standards.pdf
20. Anne Fitzpatrick and Ann Marie Halpenny, "Intergenerational Learning as a Pedagogical Strategy in Early Childhood Education Services: Perspectives from an Irish Study," *European Early Childhood Education Research Journal* 31, no. 4 (2023): 512–28.
21. Barbara Rogoff, *Apprenticeship in Thinking. Cognitive Development in Social Context* (New York: Oxford University Press, 1990).
22. Margaret Kernan and Nico van Oudenhove, "Community-Based Early Years Services. The Golden Triangle of Informal, Non-formal and Formal Approaches," presented at EUROCHILD Members Exchange Seminar, September 29–October 1, 2010, International Child Development Initiatives, Estonia.
23. Carmel Gallagher and Anne Fitzpatrick, "It's a Win-Win Situation'—Intergenerational Learning in Preschool and Elder Care Settings: An Irish Perspective," *Journal of Intergenerational Relationships* 16, no. 1–2 (2018): 26–44.
24. Verity Campbell-Barr, "Constructions of Early Childhood Education and Care Provision: Negotiating Discourses," *Contemporary Issues in Early Childhood* 15, no. 1 (2014): 5–17.
25. Fitzpatrick, "Intergenerational Learning."
26. Rogoff, *Apprenticeship in Thinking*.
27. Fitzpatrick, "Intergenerational Learning."
28. Fitzpatrick, "Intergenerational Learning."

29. Moss, "There Are Alternatives!" viii.
30. Fitzpatrick and Halpenny, "Intergenerational Learning."

Bibliography

Anderson, Lorin. W., and David R. Krathwohl. *A Taxonomy for Learning, Teaching and Assessing.* Abridged edition. Boston: Allyn and Bacon, 2001.

Bronfenbrenner, Urie. *The Ecology of Human Development.* Cambridge, MA: Harvard University Press, 1979.

Campbell-Barr, Verity. "Constructions of Early Childhood Education and Care Provision: Negotiating Discourses." *Contemporary Issues in Early Childhood* 15, no. 1 (2014): 5–17.

Fitzpatrick, Anne. "Towards a Pedagogy of Intergenerational Learning." In *Intergenerational Learning in Practice*, edited by Margaret Kernan and Guilia Cortellesi. Abingdon, UK: Routledge, 2020, 40–59.

Fitzpatrick, Anne. "Intergenerational Learning: An Exploratory Study of the Concept, Role and Potential of Intergenerational Learning (IGL) as a Pedagogical Strategy in Irish Early Childhood Education (ECE) Services." PhD diss., Technological University Dublin, 2021.

Fitzpatrick, Anne, and Ann Marie Halpenny. "Intergenerational Learning as a Pedagogical Strategy in Early Childhood Education Services: Perspectives from an Irish Study." *European Early Childhood Education Research Journal* 31, no. 4 (2023): 512–28.

Gallagher, Carmel, and Anne Fitzpatrick. "It's a Win-Win situation'—Intergenerational Learning in Preschool and Elder Care Settings: An Irish Perspective." *Journal of Intergenerational Relationships* 16, no. 1–2 (2018): 26–44.

Jobe, Rebecca, L., Jim Lenio, and Joshua Saunders. "The First Year: Bridging Content and Experience for Online Adult Learners." *Journal of Continuing Higher Education* 66, (2018): 115–21.

Jordan, Katy. "Massive Open Online Course Completion Rates Revisited: Assessment, Length and Attrition." *International Review of Research in Open and Distributed Learning* 16, no. 3 (2015): 341–58.

Kernan, Margaret, and Giulia Cortellesi. "Introduction to the TOY Approach to Intergenerational Learning." In *Intergenerational Learning in Practice: Together Old and Young*, edited by Margaret Kernan and Giulia Cortellesi. Abingdon, UK: Routledge, 2020: 1–20.

Kernan, Margaret, and Giulia Cortellesi. "Foreword." In *Intergenerational Bonds: The Contributions of Older Adults to Young Children's Lives,* Edited by Mary Renck Jalongo and Patricia A. Crawford. Educating the Young Child Series. Cham, Switzerland: Springer Nature, 2022, v–vi.

Kernan, Margaret, and Nico van Oudenhoven. "Community-Based Early Years Services. The Golden Triangle of Informal, Non-formal and Formal Approaches." Presented at EUROCHILD Members Exchange Seminar, September 29–October 1, 2010. International Child Development Initiatives, Estonia.

Kurtz, Gila, Orna Kopolovich, Elad Segev, Limor Sahar-Inbar, Lilach Gal, and Ronen Hammer. "Impact of an Instructor's Personalized Email Intervention on Completion Rates in a Massive Open Online Course (MOOC)." *Electronic Journal of e-Learning* 20, no. 3 (2022): 325–35.

Moss, Peter. "There Are Alternatives! Markets and Democratic Experimentalism in Early Childhood Education and Care." Working Papers in Early Childhood Development no. 53. The Hague: Bernard van Leer Foundation (2009), v–67.

Rogoff, Barbara. *Apprenticeship in Thinking. Cognitive Development in Social Context.* New York: Oxford University Press, 1990.

Rogoff, Barbara. "Learning by Observing and Pitching in to Family and Community Endeavours: An Orientation." *Human Development* 57, no. 3 (2014): 69–81.

Sánchez, Clyde, A., and S. Brown. "Nine Standards in Intergenerational Work. International Diploma in Intergenerational Learning." University of Granada and Generations Working Together. Accessed May 20, 2025. https://www.gu.org/app/uploads/2021/03/S%C3%A1nchezClydeBrown-9-IDILs-standards.pdf.

Serrano Dolores R., Maria Auxiliadora Dea-Ayuela, Elena Gonzalez-Burgos, Alfonso Serrano-Gil, and Aikaterini Lalatsa. "Technology-Enhanced Learning in Higher Education: How to Enhance Student Engagement through Blended Learning." *European Journal of Education* 54, no. 2 (2019): 273–86. https://doi.org/10.1111/ejed.12330.

TOY PLUS Consortium. *Together Old and Young—An Intergenerational Approach: A Handbook for Tutors and Course Developers.* Leiden, the Netherlands: TOY PLUS Project, 2018. http://www.toyproject.net/wp-content/uploads/2018/12/TOY-Course-Handbook_Sept-2018_-FINAL.pdf.

CHAPTER 20
The Development of Intergenerational Initiatives in Singapore

Leng Leng Thang

Abstract

Consensus on the need to foster intergenerational bonding has increased in recent decades. While there is already a well-established body of evidence on the benefits of intergenerational programs and their positive impact on connecting the generations, the literature on understanding developments in policy and practice to promote intergenerational bonding in society remains limited. This chapter examining the landscape of state and grassroots efforts to promote intergenerational bonding in Singapore highlights policy and socio-cultural characteristics that define the trajectories of development in intergenerational connections, including a focus on the family and *kampong* (village) creation in the community. In this chapter, the framework of the "intergenerational contact zone" undergirds the discussion as a "sensitizing" tool for exploring ways to enable and expand the creation of effective, meaningful, and sustainable spaces for desired intergenerational encounters. It further urges adoption of an intergenerational lens so that intergenerational connection is not merely an add-on but an integral part of policy and practice.

Key Words: intergenerational bonding, Singapore, kampong, intergenerational contact zone, intergenerational initiatives/programs

---

IG initiatives in Singapore

Strengths/impact
- Family- and community-centric policy and programs
- Long trajectory of efforts
- State and grassroots support and promotion
- Openness to new ideas

Limitations
- Inconsistent commitment from state in the earlier wave
- Varying depths of engagement
- Need for staff training in embracing intergenerational initiatives
- Language barriers between the young and old
- Need for sensitivity in designing shared/colocated sites for more interaction opportunities

Introduction

Background—A Rapidly Aging Society with Family-Centric Policy

Among the Asian societies experiencing an unprecedented pace of demographic aging, the small city-state of Singapore, in particular, has witnessed rapid transition from a young population half a century ago into one of the fastest-aging nations in the world today. With a large cohort of Baby Boomers born from 1947 to 1964 (about 30 percent), coupled with more than four decades of a declining fertility rate and rising life expectancy, the proportion of senior citizens has risen rapidly since 2012, from 11.7 percent in 2013 to 19.1 percent in 2023.[1] At this rate, senior citizens will comprise about 24.1 percent of the population by 2030.[2]

This trend arouses concerns about Singaporeans' capacity to provide care and support for the older population. This is exacerbated by the shrinking size of average households, which fell from 4.87 people in 1980 to 3.22 in 2020.[3] Over the last decade, older adults living in one-person households have more than doubled.[4] The shift reflects an increase in singlehood and widowhood among the older population. Baby boomers appear to prefer independent living, yet the risk of social isolation would negatively impact their life and health expectancies.[5] The changing household structure also has implications for intergenerational family bonding, with diminishing opportunities for grandparents to interact with the younger generation. Outside the family, institutional age segregation in education, work, and leisure pursuits has further resulted in widening the gap between generations, resulting in ageism, which is detrimental to social cohesion.[6]

In this chapter examining efforts to promote intergenerational bonding, Singapore serves as an interesting case study because of recent developments—in proactive state actions and grassroots community efforts that will potentially strengthen existing programs and enable more opportunities for intergenerational connections in the family and community.[7]

In general, intergenerational initiatives or programs are defined as interventions that aim "to bring people together in purposeful, mutually beneficial activities which promote greater understanding and respect between generations and contribute to building more cohesive communities. . . . [They are] inclusive, building on the positive resources that the young and old have to offer each other and those around them."[8] Conceptually, this chapter introduces the intergenerational contact zone (ICZ) framework as a "sensitizing" tool for exploring ways to enable and expand the creation of effective, meaningful, and sustainable spaces for desired intergenerational encounters. Beyond merely accommodating multiple generations in the same space, the ICZ framework is about intergenerational place-making, seeking to transform "space" to "place" with relational meaning to foster intergenerational engagement and understanding.[9]

The chapter begins with a brief note on demographic and household structural changes that unpack the rationale for family policies aimed at fostering intergenerational support and bonding. This is followed by a delineation of three waves of developments in intergenerational initiatives that define the trajectory in gradual expansion of intergenerational contact zones.

Family as the First Line of Support and Care

In Singapore, the government has long recognized the importance of strong families. "Family as basic unit of society" is one of five shared values in Singapore's social compact,[10] and Singaporeans consistently view family values as the most important value orientation, despite the changing family structure and demographic and socio-economic issues challenging the family as an institution.[11]

Social policies depicting the family as a strong pillar of support align with the guiding principles of the "many helping hands" approach. While older adults are expected to be self-reliant, the family is assumed to be the first line of care if required, followed by the community, whereas the state is to provide a framework enabling the individual, the family, and the community to play their part.[12] Nonetheless, with recent demographic shifts and changes in family structure, the emphasis is gradually moving from total family responsibility to shared support between the state and family.[13]

Zhan and Huang[14] have classified policies fostering intergenerational support between family members into three categories reflecting the apparent shift of emphasis from regulatory to supportive and complementary policies in the last four decades. Regulatory policies include the Maintenance of Parents Act passed in 1995 to legislate children's obligations to support their parents. Supportive policies encourage care and assistance for family members through housing, tax relief, and financial subsidies. Complementary policies provide direct support for seniors, mainly via assistance with health expenses and cash supplements to the income of eligible older workers.

To promote intergenerational support and bonding in Singapore families, the Inter-Ministerial Committee workgroup on cohesion and conflict in an aging society aims to propose "policy measures to strengthen our social fabric and intergenerational cohesion."[15] Policy recommendations centered on extended family ties and reciprocity include the teaching of family values in school textbooks, with illustrations of grandparents as an integral part of the family structure, giving family-based concessions based on extended family status at government-controlled recreational facilities, and giving additional incentives to public housing applicants who choose to stay in close proximity to their parents (as well as grandparents). These measures will enhance intergenerational interaction, lessen intergenerational conflict, help reinforce the role of the family in supporting senior citizens, expand the resource base of families supporting their older members, and lessen conflict between the rich and the poor.[16]

Kampong for All Ages (a Malay word meaning "village")

In 2015, with the announcement of Singapore's Action Plan for Successful Aging, efforts to strengthen intergenerational support and bonding in the family were augmented by strategies for generating intergenerational bonding in the community. The S$3 billion action plan comprises more than seventy initiatives in twelve areas, ranging from civic engagement to redefining aging. The plan's three key themes are: "opportunities for all ages," "kampong for all ages," and "city for all ages." Under "kampong for all ages," actions include housing grants to encourage families to live closer together for mutual care and support, plans for colocation of childcare and eldercare services in ten new housing developments, encouraging eldercare services to have intergenerational programs, and incorporating issues related to aging as part of the school curriculum.[17]

In 2023, a "Refreshed" Action Plan for Successful Aging was anchored on three Cs—care, contribution, and connectedness—to help Singaporeans live life to the fullest. Expanded efforts to strengthen intergenerational bonds in the family and the community came under the connectedness theme. Family-focused initiatives aim to impart family values and intergenerational bonding through immersive games and fun activity packages, "Celebrating our Grands" campaigns, and a positive parenting program to equip grandparents. Community-focused initiatives will encourage discussion of age-related themes in school subjects, create more opportunities for intergenerational engagement (such as through the common language of sports), and promote mentoring of students by older adults.[18] As will be shown, intergenerational bonding initiatives in the community are not new, and recent developments embracing intergenerational contact zones show potential for building a kampong for all ages.

Intergenerational Initiatives in Singapore—By Category

Creating opportunities for the older and younger generations to interact, intergenerational initiatives are diverse in form and depth of engagement. In general, they can be categorized in two ways. The first approach focuses on how a program is designed, that is, which population is being served: (1) children/youth serving seniors, (2) seniors serving children/youth, or (3) the old and young working together to provide a service for others.[19] The second approach, described below, gauges a program's depth of engagement.

Children/Youth Serving Seniors

Singapore initiatives in which children/youth serve seniors in old-age institutions or through home visits most often involve educational institutions and youth organizations in the community. This is partly encouraged through service-learning programs by schools and institutions of higher learning. The Ministry of Education first initiated service-learning through the Community Involvement Program in 1998 (now called Values in Action), in which interaction with seniors living in the community or senior services are common. During these visits students usually chat with residents, clean the premises, serve meals, and/or perform entertaining songs and dances. In a qualitative study of an intergenerational program involving secondary school students' interactions at a senior day-care center in Singapore, older participants reported gains in emotional support, social acceptance, self-esteem, and a sense of satisfaction. Nonetheless, a few participants cited language barriers hindering meaningful engagement, as most older participants spoke only Chinese and/or dialects, while few of the students could do so.[20]

Digitalization in recent years has further afforded opportunities for intergenerational engagement, where youth teach seniors to use digital technology, such as smartphones, Facebook, and PowerPoint. A systematic review of digital intergenerational programming found that it could reduce loneliness and increase social connectedness, including more communication with family members.[21]

Seniors Serving Children/Youth

Intergenerational programs whereby seniors serve the young are less common but are emerging as the emphasis on active aging encourages seniors to volunteer. At Singapore's Center of Excellence for Senior Volunteerism, the Retired Senior Volunteer Program (RSVP) has since 1998 played a leading role in growing senior volunteerism. In one of RSVP's most successful projects (featured in the 2023 refreshed plan), senior volunteers provide after-school care to children from low-income families, helping with homework and leisure activities. The program has benefited both the children, who received nurturing care from their senior mentors, and the senior volunteers, who found satisfaction through the act of helping others.[22]

The third category, in which both the old and young work together to provide a service for others, is less common, although changes to employment policy fostering retention of older workers will eventually lead to more intergenerational work teams in the workforce.

Depth of Intergenerational Engagement

The second categorization focuses on an intergenerational program's depth of engagement, as informed by the Depth of Engagement Continuum Scale. This scale rates the depth of engagement from low to high levels of contact as follows:

Level 1: Learning about another age group
Level 2: Seeing the other age group at a distance
Level 3: Meeting each other
Level 4: Annual or periodic activities
Level 5: Demonstration projects
Level 6: Ongoing intergenerational programs
Level 7: Ongoing natural intergenerational sharing, support, and communication

Level 7 is achieved when there is evidence that the social norms, institutional policies, and priorities of a particular site, community, or society reflect values of intergenerational reciprocity and interdependence.[23] Ideally, intergenerational interventions become redundant in settings where meaningful, ongoing "natural" intergenerational engagement is integrated into everyday life and practice. In Singapore, this resonates with the nostalgic "kampong spirit" encompassing community harmony and mutual support. Hence, terms such as "kampong for all ages" in policy statements are likened to aspirations for natural intergenerational reciprocity and interdependence.

Among the intergenerational initiatives, shared sites and colocated age-integrated centers have the potential to attain the highest levels on the engagement scale because they offer opportunities for spontaneous interaction. Intergenerational-friendly settings essentially resemble contact zones, which encourages sustainable outcomes—joint learning experiences, civic engagement, social support, and cultural continuity.[24]

Trajectories of Intergenerational Initiatives in Singapore

Wave I (1986–2006): Early Grassroots and National Efforts

Colocation sites offering childcare, after-school care, and day-care services for seniors—widely regarded as an effective model for promoting intergenerational bonding—are among the earliest intergenerational initiatives in Singapore. Two notable pioneers are the Ayer Rajah Day Care Centre, established in the West in 1986, and the Tampines 3-in-1 Family Centre, set up in the East in 1995. The latter comprises childcare, student care, and elder day-care centers located next to each other at the void decks[25] of adjacent public housing apartment blocks to enhance intergenerational contacts.[26]

Over the years, the Tampines Centre has developed a range of regular intergenerational activities, such as morning exercise in the open ground including community participation, storytelling, arts and craft, sports meets, and joint festive celebrations. Having all services nearby under the same management has greatly facilitated the smooth coordination and sustainability of the intergenerational programs.

Ayer Rajah Day Care Centre was innovative in its time. First set up by a member of parliament and grassroots leaders in a small, stand-alone single-level building with a garden, the day-care center served both generations and had a warm, family-like atmosphere. Children from child-care dropped in to the day-care center for play activities with seniors and joint festive celebrations. However, the frequency of interactions declined after relocation to a new multilevel complex twelve years later, as the services were divided between two providers. Despite close proximity, the separation of services (with children on level three and eldercare on level one) and lack of consistent management support for intergenerational interaction caused the decline. The operator of the current elder day-care center engages with other childcare centers and schools in intergenerational activities for their seniors about once a month and has recently connected with the current childcare provider above them to plan for more active collaboration.[27]

In addition to pioneering colocated sites, this wave also saw the emergence of various grassroots efforts. In the late 1990s, some social service agencies experimented with expanding their mono-age sites into interage services. For example, a family service center serving older residents added after-school care for latchkey children in the same space; a neighborhood link center situated in a public apartment block that catered to seniors created a children's corner inside the facility so that residents could visit with their grandchildren. The long-running RSVP mentoring program began bringing senior volunteers into primary school space for after-school programming during this period. These examples created contact zones that expand intergenerational engagement.

Taskforce to Promote Grandparenting and Intergenerational Bonding

National efforts dedicated to promoting intergenerational connections first emerged in 2002 when a taskforce to promote grandparenting and intergenerational bonding, initiated by the Ministry of Community Development (MCYS, now the Ministry of Social and Family Development), was formed to support the Inter-Ministerial Committee workgroup's recommendation for intergenerational cohesion.[28] The main goal of Family Matters! Singapore was to promote extended family ties, complementing existing policies and measures aimed at ensuring intergenerational interdependence and mutual support within the family. For example, the taskforce promoted the widespread celebration of Grandparents' Day and established a Grandparent of the Year Award to recognize the contributions of grandparents in the family.

Along with the family focus, the taskforce was instrumental in raising awareness of the need for and benefits of intergenerational bonding in the community. In 2003, MCYS published a guide to planning a new intergenerational program or converting an existing program into an intergenerational one. There was also funding for a variety of activities in the community[29] that represented different levels of engagement, from publication of a book on intergenerational bonding within the family (level 1), organization of monthly get-togethers for three generations of residents in a community (level 4), and a big three-generation sports carnival with a range of multigenerational games (level 4).

By 2005, state promotion of intergenerational initiatives appeared ready for an expanded platform: the taskforce was restructured and renamed G-Connect: Strengthening the Intergenerational Bond to appeal to the younger generation. National Family Week that year adopted the theme "Bonding Generations, Binding Families" and organized a Gen3 Fund interschool competition as part of its activities.

Once the need for skill building to equip social service providers for planning and implementing intergenerational programs in the community became apparent, MCYS also provided funding for organized workshops, inviting international experts in the intergenerational studies field to share with local community leaders and practitioners. As one of the early organizations to adopt an intergenerational approach, RSVP formed a committee of key leaders from child, youth, and aging services to develop an intergenerational strategy. The Association of Early Childhood Educators also enthusiastically promoted intergenerational programs in preschool settings at its 2005 seminar.

However, momentum to advance the intergenerational strategy was disrupted in 2006 by a restructuring of the Family Matters! Singapore committee and disbanding of the G-connect workgroup. Some support for intergenerational initiatives was still available under a new Golden Opportunities Fund (GO! Fund) with a focus on active aging. Although direct involvement from the state appeared to taper off with the changes, ongoing developments soon sparked a new wave of interest in expanding intergenerational connections in Singapore.

Wave 2 (2007–2014): Connecting the Generations and Promoting Active Aging

The Council for Third Age (C3A), a national independent body tasked with promoting active aging, was set up in 2007. Recognizing that intergenerational solidarity is an important tenet of active aging, C3A soon began promoting intergenerational bonding in Singapore. In 2009, it revived the Intergenerational Bonding Awards with the GO! Fund that it now administered and, significantly, added a third category, the workplace, to the first two, family and community.

Another notable effort by C3A was organization of the Fourth International Conference of the Consortium for Intergenerational Programs (ICIP) in April 2010.[30] The conference not only renewed interest in intergenerational bonding in the family and community, but it also raised awareness of the need to promote intergenerational practice in an increasingly age-diverse workplace. More older workers were expected to remain in the workforce once legislation was enacted in 2012 requiring all employers to offer reemployment to workers reaching retirement age. It would thus be necessary for the workplace to ensure inclusivity in intergenerational work teams.

Beyond work as a form of active aging, C3A promotes lifelong learning, senior volunteerism, and positive aging opportunities, with efforts to foster intergenerational bonding as a key focus.[31] It initiated a successful intergenerational learning program in 2011, pairing seniors with young people on a wide array of topics ranging from yoga, painting, and digital technology to basic coding. The intergenerational learning program has had a positive impact on the generations' perceptions of each other.[32] More recently, C3A has also started a podcast series with VintageRadio.SG called "Generations Connect!" to promote better understanding between the old and young through sharing of various topics of interest.[33]

Coupled with efforts to promote active aging, the second wave, while continuing with a variety of intergenerational initiatives organized by schools, institutions of higher learning, and youth organizations, also attracted more participation from active seniors. For example, seniors volunteered at the National Library Board's KidsRead Club to develop good reading habits among children from lower-income families. Seniors who were bilingual in English and Mandarin and dialects also became trainers in dialect learning programs, helping youth to overcome language barriers when communicating with their own grandparents and other seniors.

Activities are also organized around grandparent-grandchild bonding. Since 2008, the People's Association[34] has run intergenerational interest groups catering to the mutual interests of three generations. They included grandparent-grandchild teams for cooking and sharing recipes and a family yoga club where three generations learn yoga together.[35] In 2008, the National Library Board invited grandparents to pen letters to their grandchildren and published them in a multilingual collection. This collection provides rare opportunities to understand grandparents' hopes for their grandchildren.[36]

With the first wave as a foundation, the second wave added initiatives that harnessed the capability of active seniors—either grandparents or nonfamilial members of the community—to engage with the young, Those initiatives in turn produced more expansive bonding efforts in the subsequent wave, reflected through the creation of intergenerational contact zones in diverse settings.

Wave 3 (2015 Onward): Creating and Expanding Intergenerational Contact Zones

In this latest wave, diverse grassroots efforts to promote intergenerational bonding continue to emerge. While there are many more examples, especially youth-led initiatives that flourished during this period,[37] this section mainly focuses on spatial initiatives as intentional efforts to connect the generations. Such efforts are further abetted by emphasizing intergenerational solidarity in the community through the Action Plan for Successful Aging framework.

Development of New Shared/Colocation Sites

With the 2015 plan to colocate services for the old and young, thirteen senior care centers were said to have colocated with childcare centers by the end of 2021.[38] The first such center, set up in 2018, is situated in Kampung Admiralty, a new public housing development that received much attention for being the first public housing "retirement village" in the nation. The "vertical village" includes two blocks of a hundred studio apartments for seniors set in close proximity to amenities, healthcare, and social activity hubs.[39]

In 2017, St. Joseph's Home received wide media coverage for being the first nursing home in Singapore to turn "age-integrated" by including a childcare center at its new premises. It also has the nation's first intergenerational playground and dining area for seniors, with child-friendly seating. Despite disruptions during the COVID pandemic, the staff were committed to developing opportunities for positive intergenerational relationships.[40]

In mid-2021, another new shared site was completed during the pandemic. St. John's–St. Margaret's Village is the first purpose-built shared site in Singapore comprising a nursing home, senior care center, childcare and infant center, medical care, nursing care, and respite and home-based care for seniors. As they emerged from the pandemic, old and young have enjoyed pet therapy sessions and drumming workshops together.[41]

Efforts to link the old and young can be stymied in Singapore, especially when there are language barriers. Moreover, parents can hesitate to allow their children to interact with seniors. In shared sites, staff shortages, lack of relevant staff training, and logistical issues may impact programs' sustainability.[42] There is also a need for more sensitivity in designing shared/colocated sites that encourage spontaneous interactions across the generations. Despite increasing recognition that shared/colocated sites are uniquely suited for intergenerational bonding, there is a lack of guidelines to enhance space sharing across age groups, limiting the potential for building a community for all ages.[43]

Intergenerational Programming Model in Childcare and Day-Care Services

After the success of a year-long pilot program in 2016 held in the Health Day Centre for Seniors and My First Skool, a colocated site of the National Trade Union Congress,[44] in 2017 the childcare and eldercare services under National Trade Union Congress social enterprises creatively developed a model consisting of basic (infrequent), intermediate (monthly), and advanced (regular, intentionally planned) tiers to enable all their childcare and eldercare centers to engage in intergenerational programs on preferred intensity levels. A structured intergenerational program is woven into the childcare curriculum and eldercare activities for the advanced tier. The thoughtful programming and specially designed activities go beyond merely bringing the two generations together; they aim to enable learning, fun, and meaningful interactions that will bring purpose for seniors and inculcate good values in the children.[45]

Creating Authentic Intergenerational Community in Diverse Settings

INTERGENERATIONAL LEARNING CENTER ON A SCHOOL CAMPUS

In July 2023, the 136-year-old Methodist Girls School launched an intergenerational learning center on its school campus, the first of its kind in Singapore, creating a contact zone that will host student- and senior-led intergenerational learning activities. The school has been empowering students and seniors to initiate and collaborate—for example, in Christmas wreath-making, calligraphy, cooking classes, and a "reminiscence" autobiography project. The existence of the intergenerational learning center as a dedicated space where students and seniors can mix will imbue ownership and a sense of agency, encouraging more collaborative ideas to blossom.[46]

INTERGENERATIONAL COMMUNITY CARE SPACE WITH ASSISTED LIVING FACILITY

A new intergenerational initiative that started in July 2023, the Joo Chiat Social Club located in East Singapore is a unique, inclusive community care space launched by innovative young entrepreneurs. It houses a boutique assisted living facility and a social club for seniors, children, and persons of various abilities. It is the first-ever assisted living facility to have an intergenerational focus in Singapore.[47]

Figure 20.1 A student-initiated Chinese painting course with digital brushstrokes for older adults conducted at the IGL Centre.

Source: Image provided by Methodist Girl's School, Singapore. Photograph taken by Leng Leng Thang.

COMMUNITY LIBRARY AT THE VOID DECK

The HV Little library situated at the void deck of a public flat in an old housing estate is a community library holding more than five thousand donated books. The out-of-the-box idea originated from two neighbors living in the units who yearned for social connections during the pandemic and thought a library space would help to foster neighborliness. They started with one bookshelf in August 2022; it soon grew to more bookshelves with so many books that they now reject book donations. Besides being a twenty-four-hour lending library that operates on an honor system, the breezy space is becoming known as an intergenerational social hub where neighbors connect. The kampong spirit is alive here, as open space furnished with tables and chairs invites drop-ins and attracts all generations and ethnicities. Neighbors who register receive announcements about events such as pot-luck gatherings and festive celebrations.[48]

The third wave features the different possibilities of intergenerational contact zones (ICZs), from shared sites to a selected variety of grassroots initiatives. Many are "first

Figure 20.2 A weekday afternoon at the HV little library.
Source: Image taken by author.

of its kind" attempts, serving as examples of diverse new settings that have converged with generation-connecting and community-building properties enabling these spaces to transform into meaningful places functioning as authentic ICZs. They are, however, not without challenges. For example, another community library similarly established at the void deck in April 2023 decided to shut down six months later as a result of "complaints, messiness of the place, and a lack of community effort,"[49] highlighting the significance of kampong spirit as a necessary ingredient for making such community spaces viable.

Conclusion

For advocates of intergenerational bonding, Singapore appears to have arrived at the sweet spot where grassroots efforts match up with policy decisions to build a cohesive kampong for all ages. Moving on, there will be more exciting piloting in Singapore. For example, Queenstown, Singapore's first satellite town, became the country's first health district in 2021, a unique "model of a healthy and active community for all ages," with strategies that include the promoting of intergenerational bonding.[50] Since then, it has partnered with FaithActs, a local social service group, to establish the first community hub in Queenstown based on ibasho's principles: "creating socially integrated and sustainable communities that value their elders."[51]

More intergenerational initiatives are expected to sprout up with increasing awareness of the need for opportunities to connect the old and the young. The time is ripe for networking among those involved or interested in initiating intergenerational bonding efforts, as they could offer mutual support and share insights about relationship building and implementation issues. While it takes determination to set up a program, the challenge will be sustainability: ensuring that all who are involved in the program—seniors, young participants, staff, and management—are empowered. Program developers would do well to heed the valuable advice from Yeh et al.[52] on inserting an intergenerational program within a local, shared site: focus on the relational nature of the program and embed it as part of the organization, rather than an add-on. In fact, embedding an intergenerational lens in both practice and policy will spur the growth of more intergenerational contact zones all across Singapore.

Notes

1. In 2023, Singapore's population totaled 5.92 million, including citizens (3.61 million), permanent residents (0.54 million) and nonresidents (1.77 million). See National Population and Talent Division (NPTD) et al., *Population in Brief 2023* (Singapore: National Talent and Population Division, Strategy Group, Prime Minister's Office, Singapore Department of Statistics, Ministry of Home Affairs, Immigration & Checkpoints Authority and Ministry of Manpower, 2023).
2. NPTD et al., *Population in Brief 2023*, 10.
3. Singapore residents by age group, ethnic group, and sex, end June, annual: https://www.tablebuilder.singstat.gov.sg/publicfacing/createDataTable.action?refId=14911.
4. Ministry of Social and Family Development (MSF). "Family Trends Report 2024" (Singapore: Ministry of Social and Family Development, 2024), https://www.msf.gov.sg/docs/default-source/research-data/family-trends-report-(final).pdf?sfvrsn=8d984171_2.
5. R. Malhotra et al., "Loneliness and Health Expectancy among Older Adults: A Longitudinal Population-based Study," *Journal of the American Geriatrics Society* 69, no. 11 (2021): 3092–102.
6. G. O. Hagestad and P. Uhlenberg, "The Social Separation of Old and Young: A Root of Ageism," *Journal of Social Issues* 61, no. 2 (2005): 343–60.
7. Data for this chapter are derived mainly from secondary sources, such as policy documents, official reports, on-line and print media reports, program brochures, and research articles, including references to the chapter author's past publications, as well as her long-term participation and observations of developments in the field.
8. Beth Johnson Foundation, *A Guide to Intergenerational Practice* (Stoke-on-Trent, UK: Beth Johnson Foundation, 2011), 4.
9. M. Kaplan et al., eds., *Intergenerational Contact Zones: Place-Based Strategies for Promoting Social Inclusion and Belonging* (London: Routledge, 2020).
10. The other four shared values are nation before community and society above self; community support and respect for individuals; consensus, not conflict; and racial and religious harmony. Ministry of Social and Family Development (MSF) Office of the Director-General of Social Welfare, *Singapore Social Compact: A Quick Introduction*, October 2020, https://www.msf.gov.sg/docs/default-source/odgsw/social-compact-summary31234866-98a1-4131-912c-91937aae7eea.pdf.
11. In Tambyah et al.'s book based on the Quality of Life Study from 2011 to 2022, the seven statements in the family value orientation based on the Singapore government's Family Values Campaign (started in 1994) showed an overall decline in 2022. Despite that, the statements related to standing by one's family through ups and downs, as well as providing for one's parents, were rated as one of the most important by Singaporeans in 2022. See S. K. Tambyah et al. *Happiness and Wellbeing in Singapore: Beyond Economic Prosperity* (London: Routledge, 2024), 86.
12. Inter-Ministerial Committee on the Ageing Population, *Report of the Inter-Ministerial Committee on the Ageing Population* (Singapore: Ministry of Community Development, 1999), 37.

13. S. Zhan and L. Huang, "State Familism in Action: Aging Policy and Intergenerational Support in Singapore," *China Population and Development Studies* 7, no. 1 (2023): 200–201.
14. Zhan and Huang, "State Familism in Action."
15. See Inter-Ministerial Committee on the Ageing Population, *Report of the Inter-Ministerial Committee*, 172.
16. Inter-Ministerial Committee on the Ageing Population, *Report of the Inter-Ministerial Committee*, 177–78.
17. Ministry of Health, *I Feel Young in My Singapore! Action Plan for Successful Ageing* (Singapore: Ministry of Health, 2016), https://sustainabledevelopment.un.org/content/documents/1525Action_Plan_for_Successful_Aging.pdf, 28.
18. Ministry of Health, *Living Life to the Fullest—2023 Action Plan for Successful Ageing* (Singapore: Ministry of Health, 2023), https://isomer-user-content.by.gov.sg/3/b1fd5713-8ff9-46d5-9911-0f233f2a8b31/refreshed-action-plan-for-successful-ageing-2023.pdf.
19. J. McCrea and T. Smith, "Types and Models of Intergenerational Programs," in *Intergenerational Programs: Past, Present and Future* (Bristol, PA: Taylor and Francis, 1997), 95–114.
20. K. S. Leong et al., "Older Adults' Perspective of Intergenerational Programme at Senior Day Care Center in Singapore: A Descriptive Qualitative Study." *Health & Social Care in the Community* 30, no. 1 (2022): e222–33.
21. J. K. Phang et al., "Digital Intergenerational Program to Reduce Loneliness and Social Isolation among Older Adults: Realist Review." *JMIR Aging* 6, no. 1 (2023): e39848.
22. Refer to the RSVP website for more details: https://rsvp.org.sg/
23. M. Kaplan, "Intergenerational Programs in Schools: Considerations of Form and Function," *International Review of Education* 48 (2002): 305–34.
24. Kaplan et al. *Intergenerational Contact Zones*, 7.
25. Void decks are empty spaces on the ground level of a block of HDB flats (public apartments built by Housing and Development Board), seen commonly in older public flats built from 1970 onward. They are regarded as a space "deemed necessary to promote social cohesion and bonds among neighbors, just as there used to be in kampongs that many lived in before moving into their HDB flats." See F. Warren, *Our Homes: 50 Years of Housing a Nation* (Singapore: Housing and Development Board, 2011), 109.
26. A. Fong-Chong, "Tampines 3-in-1 Family Centre, Singapore." *Journal of Intergenerational Relationships* 1, no. 1 (2003): 169–71.
27. Information obtained from a phone conversation with the manager of the elder-care center on October 4, 2023.
28. L. L. Thang, "Promoting Intergenerational Understanding between the Young and Old: The Case of Singapore," UN Report of the Expert Group Meeting in Qatar, March 2011, https://www.un.org/esa/socdev/family/docs/egm11/EGM_Expert_Paper_Theng_Leng_Leng.pdf.
29. The funding framework for grandparenting/intergenerational programs provided 80 percent of the cost of the project up to a cap of S$20,000.
30. C3A served as the main conference organizer, partnering with the Intergenerational Consortium for Intergenerational Programs (ICIP) and National University of Singapore.
31. See C3A website: http://c3a.org.sg.
32. Council for Third Age, "An Intergenerational Learning Program in Singapore," *Journal of Intergenerational Relationships* 10, no. 1 (2012): 86–92.
33. Refer to https://www.c3a.org.sg/online-learning/ to access the series.
34. The People's Association (PA) established in 1960 is a statutory board that promotes racial harmony and social cohesion in Singapore. It runs a wide range of programs through community clubs and grassroots organizations offering social and recreational spaces for the public. See https://www.pa.gov.sg/.
35. A. Sim, "Getting Young and Old to Bond," *Straits Times*, October 28, 2009.
36. L. L. Thang, "What Do Grandfathers Value? Understanding Grandfatherhood in Asia through Chinese Grandfathers in Singapore," in *Grandfathers: Global Perspectives*, ed. Ann Buchanan and Anne Rotkirch (London: Palgrave Macmillan, 2016), 125–44.
37. See, for example, the youth-led Genlab Collective, a non-profit grassroots initiative founded in 2021: https://genlabcosg.org/.
38. Ministry of Health, *Living Life to the Fullest*, 10.
39. S. Azzali et al., "Silver Cities: Planning for an Ageing Population in Singapore. An Urban Planning Policy Case Study of Kampung Admiralty," *Archnet-IJAR: International Journal of Architectural Research* 16, no. 2 (2022): 281–306.

40. I. Yeh et al., "Development and Implementation of an Intergenerational Bonding Program in a Co-Located Model: A Case Study in Singapore," *Social Sciences* 11, no. 12 (2022): 557, https://doi.org/10.3390/socsci11120557.
41. See https://sjsmvillage.org.sg/welcome/.
42. Yeh et al., "Development and Implementation." See also S. E. Jarrott and K. Lee. "Shared-Site Intergenerational Programs: A National Profile." *Journal of Aging & Social Policy* 35, no. 3 (2023): 393–410.
43. L. L. Thang, "Promoting Intergenerational Bonding in the Family and Community: The Case of Singapore," Background paper presented at Generations United Global Conference Expert Symposium, Washington, DC, July 2023, https://www.gu.org/app/uploads/2023/11/UN_Expert_Symposium_Supplemental_Materials_Oct2023.pdf.
44. C. C. L. Lim et al., "Generativity: Establishing and Nurturing the Next Generation," *Journal of Intergenerational Relationships* 17, no. 3 (2019): 368–79.
45. P. Goy, "Inter-Generational Programme Launched to Spur Interaction between Children and the Elderly," *Straits Times*, March 27, 2017.
46. See https://www.methodist.org.sg/methodist-message/bringing-seniors-back-to-school-intergenerational-learning-at-mgs/.
47. See website of the set-up: https://joochiatsocial.club/.
48. F. W. Lim, "Kampong Is Just Downstairs Below My House," *ZB Now*, April 30, 2023 (In Chinese).
49. I. Cheng. "Boon Lay Void Deck Library to Close Due to Complaints, Messiness, Lack of Community Effort: Founder," *Straits Times*, October 20, 2023.
50. The pilot is a collaboration involving the Housing and Development Board (HDB), the National University Health System (NUHS), the National University of Singapore (NUS), and stakeholders across the public, private, and people sectors. See Cheryl Lin, "Queenstown to Become New Health District to Support Residents' Health through Life Stages," *Channel News Asia*, October 20, 2021, https://www.channelnewsasia.com/singapore/queenstown-new-health-district-residents-ageing-health-2256282.
51. See the ibasho (https://ibasho.org/and) and FaithActs (https://www.faithacts.org.sg/ibasho) websites.
52. Yeh et al., "Development and Implementation."

Bibliography

Azzali, Simona, André Siew Yeong Yew, Caroline Wong, and Taha Chaiechi. "Silver Cities: Planning for an Ageing Population in Singapore. An Urban Planning Policy Case Study of Kampung Admiralty." *Archnet-IJAR: International Journal of Architectural Research* 16, no. 2 (2022): 281–306.

Beth Johnson Foundation. *A Guide to Intergenerational Practice*. Stoke-on-Trent, UK: Beth Johnson Foundation, 2011.

Council for Third Age. "An Intergenerational Learning Program in Singapore." *Journal of Intergenerational Relationships* 10, no. 1 (2012): 86–92.

Fernandez, Warren. *Our Homes: 50 Years of Housing a Nation*. Singapore: Housing and Development Board, 2011.

Fong-Chong, Amy. "Tampines 3-in-1 Family Centre, Singapore." *Journal of Intergenerational Relationships* 1, no. 1 (2003): 169–71.

Goy, Priscilla. "Inter-Generational Programme Launched to Spur Interaction between Children and the Elderly." *Straits Times*, March 27, 2017.

Hagestad, Gunhild O., and Peter Uhlenberg. "The Social Separation of Old and Young: A Root of Ageism." *Journal of Social Issues* 61, no. 2 (2005): 343–60.

Inter-Ministerial Committee on the Ageing Population. *Report of the Inter-Ministerial Committee on the Ageing Population*. Singapore: Ministry of Community Development, 1999.

Jarrott, Shannon E., and Kathy Lee. "Shared-Site Intergenerational Programs: A National Profile." *Journal of Aging & Social Policy* 35, no. 3 (2023): 393–410.

Kaplan, Matthew S. "Intergenerational Programs in Schools: Considerations of Form and Function." *International Review of Education* 48 (2002): 305–34.

Kaplan, Matthew S., Leng Leng Thang, Mariano Sanchez, and Jaco Hoffman, eds. *Intergenerational Contact Zones: Place-Based Strategies for Promoting Social Inclusion and Belonging*. London: Routledge, 2020.

Leong, Kay See, Piyanee Klainin-Yobas, Sin Dee Fong, and Xi Vivien Wu. "Older Adults' Perspective of Intergenerational Programme at Senior Day Care Centre in Singapore: A Descriptive Qualitative Study." *Health & Social Care in the Community* 30, no. 1 (2022): e222–33.

Lim, Cheryl Ching Ling, Caymania Lay Teng Low, Soo Boon Hia, Leng Leng Thang, and Ai Ling Thian. "Generativity: Establishing and Nurturing the Next Generation." *Journal of Intergenerational Relationships* 17, no. 3 (2019): 368–79.

Lim, Fang Wei. "Kampong Is Just Downstairs below My House." *ZB Now*, April 30, 2023 (In Chinese).

Lin, Cheryl. "Queenstown to Become New Health District to Support Residents' Health through Life Stages." *Channel News Asia*, October 20, 2021. https://www.channelnewsasia.com/singapore/queenstown-new-health-district-residents-ageing-health-2256282.

Malhotra, Rahul, Md. Ismail Tareque, Yasuhiko Saito, Stefan Ma, Chi-Tsun Chiu, and Angelique Chan. "Loneliness and Health Expectancy among Older Adults: A Longitudinal Population-Based Study." *Journal of the American Geriatrics Society* 69, no. 11 (2021): 3092–102.

McCrea, James, and Thomas Smith. "Types and Models of Intergenerational Programs." In *Intergenerational Programs: Past, Present and Future*, edited by Sally Newman, Christopher R. Ward, Thomas B. Smith, Janet O. Wilson, and James M. McCrea, 95–114. Bristol, PA: Taylor and Francis, 1997.

Ministry of Health. *I Feel Young in My Singapore! Action Plan for Successful Ageing*. Singapore: Ministry of Health, 2016. https://sustainabledevelopment.un.org/content/documents/1525Action_Plan_for_Successful_Aging.pdf.

Ministry of Health. *Living Life to the Fullest—2023 Action Plan for Successful Ageing*. Singapore: Ministry of Health, 2023. https://isomer-user-content.by.gov.sg/3/b1fd5713-8ff9-46d5-9911-0f233f2a8b31/refreshed-action-plan-for-successful-ageing-2023.pdf.

Ministry of Social and Family Development. "Family Trends Report 2024." Singapore: Ministry of Social and Family Development, 2024. https://www.msf.gov.sg/docs/default-source/research-data/family-trends-report-(final).pdf?sfvrsn=8d984171_2.

National Population and Talent Division (NPTD), Singapore Department of Statistics, Ministry of Home Affairs, Immigration and Checkpoint Authority and Ministry of Manpower. *Population in Brief 2023*. Singapore: National Talent and Population Division, Strategy Group, Prime Minister's Office, Singapore Department of Statistics, Ministry of Home Affairs, Immigration & Checkpoints Authority and Ministry of Manpower, 2023.

Phang, Jie Kie, Yu Heng Kwan, Sungwon Yoon, Hendra Goh, Wan Qi Yee, Chuen Seng Tan, et al. "Digital Intergenerational Program to Reduce Loneliness and Social Isolation among Older Adults: Realist Review." *JMIR Aging* 6, no. 1 (2023): e39848.

Sim, Ashleigh. "Getting Young and Old to Bond." *The Straits Times*, October 26, 2009.

Tambyah, Siok Kuan, Soo Jiuan Tan, and Wei Lun Yuen. *Happiness and Wellbeing in Singapore: Beyond Economic Prosperity*. London: Routledge, 2024.

Thang, Leng Leng. "Promoting Intergenerational Understanding between the Young and Old: The Case of Singapore." UN Report of the Expert Group Meeting in Qatar, March 2011. https://www.un.org/esa/socdev/family/docs/egm11/EGM_Expert_Paper_Theng_Leng_Leng.pdf.

Thang, Leng Leng. "What Do Grandfathers Value? Understanding Grandfatherhood in Asia through Chinese Grandfathers in Singapore." In *Grandfathers: Global Perspectives*, edited by Ann Buchanan and Anne Rotkirch, 125–44. London: Palgrave Macmillan, 2016.

Thang, Leng Leng. "Promoting Intergenerational Bonding in the Family and Community: The Case of Singapore." Background paper presented at Generations United Global Conference Expert Symposium. Washington, DC, July 2023. https://www.gu.org/app/uploads/2023/11/UN_Expert_Symposium_Supplemental_Materials_Oct2023.pdf.

Yeh, I-Ling, Sebastian Ye Xun Wong, Lydia Safrina Binte Safaruan, Yuan Qi Kang, May S. T. Wong, and Ingrid M. Wilson. "Development and Implementation of an Intergenerational Bonding Program in a Co-Located Model: A Case Study in Singapore." *Social Sciences* 11, no. 12 (2022): 557. https://doi.org/10.3390/socsci11120557.

Zhan, Shaohua, and Lingli Huang. "State Familism in Action: Aging Policy and Intergenerational Support in Singapore." *China Population and Development Studies* 7, no. 1 (2023): 200–201. https://doi.org/10.1007/s42379-023-00135-2.

CHAPTER 21

The Power of Intergenerational Relationships to Transform Education and Promote Social Cohesion in Spain's Basque Country

Amaia Eiguren-Munitis, Naiara Berasategi-Sancho, Nahia Idoiaga-Mondragon, *and* Maitane Picaza-Gorrotxategi

Abstract

Socio-demographic changes and technological advances over the last decades reveal a constantly changing society. Life expectancy has increased and, consequently, more and more people reach their elder years. However, the distance between generations is increasing. In order to delve into the impact that intergenerational experiences have both for the participants and for society, fifteen semistructured interviews were conducted with professionals working in the intergenerational field in the Basque Country (Spain). To analyze the content, we used the Reinert method with Iramuteq software for lexical analysis. The results demonstrate the power of intergenerational experiences to break down stereotypes and strengthen relationships in favor of greater social cohesion.

Key Words: intergenerational relationships, social cohesion, education, inclusion, lifelong learning, well-being

Intergenerational relationships in the Basque Country (Spain)
Interview strengths
• Professionals from different areas
• Different intergenerational experiences
• Different years of experience
Interview limitations
• Number of interviews
• Subjectivity of professionals
• Significant differences between the programs

Introduction

The socio-demographic changes seen during recent decades highlight a society undergoing constant change.[1] Given these changes, along with increased life expectancy and the falling birth rate, it is clear that ageing societies are on the increase.[2]

Because this phenomenon is unprecedented, there is a great deal of worry in the political, social, and healthcare sectors, all of which seek different strategies for addressing it. Hence, over recent years there has been a trend toward developing and launching social policies that encourage active ageing as an alternative.[3] However, rather than older people being valued as able and experienced individuals who enrich society, they are left out and prevented from participating actively in society.

Family structures are not exempt from these changes. Historically, the family structure has been responsible for engaging people in society and for passing on social and cultural values.[4] Older people would play an important role within these structures and would be responsible for this work. According to several authors,[5] however, various changes have taken place over recent years. These include (1) fewer restrictions and new relational models, (2) changes in values and the incorporation of women into the workforce, (3) later childbearing and a decrease in the birth rate, (4) absorption of family responsibilities (health, education, and care) into the welfare state, (5) a reduction in family size, and (6) a proliferation of diverse family types. Added to these structural changes is the continuous influx of child and youth immigrants and the consequent introduction of new cultures, values, and family models into society.

The life expectancy of the population and the aforementioned changes to family structures bring social and generational changes, which lead to a larger generational gap and a loss of contact and interaction between generations.[6] This, in turn, exacerbates the negative bidirectional perspective and stereotyping that is directed toward both generations.[7] In a society with high life expectancy, people of different generations find themselves having to coexist for longer.[8] Furthermore, in recent months, the world has changed overnight due to unprecedented health events, and as demonstrated in previous epidemic situations, this has a profound social impact.[9]

Based on these considerations, intergenerational relationships take on an important role in encouraging greater social cohesion and creating shared spaces to help reduce the generational gap.[10] The formal school environment is therefore an incomparable place for encouraging intergenerational experiences.[11] The *Intergenerational Consortium for Intergenerational Programs*[12] defines intergenerational experiences as those involving people over sixty years old and children/young people under twenty-one years old during which there is mutual learning and the fostering of relationships between the different generations. In this sense, the professionals propose programs in which both the elderly and the students take an active role, beyond becoming mere consumers of activities. The participants propose intergenerational meeting activities based on their preferences and experiences, thus fostering avenues of inclusion and social cohesion for both the elderly and the participating students.

Intergenerational experiences or programs are not simply isolated experiences and programs based on one-off learning. They encourage social engagement and are experiences that may enrich the curriculum. What's more, the participants must all be willing to interact beyond the superficial.

Similarly, intergenerational experiences within formal education help to internalize the learning ideology all throughout life and foster social inclusion and intergenerational solidarity.[13] In addition, they encourage the creation of spaces for generational collaboration, which reinforce meaningful learning among participants.[14] Older participants enrich the learning process for children and young people, while children and young people enrich the lives of older people[15].

Various researchers have identified several benefits that intergenerational experiences have for students. On the one hand, students can acquire prosocial skills.[16] On the other hand, they may become more committed to school and experience increased self-esteem.[17] School motivation may also improve.[18]

Intergenerational spaces also facilitate the passing on of values, culture, and history and foster intergenerational solidarity, while knowledge transmission combats negative stereotypes.[19]

Reviews of good practice over recent years have highlighted the importance of intergenerational experiences within the school context.[20] Research into new intergenerational experiences taking place across the world via assessment of their scope and impact should be continued, given their role in achieving a more cohesive and inclusive society.

With this in mind, we investigated the value and benefits of intergenerational experiences for both participants and society.

Design of the Study—Sample

A total of fifteen professionals who have worked in direct contact with intergenerational projects and programs carried out in the school context in the Basque Country (Spain) participated in this study. In terms of gender, 73.3 percent of the sample ($n = 11$) were women and 26.7 percent ($n = 4$) were men. The participating professionals came from both public ($n = 10$, 66.7 percent) and private ($n = 5$, 33.3 percent) institutions. With respect to professional role, the interviewees were project coordinators ($n = 11$, 73.3 percent) and teachers ($n = 4$, 26.7 percent). Finally, in relation to professional experience, the majority ($n = 8$, 53.3 percent) had been working with intergenerational projects and programs for five or more years, 26.7 percent ($n = 4$) between one and two years, and 20 percent ($n = 3$) between three and four years.

Data Collection Method

In order to collect the voices of the professionals, semistructured interviews were conducted using a guide of twenty-four open-ended questions divided into four large blocks: (1) the nature of the intergenerational experiences, (2) the benefits of the intergenerational experiences for both the participants and the community, (3) personal experience, and (4) the influence of the pandemic on intergenerational relations.

We selected interviewees using the nonprobabilistic snowballing technique, which allowed one interviewee to make contact with another.[21]

To ensure participant anonymity, identifying information was determined using alphanumeric codes. All subjects participated voluntarily, received information about the research process, and gave their consent before participating in the study. This research obtained the approval of the ethics committee of the University of the Basque Country / Euskal Herriko Unibertsitatea (UPV/EHU) [file number: M10/2018/231].

Analysis of Information

Textual analysis consists of a specific type of data analysis, namely verbal materials generated in different conditions (interviews, documents, essays, etc.). This type of analysis has been commonly used in the social sciences.[22] Iramuteq software allows different types of textual data analysis, such as basic lexicography (word frequency calculation) and multivariate analysis (top-down hierarchical classification, similarity analysis). Textual analysis is carried out according to the logic of the code through elementary contextual units. On the one hand, it identifies the number of words and the average frequency of occurrence. On the other hand, it creates a small vocabulary and identifies active and complementary forms within the interviews of the professionals. Using the Reinert method,[23] all discourse is expressed from a set of words that constitute units of meaning, independent of their syntactic construction.[24] According to this method, all discourse is expressed through a system of lexical worlds that organizes rationality and gives coherence to everything said by the participants. The lexical world is made up of the sets of words that are part of the discourse. Consequently, the software algorithm aims to show lexical worlds or social manifestations from the analysis of situations, thoughts, and emotions.[25]

Therefore, by repeating word order, the software performs the quantification of the text to identify and classify the most common lexical words shared by the interviewees.[26] Following the Reinert method, a hierarchical descending distance analysis was carried out to group the elementary contextual units into classes and to find the most significant words that correspond to each of them.

Results

In the analysis of the corpus, based on the transcription of the interviews conducted with professionals, words and different forms were identified and the corpus was divided into basic contexts. Of these, 83.8 percent of the total were matched in descending rankings of text segments of different sizes, indicating the degree of similarity of topics.

Thus, the analysis identified the main ideas that professionals held about intergenerational experiences taking place within formal education. Each idea represented a cluster within the corpus of conversations—either a direct or indirect impact of intergenerational experiences and, if a direct impact, whether it was individual or social. Analysis also ascertained the methodological strategies and transmission of intergenerational experiences (see figure 21.1).

The first cluster is called methodological strategies, in which the objectives pursued by intergenerational experiences in the educational sphere and the actions used to achieve them are indicated. Thus, words such as *colloquy*, *read*, *young*, *converse*, *help*, *equality*, and *educate* appear. Most of the words refer to the personal and social influences arising from intergenerational relationships and allude to the cross-cutting action used to achieve this parallelism: "Not only were they achieving benefits for the elderly but they were also breaking stereotypes and nobody wanted to stop going to the gatherings." In the words of the professionals, at the heart of the same action is the reinforcement and development of self-esteem and personal autonomy: "When we proposed to them to do the reading support, they did not believe they were capable of doing it. They did not believe they were capable of teaching." Likewise, the professionals said that intergenerational experiences enriched participants' thinking: "Through egalitarian dialogue, the benefits are obviously significant." Interculturality is promoted when kids of fifteen different nationalities come together. "At the end of the day, we break down walls that separate people of different ages in order to grow, and we are nourished by other people and get to know other realities as there are many stereotypes related to both the old and the young."

The second and third cluster in figure 21.1 refer to the direct impact of the intergenerational experience on the participant and the immediate environment. The social impact of intergenerational experiences includes words such as *relationship*, *society*, *theme*, *objective*, *organized*, and *barter*. The professionals said that intergenerational action in the educational field involves opening up the educational community to the immediate environment: "We go beyond the neighbourhood centre because all the activity is important, all the effort we make in reweaving the network of neighbourhood relations is going to result in a greater and better quality of life for people." Creating inclusive educational models demonstrates that "older people are part of society and they cannot be excluded because of their age." Thus, whatever the degree of intensity and depth of the intergenerational experience, the professionals consider that transmission and exchange of knowledge and values are promoted through the activities: "They work in a different way with different frequency and with a different intensity at different ages, but they always have an objective to transfer." What's more, beyond mere entertainment, (reading) activities can mean an improvement in children's academic performance.

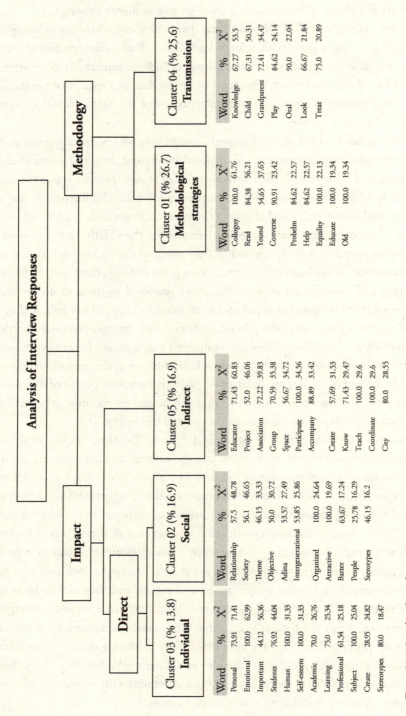

Figure 21.1 Initial analysis of interview responses.

The third cluster is where words can be found about the impact of intergenerational experiences on individual participants. Prominent words, including *personal, emotional, self-esteem, academic,* and *learning,* suggest that intergenerational experiences promote personal growth. In addition, professionals note the influence of the experiences on the emotional well-being of students: "In some cases there is emotional support when kids look for and find a reference point in older people beyond their family." Likewise, self-esteem and skills are nurtured in both directions, both in the pupils and in the older adults. "Older people feel better self-esteem and contact with the young people also helps them to pick up other types of skills that are usually of a technological nature." The professionals also believe that intergenerational experiences promote the social usefulness of the elderly: "They are capable of teaching and when they realise their value, their self-esteem rises and they move away from the idea that they are a burden." In short, they contribute to the educational process and foster lifelong learning: "We learn things to foster social cohesion, the transmission of values, and to build democracy."

In the fourth cluster, transmission of intergenerational experiences, is reflected in terms such as *knowledge, child, grandparent, look,* and *treat.* Participants view it as bidirectional: "We learn with the children and they learn with us as well, it is an exchange."

Finally, in the fifth cluster, the influence of intergenerational experiences appears indirectly. Here, words such as *educator, project, association, participation,* and *city* appear. Interviewees observe a need for coordination in the educational center and in the residential center by someone in charge if intergenerational experiences are to have an influence beyond the immediate environment. Commitment of various municipal agents (politicians in sync with the association and the educational centers) is essential.

When all the agents are united, intergenerational experiences can become a tool for building social coexistence.

Finally, with the intention of going deeper into the conversations of the professionals, we constructed a Tgen with all the words that reflect the relationship between the different generations, thus creating a subcorpus with the intergenerational text segments, and subjected the subcorpus to a lexical similarity study (see figure 21.2).

From this analysis of the words by their weight, we discerned that the different professionals place the person at the center of intergenerational relationships and, consequently, attribute strength to the partnership, the relationships, and the meeting point. The encounter that takes place between different generations enriches individual lives and society.

Discussion and Conclusions

Society has undergone significant demographic change over recent decades, and intergenerational experiences therefore take on an important role.[27] On one hand, they are a strategy against generational distancing and social isolation, and on the other, they are a means of achieving social cohesion.[28]

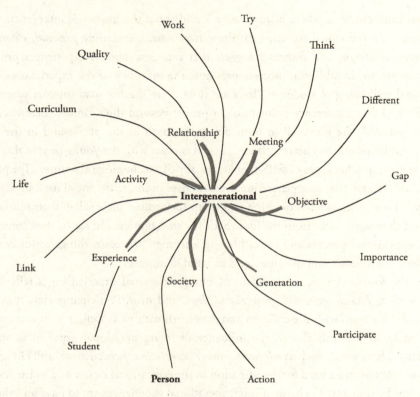

Figure 21.2 Lexical similarity analysis.

As the anthropologist Margaret Mead once said, relationships are fundamental to mental health and the stability of a country.[29] The professionals interviewed for this chapter see an "indirect" influence of the experience in the closest relational sphere beyond the main participants. However, they emphasize the need for coordination and commitment by those involved so that this can take place. Professionals in the Autonomous Community of the Basque Country whose work involves intergenerational experiences view them as valid for fostering supportive relationships and solidarity among different generations, which plays a key role in people's emotional and physical well-being.[30] They use words such as *educational*, *project*, *association*, *participation*, and *city*. They see a need to overcome the societal barriers that separate generations. Interviewees put younger and older people at the center of relationships and link them with society, intergenerational experiences, and meeting points. They also foster solidarity by reducing prejudices, and they transfer knowledge, improve mutual understanding, and encourage mutual learning.[31] Likewise, interviewees underscore how different generations coming together and actively interacting can be enriching on an individual and social level.[32] Groups and close social networks, important in addressing the loneliness associated with ageing, together with the feeling of usefulness, foster self-esteem and positive feelings. The research verified the importance of cross-generational relationships and cultural interaction employing bidirectional learning to contribute to society. Through intergenerational experiences, older people become more interested in guiding future generations, which in turn has a parallel effect on active ageing and social engagement.[33]

Beyond the education community, the interviewees have no doubt as to the positive effects of intergenerational experiences on the participants. The experience extends beyond the educational community to the social sphere, creating networks between those involved in different contexts outside the school setting. Their opinions resonate with the findings of various authors[34] who highlight the direct effects of participation in intergenerational experiences on students, both personally (self-esteem, life satisfaction, etc.) and academically.

In this sense, the experiences can be instrumental in creating inclusive models, which respond to the diversity of the education community. Moreover, the interviewees feel that intergenerational experiences should go beyond mere entertainment, given that achieving curricular objectives is the primary challenge. Intergenerational experiences enrich the curriculum by developing knowledge and transmitting and exchanging values. Therefore, the education communities supporting the experiences will be directly affected by the way of working and by the ideological change that takes place when promoting the active participation of all agents. Creating spaces in which different generations interact encourages intergenerational solidarity, social harmony, and social cohesion. In this sense, intergenerational experiences help to develop supportive relationships and intergenerational solidarity.[35]

To conclude, adjusting to the diversity of today's society will be an unavoidable challenge in the coming years. Therefore, social understanding, migratory movements of people, and attention to the diverse needs of the population will be some of the most significant lines of work in this field. In order to face these challenges, it is essential to promote research that identifies and evaluates good intergenerational practices centered on the three pillars that root intergenerational experiences, where students, elders, and community become active agents in their learning and transformative process.

In the future, in order for intergenerational experiences to enrich the educational curriculum, it will be essential to explore the potential influences they have on students. Systematized research-based guides that identify important aspects to work on would be very helpful. The voices of those who participate in the experiences should be collected in order to build knowledge about the influences and effectiveness of projects and programs and a holistic picture of the experience. Undoubtedly, program leaders will need new strategies to face the reality of social ageing and reverse the chronic exclusion of older people by promoting their active participation at a social level. Intergenerational experiences can help to meet this challenge, as they emphasize the social usefulness of older people.

Finally, on a community level, it is also important to continue promoting networking about projects and programs that are proving successful and to identify good practices in order to establish common bases for experiences and evaluation criteria. Along the same lines, it would be interesting to investigate experiences in widely differing contexts, comparing the results obtained. Furthermore, intergenerational experiences should be made visible using social networks and other tools offered by new technologies (websites, blogs, and wikis), creating shared spaces for exchanging activities and practices.

In short, as various authors have argued, the intergenerational setting must therefore be considered as a central axis around which to design the social model of the future.

Notes

1. Zygmunt Bauman, *Modernidad líquida* (México: Fondo de Cultura Económica, 2003).
2. Alan Hatton-Yeo and Toshio Ohsako, *Intergenerational Programmes: Public Policy and Research Implications; an International Perspective* (UNESCO Digital Library: Beth Johnson Foundation, UNESCO Institute for Education, 2001); Matthew S. Kaplan et al., *Intergenerational Pathways to a Sustainable Society* (New York: Springer, 2017); World Health Organization. *World Health Statistics 2019: Monitoring Health for the SDGs, Sustainable Development Goals* (Geneva: WHO, 2019).
3. Yolanda González-Rábago et al., "Envejecimiento activo en Bizkaia: situación comparada en el contexto europeo," *Zerbitzuan: Gizarte Zerbitzuetarako Aldizkaria* 59 (2015): 145–59; Alan Hatton-Yeo, "A Personal Reflection on the Definitions of Intergenerational Practice," *Journal of Intergenerational Relationships*13, no. 3 (2015): 283–84.
4. Encarnación Bas and María. V. Pérez de Guzmán, "Desafíos de la familia actual ante la escuela y las tecnologías de información y comunicación," *Educatio Siglo XXI*: Revista de La Facultad de Educación 28, no. 1 (2010): 41–68.
5. Lucia Aguado, "Familia ereduak gaurko eskolan," TANTAK 22, no. 1 (2010): 127–48; Almudena Moreno et al., "Los modelos familiares en España: reflexionando sobre la ambivalencia familiar desde una aproximación teórica," *Revista Española de Sociología* 26, no. 2 (2017): 149–67; Pedro Moreno et al., "El impacto educativo de los programas intergeneracionales: un estudio desde la escuela y las diferentes instituciones sociales implicadas," *Revista Iberoamericana de Educación* 77, no. 2 (2018): 31–54.
6. Alicia J. Beltrán and Adalver Rivas, "Intergeneracionalidad y multigeneralidad en el envejecimiento y la vejez," *Tabula Rasa* no. 18 (2013): 303–20; Valerie S. Kuehne and Julie Melville, "The State of Our Art: A Review of Theories Used in Intergenerational Program Research (2003–2014) and Ways Forward," *Journal of Intergenerational Relationships* 12, no. 4 (2014): 317–46; Carmen Orte and Marga Vives, *Compartir la infancia, Proyectos intergeneracionales en las escuelas* (Barcelona: Ediciones Octaedro, 2016).
7. Melissa S. Atkins, "How Different Can We Be? Using *Tuesdays with Morrie* and Intergenerational Interactions to Promote Positive Views of Older Adults among College Students," *Educational Gerontology* 44, no. 9 (2018): 586–94; Alma Au et al., "Proactive Aging and Intergenerational Mentoring Program to Promote the Well-being of Older Adults: Pilot Studies," *Clinical Gerontologist* 38, no. 3 (2015): 203–10.
8. Mariano Sánchez et al., *Programas Intergeneracionales. Guía introductoria* (Madrid: Instituto de Mayores y Servicios Sociales. Ministerio de Sanidad y Políticas Sociales, 2010).
9. Nahia Idoiaga et al., "Understanding an Ebola Outbreak: Social Representations of Emerging Infectious Diseases," *Journal of Health Psychology* 22, no. 7; Peter Washer, *Emerging Infectious Diseases and Society* (New York: Springer, 2010).
10. Giulia Cortellesi and Margaret Kernan, "Together Old and Young: How Informal Contact between Young Children and Older People Can Lead to Intergenerational Solidarity," *Studia paedagogica* 21, no. 2 (2016): 101–16.
11. Maria A. Gomila et al., "Proyectos educativos intergeneracionales, una perspectiva nacional e internacional: la escuela como espacio de intercambio entre generaciones," in *Vives Compartir la infancia. Proyectos intergeneracionales en las escuelas*, 31–45, ed. Carmen Orte and Marga Vives (Barcelona: Ediciones Octaedro, 2016), 31–45.
12. Matthew S. Kaplan, "School-Based Intergenerational Programs," UNESCO Institute for Education, 2001. https://unesdoc.unesco.org/ark:/48223/pf0000200481.

13. European Approaches to Inter-Generational Lifelong Learning Consortium, "Intergenerational Learning in Europe. Policies, Programmes and Practical Guidance," Institute for Innovation in Learning, 2008, http://www.menon.org/wp-content/uploads/2012/11/final-report.pdf. Łukasz Tomczyk and Andrzej Klimczuk, *Selected Contemporary Challenges of Ageing Policy*, vol. 7 (Kraków: Katedra Pedagogiki Społecznej i Andragogiki. Uniwersytet Pedagogiczny w Krakowie, 2017).
14. Carmen Orte et al., "Sharing Intergenerational Relationships in Educational Contexts: The Experience of an International Program in Three Countries (Spain, Poland and Turkey)," *Journal of Intergenerational Relationships* 16, no. 1–2 (2018): 86–103.
15. Sacramento Pinazo and Matthew S. Kaplan, "Los beneficios de los programas intergeneracionales," in *Programas intergeneracionales. Hacia una sociedad para todas las edades*, ed. Mariano Sanchez (Barcelona: Fundación La Caixa, 2007), 70–99.
16. Fiona Campbell et al., "PROTOCOL: What Is the Effect of Intergenerational Activities on the Wellbeing and Mental Health of Children and Young People?" *Campbell Systematic Reviews* 19, no. 3 (July 2023): 1–14; Marcia S. Marx et al., "Community Service Activities versus Traditional Activities in an Intergenerational Visiting Program," *Educational Gerontology* 31 (2006): 263–71; Mariano Sánchez and Matthew S. Kaplan, "Intergenerational Learning in Higher education: Making the Case for Multigenerational Classrooms," *Educational Gerontology* 40, no. 7 (2014): 473–85.
17. Nicole M. Thomas et al., "Effects of an Intergenerational Program on Adolescent Self-concept Clarity: A Pilot Study," *Journal of Personality* 90, no. 3 (2021): 476–89.
18. Rebecca Brower et al., "We Can Do This Thing Together: Intergenerational Learning and Academic Motivation among Community College Students," *Community College Journal of Research and Practice* 46, no. 12 (2022): 841–54; Linda Jucovi, *Measuring the Quality of Mentor-Youth Relationship. A Tool for Mentoring Programs* (Public/Private Ventures; Northwest Regional Educational Laboratory, 2002); Karen Vanderven, "The Road to Intergenerational Theory Is Under Construction: A Continuing Story," *Journal of Intergenerational Relationships* 9, no. 1 (2011): 22–36.
19. Matthew S. Kaplan et al., *Intergenerational Contact Zones: Place-Based Strategies for Promoting Social Inclusion and Belonging* (Nueva York: Routledge, 2020); Margaret Kernan and Giulia Cortellesi, *Intergenerational Learning in Practice: Together Old and Young* (London: Routledge, 2019); Sacramento Pinazo-Hernandis and Carolina Pinazo-Clapés, "Literatura y transmisión transgeneracional: Un proyecto intergeneracional de apadrinamiento lector en ámbito residencial," *Ocnos* 17, no. 3 (2018): 42–54.
20. Maria R. Gualano et al., "The Impact of Intergenerational Programs on Children and Older Adults: A Review," *International Psychogeriatrics* 30, no. 4 (2017): 451–68; Jennifer McAlister et al., "Intergenerational Programs in Early Childhood Education: An Innovative Approach that Highlights Inclusion and Engagement with Older Adults," *Journal of Intergenerational Relationships* 17, no. 4 (2019): 505–22.
21. Carolina Martínez, "El muestreo en investigación cualitativa. Principios básicos y algunas controversias." *Revista Ciência and Saúde Coletiva* 17, no. 3 (2012): 613–19.
22. Adriano R. A. Nascimento and Paulo R. Menandro, "Análise lexical e análise de conteúdo: Uma proposta de utilização conjugada," *Estudos e Pesquisas em Psicologia* 6, no. 2 (2006): 72–88.
23. Max Reinert, "Une méthode de classification descendante hiérarchique: application à l'analyse lexicale par contexte," *Les cahiers de l'analyse des donn*ées 8, no. 2 (1983): 187–98. Max Reinert, "Le rôle de la répétition dans la représentation du sens et son approche statistique par la méthode 'ALCESTE,'" *Semiotica* 147, no. 4 (2003): 389–420. https://doi.org/10.1515/semi.2003.100. Max Reinert, "Classification Descendante Hierarchique et Analvse Lexicale par Contexte-Application au Corpus des Poesies D'A. Rihbaud," *Bulletin of Sociological Methodology* 13, no. 1 (1987): 53–90.
24. Josué Molina, "Tutorial para el análisis de textos con el software Iramuteq," DHIGECS, Investigation Group, University of Barcelona, March 2017.
25. Nerea Larruzea-Urkixo et al., "Emozioak unibertsitateko ikasketa prozesuen ardatz: Lehen Hezkuntzako Graduaren kasua, *Tantak* 31, no. 1 (2019): 177–94. https://doi.org/10.1387/tantak.20578; Nerea Larruzea-Urkixo et al., "El alumnado del Grado de Educación ante las tareas universitarias: emoción y cognición," *Educación XII* 23, no. 1 (2019): 197–220.
26. Ariane Díaz-Iso et al., "Extracurricular Activities in Higher Education and the Promotion of Reflective Learning for Sustainability," *Sustainability* 11, no. 17 (2019): 4521; Nahia Idoiaga et al., "Communication and Representation of Risk in Health Crises: The Influence of Framing and Group Identity," *International Journal of Social Psychology* 31, no. 1 (2015): 59–74.

27. Matthew S. Kaplan et al., *Intergenerational Pathways to a Sustainable Society* (New York: Springer, 2017).
28. Sally Newman and Mariano Sánchez, "Los programas intergeneracionales: concepto, historia y modelos," in *Programas Intergeneracionales: hacia una sociedad para todas las edades*, ed. Mariano Sanchez (Barcelona: Fundación La Caixa, 2007), 7–69; Sánchez et al., *Programas Intergeneracionales*; Masashi Yasunaga et al., "Multiple Impacts of an Intergenerational Program in Japan: Evidence from the Research on Productivity through Intergenerational Sympathy Project," *Geriatrics Gerontology International* 16, no. 1 (2016): 98–109.
29. Margaret Mead, *Cultura y compromiso. Estudio sobre la ruptura generacional* (Barcelona: Gedisa, [1970] 2002).
30. Eva M. Merz et al., "Intergenerational Solidarity: An Attachment Perspective," *Journal of Aging Studies* 21, no. 2 (2007): 175–86.
31. Cythia D. Fair and Emily Delaplane, "'It Is Good to Spend Time with Older Adults. You can Teach Them, They Can Teach You.' Second Grade Students Reflect on Intergenerational Service Learning." *Early Childhood Education Journal* 43, no. 1 (2015): 19–26.
32. Angela Lavery, "Digital Storytelling and Intergenerational Collaborations: Older Adults and College Students," *Innovation in Aging* 6, no. 1 (2022): 246.
33. Bridget Laging et al., "The Delivery of Intergenerational Programmes in the Nursing Home Setting and Impact on Adolescents and Older Adults: A Mixed Studies Systematic Review," *International Journal of Nursing Studies* 133 (2022): 104281; Jennifer Petersen, "A Meta-analytic Review of the Effects of Intergenerational Programs for Youth and Older Adults," *Educational Gerontology* 49, no. 3 (2023): 175–89.
34. Brenda Krause et al., "Intergenerational Strategies Series. Making What Difference? How Intergenerational Programs Help Children and Families. Elders as Resources," Annie E. Casey Foundation, 2005; Elisa Larranaga and Santiago Yubero, "Una experiencia de aprendizaje intergeneracional con alumnos universitarios a través de la novela gráfica," *Revista de Humanidades* 32 (2017): 161–82; Jennifer Nepper, "Learning through Service: Developing an Intergenerational Project to Engage Students," *Educational Gerontology* 40, no. 9 (2014): 676–85.
35. Fan Zhang et al., "Situated Learning through Intergenerational Play between Older Adults and Undergraduates," *International Journal of Educational Technology in Higher Education* 14, no. 1 (2017): 1–16.

Bibliography

Aguado, Lucia. "Familia ereduak gaurko eskolan." *TANTAK* 22, no. 1 (2010): 127–48.

Atkins, Melissa. S. "How Different Can We Be? Using *Tuesdays with Morrie* and Intergenerational Interactions to Promote Positive Views of Older Adults among College Students." *Educational Gerontology* 44, no. 9 (2018): 586–94. https://doi.org/10.1080/03601277.2018.1516921.

Au, Alma, Eddie Ng, Belinda Garner, Simon Lai, and Kevin Chan. "Proactive Aging and Intergenerational Mentoring Program to Promote the Well-being of Older Adults: Pilot Studies." *Clinical Gerontologist* 38, no. 3 (2015): 203–10. https://doi.org/10.1080/07317115.2015.1008116.

Bas, Encarnación, and María V. Pérez de Guzmán. "Desafíos de la familia actual ante la escuela y las tecnologías de información y comunicación." *Educatio Siglo XXI: Revista de La Facultad de Educación*, 28 no. 1 (2010): 41–68.

Bauman, Zygmunt. *Modernidad líquida*. México: Fondo de Cultura Económica, 2003.

Beltrán, Alicia. J., and Adalver Rivas. "Intergeneracionalidad y multigeneralidad en el envejecimiento y la vejez." *Tabula Rasa* no. 18 (2013): 303–20.

Borrero, Lisa. "Intergenerational Service Learning: Bringing Together Undergraduate Students and Older Adult Learners to Engage in Collaborative Research." *Journal of Intergenerational Relationships* 13, no. 2 (2015): 188–92. https://doi.org/10.1080/15350770.2015.1025679.

Brower, Rebecca, Pei Hu, Hollie Daniels, Tamara Bertrand Jones, Hu Shouping. "We Can Do This Thing Together: Intergenerational Learning and Academic Motivation among Community College Students." *Community College Journal of Research and Practice* 46, no. 12 (2022): 841–54. https://doi.org/10.1080/10668926.2021.1910594.

Campbell, Fiona, Rebecca Whear, Morwenna Rogers, Anthea Sutton, Jane Barlow, Andrew Booth, et al. "PROTOCOL: What Is the Effect of Intergenerational Activities on the Well-being and Mental Health of Children and Young People?" *Campbell Systematic Reviews* 19, no. 3 (2023): 1–14. https://doi.org/10.1002/cl2.1347.

Cortellesi, Giulia, and Margaret Kernan. "Together Old and Young: How Informal Contact between Young Children and Older People Can Lead to Intergenerational Solidarity." *Studia paedagogica* 21, no. 2 (2016): 101–16.

Díaz-Iso, Ariane, Almudena Eizaguirre, and Ana García-Olalla. "Extracurricular Activities in Higher Education and the Promotion of Reflective Learning for Sustainability." *Sustainability* 11, no. 17 (2019): 4521. https://doi.org/10.3390/su11174521.

European Approaches to Inter-Generational Lifelong Learning Consortium. "Intergenerational Learning in Europe. Policies, programmes and practical guidance." Institute for Innovation in Learning, 2008. http://www.menon.org/wp-content/uploads/2012/11/final-report.pdf.

Fair, Cynthia. D., and Emily Delaplane. "'It is Good to Spend Time with Older Adults. You Can Teach Them, They Can Teach You.' Second Grade Students Reflect on Intergenerational Service Learning." *Early Childhood Education Journal* 43, no. 1 (2015): 19–26.

Gomila, María A., Joan Amer, and Carmen López. "Proyectos educativos intergeneracionales, una perspectiva nacional e internacional: la escuela como espacio de intercambio entre generaciones." In *Vives Compartir la infancia. Proyectos intergeneracionales en las escuelas*, edited by Carmen Orte and Marga Vives, 31–45. Barcelona: Ediciones Octaedro, 2016.

González-Rábago, Yolanda, Unai Martín, Amaia Bacigalupe, and Sergio Murillo. "Envejecimiento activo en Bizkaia: situación comparada en el contexto europeo." *Zerbitzuan: Gizarte Zerbitzuetarako Aldizkaria* 59 (2015): 145–59.

Gualano, Marías R., Gianluca Voglino, Bert Fabrizio, Robin Thomas, Elisa Camussi, and Roberta Siliquini. "The Impact of Intergenerational Programs on Children and Older Adults: A Review." *International psychogeriatrics* 30, no. 4 (2017): 451–68. https://doi.org/10.1017/S104161021700182X.

Gutiérrez, Marta, and Daniel Hernández. "Los beneficios de los programas intergeneracionales desde la perspectiva de los profesionales." *Pedagogía Social. Revista Interuniversitaria* 21 (2013): 213–35.

Hatton-Yeo, Alan. "A Personal Reflection on the Definitions of Intergenerational Practice." *Journal of Intergenerational Relationships* 13, no. 3 (2015): 283–84. https://doi.org/10.1080/15350770.2015.1058319.

Hatton-Yeo, Alan, and Toshio Ohsako. *Intergenerational Programmes: Public Policy and Research Implications; an International Perspective*. UNESCO Digital Library: Beth Johnson Foundation, UNESCO Institute for Education, 2001. https://unesdoc.unesco.org/ark:/48223/pf0000128018.

Idoiaga, Nahia, Lorena Gil de Montes, and Jose F. Valencia. "Communication and Representation of Risk in Health Crises: The Influence of Framing and Group Identity." *International Journal of Social Psychology* 31, no. 1 (2015): 59–74. https://doi.org/10.1080/02134748.2015.1101313.

Idoiaga, Nahia, Lorena Gil de Montes, and Jose F. Valencia. "Understanding an Ebola Outbreak: Social Representations of Emerging Infectious Diseases." *Journal of Health Psychology* 22, no. 7 (2017): 951–60. https://doi.org/10.1177/1359105315620294.

Jucovi, Linda. *Measuring the Quality of Mentor-Youth Relationship. A Tool for Mentoring Programs*. Public/Private Ventures; Northwest Regional Educational Laboratory, 2002. https://educationnorthwest.org/sites/default/files/packeight.pdf.

Kaplan, Matthew S. "School-based Intergenerational Programs." UNESCO Institute for Education, 2001. https://unesdoc.unesco.org/ark:/48223/pf0000200481.

Kaplan, Matthew S., Mariano Sánchez, and Jaco Hoffman. *Intergenerational Pathways to a Sustainable Society*. New York: Springer, 2017.

Kaplan, Matthew S., L. Thang, M. Sánchez, and J. Hoffman, eds. *Intergenerational Contact Zones: Place-Based Strategies for Promoting Social Inclusion and Belonging*. Nueva York: Routledge, 2020.

Kernan, Margaret, and Giulia Cortellesi. *Intergenerational Learning in Practice: Together Old and Young*. London: Routledge, 2019.

Krause, Brenda, David Hopping, Martha Bauman, and David Racine. "Intergenerational Strategies Series. Making What Difference? How Intergenerational Programs Help Children and Families. Elders as Resources." Annie E.Casey Foundation, 2005. https://www.anniec.org/wp-content/uploads/2016/08/AECasey-Intergenerational-Communities.pdf.

Kuehne, Valerie. S., and Julie Melville. "The State of Our Art: A Review of Theories Used in Intergenerational Program Research (2003–2014) and Ways Forward." *Journal of Intergenerational Relationships* 12, no. 4 (2014): 317–46. https://doi.org/10.1080/15350770.2014.958969.

Laging, Bridget, Grace Slocombe, Peiyuan Liu, Katrina Radford, and Alexandra Gorelik. "The Delivery of Intergenerational Programmes in the Nursing Home Setting and Impact on Adolescents and Older Adults: A Mixed Studies Systematic Review." *International Journal of Nursing Studies* 133 (2022): 104281. https://doi.org/10.1016/j.ijnurstu.2022.104281.

Larranaga, Elisa, and Santiago Yubero. "Una experiencia de aprendizaje intergeneracional con alumnos universitarios a través de la novela gráfica." *Revista de Humanidades* 32 (2017): 161–82. https://doi.org/10.5944/rdh.32.2017.18755.

Larruzea-Urkixo, Nerea, Olga Cardeñoso, and Nahia Idoiaga. "Emozioak unibertsitateko ikasketa prozesuen ardatz: Lehen Hezkuntzako Graduaren kasua." *Tantak* 31, no. 1 (2019): 177–94. https://doi.org/10.1387/tantak.20578.

Larruzea-Urkixo, Nerea, Olga Cardeñoso, and Nahia Idoiaga. "El alumnado del Grado de Educación ante las tareas universitarias: emoción y cognición." *Educación XX1* 23, no. 1 (2019): 197–220. https://doi.org/10.5944/educxx1.23453.

Lavery, Angela. "Digital Storytelling and Intergenerational Collaborations: Older Adults and College Students." *Innovation in Aging* 6, no. 1 (2022): 246.

Martínez, Carolina. "El muestreo en investigación cualitativa. Principios básicos y algunas controversias." *Revista Ciência and Saúde Coletiva* 17, no. 3 (2012): 613–19. https://doi.org/10.1590/S1413-81232012000300006.

Marx, Marcia S., Pamela Hubbard, Jiska Cohen-Mansfield, Maha Dakheel-Ali, and Khin Thein. "Community Service Activities versus Traditional Activities in an Intergenerational Visiting Program." *Educational Gerontology* 31 (2006): 263–71. https://doi.org/10.1080/03601270590916768.

McAlister, Jennifer, Esther L. Briner, and Stefania Maggi. "Intergenerational Programs in Early Childhood Education: An Innovative Approach that Highlights Inclusion and Engagement with Older Adults." *Journal of Intergenerational Relationships* 17, no. 4 (2019): 505–22. https://doi.org/10.1080/15350770.2019.1618777.

Mead, Margaret. *Cultura y compromiso. Estudio sobre la ruptura generacional*. Barcelona: Gedisa, [1970] 2002.

Merz, Eva. M., Carlo Schuengel, and Hans J. Schulze. "Intergenerational Solidarity: An Attachment Perspective." *Journal of Aging Studies* 21, no. 2 (2007): 175–86. https://doi.org/10.1016/j.jaging.2006.07.001.

Molina, Josué. "Tutorial para el análisis de textos con el software Iramuteq." March 2017. DHIGECS, Investigation Group, University of Barcelona. https://www.researchgate.net/publication/315696508_Tutorial_para_el_analisis_de_textos_con_el_software_IRAMUTEQ.

Moreno, Almudena, Marta Ortega, and Carlos Gamero. "Los modelos familiares en España: reflexionando sobre la ambivalencia familiar desde una aproximación teórica." *Revista Española de Sociología* 26, no. 2 (2017): 149–67. https://doi.org/10.22325/fes/res.2016.5.

Moreno, Pedro, Silvia Martínez de Miguel, and Andrés Escarbajal de Haro. "El impacto educativo de los programas intergeneracionales: un estudio desde la escuela y las diferentes instituciones sociales implicadas." *Revista Iberoamericana de Educación* 77, no. 2 (2018): 31–54. https://doi.org/10.35362/rie7723158.

Nascimento, Adriano R. A., and Paulo R. Menandro. "Análise lexical e análise de conteúdo: Uma proposta de utilização conjugada." *Estudos e Pesquisas em Psicologia* 6, no. 2 (2006): 72–88.

Nepper, Jennifer. "Learning through Service: Developing an Intergenerational Project to Engage Students." *Educational Gerontology* 40, no. 9 (2014): 676–85. https://doi.org/10.1080/03601277.2013.873295.

Newman, Sally, and Mariano Sánchez. "Los programas intergeneracionales: concepto, historia y modelos." In *Programas Intergeneracionales: hacia una sociedad para todas las edades*, edited by Mariano Sanchez, 7–69. Barcelona: Fundación La Caixa, 2007.

Orte, Carmen, and Marga Vives. *Compartir la infancia, Proyectos intergeneracionales en las escuelas* Barcelona: Ediciones Octaedro, 2016.

Orte, Carmen, Marga Vives, Joan Amer, Lluís Ballester, Belén Pascual, and María Antonia Gomila. "Sharing Intergenerational Relationships in Educational Contexts: The Experience of an International Program in Three Countries (Spain, Poland and Turkey)." *Journal of Intergenerational Relationships*, 16, no. 1–2 (2018): 86–103. https://doi.org/10.1080/15350770.2018.1404414.

Petersen, Jennifer. "A Meta-analytic Review of the Effects of Intergenerational Programs for Youth and Older Adults." *Educational Gerontology* 49 no. 3 (2023): 175–89. https://doi.org/10.1080/03601277.2022.2102340.

Pinazo, Sacramento, and Matthew S. Kaplan. "Los beneficios de los programas intergeneracionales." In *Programas intergeneracionales. Hacia una sociedad para todas las edades*, edited by Mariano Sanchez, 70–99. Barcelona: Fundación La Caixa, 2007.

Pinazo-Hernandis, Sacramento, and Carolina Pinazo-Clapés. "Literatura y transmisión transgeneracional: Un proyecto intergeneracional de apadrinamiento lector en ámbito residencial." *Ocnos* 17, no. 3 (2018): 42–54. https://doi.org/10.18239/ocnos_2018.17.3.1799.

Reinert, Max. "Une méthode de classification descendante hiérarchique: application à l'analyse lexicale par contexte." *Les cahiers de l'analyse des données* 8, no. 2 (1983): 187–98.

Reinert, Max. "Classification descendante hierarchique et analvse lexicale par contexte-application au corpus des poesies D'A. Rihbaud." *Bulletin of Sociological Methodology* 13, no. 1 (1987): 53–90.

Reinert, Max. "Le rôle de la répétition dans la représentation du sens et son approche statistique par la méthode 'ALCESTE.'" *Semiotica* 147, no. 4 (2003): 389–420. https://doi.org/10.1515/semi.2003.100.

Sánchez, Mariano, and Matthew S. Kaplan. "Intergenerational Learning in Higher education: Making the Case for Multigenerational Classrooms." *Educational Gerontology* 40, no. 7 (2014): 473–85. https://doi.org/10.1080/03601277.2013.844039.

Sánchez, Mariano, Matthew S. Kaplan, and Juan Sáez. *Programas Intergeneracionales. Guía introductoria*. Madrid: Instituto de Mayores y Servicios Sociales. Ministerio de Sanidad y Políticas Sociales, 2010. https://www.aepumayores.org/sites/default/files/Programas_Intergeneracionales_Coleccion_Manuales_Guias_IMSERSO_%202010.pdf.

Thomas, Nicole. M., Jan Hofer, and Dirk Kranz. "Effects of an Intergenerational Program on Adolescent Self-Concept Clarity: A Pilot Study." *Journal of Personality* 90, no. 3 (2021): 476–89. https://doi.org/10.1111/jopy.12678.

Tomczyk, Łukasz, and Andrzej Klimczuk. *Selected Contemporary Challenges of Ageing Policy*, vol. 7. Kraków: Katedra Pedagogiki Społecznej i Andragogiki. Uniwersytet Pedagogiczny w Krakowie, 2017.

Vanderven, Karen. "The Road to Intergenerational Theory Is Under Construction: A Continuing Story." *Journal of Intergenerational Relationships* 9, no. 1 (2011): 22–36. https://doi.org/10.1080/15350770.2011.544206.

Washer, Peter. *Emerging Infectious Diseases and Society*. New York: Springer, 2010.

World Health Organization. *World Health Statistics 2019: Monitoring Health for the SDGs, Sustainable Development Goals*. Geneva: WHO, 2019. https://www.who.int/publications/i/item/9789241565707.

Yasunaga, Masashi, Yoh Murayana, Tomoya Takahashi, Hiromi Ohba, Hiroyuki Suzuki, Kumiko Nonaka, et al. "Multiple Impacts of an Intergenerational Program in Japan: Evidence from the Research on Productivity through Intergenerational Sympathy Project." *Geriatrics Gerontology International* 16, no. 1 (2016): 98–109. https://doi.org/10.1111/ggi.12770.

Zhang, Fan, David Kaufman, Robyn Schell, Glaucia Salgado, Erik Tiong, and Julija Jeremic. "Situated Learning through Intergenerational Play between Older Adults and Undergraduates." *International Journal of Educational Technology in Higher Education* 14, no. 1 (2017): 1–16. https://doi.org/10.1186/s41239-017-0055-0.

CHAPTER 22

Intergenerational Programs and Places in Japan's Super-Aging Society: What Three Good Practices Can Teach Us

Masataka Kuraoka

Abstract

This chapter discusses why intergenerational programs and places have become politically and socially important in Japan, which is one of the super-aging countries. Three different types of intergenerational programs are introduced to provide background information and highlight the characteristics of each case. The first is Shibasaki Irodori Station, a community-based intergenerational place that welcomes people of all generations. The second is REPRINTS, a senior volunteer intergenerational program that involves reading aloud at local schools, kindergartens, nursery schools, and libraries. The third, Kotoen, has a long history of fostering exchanges between nursing home residents and nursery school children. These cases will provide insights into intergenerational practices in Japan and how they empower individuals engaged in those activities.

Key Words: intergenerational, Japan, long-term care, community-based, nursing home

Shibasaki Irodori Station	REPRINTS Network	Kotoen
Strengths/impact • People-centered program • Collaboration with public services • Dementia-friendly place	**Strengths/impact** • Nonprofit Organization support for each program area • Professionally designed program and management • Effect on seniors' health	**Strengths/impact** • Facility that allows frequent interaction • Trained staff members • Management and leadership
Limitations • Need for more younger-generation involvement	**Limitations** • Recruit more men • More instructors to maintain the quality of training	**Limitations** • Recovering from suspended intergenerational contact during COVID-19 • Passing skills and knowledge to younger staff

Change in Demographics and Family Structure

In the past few decades, Japan has been facing an aging population and decreasing number of young people at the same time. The total population as of March 1, 2023, was 124.5 million, continuing a downward trend since 2011. The portion under 15 years of age is 11.5 percent, and the portion 65 years old and above is 29 percent. Those proportions were 14 and 19 percent respectively, in 2003. This striking demographic change has had a significant impact on the socioeconomic system of the country and required reconstructing people's way of life.

Sazae-san is a famous Japanese TV anime that has been broadcasted every Sunday night since 1969. The main character, Sazae, lives with her husband and child and also with Sazae's parents (not parents-in-law) and her younger brother and sister in the same house. Many people have grown up watching the episodes of *Sazae-san* every Sunday and feel empathy with her family's everyday life or contrast it with their own life. On the other hand, the anime is often joked about because of the fact that the characters have never aged since the beginning of the show and the household structure of three generations seems a relic of the past. Nevertheless, many people still watch the show, as it got the highest rating in the week of September 11, 2023 of all anime in Japan.

Traditionally, the structure of many Japanese households was three-generational just like *Sazae-san*'s. In 1986, three-generation households made up 15.3 percent of all households, but that had decreased to 3.8 percent by 2022. This was mainly due to the preference for a nuclear family structure and to migration from rural areas to cities. On the other hand, single-person households have increased by about 10 percentage points in the same period, to 28.8 percent, due to the increase in unmarried people and longer life expectancy of older people.

The value placed on the intergenerational household has also changed according to an international survey of older people. In a question about how respondents want to associate with their children and grandchildren, the percentage choosing living together with children and grandchildren decreased from 59.4 percent in 1980 to 18.8 percent in 2020, whereas the percentage choosing seeing them occasionally for eating and conversation increased from 30.1 percent to 56.8 percent. It is not apparent whether intergenerational exchange among household members has somehow deteriorated in quality. However, based on the demographic change mentioned before, it is assumed that the decreasing number of children per household has made the number of opportunities for parents to see children decline, as a smaller number of children per family means the burden to visit the parents cannot be shared as widely.

Policy behind Intergenerational Programs

One of the reasons that intergenerational programs are promoted in some countries is to bridge the social or economic gap between different generations. The problem of intergenerational inequality had not been addressed in Japan in the same way as in the United

States, where local government policies and budgets can be significantly influenced by the age demographics of the population and how they vote in a given area, potentially causing the interests of one age group to conflict with those of another. In Japan, no matter where you live, the cost to individuals for everything, from nursery schools for infants to day-care services for the elderly, is relatively low and the quality is similar due to subsidies and regulations enforced by the national government. However, during the recent election, when the concept of "silver democracy" was being discussed and covered in the media, the younger generation's negative perception of the intergenerational gap was unmistakable.

In Japan, intergenerational programs gained attention when the long-term care insurance system launched in 2000. It is part of the insurance system that covers the services and costs needed to support older people with physical and mental disabilities as well as easing the burden of family care traditionally held by the daughter-in-law married to the eldest son. Since the introduction of the insurance system, the population of elderly has grown, as has the premium, the payment of which starts at the age of forty in all municipalities in Japan. As the social cost is expected to increase more in the future, some preventative measures have been implemented. For example, physical exercise programs have been promoted nationwide by municipal long-term care sections.

Later, this policy shifted to more preventative measures through community building, as the government's and professionals' involvement in local prevention programs have their limit in terms of human and monetary resources. The shift led to more *jumin shutai*, citizen-centered management of local programs, so that citizens can independently manage the program for members and newcomers. It is expected that programs under independent management by community members have better retention and are more active than groups that rely on government officials and instructors.

Thus, as preventative community measures, intergenerational programs as well as other community-based programs were expected to help meet the growing demand for long-term care in the coming years. However, the programs promoted in communities still emphasize physical exercise, and nonphysical exercise programs that are intergenerational have not been promoted as expected.

In municipalities across the country, there is a push for collaboration with diverse stakeholders and the creation of communal spaces and gathering places that involve multiple generations in care prevention, frailty prevention, and community development. Twenty years after the introduction of the long-term care insurance system, the new initiative stems from the Study Group on Promotion Strategies for General Care Prevention Projects, commissioned by the Ministry of Health, Labour, and Welfare in 2020. The study group's summary explicitly states that efforts in care prevention involving diverse and appealing communal spaces are being implemented nationwide, along with initiatives that collaborate with various private enterprises and organizations, not limited to the elderly but also encompassing intergenerational interactions.

Furthermore, the same policy emphasizes that efforts to promote participation and public relations should target not only the elderly but also their families and the active working generation. It underscores the importance of fostering understanding and enthusiasm among the elderly's families and younger generations living in the community. In essence, the policy encourages collaboration across multiple generations and diverse stakeholders while emphasizing the need to ensure that care prevention and frailty prevention are community priorities, a collective effort across all generations in community development.

In conjunction with these guidelines, a nationwide survey on implementation of the Comprehensive Support Project for Care Prevention and Daily Life Support included additional elements from 2020 onward, alongside previously existing activities (exercise, communal dining, tea gatherings, dementia prevention, and hobbies). These additions encompass farming activities, lifelong learning, volunteer work, employment-related activities, and intergenerational exchanges. However, according to the national survey of community gathering places that contributed to preventative long-term care in 2022, the number of intergenerational programs reported was only 788 out of 123,890, that is, just 0.64 percent of the total. This can be attributed to the challenges posed by the COVID-19 pandemic, which made it particularly difficult to implement intergenerational activities, resulting in underreporting. Considering that the total number of activities as of 2022 was a robust 96 percent compared to 2020, it is conjectured that the department responsible for this survey may not have recognized newly added activities like intergenerational exchanges as gathering places.[1]

Issues in Intergenerational Programs in Japan

In summer 2023, after a few years of COVID-19 restrictions, many Japanese people enjoyed traveling to their hometown during Obon period, when ancestors' spirits are believed to return to their home. Numerous cultural and traditional events, such as *bonodori* (bon dance) at local Obon festivals and fireworks shows, resumed. Many intergenerational exchanges are deeply rooted in Japanese culture. Like familial exchange in combination with cultural and seasonal events, intergenerational exchange such as Respect for the Aged Day in September is practiced at nurseries, kindergartens, schools, and community organizations. Traditional intergenerational exchanges stir up nostalgic memories, especially for the elderly. They all have significant meaning, but for the purposes of this chapter, the focus is on strategic intergenerational programs addressing challenging problems in Japanese society.

The issues the country is currently facing, such as a rapidly aging population and widening social and health disparities, have become increasingly complex and severe, alongside the fiscal constraints of local government. It is often said that family issues have become *tamondai-ka*, multiplied problems. Existing systems are struggling to cope with these challenges. Both government measures and research projects are being conducted concerning them. For example, in 2016 a Tokyo Metropolitan Institute for Geriatrics and Gerontology (TMIG) research team launched a three-year project in two towns in the Tokyo metropolitan area to build intergenerationally integrated communities targeting young parents with babies and the elderly through a campaign to promote formal greetings and multigenerational support awareness and intergenerational gathering places.[2]

Among the outcomes of this project, researchers found that, for example, *aisatsu*, greetings, is one of the most common forms of intergenerational practice promoted at local elementary schools toward people in the community in Japan; but what *aisatsu* really mean or their effect has not been recognized. The survey conducted on 1,346 elementary school students and 1,357 junior high school students shows a positive correlation between the frequency of being greeted by people in the community and the frequency of greeting by students and a positive association with community attachment and helping-others behavior.[3] The TMIG research team also conducted a baseline cross-sectional survey before the project began and a follow-up survey after the project ended in the two towns and found that promoting intergenerational exchanges significantly contributed to enhanced mental well-being, as measured by WHO-5 scores for elderly people.[4] In addition, the longitudinal survey analysis found that the impact of face-to-face contact on mental health was more significant than that of non–face-to-face contact among older adults and young adults,[5] and a higher generativity score was positively associated with maintaining higher-level functional capacity.[6]

Although the intergenerationally integrated community-building project interventions ended after three years, the volunteers who were involved in the project remain active in intergenerational efforts in both towns. Some findings reveal that intergenerational approaches are strategically important in elderly health promotion and prevention of frailty.

However, research on intergenerational exchange has long highlighted challenges related to the dissemination and sustainability of these activities. Fujiwara has pointed out factors inhibiting the widespread adoption of intergenerational exchange programs, including intergenerational conflicts, a perceived lack of necessity for such exchanges, and the administrative burdens associated with planning and execution.[7] Despite the high interest in intergenerational exchange, reports indicate that these activities do not always proceed as planned or meet expectations.[8] Furthermore, in intergenerational exchange programs involving elderly volunteers with health issues, the need for support systems and training to enable older adults with health challenges to continue participating has been emphasized.[9]

Researchers, practitioners, and local governments need to resolve these constraints on intergenerational programs and places if such measures are to be promoted widely in society. In the following section, three intergenerational cases are introduced to explore the points that good practices share.

Intergenerational Programs Practices in Japan

In Japan, there are numerous intergenerational programs and places nationwide. Whether culturally rooted or policy-rooted, programs with different purposes and settings bring generations together. In this section, three cases of intergenerational programs are introduced to illustrate the variety of intergenerational programs in Japan. The first case is Shibasaki Irodori Station, located in Tokyo. The second famous intergenerational case is REPRINTS. The third case is Kotoen.

Case 1: Shibasaki Irodori Station
BACKGROUND

Located in a corner of an old shopping street in Shibasaki in the city of Chofu, a one-hour ride from central Tokyo by train, Shibasaki Irodori Station (hereafter referred to as Irodori, which literally means "various colors") is an intergenerational community space that is located in a renovated vacant house. Irodori serves as a gathering place for a diverse range of local residents, including not only the elderly but also families with children, young generations, and even foreigners, with various activities taking place every day.

Irodori was founded in July 2019 by a physician at a local clinic and Ms. Chieko Oki, who used to work as a professional healthcare worker in the same community. They shared a belief in the importance of community building so that all community members would recognize familiar faces within the community before developing dementia. They also recognized the need for a gathering place to serve as a place for local community members to accept and connect various people's ideas and to make those ideas a reality.

Many of the visitors to Irodori are locals from the neighborhood. Some individuals even travel by bicycle or train to reach the venue. The number of elder citizens visiting Irodori is about three hundred per month, some who visit daily and those who drop by once a month. Parents and children who come to the children's cafeteria are not included in this count, meaning even more people are users of the facility. In terms of annual attendance, around eight thousand people utilized the space in 2022. Initially, the average age was around seventy, but with the addition of the children's cafeteria, young mothers and children started coming to Irodori, contributing to a more multigenerational atmosphere. The male-female ratio is roughly 2:8, but depending on the nature of the activity, male participation can also be substantial.

The primary objective of Irodori is to be a place for the community where various people's interests can be embraced, realized, and connected. To achieve this goal, the emphasis is not solely on expanding activities but on creating an environment where local residents can casually visit, fostering relationships where neighbors of different ages can connect with one another. Irodori aims for these intergenerational relationships to be carried forward, embodying the continuity of connections across generations.

ACTIVITIES

Diverse programs and events are offered at Irodori every day. The activities include physical exercise; the Orange Café, which welcomes especially people with dementia or their family members; *kodomo-shokudo*, a dining place for children; lunch meetings; a café; healthy mahjong; choral sessions; garage sales; and more. Figure 22.1 shows elderly people and elementary school students playing a game, "*taiko no tatsujin*" (taiko master), in which they compete over how accurately they drum the song shown on a monitor. This is an E-sports activity that Irodori started recently with the support of a private company that promotes E-sports in Tokyo. A monthly schedule is posted at the entrance and on the website. Irodori is open Monday through Friday and occasionally on Saturday and Sunday, and the venue also serves as a place where local residents can casually drop by for tea and conversation.

PROGRAM STRENGTHS

Irodori has several unique features and strengths. First, many businesses have closed down in the district where Irodori, a former woodworking shop, is located. Its street-facing exterior is made up of glass doors, a design that allows for activities taking place inside to be visible to pedestrians walking on the street or patients coming to the clinic next door.

Figure 22.1 Irodori Station.

The main room features tables, chairs, and a piano, creating a lively space where piano performances and singing can be heard, contributing to a vibrant atmosphere.

Irodori's diverse range of programs, described above, is another plus. People from different generations and backgrounds, including children, seniors, and foreigners, come together to participate in activities aligned with their individual interests. A driving force behind inspiring people to try new things is Ms. Oki. She believes that rather than imposing various rules and restrictions on activities, it's crucial to respond to the goals and desires of community residents.

A third distinctive feature is that the local residents themselves act as the driving force—planning, collaborating, and operating this community space. Normally, community-based programs, whether intergenerational or not, are designed by the manager or staff of an organization or by healthcare professionals as a part of government-supported initiatives. However, Ms. Oki prefers to let people come to Irodori and do what they want. If someone has musical skills, let the person run singing time; if someone used to work for a publisher and has in-depth knowledge about various books, let the person run a book club. If a woman in her eighties was a teacher for a long time and wants to teach something, she can work with the children who come to Irodori. The strength of intergenerational programs is maximized when each person involved has some role.

Fourth, it is noteworthy that around forty volunteers are involved in Irodori. They have been involved from the outset, taking on various roles such as assisting with meals and leading activities. Some volunteers come to Irodori just for cooking and leave as soon as the cooking is done. They all seem to have become involved through Ms. Oki, who is good at asking others to volunteer and keeping communications open.

Lastly, because of how Irodori started and its purpose, it has very active collaboration with external organizations, such as the Community Comprehensive Support Center (CCSC), and the Social Welfare Council. The nearest CCSC is located about a three-minute walk away, and staff members from this center often participate in various activities at Irodori. If individual users require special attention, the center may be consulted. Additionally, the CCSC sometimes introduces Irodori to individuals or leads groups directly to the Orange Café or to the muscle-training exercises. Ms. Oki, who is also a care manager, works closely with CCSC professionals, helping to maintain an interconnected safety net for the community's elderly residents.

IMPACT ON USERS AND THE COMMUNITY

A woman came to seek advice after viewing the Irodori Facebook page. Initially, she seemed withdrawn when she visited, almost as if sleeping, and didn't make eye contact with others. Now she actively participates in various activities and has even applied for long-term care insurance. Above all, the fact that she sought advice at Irodori before approaching the CCSC shows that Irodori welcomes the community and is a place people can count on when they need help.

An elderly couple with dementia, each involved in Irodori activities, see it as a place where they belong. Active involvement in Irodori activities, including by those with dementia, has produced significant positive changes. Conversely, the presence of such individuals also positively influences others. A 106-year-old former seamstress who occasionally brings homemade masks to share inspires women in their eighties. Seeing someone over a hundred years old engaging with the world outside and interacting with others encourages them to remain active. And a woman in her nineties who used to watch the local elementary school children at the crosswalk to ensure their safety every morning is delighted when children who come to Irodori to play after school recognize her in the neighborhood and greet her as "the grandmother from Irodori."

LIMITATIONS AND FUTURE CHALLENGES

Although Irodori attracts all the generations in the community, Ms. Oki believes that nurturing young people and facilitating connections among them is crucial. During child-rearing, time constraints on parents can make it difficult to focus on community involvement, but even a slight connection can blossom into something more significant later on. Therefore, cultivating connections with the young generation is a priority. Irodori aims to share its activities in various ways to become a catalyst for young people to connect, allowing the venue to serve as a place where they can gather.

Case 2: REPRINTS

BACKGROUND

REPRINTS is a senior volunteer group that reads picture books aloud to children. REPRINTS started as a research project in 2004 led by TMIG's Social Participation and Health Promotion Team. The initiative was led by the team leader, who was inspired by the Experience Corps model when he studied at Johns Hopkins University as a visiting researcher in the United States. In fact, both Experience Corps and REPRINTS were introduced together in a "World Report on Aging and Health" in 2015 as examples of social participation practices for the elderly.[10] REPRINTS literally means the English word "reprint," referencing how stories in picture books are revived, and it was named with the hope that the senior generation would shine a spotlight on their own lives and in turn contribute to community revitalization.

The REPRINTS project started in two cities in the Tokyo metropolitan area and one in Shiga Prefecture, in the western part of Japan, when the project was launched in 2004. Since the start, it has been adopted in many cities nationwide. In 2014, REPRINTS became a nonprofit organization supporting all the REPRINTS groups organized after completion of a training program. As of April 2023, there are REPRINTS groups in sixteen cities, mainly in the Tokyo metropolitan area. The number of senior volunteers per location ranges from 13 to 99, totaling 570 members. Although REPRINTS initially started as a lifelong-learning program, local governments soon saw it as a frailty-prevention program, as Japan began to take crucial steps regarding the aging population.

ACTIVITIES

Local government often introduces a program in public newsletters when it hosts seminars like "Dementia Prevention by Reading Aloud Picture Books," targeting old people who like reading picture books.

REPRINTS participants undergo a three-month training program, meeting once a week for approximately two hours. Training covers the significance of reading picture books, how to select picture books, techniques for effective storytelling, and what it means to be a school volunteer.

Upon completion of the training, the volunteers are divided into groups of six to ten and begin regular visits to read aloud picture books as an intergenerational activity in local elementary schools, kindergartens, and nurseries. The REPRINTS program emphasizes the importance of working as a group. For example, members gather to discuss what they should read next and select books in their collection or sometimes go to a local library. They practice before performing the read-aloud at the facility. Afterward, they discuss how the children reacted to their performance and how they can improve it, as figure 22.2 shows. In addition, all the small groups meet once a month and report what each group chose to read and the children's reactions to the books.

Figure 22.2 REPRINTS Network.

JAPAN'S SUPER-AGING SOCIETY | 335

PROGRAM STRENGTHS

REPRINTS has several strengths to share. First, because it originally began as a research project, implementation of the training program and group management were carefully designed and conducted with the support of diverse professionals, including medical doctors, psychologists, social welfare personnel, educators, physical therapists, and so on. TMIG still provides professional support when needed.

Second, the nonprofit organization's board consists of representatives from REPRINTS groups in each municipality. It functions as a mutual support system: volunteers can discuss their activity in depth and share experiences from practice. This is especially helpful when a new president is appointed in one area or when problems arise.

Finally, because the program is intergenerational and reaches children in the local school system and facilities, there are opportunities beyond reading aloud to engage in a facility's festival or connect with other groups. As a result, recognition from the community becomes more firmly established, and intergenerational opportunities in the daily life of the senior volunteers are enhanced.

IMPACT ON USERS AND THE COMMUNITY

In 2019 REPRINTS conducted picture book read-alouds in 212 facilities. Senior volunteers read more than twelve thousand books to about a hundred thousand children and adults. Plentiful research on REPRINTS and the volunteers from different perspectives dates back to 2004. One REPRINTS group taught sixth-grade students how to read picture books to the first-graders as one of their activities. As a result, sixth-graders who participated in the interactive lessons demonstrated improvements in both their listening skills and speaking skills compared to those who did not participate.[11]

In many Japanese schools, read-alouds by parents or the PTA used to be a common activity in the morning. However, as more parents work full-time and involvement in school is not their priority, read-alouds have no support or are a heavy burden on parents. In schools with active REPRINTS volunteers, the "physical burden" (parental time and effort) and the "psychological burden" (responsibility and sense of obligation) are reduced.[12]

Since the REPRINTS project started, regular health examinations of physical, mental, and medical status have been conducted on both REPRINTS volunteers and control group members who only participate in health checkups. Over a period of nine months, REPRINTS volunteers exhibited significant improvements in their attachment to the community, grip strength, and subjective health perception compared to older adults in the control group. Furthermore, after seven years of participation in REPRINTS, volunteers displayed significant improvements in balance maintenance, frequency of interaction with neighboring children, and intellectual proactivity (indicators of situational adaptability and intellectual curiosity).[13]

In a study involving participants from REPRINTS who underwent MRI scans during their initial assessment, as well as health monitors who participated in health surveys without engaging in read-aloud activities, the extent of hippocampal atrophy was investigated six years later among those who underwent a second MRI scan. The results for health monitors revealed gradual hippocampal atrophy within the normal range due to aging, while REPRINTS participants exhibited statistically significant suppression of hippocampal atrophy.[14]

LIMITATIONS AND FUTURE CHALLENGES

One of the biggest challenges since the start of REPRINTS is that the program has not been appealing to men: the number of male senior volunteers is usually small in each local group. As health issues are more prominent among men, particularly men living alone, REPRINTS needs to be a good option for both women and men.

There are instructors who teach the training program and support REPRINTS groups in each town. Some instructors have been instructors since 2004 and are highly respected by members of REPRINTS. However, with the growing demand for social engagement programs, many more instructors are needed in order to maintain the quality of training sessions.

Case 3: Kotoen
BACKGROUND

Kotoen is located in a residential area in Edogawa City in Tokyo. It is the best-known intergenerational facility in Japan and globally. For example, it was first introduced in "Generations in Touch: Linking the Old and Young in a Tokyo Neighborhood," by Thang.[15] In 2018 *AARP International: The Journal* had special coverage on Japan and aging, and Kotoen was one of the places featured.[16] Kotoen was founded in 1962 as an elder-care facility. In 1976, the nursery school opened, and in 1987 a nursing home and nursery school were built in the same building that began to function as an intergenerational facility, one of the first in Japan. In 2006, Kotoen opened a new integrated and intergenerational facility, called Tsubaki, a day-service center for people with mental disability as well as a nursery school and day-service center for the elderly in the same city.

As of April 2023, forty-nine residents live in the nursing home section and forty-six residents live in the special nursing home section. The average age for the nursing home is 84.8 years and is 85.3 years for the special nursing home. The oldest residents are a 101-year-old woman and a 94-year-old man. The nursery school has 126 children in total, from infants to five-year olds. According to the *AARP International Journal*, "The mission of Kotoen is to create an inclusive society, one in which people of all ages and abilities can find happiness together. That quest is obvious in the daily interactions, all designed to remove misconceptions between people and encourage communication."[17]

Author's note: The first time I visited Kotoen twenty years ago, I was overwhelmed to enter a big hall full of intergenerational interaction between elderly residents and preschool children and surprised to discover it was routine. That impression continued through forty subsequent visits, not because Kotoen practices the same routine, but because it continues to adapt to challenges and transform itself.

ACTIVITIES

The activities conducted at Kotoen are categorized by scale—small, medium, and large—according to Ms. Keiko Sugi, a Kotoen founder. Small-scale programs include a morning exercise called radio calisthenics, a physical exercise known to all Japanese since childhood, and an intergenerational exchange time, as shown in figure 22.3. Another form of small activity is the nursery school graduation ceremony. Residents attend the ceremony just like the children's parents do, and at the end of the proceedings, the elderly residents line up in the hall and make a tunnel for the children to walk through as if they are beginning a journey to a new world.

Medium-scale programs include an event in which once a month, residents and preschoolers play various games planned by staff members and have lunch together. Another program entails preschoolers visiting the elderly residents' rooms to interact with them.

Large-scale programs are significant events that involve many people once a year. These include the Sumo Festival, where Sumo wrestlers visit Kotoen, perform Sumo, and play with the children while elderly residents watch and cheer. Another big event is *undo kai*, which takes place in October. *Undo kai* is a sports festival where all preschoolers compete in running by age group and showcase gymnastic movements or dancing for family members and residents.

Figure 22.3 Kotoen.

Some intergenerational exchanges are rooted culturally and seasonally. Kotoen's concept of "big family under one roof" extends even to staff members and neighbors.[18] Residents and preschoolers can spend every day as real great-grandparents and grandchildren would.

PROGRAM STRENGTHS

Kotoen staff members are either certified care workers working in the nursing home or certified day-care teachers working in the nursery school section; some staff members hold both licenses. They collaborate in planning and executing intergenerational activities with meticulous detail. Care workers share information about the health conditions of residents participating in activities. Both sets of professionals play an equal role in these events. This collaboration has been made possible through the long history of communication between the two types of professionals, involving in-depth discussions about Kotoen's purpose and how each activity contributes to its mission. Strong leadership consistently emphasizes the values and mission of Kotoen.

Since Kotoen's founding, the organization has expanded its business and services, collaborating with various community resources, including both public and private businesses. However, the programs described earlier would not be possible without the support of neighbors. One activity that promotes community building is called the Edogawa Smile Community Activity. In this initiative, Kotoen hosts programs and events, such as a free movie showing for young parents and children, a talk event involving junior high school students and the elderly, an Edogawa Smile Community Festival, and a training event to teach people how to respond when they encounter a person with dementia walking on the street.

Ms. Sugi is an iconic figure at Kotoen, serving as the founder and manager of the facility. Her presence has rendered Kotoen unique in the intergenerational field. However, what is most impressive about her is not her leadership style or ideas for intergenerational programs, but her profound knowledge about each resident and child. Ms. Sugi understands how each person ended up at Kotoen, especially those elderly residents who lack communication with family or have no family visiting them. Her focus goes beyond the quality of intergenerational programs to ensuring that each person leads a happy life at Kotoen. This perspective is uppermost in her mind.

IMPACT ON USERS AND THE COMMUNITY

First, although the impact on residents and children at Kotoen is not scientifically monitored, Kotoen appears to foster strong generativity, resulting in good health conditions for the residents and enhanced self-esteem for the preschoolers.

Second, owing to Kotoen's extensive history, some new professional staff members were once students in Kotoen Nursery School. Ms. Sugi likens this phenomenon to salmon returning to the river. Individuals who have experienced the intergenerational culture deliberately choosing to work at Kotoen over more lucrative options is a notable decision considering the significant labor shortages in this field. Those working there every day, earning relatively low salaries, must be motivated by deeply rooted childhood values.

Lastly, Kotoen holds a symbolic place in the intergenerational field in Japan. People from all over the country who want to start an intergenerational facility or make their program or facility more attractive to all generations in their community come to visit Kotoen. They gain valuable insights into managing an intergenerational facility, implementing programs, training staff members, and most importantly, creating happiness among people.

LIMITATIONS AND FUTURE CHALLENGES

In the past few years, the pandemic forced Kotoen to suspend all intergenerational activities. The strength of Kotoen, having both a nursing home and nursery school in the same building, became a weakness. Although it is gradually resuming the exchange, it has not yet fully recovered. During this period, many residents have aged and become frail.

Moreover, newer staff members who are unfamiliar with the exchange have not developed the skills and knowledge for delivering what Kotoen's big family concept requires. Building a system to pass intergenerational skills and knowledge to the next generation in the workplace remains a challenge.

Summary

There are numerous intergenerational programs and places in Japan. Three cases introduced in this chapter provide different perspectives on intergenerational activity in the country. Although the COVID-19 pandemic led to the suspension of many intergenerational initiatives or made people reluctant to start new ones, the demographic changes and labor shortages in many fields that will continue in the future signal the importance of empowering the generations to support one another, thereby creating a new system that is sustainable for society.

With policymakers guiding Japan toward a coexistence society, more intergenerational measures are needed in the community. While the three cases in this chapter offer insights into the desired path ahead, the systems are not yet in place for long-term prevention. Believers in intergenerational connections should convey the importance of good practices and share skills and experiences widely while human resources are available and the idea of respecting different generations is still valued.

Notes

1. Masataka Kuraoka, "Exploring Sustainable 'Kayoi-no-ba': From Intergenerational and Collaborative Perspectives," *Japanese Journal of Gerontology* 45, no. 3 (2023): 268–75 (in Japanese).
2. Masataka Kuraoka, "Multigenerational Cyclical Support System: Programs in Japan for Designing a Sustainable Society through Intergenerational Co-creation," in *Intergenerational Contact Zones: Place-Based Strategies for Promoting Social Inclusion and Belonging*, ed. Matthew S. Kaplan et al. (New York: Routledge, 2020), 217–27.

3. Sachiko Murayama et al., "School Students' Greeting Behavior and its Association with their Community Attachment and Helping Behavior," *Japanese Journal of Public Health* 67, no. 7 (2020): 452–60 (in Japanese), https://doi.org/10.11236/jph.67.7_452.
4. Yuta Nemoto, et al., "The Relationship between Intra- and Inter-generational Exchange and Mental Health among Young and Older Adults," *Japanese Journal of Public Health* 65, no. 12 (2018): 719–29 (in Japanese), https://doi.org/10.11236/jph.65.12_719.
5. Yoshinori Fujiwara et al., "Influence of 'Face-to-Face Contact' and 'Non-Face-to-Face Contact' on the Subsequent Decline in Self-Rated Health and Mental Health Status of Young, Middle-Aged, and Older Japanese Adults: A Two-Year Prospective Study," *International Journal of Environmental Research and Public Health* 19, no. 4 (2022): 2218, https://doi.org/10.3390/ijerph19042218.
6. Kumiko Nonaka et al., "The Impact of Generativity on Maintaining Higher-Level Functional Capacity of Older Adults: A Longitudinal Study in Japan," *International Journal of Environmental Research and Public Health* 20, no. 11 (2023): 6015, https://doi.org/10.3390/ijerph20116015,
7. Yoshinori Fujiwara, "Present Situation and Issues for Practical Research in Intergenerational Relationships: From the Viewpoint of Gerontological Studies," *Journal of Japan Society for Intergenerational Studies* 2, no. 1 (2012): 3–8, https://doi.org/10.57559/journalofjsis.02010308.
8. Yoh Murayama et al., "Social Concern and the Present State of Intergenerational Programs: An Analysis of Newspaper Articles and a Survey of Organizations," *Japanese Journal of Public Health* 60, no. 3 (2013): 138–45, https://doi.org/10.11236/jph.60.3_138.
9. Kumiko Nonaka et al., "Exploring Factors that Affect Volunteering among the Elderly with Health Problems: Suggestions for Improvements to the Current Situation," *Journal of Japan Society for Intergenerational Studies* 3, no. 1 (2013): 19–33, https://doi.org/10.57559/journalofjsis.03011933.
10. World Health Organization, *World Report on Ageing and Health* (Geneva, Switzerland: World Health Organization, 2015).
11. Hiroyuki Suzuki et al., "The Effectiveness of an Intergenerational Relational Program Koryu-Jugyou for Elementary School Children's Communication Skills," *Journal of Japan Society for Intergenerational Studies* 5, no. 1 (2015): 21–28, https://doi.org/10.57559/journalofjsis.05012128.
12. Yoshinori Fujiwara et al., "Indirect Effects of School Volunteering by Senior Citizens on Parents through the 'REPRINTS' Intergenerational Health Promotion Program," *Nihon Koshu Eisei Zasshi, Japanese Journal of Public Health* 57, no. 6 (2010): 458–66, https://doi.org/10.11236/jph.57.6_458.
13. R. Sakurai et al., "Long-term Effects of an Intergenerational Program on Functional Capacity in Older Adults: Results from a Seven-year Follow-up of the REPRINTS Study," *Archives of Gerontology and Geriatrics* 64 (2016): 13–20, https://doi.org/10.1016/j.archger.2015.12.005.
14. R. Sakurai et al., "Preventive Effects of an Intergenerational Program on Age-Related Hippocampal Atrophy in Older Adults: The REPRINTS study," *International of Journal of Geriatric Psychiatry* 33, no. 2 (2018): e264–72, https://doi.org/10.1002/gps.4785.
15. Leng Leng Thang, *Generations in Touch: Linking the Old and Young in a Tokyo Neighborhood* (Ithaca, NY: Cornell University Press, 2001).
16. Lauren Hassani, "Caring, the Kotoen Way," *AARP International: The Journal* 11 (2018). https://www.aarpinternational.org/File%20Library/AARPTheJournal/Kotoen_AARPTheJournal2018.doi.10.26419-2Fint.00001.019.pdf.
17. Hassani, "Caring, the Kotoen Way."
18. Keiko Sugi, "Introducing Effective Intergenerational Programs in Age-Integrated Facilities at Kotoen," *Journal of Intergenerational Relationships* 7, no. 1 (2009/03/12 2009), https://doi.org/10.1080/15350770802628943.

Bibliography

Fujiwara, Yoshinori. "Present Situation and Issues for Practical Research in Intergenerational Relationships: From the Viewpoint of Gerontological Studies." *Journal of Japan Society for Intergenerational Studies* 2, no. 1 (2012): 3–8. https://doi.org/10.57559/journalofjsis.02010308.

Fujiwara, Yoshinori, Kumiko Nonaka, Masataka Kuraoka, Yoh Murayama, Sachiko Murayama, Yuta Nemoto, et al. "Influence of 'Face-to-Face Contact' and 'Non-Face-to-Face Contact' on the Subsequent Decline in Self-Rated Health and Mental Health Status of Young, Middle-Aged, and Older Japanese Adults: A

Two-Year Prospective Study." *International Journal of Environmental Research and Public Health* 19, no. 4 (2022): 2218. https://doi.org/10.3390/ijerph19042218.

Fujiwara, Yoshinori, Naoki Watanabe, Mariko Nishi, Hiromi Oba, Sangyoon Lee, Youko Kousa, et al. "Indirect Effects of School Volunteering by Senior Citizens on Parents through the 'Reprints' Intergenerational Health Promotion Program." *Nihon Koshu Eisei Zasshi, Japanese Journal of Public Health* 57, no. 6 (2010): 458–66. https://doi.org/10.11236/jph.57.6_458.

Hassani, Lauren. "Caring, the Kotoen Way." *AARP International: The Journal,* 11 (2018): 6–8. https://www.aarpinternational.org/File%20Library/AARPTheJournal/Kotoen_AARPTheJournal2018.doi.10.26419-2Fint.00001.019.pdf.

Kuraoka, Masataka. "Multigenerational Cyclical Support System: Programs in Japan for "Designing a Sustainable Society through Intergenerational Co-Creation." In *Intergenerational Contact Zones: Place-Based Strategies for Promoting Social Inclusion and Belonging*, 217–27, edited by Matt Kaplan, Leng Leng Thang, Jaco Hoffman, and Mariano Sánchez. New York: Routledge, 2020.

Kuraoka, Masataka. "Exploring Sustainable 'Kayoi-No-Ba': From Intergenerational and Collaborative Perspectives." *Japanese Journal of Gerontology* 45, no. 3 (2023): 268–75 (in Japanese).

Murayama, Sachiko, Masataka Kuraoka, Kumiko Nonaka, Motoki Tanaka, Yuta Nemoto, Masashi Yasunagawa, et al. "School Students' Greeting Behavior and Its Association with Their Community Attachment and Helping Behavior." *Japanese Journal of Public Health* 67, no. 7 (2020): 452–60 (in Japanese), https://doi.org/10.11236/jph.67.7_452.

Murayama, Yoh, Rumi Takeuchi, Hiromi Ohba, Masashi Yasunagawa, Masataka Kuraoka, Kumiko Nonaka, et al. "Social Concern and the Present State of Intergenerational Programs: An Analysis of Newspaper Articles and a Survey of Organizations." *Japanese Journal of Public Health* 60, no. 3 (2013): 138–45 (in Japanese). https://doi.org/10.11236/jph.60.3_138.

Nemoto, Yuta, Masataka Kuraoka, Kumiko Nonaka, Motoki Tanaka, Sachiko Murayama, Hiroko Matsunagawa, et al. "The Relationship between Intra- and Inter-Generational Exchange and Mental Health among Young and Older Adults." *Japanese Journal of Public Health* 65, no. 12 (2018): 719–29 (in Japanese). https://doi.org/10.11236/jph.65.12_719.

Nonaka, Kumiko, Hiroshi Murayama, Yoh Murayama, Sachiko Murayama, Masataka Kuraoka, Yuta Nemoto, et al. "The Impact of Generativity on Maintaining Higher-Level Functional Capacity of Older Adults: A Longitudinal Study in Japan." *International Journal of Environmental Research and Public Health* 20, no. 11 (2023): 6015. https://doi.org/10.3390/ijerph20116015.

Nonaka, Kumiko, Hiromi Oba, Masataka Kuraoka, Masashi Yasunaga, Yoh Murayama, Rumi Takeuchi, et al. "Exploring Factors That Affect Volunteering among the Elderly with Health Problems: Suggestions for Improvements to the Current Situation." *Journal of Japan Society for Intergenerational Studies* 3, no. 1 (2013): 19–33. https://doi.org/10.57559/journalofjsis.03011933.

Sakurai, R., Kenji Ishii, Naoko Sakuma, Masashi Yasunaga, Hiroyuki Suzuki, Yoh Murayama, et al. "Preventive Effects of an Intergenerational Program on Age-Related Hippocampal Atrophy in Older Adults: The Reprints Study." *International of Journal of Geriatric Psychiatry* 33, no. 2 (2018): e264–72. https://doi.org/10.1002/gps.4785.

Sakurai, R., Masashi Yasunaga, Yoh Murayama, Hiromi Ohba, Kumiko Nonaka, Hiroyuki Suzuki, et al. "Long-Term Effects of an Intergenerational Program on Functional Capacity in Older Adults: Results from a Seven-Year Follow-up of the Reprints Study." *Archives of Gerontology and Geriatrics* 64 (2016): 13–20. https://doi.org/10.1016/j.archger.2015.12.005.

Sugi, Keiko. "Introducing Effective Intergenerational Programs in Age-Integrated Facilities at Kotoen." *Journal of Intergenerational Relationships* 7, no. 1 (2009): 40–44. https://doi.org/10.1080/15350770802628943.

Suzuki, Hiroyuki, Hiromi Ohba, Masashi Yasunaga, and Yoshinori Fujiwara. "The Effectiveness of an Intergenerational Relational Program Koryu-Jugyo for Elementary School Children's Communication Skills." *Journal of Japan Society for Intergenerational Studies* 5, no. 1 (2015): 21–28. https://doi.org/10.57559/journalofjsis.05012128.

Thang, Leng Leng. *Generations in Touch: Linking the Old and Young in a Tokyo Neighborhood*. Ithaca, NY: Cornell University Press, 2001.

"Weekly High Rating of TV Programs." Accessed September 14, 2023. https://www.videor.co.jp/tvrating/.

World Health Organization. *World Report on Ageing and Health*. Geneva, Switzerland: World Health Organization. Geneva, Switzerland: World Health Organization, 2015.

CHAPTER 23

Embedding Intergenerational Practice and Approaches in Northern Ireland—The Story So Far

Vicki Titterington *and* Alan Hatton-Yeo

> **Abstract**
>
> This chapter highlights some of the developments in the United Kingdom that underpinned the establishment of Linking Generations Northern Ireland under the auspices of The Beth Johnson Foundation and then reflects on how it evolved with the support of Atlantic Philanthropies in 2009. The work of Linking Generations Northern Ireland has always been rooted in the wider international development of the intergenerational field This chapter tells the story of LGNI's catalyst approach to supporting the development of intergenerational practice across Northern Ireland by taking a capacity building approach.
>
> **Key Words:** intergenerational, Linking Generations, age-friendly, Northern Ireland, ageism, older people, young people

Intergenerational Digital Age Project	Intergenerational Safer Communities Project
Strengths/impact • Relationships • Intergenerational learning • Sharing of skills • Utilizing existing resources • Partnership working • Scalable program • Strategic and applicable • Mutually beneficial • Evaluation data • Social inclusion • Positive promotion for Linking Generations Northern Ireland awareness of intergenerational work • Validity with funders • Legacy resource created	**Strengths/Impact** • Relationships • Challenged attitudes and perceptions • Increased feelings of community safety • Positive approach to negative issue • Evaluation data and evidence • Strategically placed and supported • Legacy and long-term change embedding of intergenerational approach to addressing community safety

Intergenerational Digital Age Project	Intergenerational Safer Communities Project
Limitations • Setup dependent on staffing • Short-term funded • Required venue and equipment	**Limitations** • Not a panacea to creating safe communities • Intergenerational element is a contribution to other factors • Funding for activities

The Beth Johnson Foundation

Twenty-five years ago, The Beth Johnson Foundation (BJF) became involved in intergenerational work to challenge the negative discourse that described older people as needy and passive. Instead, BJF saw older people as vital contributors to the well-being of those around them. In thinking about the need to take an asset-based approach to older people, we also became aware of how disconnected the generations were becoming from one another and how young people needed opportunities for positive engagement and to be part of mutually supportive networks.

As we tried to decide on the best way forward, it quickly became apparent that although intergenerational practice wasn't new and a lot of people in the United Kingdom were interested in it, initiatives took place largely in isolation from one another. In addition, the short-term project nature of much of the work meant that it was rarely written up and rigorously evaluated, let alone built upon. Taking the first steps to understand intergenerational work, BJF was fortunate to become involved in the developing international, intergenerational movement. Professor Sally Newman came to England in 1998 and spent a week with BJF sharing her knowledge and experience. This was a catalyst for meetings that led to the founding of the International Consortium for Intergenerational Programmes (ICIP) and collaboration with colleagues from around the world.

Within the United Kingdom, government and professional structures have traditionally been very compartmentalized, creating a fragmented approach to social policy. Policy has followed a deficit model addressing what are seen as problems rather than seeking to strengthen the social fabric of our communities. Much of the debate about our youth and older people was based on negative stereotypes and, as in many western societies, there was decreasing contact and understanding between the generations.

During 1999 and 2000 BJF consulted widely in the United Kingdom about how we could support the development of intergenerational work. We received one of only fifty National Health Action Zone Innovation Grants to develop intergenerational volunteering in schools—older volunteers working with young people at risk of failure. This project was evaluated externally and developed into a model that was copied globally.

Following a roundtable with all the key U.K. organizations interested in this work, BJF was given a mandate to lead development of the Centre for Intergenerational Practice (CIP). From the beginning, CIP's vision was to build networks, resources, understanding, and influence to create a policy and funding environment that would promote interdependence and exchange between the generations. At the same time, it was important for BJF to ask critical questions about the nature and impact of intergenerational work. BJF was always mindful of the dangers of overclaiming the impact of intergenerational work because of its power to capture people's imaginations. We also realized that intergenerational work is only one part of the answer to the question of how to build fair and just societies and communities where all can age well together, but it is an essential part. For societies to flourish, there needs to be recognition of people's human rights, freedom of speech and thought, and equality of access to education, employment, and services.

At the end of 2000, BJF obtained grants from the then U.K. Lottery and the Lloyds TSB Foundation for England and Wales and, on April 1, 2001, launched the U.K. Centre for Intergenerational Practice. The success and achievements of the Centre, more than anything, encapsulate the power of the intergenerational idea. For significant periods of its existence it had only one paid staff member, but the ideas it represented created partnerships, relationships, and opportunities bound together by people's desire to better understand and promote intergenerational work. Fittingly, the first major conference the Centre organized was the inaugural International Consortium for Intergenerational Practice Conference held in 2002 in Keele, England. Many of those who met at that conference are still collaborating.

For example, the Centre was pivotal in the Welsh government's identifying intergenerational practice as a funded part of its National Strategy for Older People in 2003 and its launch of a National Intergenerational Strategy in 2008 that looked at the implications of intergenerational work across a broad policy perspective.

We also worked with the Scottish government on development of its 2007 Strategy for an Ageing Population, which led to funding for the Scottish Centre for Intergenerational Practice, based on the U.K. CIP model. Since that early start, intergenerational work in Scotland has gone from strength to strength and grown into the highly influential and successful Generations Working Together Programme (see *Handbook* chapter 18).

Next, BJF worked in partnership with Age Concern Northern Ireland to raise the profile of the work and employ dedicated paid staff. BJF proposed a model by which all four U.K. countries would host their own dedicated centers and in 2009 was successful in obtaining funding from Atlantic Philanthropies for the Linking Generations Northern Ireland (LGNI) program—initially as part of BJF's work but with a clear aim to be an independent identity.

In England, one of BJF's most significant successes was facilitating the establishment of the interministerial group that brought five government departments together to fund the Generations Together Programme through which twelve local authorities developed substantial demonstration programs to explore the impacts and effectiveness of different intergenerational activities. The legacy and learning from this were taken forward by the Inspiring Communities Programme, which explored how the community needed to come together to promote the achievements of young people.

Equally important, BJF worked with fifty local authorities and five thousand organizations to help them develop their understandings and practices of intergenerational work. As BJF's work in the United Kingdom advanced, it was mirrored by a growing interest in intergenerational projects in Europe. Since 2009, April 29 has been designated as the European Day of Intergenerational Solidarity, and 2012 was the European Year of Active Ageing and Intergenerational Solidarity.

With the support of the Calouste Gulbenkian Foundation and our many European partners, in 2013 BJF launched the European Network EMIL (European Map of Intergenerational Learning) to create opportunities for cross-cultural comparisons of intergenerational work. Inevitably, the changing economic and political climate in the United Kingdom and nationally has impacted and reshaped these initiatives, and the intergenerational movement has found new partners to develop and influence this work.

The great evils that beset us, both in the more developed as well as in the less well-developed parts of the world, are poverty, inequality, and disadvantage. These cannot be challenged from a mono-generational perspective. They are endemic in our society, and if we want to create places that value social justice and generational equity, they have to be addressed from an intergenerational perspective that promotes the aspirational achievements and value of all. For BJF, the challenge was to explore (beyond discrete projects) how intergenerational thinking and approaches can build the strong, mutually beneficial relationships needed to underpin a fair and equitable society in the future. Here's how LGNI addresses many of these challenges.

LGNI—The History and Background

Linking Generations Northern Ireland (LGNI) was officially launched in 2009 with a grant from the Atlantic Philanthropies. This funding was allocated because of the successes of pilot initiatives supported by and involving Age Concern Northern Ireland and the NI Intergenerational Steering Group, The Beth Johnson Foundation (BJF), Belfast City Council, Ards Borough Council, and the South Eastern Health and Social Care Trust. These intergenerational pilot activities identified the potential impact that intergenerational approaches could have on challenging ageism, addressing community safety, and improving health and well-being. They also highlighted the importance of practitioner support for the delivery of these activities. Today, LGNI although small, has a consistent and recognized brand that is supported and trusted.

Intergenerational Practice as a Professional Approach

LGNI has led the way in connecting generations in communities across Northern Ireland since 2009 and is the only organization solely focusing on the development and promotion of intergenerational approaches to address societal issues. LGNI's small but dedicated team has worked to ensure that "Northern Ireland will be a place where all generations are respected, understood, connected, and engaged together in their communities." To achieve this vision, LGNI brings generations together in lots of different places for lots of different reasons by working at three levels: bringing generations together in communities, influencing and supporting intergenerational practice within organizations, and using evidence to influence policy (see figure 23.1.)

LGNI uses BJF's definition of intergenerational practice, which continues to be the most commonly used definition by those involved in the intergenerational movement across the globe: "Intergenerational practice aims to bring people together in purposeful, mutually beneficial activities which promote greater understanding and respect between generations and contributes to building more cohesive communities. Intergenerational practice is inclusive and builds on the positive resources that the young and old have to offer each other and those around them."[1] In promoting the development and raising awareness of intergenerational practice across Northern Ireland, LGNI has placed specific emphasis on key terms within this definition, as highlighted in italics below:

Figure 23.1 All ages approaches.
Source: LGNI.

- Intergenerational practice promotes activities that bring people *together* and are *mutually* beneficial.
- By taking part in activities, there is greater *understanding* and *respect* between generations (individual/community level) and more *cohesive* communities (societal level).
- As an approach, intergenerational practice is *inclusive* and builds on the positive *resources* of young and old for each other and those around them (all levels).

Alongside the definition of intergenerational practice, LGNI promotes a set of fundamental principles that guide the development and delivery of intergenerational activities and programs. The principles were developed as part of a European Union–funded project involving BJF in 2009 (MATES [Mainstreaming Intergenerational Solidarity]) and published in the *Guide of Ideas for Planning and Implementing Intergenerational Projects*.[2] An explanatory list of these core principles is included below and, if adhered to by those developing intergenerational activities/programs, provides an opportunity to maximize the success and impact achieved for individuals, future practice, and policy.

- **Mutual and Reciprocal Benefit:** Intergenerational projects are strategically designed so that all participating generations derive equal advantages. The approach is rooted in the aspirations of the involved generations. The key question is what the participants hope to achieve and how their expectations are managed, all with the aim of attaining their desired outcomes.

- **All-Age-Friendly Communities and Services:** Intergenerational projects operate on an asset-based model. Unlike the traditional approach that identifies problems and seeks to eliminate them, intergenerational projects work with the generations to identify and amplify their strengths. This strategy fosters success, understanding, and mutual respect.
- **Well-Planned Structure:** Intergenerational projects are not meant to replace natural connections; rather, they deliberately aim to introduce positive changes alongside existing processes. These projects are built on structured programs or initiatives, and evidence shows that the principles of effective program design are just as crucial to successful intergenerational projects as they are to any other project.
- **Cultural Sensitivity:** Given the diverse cultural landscape across Europe, there cannot be one-size-fits-all programs that work universally. While the underlying principles remain consistent, the needs, context, and attitudes of people can vary widely across different settings.
- **Strengthening Community Bonds and Encouraging Active Citizenship:** Intergenerational projects encourage interaction between people of different generations and those in their surroundings. By emphasizing positive connections and capitalizing on people's strengths, these projects are highly effective in building resilient, well-connected communities with increased social capital. This, in turn, leads to greater engagement of citizens in local democracy and social issues.
- **Addressing Ageism:** Ageist attitudes affect both the young and the old to various degrees. Intergenerational projects provide a platform for different generations to meet, collaborate, and explore together. Through these experiences, they can rediscover the true nature of each age group, challenging preconceived notions and stereotypes.

Applying an Intergenerational Lens in Northern Ireland

Northern Ireland has a population of 1.8 million people and is a society in the process of recovering from the "Troubles." The legacy of the Troubles, a history of violent community conflict and division, is still evident in communities and also at a government level. The continuous instability and lack of a Northern Ireland government over the last few years has posed significant challenges for progressing intergenerational practice in a sustainable and strategic manner due to a lack of decision-making and funding for the community and voluntary sectors. The focus of LGNI's approach to outcomes like respect, cohesion, and inclusion holds great relevance for addressing broader needs within Northern Ireland and crosscuts a range of agendas and sectors. LGNI views intergenerational practice as an approach—as opposed to an activity—and advocates for its use in achieving positive outcomes for people, communities, practice, and policy. The above-mentioned principles informing LGNI's work guide the use of intergenerational practice to address issues and build on existing assets, for it works best when adding value to existing resources, agendas, and activities.

Over the years LGNI's alignment of intergenerational activity with wider societal concerns has helped to demonstrate the wide-ranging applicability of an intergenerational approach and has provided evidence to support this. LGNI benefitted from the Communities for All Ages model developed by the Intergenerational Center at Temple University in the United States[3] to promote viewing society and community issues through an intergenerational lens. In 2015, Nancy Henkin, from Temple University, visited Northern Ireland and produced a paper with LGNI stating, "An all-age lens has the great potential to support efforts that address a wide range of community issues and help move toward a vision of an inclusive society."[4] LGNI, alongside intergenerational practitioners across the world, works hard to change the narrative on intergenerational practice so that it can be viewed as necessary, as opposed to something that is nice to do. The constant challenge with intergenerational practice in Northern Ireland and probably across the globe is convincing people that intergenerational practice is intentional and that well-planned application of an intergenerational lens requires support and must be guided by the core principles outlined previously.

LGNI's initial Atlantic Philanthropies grant paved the way for the growth of intergenerational practice across Northern Ireland by creating an awareness of the concept, brand and position for LGNI in the sector, development, and delivery of demonstration projects, and in turn, an evidence base for IG highlighting its potential benefits. Our initial local council pilot program, which provided small grants with a community safety focus, demonstrated a positive approach to addressing older people's fear of crime and negative perceptions of young people. Many innovative funding programs have followed that have both organically and intentionally begun to position intergenerational work within a range of agendas and sectors—for example, community safety, education, housing, digital inclusion, and care homes. Today we place social issues at the center of our work to ensure a robust and tailored narrative for intergenerational approaches, applicability, and potential outcomes. Some of LGNI's flagship projects and examples that have helped validate and position intergenerational practice over the years have included those described in the following sections.

The Intergenerational Safer Communities Project, 2013–2015

Following the success of LGNI's local community safety small grant schemes, a strong relationship was established with the Northern Ireland Department of Justice (DOJ). The DOJ Building Safer, Shared, and Confident Communities Strategy 2012–2017 committed to "promote intergenerational projects to bring young and old together to increase confidence" and

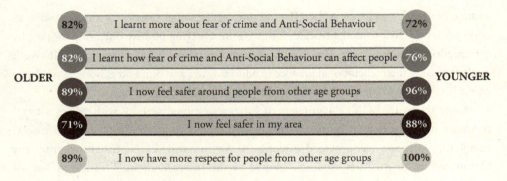

Figure 23.2 Participants' personal experiences of the project.
Source: LGNI.

"reduce fear of crime and make older and vulnerable people feel safer." LGNI received DOJ funding to provide expertise regarding intergenerational approaches to community safety in conjunction with local council Policing and Community Safety Partnerships (PCSPs).

In September 2013 LGNI started the Intergenerational Safer Communities project, which involved engaging local experts and listening to the needs of a range of community stakeholders and helping them to develop intergenerational thinking. LGNI delivered workshops to build capacity and supported the delivery of projects and initiatives through their services. Participants included PCSP staff and members, Police Service of Northern Ireland neighborhood officers, community leaders, organizations, and institutions.

Following meetings with PCSP managers, activities in nineteen council areas were supported, more than doubling the original target of nine. In total, LGNI supported the delivery of twenty-two projects/initiatives across Northern Ireland. Figure 23.2 illustrates some of the outcomes. A full evaluation report of the project was completed.[5]

Although DOJ support for LGNI's work ceased at the end of this project, all local council PCSP plans continue to acknowledge and support intergenerational practice and provide opportunities for local people to have their intergenerational community safety ideas funded on a small scale.

The Digital Age Project, 2012–2017

LGNI was delighted to be included in this partnership project led by the Workers Educational Authority in Northern Ireland. The Digital Age Project was awarded £500,000 by the Big Lottery Fund Northern Ireland's Reaching Out: Connecting Older People program aimed at enabling older people at risk of exclusion or isolation to lead fuller, connected lives as valued members of the community. It was intended to increase internet access and develop the digital capabilities of older people living in sheltered housing and connect them with young people in their communities. Initially, LGNI had a small role. Then, in early 2014 the Workers Educational Authority (lead partner) became insolvent and left the project uncompleted and partners unpaid. LGNI took charge of the project, which in a difficult funding period for LGNI ultimately stabilized our future. This important milestone took LGNI from having a small role to validation of our work, respect, and position. Over the next two years, the project served 409 older people in three dozen Northern Ireland housing schemes and intergenerational digital projects involving 135 older people and 219 young people.

Evidence of the project's success came in an extra year of Big Lottery Fund Northern Ireland funding occasioned by very positive feedback for the intergenerational element of the project. Ninety-one percent of older people reported that taking part in an intergenerational project helped increase their confidence in using technology, while 87 percent reported that they had developed their digital skills and knowledge. Eighty-seven percent said that they were now more interested in technology. A full evaluation report is available.[6] We transformed the project into a stand-alone intergenerational program, a strong model for school pupils and older people to exchange skills and build relationships. The intergenerational learning approach and connections not only empowered older people as intended but also achieved educational outcomes for young people, as illustrated in figure 23.3:

This projects' legacy continues today and has provided abundant data, as reported in "An Intergenerational Approach to Improving Skills and Educational Outcomes for Children and Young People in Northern Ireland," collated by Juniper Consulting NI.[7]

Finding a Home for Intergenerational Practice in Northern Ireland—The Age-Friendly Movement

When the need for a more strategic approach to developing intergenerational practice across Northern Ireland was identified, the LGNI team drew on the evidence base, relationships with key stakeholders and funders, and learning from their Scottish colleagues, Generations Working Together (GWT; see *Handbook* chapter 18) to create a business case proposing the development and coordination of a Northern Ireland–wide intergenerational network. The network would inspire, support, and connect those interested in intergenerational practice across a range of sectors and communities. It would replicate the Scottish GWT model (funded by the Scottish government) by developing intergenerational champions across Northern Ireland and providing support services, including network meetings, training, demonstration projects, partnerships, and lobbying.

Harnessing the impact and successful intergenerational activities and aligning them with key agendas and high-level societal issues have been important tactics in the progression of LGNI's work. Alignment with the World Health Organization's global age–friendly movement, for example, has drawn attention to LGNI's work and recognition from the Northern Ireland central government (Department for Communities Active Ageing Strategy), local government via councils (older people and community planning), key age-sector stakeholders (Age NI), and financially, from the Public Health Agency for Northern Ireland. The World Health Organization believes that a key strategy to facilitate the inclusion of older persons is to make our world more age-friendly. "An age-friendly world enables people of all

Figure 23.3 Benefits of intergenerational connections.

Source: LGNI.

ages to actively participate in community activities and treats everyone with respect, regardless of their age. It is a place that makes it easy for older people to stay connected to people that are important to them. And it helps people stay healthy and active even at the oldest ages and provides appropriate support to those who can no longer look after themselves."[8]

The designation of 2012 as the European Union Year of Active Ageing and Intergenerational Solidarity and April 29 as the European Union Day of Solidarity between generations presented a significant opportunity for LGNI to raise awareness of the importance of intergenerational practice and also their role in its development in Northern Ireland. The president of Age Platform Europe said at the launch of EY2012 (the European Year of Active Ageing and Intergenerational Solidarity 2012) that "creating an Age-Friendly European Union means fostering solidarity between generations and enabling the active participation and involvement of all age groups in society while providing them with adequate support and protection. This cannot be achieved through isolated initiatives. It requires a commitment and a common vision."

The European Union set a goal for Europe to be age-friendly by 2020, and LGNI benefited from the knowledge base and involvement of The Beth Johnson Foundation with its partner Manchester in the UK Age-Friendly Cities Network. The direct links made by the European Union between Active Ageing and intergenerational solidarity opened the doors for LGNI to engage with the office of the first and deputy first ministers in Northern Ireland and to reach out to policy-makers in the Department for Communities Active Ageing team to influence the inclusion of intergenerational practice as a key approach to building an age-friendly Northern Ireland.

Northern Ireland's neighbor Ireland was the first country to define itself as an age-friendly nation, with all local authorities in Ireland having an age-friendly process in place—consultation, an alliance of people and partnerships, and an action plan. The Belfast City Council led the way, working with LGNI on an intergenerational toolkit as part of its delivery activity[9]. In 2015 LGNI partnered with the Belfast City Council, Ark Ageing at Queens, and visiting fellow Nancy Henkin (mentioned previously) to host the Collaborating Towards an Age-Friendly NI event at which intergenerational and age-friendly experts from across the United Kingdom and Ireland highlighted their achievements. This event opened the doors for LGNI's relationship with the Public Health Agency NI and was a significant milestone in accessing funding support for our infrastructure today. A paper of the event was published.[10]

Developing an Infrastructure for Intergenerational Practice in NI

After many years of lobbying, in 2018 Public Health Agency NI and the UK Lottery Fund financed the new network to support high-quality delivery of intergenerational work across Northern Ireland and utilize the age-friendly concept to embed intergenerational practice within local government policy by means of awareness raising, information, advice, advocacy, training, seed funding, and research. LGNI's network has over 870 members, and its numbers are steadily growing. However, at the end of the UK Lottery Fund grant and with continuing government instability, support for LGNI's network infrastructure has been greatly reduced. The Public Health Agency still funds LGNI and provides stability, sustainability, and strategic direction. The network and their support services are at the core of everything that LGNI does. This has been a very useful approach for LGNI and has enabled them to continue to meet their core objectives by packaging and aligning their work activities for other funders with an overarching aim. (An external evaluation of the Engage Together Project[11] provides a snapshot of LGNI's activities, progress, and important milestones. An up-to-date LGNI impact report on activities and resources can be accessed on the LGNI website at www.linkinggenerationsni.com.)

The growth of LGNI's network and wider support have been key steps in the positioning for intergenerational practice in Northern Ireland and also for LGNI. Working with a small team and limited capacity, LGNI has utilized the network membership as advocates for IG, provided support for practitioners and community leaders to take the lead on developing IG through training offerings and resources, and has acted as a hub for the promotion of intergenerational stories and work to inspire others. Grasping the digital world has enabled LGNI to streamline, promote, and garner support for the work. LGNI uses digital marketing to spread messages and services across social media channels, thereby growing the numbers of supporters and directing interest to the website and resources. This catalyst for intergenerational practice in Northern Ireland has been an important factor in LGNI's success bringing people, practitioners, and policy-makers along with them and creating an intergenerational movement.

Acting as a Catalyst for Intergenerational Practice in Northern Ireland—Building Capacity

The development of LGNI's support infrastructure and intergenerational network was designed to align with LGNI's goal of increasing capacity so that, ultimately, everyone can experience the benefits of intergenerational practice. LGNI evaluator BMK Consulting developed this chain of outcomes as part of the EngAge Together Project (2018–2021), which illustrates the link between the project's immediate outcomes and the core outcomes we are pursuing. LGNI's core outcomes, shown in the right-hand column of figure 23.4, underpinned the EngAge Together Project outcomes (on the left). As mentioned previously, placing these outcomes at the center of all of our work has been a key tactic in sustainability, strategic focus, and funding efforts.

More about the LGNI Network

LGNI's intergenerational network has become an established community of practice that brings together people across Northern Ireland who are interested in developing and supporting connections between generations where they live, work, and go to school. Members come from a wide range of communities and sectors across Northern Ireland and

Population Outcome	Our citizens benefit from IP outcomes: This can only be achieved by many agents and actions over time
Goal	There is greater community capacity to sustain IP
	Project outcomes / **LGNI core outcomes**
Client Outcomes	Influence on practice and policy at local and regional level. / **Stronger IP infrastructure:** There is a stronger infrastructure supporting access to IP tools, research, evidence, professional and policy development.
	Increased skills and self-esteem amongst young people. / **More IP delivered and evidenced:** People have improved access to advice, support and funds to apply their IP learning and demonstrate IP benefits by delivering more intergenerational projects.
	Increased levels of social engagement amongst older and younger people. / **Improved IP knowledge:** People learn about IP, its uses, outcomes and principles.
	Increased IP capacity within communities and organisations. / **Better connections:** People have connections to hear of IP and learn from one another.
Activities	The work that will create the outcomes: • Local IP Networks • IP Training • IP Project Support • Embedding IP
Tactic	Generate project outcomes that create and support a skilled and supportive *Community of Practice* with a supportive infrastructure.

Figure 23.4 Project outcomes and core outcomes.

Source: Outcomes chain created by BMK Consulting for LGNI EngAge Together Project.

also internationally, including individuals, community leaders, practitioners in community organizations, teachers, care home staff, housing staff, academics, and central and local government officials. Members of LGNI's small staff act as local network area contacts for specific council areas to provide advice and support and also attend local meetings and events of relevance. The network is designed to grow organically and enable members to engage at all stages of their intergenerational journeys and for a range of purposes. New members can connect with others via the network, be inspired by the stories of other members, get support to develop their intergenerational work, and in turn promote their work to inspire others. LGNI hosts four network meetings twice per year, inviting all council areas to share learning and practice. When LGNI asked network members to rate different aspects of the 2022–2023 meetings, well over three-quarters of them replied positively in every category.

Seed Grant Funding

Seed grants give an incentive for small local groups to develop intergenerational ideas where they live, work, and go to school. They help LGNI reach deep into communities and connect with people who are often disadvantaged by age, isolation, or other life circumstances. LGNI's latest All Ages April 2023 evaluation report details how successful this approach is in developing intergenerational activity across Northern Ireland.[12]

LGNI Training

Training, support, and advice have been central to LGNI's approach from the early days of The Atlantic Philanthropies funding program, with an emphasis on building capacity for intergenerational practice. We drew on the expertise and resources developed by The Beth Johnson Foundation's Centre for Intergenerational Practice, the European Certificate of Intergenerational Learning, the Pittsburgh University Intergenerational Specialist Award, and members of the Northern Ireland Intergenerational Steering Committee. Training resources were shared across the four partners that CIP supported and live on today as legacies—the International Certificate in Intergenerational Practice and Generations Working Together Training.

LGNI envisioned intergenerational training as a professional tool for practitioners across sectors—care home staff, teachers/educators, young people—and also as a potential income generator. In early 2019 LGNI accessed accreditation for the three-module course, "An Introduction to Intergenerational Practice for Community Leaders & Practitioners," and began marketing it for a fee and packaging it as an offering within funding bids. Trainees are supported from generating an intergenerational idea through to all the stages of developing, delivering, evaluating, and sustaining a project. For example, with funding from the LFT Trust, LGNI developed a Zoom training and support program with a toolkit specifically tailored for care home activity coordinators.[13] Along similar lines, housing associations across Northern Ireland are keen to equip housing coordinators with the skills to engage their older tenants in intergenerational activities and connections.

LGNI's vast experience of developing and delivering intergenerational projects in schools and the education research mentioned previously in this chapter underpin an intergenerational training offering for teachers. Relevant curricular topics and links include health and social care, personal development and mutual understanding, communication and listening, Department of Education community engagement policy, and skills for life and work.

LGNI also developed training that could support young people to take the lead in developing their own intergenerational ideas—college students studying health and social care and early years education, secondary education students, and young people not in education and employment. All of these training approaches have provided skill development and practice-based learning and leadership skills for the young people, thereby helping to develop their intergenerational ideas. Figure 23.5 shows the journey of the secondary education pupils supported by LGNI from 2022 to 2023.

Forming Partnerships Locally and Internationally

In 2012 LGNI joined the TOY Plus Project based on the expertise of The Beth Johnson Foundation in the intergenerational field. This large Erasmus+–funded project led by

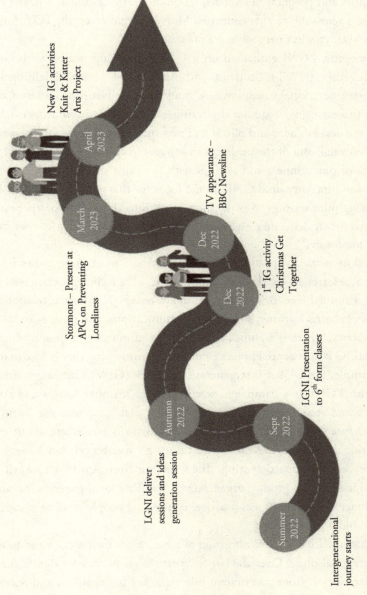

Figure 23.5 The New-Bridge College intergenerational journey.

Source: LGNI.

international child care development initiatives in the Netherlands included partners from the United Kingdom, Ireland, Slovenia, Italy, Greece, and Spain. The focus was on nurturing the skills and competencies to develop and deliver intergenerational learning programs involving young adults and older people. Project outputs included a handbook for tutors and program developers, an online learning course, and the piloting of these resources across the partner countries. More information on the TOY Project can be found via www.toyproject.net and in *Handbook* chapter 19.

More recently, LGNI embarked on a U.K. partnership project with Generations Working Together (GWT) Scotland and Apples and Honey Nightingale House, Creating Intergenerational Communities, funded by the National Lottery Community Fund. This project brings together the training expertise and resources of all partners and entails the development and piloting of new quality indicators for intergenerational practice. The overall aim of the project is to support quality and sustainability by equipping a range of practitioners and settings with the skills and knowledge to embed IG within the work that they do. LGNI's initial focus for this project is with the early years sector, assisting pilot settings to make intergenerational links with partner settings and work collectively on delivering high-quality intergenerational practice that can be sustained into the future.[14]

Partnership work by participants, communities, practitioners, funders, policymakers, and researchers is the key component of an intergenerational approach. Whether at a funded level or merely a mutually beneficial informal relationship, such alliances foster shared learning, practice, communications, and promotion of intergenerational practice. There is significant strength in numbers and in spreading a global narrative that IG is an essential practice rather than something that is nice to do. To this end, for example, the Global Intergenerational Week (GIW) Campaign, led by GWT Scotland with LGNI as a campaign executive team member fosters and strengthens the narrative and recognition of intergenerational practice across the world (see also *Handbook* chapter 18). GIW connects everyone who is passionate about everything intergenerational. The fourth year of the campaign was bigger and better than ever, with fourteen countries participating. The week ran from April 24 to April 30, 2023 and inspired individuals, groups, organizations, local/national government, and NGOs to fully embrace intergenerational practice, connecting people of all ages, especially the younger and older generations.[15]

LGNI has utilized the GIW campaign to advance our own agenda and to make a lot of intergenerational noise. Over the last few years it has provided a significant opportunity to garner support from government ministers, key stakeholders, and policy makers; develop partnership resources, initiatives, and messaging; and inspire the delivery of grassroots activity. Social media and online communications as well as local press have played an important role in the campaign, with a focus on celebrating the week by sharing, tagging, posting, and ultimately supporting the work. Highlights include

- **All-ages April grants:** Forty small grants allocated by LGNI to communities, groups, and settings across Northern Ireland to support intergenerational activity. Over a thousand participants took part, and a vast amount of intergenerational good news filled social media and local press and was recognized by Northern Ireland policy makers.
- **Council building light-ups:** LGNI's request to light up council buildings with our logo color (pink) for the week was fulfilled by nine of the eleven local councils in Northern Ireland. All of the participating councils posted photos of their buildings on their social media channels, promoting intergenerational week and linking to LGNI's website.
- **GIW Photo Competition:** LGNI teamed up with the Commissioners for Older and Younger People Northern Ireland to promote a photo competition with the theme Connecting Generations.
- LGNI teamed up with Twinkl Northern Ireland and the Soil Association to develop GIW resources focused on education and grandparents gardening.

The joint promotion activity generated as part of these activities by these respected influencers and organizations had a massive impact on raising awareness for GIW locally, for intergenerational practice, and for LGNI.[16]

Conclusions—LGNI as a Center of Excellence for Intergenerational Practice in Northern Ireland

As mentioned throughout this chapter, LGNI's aim (and challenge) is to strategically place intergenerational practice and embed it as an approach within Northern Ireland society by increasing funding and support for its delivery and infrastructure. Although we are a very small team, we have aligned the intergenerational lens and intergenerational approach with our various activities to raise awareness of the potential benefits and applicability of intergenerational practice and to garner support for it across all sectors and at all levels. Northern Ireland's small geographic area and population, the reorganization of local government from twenty-eight council areas to eleven, and unique work focus have been a real advantage in forming partnerships and relationships on a Northern Ireland–wide scale. We have greatly benefited from ease of access to important and influential people (policy-makers, government officials, and politicians), engaging locally with supporters and being an intergenerational voice on a range of multiagency strategic meetings and through lobbying activities. With original staff members still on board today, continuity has been a valuable asset to LGNI, fostering a raft of relationships, pushing the same core messages, and building trust in LGNI's work.

LGNI is widely recognized as Northern Ireland's intergenerational expert organization within the community voluntary sector, education sector, local and central government, and health and social care, and we utilize this reputation to grow support for our work. The grassroots work has developed local intergenerational champions who act as advocates for intergenerational practice and support the promotion of intergenerational practice by sharing their good news stories and recognizing the support they have received from LGNI in their intergenerational journey. This positioning has enabled LGNI to secure a seat and voice at a wide range of tables, including local council age-friendly alliances across Northern Ireland, the Northern Ireland Policy Action Group on Loneliness, local housing advisory groups, Northern Ireland Care Home ECHO group, education, and active ageing consultations. This important advocacy role for intergenerational practice has in return opened up many doors for LGNI to contribute to conversations and partnerships that create new work opportunities and foster intergenerational practice at the community, practice, and policy levels—for example, presenting to politicians and government officials, speaking at a range of conferences, linking in with academic research and projects, providing facilitation for partner organizations, and being promoted by Northern Ireland media via newspapers, radio, and TV.

The story so far of intergenerational practice in Northern Ireland and LGNI suggests that there will continue to be many challenges and opportunities along the way, but the focus will always remain on building local intergenerational capacity that will hopefully take Northern Ireland one step closer to becoming truly all-age friendly.

Notes

1. "Working with Others," Beth Johnson Foundation, 2009, https://www.bjf.org.uk.
2. T. Almeida Pinto et al., *Guide of Ideas for Planning and Implementing Intergenerational Projects* (Portugal: Association VIDA, 2009).
3. C. Brown and N. Henkin, *Communities for All Ages, Intergenerational Community Building: Resource Guide* (Philadelphia: Intergenerational Centre Temple University, 2012).
4. N. Henkin, "Communities for All Ages: A Life Course Approach to Strengthening Communities in Northern Ireland," Ark Ageing Programme, February, 2015, https://www.ark.ac.uk/ARK/sites/default/files/2018-08/cfaa.pdf, 4.
5. Linking Generations Northern Ireland, *Evaluation of the Intergenerational Safer Communities Project* (Belfast: LGNI, 2015).
6. Linking Generations Northern Ireland, *Evaluation of the Digital Age Project* (Belfast: LGNI, 2018).
7. Juniper Consulting, *An Intergenerational Approach to Improving Skills and Educational Outcomes for Children and Young People in Northern Ireland* (Belfast: LGNI, 2021). https://www.linkinggenerationsni.com/wp-content/uploads/2021/06/LGNI-Intergenerational-Education-Research-Branded.pdf.
8. https://www.emro.who.int/fr/elderly-health/elderly-news/age-friendly-world-adding-life-to-years.html.
9. Belfast City Council, *Age-friendly Belfast Intergenerational Toolkit* (Belfast: Belfast City Council, 2015).
10. ARK Ageing Programme, *Collaborating towards an Age-Friendly Northern Ireland* (Belfast: ARK Ageing Programme, 2014).
11. Linking Generations Northern Ireland, *Evaluation of the Engage Together Project* (Belfast: LGNI, 2021).
12. Linking Generations Northern Ireland, *All Ages April 2023 Report* (Belfast: LGNI, 2023).
13. Further information about LGNI's LFT project can be accessed via https://www.linkinggenerationsni.com/project/care-homes-connect-intergenerationally/.
14. For more information, go to https://generationsworkingtogether.org/news/creating-intergenerational-communities.
15. Further information on the GIW campaign and participating countries is available via https://generationsworkingtogether.org/global-intergenerational-week.
16. Go to https://www.linkinggenerationsni.com/global-intergenerational-week/ for more information.

Bibliography

ARK Ageing Programme. *Collaborating towards an Age-friendly Northern Ireland*. Belfast: ARK Ageing Programme, 2014.

Belfast City Council. *Age-friendly Belfast Intergenerational Toolkit*. Belfast: Belfast City Council, 2015.

Beth Johnson Foundation. "Working with Others." 2009. https://www.bjf.org.uk.

Brown, C., and N. Henkin. *Communities for All Ages, Intergenerational Community Building: Resource Guide*. Philadelphia: Intergenerational Center Temple University, 2012).

Henkin, N. "Communities for All Ages: A Life Course Approach to Strengthening Communities in Northern Ireland." Ark Ageing Programme. February 2015. https://www.ark.ac.uk/ARK/sites/default/files/2018-08/cfaa.pdf, 4.

Juniper Consulting. *An Intergenerational Approach to Improving Skills and Educational Outcomes for Children and Young People in Northern Ireland*. Belfast: LGNI, 2021. https://www.linkinggenerationsni.com/wp-content/uploads/2021/06/LGNI-Intergenerational-Education-Research-Branded.pdf.

Linking Generations Northern Ireland. *Evaluation of the Intergenerational Safer Communities Project*. Belfast: LGNI, 2015.

Linking Generations Northern Ireland. *All Ages April 2023 Report*. Belfast: LGNI, 2023.

Pinto, T. Almeida, Iris Marreel, and Alan Hatton-Yeo. *Guide of Ideas for Planning and Implementing Intergenerational Projects*. Portugal: Association VIDA, 2009.

CHAPTER 24

Shaping the Future of Work—Intergenerational Growing Pains and Gains in Canada's Workplaces

Lisa Taylor *and* Emily Schmidt

Abstract

This chapter discusses the importance of intergenerational approaches to social, workforce, and economic challenges in Canadian workplaces. While policy spheres are gradually recognizing the need for an intergenerational mindset, workplaces have yet to fully embrace it. Therefore, this chapter explores three case studies of current workplace programs engaging diverse age groups to present a better understanding of the benefits and barriers these programs face. Using Challenge Factory's Broken Talent Escalator® model, the findings point to recognition that generations work together but few organizations explicitly tie intergenerational initiatives or metrics to business outcomes. Even in Canadian workplaces with strong commitment to diversity, age is often not considered. The lack of specifically age-aware initiatives within Canada's workspaces reflects the challenge of addressing workplace ageism. If it isn't recognized, it can't be addressed.

Key Words: intergenerational, ageism, demographics, workplace, workforce, career, talent

Centre for Social Innovation Community Animator Program	Canada Free Agents Program	Vancity Employee Resource Programs
Strengths/impact Gives newcomers and young people experience, leading to permanent employment offers.	**Strengths/impact** Offers public servants freedom and support to select work that matches their skills and interests. Also helps managers acquire talent quickly, on a short-term basis.	**Strengths/impact** Community focus provides a safe space and opportunity to build connections and a sense of belonging for people who share similar elements of identity. Also creates opportunity to provide feedback to the company.
Limitations Funding constraints and limited selection of experiences for program participants (front desk and administrative work).	**Limitations** Evaluation and impact measurements for the program need development.	**Limitations** Attempting to refine their programs while simultaneously expanding.

Introduction

Canada is at a pivotal moment in recognizing the importance of intergenerational approaches to social, workforce, and economic issues. Formal structures, such as political spending priorities, pensions, and housing, are currently designed to benefit older people. At the research and policy levels, there is growing awareness that how one generation is treated has a direct impact on other generations. However, this intergenerational mindset has not yet permeated workplaces, where programs designed for new graduate hires or next-generation leaders make investment bets based on a specific career stage. This lack of an intergenerational, systemic approach to workforce management leads to unanticipated consequences and challenges with hiring, employee engagement, and recognition programs.

This chapter considers the importance and potential of intergenerational programs and examines three case studies. Currently, awareness that challenging social and economic conditions require intergenerational thinking has permeated policy spheres but is not yet explicitly evident in how workplaces support and address employee needs.

While other nations, such as Wales, have created formal positions within government to monitor the impact of current decisions on future generations, Canada has moved more slowly in developing intergenerational policy or mandates. In March 2022, Statistics Canada announced their Quality of Life Framework that tracks the well-being of Canadians across more than a hundred indicators, with particular focus on disparities across diverse populations, including generations.[1] Through an analysis of nine indicators from the Quality of Life Framework, Statistics Canada has quantified a difference in perceived well-being between younger and older Canadians.[2] While these efforts to collect data, track, and report on intergenerational fairness are in their early stages, their existence alone shines a light on areas of impact, and they are making their way into discussions within major policy areas that affect workers, such as health, child care, and housing. Intergenerational approaches can lead to better short- and long-term economic and social outcomes for all generations. One environment where all generations interact is the workplace, yet advancements seen in the policy spheres have not yet become commonplace there. While there is a recognition that many generations work together, there are few explicitly intergenerational initiatives or metrics tied to business outcomes the way the Quality of Life Framework links to social outcomes.

By turning to the wisdom of Indigenous Peoples, we can learn more about how intergenerational awareness shapes society. The Anishanaabe Seven Generations tradition can help inform strong intergenerational approaches. This Indigenous teaching tells us, "What we do today will affect the seventh generation and because of this we must bear in mind our responsibility to them today and always."[3] All actions, decisions, and opportunities are positioned within the context of what past generations have intended and what future generations will need. This powerful lens teaches generations across a long time horizon to be good stewards of life, land, and each other.

Understanding Intergenerational Workplaces

Currently, many traditional workplace constructs and systems are being challenged and overturned. The novel concept and mindset of "intergenerational fairness" call for acknowledgment of and action to change structures that were originally designed to address the needs of older workers by placing future burdens on younger workers. Yet society continues to prioritize and value messages and images of youth, discounting the vitality, wisdom, and competence of older people. Altogether, doing so creates the perfect conditions for generational resentment and divisiveness.

Workplaces are microcosms of society, and today's Canadian workplaces demonstrate how vital and complex intergenerational relationships can be. Unlocking their value is complicated. Overt, subtle, and self-imposed ageism prevents many leadership teams from identifying what's trapped within its own workforce. In an era where leaders struggle to address skill gaps and tight labor markets, meaningful and powerful solutions to common talent issues often lie within their own organizations. However, perceptions, misperceptions, and myths about generational cohorts keep the true value of an intergenerational workforce from being tapped.

In Canada, the demographic profile of the workforce serves as an early warning system (or early opportunity alert) for how the world of work will continue to change. While there are many shifting aspects of the world of work, from artificial intelligence (AI) and technological change to globalization and climate change, none is more predictable than lifespans, working lifespans, and demographics.

Mainstream and social media provide a continuous stream of stories reinforcing the differences between generations. While distinctions between generations may exist, there are few truly universal differences based on year of birth. Not all boomers are the same, and when it comes to workplace values, boomers and millennials have more in common than differences. (See *Handbook* chapters 27 and 28.) An examination of workplace programs and case studies can shine a light on intergenerational initiatives overcoming the narrative that says what's meaningful about five generations in the workforce is what divides them. Instead, it can help rewrite the story of a successful workforce and "workspan" (the period of time during which an individual is actively engaged in work or career).

Snapshot of Canadian Demographics and Ageism

Canada is one of the most diverse countries in the world, with 27.5 percent of its population composed of newcomers and first-generation Canadians.[4] But discussions about the strength of diversity, how it contributes to Canada's role in the world, and the success of individual industries and sectors often overlook the dimension of age diversity.

Bolstering the strength of the diverse talent within Canada's labor force is the emphasis placed on education. According to the Organisation for Economic Co-operation and Development, Canada is one of the most educated countries in the world, second only to Korea, including within the fifty-five- to sixty-four-year-old age cohort.

In recent years, reports have indicated that Canada's labor market is experiencing significant labor and skills shortages, although the accuracy of these reports is not certain. Working-age Canadians are considered to be eighteen to sixty-four years of age, despite a significant proportion of older workers remaining connected in some fashion to the paid workforce past the age of sixty-five. By not including Canadians aged sixty-five and older in workforce measurements, systemic ageism is perpetuated in how workforce issues are defined and how interventions and solutions are presented. As a result, older workers remain a hidden talent pool in the larger labor market as well as within organizations.

Workforce demographics in Canada are reported according to age brackets, with eighteen to twenty-four representing students or early careerists, followed by ten-year cohorts (twenty-five to thirty-four etc.). In addition, characteristics related to age are often attributed to specific generations. For example, as cohorts passed through the twenty-five- to thirty-four-year-old segment of life, they were labeled "hippies" (Boomers), "slackers" (Gen X), or "entitled" (Millennials). These labels, once assigned, are difficult to shake and obscure true differences associated with aspects of youth and development over time.

Labels and general workforce reporting based on discrete age-based segments also serve to keep generations separated, with little incentive to systematically explore interdependence between workers of different ages. As a result, anecdotal studies abound that highlight the presence of intergenerational conflict in the workplace, with emphasis on how both younger and older workers dismiss each other's capabilities and potential.[5] While discrimination on the basis of age is prohibited in Canada under the Charter of Rights and Freedoms, it can be seen in everyday interactions, in mainstream media depictions of populations, and in workplaces. A recent Canadian survey found that ageism remains a form of discrimination whose study continues to be neglected by researchers. Initiatives tend to focus on psycho-social impacts on older workers as opposed to intergenerational impacts and potential across generations.[6] Despite intergenerational indicators being created for overall well-being and social cohesion, workplaces continue to foster age-based divisions, myths, and stereotypes.

The Broken Talent Escalator® that is Costing Organizations and Employees

Fortunately, there is good reason for optimism in how Canada and its workplaces will navigate this messy moment. Challenge Factory, a Certified B Corporation and Future of Work research and advisory services firm that helps clients achieve productivity gains and positive social impact, developed a useful model called the Broken Talent Escalator for discovering where the value of intergenerational workforces is trapped within traditional talent management systems and where leadership teams should focus energy and resources to create new approaches allowing talent, productivity, and profitability to flow.

The Broken Talent Escalator® highlights the interconnectedness of employees at various stages of their careers. While many organizations are focused on initiatives to retain and engage younger employees, few have effective programs to foster strong connections with and lifelong career development for older employees. As a result, organizations become places where it is not good to become too old. Younger workers see how older workers are treated and set a time limit for their tenure with the company. By failing to address issues related to later needs, younger employees make career choices that lead to midcareer attrition and high recruitment costs, both of which are detrimental to the business and culture of the organization.[7]

Workforces operate as a system. Attempts to address one cohort in isolation, such as new graduates or Millennial high-potential employees, without consideration for how all generations work together, are destined to lead to incomplete solutions and unintended consequences. In modeling workforces from within organizations as disparate as law firms and steel manufacturers, a consistent pattern has emerged revealing employees on the Broken Talent Escalator. Mistreatment or isolation of employees higher up on the escalator, who are later in their career, leads to real costs and pains for employees earlier in their career and for the business overall (see figure 24.1.)

Challenge Factory's Broken Talent Escalator model identifies how organizations can shape stronger workforces that align across generations. Organizations often focus career development efforts exclusively on younger workers. After age forty-nine, Canadian workers experience a sharp decline in the frequency and quality of career conversations and training opportunities.

The Broken Talent Escalator models the real costs businesses incur when intergenerational approaches are not part of workforce planning. Many companies ignore the career needs of older workers, leaving them to languish or find their own way into later-life work opportunities. Uncertain of what work possibilities might exist outside their current role, individuals at or nearing the traditional age of retirement are reluctant to step out of work completely. The lack of role models and formal career development for this cohort leads them to remain in place long after they have become bored in their roles or their needs related to work have changed. The result is a bunching effect of older employees operating as if on treadmills. They are capable, but disengaged, invisible, and exhausted.

Many organizations initiate intergenerational programming by assigning older workers to mentor younger workers, with the expectation that knowledge transfer will occur. These types of initiatives are designed to maximize the benefit that younger employees gain from being connected to those with more experience. Often, benefit and support for the older worker in the relationship is accidental or overlooked. As a result, younger workers gain access to a qualified and experienced role model, but that role model also needs—and does not receive—direction, validation, and support to shift into a new career stage.

As mentioned above, organizations typically prioritize particular challenges that relate to one part of the overall career lifecycle rather than taking a systems approach to employee engagement, retention, and quality issues. For example, in any given year, organizations might identify recruitment and brand awareness among new graduates as a key

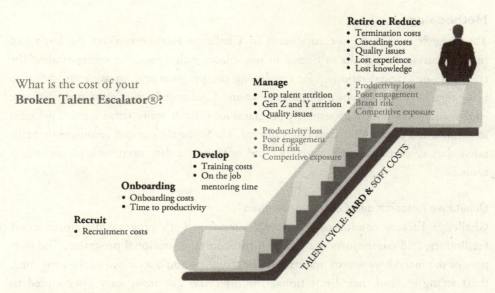

Figure 24.1 The Broken Talent Escalator®.
Source: Challenge Factory

priority. Early-stage career retention is also a common area of focus as organizations incur the costs associated with new employees joining and becoming trained. It is expensive and disruptive to have high turnover during the early career years after investing heavily in individuals. Sometimes the major challenge is identifying next-generation leadership, especially while recognizing the need for diversity, equity, and inclusion (DEI) at all levels within the organization. Across the various employee lifecycle stages, if one step on the Talent Escalator is costing the organization too much time or money, that becomes a strategic priority for the year.

By modeling root causes versus contributing symptoms, risk-, financial-, and engagement-related concerns associated with any generational group inside an organization typically indicate gaps in career development and talent management among employees one or two steps higher up on the Talent Escalator (see figure 24.1). Thus, the challenges (and opportunities) employees face at different stages of their careers are best addressed through intergenerational rather than generation-specific initiatives. By building systemic solutions to issues related to recruitment, onboarding, engagement, skill development, career management, and postcareer activities, organizations can solve problems in unique and creative ways. Work is not divided by age. Work tasks are not assigned only to employees under the age of forty-five. Departments are intergenerational by default, and, as a result, approaching talent management with an eye to workplace realities creates better opportunities for employees of all ages. The case studies selected for this chapter demonstrate how systemic and intergenerational approaches can be put into practice.

Methodology

The research in this chapter, conducted by Challenge Factory, explores the impact of intergenerational programs in Canadian workplaces with a focus on understanding the core issue or original rationale for developing the program and assessing its ability to bring together employees of multiple generations. Challenge Factory examined eight case studies and chose three representative programs for their diversity across sectors, program structures, and the depth of detail they offered. The following sections present both qualitative data gathered through interviews and quantitative data from multiple secondary sources.

Qualitative Research and Case Study Analysis

Challenge Factory conducted structured interviews with program directors, senior facilitators, and community managers of three intergenerational programs. The purpose of the interviews was to understand the structure and operations of the programs, their strengths, and their limitations. The interview questions were open-ended to allow participants to share their observations without restraint. Interviewees were asked for program details, the tools they used to measure success, and the impact on program participants. Interviewees also spoke about the future of the programs and areas of concern. Each interview lasted approximately thirty minutes and was transcribed for analysis. Thematic analysis was used to identify core themes in the interview results, and the overall case study analysis approach provided rich insights into the specific circumstances, experiences, and implications of these programs in Canadian workplaces.

Quantitative Research

We also collected secondary data from a variety of sources to assess general demographics and labor market trends in Canada. These sources included reports and publications from the Organisation for Economic Co-operation and Development, Canadian government databases, and peer-reviewed research papers. Data on a range of indicators were collected, such as diversity, unemployment, and employment rates; labor force participation; and education levels. Quantitative analysis was conducted to identify patterns in the data and to confirm consistency between the qualitative and quantitative findings.

Ethical Considerations

All participants in this study were informed about the research's purpose, and their informed consent was obtained.

The combination of research methods allowed for comprehensive understanding of the impact that intergenerational programs could have in the Canadian workplace and their ability to promote interactions and build connections between generations for better business outcomes.

Case Studies

The case studies included in this chapter are not intended to be exhaustive. Rather, they are representative of the types of initiatives that can be found in organizations across the country. There is often an element of new or novel approaches, either in the mission or mandate of the program or in how participants are recruited or included. After Challenge Factory reviewed top employer lists and considered various types of employer and employment initiatives, we selected three case studies representing public sector, nonprofit, and private sector approaches.

The case studies illustrate where ageism and generational bias had the best opportunity to be addressed within program parameters, even if they were not explicit goals of the initiative. Over the course of multiple discussions with program leaders, human resources professionals, and executives, it became clear that while these programs are intergenerational, they were not intentionally designed to be so. This accidental approach to blending generational experience and wisdom means that until our interviews, many organizations had not considered how to track or amplify the intergenerational benefits and impact of their programs.

As we present the three case studies, we discuss the design of the program and how it maps to the Broken Talent Escalator. Finally, we pose questions that delve deeper into how the program might contribute to stronger intergenerational fairness and structural change.

Canada Free Agents

Canada Free Agents operates across several departments and agencies of the government of Canada. It has a dedicated team supported through human resources. It is a lateral mobility program that allows employees of the federal public service to smoothly transition into short-term positions within the government, with the potential to lead to longer-term placements. The positions are outside regular headcount and performance management structures (treated as a separate entity). The program was launched in 2016 by Natural Resources Canada before expanding to additional departments. As of the summer of 2023, it has 101 active free agents and 39 alumni.

Program participants select a work assignment from one of fifty departments and agencies to develop new skills and gain experience. The program does not explicitly target a specific age cohort, but many of the participants are in the last five years of their career. It is a good example of how experiential career development programs for older employees can shift them into new modes and roles of working while also providing ways for their wisdom and experience to reach new networks and areas of complex organizations.

MAJOR RESULTS/LEARNINGS

The program was established in reaction to employees feeling "stuck" in their positions, an indicator of the Broken Talent Escalator treadmill effect. Having spent decades in the same type of role or department, mid- and late-career civil servants were interested in finding ways to remain employed by the public service while developing new skills, establishing new networks, and exploring different career options. The goal of the Free Agents program is to unlock job opportunities for employees and support them in navigating the career obstacles they face. Free Agents provides a creative and nonlinear approach to how public servants can develop and manage their career. The program offers participants mentorship and provides job opportunities where they tackle opportunities to improve government operations in a variety of different departments. It assumes that later-life career transitions are possible and provides a way for long-time employees to experiment. As a result, it reengages staff who otherwise might become disaffected and addresses key issues of top talent attrition.

There is a "natural mentorship" element to this program because the normal boundaries of office politics are absent. Free agents are outside the usual headcount and performance management systems, which means that they are not in direct competition for roles and recognition, as regular staff might be. Additionally, program alumni remain engaged with current participants, extending the benefits of continued skills development, network building, and community inclusion year over year.

Participants have completed more than seven hundred assignments, and the program now has a very strong and active community. Members note that they find relationships within the free agent community to be easier than other workplace relationships and that there are fewer political barriers and issues with interpersonal office dynamics. This program is not only helping free agents in the program. It models for all employees who interact with free agents that career options can be reconsidered, including the need to learn new skills at any stage in a person's career within the Canadian federal public service. In sum, the Free Agents program offers a model of incorporating natural career exploration as standard practice throughout a career, encouraging skill diversification and lifelong learning and development. This approach encourages individuals to step into new career paths at various career stages. By training managers to be open and supportive during career conversations that lean toward nontraditional pathways, any organization adopting this model can expect to see enhanced skill development and increased employee engagement and satisfaction.

QUESTIONS FOR THE FUTURE

Looking ahead, this program is now aiming to move from 'startup' status to a more mature organization. Program facilitators are establishing more measures to track who they serve and how to support them. Challenge Factory encourages them to consider the following: How might this type of natural career exploration later in life become a standard part of career paths, rather than a special program with a set intake number each year? What if managers were better trained to have career conversations that included non-traditional opportunities for career exploration and growth? How might the benefit of such approaches to life-long career development be realized and reported?

Community Animator Program (CAP)

Sponsored by the Centre for Social Innovation (CSI), Toronto, Ontario, the Community Animator Program provides experience and training in community building within the context of social innovation and social purpose. CSI is an organization that provides a platform for organizations from all sectors that have a social purpose. The platform includes physical workspaces (as one of Canada's oldest coworking organizations), community building, learning, and innovation.[8]

The CAP program was created in 2009 to support CSI's members at their physical coworking spaces. These spaces offer more than just workspace and business equipment. Members know each other, and the community is active at each location, designed to ensure that creative collisions and collaborations between members occur. Community animators are a critical part of CSI's success. Early in the program, this role was recognized as an exceptional opportunity to expose young entrepreneurs, newcomers, and older workers in transition to a wide variety of organizations, gain community-building skills, and establish a work routine or stability in times of career uncertainty.

The program provides training and peer support as participants join the CSI organization. While they may only stay within CSI for the three-month duration of the program, they benefit from having an exceptional onboarding experience. The focus is on ensuring smooth and rapid transition into a new role, without assuming new staff are young. Participants are not expected to join CSI as permanent staff members. Rather, they act as community hosts for three months while working to determine their next steps into entrepreneurship or employment. They are part of experiential learning initiatives related to networking, culture building, and animation in busy spaces that service hundreds of social purpose organizations daily.

There is no age requirement for participants, who range from students to retirees. Most applicants come to the program during a career change or another life transition. The program provides a new peer group for participants, with a new cohort starting every three months. It is common to see a new entrepreneur in their early sixties working beside a recently graduated student or newcomer to Canada in their early thirties. These intergenerational cohorts provide natural support, mentoring, and networking with each other.

MAJOR RESULTS/LEARNINGS

Many CAP program participants go on to find employment after gaining relevant experience. This is one of the program's main measures of success. Additionally, participants are key to creating an inclusive CSI culture and identity. They provide community animation that identifies the needs of members to take full advantage not only of the physical space available but also all possible relationships and connections. CAPs deliver practical and logistical support to members, are often the first and main face visitors see, lead rituals and organization events that are core to CSI's culture, and work with the permanent staff to deliver exceptional experiences to anyone in the building.

While intergenerational engagement and relationships are common within the program, they had not been documented or prioritized prior to our interview. CSI values and actively works to build the diversity of its staff and community members. It shares intergenerational stories but has not showcased the CAP program as an "intergenerational opportunity."

CSI's approach to measuring outcomes focuses mainly on using "soft touch" supports. Relationships are supported intentionally: identity differences and communication styles are discussed and considered as part of the ongoing evolution of the overall structure of the program. Open dialogue is a priority, with everyone's needs shared, as well as recognizing individuality as a strength. Space is valued as an opportunity for people to be cared for, which is viewed as facilitating stronger team cohesion.

The CAP program offers the structure and support to gain experience and build new community networks, especially during times of career change or life transition. While not intentionally intergenerational, many aspects of this program encourage mentorship and collaboration between participants of different generations. The program models the type of community CSI wants to foster and demonstrates to its community members positive, intersectional collaboration. The program has the potential to help participants develop a deeper understanding of inclusivity while expanding the organization's culture of acceptance and respect.

Community animator programs serve an important function in public spaces, engaging with members and fostering inclusive and productive relationships. The CAPS participants achieve these aims by encouraging discussions on key social, economic, and environmental topics through an intergenerational lens. Bringing members of different age groups and backgrounds together to work on common issues accelerates knowledge exchange and the development of trust-based relationships that can bridge generational gaps.

QUESTIONS FOR THE FUTURE
Challenge Factory encourages CSI to consider the following: What if ageism and longevity awareness was an explicit part of the training curriculum provided to new cohorts of the CAP program? How might CAP participants intentionally foster intergenerational collaboration across CSI's member organizations on key social, economic, and environmental topics?

Vancity Employee Resource Programs
Sponsored by Vancity Credit Union, British Columbia, each of the Vancity Employee Resource Programs has a specific budget and an executive sponsor who advocates for

their program participants within the company. Vancity is Canada's largest community credit union, a financial cooperative that operates within the territories of the Coast Salish and Kwakwaka'wakw people. The company is a member-owned, community-based, full-service financial institution with branches.[9]

Vancity's six Employee Resource Programs provide opportunities for staff to make connections and foster a sense of belonging within cohorts who share similar elements of identity. Each program is named for the intergenerational community of employees who participate:

- 2SLGBTQIA+ Group
- Indigenous Group
- Mental Health Group
- Persons with Disabilities Group
- Racial Equity Group
- Women's Equity Group

The important conversations that occurred in the aftermath of George Floyd's death served as the catalyst for the programs. Two key purposes in establishing the programs in 2020 were to offer a safe space within the company and improve awareness of issues that are important to staff. Each year, the six groups receive budget and executive sponsorship support to tackle important issues and increase their involvement in local community-based events. Two examples illustrate how the programs have fostered stronger culture and better employee-focused practices within Vancity related to racial equity and Indigenous employee support:

> The Racial Equity Group contributed to a formal racial equity employee audit by conducting interviews and validating the data.
>
> The Indigenous Group advocated for, supported, and received funding to create a reconciliation budget. The group uses these funds for efforts toward healing processes, naming ceremonies, and other initiatives that support meaningful reconciliation between settler and Indigenous employees.

Vancity recognizes the role these programs play in developing and retaining staff, and they look to the quality of the employee experience as a key measure of success. Specific trainings are offered, led by the expressed interests and needs of the groups. Participation provides support and opportunity outside formal company structures and hierarchy.

Like many initiatives, Vancity does not track the age of program participants but reports that all groups are age diverse, forming natural intergenerational networks and relationships based on trust. Intersectional understanding of how ageism exacerbates prejudice and compounds the negative experiences of marginalized groups is an interesting area for future exploration.

MAJOR RESULTS/LEARNINGS

According to anecdotal observations, age-diverse discussions do take place within each group, despite their not focusing on age. Vancity has developed key performance indicators for each group and sets goals with the chair of each group annually. There is great value in taking this intentional approach to goal development and monitoring of metrics not only in how it informs future program development, but also in the commitment it communicates to the broader employee community that each group's initiatives matter.

Group chairs and cochairs are compensated for their time; term length is two years. Groups also ask for recommitment every year from their executive sponsors, ensuring intentional participation and engagement, rather than passive support. These features contribute to the sustainability of the groups rather than requiring them to be operated "off the side of someone's desk" or in addition to expected work duties.

Vancity's approach to fostering inclusivity through its Employee Resource Programs is one way it fosters psychological workplace safety for employees. The importance placed on mutual goal development and measurement of metrics differentiates these programs from traditional social clubs.

QUESTIONS FOR THE FUTURE

How might Vancity build upon what it has started with a focus on broader community impact and sound evaluation frameworks? If Vancity wants to transfer this type of program into other workplaces within its community, Challenge Factory suggests adapting the metrics outlined in the federal Quality of Life Framework to offer unique opportunities for marginalized groups to speak about their experiences, both pains and gains, with an intergenerational lens. This measured and evidence-based approach would allow for a more comprehensive understanding of the diverse employee experience and provide robust data to create more informed, sustainable programming. In addition, how might Vancity make the intersectionality of age and identity-based marginalization more explicit and overt so that the safe spaces created within the employee groups become places for intentional intergenerational innovation?

Conclusions and a Way Forward

Canada is at a threshold moment in recognizing the value of understanding intergenerational dynamics and impacts in policy development. Often, maturity and access to data mirror the level of understanding and importance placed upon what is being measured. Applying this logic, the creation of the federal Quality of Life Framework is significant. It indicates a shift from anecdotal interest in age-based implications of existing policy toward a measured and evidence-based approach to considering intergenerational fairness in new policy development.

The case studies examined within this study indicate that Canadian workplaces are not yet at this level of age-aware maturity. Many of the innovative initiatives explored have age-diverse cohorts at the core of their success, yet the focus on implications of age, ageism, and intergenerational opportunity remains weak. As a result, data on age and intergenerational pains and gains are not formally tracked.

A key finding from this study results from examining what data are tracked and used. In all cases, robust reporting systems exist to ensure that the program participant experience meets both expectations and organizational design goals. In some organizations, these metrics lead to the assignment of financial resources, allocation of executive sponsorship, and compensation to participants to ensure program sustainability and commitment.

While the federal Quality of Life Framework signifies a positive shift toward evidence-based policy development and intergenerational fairness, Canadian workplaces are slow to recognize the significance of age-related opportunities, with limited formal tracking of age and intergenerational dynamics.

At the time of writing, it is important to note two nascent initiatives that aim to bring generations together and shape a better future of work for everyone: Challenge Factory's InterGen Lab[10] and Generation Squeeze's campaign for a federal "task force" on generational fairness.[11]

Generation Squeeze advocates for policies and initiatives that will create a more equitable and sustainable society for all generations. They focus on issues of housing, education, and the general well-being of Canadians and call for a federal task force on generational fairness. This task force will serve as a "checkpoint" for government decision-making, acting as an intergenerational lens to ensure that new policies are designed to benefit all generations. Generation Squeeze has already worked with the Canadian government on the application of intergenerational analysis in a Canadian federal budget, and they are committed to continually advocating for generational fairness in policy to create a more equitable future.[12]

Challenge Factory's InterGen Lab launched in September 2023 with an invitation to organizations with large and complex workforces to consider a new approach to planning for the future. Using a scientific approach, the InterGen Lab encourages organizations to bring forward social, economic, and political issues that impede (or threaten to impede) business success. For example, the current housing shortage that most of Canada's major cities are experiencing presents specific challenges for organizations that wish to have workforces living in close proximity to offices. While housing is not typically an employer's problem to solve, the current situation is causing workforce shortages and impeding the path to productivity and growth. Within the InterGen Lab, this challenge is championed by a lead company that is setting out specific hypotheses for how an intergenerational lens might lead to different thinking and resource allocation. During the six-month experimentation period, intergenerational approaches will explore how the company might offer different employee benefits and use its power to advocate for political change in its local region.

This initiative is one example of one company's project within the InterGen Lab. At any point in time, up to nine organizations are pursuing their own project and sharing the learnings and results across all participating organizations. Since intergenerational approaches and tools are at the core of how the experiments unfold, this growing community of business, academic, and nonprofit leaders demonstrates the impact and importance of intergenerational literacy.

There is no shortage of examples of initiatives in Canadian workplaces that provide the opportunity for employees from different age cohorts to collaborate. Workplaces are intergenerational communities by nature. The fact that few specifically age-aware initiatives exist within Canada's workspaces indicates that the economic, social, and personal costs and implications of ageism are still not well understood. On a more optimistic note, this study impacted each of the organizations that participated in interviews by raising awareness of how age might impact their showcase workplace programs, while also opening up new opportunities to explore, measure, and report on intergenerational successes.

Canada's diverse population establishes a strong rationale for including age diversity. Policy and research-based institutions are advancing concepts, metrics, and reporting on intergenerational impacts. Now is the time for every organization to take up more intentional intergenerational approaches to managing the Talent Escalator.

Notes

1. "Infosheet: Quality of Life Framework for Canada," Statistics Canada, February 28, 2023, https://www160.statcan.gc.ca/infosheet-infofiche-eng.htm.
2. "Younger Canadians Experience Lower Perceived Well-Being: Insights from the Canadian Social Survey," Statistics Canada, February 14, 2023, https://www150.statcan.gc.ca/n1/daily-quotidien/230214/dq230214b-eng.htm.
3. Linda Clarkson et al., "Our Responsibility to The Seventh Generation: Indigenous Peoples and Sustainable Development," 1992, 24, https://www.iisd.org/system/files/publications/seventh_gen.pdf.
4. "2021 Census of Population," Statistics Canada, March 29, 2023, https://www12.statcan.gc.ca/census-recensement/2021/dp-pd/prof/index.cfm?Lang=E.
5. "Harnessing the Power of a Multigenerational Workforce: Thought Leaders Solutions Forum," SHRM Foundation, 2017, https://www.shrm.org/content/dam/en/shrm/foundation/2017%20TL%20Executive%20Summary-FINAL.pdf.
6. Martine Lagacé, "An Examination of the Social and Economic Impacts of Ageism," July 29, 2022, https://www.canada.ca/en/employment-social-development/corporate/seniors/forum/reports/ageism-social-economic-impacts.html#h2.14.
7. Lisa Taylor and Fern Lebo, *The Talent Revolution: Longevity and the Future of Work* (Toronto: University of Toronto Press, 2019).
8. "Home: Centre for Social Innovation," Centre for Social Innovation, 2022, https://socialinnovation.org.
9. "Personal Banking: Vancity," Vancity, 2023, https://www.vancity.com.
10. "InterGen Lab," Challenge Factory, 2023, https://challengefactory.ca/services/intergen-lab.
11. "Homepage: Generation Squeeze," Generation Squeeze, accessed January 20, 2025, https://www.gensqueeze.ca.
12. Andrea Long, "Five Reasons Canada Needs a Generational Fairness Task Force," October 18, 2023, https://www.gensqueeze.ca/five_reasons_for_generational_fairness_task_force.

Bibliography

AARP International. "Issue Brief: Global Insights on the Multigenerational Workforce." AARP, 2020. https://www.aarpinternational.org/File%20Library/Future%20of%20Work/2020-Global-Insights-Multigenerational-Workforce-IssueBrief.doi.10.26419-2Fres.00399.001.pdf.

Centre for Social Innovation. "Home: Centre for Social Innovation." 2023. https://socialinnovation.org.

Challenge Factory. "InterGen Lab." 2023. https://challengefactory.ca/services/intergen-lab.

Clarkson, Linda, Vern Morrissette, and Gabriel Régallet. "Our Responsibility to the Seventh Generation: Indigenous Peoples and Sustainable Development." 1992, 24. https://www.iisd.org/system/files/publications/seventh_gen.pdf.

Dixon-Fyle, Sundiatu, Kevin Dolan, Dame Vivian Hunt, and Sara Prince. "Diversity Wins: How Inclusion Matters." McKinsey. May 19, 2020. https://www.mckinsey.com/featured-insights/diversity-and-inclusion/diversity-wins-how-inclusion-matters.

Employment and Social Development Canada. "Age-Friendly Workplaces: Promoting Older Worker Participation." Government of Canada. October 2016. https://www.canada.ca/en/employment-social-development/corporate/seniors/forum/older-worker-participation.html#tc7.

Generation Squeeze. "Homepage: Generation Squeeze." Accessed January 20, 2025. https://www.gensqueeze.ca.

Hill, Tegan, Milagros Palacios, and Alex Whalen. "An Aging Population: The Demographic Drag on Canada's Labour Market." Fraser Institute. August 2022. https://www.fraserinstitute.org/sites/default/files/an-aging-population-the-demographic-drag-on-canadas-labour-market.pdf.

Immigration, Refugees, and Citizenship Canada. "An Immigration Plan to Grow the Economy." Government of Canada. November 1, 2022. https://www.canada.ca/en/immigration-refugees-citizenship/news/2022/11/an-immigration-plan-to-grow-the-economy.html.

International Federation on Ageing. "Revera Report on Ageism." International Federation on Ageing. March 2013. https://ifa.ngo/wp-content/uploads/2013/03/Revera-IFA-Ageism-Report.pdf.

Kostoulas, John. "Technologies Are Critical for Inclusion in the Workplace." Gartner. August 30, 2018). https://blogs.gartner.com/john-kostoulas/2018/08/30/technologies-critical-for-inclusion/.

Lagacé, Martine. "An Examination of the Social and Economic Impacts of Ageism." Government of Canada. July 29, 2022. https://www.canada.ca/en/employment-social-development/corporate/seniors/forum/reports/ageism-social-economic-impacts.html#h2.14.

Long, Andrea. "Five Reasons Canada needs a Generational Fairness Task Force." Generation Squeeze. October 18, 2023. https://www.gensqueeze.ca/five_reasons_for_generational_fairness_task_force.

Notre Dame of Maryland University. "The Evolution of Communication across Generations." Notre Dame of Maryland University. February 6, 2022. https://online.ndm.edu/news/communication/evolution-of-communication/.

OECD. "Population with Tertiary Education." OECD. 2023. https://data.oecd.org/eduatt/population-with-tertiary-education.htm#indicator-chart.

Pew Research Center. "State of the News Media 2016." Pew Research Center. June 2016. https://assets.pewresearch.org/wp-content/uploads/sites/13/2016/06/30143308/state-of-the-news-media-report-2016-final.pdf.

Randstad. "Global Report Randstad Workmonitor Q2 2018." Randstad. 2018. https://www.randstad.com.sg/s3fs-media/sg/public/2021-08/randstad-workmonitor-q2-2018-global-report.pdf.

Sabatini, Debra, and Bradley Schurman. "Bridging Generational Divides in Your Workplace." *Harvard Business Review*, January 5, 2023. https://hbr.org/2023/01/bridging-generational-divides-in-your-workplace.

SHRM Foundation. "Harnessing the Power of a Multigenerational Workforce: Thought Leaders Solutions Forum." 2017. https://www.shrm.org/content/dam/en/shrm/foundation/2017%20TL%20Executive%20Summary-FINAL.pdf.

Statistics Canada. "2021 Census of Population." Government of Canada. March 29, 2023. https://www12.statcan.gc.ca/census-recensement/2021/dp-pd/prof/index.cfm?Lang=E.

Statistics Canada. "Infosheet: Quality of Life Framework for Canada." Government of Canada. February 28, 2023. https://www160.statcan.gc.ca/infosheet-infofiche-eng.htm.

Statistics Canada. "Younger Canadians Experience Lower Perceived Well-Being: Insights from the Canadian Social Survey." Government of Canada. February 14, 2023. https://www150.statcan.gc.ca/n1/daily-quotidien/230214/dq230214b-eng.htm.

Taylor, Lisa, and Fern Lebo. *The Talent Revolution: Longevity and the Future of Work*. Toronto: University of Toronto Press–Rotman Imprint, 2019.

Vancity. "Personal Banking: Vancity." 2023. https://www.vancity.com.

CHAPTER 25
Understanding Age-Diverse Knowledge Exchange through Social Comparison

Laura Rinker, Ulrike Fasbender, *and* Fabiola H. Gerpott

Abstract

This chapter outlines social comparison dynamics and age-diverse knowledge exchange within the workplace. It provides an overview of three relevant theories (i.e., social comparison theory, social identity theory, and intergroup contact theory) that serve as theoretical frameworks for the chapter, and it identifies three key areas for future research in the context of age-diverse knowledge exchange from a social comparison lens: (1) employee use of social comparisons to identify suitable knowledge exchange partners and role distribution within knowledge exchange relationships by employees of different ages, especially in the context of evolving expertise dynamics; (2) the dilemma associated with age-diverse knowledge exchange including the potential competence-related gains and costs younger and older employees must consider when engaging in knowledge exchange; and (3) how social comparisons may improve intergroup contact quality by fostering perspective-taking and, building on this, by capitalizing on the social comparison tendencies of particular age groups.

Key Words: social comparison, age diversity, knowledge exchange, social identity, intergroup contact

Introduction

The exchange of knowledge between age groups has emerged as a vital asset for organizations striving to remain competitive in the face of developments such as retirement brain drain and the downsizing of the workforce due to lower birthrates.[1] Considering the ongoing societal aging of industrialized countries and the associated postponement of retirement,[2] workplaces are rapidly transforming into melting pots for workers of different ages. While, in theory, this development creates excellent conditions for age-diverse knowledge exchange (referring to the transfer of unique knowledge between younger and older employees[3]), employees of different ages face various challenges.

One such challenge involves managing the social dynamics between different age groups—in particular, social comparison (i.e., assessing oneself through comparison with others),[4] which may both hinder and foster age-diverse knowledge exchange. It is important to foster age-diverse knowledge exchange due to its immense potential for increasing innovation,[5] enhancing employee development,[6] and ensuring the preservation of organizational memory.[7] With each age group providing unique perspectives and expertise,[8] age-diverse knowledge exchange contributes not only to knowledge retention but also to the creation of new knowledge.

Within the knowledge exchange literature, social comparisons have recently garnered attention as a crucial lens through which to understand the social dynamics of age-diverse knowledge exchange.[9] They provide a nuanced perspective for comprehending how employees of different ages perceive their relative standing within the social organizational hierarchy and how this perception influences their engagement in knowledge exchange. In this regard, Fasbender and Gerpott suggest that anticipated current and future status differences may shape knowledge exchange between different age groups.[10] This is because older employees may rank higher than their younger counterparts at a given time but may be out-competed by their younger colleagues in the future. As a result, tensions and competition between age groups can emerge,[11] which may impede knowledge exchange.

Alternatively, a more positive scenario is also plausible, in which status or knowledge differences between age-diverse colleagues encourage them to share their respective expertise, experiences, and insights. In this case, older—and often more experienced—employees may be motivated by the desire to cement their perceived status and legacy within an organization by imparting wisdom to younger colleagues.[12] Likewise, a younger employee may aspire to climb the organizational ladder, learn from more experienced colleagues, and demonstrate up-to-date knowledge.[13] Therefore, it is fitting and valuable to provide an overview of relevant theories and the current empirical evidence to showcase how social comparison shapes age-diverse knowledge exchange and how future research can contribute to further understanding of this phenomenon.

By shedding light on the interplay between age-diverse knowledge exchange and social comparison dynamics at work, the chapter will make three contributions: (1) a comprehensive overview of pertinent theories that help explain the multifaceted relationship between social comparison and knowledge exchange in an age-diverse context (i.e., social comparison theory, social identity theory, and intergroup contact theory); (2) examples of how social comparisons may play a role in age-diverse knowledge exchange based on these theoretical frameworks and the existing tentative and adjacent empirical insights; and (3) promising areas for future research in the domain of social comparisons and age-diverse knowledge exchange. Figure 25.1 provides an overview of the existing research within three theoretical perspectives and suggested future research areas emerging from their integration.

Theoretical Frameworks and Empirical Findings: Linking Social Comparison and Knowledge Exchange in an Age-Diverse Context

To unravel the interplay of social comparisons among younger and older employees in age-diverse knowledge exchange, it is helpful to review Festinger's theory of social

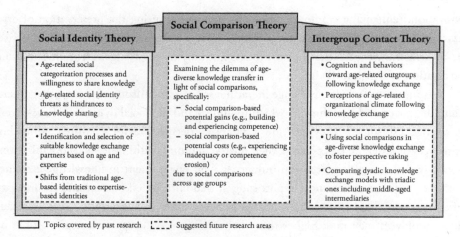

Figure 25.1 Past and future age-diverse knowledge exchange research from the (joint) perspectives of social comparison theory, social identity theory, and intergroup contact theory.

Source: Rinker, Fasbender, and Gerpott, 2023

comparisons[14] and Zell and Alicke's temporal social comparison theorizing,[15] as well as the underlying principles and empirical findings of social identity theory[16] and intergroup contact theory[17]—two perspectives that scholars have used to examine the social dynamics of age-diverse knowledge exchange.[18]

Social Comparison Theory

Festinger introduced social comparison theory in 1954, positing that individuals have an inherent tendency to evaluate themselves by comparing their attributes, skills, and achievements with those of others. Rooted in the desire for accurate self-assessment and identity formation,[19] social comparison shapes individuals' perceptions of their place in the social hierarchy and informs affective, cognitive, and behavioral responses.[20] Social comparisons can be characterized by their directionality: they can be upward (i.e., with others who are better than oneself), lateral (i.e., with others who are equal to oneself), or downward (i.e., with others who are worse than oneself). To differentiate further, scholars also discern whether one feels more similar or less similar to the other person in response to social comparison.[21]

While researchers have tended to view social comparisons as static or singular events, Zell and Alicke encourage a more dynamic view of social comparisons over time[22] by examining how relative differences in various domains (e.g., status, experience, or salary) evolve. This temporal perspective provides an opportunity to consider relative gains and losses compared to comparison targets. Fasbender and Gerpott note that this perspective is particularly applicable to age-diverse colleagues—older employees often have higher current status due to longer work history, and younger counterparts have more space to rise in the ranks owing to their relatively lower status.[23] This circumstance could have both positive and negative effects on knowledge exchange, as it has a motivating potential but may also trigger fears among age-diverse colleagues.

Social Identity Theory

Tajfel and Turner's social identity theory explains how people form and maintain social identities,[24] stating that individuals classify themselves and others into groups based on shared characteristics (e.g., age, gender, ethnicity, or religion). Then, individuals evaluate these groups in terms of social status and their own identity, which influences their self-concept and behavior. As a result, social identities are those parts of the self-concept that stem from membership in social groups. Social identity formation and social comparison processes intersect through their mutual influence on how individuals perceive themselves as well as the social groups to which they assign themselves.[25] The theory explains the formation of social identities based on group membership, while comparisons contribute to maintaining those identities and the dynamics between different social groups.[26] In this context, social comparisons are a cognitive process through which individuals ascertain distinct and shared social identities.[27]

Empirical findings support social identity theory in the context of age-diverse knowledge exchange. For instance, age plays a pivotal role in shaping social groupings among employees[28] when it affects the willingness to share knowledge with colleagues of other age groups.[29] Age, compared to other demographic characteristics, is a particularly salient characteristic for subgroup formation.[30] Specifically, drawing on social identity theory, Gerpott and colleagues argued that age diversity fosters the formation of subgroups through social categorizations and increases the risk that shared knowledge is seen as outdated or inadequate, which can threaten one's identity. In light of this, they empirically showed that perceptions of age diversity in training groups obstruct learning through decreased knowledge sharing among group members.[31] In addition, older employees are apt to share less knowledge with younger colleagues if they perceive a threat to their social identity (i.e., perceived age discrimination).[32]

Intergroup Contact Theory

The concept of intergroup contact theory stems from Allport's contact hypothesis,[33] which proposes that interactions between members of diverse groups can mitigate biases and encourage constructive relationships between these groups.[34] Group interaction can lead to greater understanding and awareness, along with diminishing feelings of apprehension. To achieve this, the interactions are ideally based on equal standing, shared objectives, and collaborative efforts. Yet, the intersection of intergroup contact and social comparisons has rarely been studied in the context of age diversity, despite initial conceptual considerations[35] and promising tentative findings[36] showing that social comparisons between age groups as part of age-diverse knowledge exchange can improve contact and understanding between groups by fostering perspective-taking and a sense of shared identity.

Empirical findings support the theoretical notions of intergroup contact theory within the context of age-diverse knowledge exchange: intergroup contact as part of knowledge exchange fosters positive age-diverse interactions, enhances the quality of connections between different age groups, and positively shapes attitudes and behaviors toward older employees.[37] For example, younger workers empathize more with older colleagues when they engage in knowledge exchange.[38] For older employees, knowledge exchange is associated with positive perceptions of an organization's intergenerational climate.[39] In sum, the quality and quantity of contact between age groups promotes positive views of older workers and reduces ageism through knowledge exchange.[40]

Social Comparison in Age-Diverse Knowledge Exchange: Areas for Future Research

Whereas research on social comparisons at work[41] and research on age-diverse knowledge sharing from the perspectives of social identity and intergroup contact theory[42] have received considerable scholarly attention in the past,[43] research advocating the integration of these theoretical perspectives is still in its infancy.[44] Therefore, the following section draws on existing theoretical considerations and empirical findings from both fields to offer ideas for future research. Specifically, it suggests three possible research areas to shed light on social comparisons in age-diverse knowledge exchange processes.

The first considers how social comparisons may be used by employees of different ages to identify and select suitable knowledge exchange partners. The second advocates for research contrasting the potential gains and costs that employees of different age groups have to weigh during knowledge exchange. The third elaborates on how social comparisons can help to build bridges between age groups in light of age-diverse knowledge exchange.

Identification and Selection of Suitable Knowledge Exchange Partners

Before employees can engage in knowledge exchange, they must identify suitable partners for the process. Age, as a distinguishing demographic factor between employees, can significantly influence how individuals perceive and choose their exchange counterparts. The interplay between age and expertise offers room for social identities and social comparison dynamics to shape the formation of knowledge-exchange partnerships.

Traditionally, age has been associated with accumulated expertise and experience, as older employees often possess deep-rooted organizational knowledge, garnered through years of immersion in company practices and industry developments.[45] This accumulation of knowledge makes older employees indispensable actors in organizational knowledge exchange, especially when considering the preservation of organizational memory as an important goal. Younger employees, by contrast, are traditionally assigned to the receiving party in the source-recipient model of knowledge transfer.[46] Nevertheless, research has found that they may contribute fresh insights and up-to-date knowledge from their education to invigorate established practices[47] along the lines of a mutual exchange model.[48] In particular, the advent of the digital age has introduced a critical shift in the traditional expert-novice relationship between older and younger employees. In combination, the attributes of both age groups foster an environment in which they can complement each other through collaboration.

Employees use social comparisons to evaluate their strengths and shortcomings in light of what colleagues belonging to other age groups bring to the table. For instance, older employees can contribute company-specific knowledge or strategies for dealing with social situations, whereas younger employees can offer systematic learning strategies or methods to obtain information.[49] Thus, while age can serve as an initial marker of accumulated experience, the shifting dynamics of expertise in the digital age may reshape traditional perceptions of who sends knowledge and who receives knowledge.[50] Such changes in role distribution may also affect older and younger employees' social identity as knowledge senders and knowledge receivers.

Therefore, researchers are encouraged to explore the role of social comparisons in the context of age- versus experience-based identities for identifying knowledge exchange partners for employees of different ages. For instance, scholars could explore interactions between age and expertise in partner selection by investigating whether older individuals place a higher value on certain types of expertise due to their experience and whether younger individuals prioritize different domains of expertise due to their digital literacy and familiarity with emerging technologies. Research could also inquire into how these priorities differ in employees when selecting knowledge recipients versus knowledge sources. Furthermore, scholars could examine whether the traditional age-based identities (i.e., "older workers," "younger workers") are giving way to more expertise-based identities (e.g., "digital natives," "digital pioneers") as a consequence of redefining one's identity through social comparisons. Lastly, research could also investigate whether such shifts in the relevance of age-based and expertise-based identities create new opportunities for collaboration and understanding between younger and older employees by shaping knowledge exchange partner identification and selection.

Knowledge Exchange as an Age-Diverse Dilemma: Potential Gains and Costs

Cabrera and Cabrera compare knowledge sharing among colleagues to a public goods dilemma,[51] a situation in which individuals must decide whether to contribute to a shared resource that benefits everyone or withhold their contribution for personal gain. Such a dilemma manifests in the workplace when individuals must decide whether to share their knowledge (and potentially risk the loss of personal recognition, power, or unique expertise) or withhold it.

The potential gains and costs feeding into this dilemma for workplace colleagues of different ages are at least partly rooted in social comparisons. Social comparisons in age-diverse knowledge exchange can either fulfill or compromise employees' fundamental human need for competence.[52] This need (i.e., psychological desire to feel effective, capable, and successful in one's activities and endeavors)[53] persists across the lifespan but may vary depending on one's life stage.[54]

Age-diverse knowledge exchange can fulfill employees' need for competence in two ways. First, it allows employees to identify and strategically seek out unique knowledge from colleagues in other age groups to enhance their own knowledge repertoire.[55] Second, it can foster employees' sense of competence by providing younger and older employees alike with a platform to share their unique knowledge. In turn, sharing knowledge may promote employees' experience as competent professionals,[56] which is important for younger employees seeking to establish themselves professionally as well as for older employees striving to consolidate their professional standing.

On the flip side, social comparisons with colleagues of other age groups can also be detrimental to employees' competence need fulfillment. Younger employees may feel inadequate when they compare their knowledge and skills to those of older, more experienced colleagues, especially if they perceive a substantial discrepancy with their older colleagues that they cannot resolve in the future. Older employees engaging in age-diverse knowledge exchange may encounter perceptions of competence erosion, a concern that their knowledge is outdated. If older employees feel sidelined, their sense of competence is jeopardized, and this may discourage knowledge exchange altogether.[57] Future research examining these potential gains and costs associated with social comparisons for younger and older employees can lay a foundation for solving the knowledge exchange dilemma in the context of age-diverse knowledge transfer.

Bridging Age-Related Divides through Social Comparisons

While social comparisons can create a barrier to age-diverse knowledge exchange if they involve costs, they also can provide an opportunity to build bridges between different age groups in line with intergroup contact theory.[58] Specifically, social comparison can facilitate intergroup contact by serving as a psychological mechanism that drives individuals from different age groups to interact, engage, and find common ground during and after knowledge exchange.

For instance, social comparison encourages individuals to consider the viewpoints and experiences of others.[59] As employees of different ages compare their strengths and weaknesses during knowledge exchange, they gain insights into each other's unique circumstances. This perspective-taking can lay the foundation for positive intergroup contact as it fosters positive interactions and cultivates social connections.[60]

Suls and Mullen argue that middle-aged individuals (i.e., between forty and sixty-five years) show an increased preference for social comparisons with dissimilar others, especially in a work context.[61] Thus, middle-aged employees could act as ideal intermediaries between younger and older age groups in the workplace. As an additional benefit of social comparisons in the context of intergroup contact, Sharp et al. reported that the tendency to engage in social comparison moderated the impact of extended contact with outgroups.[62] Specifically, they observed that White, heterosexual individuals with a greater tendency to engage in social comparison experienced more pronounced positive effects (i.e., more favorable attitudes) of extended contact with both Asian and gay groups. In sum, this reasoning suggests that social comparison and subsequent cognitive processes such as perspective-taking may enhance contact between age groups following age-diverse knowledge exchange.

Future research should investigate the potential synergies of social comparisons and knowledge exchange processes in bridging age-related divides. For instance, leveraging social comparison as a psychological mechanism, intervention studies could explore how social comparisons drive individuals from different age groups to interact, engage, and find common ground during and after knowledge exchange. To illustrate, interventions might encourage employees of varying ages to display structured knowledge exchange activities that explicitly involve social comparison processes. These activities could be designed to foster perspective-taking and empathy by encouraging participants to reflect on their strengths and weaknesses in comparison to their colleagues of different age groups.[63] Moreover, scholars could ascertain whether middle-aged employees' social comparison preferences enable them to act as facilitators of high-quality intergroup contact in age-diverse knowledge exchange. In this way, middle-aged employees could act as mediators between younger and older colleagues, bridging the two ends of the age spectrum. Specifically, this triadic model of age-diverse knowledge exchange should be compared with the prevailing dyadic approach.[64]

Conclusion

This chapter explored knowledge exchange between employees of different age groups by integrating a social comparison perspective with two theoretical frameworks commonly used in age-diverse knowledge exchange research (i.e., social identity theory and intergroup contact theory) and outlining extant empirical findings. It presented three future research areas to better connect social comparison and age-diverse knowledge exchange perspectives. First, the chapter suggested that social comparisons may influence the identification of suitable knowledge exchange partners and the distribution of roles within knowledge exchange relationships, especially in the context of evolving expertise dynamics. Second, it discussed the dilemma associated with age-diverse knowledge exchange, drawing attention to the potential competence-related gains and costs employees must weigh. Last, the chapter outlined how social comparisons may improve intergroup contact quality by encouraging perspective-taking and, building on this, by capitalizing on the social comparison tendencies of particular age groups.

As organizations become increasingly age-diverse, understanding how social comparisons influence the exchange of knowledge among employees of different ages is crucial for leveraging the unique advantages that age diversity can bring to an organization.

Continued research on the intersection of social comparisons and age-diverse knowledge exchange holds the promise of providing valuable insights and practical strategies for organizations seeking to navigate the challenges and opportunities presented by an increasingly age-diverse workforce.

Author Note

We have no known conflict of interest to disclose. This research was funded by the Deutsche Forschungsgemeinschaft (DFG, German Research Foundation: FA 1593/4-1).

Notes

1. Moria Levy, "Knowledge Retention: Minimizing Organizational Business Loss," *Journal of Knowledge Management* 15, no. 4 (2011): 582–600, https://doi.org/10.1108/13673271111151974.
2. Xenia Schmidt and Katrin Muehlfeld, "What's So Special about Intergenerational Knowledge Transfer? Identifying Challenges of Intergenerational Knowledge Transfer," *Management Revu* 28, no. 4 (2017): 375–411, https://doi.org/10.5771/0935-9915-2017-4-375.
3. Laura Dietz et al., "Age and Knowledge Exchange," in *Age and Work: Advances in Theory, Methods, and Practice*, 1st ed., ed. Hannes Zacher and Cort W. Rudolph, 259–76, SIOP Organizational Frontiers Series (New York: Routledge: 2022).
4. Leon Festinger, "A Theory of Social Comparison Processes," *Human Relations* 7, no. 2 (1954): 117–40, https://doi.org/10.1177/001872675400700202.
5. Changyu Wang et al., "Linking Online and Offline Intergenerational Knowledge Transfer to Younger Employees' Innovative Work Behaviors: Evidence from Chinese Hospitals," *Journal of Knowledge Management* 27, no. 3 (2023): 762–84, https://doi.org/10.1108/JKM-11-2021-0839.
6. Constantin Bratianu and Ramona Diana Leon, "Strategies to Enhance Intergenerational Learning and Reducing Knowledge Loss," *VINE* 45, no. 4 (2015): 551–67, https://doi.org/10.1108/VINE-01-2015-0007.
7. Jean-François Harvey, "Managing Organizational Memory with Intergenerational Knowledge Transfer," *Journal of Knowledge Management* 16, no. 3 (2012): 400–17, https://doi.org/10.1108/13673271211238733.
8. Fabiola Heike Gerpott et al., "A Phase Model of Intergenerational Learning in Organizations," *Academy of Management Learning & Education* 16, no. 2 (2017): 193–216, https://doi.org/10.5465/amle.2015.0185.
9. Ulrike Fasbender and Fabiola H. Gerpott, "Why Do or Don't Older Employees Seek Knowledge from Younger Colleagues? A Relation-Opportunity Model to Explain How Age-Inclusive Human Resources Practices Foster Older Employees' Knowledge Seeking from Younger Colleagues," *Applied Psychology* 71, no. 4 (2022): 1385–1406, https://doi.org/10.1111/apps.12362.
10. Fasbender and Gerpott, "Why Do or Don't Older Employees."
11. Michael J. Urick et al., "Understanding and Managing Intergenerational Conflict: An Examination of Influences and Strategies," *Work, Aging and Retirement* 3, no. 2 (2016): waw009, https://doi.org/10.1093/workar/waw009.
12. Jisung Park et al., "The Need for Status as a Hidden Motive of Knowledge-Sharing Behavior: An Application of Costly Signaling Theory," *Human Performance* 30, no. 1 (2017): 21–37, https://doi.org/10.1080/08959285.2016.1263636.
13. Ulrike Fasbender et al., "Give and Take? Knowledge Exchange between Older and Younger Employees as a Function of Generativity and Development Striving," *Journal of Knowledge Management* 25, no. 10 (2021): 2420–43, https://doi.org/10.1108/JKM-11-2020-0856.
14. Festinger, "A Theory of Social Comparison."
15. Ethan Zell and Mark D. Alicke, "Comparisons over Time: Temporal Trajectories, Social Comparison, and Self-Evaluation," *European Journal of Social Psychology* 40, no. 3 (2010): 375–82, https://doi.org/10.1002/ejsp.737.
16. H. Tajfel and J. C. Turner, "The Social Identity Theory of Intergroup Behaviour," in *Psychology of Intergroup Relations*, ed. S. Worchsel and W. G. Austin, 7–24 (Chicago: Nelson-Hall, 1986).

17. Gordon W. Allport, *The Nature of Prejudice* (Cambridge, MA: Addison-Wesley, 1954).
18. Anne Burmeister et al., "Understanding the Motivational Benefits of Knowledge Transfer for Older and Younger Workers in Age-Diverse Coworker Dyads: An Actor-Partner Interdependence Model," *Journal of Applied Psychology* 105, no. 7 (2020): 748–59, https://doi.org/10.1037/apl0000466; Sarah De Blois and Martine Lagacé, "Understanding Older Canadian Workers' Perspectives on Aging in the Context of Communication and Knowledge Transfer," *Canadian Journal of Communication* 42, no. 4 (2017): 631–44, https://doi.org/10.22230/cjc.2017v42n4a3071; Ulrike Fasbender and Fabiola Heike Gerpott, "To Share or Not to Share: A Social-Cognitive Internalization Model to Explain How Age Discrimination Impairs Older Employees' Knowledge Sharing with Younger Colleagues," *European Journal of Work and Organizational Psychology* 30, no. 1 (2021): 125–42, https://doi.org/10.1080/1359432X.2020.1839421; Kendra Geeraerts et al., "Teachers' Perceptions of Intergenerational Knowledge Flows," *Teaching and Teacher Education* 56 (2016): 150–61, https://doi.org/10.1016/j.tate.2016.01.024.
19. Festinger, "A Theory of Social Comparison."
20. Jerald Greenberg et al., "Social Comparison Processes in Organizations," *Organizational Behavior and Human Decision Processes* 102, no. 1 (2007): 22–41, https://doi.org/10.1016/j.obhdp.2006.09.006.
21. Bram Pieter Buunk and Jan Fekke Ybema, "Social Comparison and Occupational Stress: The Identification-Contrast Model," in *Health, Coping, and Well-Being: Perspectives from Social Comparison Theory*, ed. Bram P. Buunk and Frederick X. Gibbons, 359–88 (Hillsdale, NJ: Erlbaum, 1997); Thomas Mussweiler, "'Seek and Ye Shall Find': Antecedents of Assimilation and Contrast in Social Comparison," *European Journal of Social Psychology* 31, no. 5 (2001): 499–509, https://doi.org/10.1002/ejsp.75.
22. Zell and Alicke, "Comparisons over Time," 375.
23. Fasbender and Gerpott, "Why Do or Don't Older Employees."
24. Tajfel and Turner, "The Social Identity Theory."
25. Michael A. Hogg, "Social Identity and Social Comparison," in *Handbook of Social Comparison*, ed. Jerry Suls and Ladd Wheeler, 401–21 (Boston: Springer U.S., 2000).
26. John C. Turner, "Social Comparison and Social Identity: Some Prospects for Intergroup Behaviour," *European Journal of Social Psychology* 5, no. 1 (1975): 1–34, https://doi.org/10.1002/ejsp.2420050102.
27. Blake E. Ashforth and Fred Mael. "Social Identity Theory and the Organization," *Academy of Management Review* 14, no. 1 (1989): 20, https://doi.org/10.2307/258189; Tajfel and Turner, "The Social Identity Theory."
28. Kendra Geeraerts et al., "Teachers' Perceptions."
29. Michael J. Urick et al., "Understanding and Managing Intergenerational Conflict: An Examination of Influences and Strategies," *Work, Aging and Retirement* 3, no. 2 (2016): waw009, https://doi.org/10.1093/workar/waw009.
30. Fabiola H. Gerpott et al., "Age Diversity and Learning Outcomes in Organizational Training Groups: The Role of Knowledge Sharing and Psychological Safety," *International Journal of Human Resource Management* 32, no. 18 (2021): 3777–804, https://doi.org/10.1080/09585192.2019.1640763.
31. Gerpott et al., "Age Diversity and Learning Outcomes."
32. Ulrike Fasbender and Fabiola Heike Gerpott, "To Share or Not to Share: A Social-Cognitive Internalization Model to Explain How Age Discrimination Impairs Older Employees' Knowledge Sharing with Younger Colleagues," *European Journal of Work and Organizational Psychology* 30, no. 1 (2021): 125–42, https://doi.org/10.1080/1359432X.2020.1839421.
33. Allport, *The Nature of Prejudice*.
34. Ulrike Fasbender and Mo Wang, "Intergenerational Contact and Hiring Decisions about Older Workers," *Journal of Managerial Psychology* 32, no. 3 (2017): 210–24, https://doi.org/10.1108/JMP-11-2016-0339.
35. Diana Onu, Thomas Kessler, and Joanne R. Smith, "Admiration: A Conceptual Review," *Emotion Review* 8, no. 3 (2016): 218–30, https://doi.org/10.1177/1754073915610438.
36. Melanie Sharp et al., "Individual Difference Variables as Moderators of the Effect of Extended Cross-Group Friendship on Prejudice," *Group Processes & Intergroup Relations* 14, no. 2 (2011): 207–21, https://doi.org/10.1177/1368430210391122.
37. Fasbender and Gerpott, "Why Do or Don't Older Employees"; Martine Lagacé et al., "Building on Intergenerational Climate to Counter Ageism in the Workplace? A Cross-Organizational Study," *Journal of Intergenerational Relationships* 17, no. 2 (2019): 201–19, https://doi.org/10.1080/15350770.2018.1535346..

38. Najat Firzly et al., "Let's Work Together: Assessing the Impact of Intergenerational Dynamics on Young Workers' Ageism Awareness and Job Satisfaction," *Canadian Journal on Aging/ La revue canadienne du vieillissement* 40, no. 3 (2021): 489–99, https://doi.org/10.1017/S0714980820000173.
39. Lagacé et al., "Building on Intergenerational Climate."
40. Martine Lagacé et al. "Fostering Positive Views about Older Workers and Reducing Age Discrimination: A Retest of the Workplace Intergenerational Contact and Knowledge Sharing Model," *Journal of Applied Gerontology* 42, no. 6 (2023): 1223–33, https://doi.org/10.1177/07334648231163840.
41. Jerald Greenberg et al., "Social Comparison Processes in Organizations," *Organizational Behavior and Human Decision Processes* 102, no. 1 (2007): 22–41, https://doi.org/10.1016/j.obhdp.2006.09.006.
42. Schmidt and Muehlfeld, "What's So Special."
43. Gerpott et al., "Age Diversity and Learning Outcomes"; Lagacé et al., "Building on Intergenerational Climate"; Lagacé et al. "Fostering Positive Views"; Urick et al., "Understanding and Managing Intergenerational Conflict."
44. Fasbender and Gerpott, "Why Do or Don't Older Employees."
45. Gerpott et al., "A Phase Model of Intergenerational Learning."
46. Harvey, "Managing Organizational Memory."
47. Gerpott et al., "A Phase Model of Intergenerational Learning."
48. Harvey, "Managing Organizational Memory"; Ulrike Fasbender et al., "Give and Take?"
49. Gerpott et al., "A Phase Model of Intergenerational Learning."
50. Anne Burmeister et al., "Being Perceived as a Knowledge Sender or Knowledge Receiver: A Multi-study Investigation of the Effect of Age on Knowledge Transfer," *Journal of Occupational and Organizational Psychology* 91, no. 3 (2018): 518–45, https://doi.org/10.1111/joop.12208.
51. Angel Cabrera and Elizabeth F. Cabrera, "Knowledge-Sharing Dilemmas," *Organization Studies* 23, no. 5 (2002): 687–710, https://doi.org/10.1177/0170840602235001.
52. cf. Fasbender and Gerpott, "Why Do or Don't Older Employees."
53. Richard M. Ryan and Edward L. Deci. *Self-Determination Theory: Basic Psychological Needs in Motivation, Development, and Wellness* (New York: Guilford Press, 2017). https://doi.org/10.1521/978.14625/28806.
54. Richard M. Ryan and Jennifer G. La Guardia, "What Is Being Optimized? Self-Determination Theory and Basic Psychological Needs," in *Psychology and the Aging Revolution: How We Adapt to Longer Life*, ed. Sara H. Qualls and Norman Abeles, 145–72 (Washington: American Psychological Association, 2000).
55. Stephen P. Borgatti and Rob Cross, "A Relational View of Information Seeking and Learning in Social Networks," *Management Science* 49, no. 4 (2003): 432–45; Peter H. Gray and Darren B. Meister, "Knowledge Sourcing Effectiveness," *Management Science* 50, no. 6 (2004): 821–34, https://doi.org/10.1287/mnsc.1030.0192.
56. Svetlana Šajeva, "Encouraging Knowledge Sharing among Employees: How Reward Matters," *Procedia - Social and Behavioral Sciences* 156 (2014): 130–34, https://doi.org/10.1016/j.sbspro.2014.11.134.
57. Soohyun Lee, "The Bright and Dark Sides of Upward Social Comparison: Knowledge Sharing and Knowledge Hiding Directed at High Performers" (Dissertation, Graduate Faculty in Psychology, City University of New York), 2022, https://academicworks.cuny.edu/gc_etds/4928/.
58. Allport, *The Nature of Prejudice*.
59. Alain Morin, "A Neurocognitive and Socioecological Model of Self-Awareness," *Genetic, Social, and General Psychology Monographs* 130, no. 3 (2004): 197–222, https://doi.org/10.3200/MONO.130.3.197-224.
60. Cynthia S. Wang et al., "Perspective-Taking Increases Willingness to Engage in Intergroup Contact," *PLoS One* 9, no. 1 (2014): e85681, https://doi.org/10.1371/journal.pone.0085681.
61. Jerry Suls, "From the Cradle to the Grave: Comparison and Self-Evaluation across the Life-Span," in *Psychological Perspectives on the Self*, ed. Jerry M. Suls, 97–125 (Hillsdale, NJ: Lawrence Erlbaum, 1982).
62. Sharp et al., "Individual Difference Variables."
63. cf. Anne Burmeister et al., "Reaching the Heart or the Mind? Test of Two Theory-Based Training Programs to Improve Interactions between Age-Diverse Coworkers," *Academy of Management Learning & Education* 20, no. 2 (2021): 203–32, https://doi.org/10.5465/amle.2019.0348.
64. Harvey, "Managing Organizational Memory."

Bibliography

Allport, Gordon W. *The Nature of Prejudice*. Cambridge, MA: Addison-Wesley, 1954.

Ashforth, Blake E., and Fred Mael. "Social Identity Theory and the Organization." *Academy of Management Review* 14, no. 1 (1989): 20. https://doi.org/10.2307/258189.

Borgatti, Stephen P., and Rob Cross. "A Relational View of Information Seeking and Learning in Social Networks." *Management Science* 49, no. 4 (2003): 432–45.

Bratianu, Constantin, and Ramona Diana Leon. "Strategies to Enhance Intergenerational Learning and Reducing Knowledge Loss." *VINE* 45, no. 4 (2015): 551–67. https://doi.org/10.1108/VINE-01-2015-0007.

Burmeister, Anne, Ulrike Fasbender, and Jürgen Deller. "Being Perceived as a Knowledge Sender or Knowledge Receiver: A Multi-study Investigation of the Effect of Age on Knowledge Transfer." *Journal of Occupational and Organizational Psychology* 91, no. 3 (2018): 518–45. https://doi.org/10.1111/joop.12208.

Burmeister, Anne, Fabiola H. Gerpott, Andreas Hirschi, Susanne Scheibe, Karen Pak, and Dorien Kooij. "Reaching the Heart or the Mind? Test of Two Theory-Based Training Programs to Improve Interactions between Age-Diverse Coworkers." *Academy of Management Learning & Education* 20, no. 2 (2021): 203–32. https://doi.org/10.5465/amle.2019.0348.

Burmeister, Anne, Mo Wang, and Andreas Hirschi. "Understanding the Motivational Benefits of Knowledge Transfer for Older and Younger Workers in Age-Diverse Coworker Dyads: An Actor-Partner Interdependence Model." *Journal of Applied Psychology* 105, no. 7 (2020): 748–59. https://doi.org/10.1037/apl0000466.

Buunk, Bram Pieter, and Jan Fekke Ybema. "Social Comparison and Occupational Stress: The Identification-Contrast Model." In *Health, Coping, and Well-Being: Perspectives from Social Comparison Theory*. Edited by Bram P. Buunk and Frederick X. Gibbons, 359–88. Hillsdale, NJ: Erlbaum, 1997.

Cabrera, Angel, and Elizabeth F. Cabrera. "Knowledge-Sharing Dilemmas." *Organization Studies* 23, no. 5 (2002): 687–710. https://doi.org/10.1177/0170840602235001.

De Blois, Sarah, and Martine Lagacé. "Understanding Older Canadian Workers' Perspectives on Aging in the Context of Communication and Knowledge Transfer." *Canadian Journal of Communication* 42, no. 4 (2017): 631–44. https://doi.org/10.22230/cjc.2017v42n4a3071.

Dietz, Laura, Anne Burmeister, and Ulrike Fasbender. "Age and Knowledge Exchange." In *Age and Work: Advances in Theory, Methods, and Practice*. Edited by Hannes Zacher and Cort W. Rudolph. 1st ed., 259–76. SIOP Organizational Frontiers Series. New York: Routledge, 2022.

Fasbender, Ulrike, and Fabiola Heike Gerpott. "To Share or Not to Share: A Social-Cognitive Internalization Model to Explain How Age Discrimination Impairs Older Employees' Knowledge Sharing with Younger Colleagues." *European Journal of Work and Organizational Psychology* 30, no. 1 (2021): 125–42. https://doi.org/10.1080/1359432X.2020.1839421.

Fasbender, Ulrike, and Fabiola H. Gerpott. "Knowledge Transfer between Younger and Older Employees: A Temporal Social Comparison Model." *Work, Aging and Retirement* 8, no. 2 (2022): 146–62. https://doi.org/10.1093/workar/waab017.

Fasbender, Ulrike, and Fabiola H. Gerpott. "Why Do or Don't Older Employees Seek Knowledge from Younger Colleagues? A Relation-Opportunity Model to Explain How Age-Inclusive Human Resources Practices Foster Older Employees' Knowledge Seeking from Younger Colleagues." *Applied Psychology* 71, no. 4 (2022): 1385–1406. https://doi.org/10.1111/apps.12362.

Fasbender, Ulrike, Fabiola H. Gerpott, and Dana Unger. "Give and Take? Knowledge Exchange between Older and Younger Employees as a Function of Generativity and Development Striving." *Journal of Knowledge Management* 25, no. 10 (2021): 2420–43. https://doi.org/10.1108/JKM-11-2020-0856.

Fasbender, Ulrike, and Mo Wang. "Intergenerational Contact and Hiring Decisions about Older Workers." *Journal of Managerial Psychology* 32, no. 3 (2017): 210–24. https://doi.org/10.1108/JMP-11-2016-0339.

Festinger, Leon. "A Theory of Social Comparison Processes." *Human Relations* 7, no. 2 (1954): 117–40. https://doi.org/10.1177/001872675400700202.

Firzly, Najat, Lise van de Beeck, and Martine Lagacé. "Let's Work Together: Assessing the Impact of Intergenerational Dynamics on Young Workers' Ageism Awareness and Job Satisfaction." *Canadian Journal on Aging/ La revue canadienne du vieillissement* 40, no. 3 (2021): 489–99. https://doi.org/10.1017/S0714980820000173.

Geeraerts, Kendra, Jan Vanhoof, and Piet van den Bossche. "Teachers' Perceptions of Intergenerational Knowledge Flows." *Teaching and Teacher Education* 56 (2016): 150–61. https://doi.org/10.1016/j.tate.2016.01.024.

Gerpott, Fabiola H., Nale Lehmann-Willenbrock, Ramon Wenzel, and Sven C. Voelpel. "Age Diversity and Learning Outcomes in Organizational Training Groups: The Role of Knowledge Sharing and Psychological

Safety." *International Journal of Human Resource Management* 32, no. 18 (2021): 3777–804. https://doi.org/10.1080/09585192.2019.1640763.

Gerpott, Fabiola Heike, Nale Lehmann-Willenbrock, and Sven C. Voelpel. "A Phase Model of Intergenerational Learning in Organizations." *Academy of Management Learning & Education* 16, no. 2 (2017): 193–216. https://doi.org/10.5465/amle.2015.0185.

Gray, Peter H., and Darren B. Meister. "Knowledge Sourcing Effectiveness." *Management Science* 50, no. 6 (2004): 821–34. https://doi.org/10.1287/mnsc.1030.0192.

Greenberg, Jerald, Claire E. Ashton-James, and Neal M. Ashkanasy. "Social Comparison Processes in Organizations." *Organizational Behavior and Human Decision Processes* 102, no. 1 (2007): 22–41. https://doi.org/10.1016/j.obhdp.2006.09.006.

Harvey, Jean-François. "Managing Organizational Memory with Intergenerational Knowledge Transfer." *Journal of Knowledge Management* 16, no. 3 (2012): 400–17. https://doi.org/10.1108/13673271211238733.

Hogg, Michael A. "Social Identity and Social Comparison." In *Handbook of Social Comparison*. Edited by Jerry Suls and Ladd Wheeler, 401–21. Boston: Springer U.S., 2000.

Lagacé, Martine, Anna Rosa Donizzetti, Lise Van de Beeck, Caroline D. Bergeron, Philippe Rodrigues-Rouleau, and Audrey St-Amour. "Testing the Shielding Effect of Intergenerational Contact against Ageism in the Workplace: A Canadian Study." *International Journal of Environmental Research and Public Health* 19, no. 8 (2022). https://doi.org/10.3390/ijerph19084866.

Lagacé, Martine, Lise van de Beeck, Caroline D. Bergeron, and Philippe Rodrigues-Rouleau. "Fostering Positive Views about Older Workers and Reducing Age Discrimination: A Retest of the Workplace Intergenerational Contact and Knowledge Sharing Model." *Journal of Applied Gerontology* 42, no. 6 (2023): 1223–33. https://doi.org/10.1177/07334648231163840.

Lagacé, Martine, Lise van de Beeck, and Najat Firzly. "Building on Intergenerational Climate to Counter Ageism in the Workplace? A Cross-Organizational Study." *Journal of Intergenerational Relationships* 17, no. 2 (2019): 201–19. https://doi.org/10.1080/15350770.2018.1535346.

Lee, Soohyun. "The Bright and Dark Sides of Upward Social Comparison: Knowledge Sharing and Knowledge Hiding Directed at High Performers." Dissertation, Graduate Faculty in Psychology, City University of New York, 2022. https://academicworks.cuny.edu/gc_etds/4928/.

Levy, Moria. "Knowledge Retention: Minimizing Organizational Business Loss." *Journal of Knowledge Management* 15, no. 4 (2011): 582–600. https://doi.org/10.1108/13673271111151974.

Morin, Alain. "A Neurocognitive and Socioecological Model of Self-Awareness." *Genetic, Social, and General Psychology Monographs* 130, no. 3 (2004): 197–222. https://doi.org/10.3200/MONO.130.3.197-224.

Mussweiler, Thomas. "'Seek and Ye Shall Find': Antecedents of Assimilation and Contrast in Social Comparison." *European Journal of Social Psychology* 31, no. 5 (2001): 499–509. https://doi.org/10.1002/ejsp.75.

Onu, Diana, Thomas Kessler, and Joanne R. Smith. "Admiration: A Conceptual Review." *Emotion Review* 8, no. 3 (2016): 218–30. https://doi.org/10.1177/1754073915610438.

Park, Jisung, Heesun Chae, and Jin Nam Choi. "The Need for Status as a Hidden Motive of Knowledge-Sharing Behavior: An Application of Costly Signaling Theory." *Human Performance* 30, no. 1 (2017): 21–37. https://doi.org/10.1080/08959285.2016.1263636.

Ryan, Richard M., and Edward L. Deci. *Self-Determination Theory: Basic Psychological Needs in Motivation, Development, and Wellness*. New York: Guilford Press, 2017. https://doi.org/10.1521/978.14625/28806.

Ryan, Richard M., and Jennifer G. La Guardia. "What Is Being Optimized? Self-Determination Theory and Basic Psychological Needs." In *Psychology and the Aging Revolution: How We Adapt to Longer Life*. Edited by Sara H. Qualls and Norman Abeles, 145–72. Washington: American Psychological Association, 2000.

Šajeva, Svetlana. "Encouraging Knowledge Sharing among Employees: How Reward Matters." *Procedia - Social and Behavioral Sciences* 156 (2014): 130–34. https://doi.org/10.1016/j.sbspro.2014.11.134.

Schmidt, Xenia, and Katrin Muehlfeld. "What's So Special about Intergenerational Knowledge Transfer? Identifying Challenges of Intergenerational Knowledge Transfer." *Management Revu* 28, no. 4 (2017): 375–411. https://doi.org/10.5771/0935-9915-2017-4-375.

Sharp, Melanie, Alberto Voci, and Miles Hewstone. "Individual Difference Variables as Moderators of the Effect of Extended Cross-Group Friendship on Prejudice." *Group Processes & Intergroup Relations* 14, no. 2 (2011): 207–21. https://doi.org/10.1177/1368430210391122.

Suls, Jerry. "From the Cradle to the Grave: Comparison and Self-Evaluation across the Life-Span." In *Psychological Perspectives on the Self*. Edited by Jerry M. Suls, 97–125. Hillsdale, NJ: Lawrence Erlbaum, 1982.

Tajfel, H., and J. C. Turner. "The Social Identity Theory of Intergroup Behaviour." In *Psychology of Intergroup Relations*. Edited by S. Worchsel and W. G. Austin, 7–24. Chicago: Nelson-Hall, 1986.

Turner, John C. "Social Comparison and Social Identity: Some Prospects for Intergroup Behaviour." *European Journal of Social Psychology* 5, no. 1 (1975): 1–34. https://doi.org/10.1002/ejsp.2420050102.

Urick, Michael. "Generational Differences and COVID-19: Positive Interactions in Virtual Workplaces." *Journal of Intergenerational Relationships* 18, no. 4 (2020): 379–98. https://doi.org/10.1080/15350770.2020.1818662.

Urick, Michael J., Elaine C. Hollensbe, Suzanne S. Masterson, and Sean T. Lyons. "Understanding and Managing Intergenerational Conflict: An Examination of Influences and Strategies." *Work, Aging and Retirement* 3, no. 2 (2016): waw009. https://doi.org/10.1093/workar/waw009.

Wang, Changyu, Yihong Dong, Zixi Ye, and Jiaojiao Feng. "Linking Online and Offline Intergenerational Knowledge Transfer to Younger Employees' Innovative Work Behaviors: Evidence from Chinese Hospitals." *Journal of Knowledge Management* 27, no. 3 (2023): 762–84. https://doi.org/10.1108/JKM-11-2021-0839.

Wang, Cynthia S., Tai Kenneth, Gillian Ku, and Adam D Galinsky. "Perspective-Taking Increases Willingness to Engage in Intergroup Contact." *PLoS One* 9, no. 1 (2014): e85681. https://doi.org/10.1371/journal.pone.0085681.

Zell, Ethan, and Mark D. Alicke. "Comparisons over Time: Temporal Trajectories, Social Comparison, and Self-Evaluation." *European Journal of Social Psychology* 40, no. 3 (2010): 375–82. https://doi.org/10.1002/ejsp.737.

CHAPTER 26

Bridging Generations and Disciplines: Exploring How Interprofessional Conversations and Circle of Change Revisited Can Improve Intergenerational Practice Experience and Outcomes in Australia

Xanthe Golenko, Jennifer Cartmel, Gaery Barbery, *and* Anneke Fitzgerald

Abstract

Intergenerational practice focuses on building connections and understanding between different age groups, which often requires collaboration between professionals from various disciplines to achieve common goals. However, challenges associated with cross-disciplinary collaboration can create barriers that can severely impact the development, implementation, and evaluation of intergenerational programs. Becoming aware of potential challenges and strategies to overcoming them can enhance the experience of intergenerational programs for facilitators and practitioners, as well as improve outcomes for participants. In this chapter, we introduce the concepts of interprofessional conversations and circle of change revisited and discuss them in the context of intergenerational practice. We then provide case study examples of how these concepts can be applied to improve experience and outcomes for all.

Key Words: intergenerational practice, cross-disciplinary collaboration, interprofessional conversations, circle of change revisited, collaboration, decision-making, problem solving

Interprofessional conversations	Circle of change revisited
Strengths/impact	**Strengths/impact**
• Collaborative approach to problem solving and decision-making	• Collaborative problem solving, diverse perspectives, sense of community engagement
• Professionals from various backgrounds working together to address complex issues and achieve common goals	• Sustained positive transformations in social dynamics and systems.
	• Adaptable framework that enables tailored interventions
	• Empowering individuals to enact meaningful change within their unique contexts

Interprofessional conversations	Circle of change revisited
Limitations	**Limitations**
• Different professional terminology, jargon, or communication styles that can lead to miscommunication, misunderstandings, errors, or inefficiencies • Varying perspectives, objectives, and priorities of professionals from different disciplines, which can deter reaching agreement on common goals • Hierarchical structures and logistical challenges that can impede collaboration	• Potential challenges in ensuring widespread adoption and scalability • Continuous adaptation to evolving societal dynamics that may pose difficulties in maintaining the model's effectiveness over time • Possible need for ongoing refinement and strategic adjustments to address systemic barriers and achieve comprehensive change

Introduction

Intergenerational practice involves bringing together individuals from different age groups to promote mutual understanding, collaboration, and learning.[1] It recognizes the value of meaningful interactions between generations that are mutually beneficial.[2] Intergenerational practice fosters social cohesion, empathy, and the sharing of diverse perspectives and experiences among individuals of different ages.[3]

Intergenerational practice programs have gained recognition as a way of breaking down ageism stereotypes,[4] improving social connection,[5] improving adolescents' self-efficacy scores,[6] improving children's reading outcomes,[7] and decreasing the likelihood of children participating in deviant or delinquent behavior later in life.[8] Programs can occur in schools,[9] community centers,[10] aged and healthcare facilities,[11] and other spaces where generations interact.

Intergenerational practice is inherently multidisciplinary and requires collaboration between professionals from various industries (e.g., education, healthcare and aged care, research) and disciplines (e.g., early childhood education, primary and secondary education, nursing, lifestyle) to achieve common goals. However, collaboration between professionals from various industries and disciplines, often referred to as interdisciplinary or cross-disciplinary collaboration, can come with a number of challenges[12] that can undermine the potential benefits of intergenerational programs.

Challenges Associated with Interprofessional Collaboration

Professionals from diverse backgrounds may use different terminology, jargon, or communication styles, making it challenging to understand one another. Miscommunication or misunderstandings can lead to errors or inefficiencies.[13] In addition, professionals may have various perspectives, objectives, and priorities based on their disciplines, which can create conflicts when trying to agree on common goals.[14] Effective conflict resolution strategies must be in place to address these issues constructively.

In some organizations, hierarchical structures can impede collaboration, as professionals may be accustomed to following the direction of their own discipline's leaders, which can hinder open and equitable participation.[15] Also, professionals without training in interdisciplinary collaboration are ill-equipped to navigate the challenges that arise when working with individuals from different fields. Determining leadership roles and decision-making processes within interdisciplinary teams can be complex, especially if there is a lack of clarity regarding who has the final say on certain matters. Professionals may also encounter legal and ethical dilemmas when collaborating across disciplines, such as confidentiality concerns or ethical standards that differ between fields.

Collaboration across various disciplines can be complex, and professionals may face logistical challenges related to scheduling, project management, and data sharing.[16] Collaborative projects may also require additional resources, such as funding, personnel, or equipment, which can be hard to secure and allocate across multiple disciplines or departments.[17] Therefore, collaborative efforts often require additional time for planning, coordination, and meetings. Building trust and mutual respect among professionals from different disciplines can take time on top of regular workloads, and preconceived biases or stereotypes about other disciplines can hinder the development of strong working relationships.[18] It requires strategic consideration.

Measuring and evaluating the outcomes of interdisciplinary collaboration can also be challenging. It may be difficult to assess the specific contributions of each discipline and demonstrate the value of collaboration,[19] but understanding its value adds to the effectiveness of interprofessional collaboration.

Overcoming these challenges requires a commitment to building a collaborative culture, effective communication strategies, strong leadership, ongoing training and education, and clear processes for conflict resolution and decision-making. Despite the difficulties, interdisciplinary collaboration can yield innovative solutions and improved outcomes in various fields, making it a valuable endeavor when managed effectively. In this chapter, we present two strategies that address these challenges: (1) interprofessional conversations; and (2) circle of change revisited (COCR). We discuss these two important concepts and provide case study examples of how they can be applied to improve both experience and outcomes of intergenerational practice.

Interprofessional Conversations

Interprofessional conversations refer to collaborative and communicative interactions between professionals from different disciplines or fields of expertise. The primary goal of these conversations is to improve the quality of care, education, or services provided by leveraging the unique skills, knowledge, and perspectives of each professional involved.

Interprofessional conversations emphasize a collaborative approach to problem solving and decision-making. Professionals from various backgrounds work together as a team to address complex issues and achieve common goals. These conversations can involve professionals from diverse disciplines, such as healthcare, aged care, child care, education, social work, or business, who come together to contribute their specialized expertise to a shared endeavor. Interprofessional conversations require the sharing of information and knowledge among team members. This exchange helps build a comprehensive understanding of the issues at hand and enables informed decision-making.

Effective communication is a key component of interprofessional conversations. Professionals must communicate clearly and respectfully to ensure that everyone's input is valued and understood. Active listening is crucial in this context. In intergenerational programs, interprofessional conversations promote a holistic approach to program design that benefit both the older and younger generations. They recognize that individuals may have multifaceted needs that require input from professionals with different areas of expertise. Interprofessional collaboration often leads to improved outcomes in terms of participant satisfaction, educational success, or effective problem resolution. By pooling resources and knowledge, professionals can develop more comprehensive solutions.

Interprofessional conversations help break down the silos that can exist between different professional groups or departments within organizations. This integration of perspectives can lead to more efficient and effective services. In situations where conflicts or disagreements arise, interprofessional conversations provide a platform for constructive conflict resolution. Professionals can work through differences to reach mutually agreeable solutions.

In intergenerational programs, interprofessional conversations ensure that decisions are made with the interests of both generations in mind and promote the active involvement of participants in the decision-making process. These conversations offer opportunities for ongoing professional development where professionals can learn from one another, broaden their understanding of other disciplines, and enhance their own skills and knowledge. Ethical discussions are common in interprofessional conversations as professionals navigate complex ethical dilemmas and make decisions that align with their respective ethical codes.

Overall, interprofessional conversations play a vital role in promoting collaboration, enhancing the quality of the program, and breaking down barriers between professional disciplines. They are essential in intergenerational programs where diverse expertise is required to address complex challenges and are characterized by effective communication, shared decision-making, and a commitment to improving outcomes for individuals and communities.

Circle of Change Revisited
Circle of change revisited (COCR)[20] is a model of critical thinking that emphasizes a participatory and collaborative approach used in various settings to facilitate open dialogue, foster collaboration, and drive transformative change. This concept is rooted in principles of inclusivity, shared leadership, and the belief that diverse perspectives and experiences

are essential for addressing complex issues and achieving positive outcomes. COCR is designed to create inclusive spaces where individuals from diverse backgrounds, including different cultures, professional disciplines, and perspectives, come together to engage in meaningful conversations. The goal is to ensure that all voices are heard and valued. The COCR model of critical thinking is presented in figure 26.1.

The four key steps in the COCR process are as follows:

1. Deconstruct: Describe the phenomenon.
2. Confront: Clarify perspectives about the phenomenon and challenge personal values and beliefs.

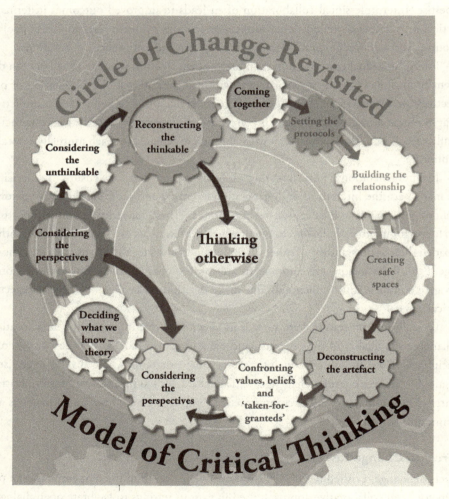

Figure 26.1 Circle of change revisited.

Source: Cartmel, J., et al. *Leading Learning Circles: For Educators Engaged in Study.* Canberra, ACT: Australian Government Department of Education, 2015.

3. Theorize: Examine characteristics of the phenomenon from different professional and theoretical perspectives.
4. Think otherwise: Review the dominant perspective and consider the impact of the practice.

Central to the COCR model is the concept of dialogue that emphasizes equality and the absence of hierarchy. Participants engage in open and honest conversations, often using facilitation techniques to ensure respectful communication. Rather than relying on traditional hierarchical structures, COCR promotes shared leadership. (See also *Handbook* chapter 5.) Participants are encouraged to take on leadership roles as needed, and decision-making is often a collective process. Given that this approach is often used to address complex issues and challenges, participants work together to identify problems, generate innovative solutions, and plan actions for change through dialogue and collaboration.

COCR can be applied in a wide range of contexts, including community development, organizational change, and social justice initiatives. It is often used in situations where diverse stakeholders need to come together to address shared concerns or achieve common goals, as in intergenerational programs. It explores how personal reflection, communication, and transformational change can impact practice.

Effective facilitation is essential for the success of COCR; facilitators guide the conversation, ensure that participants follow agreed-upon processes, and create a safe and respectful environment for dialogue. While consensus is not always the goal, COCR often aims to reach a shared understanding or agreement among participants. This can involve finding common ground, building trust, and creating a sense of collective ownership of the issues and solutions. The ultimate aim of COCR is to bring about transformative change. This change may be personal, organizational, or societal, depending on the context in which it is applied. The process itself can be transformative, as it challenges traditional power structures and encourages reflection and growth.

The COCR model has gained recognition as a powerful tool for promoting inclusivity, collaboration, and problem solving across diverse groups. In turn, it emphasizes the importance of dialogue and collective wisdom in addressing complex challenges and creating positive outcomes. This concept continues to evolve and adapt to different contexts, making it a valuable approach in various fields, including community development, social justice, and organizational change.

Theoretical Underpinnings of Interprofessional Conversations and COCR Model of Critical Thinking

Interprofessional conversations and circle of change revisited (COCR) theories share some common principles related to collaboration, communication, and teamwork, but they also have distinct characteristics that set them apart. Interprofessional conversation theories are primarily applied in healthcare and social services to improve patient/client outcomes, while COCR theories are versatile and can be used in various contexts to drive broader social or organizational transformation, as presented in table 26.1.

Theoretical frameworks that inform interprofessional conversations contribute to promoting collaboration, understanding, and communication among professionals from different disciplines. Similarly, the theoretical frameworks that inform COCR emphasize

Table 26.1 Theoretical underpinnings of interprofessional COCR

Theoretical frameworks that inform interprofessional conversations	Theoretical frameworks that inform COCR
Interprofessional education promotes a culture of teamwork, mutual respect, and effective communication among professionals from diverse backgrounds.	*Participatory action research (PAR)* emphasizes collaboration between researchers and participants to identify and address real-world problems. COCRs often incorporate elements of PAR—collaborative inquiry, problem-solving, and action planning.
Communication theories, such as the communication accommodation theory and the Gricean maxims of communication, inform interprofessional conversations by highlighting the importance of clear and effective communication and emphasize adaptability in communication styles to ensure that information is conveyed and received accurately among team members.	*Dialogical communication theories*, influenced by scholars like Mikhail Bakhtin and Martin Buber, underscore the importance of open and authentic dialogue in fostering understanding and shared meaning when exploring diverse perspectives and cocreating solutions.
Teamwork Theory: The Tuckman model of team development (forming, storming, norming, performing) and Belbin's team role theory are examples of teamwork theories that inform interprofessional conversations. These theories help professionals understand the stages of team development, transition from one to the next, and navigate challenges and conflicts effectively.	*Asset-based community development (ABCD)* is a community-focused framework that emphasizes leveraging existing strengths and assets within a community to drive change. COCR often incorporate ABCD principles by engaging community members and stakeholders in identifying and utilizing their assets to address challenges.
Shared decision-making and person-centered care: The shared decision-making model and the principles of patient-centered care emphasize the importance of involving participants in decision-making processes and considering their values, preferences, and priorities.	*Appreciative inquiry* that focuses on exploring and amplifying the positive aspects of a system or situation. COCR integrates appreciative inquiry by encouraging participants to envision and work toward desired future states rather than solely focusing on problems and deficits.
Conflict resolution theories: Conflict resolution frameworks, such as principled negotiation (based on the work of Roger Fisher and William Ury) and interest-based negotiation, provide strategies for addressing conflicts and disagreements constructively within interprofessional teams—active listening, problem-solving, and mutual respect.	*Systems thinking* theories inform COCR by helping participants to understand the interconnectedness of issues and systems and to consider the broader context and identify root causes rather than only addressing symptoms.

the importance of collaboration, inclusivity, dialogue, and a holistic understanding of complex issues. Integrating these theories into practice can collectively enhance teamwork, improve participant outcomes, and promote transformative change within various contexts, including intergenerational programs.

Case Study Examples of Intergenerational Programs in Australia and the Application of Interprofessional Conversations and COCR

In this section, we present three case study examples of intergenerational programs that have been conducted in Australia.

1. The Intergenerational Care Project
2. Creating connections across the generations through digital storytelling
3. Intergenerational practice in Southeast Queensland

We explain how interprofessional conversations and the COCR methodology were applied and contributed to successful implementation and effectiveness.

Table 26.2 presents a comparative summary of strengths and limitations of the case study examples.

Case Study 1: The Intergenerational Care Project

The Intergenerational Care Project was conducted across four research sites located in Southeast Queensland and New South Wales from 2017 to 2019. The aim of the project was to prepare, pilot, and evaluate two models of intergenerational practice in Australia. One was a colocation model, where aged care and child care centers were located on the same property. The other was a visitation model, where the centers were located separately and people from one center were transported to the other center.[21]

The study involved a sixteen-week intergenerational learning program where preschool aged children (three to five years) and older adults came together every week for one to two hours to engage in meaningful activities.[22] An intergenerational learning framework was developed through consultation with stakeholders and experts and was informed by three emergent theories around early learning and play: the Belonging, Being and Becoming: Early Years Learning Framework;[23] circle of change;[24] and a neurosequential model of education.[25] The key concept of the intergenerational learning framework was that both generations can learn from each other. This led to the development of five principles of learning that were the critical core components for program design: (1) respectful and reciprocal relationships, (2) partnerships, (3) high expectations and equity, (4) respect for diversity, and (5) ongoing learning and reflective practices.[26]

Workforce participants from each site (aged care and child care) were involved in a series of workshops prior to commencing the program. The workshops were facilitated by experts in intergenerational practice and members of the research team and covered topics

Table 26.2 Summary of the strengths and limitations of case study examples

Program name	The Intergenerational Care Project	Creating connections across the generations through digital storytelling	Intergenerational practice in Southeast Queensland
Program strengths/impact	• Development, implementation, and evaluation of an intergenerational learning program across four sites • Underpinned by the early years learning framework • 16-week program of activities codesigned with each site to suit the needs of participants, the environment, and available resources and equipment • Evaluation included participant outcomes (older adults and children), workforce and learning (intergenerational engagement), economic and process evaluations	• 170 year 7 students from one school and 35 older adults living in retirement villages and the community • Small groups of students worked with individual older adults to create a digital story about a shared interest (e.g., sports, music, farming, outdoors) • Weekly meetings with key stakeholders (teachers, Retirement Village managers, and researchers) to codesign activities to enhance engagement and participant experience	• Development, implementation, and evaluation of an intergenerational program involving two child care centers and older residents from the local community • Weekly excursion to community venues where the program was held • Underpinned by the early years learning framework • Program of activities prepared by early childhood educators
Program limitations	• Ensuring time was available for the early childhood and aged care staff to engage in planning and reflective thinking about their practice.	• COVID interruptions, challenges with technology, and managing/coordinating a large cohort	• Ensuring time was available for the early childhood staff to engage in reflective thinking about their practice • Weekly transport of all resources to community venues.

including the theoretical frameworks, intergenerational practice and facilitation, and evaluation. An important part of the workshops was ensuring opportunities for interprofessional conversations. Aged care staff and early childhood educators spent time working collaboratively to set common goals and plan activities that were mutually beneficial and linked with the five principles of learning and intended outcomes. Reflection on the previous session as well as planning and preparing the following session were part of the collaborative process during the sixteen weekly meetings.

Evaluation of the intergenerational learning program consisted of three key components: (1) outcomes (participant, workforce, learning), (2) economic evaluation, and (3) process evaluation (see table 26.3.)

Table 26.3 Evaluation framework components linked with objectives, indicators, and data sources

Evaluation component	Objectives	Indicators	Data sources
Outcome evaluation			
Participant outcomes	1. To examine how an intergenerational learning program impacts on the health and well-being of participants	• Health • Well-being • Mood	• Surveys • Mood scales
Education outcomes	2. To examine the impact of an intergenerational learning program on engagement and program satisfaction	• Level of engagement • Program satisfaction	• Video ethnography • Engagement scale • Leuven scale • Reflective journal (program reflections) • Follow-up interviews with participants (children and older people)
Workforce outcomes	3. To examine the impact on workforce in terms of staff retention and career development	• Job stress inventory • Career development opportunities • Program satisfaction	• Reflective journal (individual practice) • Job stress inventory (pre and post) • Session satisfaction • Reflective journal (program reflections) • Workforce interviews (pre and post)
Economic evaluation			
Socioeconomic outcomes	4. To examine the costs and benefits associated with implementing an intergenerational learning program	• Cost analysis • Willingness to pay • Cost-benefit analysis	• Surveys • Cost data spreadsheet
Process evaluation			
Program fidelity and sustainability	5. To identify the core components of the program that are critical to its success and other components that can be adapted to suit different contexts	• Did we do as planned? • Why/why not? • What would we do differently?	All

Source: Golenko, Radford

[a] Golenko et al., "Uniting Generations."

To assess the education and workforce outcomes, the research team developed two reflective journals for the workforce participants to complete. One program reflections journal was completed collaboratively by the participating workforce at each site after each session. Each session was described in detail, including the program planning and delivery aspects, such as preparation of the space and learning materials, the activities that were conducted during the sessions, and what was successful and what could have been done differently. In addition, each workforce participant completed an individual reflective journal that used the circle of change revisited (COCR) model as previously described.

Through the purposeful application of interprofessional conversations and the COCR, the workforce participants were able to clearly describe what happened during each session and critically assess what happened by challenging personal and professional assumptions. In doing so, they were able to engage in collaborative decision-making and problem solving, to design and deliver meaningful activities that were mutually beneficial for both older and younger participants, and maximize the benefits for all involved.

Case Study 2: Creating Connections across the Generations through Digital Storytelling

The Creating Intergenerational Connections through Digital Storytelling project was a partnership between Bolton Clarke, Faith Lutheran College Plainland, and Swinburne University and was conducted in 2022. The aim of the research project was to enhance the psychological and emotional well-being of older adults living in the community and improve teenagers' attitudes toward older adults. The project involved bringing 170 year 7 students together with 35 older adults, including residents from Bolton Clarke Retirement Villages and Faith Lutheran College grandparents, to create a digital story about a shared topic of interest. Small groups of students worked with individual seniors or couples to create a three-minute digital story using images, video, sound, music, and narration.

The intergenerational digital storytelling program was built into the year 7 Integrated Studies curriculum. It involved ten sessions that were held during school time for one hour and thirty minutes from April to July, across school terms 2 and 3. Sessions were held in person, alternating between older adults traveling to the school and students traveling to the retirement villages. One session was held online via video conferencing.

Prior to commencing the program, the researchers and an expert in digital storytelling held a series of online seminars and discussions with the workforce participants, which included staff from the participating retirement villages along with senior staff and teachers from the school. Topics covered during these sessions included an introduction to intergenerational practice and facilitation, digital storytelling, and program evaluation. In addition, an initial program schedule and session activity plan with specified outputs and outcomes was developed. Initially, the plan was quite structured and was designed to align with curriculum requirements and predetermined outputs and outcomes that supported the interests of each participant group. However, several unexpected challenges and disruptions occurred during the program delivery phase. These included COVID outbreaks, buses breaking down, and issues with technology, as well as coordinating and managing a large cohort totaling over two hundred people.

In response to these challenges, the team of researchers, experts, teachers, and aged care staff met regularly (at least weekly) to discuss issues that arose and come up with innovative solutions to ensure that the program could continue and that it would be beneficial to all involved. Through this process of interprofessional conversation and learning, the team developed a strong bond with high levels of trust and mutual respect. The planning and preparation of session activities became a more iterative process, and the delivery of the sessions was more organic and emergent. While the team did not formally engage in the COCR process through reflexive journaling, they completed each step of reflecting, challenging personal assumptions and beliefs, considering the perspectives of other participant groups, and proposing solutions that would benefit all.

Students and older adults successfully created twenty-eight digital stories across a range of topics including farming, horses, dancing, skating, and music. The program culminated in a screening and presentation event held at the school that was attended by over four hundred people. Attendees enjoyed a student choir performance, a poetry recital by the older adults, and a screening of selected digital stories. Findings from the research demonstrated a statistically significant difference in attitudes toward older adults among the students. While quantitative data from the older adults did not show a statistically significant difference in psychological and emotional well-being, qualitative data indicated that the older adults enjoyed the program and relished spending time with the teens.

Case Study 3: An Intergenerational Practice Project in Southeast Queensland

This case study explores a successful initiative that brought preschool children together with older adults in a community setting in Southeast Queensland. The younger participants were recruited from an early childhood center, and the older adults were recruited from a community center that provided social and other support to older adults living independently in the community. The two sites were within close proximity of each other in Southeast Queensland. The program took place weekly for eight weeks to fit within the Queensland school term. Twenty-two older adults with an age range of fifty-four to ninety-one years participated in the program. These older adults had varied backgrounds; there were retired teachers, other professionals, and women who had raised and educated their families. The program also included twenty-six children, aged three to five years, who attended the early childhood center. Our approach involved four stages:

Stage one entailed development of an intergenerational practice program and participant recruitment. In this initial stage, information and Q&A sessions were held at the community center to assist in the recruitment of the older participants. All people who work with children in Queensland require a "blue card" to ensure the safety of the children. Obtaining a blue card for all older adult participants created a barrier, as many did not have the required identification, such as a passport or driver's license.

Stage two involved training those involved in facilitating the program and codesigning the program activities. As the older adults lived within the community, the main staff involved in facilitating the program were the early childhood educators. Training consisted of three half-day workshops that covered topics such as understanding what constitutes an intergenerational practice, death and dying, and awareness of older people's needs. The process of codesigning the program activities involved bringing staff from the organizations together with older people to discuss program elements (layout of the rooms, safety concerns for older people, risk assessments) and brainstorm the types of activities that were consistent with available resources and were within the current early childhood curriculum. Similar to case study one, this training used the COCR strategy to allow the educators to develop and reflect on their practice throughout the program.

Stage three saw implementation of the eight-week intergenerational program. The weekly sessions included activities such as arts and crafts, music, dance, and storytelling, which provided opportunities for older adults and children to interact and engage in fun and meaningful activities together. For example, flowerpots were decorated and then planted with herbs, picture frames were decorated to be used as mementos, activity games were chosen to foster movement and balance, and dance was added simply to create fun and laughter. Upon completion of the eight-week program, a celebration was jointly organized and attended by both groups, carers, and parents, to enhance a sense of community.

Stage four involved evaluating the outcomes of the program.

Program Outcomes
Overall, the program achieved remarkable results for both groups of participants. Observations from parents and staff noted improvements in children's maturity, social competence, behavior, and overall confidence. While many of the experiences provided in the intergenerational program were similar to those available to the children at their early childhood center, the children's positive outcomes seemed to reflect the one-on-one time they had with the older adults and the connections that were formed through those interactions. As for the older adults, some were anxious and unsure in the initial stages about how they should behave and interact with young children. However, they soon relaxed and, while they often felt a little fatigued afterward due to the activity levels, all looked forward to returning the following week. A significant finding was the improvement in the physical capabilities and confidence in the older adults during the program. For example, participants found it easier to get in and out of chairs and there was less need for support from walking aids. While some activities like dancing were challenging for individual adults, they modified or adapted their movements by doing them seated or walking slowly, and but they did not want to stop participating with the others.

Some unintended outcomes from the program were other connections made. First, connections were made between the older adults themselves. Most older adults lived independently, and the weekly meetings led to chatting after the session, helping one another when needed, or encouraging participation in an activity. Second, connections were made between the older adults and the parents of the children. In today's society there are many families who lack familial support, whether this is due to immigrating to Australia, having moved from another state, or being a single parent. When children talked about their experiences and the elders they were connecting with, parents struck up conversations with the older adults and invited them to their home for BBQs, dinner, and picnics. Lastly was the impact that the intergenerational program had on the staff facilitating the program. They reported that seeing firsthand the growth in both the children (whose behaviors they knew very well) and the older adults during the eight weeks made for the most rewarding program they had ever been involved in, had invigorated their work life, and had changed how they now worked with the children and how they might approach life.

While the program has been largely successful, it faces certain future challenges, including adapting to the changing needs of both older adults and young children, maintaining a delicate balance in activities, and addressing the health concerns of seniors. Nevertheless, the benefits of bringing old and young together strongly outweigh the challenges. Continuous improvement utilizing codesign of programs and professional development of program facilitators will enhance the chances for program sustainability.

The intergenerational practice project in Southeast Queensland serves as a testament to the potential of intergenerational practice programs to create enriching and supportive environments for both older adults and young children. This case study illustrates the positive impact of bridging generations, fostering relationships, and building stronger and more inclusive communities.

Conclusion

Intergenerational practice is a powerful approach that brings individuals from different age groups together to foster mutual understanding, collaboration, and learning. It recognizes the value of meaningful interactions between generations, promoting social cohesion, empathy, and the exchange of diverse perspectives and experiences. However, the multidisciplinary nature of intergenerational practice demands collaboration between professionals from various industries and disciplines, which can present challenges. These challenges include differences in terminology and communication styles, conflicting objectives and hierarchical structures within organizations, a lack of interdisciplinary training; legal and ethical dilemmas, logistical issues, and the need for additional resources. Overcoming these challenges requires a commitment to building a collaborative culture, effective communication strategies, strong leadership, ongoing training and education, and clear processes for conflict resolution and decision-making.

Despite the difficulties, interdisciplinary collaboration can yield innovative solutions and improved outcomes across different fields when effectively managed. To address these challenges, we have presented two key strategies in this chapter: (1) interprofessional conversations and (2) circle of change revisited. These strategies, along with case study examples, offer a pathway to enhance the experience and outcomes of intergenerational practice.

Notes

1. S. E. Jarrott et al., "Implementation of Evidence-Based Practices in Intergenerational Programming: A Scoping Review," *Research on Aging* 43, no. 7–8 (2021): 283–93.
2. S. Hatzifilalithis and A. M. Grenier, "Understanding Intergenerationality: Theories, Reflections, and Experiences," *Innovation in Aging* 3, no. Suppl. 1 (2019): S154.
3. A. Hatton-Yeo and C. Batty, "Twelve: Evaluating the Contribution of Intergenerational Practice to Achieving Social Cohesion," in *Promoting Social Cohesion*, ed. I. Newman and P. Ratcliffe (Bristol, UK: Policy Press, 2011), 242–57; T. Buffel et al. "Promoting Sustainable Communities through Intergenerational Practice," *Procedia - Social and Behavioral Sciences* 116 (2014): 1785–91.
4. A. Lytle, J. Macdonald, and S. R. Levy, *An Experimental Investigation of a Simulated Online Intergenerational Friendship Gerontology & Geriatrics Education* 44, no. (2 (2023): 286–97.
5. U. Suragarn et al., "Approaches to Enhance Social Connection in Older Adults: An Integrative Review of Literature," *Aging and Health Research* 1, no. 3 (2021): 100029.
6. Y. Murayama et al., "Effects of Participating in Intergenerational Programs on the Development of High School Students' Self-efficacy," *Journal of Intergenerational Relationships* 20, no. 4 (2022): 406–23.
7. G. W. Rebok et al., "Short-Term Impact of Experience Corps® Participation on Children and Schools: Results from a Pilot Randomized Trial," *Journal of Urban Health* 81 (2004): 79–93.
8. M. L. Ohmer, "Youth-Adult Partnerships to Prevent Violence," *Journal of Intergenerational Relationships* 20, no. 1 (2022): 105–26.
9. J. Cohen-Mansfield and B. Jensen, "Intergenerational Programs in Schools: Prevalence and Perceptions of Impact," *Journal of Applied Gerontology* 36, no. 3 (2017): 254–76.
10. X. Golenko et al., "Uniting Generations: A Research Protocol Examining the Impacts of an Intergenerational Learning Program on Participants and Organisations," *Australasian Journal on Ageing* 39, no. 3 (2020): e425–35.
11. R. Fukuoka et al., "Effectiveness of Intergenerational Interaction on Older Adults Depends on Children's Developmental Stages; Observational Evaluation in Facilities for Geriatric Health Service," *International Journal of Environmental Research and Public Health* 20, no. 1 (2023): 836.
12. E. Larkin and S. Newman, "Intergenerational Studies: A Multi-disciplinary Field," in *Intergenerational Approaches in Aging*, ed. K. Brabazon and R. Disch (New York: Routledge, 2013), 5–16; A. Lavery et al., "Interprofessional Collaboration to Address Social Isolation and Facilitate Intergenerational Service Learning within Graduate Education," *Journal of Community Engagement & Higher Education* 15, no. 1 (2023): 14.
13. J. Thistlethwaite et al., "Interprofessional Collaborative Practice: A Deconstruction," *Journal of Interprofessional Care* 27, no. 1 (2013): 50–56.
14. D. Nicolini et al., "Understanding the Role of Objects in Cross-Disciplinary Collaboration," *Organization Science* 23 (2012): 612–29, https://doi.org/10.1287/orsc.1110.0664; S. Prins, "From Competition to Collaboration: Critical Challenges and Dynamics in Multiparty Collaboration," *Journal of Applied Behavioral Science* 46, no. 3 (2010): 281–312.
15. A. Buanes and S. Jentoft, "Building Bridges: Institutional Perspectives on Interdisciplinarity," *Futures* 41, no. 7 (2009): 446–54.
16. Nicolini et al., "Understanding the Role."
17. Nicolini et al., "Understanding the Role."
18. Prins, "From Competition to Collaboration."
19. S. E. Jarrott, "Where Have We Been and Where Are We Going? Content Analysis of Evaluation Research of Intergenerational Program," *Journal of Intergenerational Relationships* 9, no. 1 (2011): 37–52.

20. J. Cartmel et al., *Leading Learning Circles: For Educators Engaged in Study* (Canberra, ACT: Australian Government Department of Education, 2015).
21. K. Radford et al., *Intergenerational Care Project Research Report* (Southport, Queensland: Griffith University, 2019).
22. Golenko et al., "Uniting Generations."
23. Australian Government Department of Education, *Belonging, Being and Becoming: The Early Years Learning Framework for Australia*, V2.0, (Canberra, Australia: Australian Government Department of Education for the Ministerial Council, 2002).
24. K. Macfarlane and J. Cartmel, Circles of Change Revisited: Building Leadership, Scholarship and Professional Identity in the Children's Services Sector," *Professional Development in Education* 38, no. 5 (2012): 845–61.
25. B. D. Perry and E. P. Hambrick, "The Neurosequential Model of Therapeutics," *Reclaiming Children and Youth* 17, no. 3 (2008): 38–43.
26. Golenko et al., "Uniting Generations."

Bibliography

Australian Government Department of Education. *Belonging, Being and Becoming: The Early Years Learning Framework for Australia*." V2.0. Canberra, Australia: Australian Government Department of Education for the Ministerial Council, 2002.

Buanes, A., and S. Jentoft. "Building Bridges: Institutional Perspectives on Interdisciplinarity." *Futures* 41, no. 7 (2009): 446–54.

Buffel, T., J. Cartmel, K. Macfarlane, M. Casley, and K. Smith. "Promoting Sustainable Communities through Intergenerational Practice." *Procedia - Social and Behavioral Sciences* 116 (2014): 1785–91.

Cartmel, J., K. Macfarlane, M. Casley, and K. Smith. *Leading Learning Circles: For Educators Engaged in Study*. Canberra, ACT: Australian Government Department of Education, 2015.

Cohen-Mansfield, J., and B. Jensen. "Intergenerational Programs in Schools: Prevalence and Perceptions of Impact." *Journal of Applied Gerontology* 36, no. 3 (2017): 254–76.

Fukuoka, R., S. Kimura, and T. Nabika. "Effectiveness of Intergenerational Interaction on Older Adults Depends on Children's Developmental Stages; Observational Evaluation in Facilities for Geriatric Health Service." *International Journal of Environmental Research and Public Health* 20, no. 1 (2023): 836.

Golenko, X., K. Radford, J. A. Fitzgerald, N. Vecchio, J. Cartmel, and N. Harris. "Uniting Generations: A Research Protocol Examining the Impacts of an Intergenerational Learning Program on Participants and Organisations." *Australasian Journal on Ageing* 39, no. 3 (2020): e425–35.

Hatton-Yeo, A., and C. Batty. "Twelve: Evaluating the Contribution of Intergenerational Practice to Achieving Social Cohesion." In *Promoting Social Cohesion*, edited by I. Newman and P. Ratcliffe, 242–57. Bristol, UK: Policy Press, 2011.

Hatzifilalithis, S., and A. M. Grenier. "Understanding Intergenerationality: Theories, Reflections, and Experiences." *Innovation in Aging* 3, Suppl. 1 (2019): S154.

Jarrott, S. E. "Where Have We Been and Where Are We Going? Content Analysis of Evaluation Research of Intergenerational Program." *Journal of Intergenerational Relationships* 9, no. 1 (2011): 37–52.

Jarrott, S. E., R. M. Scrivano, C. Park, and A. N. Mendoza. "Implementation of Evidence-Based Practices in Intergenerational Programming: A Scoping Review." *Research on Aging* 43, no. 7–8 (2021): 283–93.

Larkin, E., and S. Newman. "Intergenerational Studies: A Multi-disciplinary Field." In *Intergenerational Approaches in Aging*, edited by K. Brabazon and R. Disch, 5–16. New York: Routledge, 2013.

Lavery, A., E. Knight, S. Cole, and S. Metz. "Interprofessional Collaboration to Address Social Isolation and Facilitate Intergenerational Service Learning within Graduate Education." *Journal of Community Engagement & Higher Education* 15, no. 1 (2023): 14.

Lytle, A., J. Macdonald, and S. R. Levy. "An Experimental Investigation of a Simulated Online Intergenerational Friendship." *Gerontology & Geriatrics Education*, 44, no. 2 (2023): 286–97.

Macfarlane, K., and J. Cartmel. "Circles of Change Revisited: Building Leadership, Scholarship and Professional Identity in the Children's Services Sector." *Professional Development in Education* 38, no. 5 (2012): 845–61.

Murayama, Y., J. Yamaguchi, M. Yasunaga, M. Kuraoka, and Y. Fujiwara. "Effects of Participating in Intergenerational Programs on the Development of High School Students' Self-efficacy." *Journal of Intergenerational Relationships* 20, no. 4 (2022): 406–23.

Nicolini, D., J. Mengis, and J. Swan. "Understanding the Role of Objects in Cross-Disciplinary Collaboration." *Organization Science* 23 (2012): 612–29. https://doi.org/10.1287/orsc.1110.0664.

Ohmer, M. L. "Youth-Adult Partnerships to Prevent Violence." *Journal of Intergenerational Relationships* 20, no. 1 (2022): 105–26.

Perry, B. D., and E. P. Hambrick. "The Neurosequential Model of Therapeutics." *Reclaiming Children and Youth* 17, no. 3 (2008): 38–43.

Prins, S. "From Competition to Collaboration: Critical Challenges and Dynamics in Multiparty Collaboration." *Journal of Applied Behavioral Science* 46no. 3 (2010): 281–312.

Radford, K., J. Fitzgerald, N. Vecchio, J. Cartmel, N. Harris, and X. Golenko. *Intergenerational Care Project Research Report*. Southport, Queensland: Griffith University, 2019.

Rebok, G. W., M. C. Carlson, T. A. Glass, S. McGill, J. Hill, B. A. Wasik, et al. "Short-Term Impact of Experience Corps® Participation on Children and Schools: Results from a Pilot Randomized Trial." *Journal of Urban Health* 81 (2004): 79–93.

Suragarn, U., D. Hain, and G. Pfaff. "Approaches to Enhance Social Connection in Older Adults: An Integrative Review of Literature." *Aging and Health Research* 1, no. 3 (2021): 100029.

Thistlethwaite, J., A. Jackson, and M. Moran. "Interprofessional Collaborative Practice: A Deconstruction." *Journal of Interprofessional Care* 27, no. 1 (2013): 50–56.

PART V

Challenges to Generational Thinking, A Research Overview, and Recommendations for Strengthening and Sustaining the Intergenerational Movement

PART

V

Challenges to
Ceremonial
Thinking: A Research
Overview and
Recommendations
for Strengthening
and Sustaining the
Intergenerational
Movement

CHAPTER 27

Generations and Generational Differences: A Thought Experiment

Cort W. Rudolph *and* Hannes Zacher

Abstract

Generations do not objectively exist, because they cannot; this is the consensus reached by psychological science and recognized long ago by statisticians, who faced similar questions about whether chronological age and birth cohort effects could be uniquely identified in cross-sectional research. This reality has not stopped researchers and practitioners from exploiting this socially constructed phenomenon for their professional gains. The generations industry is thriving because it successfully makes people believe in generations and generational differences. This chapter presents a thought experiment and several conceptual replications that clarify why, even if generations did exist, it would be impractical if not impossible to study them in a way that approaches minimum standards for valid inference. We hope to impress upon readers that generations are, at best, a misunderstanding regarding basic principles of human development and linear dependency and, at worst, a denial of reality and science.

Key Words: generations, generational differences, thought experiment, pseudoscience, generationalism

Generations and Generational Differences

There is now consensus in psychological science that the concept of generations (i.e., distinct groupings of multiple successive birth cohorts that accompany meaningful group differences in characteristic patterns of feeling, thinking, and acting) does not hold up to logical and empirical scrutiny.[1] That is to say, the common notion of "generations" and assumptions about the existence of "generational differences" are, simply put, wrong.[2] We (the authors) and others[3] have dedicated quite a bit of effort over the past several years to unpacking the flawed logic of generations and the methodological problems associated with studies claiming to demonstrate evidence for or against generational differences.[4] To this end, our previous work[5] has reviewed and "busted" ten common myths regarding generations and generational differences (e.g., the myth that generational "theory" was meant to be tested, the myth that generational explanations are obvious, the myth the statistical models can help disentangle generational differences).

One of the most important, and somewhat ancillary, takeaway lessons from our research in this area is that, despite evidence to the contrary, many still hold onto a stubborn reliance on "generational thinking" to offer explanations for a wide-variety of expressed attitudes, values, and behaviors observed in daily life. For example, some practitioners trained in organizational psychology offer advice regarding how to manage members of different generations; educational psychologists may base pedagogical choices on assumptions about generational differences; and demographers—often in collaboration with media outlets and in popular books—attempt to identify and demarcate "new" generations. Indeed, "generationalism," referring to the belief that members of various generations possess discernable characteristics that are specific to that generation and then drawing distinctions between them, often for the purposes of comparison, and often at the expense of denigrating one group versus another, is a pervasive concern.[6]

Given the ubiquity of generational thinking in the face of evidence suggesting otherwise, psychological science would benefit from a critical approach to this topic that can help explain why the study of generations is, and will always be, a proverbial "dead end."[7] Thought experiments, which "take place in a unique setting: the laboratory of the mind" are well geared to achieve such goals "by presenting hypothesized alternate explanations, extending extant theory to include new contexts, and providing counterexamples for prevailing theories."[8]

This chapter focuses on developing a thought experiment to address perhaps the most common misunderstanding that researchers adopt when they make the argument that generations are "real" and that they have an important, knowable, and observable influence on people's behavior. Specifically, we focus on the assumption that generations can be understood and studied by characterizing people of different ages (and, by definition, different birth cohorts) with qualities assumed to follow from our understanding of artificially defined generational groups (i.e., through a process of combining multiple birth cohorts with one another and comparing them). Our thought experiment is thus designed with the goal of explaining, through metaphor, why the most common way of conceptualizing the existence of generations is both untenable and untestable. By corollary, we consider the type of evidence that would be needed to shift the consensus on generations and generational differences among both scientists and practitioners. That is, our thought experiment helps refocus attention on what it would take to unambiguously identify generations and demonstrate differences between them. As readers will see, the conditions necessary to achieve this goal are impractical and are very likely to be impossible given the necessary time and resource constraints.

We start by outlining key features of thought experiments in general and then discuss the "design" of our thought experiment by explaining the specific assumptions that underlie our arguments. Then we present the arguments that define our focal thought experiment and introduce variations on this experiment as "conceptual replications" to show how this general framework could be applied to a wide variety of related arguments that are commonly held up in favor of defining generational groups.

Thought Experiments

The term "thought experiment" refers to "judgments about what would happen if an imagined scenario were real."[9] Thought experiments have a long and rich history as a tool for philosophical inquiry in science (e.g., Sir Isaac Newton's cannonball thought experiment[10]) but are used much less frequently in psychological science compared to other approaches, such as laboratory experiments or survey studies. A recent paper,[11] a series of steps, and associated best practice recommendations are outlined that should be undertaken to perform thought experiments. We adopt such suggestions here to support our arguments.

The first step in building a thought experiment requires positioning one's study within a four-part taxonomy that can be applied to either (1) early- or late-stage theories, with the goals of either (2) theory confirmation or disconfirmation.[12] Arguably, given the lack of well-formalized theories of generations and generational differences, these are early stage theories. However, given that applied fields of psychological science tend to emphasize verbal over formal theories, it could be well argued that most theory in such fields is early stage. Moreover, given our stated position and based on our previous work in this area, our goal is theory disconfirmation, rather than confirmation. However, through various (counter) examples, we explore the necessary conditions by which generations "theory" could be supported empirically by pointing out that such conditions would generally be unreasonable to obtain.

Theoretical Considerations

As suggested, there is no strong (e.g., comprehensive, falsifiable) theory of generations, in the sense of a well-regarded and formalized model that makes specific, testable predictions regarding the functional relations among variables.[13] However, there is no shortage of "verbal theories" that have attempted to describe generations and generational phenomena, including the supposed mechanisms of their formation (e.g., epochal events[14]) and their consequences (e.g., various contrived typologies of generations and assumed differences in attitudes, values, and behaviors among them[15]). At this point in a chapter such as this, readers may expect to see a listing of various generational groups and qualities that are typically ascribed to them (e.g., "Members of generation *whatever* act in these various ways..."). We have purposefully omitted such discussions here, as this practice legitimizes these misguided ideas.

We doubt that it would be possible to develop a well-formalized theory that can explain the functional mechanism(s) by which generations form, and do not wish to encourage such folly. A key challenge to such an endeavor includes, but is by no means limited to, issues with establishing a clear understanding of the data-generating mechanism(s) that would give rise to distinct generations and differences between one assumed generation and another. Such mechanisms would need to address how generations form in terms of well-defined psychosocial mechanisms (e.g., through personality development, through social interactions, through culture formation, through contextual factors) and address the manifestation of generations against typically studied outcome variables (e.g., narcissism, work motivation), which would likely vary for each possible generation-outcome combination. Such a task would indeed be a fool's errand. For example, one would need a clear understanding of whether membership in a specific generation affects observed means (i.e., average levels of a phenomenon), variability (i.e., within- vs. between-generation variance), or act as a "third variable" (e.g., as moderators, modifying the strength of the relation between two or more variables, or as confounders/colliders, obfuscating other modeled or unmodeled causal paths between generations and modeled outcomes). More importantly, perhaps, one would need to define why this occurs, by understanding both mechanisms and boundary conditions that explain (directly and conditionally) the formation of generations.

Assumptions

The most important assumption that underlies this thought experiment is a long-known[16] and well understood[17] linear dependency between three co-occurring sources of variance that are present anytime one attempts to study time-graded processes—that is, for any given person i, age, period, and cohort (i.e., APC confounding). Age (A_i) simply refers to an individual's chronological age, as indexed (typically) as time since birth, in years. Period (P_i) reflects contemporaneous time (i.e., the current year) and refers to a given time period (e.g., the current year) in which data are collected. Finally, (birth) cohort (C_i) refers to one's year of birth. Importantly, the concept of a generation as it is typically understood most closely aligns with the definition of cohort but goes beyond it by artificially grouping together people born within a more or less wide range of birth years (e.g., fifteen or twenty years). However, in biological terms, each successive birth cohort represents a single generation. Only through the process of imposing value on artificially constructed *groups* of birth cohorts do our typical and common understandings of different generational groups emerge. To clarify, the following sentence, "Grier was born in 2015 (cohort), and he is eight years old (age) in the year 2023 (period)" highlights the problem of confounding alluded to earlier, which is that

(1) $C_i = P_i - A_i$

Applying this formula (1) to the previous example, we can illustrate further:

(2) $2015_{Cohort} = 2022_{Period} - 8_{Age}$

That is, cohort effects are derived by taking age from period effects. This formula (1) can be arranged variously, for example,

(3) $A_i = P_i - C_i$

That is, age effects are derived by taking cohort from period effects. This is the essence of the challenge that researchers face when trying to identify cohort effects (or age effects, for that matter), which filter into the study of generations. If period is held constant, which is the case in most of the research on generations and generational differences that adopt cross-sectional research designs,[18] there is no means of decoupling age and cohort effects because they are completely confounded; knowing one tells you the other.

As suggested, this linear dependency has long been known, and although it is remarkably easy to understand, it is generally considered to be an intractable problem in the study of time-graded processes where one wishes to make separate inferences about one or more of these (generally assumed to be theoretically relevant) sources of variance. Although various methodologies and analytic strategies have been developed over time in attempts to decouple these sources of variance, each one falls short in terms of truly and unambiguously separating age, period, and cohort effects from one another.[19] This issue has been characterized as "a futile quest."[20] Moreover, this confounding, even when recognized by researchers, has largely been ignored in cross-sectional studies of age and/or cohort effects, arguing that the strength of theory is sufficient to rule out one particular cause versus another.[21] The problem with this is that to advance both empirical and theoretical models of human development, one needs unambiguous definitions of the concepts under study. The concept of generations as typically understood does not meet this minimum standard of acceptable science.

Our Thought Experiment

A useful strategy[22] for developing thought experiments is to model them on existing thought experiments.[23] We thus invoke the classic thought experiment of Schrödinger's cat to inform our work.[24] Briefly, Schrödinger's thought experiment unfolds as such: "The fate of a (hypothesized) cat hinges on a subatomic event that may or may not occur according to the Copenhagen interpretation of quantum mechanics, which implies that the cat would be simultaneously alive and dead. However, someone observing the cat in the box would observe it to be alive or dead."[25] With our inspiration for this work clarified, let us proceed to the thought experiment on generations.

Imagine the following hypothetical scenario: You are a researcher tasked with identifying whether a specific behavior exhibited by a single research participant is caused by either chronological age or birth cohort. That is to say, your job is to determine whether "age" or "generational" effects are driving such behavior. For the purposes of this thought experiment, the particular behavior in question is of little consequence (e.g., checking social media on a cellphone). More importantly, the only means by which you can ascertain the cause is by seeing the results of the specific behavior exhibited by this research participant. You enter a specially designed research laboratory (see figure 27.1, panel A) and are seated at a desk. On the desk is a piece of paper that provides basic descriptive

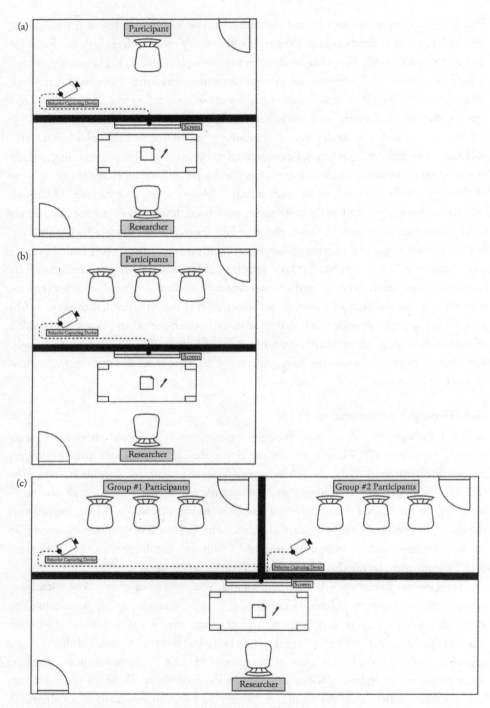

Figure 27.1 "Blueprint" of hypothetical research laboratory.

information about the research participant, including chronological age and year of birth; today's date is also printed on the sheet. In front of the desk is a screen that only displays text describing the specific behavior in question. The screen hangs on a solid partition that divides the room. On the other side of the partition sits a research participant whose behavior is observed and processed through a device that translates actions into a succinct written description of behavior that you are tasked with evaluating. After reading the information sheet, you look up at a description of the behavior in question. Using a pen, you attempt to record the supposed cause of the behavior (i.e., age or cohort) on the sheet. Which should be selected?

Given the age, period, and cohort-confounding problem outlined above, the specific cause of the behavior in question could be *either* age or cohort (i.e., as period is held constant in this case). However, an underappreciated consequence of the noted confounding between age and cohort is that it would also be equally correct to conclude that the behavior in question is caused by *both* age and cohort, as each is an equally likely cause of the behavior in question. Moreover, this conclusion would not change if you were given only information about the research participant's chronological age *or* their birth year. Again, given the confounding of age and cohort when period is held constant, knowledge about only two sources of variation (e.g., age and period, or cohort and period) completely determines the third.

Conceptual Replications

The ultimate goal of psychological theory, broadly defined, is to explain behavior at different conceptual levels of analysis. We have focused on a single actor in our thought experiment, but this setup could be altered slightly to account for inferences across such levels to the same end. That is, given the basic setup of our thought experiment, we can test several alternative specifications of these variables to approximate the idea of "conceptual replications" as understood in the traditional empirical sense of the phrase.[26] For example, the basic setup could be expanded to include more than a single research participant—for example, by focusing on one or more groups of research participants of similar or different ages.

In an expanded version of our thought experiment, imagine that a group ($n > 1$) of same-aged people are seated behind the partition (see figure 27.1, panel B). As before, you have access to summary information about their ages, birth years, and the current date. Likewise, the behavior of the group is observed and processed through the same device that translates their actions into a description of the observed behavior. However, what appears on the screen is a summary of the group's *collective* behavior (e.g., a mean, a standard deviation, etc.) rather than the behavior of a single research participant. Your task is the same in this scenario, to determine the cause of the behavior as either age or cohort. In this case, as before, the cause cannot be unambiguously determined because moving from the $n = 1$ to the $n > 1$ case does nothing to change or clarify these confounded inferences.

In a further expanded version, imagine that *two* groups (both $n > 1$) of same-aged people are seated behind separate partitions that further subdivide the laboratory (see figure 27.1, panel C). As before, you have access to summary information about the ages and birth years of both groups and the current date. In this case, the two groups differ in terms of their ages. As before, the behavior of both groups is observed and processed through the same devices that translate their actions into descriptions of the behavior. Much like in the previous replication, what appears on the screen are separate summaries of both group's collective behavior. However, now the task shifts somewhat from attributing individual or group behavior to either age or cohort to determining if any differences in the behavior observed between the two groups is attributable to age or cohort. Of note, this particular scenario is closely aligned with typical cross-sectional research that attempts to identify generations and differences between them.

Importantly, as in the cases presented above, the task is impossible, because you cannot unambiguously determine this cause. Moving from one individual to one group to multiple groups does nothing to change the confounded inferences you can make in any of these scenarios. Additionally, in the third scenario, this task is made more complex because you are considering (assumed) differences between *two* group's behaviors, which calls for an additional inferential step not previously required. This step requires researchers to impose their own value and meaning onto both group's behaviors for the purposes of comparison. Moreover, consider that even if one or both groups' behavior was *actually* driven by cohort (or age, for that matter), you still would not be able to ascertain whether any observed difference between these groups was due to either age or cohort.

Discussion

Despite a consensus in psychological science that the concept of generations does not meet basic scientific standards, many researchers and practitioners hold on to generational thinking and/or perceive incentives to create, train, or manage generations. The goal of this chapter was to present a thought experiment and several conceptual replications to explore the notions of generations and generational differences. Based on recent criticisms of these concepts and the long-known APC confounding assumption, we demonstrate that, even if generations and generational differences did exist, it would be impossible to study them in a scientific way.

In the focal thought experiment, and across two conceptual replications, the behavior that a hypothetical researcher observes is viewed through a biased lens regarding how people "ought" to act, given socially constructed views of age and generations.[27] Any conclusions drawn by the researcher in the thought experiment (and, indeed, any "real" researcher faced with a similar task) is thus influenced by knowing how such generations are socially constructed and by interpreting the situation as being reflective of one source of variance versus another. Importantly, because age and, by consequence, cohort are not causal variables (i.e., they cannot be reasonably manipulated), either explanation for observed behavior needs to be understood through an intervening variable that is sensitive to age or cohort-related change.[28] Thus, what is captured when studying age could be due to developmental processes or to any number of things that covary along with age but are generally left unmodeled.

These ideas, reflected clearly in the thought experiment, embody various long-known general methodological challenges in studying human development.[29] If one is interested in studying ageing, longitudinal methodologies are most appropriate. Of note, such methodologies can hold the cohort constant, although this is not necessary, but most allow variation over periods, by definition). To study cohorts, one needs a means to hold both age and period effects constant, which can be partially addressed in various forms of longitudinal sequential designs (e.g., "cohort-sequential" designs). In such designs, multiple longitudinal sequences are collected over a period of time from individuals of the same age.[30] By doing so, the influence of age and cohort effects are decoupled from one another (e.g., forty-year-olds in 2000 can be compared to forty-year-olds in 2010). However, and importantly, this approach does nothing to address how generations, defined as contrived groupings of a more or less broad range of birth years, are understood. Thus, while there is some value to be gained from controlling for birth cohort effects when studying long-term and contemporaneous developmental processes, longitudinal sequential designs do not address the fundamental concerns about the meaning and value that are artificially placed on generational groups when they are constructed.

Moreover, the challenges associated with "pulling off" such designs largely make them impractical for researchers to attempt without a vast array of resources, including time, at their disposal.[31] Additionally, the limitations of theory with regard to such studies must be considered, as they do not help clarify the common understanding of generations as artificial groupings of birth cohorts. More importantly to this end, there is no good (i.e., clear, unambiguous) guidance for how to accomplish this in the literature, as such groupings are largely understood to be "moving targets" that vary from study to study. Consider the absence of agreed-upon timeframes by which generational effects are supposed to emerge. Common groupings posit that a new generation "emerges" approximately every fifteen years.[32] Thus, to compare three generations to one another, at least forty-five years of time—the length of a typical research career—would need to be set aside (with appropriate funds and resources to support such efforts). For such a poorly formed idea, resources are surely better spent on bigger issues facing our society. Accordingly, the authors suggest that such an effort would be simultaneously unnecessary and impossible.

The applications of this thought experiment beyond "the laboratory of the mind" bear additional considerations as well. For example, the concept of generations and discussions of generational differences are very common in organizational settings, and researchers in organizational psychology and related fields (e.g., human resources management, organizational behavior) often invoke these ideas to study age-related processes using methodologies that are not unlike those we describe here.[33] The substantial body of published research in this area lends an air of legitimacy to misguided practice, for example, by organizational consultants who sustain a thriving "generations industry."[34] Moreover, educational researchers and practitioners (e.g., administrators at various primary, secondary, and postsecondary institutions) have variously applied the concepts of generations and discussions of generational differences to base policy recommendations and to guide pedagogical choices.[35] In cases such as those presented here, decisions about generations are made under the guise of "evidence-based practice."[36] Given the clear shortcomings of the evidence base regarding generations, their existence, and our ability to identify difference between them, there are clear challenges to such practices.

Thought experiments are useful tools for exploring specific boundaries around commonly accepted ideas in the absence of appropriate theory, data, methods, or needed resources. Indeed, Mannheim's[37] original conceptualization of generations was the product of a thought experiment, which simply asked whether social change was possible in a contrived situation where there were no new ideas brought to bear on society by members of successive birth cohorts. However, like any study, our thought experiment is not without its limitations. Indeed, it focused on a rather simplistic and narrow, yet pervasive and commonly encountered issue in the identification of generations—the confounding of age, period, and cohort. Because most research that attempts to study generations and related phenomena relies on a single time point in cross-sectional research designs, the concerns raised here apply to the vast majority of research on this topic.[38]

Relatedly, we have arguably adopted a rather positivist view on the means of studying generations and generational differences. Importantly, even nonpositivist approaches (e.g., phenomenological approaches) would suffer from the same concerns outlined here. The linear dependency between age, period, and cohort is not only a concern for positivists, as it reflects the socially constructed view of how we have defined the sequence of time as successions of years and organized age as the passage of time since birth.[39] Any empirical effort aimed at identifying generational issues, from any epistemological point of view, suffers from the same concern. In this way, the concerns raised here are arguably the most general issue faced by researchers who seek to understand these specific nuances of human development.

Conclusions

This chapter argues that the most common way of understanding and studying the idea of generations and generational differences is deeply flawed. We present a thought experiment and several conceptual replications to further clarify this point. Our hope is that, by explaining these concerns through metaphor, researchers and various consumers of research (e.g., students, consultants, media representatives, policy-makers) will see the folly in these approaches. We have struck a purposefully critical and hyperbolic tone throughout to inspire such stakeholders to read and deeply consider our arguments. If a moratorium was placed on research on generations, scholars could invest their time and energy into answering more important and meaningful questions about human experience and development.

Notes

1. N.A.S.E.M., *Are Generational Categories Meaningful Distinctions for Workforce Management?* (Washington, DC: National Academies Press, 2020). https://doi.org/10.17226/25796.
2. C. W. Rudolph et al., "Generations and Generational Differences: Debunking Myths in Organizational Science and Practice and Paving New Paths Forward," *Journal of Business and Psychology* 36, no. 6 (2021): 945–67, https://doi.org/10.1007/s10869-020-09715-2.
3. M. Schröder, "Der Generationenmythos (The generation myth)," *Kölner Zeitschrift für Soziologie und Sozialpsychologie* 70, no. 3 (2018): 469–94, https://doi.org/10.1007/s11577-018-0570-6; L. Stassen, F. Anseel, and K. Levecque, "Generatieverschillen op de werkvloer: 'What people believe is true is frequently wrong,'" *Gedrag & Organisatie* 29, no. 1 (2016): 86–92, https://doi.org/10.5117/2016.029.001.005; C. W. Rudolph and H. Zacher, "Considering Generations from a Lifespan Developmental Perspective," *Work, Aging and Retirement* 3, no. 2 (2017): 113–29, https://doi.org/10.1093/workar/waw019.
4. C. W. Rudolph et al., "Leadership and Generations at Work: A Critical Review," *Leadership Quarterly* 29, no. 1 (2018): 44–57, https://doi.org/10.1016/j.leaqua.2017.09.004; C. W. Rudolph et al., "Answers to 10 Questions about Generations and Generational Differences in the Workplace," *Public Policy & Aging Report* 30, no. 3 (2020): 82–88, https://doi.org/10.1093/ppar/praa010; Rudolph and Zacher, "Considering Generations."
5. Rudolph et al., "Generations and Generational Differences."
6. R. S. Rauvola et al., "Generationalism: Problems and Implications," *Organizational Dynamics* 48, no. 4 (2018): 100664, https://doi.org/10.1016/j.orgdyn.2018.05.006; J. White, "Thinking Generations," *British Journal of Sociology* 64, no. 2 (2013): 216–47, https://doi.org/10.1111/1468-4446.12015.
7. C. W. Rudolph and H. Zacher, "Generations, We Hardly Knew Ye: An Obituary," *Group & Organization Management* 47, no. 5 (2022): 928–35, https://doi.org/10.1177/10596011221098307.
8. H. Aguinis et al., "Thought Experiments: Review and Recommendations," *Journal of Organizational Behavior* 44, no. 3 (2023): 545–46, https://doi.org/10.1002/job.2658.
9. Aguinis et al., "Thought Experiments," 545.
10. I. Newton, *A Treatise of the System of the World* (North Chelmsford, MA: Courier Corporation, 1728).
11. Aguinis et al., "Thought Experiments."
12. Aguinis et al., "Thought Experiments."
13. J. P. Campbell and M. P. Wilmot, "The Functioning of Theory in Industrial, Work and Organizational Psychology (IWOP)," in *The SAGE Handbook of Industrial, Work and Organizational Psychology: Personnel Psychology and Employee Performance*, ed. D. S. Ones, et al. (New York: Sage, 2018), 3–37.
14. W. Strauss and N. Howe, *Generations: The History of America's Future, 1584 to 2069* (New York: William Morrow, 1991).
15. R. D. Debard, "Millennials Coming to College," in *Serving the Millennial Generation: New Directions for Student Services*, ed. R. D. Debard and M.D. Coomes (San Francisco: Jossey-Bass, 2004), 33–45; L. C. Lancaster and D. Stillman, *When Generations Collide. Who They Are. Why They Clash. How to Solve the Generational Puzzle at Work* (New York: Collins Business, 2002).
16. N. D. Glenn, "Cohort Analysts' Futile Quest: Statistical Attempts to Separate Age, Period and Cohort Effects," *American Sociological Review* 41, no. 5 (1976): 900–904, https://doi.org/10.2307/2094738; N. D. Glenn, *Cohort Analysis* (New York: SAGE, 2005).
17. A. Bell and K. Jones, "The Impossibility of Separating Age, Period, and Cohort Effects." *Social Science & Medicine* 93 (2013): 163–65.
18. D. P. Costanza et al., "Generational Differences in Work-Related Attitudes: A Meta-Analysis," *Journal of Business and Psychology* 27 (2012): 375–94, https://doi.org/10.1007/s10869-012-9259-4; Rudolph et al., "Leadership and Generations at Work."
19. D. P. Costanza et al., "A Review of Analytical Methods Used to Study Generational Differences: Strengths and Limitations," *Work, Aging and Retirement* 3, no. 2 (2017): 149–65, https://doi.org/10.1093/workar/wax002; C. W. Rudolph et al., "Cross-Temporal Meta-Analysis: A Conceptual and Empirical

Critique," *Journal of Business and Psychology* 35, no. 6 (2020): 733–50, https://doi.org/10.1007/s10 869-019-09659-2.
20. Glenn, "Cohort Analysts' Futile Quest."
21. Rudolph and Zacher, "Considering Generations."
22. Aguinis et al., "Thought Experiments."
23. R. Harre and H. T. Wang, "Setting Up a Real 'Chinese Room': An Empirical Replication of a Famous Thought Experiment," *Journal of Experimental & Theoretical Artificial Intelligence* 11, no. 2 (1999): 153–54, https://doi.org/10.1080/095281399146517; B. Wempe, "Contractarian Business Ethics: Credentials and Design Criteria," *Organization Studies* 29, no. 10 (2008): 1337–55, https://doi.org/10. 1177/ 0170840608093546.
24. E. Schrödinger, "Die gegenwärtige Situation in der Quantenmechanik," *Naturwissenschaften* 23, no. 48 (1935): 807–12. https://doi.org/10.1007/BF01491891.
25. Aguinis et al., "Thought Experiments," 547.
26. M. Derksen and J. Morawski, "Kinds of Replication: Examining the Meanings of 'Conceptual Replication' and 'Direct Replication,'" *Perspectives on Psychological Science* 17, no. 5 (2022): 1490–505, https://doi.org/ 10.1177/17456916211041116.
27. Rudolph et al., "Generations and Generational Differences"; C. W. Rudolph and H. Zacher, "Intergenerational Perceptions and Conflicts in Multi-Age and Multigenerational Work Environments," in *Facing the Challenges of a Multi-Age Workforce: A Use Inspired Approach*, ed. L. M. Finkelstein, et al. (New York: Taylor and Francis, 2015): 253–82.
28. C. Bohlmann et al., "Methodological Recommendations to Move Research on Work and Aging Forward," *Work, Aging and Retirement* 4, no. 3 (2018): 225–37. https://doi.org/10.1093/workar/wax023.
29. P. B. Baltes et al., *Life-Span Developmental Psychology: Introduction to Research Methods* (East Sussex England: Psychology Press, 1988).
30. Rudolph and Zacher, "Considering Generations."
31. K.W. Schaie and C. Hertzog, "Fourteen-Year Cohort-Sequential Analyses of Adult Intellectual Development," *Developmental Psychology* 19, no. 4 (1983): 531–43. https://doi.org/10.1037/0012-1649.19.4.531; Costanza et al., "Generational Differences in Work-Related Attitudes."
32. M. Dimock, "Defining Generations: Where Millennials End and Generation Z Begins," Pew Research Center, 2019, https://www.pewresearch.org/short-reads/2019/01/17/where-millennials-end-and-generat ion-z-begins/.
33. Rudolph et al., "Answers to 10 Questions."
34. Rudolph et al., "Generations and Generational Differences."
35. D. H. Roberts et al., "Twelve Tips for Facilitating Millennials' Learning," *Medical Teacher* 34, no. 4 (2012): 274–78. https://doi.org/10.3109/0142159X.2011.613498.
36. "Critically Appraised Topic: Generational Differences," Center for Evidence Based Management (CEBMa), https://www.cebma.org/wp-content/uploads/CAT-Generational-Differences.pdf.
37. K. Mannheim, "The Problem of Generations," in *Essays on the Sociology of Knowledge*, ed. K. Mannheim (London: Routledge, 1952): 276–322.
38. Costanza, et al., "A Review of Analytical Methods"; Rudolph et al., "Cross-Temporal Meta-Analysis."
39. S. Fineman, *Organizing Age* (New York: Oxford University Press, 2011).

Bibliography

Aguinis, H., J. R. Beltran, E. E. Archibold, E. L. Jean, and D. B. Rice. "Thought Experiments: Review and Recommendations." *Journal of Organizational Behavior* 44, no. 3 (2023): 544–60. https://doi.org/10.1002/ job.2658.

Baltes, P. B., H. W. Reese, and J. R. Nesselroade. *Life-Span Developmental Psychology: Introduction to Research Methods*. East Sussex, England: Psychology Press, 1988.

Bell, A., and K. Jones. "The Impossibility of Separating Age, Period, and Cohort Effects." *Social Science & Medicine* 93 (2013): 163–65.

Bohlmann, C., C. W. Rudolph, and H. Zacher. "Methodological Recommendations to Move Research on Work and Aging Forward." *Work, Aging and Retirement* 4, no. 3 (2018): 225–37. https://doi.org/10.1093/ workar/wax023.

Campbell, J. P., and M. P. Wilmot. "The Functioning of Theory in Industrial, Work and Organizational Psychology (IWOP)." In *The SAGE Handbook of Industrial, Work and Organizational Psychology: Personnel Psychology and Employee Performance*, edited by D. Ones, N. Anderson, C. Viswesvaran, and H. Sinangil. New York: Sage, 2018, 3–37.

CEBMa. "Critically Appraised Topic: Generational Differences." Center for Evidence Based Management (CEBMa). Accessed September 23, 2023. https://www.cebma.org/wp-content/uploads/CAT-Generational-Differences.pdf.

Costanza, D. P., Jessica M. Badger, Rebecca L. Fraser, Jamie B. Severt, and Paul A. Gade. "Generational Differences in Work-Related Attitudes: A Meta-Analysis." *Journal of Business and Psychology* 27 (2012): 375–94. https://doi.org/10.1007/s10869-012-9259-4.

Costanza, D. P., Jessica Badger Darrow, Allison B. Yost, and Jamie B. Severt. "A Review of Analytical Methods Used to Study Generational Differences: Strengths and Limitations." *Work, Aging and Retirement* 3, no. 2 (2017): 149–65. https://doi.org/10.1093/workar/wax002.

Debard, R. D. "Millennials Coming to College." In *Serving the Millennial Generation: New Directions for Student Services*, edited by R. D. Debard and M. D. Coomes. San Francisco, CA: Jossey-Bass, 2004, 33–45.

Derksen, M., and J. Morawski. "Kinds of Replication: Examining the Meanings of 'Conceptual Replication' and 'Direct Replication.'" *Perspectives on Psychological Science* 17, no. 5 (2022): 1490–505. https://doi.org/10.1177/17456916211041116.

Dimock, M. "Defining Generations: Where Millennials End and Generation Z Begins." Pew Research Center. 2019. https://www.pewresearch.org/short-reads/2019/01/17/where-millennials-end-and-generation-z-begins/.

Fineman, S. *Organizing Age*. New York: Oxford University Press, 2011.

Glenn, N. D. "Cohort Analysts' Futile Quest: Statistical Attempts to Separate Age, Period and Cohort Effects." *American Sociological Review* 41, no. 5 (1976): 900–904. https://doi.org/10.2307/2094738.

Glenn, N. D. *Cohort Analysis*. New York: SAGE, 2005.

Harre, R., and H. T. Wang. "Setting Up a Real 'Chinese Room': An Empirical Replication of a Famous Thought Experiment." *Journal of Experimental & Theoretical Artificial Intelligence* 11, no. 2 (1999): 153–54. https://doi.org/10.1080/095281399146517.

Lancaster, L. C., and D. Stillman. *When Generations Collide. Who They Are. Why They Clash. How to Solve the Generational Puzzle at Work*. New York: Collins Business, 2002.

Mannheim, K. "The Problem of Generations." In *Essays on the Sociology of Knowledge*, edited by K. Mannheim. London: Routledge, 1952, 276–322.

N.A.S.E.M. *Are Generational Categories Meaningful Distinctions for Workforce Management?* Washington, DC: National Academies Press, 2020. https://doi.org/10.17226/25796.

Newton, I. *A Treatise of the System of the World*. North Chelmsford, MA: Courier Corporation, 1728.

Rauvola, R. S., C. W. Rudolph, and H. Zacher. "Generationalism: Problems and Implications." *Organizational Dynamics* 48, no. 4 (2018): 100664. https://doi.org/10.1016/j.orgdyn.2018.05.006.

Roberts, D. H., L. R. Newman, and R. M. Schwartzstein. "Twelve Tips for Facilitating Millennials' Learning." *Medical Teacher* 34, no. 4 (2012): 274–78. https://doi.org/10.3109/0142159X.2011.613498.

Rudolph, C. W., David P. Costanza, Charlotte Wright, and Hannes Zacher. "Cross-Temporal Meta-Analysis: A Conceptual and Empirical Critique." *Journal of Business and Psychology* 35, no. 6 (2020): 733–50. https://doi.org/10.1007/s10869-019-09659-2.

Rudolph, C. W., Rachel S. Rauvola, David P. Costanza, and Hannes Zacher. "Answers to 10 Questions about Generations and Generational Differences in the Workplace." *Public Policy & Aging Report* 30, no. 3 (2020): 82–88. https://doi.org/10.1093/ppar/praa010.

Rudolph, C. W., Rachel S. Rauvola, David P. Costanza, and Hannes Zacher. "Generations and Generational Differences: Debunking Myths in Organizational Science and Practice and Paving New Paths Forward." *Journal of Business and Psychology* 36, no. 6 (2021): 945–67. https://doi.org/10.1007/s10869-020-09715-2.

Rudolph, C. W., R. S. Rauvola, and H. Zacher. "Leadership and Generations at Work: A Critical Review." *The Leadership Quarterly* 29, no. 1 (2018): 44–57. https://doi.org/10.1016/j.leaqua.2017.09.004.

Rudolph, C. W., and H. Zacher. "Intergenerational Perceptions and Conflicts in Multi-Age and Multigenerational Work Environments." In *Facing the Challenges of a Multi-Age Workforce: A Use Inspired Approach*, edited by L. M. Finkelstein, Donald M. Truxillo, Franco Fraccaroli, and Ruth Kanfer, New York: Taylor and Francis, 2015: 253–82.

Rudolph, C. W., and H. Zacher. "Considering Generations from a Lifespan Developmental Perspective." *Work, Aging and Retirement* 3, no. 2 (2017): 113–29. https://doi.org/10.1093/workar/waw019.

Rudolph, C. W., and H. Zacher. "Generations, We Hardly Knew Ye: An Obituary." *Group & Organization Management* 47, no. 5 (2022): 928–35. https://doi.org/10.1177/10596011221098307.

Schaie, K.W., and C. Hertzog. "Fourteen-Year Cohort-Sequential Analyses of Adult Intellectual Development." *Developmental Psychology* 19, no. 4 (1983): 531–43. https://doi.org/10.1037/0012-1649.19.4.531.

Schröder, M. "Der Generationenmythos: The Generation Myth." *Kölner Zeitschrift für Soziologie und Sozialpsychologie* 70, no. 3 (2018): 469–94. https://doi.org/10.1007/s11577-018-0570-6.

Schrödinger, E. "Die gegenwärtige Situation in der Quantenmechanik." *Naturwissenschaften* 23, no. 48 (1935): 807–12. https://doi.org/10.1007/BF01491891.

Stassen, L., F. Anseel and K. Levecque. "Generatieverschillen op de werkvloer: 'What people Believe Is True Is Frequently Wrong.'" *Gedrag & Organisatie* 29, no. 1 (2016): 86–92. https://doi.org/10.5117/2016.029.001.005.

Strauss, W., and N. Howe. *Generations: The History of America's Future, 1584 to 2069*. New York: William Morrow, 1991.

Wempe, B. "Contractarian Business Ethics: Credentials and Design Criteria." *Organization Studies* 29, no. 10 (2008): 1337–55. https://doi.org/10. 1177/0170840608093546.

White, J. "Thinking Generations." *British Journal of Sociology* 64, no. 2 (2013): 216–47. https://doi.org/10.1111/1468-4446.12015.

CHAPTER 28

The Sociology of Age Diversity

Sasha Johfre

Abstract

A person's age is important social information: age is a central way people make sense of one another, and it helps determine a person's status within social interactions and institutions. In part because of this, mixed-age relationships are common and can be powerful influences on people's lives: they can be welcome sources of diversity or harmful vehicles for mistreatment. This chapter considers how age orders society and the implications that has for the costs, benefits, and barriers to intergenerational connection. It further discusses how the social meaning of age goes well beyond a number and explores implications for conceptualizing age as a multidimensional construct. Future research and application may benefit from considering how connections between people of different ages, conceptualized chronologically as well as through other dimensions (e.g., related to bodies, social roles, or psychology), can promote positive social outcomes.

Key Words: age, power, intersectionality, structure, culture

Introduction

Social connection is necessary for humans from the day they are born until the day they die: people need other people to physically survive, to feel happy and purposeful, and even to define who they are as individuals. For people of all ages, being socially connected, rather than socially isolated, is one of the strongest predictors of life satisfaction and both cognitive and physical health.[1] Yet the way that that cultures around the world sort people into buckets of belonging can make it challenging for everybody to have access to meaningful connections with whomever they want and therefore to feel like they truly belong in society. In a world with access to increasingly longer lives, it is crucial to figure out ways to foster meaningful connections between people across the life course and to value age diversity.

Within half a second of meeting a new person, an actor has classified the other person into gender, age, and (in the United States) race categories.[2] This classification normally happens unconsciously. Humans classify each other into social categories because those categories are useful: in order to have any sort of social interaction, people must have a shared understanding of what their social status is in relation to their interaction partner.[3]

American culture has therefore developed a set of (largely unspoken) heuristics that help people absorb disparate pieces of information about a person (e.g., their skin color, wrinkles, clothing style, and social role) and use them to classify that person into a gender, race, and age category. The particular categories in use, while seemingly inherent and absolute, are in reality specific to time and culture: for example, the category "Hispanic" didn't emerge in the United States until about thirty years ago,[4] and the category "child" was invented in the seventeenth century.[5] Once an actor does classify another person into social categories, they use that information to make sense of them and their behavior.[6] They also use the information to judge how they should treat the person, what they should expect of them, and what status they should have in society.[7] The classification of human beings into buckets of belonging therefore structures the social world and people's experiences of it.

This chapter interrogates one aspect of this type of social ordering: age. The family roles people take on, the jobs they have access to, their status in the workplace, the clothes they choose to wear, the activities they engage in, their legal rights like voting and obtaining government benefits, and their social networks all depend on how old or young they are. The logic of age as an axis of social difference orders nearly every aspect of society.

This age structuring occurs within a new demographic context: the most chronologically age-diverse society of all time. At the turn of the last century, 44 percent of the U.S. population was under 20 years old, and 6 percent was over 60. About 120 years later, only 25 percent of people are under 20, and 23 percent are over 60. This type of demographic change is what has led many to claim that many present-day nations are "aging societies." What is more rarely discussed, but historically unique and socially profound, is the amount of chronological age diversity the world now has. As shown in figure 28.1, the U.S. population is now evenly distributed across chronological ages through the eighth decade of life; similar patterns can be seen in other highly developed nations.

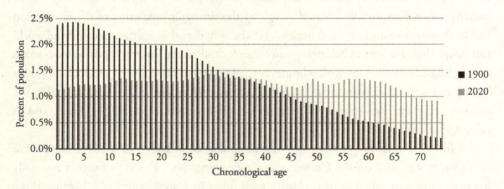

Figure 28.1 Chronological age distribution of the U.S. population, zero to seventy-four years old, in 1900 and 2020.

Note: Data from U.S. Census Bureau population counts and estimates; analysis by the author.

This demographic shift has monumental consequences for intergenerational relationships. A century ago, a person would have been unlikely to interact with anybody more than fifty years older or younger, because the average life expectancy in the United States was forty-eight years old.[8] Now, with life expectancy at birth reaching seventy-nine years old, opportunities abound to meet, befriend, and learn from people who were born a half-century or more before or after.[9] These cross-age interactions happen in families, communities, and the workforce. In 1900, only 6 percent of American children had four living grandparents; one hundred years later, 40 percent of American children do.[10] Adults are more likely than in the past to rely on their relationship with their parents, in part because delays in marriage timing and increasing divorce rates make spouses a less ubiquitously reliable family bond.[11] Among current U.S. young adults aged twenty-five to thirty-two years old, 98 percent report having regular contact with at least one parent,[12] reflecting a trend since at least the 1990s toward more frequent contact between generations in the same family.[13] Outside the immediate family, many neighborhoods have people of different ages shopping at the same grocery stores; going to the same community centers, parks, and churches; and living on the same block. Workforces frequently have members of the Gen Z, Millennial, Gen X, Baby Boomer, and Silent Generations all working toward the same goal. The unprecedented demographic shift toward longevity and therefore age diversity creates new opportunities for people to connect with and learn from people who grew up in different economic, social, and technological contexts than themselves.

In this chapter, I will start by describing a sociological perspective on age as a central ordering principle of society that is associated with status and power. Then, I will use this perspective to explain why there might be several benefits, costs, and barriers to intergenerational relationships, and I will review existing research on these features of cross-age connection and how they can be changed. Next, I will address the question of what "age" really means in the first place and why a multidimensional perspective on the meaning of age may be most effective for researchers and practitioners working on intergenerational connection. Age diversity can be powerful, and understanding how to harness it for good requires an understanding of the social processes of age and age diversity.

Age Is a Status Characteristic

Age is not as natural a characteristic as it may seem at first glance; rather, age categories, and the meanings we assign them, are products of the social world. For example, people today might feel that teenagers experience a uniquely challenging developmental period; but the concept of adolescence didn't enter the public consciousness until psychologists began labeling it as such in the last hundred years.[14] Even the concept of childhood didn't appear in Europe until the 1600s; before that, children were thought of as smaller versions of adults.[15] The stage of life now called old age only appeared after the rise of wage labor around the turn of the twentieth century, which measured the life course through productive ability and set in motion the idea of retirement; before that, people over sixty years old were not seen as fundamentally different than those younger than them.[16] Once these age categories became salient to people, they became even more "real" because people expected them to happen. For example, most people under eighteen are considered children in part because they are in school rather than the workforce; people over sixty-five might be considered old because they retired from a primary career; and developmental milestones in adolescence have continued to push back in the life course, such that even twenty-five-year-olds now are often materially dependent on their parents. The changing meaning of age categories and life transitions therefore has also changed the meaning of intergenerational relationships over time.[17] This arbitrariness of age categories shows how the meaning associated with age is not a fixed part of the human condition; rather, it has been created, and it can be recreated with different meanings and implications.

People of different ages are assumed to be fundamentally different, and those differences have implications for how they are conceptualized and treated. Age is an example of a *status characteristic*: an apparent trait of a person that determines their position relative to others.[18] The most universally salient status characteristics across the world are age and gender; in the United States, race is added to this list.[19] These "master statuses" move with people across every social context and help others set expectations about a person's behavior and decide how to treat them in return.[20] Once age is assigned to a person in an interaction, it can determine who gets respect and resources: this is evident in contexts as diverse as which sibling is likely to get to ride in the front seat in the car, the fact that people under eighteen years old cannot vote or be on juries, and whether an older or younger colleague's comment in a meeting is most likely to be listened to.

Ageism as a concept refers to the way that many people believe and act as though people of different ages are fundamentally different and deserve different levels of respect or resources. It is something people do to others, such as when somebody decides an older worker is too slow or too expensive for a job, when a person teases a friend for listening to old music, or an activist claims that COVID is no big deal because frail elderly members of society are expendable. However, it is also something people do to themselves, such as when fretting over developing wrinkles, determining they are too young or too old to try a new hobby, or deciding not to engage in a conversation with somebody sixty years their junior or senior. In many cases, ageism harms older adults, who face the most negative stereotypes toward their stage of life. However, ageism can just as easily be directed toward younger people, such as when a political candidate is seen as too inexperienced (case in point: the average age of Senate members is sixty-five years).

The assumed social difference we attribute to age is part of what makes intergenerational connection meaningful in the first place. As further described in the next section, cross-age relationships bring together people who are seen by society as different; this bridges divides and brings opportunities for learning, for sharing otherwise one-sided resources, and for more creative and innovative problem-solving. It also presents opportunities for harm, such as in the cases of child or elder abuse, where (because of being very young or very old) the victim has less power than the abuser.

The age ordering of society is complicated by the fact that the status value of age is intermixed with the status value of gender, race, and class. For example, research shows that youth of color are seen as older, and therefore more responsible and sexually mature, than their White counterparts. This interaction between race, gender, and age is part of why boys of color are so much more likely than White boys in the criminal justice system to be tried in adult rather than juvenile court, and why girls of color are often sexualized by people such as teachers at earlier ages than White girls.[21] Age and race interact in other stereotypes as well, such as the "mammy" archetype referring to old (but not young) Black women, the assumed aggression of young (but not old) Black men, and idioms such as "Black don't crack," which shows that White skin is the assumed baseline metric of aging. In the workforce, older women often feel invisible, whereas some older men are able to achieve status as wise and sought-after mentors;[22] although simultaneously, some research suggests that older women may be *less* discriminated against in hiring than older men, possibly because the stereotypes about older people are overall more aligned with stereotypes about women (e.g., having high warmth) than those about men (e.g. having high competence).[23] In intergenerational relationships, women might have both more access and more burdens: because of gendered stereotypes of care work and structural labor market inequalities, it is much more standard for women than for men to care for children, grandchildren, parents, and grandparents in the family. In some cultures, daughters are not only responsible for their own parents and grandparents, but also for their spouse's.[24] These responsibilities might make intergenerational family relationships both more common but also potentially more burdensome for women than for men.[25] The way that age governs identities, interactions, organizations, and culture is deeply connected with the way that systems such as gender, race, and class also help order society.

Benefits, Costs, and Barriers to Intergenerational Connections

Intergenerational connection can be transformative, but it is not necessarily so. The role that age has in society, and in particular its associations with status and power, helps explain why cross-age relationships can be so beneficial but also why they can be costly as well as hard to implement effectively. Each of these issues will be discussed in turn, followed by evidence-based ways to foster positive intergenerational connection.

Benefits of Intergenerational Connection

Within families, research suggests that when older adults help their children and grandchildren, they experience mental and physical health benefits.[26] These benefits include increased feelings of usefulness,[27] self-esteem,[28] mental health,[29] and overall self-rated health.[30] Even among older adults with functional disabilities, such as vision loss or mobility impairment, giving emotional support to younger family members is common. This type of support can be deeply meaningful to both parties, perhaps explaining why older adults with disabilities actually report more positive physical and mental benefits than do their able-bodied counterparts when they engage in such cross-generational support behaviors.[31]

Developing social ties with midlife and older adults is good for young people as well, and for relationships outside of the family context. For example, young people who have a meaningful relationship with a nonparental adult (such as another family member, sports coach, or minister) are more likely to do better in school, display less risky "problem" behaviors, be more independent, and have fewer depressive symptoms than those without.[32] Among youth who do have these relationships, the quality matters: young people who experience more warmth, closeness, and acceptance from the adults around them have better outcomes.[33] These relationships seem to be most impactful for otherwise at-risk youth, who face barriers to success due to limited resources in their family or community.[34]

Within the work context, research suggests that intergenerational relationships may be good for the economy. Among companies engaged in creativity-focused tasks (rather than routine tasks), age-diverse workforces are more innovative and productive than age-segregated ones.[35] In general, when workforces can reduce within-workforce segregation and alienation, diversity across nearly any dimension has been shown to be beneficial because it increases the likelihood that new ideas or skills are available to the group.[36] For people early in their careers, having multiple older mentors predicts career success, satisfaction, commitment, and feelings of belonging.[37] Even later-career workers experience benefits from being mentored by colleagues both older and younger than themselves.[38]

Costs of Intergenerational Connection

Intergenerational relationships may also impose several types of negative costs. For example, in families, grandparents who are primary caregivers for their grandchildren have poorer health, more functional limitations, and higher rates of depression, compared to grandparents who are not the primary caregivers.[39] However, this effect is confounded by the fact that having a grandparent as the primary caregiver for children is more common among poorer families, who also often face higher barriers to good health.[40] For people of all economic backgrounds, intergenerational relationships may also be costly to young people who feel rejected by adults who aren't accepting of their identities or interests. For example, queer youth are more than twice as likely to be homeless due to familial rejection and to experience discrimination at school, leading to higher rates of depression and suicidality compared to straight- and cis-gendered youth.[41] Within community programs, older volunteers (who in many cases are predominantly White and middle- or upper-class) may struggle to understand the experiences of the youth they work with (who may be lower-class youth of color), potentially undermining the value of the relationship in the first place.[42]

Finally, abuse within close relationships is disturbingly common; the CDC estimates that at least one in seven children and one in ten older adults experience sexual, physical, or emotional abuse from a caregiver;[43] the WHO estimates that worldwide, six out of every ten children and one out of six older adults face physical or emotional violence.[44] The experience of abuse by a caregiver is fundamentally about a harmful intergenerational relationship; because age is linked with status and power (with the very young and old losing out, as mentioned above), many intergenerational relationships have asymmetric power dynamics and therefore room for abuse and mistreatment. Abuse and other dynamics may make some intergenerational relationships, especially ones like those within families that may seem potentially very beneficial, deeply harmful in reality.[45]

Costs can also appear in work contexts. Research suggests that more age-diverse workforces sometimes also face challenges, including higher levels of reported ageism, resentment, absenteeism, and turnover intention.[46] One study examining over 8,500 workers across 128 companies found that workplaces perceived to have greater age diversity were also more likely to be perceived as having more age discrimination, which was associated with lower employee commitment and subsequent performance.[47] These findings show the importance of cultural contexts that change the *meaning* of age diversity and age difference: workplaces that are both age diverse and successfully value age diversity are among the most productive, whereas those that are age diverse but don't successfully value that diversity face challenges and detrimental effects. Intergenerational relationships are a tool that organizations can use to foster a productive and creative workforce, but it requires a commitment from leaders to create the formal policies and informal organizational culture that successfully values those relationships in order for them to realize their potential.[48]

Barriers to Intergenerational Connection

Despite the potential transformative effects of positive intergenerational connection, intergenerational relationships are not widespread. The fact that age is associated with status and is involved in social structuring helps explain some of the largest barriers to positive intergenerational connection. This section describes three types of barriers—age segregation, age stereotypes, and age discrimination—and then suggests some evidence-based ways to reduce those barriers.

Many institutions are strongly *age segregated*: for example, primary and secondary schools generally only have young people as students, and even within any given school, students are split into classes and grades based on their birth year. Residentially, although less extreme in extent than segregation by race or class, neighborhoods are highly age-segregated. This is both because of the existence of explicitly age-specific residences such as college dorms and retirement communities, as well as age segregation that occurs organically in neighborhoods and cities across the United States. One study found that in order to achieve perfectly age-integrated neighborhoods, nearly half of Americans (43%) would have to move to a new area.[49]

Perhaps in part because of this, friendship and social networks are often extremely age-homogenous. One large study of people across Europe in 2015 found that fewer than one in ten older adults had a close relationship with somebody outside their family who is more than ten years younger or older than themselves.[50] In the United States, research suggests that social networks are even more structured by age than they are by gender, and apart from relationships with direct descendants or parents/grandparents, age segregation in social networks is on par with segregation based on religion.[51] Furthermore, although social networks have become more gender-integrated in recent decades, they are just as age-segregated today as they were forty years ago.[52] A primary explanation for this, according to researchers, is segregation in institutions such as schools, workplaces, and churches.[53] A person is unlikely to run into somebody much older or younger when pursuing daily life and interests and therefore is unlikely to develop friendships with people who are not their own age.[54]

A second barrier to intergenerational connection is *age stereotypes*, or any belief about a person's ability or traits based on their age. People use age stereotypes when they are deciding on their own age identity, when they determine how to interact with another person based on their age, and when institutions structure their organization based on age difference. Some of the most common age stereotypes insist that children are too naive to learn about certain topics and that older people are slow to learn new technology.[55] The sticky thing about stereotypes is that they are also often rooted in some truth; however, they often distort the truth, and sometimes that "truth" may be a product rather than a cause of the stereotype. This is because once a stereotype becomes dominant in culture, it also can become a self-fulfilling prophecy given that people expect others to behave in stereotypical ways. In the case of age stereotypes, many have been found to be either overstated or false—for example, the idea that older workers cost more to employers than younger workers is not true. Although they do tend to have higher salaries, older workers also have lower absenteeism and lower turnover than younger workers, leading to overall lower company costs.[56] Age stereotypes can be powerfully detrimental, because they can be used to seemingly justify mistreatment and inequity.[57]

A third type of barrier is *age discrimination*, or when somebody treats another person as less worthy based on their age. Research shows that age discrimination, toward both older and younger people, is rampant and harmful. For example, one study sent two fictional candidate resumes to nearly four thousand firms in the Boston area that were rated by experienced hiring managers as identically hirable except for one thing: the chronological age of the hypothetical candidate. The younger candidate was 40 percent more likely to be called back for an interview than the older identically skilled candidate.[58] This type of age discrimination is well-documented and occurs across industries, job types, skill levels, and even beyond the employment context.[59]

Ways to Reduce Barriers

People in the United States and around the world need permission and opportunity to develop friendships (and other meaningful relationships) with people much older or younger than themselves. This requires two things: (1) cultural change to dismantle age stereotypes and raise awareness about the value of age diversity and (2) concrete policies to counter segregation and discrimination. There are several evidence-based ways to approach each of these goals.

While changing culture takes the involvement of many people over time in order to be effective, it is possible and important. One way to start is to develop campaigns that raise awareness, share insights, and change incentive structures in order to prioritize age equity and intergenerational connection. In one example, Changing the Narrative, a Colorado-based nonprofit dedicated to reducing ageism, commissioned artists to create antiageist birthday cards and sell them on their website. Rather than reify negative stereotypes of aging, these cards prioritize positive messages about growing older. Although it is a small initiative in the grand scale of things, this type of program creates opportunities for culture to "catch up" to antiageist attitudes by providing alternative cultural scripts. Such antiageism campaigns are examples of "consciousness-raising" projects, which are highly effective strategies that have been used in social change initiatives from identity politics[60] to road safety.[61] In the case of ageism, awareness-raising may be particularly important, given research suggesting that younger people who say they prioritize gender and racial equality are actually more likely to also be openly ageist.[62] Ageism is a form of oppression that is linked to racism, sexism, and classism, and it's time for antiageism to be part of an intersectional egalitarian ideology. Intergenerational relationships may even be a tool for organizers to use to promote gender- and race-based justice in the United States and around the world. Providing laypeople and influencers with key concepts related to the sociology of age in order to help them better understand their world can be transformative and is crucial for effecting social change.

Faster to effect are concrete policies and programs, within nations, organizations, and communities, that can reduce barriers to intergenerational connection. For example, laws prohibiting age discrimination began to be enacted in the second half of the twentieth century.[63] Research suggests that on the whole, anti–age discrimination laws are effective in reducing age discrimination in hiring,[64] and states with stronger laws see lower levels of discrimination against older workers.[65] However, the laws clearly are not fully effective, given the continued high rate of age discrimination overall and the effort and concern they generate within firms about developing age-related workplace initiatives.[66] Federal, state, and local laws against age discrimination are a crucial tool to create healthy intergenerational workplaces, but they must be combined with policies and programs that incentivize healthy age-related conversations and diversity among colleagues.

Luckily, those organizational inclusion policies and programs have evidence-based precedents. Research shows that companies that enact policies promoting age diversity, as well as intentionally embracing diversity on teams, experience better firm-level performance, lower turnover among employees, and more innovative intergenerational teams.[67] Such age-inclusive polices can include age-neutral recruiting activities, equal access to training and education for all age groups, and an open-minded and welcoming intellectual culture.[68] For hiring, research shows that when organizations implement clear hiring and evaluation systems, such as with standardized metrics and clear instructions, they not only hire and retain more talented workers, but they do so with less status-based discrimination.[69] Furthermore, age diversity in the workplace can actually help create a positive feedback loop to reduce barriers to intergenerational connection. For example, one study found that managers who had more frequent positive contact with people of very different ages than themselves were less biased in hiring decisions, thereby recruiting the most talented candidates.[70] These findings suggest that engaging older and younger workers on the same teams can actually feed the very culture necessary to make intergenerational connections more common and more effective at work.

Age Is Multidimensional

The fact that age orders society raises important questions: What does "age" really mean to people and culture? In mixed-age relationships, what is it about people that is varying? What are we really talking about when we discuss people of different "generations," such as in the very title of this handbook (*Intergenerational Connections*)?

The most straightforward answer to this question is that age equals chronology: it is the amount of time a person has lived since birth. Intergenerational relationships, then, would mean any relationship with somebody of a very different chronological age, such as a seven-year-old with a seventy-seven-year old. Extending this perspective, the age ordering of society would operate through differences in the amount of time since people's births.

There is obvious truth to this possible framework: check any dictionary and find chronology as the central definition of the word "age." Chronological age is also clearly involved in social ordering, in that it is baked into public and private institutions: for example, seventeen-year-olds and eighteen-year-olds have vastly different legal rights, forty-year-olds (but not thirty-nine-year-olds) are protected by the Age Discrimination in Employment Act, and people sixty-two years and older can purchase a Senior Pass to U.S. National Parks. In social scientific and medical research, age is nearly always operationalized in terms of one's chronological age. To a certain degree, it is perhaps painfully obvious that "age" means time since birth; after all, as the saying goes, "age is just a number."

Yet, it is also evident that age can take on meanings above and beyond chronology.[71] Whenever somebody proclaims on a dating app that they "feel younger" than they are, when a doctor measures a medical patient's "biological age," or when a young adult derides a friend's fashion choices as "grandma clothes," they are behaving in ways that suggest that a person's "age" in fact encompasses several dimensions. This tension has shown up in research as well: in the 1960s, health researchers struggled with the challenge that chronological age, while important, was not a reliable predictor of morbidity and well-being outcomes. Particularly for older adults, the variance in health status is greater within a chronological age than between ages; for example, the health difference between an infirm seventy-five-year old and a healthy adult of the same chronological age is much wider than the difference between any given seventy-five- vs. eighty-five-year old.[72] Defining chronological age as the most important and fundamental aspect of a person's age, a perspective I have called *chronological essentialism*,[73] is therefore culturally and empirically incorrect: age truly is "more than a number."

Research suggests that a more useful framework of the meaning of "age" considers age to be multidimensional.[74] Chronological age is a piece of the broader construct of age, but so too are attributes like appearance, emotional maturity, aesthetic preferences, and how long a person has worked at a particular job. Chronological age is actually quite a poor predictor of several important health and well-being outcomes compared to alternate age operationalizations, including measures of biological and identity age.[75] People often experience their life course through major life milestones (e.g., getting a first job or having children) and time horizons (e.g., believing they have a long vs. short time left to live) more so than their chronological age.[76]

Management scholars have also shown that in order to retain and utilize older workers, managers must take into account multiple types of age,[77] including generation, (chronological) age, tenure, and experience (collectively known as GATE).[78] A recent review article[79] synthesized past research on the meanings of an individual's age and found there to be at least eight broad dimensions, each with multiple subdimensions. Each subdimension could be measured within social scientific contexts (such as through surveys, interviews, or medical exams) to increase the theoretical and empirical precision of a researcher's operationalization of age. This typology is represented in table 28.1 with an adapted list of subdimensions that are particularly relevant for intergenerational connection.

The perspective that "age" refers to more than one dimension of variation has real implications for culture and policy. It suggests that whenever people (in the academy and beyond) use the word "age," they should be aware that the word itself means more than just chronology; it means all the things displayed in table 28.1 (and potentially more). It suggests that workplace age diversity initiatives should consider how to make welcoming and productive environments for dimensions of age beyond chronology, including health, family roles, and expertise. It also suggests that the very meaning of "intergenerational" connection refers not just to relationships between people of different chronological ages, but also between people who differ across other dimensions of age, such as an intern with an executive, an avocado toast fan with a prime rib connoisseur, and an agile athlete with somebody who has limited mobility. Regardless of these people's chronological ages, their social position due to their jobs, hobbies, and bodies vary in ways that are themselves dimensions of the broader construct of age. That variation is important to consider in

Table 28.1 A nonexhaustive list of multiple dimensions of age

Dimension of age	Example subdimensions
Chronological	Time since birth
	Life expectancy at age X
	Healthy life expectancy at age X
Generation	Generation/cohort
	Institutional cohort (e.g., grade in school)
Physical	Biomarkers (cellular or physiological)
	Health
	Mobility and fitness
	Appearance
Psychological	Cognitive ability (e.g., reaction time, memory, etc.)
	Emotional maturity (e.g., impulsiveness, distractibility, etc.)
Life stage	Age category (e.g., child, older adult, etc.)
	Stage in life transitions (e.g., marriage, retirement status, etc.)
Responsibility	Family role (e.g., child, parent, or grandparent)
	Civic rights and responsibilities (e.g., whether the person can drive, buy alcohol, or use Medicare)
	Workplace responsibility (e.g., whether a person is in a managerial role)
Experience	Tenure within an institution (e.g., workplace or volunteer organization)
	Expertise with a specific activity
	Wisdom and competence
Cultural consumption	Aesthetic preferences (e.g., clothing, music, slang, etc.)
	Activities and interests (e.g., hobbies or behaviors)

Adapted from Johfre & Saperstein, "The Social Construction of Age," *Annual Review of Sociology*, 2023.

its own right when thinking about what age diversity will mean in a new era of century-long lives.

The multidimensionality of age also has implications for future research on intergenerational connection. For example, beyond what this chapter has summarized, there is currently little known about the mechanisms of why cross-age relationships can be so meaningful to people's lives. One possible avenue for research could be to investigate whether variation in intergenerational relationships based on multiple dimensions of age is predictive of outcomes. Are relationships that vary based on some dimensions of age (e.g., aesthetic preferences or experience) more valuable to one or both people compared to relationships that vary based on other dimensions of age (e.g., chronology or their civic rights and responsibilities)? Extending this question to mixed-age groups (e.g., at work),

Are some forms of age diversity more beneficial than others? Using multiple dimensions of age as a way to operationalize variation in intergenerational connection could be fruitful for research seeking to understand the links between cross-age interactions and various individual and societal outcomes.

While operationalizing age through multiple dimensions may be highly effective in research and in cultural conversations, there is reason to be cautious about extending definitions of age in policy because it could open the door for new forms of bias and discrimination. While chronological age may not be the most accurate way to measure a person's age, it is accepted as a universal truth, which makes it possible to make reproducible decisions. In most nations, citizens have a concrete date of birth, tracked by their government and therefore legitimized on birth certificates, driver's licenses, and passports. It is challenging to manipulate one's chronological age beyond just waiting for it to change with time (although plenty of people try to do this, including minors using fake IDs to buy alcohol, people lying about their chronological age on dating websites or immigration applications, or even people attempting to legally change their chronological age). The benefit of this cultural acceptance of the "truth" of chronological age is that it allows for a measure of age that can help eliminate age-related bias. Deciding whether somebody is allowed to drive, vote, consume alcohol, run for president, or access social security is not up to anybody's subjective decision about how old somebody seems across more fluid dimensions of age like emotional maturity or mobility; rather, it is up to the government's determination of when exactly in the past that person was born. This allows for an objective[80] (although not necessarily fair) distribution of age-based benefits.

This is especially important because many nonchronological dimensions of age, such as perceived maturity, appearance, and health status, are intricately intertwined with systems of race, gender, and social class. This intersectionality means that decision-making based on nonchronological dimensions of age is more likely to pick up other forms of bias than is decision-making based on chronological age. For example, past attempts to limit voting rights to those who could pass a "literacy test" (which could theoretically be more objective a measure of voting ability than chronological age) were in reality a way for White supremacists to deny Black people their citizenship rights by relying on unequal access to schooling and corrupt examiners. While it therefore currently still makes sense to have some chronological-age-based rights, in order to truly embrace the full benefits of century-long lives, future research and thought leadership must consider how to build fair policies and programs of research (both public and private) that center nonchronological dimensions of age. Chronological age is, in truth, neither universal nor objective: it is a product of longstanding and power-laden social processes.

Conclusion

We are living in an era of unprecedented opportunities for long life, and with them, the most chronologically age-diverse planet our species has ever experienced. Opportunities for intergenerational connection abound and can meaningfully impact people's lives for both good and bad. Age is a status characteristic that is deeply meaningful in society: it helps structure individual experience, interpersonal interactions, institutions, and culture. It is associated with power and resource differences, with the young benefitting in some realms (e.g., being seen as more beautiful and energetic) and the old benefitting in others (e.g., access to political power, assumed legitimacy, and financial resources). The fact that age is so salient in society helps explain several things about intergenerational connections: why they can be beneficial (e.g., sharing power and resources between young and old people), why they can be harmful (e.g., abusing that power differential), and why they face barriers to success due to age segregation, stereotypes, and discrimination. The dominant cultural framework of *chronological essentialism* reifies the idea that the number of years a person has lived is a true and accurate description of how old they are, without taking into account other types of age, such as experience, health, and social role. "Age" is in reality a multidimensional construct, and cross-age relationships are meaningful in part because they bring together people who are similar or different from each other across several age dimensions (e.g., physical abilities, hobbies, or expertise). Fostering meaningful age diversity in workplaces, families, and communities is crucial to ensure that all people have access to growth, resources, and opportunities.

Notes

1. Robert J. Waldinger et al., "Security of Attachment to Spouses in Late Life: Concurrent and Prospective Links with Cognitive and Emotional Well-being," *Clinical Psychological Science* 3, no. 4 (2015): 516–29, https://doi.org/10.1177/2167702614541261; M. Maria Glymour et al., "Social Ties and Cognitive Recovery after Stroke: Does Social Integration Promote Cognitive Resilience?" *Neuroepidemiology* 31, no. 1 (2008): 10–20, https://doi.org/10.1159/000136646.
2. Marilynn B. Brewer and Layton N. Lui, "The Primacy of Age and Sex in the Structure of Person Categories," *Social Cognition* 7, no. 3 (1989): 262–74, https://doi.org/10.1521/soco.1989.7.3.262.
3. Cecilia L. Ridgeway, *Status: Why Is It Everywhere? Why Does It Matter?* (New York: Russell Sage Foundation, 2019).
4. G. Cristina Mora, *Making Hispanics: How Activists, Bureaucrats, and Media Constructed a New American* (Chicago, IL: University of Chicago Press, 2014).
5. Hugh Cunningham, *The Invention of Childhood* (New York: Random House, 2012).
6. Joseph Berger and David G. Wagner, "Expectation States Theory," in *The Blackwell Encyclopedia of Sociology*, ed. George Ritzer (John Wiley & Sons, Inc., 2007), 1–5, https://doi.org/10.1002/9781405165518.wbeose084.pub2.
7. Cecilia L. Ridgeway, "The Social Construction of Status Value: Gender and Other Nominal Characteristics," *Social Forces* 70, no. 2 (1991): 367–86, https://doi.org/10.1093/sf/70.2.367.
8. Centers for Disease Control, "Life Expectancy at Birth Trend Tables," 2010. https://www.cdc.gov/nchs/products/life_tables.htm
9. Centers for Disease Control, "Life Expectancy at Birth."
10. Peter Uhlenberg, "Mortality Decline in the Twentieth Century and Supply of Kin Over the Life Course," *Gerontologist* 36, no. 5 (1996): 681–85.
11. Vern L. Bengtson, "Beyond the Nuclear Family: The Increasing Importance of Multigenerational Bonds," *Journal of Marriage and Family* 63, no. 1 (2001): 1–16, https://doi.org/10.1111/j.1741-3737.2001.00001.x; Teresa Toguchi Swartz, "Intergenerational Family Relations in Adulthood: Patterns, Variations, and Implications in the Contemporary United States," *Annual Review of Sociology* 35 (2009): 191–212, https://doi.org/10.1146/annurev.soc.34.040507.134615.

12. Caroline Sten Hartnett et al., "Without the Ties That Bind: U.S. Young Adults Who Lack Active Parental Relationships," *Advances in Life Course Research* 35 (2018): 103–13, https://doi.org/10.1016/j.alcr.2018.01.004.
13. Karen L. Fingerman et al., "Helicopter Parents and Landing Pad Kids: Intense Parental Support of Grown Children," *Journal of Marriage and Family* 74, no. 4 (2012): 880–96, https://doi.org/10.1111/j.1741-3737.2012.00987.x; T. K. Hareven, "Aging and Generational Relations: A Historical and Life Course Perspective," *Annual Review of Sociology* 20 (1994): 437–61, https://doi.org/10.1146/annurev.soc.20.1.437; Diane N. Lye, "Adult Child-Parent Relationships," *Annual Review of Sociology* 22 (1996): 79–102.
14. Kent Baxter, *The Modern Age: Turn-of-the-Century American Culture and the Invention of Adolescence* (Tuscaloosa: University of Alabama Press, 2008).
15. Cunningham, *The Invention of Childhood*.
16. W. Andrew Achenbaum, *Old Age in the New Land: The American Experience since 1790* (Baltimore: Johns Hopkins University Press, 1978).
17. Hareven, "Aging and Generational Relations."
18. Christopher P. Kelley et al., "The Status Value of Age," *Social Science Research* 66 (2017): 22–31, https://doi.org/10.1016/J.SSRESEARCH.2017.05.001; Joseph Berger et al., "Status Characteristics and Social Interaction," *American Sociological Review* 37, no. 3 (1972): 241, https://doi.org/10.2307/2093465.
19. Brewer and Lui, "The Primacy of Age and Sex."
20. Ridgeway, *Status: Why Is It Everywhere?*
21. David L. Myers, *Boys among Men: Trying and Sentencing Juveniles as Adults* (Westport, CT: Greenwood Publishing Group, 2005); Eileen L. Zurbriggen and T. Roberts, *The Sexualization of Girls and Girlhood: Causes, Consequences, and Resistance.* (New York: Oxford University Press, 2013).
22. Toni M. Calasanti and Kathleen F. Slevin, *Gender, Social Inequalities, and Aging* (Walnut Creek: AltaMira Press, 2001).
23. Ashley E. Martin et al., "Intersectional Escape: Older Women Elude Agentic Prescriptions More Than Older Men," *Personality and Social Psychology Bulletin* 45, no. 3 (2019): 342–59, https://doi.org/10.1177/0146167218784895; Enrica N. Ruggs et al., "Selection Biases That Emerge When Age Meets Gender," *Journal of Managerial Psychology* 29, no. 8 (2014): 1028–43, https://doi.org/10.1108/JMP-07-2012-0204.
24. Evelyn Nakano Glenn, *Forced to Care* (Harvard University Press, 2012).
25. Lye, "Adult Child-Parent Relationships."
26. Karen L. Fingerman et al., "A Decade of Research on Intergenerational Ties: Technological, Economic, Political, and Demographic Changes," *Journal of Marriage and Family* 82, no. 1 (2020): 383–403, https://doi.org/10.1111/jomf.12604.
27. T. L. Gruenewald et al., "Feelings of Usefulness to Others, Disability, and Mortality in Older Adults: The MacArthur Study of Successful Aging," *Journals of Gerontology Series B: Psychological Sciences and Social Sciences* 62, no. 1 (2007): P28–37, https://doi.org/10.1093/geronb/62.1.P28.
28. N. Krause and B. A. Shaw, "Giving Social Support to Others, Socioeconomic Status, and Changes in Self-Esteem in Late Life," *Journals of Gerontology Series B: Psychological Sciences and Social Sciences* 55, no. 6 (2000): S323–33, https://doi.org/10.1093/geronb/55.6.S323.
29. Courtney A. Polenick et al., "Relationship Quality between Older Fathers and Middle-Aged Children: Associations with Both Parties' Subjective Well-Being," *Journals of Gerontology Series B: Psychological Sciences and Social Science* 73, no. 7 (2016): 1203–213, https://doi.org/10.1093/geronb/gbw094; Jeong Shin An and Teresa M. Cooney, "Psychological Well-Being in Mid to Late Life: The Role of Generativity Development and Parent–Child Relationships across the Lifespan," *International Journal of Behavioral Development* 30, no. 5 (2006): 410–21, https://doi.org/10.1177/0165025406071489.
30. Polenick et al., "Relationship Quality Between Older Fathers."
31. Meng Huo et al., "Aging Parents' Disabilities and Daily Support Exchanges with Middle-Aged Children," *Gerontologist* 58, no. 5 (2018): 872–82, https://doi.org/10.1093/geront/gnx144.
32. Steven M. Kogan and Gene H. Brody, "Linking Parenting and Informal Mentor Processes to Depressive Symptoms among Rural African American Young Adult Men," *Cultural Diversity and Ethnic Minority Psychology* 16, no. 3 (2010): 299–306, https://doi.org/10.1037/a0018672; David L. DuBois and Naida Silverthorn, "Natural Mentoring Relationships and Adolescent Health: Evidence from a National Study," *American Journal of Public Health* 95, no. 3 (2005): 518–24, https://doi.org/10.2105/AJPH.2003.031476;

Ellen Greenberger et al., "The Role of 'Very Important' Nonparental Adults in Adolescent Development," *Journal of Youth and Adolescence* 27, no. 3 (1998): 321–43, https://doi.org/10.1023/A:1022803120166.

33. David L Dubois and Naida Silverthorn, "Characteristics of Natural Mentoring Relationships and Adolescent Adjustment: Evidence from a National Study," *Journal of Primary Prevention* 26, no. 2 (2005): 69–92, https://doi.org/10.1007/s10935-005-1832-4.

34. Junlei Li and Megan M. Julian, "Developmental Relationships as the Active Ingredient: A Unifying Working Hypothesis of 'What Works' across Intervention Settings," *American Journal of Orthopsychiatry* 82, no. 2 (2012): 157–66, https://doi.org/10.1111/j.1939-0025.2012.01151.x.

35. Uschi Backes-Gellner and Stephan Veen, "Positive Effects of Ageing and Age Diversity in Innovative Companies: Large-Scale Empirical Evidence on Company Productivity," *Human Resource Management Journal* 23, no. 3 (2013): 279–95, https://doi.org/10.1111/1748-8583.12011.

36. Cedric Herring, "Does Diversity Pay? Race, Gender, and the Business Case for Diversity," *American Sociological Review* 74, no. 2 (2009): 208–24, https://doi.org/10.1177/000312240907400203; Payam Aminpour et al., "The Diversity Bonus in Pooling Local Knowledge about Complex Problems," *Proceedings of the National Academy of Sciences of the United States of America* 118, no. 5 (2021), https://doi.org/10.1073/pnas.2016887118.

37. S. Gayle Baugh and Terri A. Scandura, "The Effect of Multiple Mentors on Protege Attitudes toward the Work Setting," *Journal of Social Behavior and Personality* 14, no. 4 (1999): 503–21; Ronald J. Burke, "Mentors in Organizations," *Group & Organization Studies* 9, no. 3 (1984): 353–72, https://doi.org/10.1177/105960118400900304.

38. Finkelstein, Lisa M. et al., "An Examination of the Role of Age in Mentoring Relationships," *Group & Organization Management* 28, no. 2 (2003): 249–81. https://doi.org/10.1177/1059601103028002004.

39. Meredith Minkler and Esme Fuller-Thomson, "The Health of Grandparents Raising Grandchildren: Results of a National Study," *American Journal of Public Health* 89, no. 9 (1999): 1384–89, https://doi.org/10.2105/AJPH.89.9.1384; Meredith Minkler et al., "Depression in Grandparents Raising Grandchildren Results of a National Longitudinal Study," *Arch Family Medicine* 6 (1997): 445–52.

40. E. Fuller-Thomson et al., "A Profile of Grandparents Raising Grandchildren in the United States," *Gerontologist* 37, no. 3 (1997): 406–11, https://doi.org/10.1093/geront/37.3.406; Molly N. Williams, "The Changing Roles of Grandparents Raising Grandchildren," *Journal of Human Behavior in the Social Environment* 21, no. 8 (2011): 948–62, https://doi.org/10.1080/10911359.2011.588535.

41. Joanna Almeida et al., "Emotional Distress among LGBT Youth: The Influence of Perceived Discrimination Based on Sexual Orientation," *Journal of Youth and Adolescence* 38, no. 7 (2009): 1001–14, https://doi.org/10.1007/s10964-009-9397-9; Sabra L. Katz-Wise et al., "Lesbian, Gay, Bisexual, and Transgender Youth and Family Acceptance," *Pediatric Clinics of North America* 63, no. 6 (2016): 1011–1025, https://doi.org/10.1016/j.pcl.2016.07.005; Matthew H. Morton et al., "Prevalence and Correlates of Youth Homelessness in the United States," *Journal of Adolescent Health* 62, no. 1 (2018): 14–21, https://doi.org/10.1016/j.jadohealth.2017.10.006.

42. Corita Brown and Nancy Henkin. "Building Communities for All Ages: Lessons Learned from an Intergenerational Community-Building Initiative." *Journal of Community & Applied Social Psychology* 24, no. 1 (2014): 63–68. https://doi.org/10.1002/casp.2172.

43. "Preventing Elder Abuse," Centers for Disease Control, 2021, https://www.cdc.gov/violenceprevention/elderabuse/fastfact.html; "Preventing Child Abuse & Neglect," Centers for Disease Control, 2021, https://www.cdc.gov/violenceprevention/childabuseandneglect/fastfact.html.

44. "Child Maltreatment," World Health Organization, 2021, https://www.who.int/news-room/fact-sheets/detail/child-maltreatment; "Elder Abuse," World Health Organization, 2021, https://www.who.int/news-room/fact-sheets/detail/elder-abuse.

45. Joseph H. Beitchman et al., "A Review of the Long-Term Effects of Child Sexual Abuse," *Child Abuse and Neglect* 16, no. 1 (1992): 101–18, https://doi.org/10.1016/0145-2134(92)90011-F; Jennifer J. Freyd, *Betrayal Trauma: The Logic of Forgetting Childhood Abuse* (Cambridge, MA: Harvard University Press, 1998).

46. Aparna Joshi and Hyuntak Roh, "The Role of Context in Work Team Diversity Research: A Meta-Analytic Review," *Academy of Management Journal* 52, no. 3 (2009): 599–627, https://doi.org/10.5465/AMJ.2009.41331491; Lynn M. Shore et al., "Diversity in Organizations: Where Are We Now and Where Are We Going?" *Human Resource Management Review* 19, no. 2 (2009): 117–33, https://doi.org/10.1016/j.hrmr.2008.10.004; Hans Van Dijk et al., "Defying Conventional Wisdom: A Meta-Analytical

Examination of the Differences between Demographic and Job-Related Diversity Relationships with Performance," *Organizational Behavior and Human Decision Processes* 119, no. 1 (2012): 38–53, https://doi.org/10.1016/j.obhdp.2012.06.003; Daan Van Knippenberg et al., "Work Group Diversity and Group Performance: An Integrative Model and Research Agenda," *Journal of Applied Psychology* 89, no. 6 (2004): 1008–22, https://doi.org/10.1037/0021-9010.89.6.1008.

47. Florian Kunze et al., "Age Diversity, Age Discrimination Climate and Performance Consequences: A Cross Organizational Study," *Journal of Organizational Behavior* 32, no. 2 (2011): 264–90, https://doi.org/10.1002/job.698.

48. Stephan A. Boehm and Florian Kunze, "Age Diversity and Age Climate in the Workplace," in *Aging Workers and the Employee-Employer Relationship,* ed. P. Matthijs Bal, Dorien T.A.M. Kooij, and Denise M. Rousseau (Cham, Switzerland: Springer International Publishing, 2015), 33–55, https://doi.org/10.1007/978-3-319-08007-9_3.

49. Richelle Winkler and Rozalynn Klaas, "Residential Segregation by Age in the United States," *Journal of Maps* 8, no. 4 (2012): 374–78, https://doi.org/10.1080/17445647.2012.739099.

50. Haosen Sun and Markus H. Schafer, "Age Integration in Older Europeans' Non-Kin Core Networks: Does Formal Social Participation Play a Role?" *European Journal of Ageing* 16, no. 4 (2019): 455–72, https://doi.org/10.1007/S10433-019-00507-Z.

51. Jeffrey A. Smith et al., "Social Distance in the United States: Sex, Race, Religion, Age, and Education Homophily among Confidants, 1985 to 2004," *American Sociological Review* 79, no. 3 (2014): 432–56, https://doi.org/10.1177/0003122414531776; Miller Mcpherson et al., "Birds of a Feather: Homophily in Social Networks," *Annual Review of Sociology* 27 (2001): 415–44.

52. Smith et al., "Social Distance in the United States."

53. Smith et al., "Social Distance in the United States"; Peter Uhlenberg and Jenny de Jong Gierveld, "Age-Segregation in Later Life: An Examination of Personal Networks," *Ageing & Society* 24, no. 1 (2004): 5–28, https://doi.org/10.1017/S0144686X0300151X.

54. Smith, et al, "Social Distance in the United States."

55. Warren C. K. Chiu et al., "Age Stereotypes and Discriminatory Attitudes towards Older Workers: An East-West Comparison," *Human Relations* 54, no. 5 (2001): 629–61, https://doi.org/10.1177/0018726701545004; Mary E. Kite et al., "Stereotypes of Young and Old: Does Age Outweigh Gender?" *Psychology and Aging* 6, no. 1 (1991): 19–27, https://doi.org/10.1037/0882-7974.6.1.19.

56. Richard A. Posthuma and Michael A. Campion, "Age Stereotypes in the Workplace: Common Stereotypes, Moderators, and Future Research Directions," *Journal of Management* 35, no. 1 (2009): 158–88, https://doi.org/10.1177/0149206308318617; Uta Schloegel et al., "Age Stereotypes in Agile Software Development: An Empirical Study of Performance Expectations," *Information Technology and People* 31, no. 1 (2018): 41–62, https://doi.org/10.1108/ITP-07-2015-0186.

57. Andreas Kruse and Eric Schmitt, "A Multidimensional Scale for the Measurement of Agreement with Age Stereotypes and the Salience of Age in Social Interaction," *Ageing and Society* 26, no. 3 (2006): 393–411, https://doi.org/10.1017/S0144686X06004703; Michael S. North and Susan T. Fiske, "Subtyping Ageism: Policy Issues in Succession and Consumption," *Social Issues and Policy Review* 7, no. 1 (2013): 36–57, https://doi.org/10.1111/j.1751-2409.2012.01042.x; V. J. Roscigno et al., "Age Discrimination, Social Closure and Employment," *Social Forces* 86, no. 1 (2007): 313–34, https://doi.org/10.1353/sof.2007.0109; Benson Rosen and Thomas H. Jerdee, "The Influence of Age Stereotypes on Managerial Decisions," *Journal of Applied Psychology* 61, no. 4 (1976): 428–32, https://doi.org/10.1037/0021-9010.61.4.428.

58. Joanna N. Lahey, "Age, Women, and Hiring," *Journal of Human Resources* 43, no. 1 (2008): 30–56, https://doi.org/10.3368/jhr.43.1.30; see also a replication in David Neumark et al., "Age Discrimination and Hiring of Older Workers," February 27, 2017.

59. Boehm and Kunze, "Age Diversity and Age Climate in the Workplace"; Eva Derous and Jeroen Decoster, "Implicit Age Cues in Resumes: Subtle Effects on Hiring Discrimination," *Frontiers in Psychology* 8 (2017): 1–15, https://doi.org/10.3389/fpsyg.2017.01321; Ulrike Fasbender and Mo Wang, "Intergenerational Contact and Hiring Decisions about Older Workers," *Journal of Managerial Psychology* 32, no. 3 (2017): 210–24, https://doi.org/10.1108/JMP-11-2016-0339; Hannah L. Giasson et al., "Age Group Differences in Perceived Age Discrimination: Associations With Self-Perceptions of Aging," *The Gerontologist* 57, no. 2 (2017): S160–68, https://doi.org/10.1093/geront/gnx070; Michèle C. Kaufmann, et al., "Looking Too Old? How an Older Age Appearance Reduces Chances of Being Hired," *British Journal of Management* 27,

no. 4 (2016): 727–39, https://doi.org/10.1111/1467-8551.12125; Franciska Krings et al., "Stereotypical Inferences as Mediators of Age Discrimination: The Role of Competence and Warmth," *British Journal of Management* 22, no. 2 (2011): 187–201, https://doi.org/10.1111/j.1467-8551.2010.00721.x; Kunze et al., "Age Diversity, Age Discrimination"; Elissa L. Perry et al., "Talkin' 'bout Your Generation: The Impact of Applicant Age and Generation on Hiring-Related Perceptions and Outcomes," *Work, Aging and Retirement* 3, no. 2 (2017): 186–99, https://doi.org/10.1093/workar/waw029.

60. Nancy Whittier, "Identity Politics, Consciousness Raising, and Visibility Politics," in *The Oxford Handbook of U.S. Women's Social Movement Activism*, ed. Holly J. McCammon, Verta Taylor, Jo Reger, and Rachel L. Einwohner (Oxford, UK: Oxford University Press, 2017), 376–97.

61. Tamara Hoekstra and Fred Wegman, "Improving the Effectiveness of Road Safety Campaigns: Current and New Practices," *IATSS Research* 34, no. 2 (2011): 80–86, https://doi.org/10.1016/j.iatssr.2011.01.003.

62. Ashley E. Martin and Michael S. North, "Equality for (Almost) All: Egalitarian Advocacy Predicts Lower Endorsement of Sexism and Racism, but Not Ageism," *Journal of Personality and Social Psychology* 123, no. 2 (2022): 373–99, https://doi.org/10.1037/PSPI0000262.

63. Joanna N. Lahey, "International Comparison of Age Discrimination Laws," *Research on Aging* 32, no. 6 (2010): 679–97, https://doi.org/10.1177/0164027510379348.

64. David Neumark et al., "Does Protecting Older Workers from Discrimination Make It Harder to Get Hired? Evidence from Disability Discrimination Laws," *Research on Aging* 39, no. 1 (2017): 29–63, https://doi.org/10.1177/0164027516656142.

65. David Neumark et al., "Do State Laws Protecting Older Workers from Discrimination Reduce Age Discrimination in Hiring? Evidence from a Field Experiment," *Journal of Law and Economics* 62, no. 2 (2019): 373–402, https://doi.org/10.1086/704008.

66. Robert J. Grossman, "The Under-Reported Impact of Age Discrimination and Its Threat to Business Vitality," *Business Horizons* 48, no. 1 (2005): 71–78, https://doi.org/10.1016/j.bushor.2004.10.007.

67. Stephan A. Boehm et al., "Spotlight on Age-Diversity Climate: The Impact of Age-Inclusive HR Practices on Firm-Level Outcomes," *Personnel Psychology* 67, no. 3 (2013): 667–704, https://doi.org/10.1111/peps.12047.

68. Boehm et al., "Age Diversity, Age Discrimination."

69. James N. Baron et al., "In the Company of Women: Gender Inequality and the Logic of Bureaucracy in Start-Up Firms," *Work and Occupations* 34, no. 1 (2007): 35–66, https://doi.org/10.1177/0730888406296945; Emilio J. Castilla, "Accounting for the Gap: A Firm Study Manipulating Organizational Accountability and Transparency in Pay Decisions," *Organization Science* 26, no. 2 (2015): 311–33, https://doi.org/10.1287/orsc.2014.0950; Barbara F. Reskin and Debra B. McBrier, "Why Not Ascription? Organizations' Employment of Male and Female Managers," *American Sociological Review* 65, no. 2 (2000): 210–33, https://doi.org/10.2307/2657438.

70. Fasbender and Wang, "Intergenerational Contact and Hiring Decisions."

71. Sasha Johfre and Aliya Saperstein, "The Social Construction of Age: Concepts and Measurement," *Annual Review of Sociology* 49 (2023): 339–58.

72. Angela M. O'Rand and John C. Henretta, *Age and Inequality: Diverse Pathways through Later Life* (Boulder, CO: Westview Press, 1999).

73. Sasha Johfre, "It's Been 50 Years Since the Voting Age Was Lowered. It's Time to Do It Again," *Newsweek*, July 3, 2021.

74. Sasha Johfre and Aliya Saperstein, "The Social Construction of Age."

75. Sara Ahadi, "Personal Aging Markers and Ageotypes Revealed by Deep Longitudinal Profiling," *Nature Medicine* 26 (2020): 83–90. https://doi.org/10.1038/s41591-019-0719-5.; Warren C. Sanderson and Sergei Scherbov, "The Characteristics Approach to the Measurement of Population Aging," *Population and Development Review* 39, no. 4 (2013): 673–85, https://doi.org/10.1111/j.1728-4457.2013.00633.x.; Richard Settersten and Karl Ulrich Mayer, "The Measurement of Age, Age Structuring, and the Life Course," *Annual Review of Sociology* 23 (1997): 233–61, https://doi.org/10.1146/annurev.soc.23.1.233.

76. Glen H. Elder, et al., "The Emergence and Development of Life Course Theory," in *Handbook of the Life Course*, ed. Jeylan T. Mortimer and Michael J. Shanahan (Boston, MA: Springer US, 2003), 3–19, https://doi.org/10.1007/978-0-306-48247-2_1; Glen H. Elder, "The Life Course as Developmental Theory," *Child Development* 69, no. 1 (1998): 1–12, https://doi.org/10.1111/j.1467-8624.1998.tb06128.x; Laura Carstensen, "Selectivity Theory: Social Activity in Life-Span Context," *Annual Review of Gerontology and*

Geriatrics 1, (1991): 195–217; Karl Ulric Mayer and Nancy Brandon Tuma, eds., *Event History Analysis in Life Course Research* (Madison, WI: University of Wisconsin Press, 1990).
77. Marcie Pitt-Catsouphes et al., *Through a Different Looking Glass: The Prism of Age* (Chestnut Hill, MA: Sloan Center on Aging & Work at Boston College, 2012).
78. Michael S. North, "A Gate to Understanding 'Older' Workers: Generation, Age, Tenure, Experience," *Academy of Management Annals* 13, no. 2 (2019): 414–43, https://doi.org/10.5465/annals.2017.0125; Michael S. North and Angela Shakeri, "Workplace Subjective Age Multidimensionality: Generation, Age, Tenure, Experience (GATE)," *Work, Aging and Retirement* 5, no. 4 (2019): 281–86, https://doi.org/10.1093/workar/waz020.
79. Sasha Johfre and Aliya Saperstein, "The Social Construction of Age."
80. In truth, it may be more accurate to describe chronological age as "nearly objective" than truly "objective" because while chronological age may seem like a universal truth in developed nations, it has not always been the case, and it is still not worldwide. Not all people in the world have reliable birth records, and therefore whole communities of people don't know their chronological age. In American history, enslaved people were often not told their birthday and therefore never were never sure of their chronological age. In his memoir, Frederick Douglass poignantly described that this denial of knowledge was a tool that slaveowners could use to further subjugate personhood through making enslaved people unable to engage in some standard social interactions and bureaucratic institutions. Vital statistics such as birth year therefore help create the significance of the variation being measured in the first place. See John Cleland, "Demographic Data Collection in Less Developed Countries 1946–1996," *Population Studies* 50, no. 3 (1996): 433–50, https://doi.org/10.1080/0032472031000149556; Philip W. Setel et al., "A Scandal of Invisibility: Making Everyone Count by Counting Everyone," *Lancet* 370, no. 9598 (2007): 1569–77, https://doi.org/10.1016/S0140-6736(07)61307-5; Frederick Douglass, *Narrative of the Life of Frederick Douglass, an American Slave* (Anti-Slavery Office, 1845); David Kertzer and Dominique Arel, eds., *Census and Identity* (Cambridge University Press, 2001); Paul Starr, "The Sociology of Official Statistics," in *The Politics of Numbers*, ed. William Alonso and Paul Starr (New York: Russell Sage Foundation, 1987), 7–57.

Bibliography

Achenbaum, W. Andrew. *Old Age in the New Land: The American Experience since 1790.* Baltimore: Johns Hopkins University Press, 1978.

Ahadi, Sara, Wenyu Zhou, Sophia Miryam Schüssler-Fiorenza Rose, M. Reza Sailani, Kévin Contrepois, Monika Avina, et al. "Personal Aging Markers and Ageotypes Revealed by Deep Longitudinal Profiling." *Nature Medicine* 26 (2020): 83–90. https://doi.org/10.1038/s41591-019-0719-5.

Almeida, Joanna, Renee M. Johnson, Heather L. Corliss, Beth E. Molnar, and Deborah Azrael. "Emotional Distress among LGBT Youth: The Influence of Perceived Discrimination Based on Sexual Orientation." *Journal of Youth and Adolescence* 38, no. 7 (2009): 1001–14. https://doi.org/10.1007/s10964-009-9397-9.

Aminpour, Payam, Steven A. Gray, Alison Singer, Steven B. Scyphers, Antonie J. Jetter, Rebecca Jordan, et al. "The Diversity Bonus in Pooling Local Knowledge about Complex Problems." *Proceedings of the National Academy of Sciences of the United States of America* 118, no. 5 (2021): e2016887118. https://doi.org/10.1073/pnas.2016887118.

An, Jeong Shin, and Teresa M. Cooney. "Psychological Well-Being in Mid to Late Life: The Role of Generativity Development and Parent–Child Relationships across the Lifespan." *International Journal of Behavioral Development* 30, no. 5 (2006): 410–21. https://doi.org/10.1177/0165025406071489.

Backes-Gellner, Uschi, and Stephan Veen. "Positive Effects of Ageing and Age Diversity in Innovative Companies: Large-Scale Empirical Evidence on Company Productivity." *Human Resource Management Journal* 23, no. 3 (2013): 279–95. https://doi.org/10.1111/1748-8583.12011.

Baron, James N., Michael T. Hannan, Greta Hsu, and Özgecan Koçak. "In the Company of Women: Gender Inequality and the Logic of Bureaucracy in Start-Up Firms." *Work and Occupations* 34, no. 1 (2007): 35–66. https://doi.org/10.1177/0730888406296945.

Baugh, S. Gayle, and Terri A. Scandura. "The Effect of Multiple Mentors on Protege Attitudes toward the Work Setting." *Journal of Social Behavior and Personality* 14, no. 4 (1999): 503–21.

Baxter, Kent. *The Modern Age: Turn-of-the-Century American Culture and the Invention of Adolescence.* Tuscaloosa: University of Alabama Press, 2008.

Beitchman, Joseph H., Kenneth J. Zucker, Jane E. Hood, Granville A. DaCosta, Donna Akman, and Erika Cassavia. "A Review of the Long-Term Effects of Child Sexual Abuse." *Child Abuse and Neglect* 16, no. 1 (1992): 101–18. https://doi.org/10.1016/0145-2134(92)90011-F.

Bengtson, Vern L. "Beyond the Nuclear Family: The Increasing Importance of Multigenerational Bonds." *Journal of Marriage and Family* 63, no. 1 (2001): 1–16. https://doi.org/10.1111/j.1741-3737.2001.00001.x.

Berger, Joseph, Bernard P. Cohen, and Morris Zelditch. "Status Characteristics and Social Interaction." *American Sociological Review* 37, no. 3 (1972): 241–55.

Berger, Joseph, and David G. Wagner. "Expectation States Theory." In *The Blackwell Encyclopedia of Sociology*, edited by George Ritzer, 1–5. John Wiley & Sons, Inc., 2007. https://doi.org/10.1002/9781405165518.wbeose084.pub2.

Boehm, Stephan A., and Florian Kunze. "Age Diversity and Age Climate in the Workplace." In *Aging Workers and the Employee-Employer Relationship*, edited by P. Matthijs Bal, Dorien T.A.M. Kooij, and Denise M. Rousseau, 33–55. Cham, Switzerland: Springer International Publishing, 2015. https://doi.org/10.1007/978-3-319-08007-9_3.

Boehm, Stephan A., Florian Kunze, and Heike Bruch. "Spotlight on Age-Diversity Climate: The Impact of Age-Inclusive HR Practices on Firm-Level Outcomes." *Personnel Psychology* 67, no. 3 (2013): 667–704. https://doi.org/10.1111/peps.12047.

Brewer, Marilynn B., and Layton N. Lui. "The Primacy of Age and Sex in the Structure of Person Categories." *Social Cognition* 7, no. 3 (1989): 262–74. https://doi.org/10.1521/soco.1989.7.3.262.

Brown, Corita, and Nancy Henkin. "Building Communities for All Ages: Lessons Learned from an Intergenerational Community-Building Initiative." *Journal of Community & Applied Social Psychology* 24, no. 1 (2014): 63–68. https://doi.org/10.1002/casp.2172.

Burke, Ronald J. "Mentors in Organizations." *Group & Organization Studies* 9, no. 3 (1984): 353–72. https://doi.org/10.1177/105960118400900304.

Calasanti, Toni M., and Kathleen F. Slevin. *Gender, Social Inequalities, and Aging*. Walnut Creek: AltaMira Press, 2001.

Carstensen, Laura. "Selectivity Theory: Social Activity in Life-Span Context." *Annual Review of Gerontology and Geriatrics* 1 (1991): 195–217.

Castilla, Emilio J. "Accounting for the Gap: A Firm Study Manipulating Organizational Accountability and Transparency in Pay Decisions." *Organization Science* 26, no. 2 (2015): 311–33. https://doi.org/10.1287/orsc.2014.0950.

Centers for Disease Control. "Life Expectancy at Birth Trend Tables," 2010. https://www.cdc.gov/nchs/products/life_tables.htm.

Centers for Disease Control. "Preventing Child Abuse & Neglect," 2021. https://www.cdc.gov/violenceprevention/childabuseandneglect/fastfact.html.

Centers for Disease Control. "Preventing Elder Abuse," 2021. https://www.cdc.gov/violenceprevention/elderabuse/fastfact.html.

Chiu, Warren C. K., Andy W. Chan, Ed Snape, and Tom Redman. "Age Stereotypes and Discriminatory Attitudes towards Older Workers: An East-West Comparison." *Human Relations* 54, no. 5 (2001): 629–61. https://doi.org/10.1177/0018726701545004.

Cleland, John. "Demographic Data Collection in Less Developed Countries 1946–1996." *Population Studies* 50, no. 3 (1996): 433–50. https://doi.org/10.1080/0032472031000149556.

Cunningham, Hugh. *The Invention of Childhood*. New York: Random House, 2012.

Derous, Eva, and Jeroen Decoster. "Implicit Age Cues in Resumes: Subtle Effects on Hiring Discrimination." *Frontiers in Psychology* 8 (2017): 1–15. https://doi.org/10.3389/fpsyg.2017.01321.

Dijk, Hans Van, Marloes L. Van Engen, and Daan Van Knippenberg. "Defying Conventional Wisdom: A Meta-Analytical Examination of the Differences between Demographic and Job-Related Diversity Relationships with Performance." *Organizational Behavior and Human Decision Processes* 119, no. 1 (2012): 38–53. https://doi.org/10.1016/j.obhdp.2012.06.003.

Douglass, Frederick. *Narrative of the Life of Frederick Douglass, an American Slave*. Anti-Slavery Office, 1845.

Dubois, David L., and Naida Silverthorn. "Characteristics of Natural Mentoring Relationships and Adolescent Adjustment: Evidence from a National Study." *Journal of Primary Prevention* 26, no. 2 (2005): 69–92. https://doi.org/10.1007/s10935-005-1832-4.

DuBois, David L., and Naida Silverthorn. "Natural Mentoring Relationships and Adolescent Health: Evidence from a National Study." *American Journal of Public Health* 95, no. 3 (2005): 518–24. https://doi.org/10.2105/AJPH.2003.031476.

Elder, Glen H. "The Life Course as Developmental Theory." *Child Development* 69, no. 1 (1998): 1–12. https://doi.org/10.1111/j.1467-8624.1998.tb06128.x.

Elder, Glen H., Monica Kirkpatrick Johnson, and Robert Crosnoe. "The Emergence and Development of Life Course Theory." In *Handbook of the Life Course,* edited by Jeylan T. Mortimer and Michael J. Shanahan, 3–19. Boston, MA: Springer US, 2003. https://doi.org/10.1007/978-0-306-48247-2_1.

Fasbender, Ulrike, and Mo Wang. "Intergenerational Contact and Hiring Decisions about Older Workers." *Journal of Managerial Psychology* 32, no. 3 (2017): 210–24. https://doi.org/10.1108/JMP-11-2016-0339.

Fingerman, Karen L., Yen-Pi Cheng, Eric D. Wesselmann, Steven Zarit, Frank Furstenberg, and Kira S. Birditt. "Helicopter Parents and Landing Pad Kids: Intense Parental Support of Grown Children." *Journal of Marriage and Family* 74, no. 4 (2012): 880–96. https://doi.org/10.1111/j.1741-3737.2012.00987.x.

Fingerman, Karen L., Meng Huo, and Kira S. Birditt. "A Decade of Research on Intergenerational Ties: Technological, Economic, Political, and Demographic Changes." *Journal of Marriage and Family* 82, no. 1 (2020): 383–403. https://doi.org/10.1111/jomf.12604.

Finkelstein, Lisa M., Tammy D. Allen, and Laura A. Rhoton. "An Examination of the Role of Age in Mentoring Relationships." *Group & Organization Management* 28, no. 2 (2003): 249–81. https://doi.org/10.1177/1059601103028002004.

Freyd, Jennifer J. *Betrayal Trauma: The Logic of Forgetting Childhood Abuse.* Cambridge, MA: Harvard University Press, 1998.

Fuller-Thomson, E., M. Minkler, and D. Driver. "A Profile of Grandparents Raising Grandchildren in the United States." *The Gerontologist* 37, no. 3 (1997): 406–11. https://doi.org/10.1093/geront/37.3.406.

Giasson, Hannah L., Tara L. Queen, Marina Larkina, and Jacqui Smith. "Age Group Differences in Perceived Age Discrimination: Associations with Self-Perceptions of Aging." *Gerontologist* 57, no. 2 (2017): S160–68. https://doi.org/10.1093/geront/gnx070.

Glenn, Evelyn Nakano. *Forced to Care.* Harvard University Press, 2012.

Glymour, M. Maria. "Social Ties and Cognitive Recovery after Stroke: Does Social Integration Promote Cognitive Resilience?" *Neuroepidemiology* 31, no. 1 (2008): 10–20. https://doi.org/10.1159/000136646.

Greenberger, Ellen, Chuansheng Chen, and Margaret R. Beam. "The Role of 'Very Important' Nonparental Adults in Adolescent Development." *Journal of Youth and Adolescence* 27, no. 3 (1998): 321–43. https://doi.org/10.1023/A:1022803120166.

Grossman, Robert J. "The Under-Reported Impact of Age Discrimination and Its Threat to Business Vitality." *Business Horizons* 48, no. 1 (2005): 71–78. https://doi.org/10.1016/j.bushor.2004.10.007.

Gruenewald, T. L., Arun S. Karlamangla, Gail A. Greendale, Burton H. Singer, and Teresa E. Seeman. "Feelings of Usefulness to Others, Disability, and Mortality in Older Adults: The MacArthur Study of Successful Aging." *Journals of Gerontology Series B: Psychological Sciences and Social Sciences,* 62 no. 1 (2007): P28–37. https://doi.org/10.1093/geronb/62.1.P28.

Hareven, T. K. "Aging and Generational Relations: A Historical and Life Course Perspective." *Annual Review of Sociology* 20 (1994): 437–61. https://doi.org/10.1146/annurev.soc.20.1.437.

Hartnett, Caroline Sten, Karen L. Fingerman, and Kira S. Birditt. "Without the Ties That Bind: U.S. Young Adults Who Lack Active Parental Relationships." *Advances in Life Course Research* 35 (2018): 103–13. https://doi.org/10.1016/j.alcr.2018.01.004.

Herring, Cedric. "Does Diversity Pay? Race, Gender, and the Business Case for Diversity." *American Sociological Review* 74, no. 2 (2009): 208–24. https://doi.org/10.1177/000312240907400203.

Hoekstra, Tamara, and Fred Wegman. "Improving the Effectiveness of Road Safety Campaigns: Current and New Practices." *IATSS Research* 34, no. 2 (2011): 80–86. https://doi.org/10.1016/j.iatssr.2011.01.003.

Huo, Meng, Jamie L. Graham, Kyungmin Kim, Steven H. Zarit, and Karen L. Fingerman. "Aging Parents' Disabilities and Daily Support Exchanges with Middle-Aged Children." *Gerontologist* 58, no. 5 (2018): 872–82. https://doi.org/10.1093/geront/gnx144.

Johfre, Sasha. "It's Been 50 Years Since the Voting Age Was Lowered. It's Time to Do It Again." *Newsweek,* July 3, 2021.

Johfre, Sasha, and Aliya Saperstein. "The Social Construction of Age: Concepts and Measurement." *Annual Review of Sociology* 49 (2023): 339–58.

Joshi, Aparna and Hyuntak Roh. "The Role of Context in Work Team Diversity Research: A Meta-Analytic Review." *Academy of Management Journal* 52, no. 3 (2009): 599–627. https://doi.org/10.5465/AMJ.2009.41331491.

Katz-Wise, Sabra L., Margaret Rosario, and Michael Tsappis. "Lesbian, Gay, Bisexual, and Transgender Youth and Family Acceptance." *Pediatric Clinics of North America* 63, no. 6 (2016): 1011–1025. https://doi.org/10.1016/j.pcl.2016.07.005.

Kaufmann, Michèle C., Franciska Krings, and Sabine Sczesny. "Looking Too Old? How an Older Age Appearance Reduces Chances of Being Hired." *British Journal of Management* 27, no. 4 (2016): 727–39. https://doi.org/10.1111/1467-8551.12125.

Kertzer, David, and Dominique Arel, eds. *Census and Identity. Census and Identity*. Cambridge, UK: Cambridge University Press, 2001.

Kite, Mary E., Kay Deaux, and Margaret Miele. "Stereotypes of Young and Old: Does Age Outweigh Gender?" *Psychology and Aging* 6, no. 1 (1991): 19–27. https://doi.org/10.1037/0882-7974.6.1.19.

Knippenberg, Daan Van, Carsten K.W. De Dreu, and Astrid C. Homan. "Work Group Diversity and Group Performance: An Integrative Model and Research Agenda." *Journal of Applied Psychology* 89, no. 6 (2004): 1008–22. https://doi.org/10.1037/0021-9010.89.6.1008.

Kogan, Steven M., and Gene H. Brody. "Linking Parenting and Informal Mentor Processes to Depressive Symptoms among Rural African American Young Adult Men." *Cultural Diversity and Ethnic Minority Psychology* 16, no. 3 (2010): 299–306. https://doi.org/10.1037/a0018672.

Krause, N., and B. A. Shaw. "Giving Social Support to Others, Socioeconomic Status, and Changes in Self-Esteem in Late Life." *Journals of Gerontology Series B: Psychological Sciences and Social Sciences* 55, no. 6 (2000): S323–33. https://doi.org/10.1093/geronb/55.6.S323.

Krings, Franciska, Sabine Sczesny, and Annette Kluge. "Stereotypical Inferences as Mediators of Age Discrimination: The Role of Competence and Warmth." *British Journal of Management* 22, no. 2 (2011): 187–201. https://doi.org/10.1111/j.1467-8551.2010.00721.x.

Kruse, Andreas, and Eric Schmitt. "A Multidimensional Scale for the Measurement of Agreement with Age Stereotypes and the Salience of Age in Social Interaction." *Ageing and Society* 26, no. 3 (2006): 393–411. https://doi.org/10.1017/S0144686X06004703.

Kunze, Florian, Stephan A. Boehm, and Heike Bruch. "Age Diversity, Age Discrimination Climate and Performance Consequences-a Cross Organizational Study." *Journal of Organizational Behavior* 32, no. 2 (2011): 264–90. https://doi.org/10.1002/job.698.

Lahey, Joanna N. "Age, Women, and Hiring." *Journal of Human Resources* 43, no. 1 (2008): 30–56. https://doi.org/10.3368/jhr.43.1.30.

Lahey, Joanna N. "International Comparison of Age Discrimination Laws." *Research on Aging* 32, no. 6 (2010): 679–97. https://doi.org/10.1177/0164027510379348.

Li, Junlei, and Megan M. Julian. "Developmental Relationships as the Active Ingredient: A Unifying Working Hypothesis of 'What Works' across Intervention Settings." *American Journal of Orthopsychiatry* 82, no. 2 (2012): 157–66. https://doi.org/10.1111/j.1939-0025.2012.01151.x.

Lye, Diane N. "Adult Child-Parent Relationships." *Annual Review of Sociology* 22 (1996): 79–102.

Martin, Ashley E., and Michael S. North. "Equality for (Almost) All: Egalitarian Advocacy Predicts Lower Endorsement of Sexism and Racism, but Not Ageism." *Journal of Personality and Social Psychology* 123, no. 2 (2022): 373–99. https://doi.org/10.1037/PSPI0000262.

Martin, Ashley E., Michael S. North, and Katherine W. Phillips. "Intersectional Escape: Older Women Elude Agentic Prescriptions More Than Older Men." *Personality and Social Psychology Bulletin* 45, no. 3 (2019): 342–59. https://doi.org/10.1177/0146167218784895.

Mayer, Karl Ulric, and Nancy Brandon Tuma, eds. *Event History Analysis in Life Course Research*. Madison, WI: University of Wisconsin Press, 1990.

Mcpherson, Miller, Lynn Smith-Lovin, and James M. Cook. "Birds of a Feather: Homophily in Social Networks." *Annual Review of Sociology* 27 (2001): 415–44.

Minkler, Meredith, and Esme Fuller-Thomson. "The Health of Grandparents Raising Grandchildren: Results of a National Study." *American Journal of Public Health* 89, no. 9 (1999): 1384–89. https://doi.org/10.2105/AJPH.89.9.1384.

Minkler, Meredith, Esme Fuller-Thomson, Doriane Miller, and Diane Driver. "Depression in Grandparents Raising Grandchildren: Results of a National Longitudinal Study." *Arch Family Medicine* 6 (1997): 445–52.

Mora, G. Cristina. *Making Hispanics: How Activists, Bureaucrats, and Media Constructed a New American*. Chicago, IL: University of Chicago Press, 2014.

Morton, Matthew H., Amy Dworsky, Jennifer L. Matjasko, Susanna R. Curry, David Schlueter, Raúl Chávez, et al. "Prevalence and Correlates of Youth Homelessness in the United States." *Journal of Adolescent Health* 62, no. 1 (2018): 14–21. https://doi.org/10.1016/j.jadohealth.2017.10.006.

Myers, David L. *Boys among Men: Trying and Sentencing Juveniles as Adults*. Westport, CT: Greenwood Publishing Group, 2005.

Neumark, David, Ian Burn, and Patrick Button. "Age Discrimination and Hiring of Older Workers." *Research from the Federal Reserve Bank of San Francisco*. February 27, 2017. https://www.frbsf.org/wp-content/uploads/el2017-06.pdf

Neumark, David, Ian Burn, Patrick Button, and Nanneh Chehras. "Do State Laws Protecting Older Workers from Discrimination Reduce Age Discrimination in Hiring? Evidence from a Field Experiment." *Journal of Law and Economics* 62, no. 2 (2019): 373–402. https://doi.org/10.1086/704008.

Neumark, David, Joanne Song, and Patrick Button. "Does Protecting Older Workers from Discrimination Make It Harder to Get Hired? Evidence from Disability Discrimination Laws." *Research on Aging* 39, no. 1 (2017): 29–63. https://doi.org/10.1177/0164027516656142.

North, Michael S. "A Gate to Understanding 'Older' Workers: Generation, Age, Tenure, Experience." *Academy of Management Annals* 13, no. 2 (2019): 414–43. https://doi.org/10.5465/annals.2017.0125.

North, Michael S., and Susan T. Fiske. "Subtyping Ageism: Policy Issues in Succession and Consumption." *Social Issues and Policy Review* 7, no. 1 (2013): 36–57. https://doi.org/10.1111/j.1751-2409.2012.01042.x.

North, Michael S., and Angela Shakeri. "Workplace Subjective Age Multidimensionality: Generation, Age, Tenure, Experience (GATE)." *Work, Aging and Retirement* 5, no. 4 (2019): 281–86. https://doi.org/10.1093/workar/waz020.

O'Rand, Angela M., and John C. Henretta. *Age and Inequality: Diverse Pathways through Later Life*. Boulder, CO: Westview Press, 1999.

Perry, Elissa L., Frank D. Golom, Lauren Catenacci, Megan E. Ingraham, Emily M. Covais, and Justin J. Molina. "Talkin' 'bout Your Generation: The Impact of Applicant Age and Generation on Hiring-Related Perceptions and Outcomes." *Work, Aging and Retirement* 3, no. 2 (2017): 186–99. https://doi.org/10.1093/workar/waw029.

Pitt-Catsouphes, Marcie, Christina Matz-Costa, and Jacquelyn James. *Through a Different Looking Glass: The Prism of Age*. Chestnut Hill, MA: Sloan Center on Aging & Work at Boston College, 2012.

Polenick, Courtney A., Nicole DePasquale, David J. Eggebeen, Steven H. Zarit, and Karen L. Fingerman. "Relationship Quality between Older Fathers and Middle-Aged Children: Associations with Both Parties' Subjective Well-Being." *Journals of Gerontology Series B: Psychological Sciences and Social Sciences* 73, no. 7 (2016): 1203–213 https://doi.org/10.1093/geronb/gbw094.

Posthuma, Richard A., and Michael A. Campion. "Age Stereotypes in the Workplace: Common Stereotypes, Moderators, and Future Research Directions." *Journal of Management* 35, no. 1 (2009): 158–88. https://doi.org/10.1177/0149206308318617.

Reskin, Barbara F., and Debra B. McBrier. "Why Not Ascription? Organizations' Employment of Male and Female Managers." *American Sociological Review* 65, no. 2 (2000): 210–33. https://doi.org/10.2307/2657438.

Ridgeway, Cecilia L. "The Social Construction of Status Value: Gender and Other Nominal Characteristics." *Social Forces* 70, no. 2 (1991): 367–86. https://doi.org/10.1093/sf/70.2.367.

Ridgeway, Cecilia L. *Status: Why Is It Everywhere? Why Does It Matter?* New York: Russell Sage Foundation, 2019.

Roscigno, V. J., S. Mong, R. Byron, and G. Tester. "Age Discrimination, Social Closure and Employment." *Social Forces* 86, no. 1 (2007): 313–34. https://doi.org/10.1353/sof.2007.0109.

Rosen, Benson, and Thomas H. Jerdee. "The Influence of Age Stereotypes on Managerial Decisions." *Journal of Applied Psychology* 61, no. 4 (1976): 428–32. https://doi.org/10.1037/0021-9010.61.4.428.

Ruggs, Enrica N., Michelle R. Hebl, Sarah Singletary Walker, and Naomi Fa-Kaji. "Selection Biases That Emerge when Age Meets Gender." *Journal of Managerial Psychology* 29, no. 8 (2014): 1028–43. https://doi.org/10.1108/JMP-07-2012-0204.

Sanderson, Warren C., and Sergei Scherbov. "The Characteristics Approach to the Measurement of Population Aging." *Population and Development Review* 39, no. 4 (2013): 673–85. https://doi.org/10.1111/j.1728-4457.2013.00633.x.

Schloegel, Uta, Sebastian Stegmann, Alexander Maedche, and Rolf Van Dick. "Age Stereotypes in Agile Software Development: An Empirical Study of Performance Expectations." *Information Technology and People* 31, no. 1 (2018): 41–62. https://doi.org/10.1108/ITP-07-2015-0186.

Setel, Philip W., Sarah B. Macfarlane, Simon Szreter, Lene Mikkelsen, Prabhat Jha, Susan Stout, et al. "A Scandal of Invisibility: Making Everyone Count by Counting Everyone." *Lancet* 370, no. 9598 (2007): 1569–77. https://doi.org/10.1016/S0140-6736(07)61307-5.

Settersten, Richard, and Karl Ulrich Mayer. "The Measurement of Age, Age Structuring, and the Life Course." *Annual Review of Sociology* 23 (1997): 233–61. https://doi.org/10.1146/annurev.soc.23.1.233.

Shore, Lynn M., Beth G. Chung-Herrera, Michelle A. Dean, Karen Holcombe Ehrhart, Don I. Jung, Amy E. Randel, et al. "Diversity in Organizations: Where Are We Now and Where Are We Going?" *Human Resource Management Review* 19, no. 2 (2009): 117–33. https://doi.org/10.1016/j.hrmr.2008.10.004.

Smith, Jeffrey A., Miller McPherson, and Lynn Smith-Lovin. "Social Distance in the United States: Sex, Race, Religion, Age, and Education Homophily among Confidants, 1985 to 2004." *American Sociological Review* 79, no. 3 (2014): 432–56. https://doi.org/10.1177/0003122414531776.

Starr, Paul. "The Sociology of Official Statistics." In *The Politics of Numbers*. Edited by William Alonso and Paul Starr, 7–57. New York: Russell Sage Foundation, 1987.

Sun, Haosen, and Markus H. Schafer. "Age Integration in Older Europeans' Non-Kin Core Networks: Does Formal Social Participation Play a Role?" *European Journal of Ageing* 16, no. 4 (2019): 455–72. https://doi.org/10.1007/S10433-019-00507-Z.

Swartz, Teresa Toguchi. "Intergenerational Family Relations in Adulthood: Patterns, Variations, and Implications in the Contemporary United States." *Annual Review of Sociology* 35 (2009): 191–212. https://doi.org/10.1146/annurev.soc.34.040507.134615.

Uhlenberg, Peter. "Mortality Decline in the Twentieth Century and Supply of Kin over the Life Course." *Gerontologist* 36, no. 5 (1996): 681–85.

Uhlenberg, Peter, and Jenny de Jong Gierveld. "Age-Segregation in Later Life: An Examination of Personal Networks." *Ageing & Society* 24, no. 1 (2004): 5–28. https://doi.org/10.1017/S0144686X0300151X.

Waldinger, Robert J., Shiri Cohen, Marc S. Schulz, and Judith A. Crowell. "Security of Attachment to Spouses in Late Life: Concurrent and Prospective Links with Cognitive and Emotional Wellbeing." *Clinical Psychological Science* 3, no. 4 (2015): 516–29. https://doi.org/10.1177/2167702614541261.

Whittier, Nancy. "Identity Politics, Consciousness Raising, and Visibility Politics." In *The Oxford Handbook of US Women's Social Movement Activism*, edited by Holly J. McCammon, Verta Taylor, Jo Reger, and Rachel L. Einwohner, 376–97. Oxford, UK: Oxford University Press, 2017.

Williams, Molly N. "The Changing Roles of Grandparents Raising Grandchildren." *Journal of Human Behavior in the Social Environment* 21, no. 8 (2011): 948–62. https://doi.org/10.1080/10911359.2011.588535.

Winkler, Richelle, and Rozalynn Klaas. "Residential Segregation by Age in the United States." *Journal of Maps* 8, no. 4 (2012): 374–78. https://doi.org/10.1080/17445647.2012.739099.

World Health Organization. "Child Maltreatment," 2021. https://www.who.int/news-room/fact-sheets/detail/child-maltreatment.

World Health Organization. "Elder Abuse," 2021. https://www.who.int/news-room/fact-sheets/detail/elder-abuse.

Zurbriggen, Eileen L., and T. Roberts. *The Sexualization of Girls and Girlhood: Causes, Consequences, and Resistance*. New York: Oxford University Press, 2013.

CHAPTER 29

Evaluating Intergenerational Strategies to Enhance Individual and Community Development

Shannon E. Jarrott

> **Abstract**
>
> This chapter addresses evaluation strategies to enhance understanding of intergenerational programs that support diverse goals for varied stakeholder groups. It describes how intergenerational program evaluation has developed. As innovative programs continue to emerge, evaluation methods and documented outcomes have expanded, while some challenges persist. The chapter offers a call to action for current program evaluators, providing strategies to enhance understanding, success, and sustainability of intergenerational programs. Partnerships are emphasized to include participants, families, and staff. Resources to improve the trustworthiness of evaluation results are offered. Methods for communicating findings to partners strengthen partnerships to enhance evaluation data and program stability. Documenting responsive, creative intergenerational programs with appropriate evaluation methods will strengthen and extend intergenerational strategies into other communities.
>
> **Key Words:** program evaluation, community-based participatory methods, measurement, intergenerational program, contact theory

Introduction

With the previous *Handbook* chapters demonstrating the range of needs and opportunities that can be addressed with youth and older adults of vastly different ages, abilities, and backgrounds, a concluding chapter on evaluating these programs could take many directions. This chapter provides context on how intergenerational program evaluation has developed. Next, specific intergenerational program evaluation strategies are described and illustrated. The chapter concludes with a call to action for program practitioners, funders, and evaluators invested in comprehending intergenerational program processes and outcomes for different groups.

Background on Intergenerational Program Evaluation

Early program evaluation research commonly involved young children in preschool through primary school and independent older adults.[1] Foster Grandparents is one of the oldest intergenerational programs, placing independent community adults in elementary schools since 1965. The older volunteers could complete surveys or interviews, and age-appropriate measures were developed for the children. An early paper by Rybak and colleagues described foster grandparents serving in a nursery; the older adults described feeling more youthful, financially secure, and happier after six months of participation.[2]

Programming also took place in nursing homes and adult day service programs, but information was rarely gathered on adult participants due to their limited ability, actual or anticipated, to provide reliable self-report.[3] Observational scales were introduced by Newman and colleagues[4] to represent social behaviors of young and older participants. A recent review of intergenerational studies involving adults with dementia noted outcomes such as mental health indicators, including depression and loneliness, attitudes, and functional health indicators, such as activities of daily living.[5]

Early evaluations painted a consistent, if limited, picture of intergenerational programs in which benefits predominated.[6] Studies shaped expectations of who participated in intergenerational programs, whose experiences were worth evaluating, and what outcomes could be achieved. A deficit orientation is reflected in studies that assessed only one participant group or that relied on proxy rather than direct reporting. Scholars perpetuated this perspective by categorizing programs as youth serving older adults, adults serving youth, and youth and older adults receiving services jointly.[7] While the typology was created to simplify categorization of programs, it reinforced a deficit view of most intergenerational programming.

Fortunately, intergenerational programs are extraordinarily adaptive to different community needs and resources. With the 1990s asset-based community development (ABCD) model, a strengths-based orientation emerged.[8] Kretzman and McKnight's community model was complimented by the Reggio Emilia child development model and Baltes and Baltes' lifespan perspective and selective optimization with compensation models of adult development.[9] These emphasized individuals as adaptive, competent learners developing throughout the life course. With this shift to strengths-based views of participants, intergenerational programming expanded. Groups like Generations United responded with programming and evaluation resources such as the Under One Roof guide.[10] Generations Together, which operated out of the University of Pittsburgh from 1979 into the early 2000s facilitated an Intergenerational Specialist Certificate that included training on setting goals and evaluating program outcomes.[11]

Intergenerational program evaluation has evolved to reflect the growing knowledge base. The expansion of information has its benefits and drawbacks for any evaluator or practitioner. Examples abound for different programs delivered in varied contexts, thereby providing numerous models to inspire others. However, resources to guide implementation and evaluation of these different programs remain limited. Systematic reviews of program evaluations revealed a common practice in which evaluators created a new measure specific to their intergenerational program.[12] Study authors rarely reported indicators of the instrument's psychometrics.[13] Thus, despite having diverse programming examples, intergenerational professionals find limited choices of reliable, valid instruments appropriate for the intergenerational context.

Still, noteworthy changes in intergenerational program evaluation reflect the growing diversity of programs, including participants, program content, and settings. For example, responding to the growing call for environmental action shared by members of all generations, Ayalon and colleagues developed a measure of older adults' perceptions of young people's role in climate action.[14] They are confident that the instrument can help practitioners facilitate and assess programming that unites young and older people in climate action.

Relatedly, measured outcomes have diversified. Whereas measurement of attitudes about older adults predominated in early evaluations, outcomes now include indicators of physical, cognitive, social, and mental health; knowledge; and behaviors.[15] The increasing range of outcomes evaluated reflects the increasing disciplinary breadth represented within intergenerational programs. For example, a recent evaluation of children's perceptions of an intergenerational shared-site program focused on design features that impact intergenerational exchange.[16] Norouzi and colleagues demonstrated the value of inviting young people to offer input on the design of spaces they will use and highlighted the physical environment's influence on intergenerational program outcomes.

The experiences of multiple participant groups are represented more frequently in contemporary evaluations than previously, when youth were commonly the sole group represented.[17] Evaluations of different perspectives include program staff.[18] In Weaver and colleagues' evaluation, staff members offered feedback about learning to implement evidence-based intergenerational practices.[19] Themes related to practice-evaluation partnerships included needs for support from supervisors, equal status with program evaluators, cooperation with program evaluators, and positive communication with the evaluation team. Evaluators modified their strategies based on these findings, which supported enhanced programming and evaluation outcomes.[20]

Although intergenerational research findings were predominantly positive, some findings were equivocal. Evaluations in which preschoolers demonstrated no change or poorer attitudes toward older adults following intergenerational program participation led practitioners to raise concerns about involving young children or frail older adults in programming.[21] Fortunately, scholars and practitioners partnered to study the mechanisms by which change occurs in the intergenerational setting.[22] As chapters in this text reflect, how youth and older adults are brought together is as or more important than what they do together.[23] Associating specific practices with program outcomes reflects and should inform program evaluation. For example, Jarrott and colleagues linked practices that paired participants with higher levels of intergenerational interaction compared to activities when these practices were not used.[24] Such findings speak to the value of evaluation that documents outcomes and the practices that support their achievement.

Finally, press from funders contributes to the development of intergenerational program evaluation. Programs increasingly find that grant applications are stronger if they can share evaluation data to demonstrate need and past successes. Also, funders are likely to specify that funded projects implement an evaluation plan and report outcome results.

Despite all the developments in intergenerational program evaluation, some things have not changed. Colleagues repeatedly cite limitations associated with small, homogenous samples, simple pre-post measures without follow-up, and use of measures lacking indicators of reliability or validity.[25] The next section offers evaluation strategies that can enhance the process and utility of program evaluation and reduce the challenges evaluators frequently face.

Intergenerational Program Evaluation Strategies

Establish Evaluation-Practice Partnerships

Evaluation and practice experts need each other—always. An evaluation/practice partnership offers several advantages and is supported by a few simple steps. A benefit to programs working with an evaluator is that evaluators can offer best evaluation practices and contemporary knowledge of intergenerational program evidence that most organizations do not have on staff. Evaluators also benefit from collaborating with program staff who possess invaluable contextual expertise. They can share program history, licensing and organizational policy, programming logistics, and recent events that impact evaluation efforts. The partnership should also involve organizational stakeholders. Sharing evaluation plans and inviting questions and feedback from stakeholders, including staff and participants, honors the expertise that each stakeholder group represents. As a result, investment in the evaluation grows, contributing to a more reliable outcome.

Engaging different groups reflects the intergroup contact theory tenet of *secure support from authority figures, custom, or law.*[26] Designed to promote positive contact between disparate groups, contact theory is the most widely cited theory guiding intergenerational programs and can also be applied to collaborations among evaluation partners.[27] When evaluators leave out groups, tension and distrust can negatively impact the relationship and evaluation process.[28] Engaging organizational shareholders is especially important when shareholders belong to groups frequently disenfranchised from planning that affects them, such as low-wage workers, persons from minoritized groups, and the focal participants of intergenerational programs—youth and older adults.[29]

Collaborative program evaluation partnerships should balance context, needs, and resources. For example, leaders of a program serving primarily teens and independent older adults of color in an under-resourced community might find a participatory method appropriate, as it recognizes member expertise and invites their input at each stage of the process. As in this example, the participatory method can be especially powerful when it involves groups often excluded from decision-making. In other settings, such intensive collaboration may be neither necessary nor appropriate. Considering a shared-site day program providing preschool and adult day services, partners may lack the resources to engage all stakeholders, such as family caregivers and staff, in co-construction of the program evaluation. In these cases, advisory councils may be formed with a few representatives from each stakeholder group.[30] The evaluator can create accessible communications about the process and provide windows of time for stakeholders to offer input and ask questions.

The evaluation and program partners should have a contract or memorandum of understanding that specifies evaluation goals and guides the evaluation and communication of findings. An example for intergenerational partners can be found in a resource created by Henkin and Patterson.[31] The clear statement of program goals enables evaluators to align their efforts with these goals. This seems obvious, but reports of intergenerational program outcomes do not always reflect program goals. To illustrate, intergenerational program reports typically address change in young persons' attitudes about older adults even though different reasons for implementing the program are articulated by report authors.[32] Clarity of program goals can and should guide program evaluators.

Prepare for Program Evaluation
VERIFY INTENDED PROGRAM GOALS
Evaluators can start their evaluation planning with the intergenerational program's mission statement; if this does not exist, the organization's mission statement offers a useful guide. Communicating with partners, including administrators and programming staff, about why their organization offers the intergenerational program should shed light on its purpose. Responses will likely reflect shared and distinct goals for multiple groups, including young and older participants and other groups like family members of participants or program staff. Evaluators can check their understanding of program goals with partners to represent them in the evaluation plan.

ALIGN EVALUATION PLANS WITH PROGRAM GOALS
Programming goals drive the evaluation. Goals inform what is evaluated, who is evaluated, and how the evaluation is conducted. Evaluation plans must also account for context and available resources. Balancing this tension requires communication among partners and a healthy dose of perspective.

Commonly, evaluators report on output, outcome, and process indicators. Output represents exposure to the program, such as a count of the number of intergenerational competitors in the local intergenerational Olympics. This information reflects program implementation and should help shape future events. Another common output indicator involves the number of intergenerational sessions attended. With these numbers, evaluators can estimate the cost of delivering programming per person or per activity, which may be useful for budgeting.

Outputs are important, but they rarely capture the impact of programming. To do this, *outcomes* need to be assessed. Outcomes indicate the influence of program participation on some phenomenon of interest, such as a child's empathy or an older adult's report of loneliness. It is common to distinguish the two by describing output as the "what" and outcome as the "why." These connotations point to the value of knowing the purpose and goals of the intergenerational program, which typically describes what the program does *and* why.

In addition to knowing the "what" and "why" of intergenerational programs, evaluators should represent the "how" by capturing process and contextual indicators of the program. Process indicators might include the steps taken to implement an intergenerational program. For example, scholars emphasize the importance of preparing staff and participants for programming;[33] thus, process indicators could describe who completed preparatory training and what it entailed. Other process indicators might include identification of specific practices used during programming.[34] An observational tool that captures those practices used in conjunction with an outcome measure can help practitioners understand "how" programming supported outcomes.

Contextual indicators document unique characteristics or events that may influence outcomes. An example comes from an early study by Seefeldt.[35] Preschool children who joined programming with nursing home residents demonstrated more negative attitudes about older adults at the end of the program than a group of age peers who had not participated in organized intergenerational activities. These outcome data could indicate that intergenerational programs are harmful or that they shouldn't be conducted in older adult care settings. However, the authors provided an important contextual indicator; they described that participating older adults were largely unresponsive and could not interact with the children due to their health conditions. This contextual information highlights the importance of involving participants who can interact with their intergenerational partners. Since this early evaluation, numerous evaluations of programs involving young children and frail older adults have demonstrated positive outcomes for youth and adults alike.[36]

Evaluators are encouraged to capture output, outcome, process, and contextual data that reflect intergenerational program goals. Gathering just one source of information will leave stakeholders without a full picture of the program's value. Knowing that a program reached a thousand people may be impressive but is meaningless if participation did not advance program goals. Demonstrating impact without information on how it was achieved challenges sustainability and replication of the positive effects. Methods exist to support efficient collection, analysis, and reporting of intergenerational output, outcome, and process evaluation data. The next section addresses some of these strategies.

Conduct the Program Evaluation—Recommendations

Program evaluators and community-based researchers are interested in collecting evaluation data over time. Working with community partners, however, evaluators should be mindful of the burden that evaluation places on stakeholders. Whether it's inviting families to complete a survey or asking staff to remind families to complete those surveys, evaluation places demands on all involved. When considering these demands, evaluators need to recall the golden rule of evaluation: align evaluation efforts with program goals.

To demonstrate progress toward goals, evaluation data may need to be gathered at different intervals. Daily evaluation records might indicate how many older adults and youth choose to sit at the intergenerational lunch table offered Monday through Friday. Periodic assessments could address the question "Do new program leaders use 80 percent of the intergenerational best practices within two months of onboarding?" Evaluation data may be recorded before and after a period of programming to reflect change (e.g., "How are students' reading scores different after six months of twice weekly sessions with a trained older adult helper?"). Partners might contribute to assessments annually, such as having older residents recommend features for next year's intergenerational program. Even longitudinal data, woefully underrepresented in intergenerational program evaluations, could figure into evaluation plans to demonstrate progress toward goals (e.g., "What are the long-term effects on attitudes toward one's own aging among youth participants in shared-site preschool programs?").

Frequently collected evaluation data often falls short of demonstrating progress toward goals. Satisfaction surveys, commonly collected at the end of an intergenerational program, may address one goal of programming—to offer a satisfying experience to participants—but are a poor means to detect change resulting from joining the program. Pre-post evaluation methods, in which an assessment is administered before programming and at the end of programming, offer an opportunity to note change during this window of time, but they also face limitations. The immediate benefits of program participation may not indicate long-term effects. Aday and colleagues offered a rare one-year and five-year follow-up evaluation that indicated sustained improvement in attitudes toward older adults among youth who participated in a nine-month intergenerational program.[37] Collecting such data is difficult, whether due to participant mobility that makes tracking difficult or because program funding will not sustain longitudinal data collection. Here, too, the value of evaluation-practice partnerships proves important, as partners may collaborate to conduct follow-up investigations beyond the period of a grant-funded project, thereby adding to comprehension of program impact.

Evaluators can also err on the side of gathering too much data, which can diminish reliability and support of the evaluation effort among involved stakeholders. To illustrate, evaluators of a shared-site intergenerational program[38] asked program leaders to complete a form every time they led an intergenerational activity, which was typically two times per week, for about two years. Some program leader supported the effort diligently, completing the form shortly after each activity. Others sometimes let weeks go by before completing a batch of forms all at once. Their other duties made it difficult to complete the form after each activity. Completing the tool weeks after an activity, the program leader may not have accurately recalled which practices were used during different activities, thereby affecting the quality of the evaluation data. In focus group interviews at the end of the evaluation, program leaders suggested that the tool might still be useful if administered less frequently—such as when new programming was initiated or when a new program leader was starting their intergenerational practice. This would reduce the burden on program leaders and would likely increase the reliability of reported evaluation data.

Take Perspective on all Stakeholders Involved to the Fullest Extent Possible

Contact theory offers guidance on who to include in an intergenerational program evaluation.[39] As support from authority figures is essential to program success, the range of authority figures should be represented as much as possible. While the term "authority figure" commonly conjures up images of parents, police officers, and school principals, in this case they are persons with the power to impact the operation—even the existence—of an intergenerational program. Thus, authority figures include participants, staff or volunteers who facilitate programming, and administrators who designate space, staff time, and other resources to the program. It may include participants' family members if the youth are minors and the adult participants are in care settings. Other authority figures may include advisory board members, regulators responsible for ensuring compliance with safety and operational codes, and staff indirectly impacted by program operations—such as custodians who find themselves cleaning up after additional people. Representing all these voices lends richness and validity to evaluation results, and it creates logistical complexity. These additional steps are prohibitive for some projects, as reflected in the limited number of published evaluations that include perspectives of persons other than participants.[40]

Different perspectives can be represented in varied ways. A single measure may be appropriate for different partner groups if it captures a goal shared by the groups and is valid for the groups' ages and abilities. For example, a service-learning program involving university students and retirees designed to enhance social connection and reduce loneliness among both groups might administer the UCLA loneliness scale to young and older participants.[41] Often, multiple evaluation tools will be needed to demonstrate progress toward common and distinct goals for participants and other partner groups. For example, in a scoping review of intergenerational programs involving adolescents and residents of aged care homes, DeBellis and colleagues reported a range of outcomes that would require different measurements reflecting the varied goals and focal population, such as youth interpersonal skills and attitudes toward aging, and older adult engagement and adaptation to the residential care setting.[42]

Outcomes of interest for other partner groups should reflect their unique perspective. A parent might describe a child's comfort interacting with grandparents or other older adults outside of the intergenerational program setting.[43] An administrator could address whether the intergenerational program supports the organization's mission and helps to recruit new clients.[44] A teacher or staff member might speak to their confidence facilitating intergenerational programming. When achievement of intergenerational program goals depends on the support of others, which it always does, those perspectives should be represented in the evaluation.

Use Reliable Measures

Systematic and scoping reviews of intergenerational research involving different groups of youth and older adult participants frequently present measures created by the authors for the study.[45] Creating a new measure for a project may be the best way to align evaluations with program goals. However, using evaluation instruments lacking evidence of reliability and validity leaves stakeholders to question the accuracy of findings.

Reliable, valid measures are frequently used in intergenerational research.[46] Many of these have been compiled in the Intergenerational Evaluation Toolkit, which provides instruments used in published, peer-reviewed research evaluating intergenerational programs. The researchers described the psychometrics of the instruments, which were used with early childhood, youth, older adults, and activity leader partners. Measurement outcomes ranged from attitudinal measures to developmental indicators like ego integrity and generativity, to socioemotional indicators like anxiety, loneliness, and morale. For each curated instrument, the toolkit describes (1) target population, (2) construct measured, (3) instrument length, (4) procedures for using the scale, (5) psychometric indicators, (6) the citation(s) for the instrument, including its application to intergenerational evaluation, and (7) a print-friendly copy of the instrument or link to access the instrument.

Also in the Intergenerational Program Evaluation Toolkit, readers can access the Intergenerational Program Evaluation Tool (IPET).[47] The authors created the IPET to shine light on the "black box" of intergenerational programming.[48] Guided by contact theory, the IPET developers identified observable indicators of relationship building (interaction and positive affect). Finding that program leaders' practices impact the response to programming, they also wanted to identify practices that promote these indicators.[49] The scale was developed in a setting where children and older adults receiving care often had difficulty self-reporting their experiences; thus, the instrument uses an observational method to represent participant experiences.

The tool consists of two parts. Part 1 of the IPET represents program leaders' use of practices before, during, and after individual activities.[50] Additionally, part 1 captures basic information to support activity tracking, a summary indicator of youth and older adult participant engagement and affect, and facilitator notes. Facilitators can read about the practices and then use this tool to note which practices they used. In this manner, activity leaders can build their skills using evidence-based practices and understand which practices are important for their participant and program context. Evaluators might use the IPET in conjunction with other outcome measures, such as youth self-efficacy or older adult morale.

Part 2 of the IPET is designed for in-house program evaluation when persons conducting the evaluation have limited evaluation experience. In the part 2 worksheet, program leaders identify goals for their youth and older adult participants and note progress toward those goals. Unlike part 1, which reflects a single intergenerational activity, adopters of part 2 are encouraged to review progress toward goals periodically, such as monthly.

The IPET will suit some intergenerational programs, but evaluators may need additional tools to reflect their program goals. The Intergenerational Evaluation Toolkit emphasizes quantitative measures; validity and reliability can be calculated for these, and they can be an efficient way to gather information consistently.[51] Qualitative evaluation data, such as observational notes and stakeholder interviews, are also sources of potentially rich data that can be gathered on an ongoing or periodic basis.

Evaluators are encouraged to adopt instruments and methods that have proven effective in the intergenerational field. Using established measures can save evaluators time and increase confidence in evaluation results.

Align Evaluation Plans with Resources

Organizations must be mindful of their resources and balance the desire to generate new knowledge with work demanded of staff/participants to support the effort.[52] Professional evaluators can recommend any number of evidence-based practices, including those in this chapter, to improve the quality of evaluation data and enhance understanding of a program's impact. While evaluation plans need to align with program goals and reflect evidence-based practices, they should also honor available resources. This section addresses strategies to balance evaluation requirements and associated demands on stakeholders.

Most organizations are already gathering data, some of which may be useful for program evaluation procedures. For example, care agencies like child care centers and residential care settings collect indicators for licensing and accreditation that may offer insight into intergenerational program outcomes. For example, Turner and colleagues combined data on participation in intergenerational programming among adult day service participants with regulatory data on meal and fluid consumption.[53] They determined that adults who joined intergenerational activities before lunch consumed greater proportions of their meal, a valuable indicator of the goal to offer intergenerational programming to improve participant health. In this way, evaluators leveraged access to standard data collection (meal and fluid consumption) with a simple activity-tracking measure to enhance understanding of intergenerational program impact. Other groups, such as schools, might combine data on participation in a mentoring program with the school's standardized learning and socioemotional skills assessments, as Experience Corps has done.[54] In this way, the only new data to be tracked is participation in the mentoring program. Evaluators should learn what data are available that align with intergenerational program goals and could support the evaluation. Then, evaluators should confirm that information is gathered in a manner consistent with administration guidelines. Working with available data can help minimize collection of additional evidence.

When evaluators have identified gaps between data being gathered and evidence needed to demonstrate progress toward program goals, they should explore options for integrating collection of this information with routine documentation. For example, if a community center routinely administers an annual satisfaction and interest survey, they might add two to three items about respondents' experience and interest related to intergenerational programming at the center. If an intergenerational theater program concludes with discussion of what worked well and what the group might try differently next time, these conversations could be documented and reviewed on a periodic basis to see how experiences change across the project. Streamlining data collection can help invest partners in the evaluation process. They can support the evaluation's data collection and interpretation while helping to contain demands on time and finances.

When assessment of progress toward program goals demands resources (time, expertise, or materials) not present in the organization, organizations may find value in building partnerships with secondary and higher education programs. These groups may welcome an opportunity for students to learn and practice skills that could support evaluation efforts. For example, students might receive training and conduct participant interviews or prepare a standardized assessment in a format that respondents can complete on their phones. Faculty and/or students may be interested in opportunities to build experience gathering observational assessments, analyzing survey data, or crafting infographics representing the data. Through such partnerships, organizations may gain access to affordable evaluation expertise, and the evaluators can build skills and disseminate their findings, such as through student honors theses, conference presentations, and research publications.

Even when evaluations are conducted by program staff or students who earn course credit instead of wages to support the effort, there is a cost. Staff direct attention from other tasks, and research partnerships require time from the organizational partner. Evaluation costs should be built into a program's budget, whether these come from grant funding for a new intergenerational program or standard operating expenses. Increasingly, current and potential funders want evidence of program practices and outcomes. Thus, to secure funding and comply with funding requirements, organizations benefit from conducting program evaluations.

Allocating resources (time and money) to program evaluation protects organizational investments in the intergenerational program. Organizations can use findings to identify effective practices to sustain and ineffective practices to discontinue. They should promote results to potential participants, partners, and funders. Some tasks may be managed in-house, but contracting with outside agencies to conduct interviews, surveys, or observations and work with the resultant data can ultimately save an organization money if it allows organization staff to focus on their primary responsibilities. Building relationships where each representative has value to add to the evaluation process is effective and mutually beneficial—much like a good intergenerational relationship.

Communicate Evaluation Outcomes

Program leaders are responsible for sharing evaluation results with their partners, from participants to board members to staff to funders. This presents challenges because different groups have varied needs and preferences to access and interpret findings. Some will need or want information presented at an intermediate reading level, in different languages, or in small nuggets oriented to visual and other formats. Others will want a standard, executive summary with detailed methods, findings, figures, and tables. Evaluators are building experience translating standard reports into different products. For example, infographics enhance comprehension via visual depiction of information. Infographics can be shared in toto or be broken up into a series of posts to social media outlets. While programs like Canva and PowerPoint are powerful even in the hands of novices, organizations may find paying a professional to develop communication products worthwhile. In addition to design, writing, and editing skills, a media specialist will likely have access to valuable software and stock images that organizations lack.

Professionals developing and disseminating evaluation findings should receive training on antiageist communication, and products should be reviewed for ageist depictions of younger or older participants. The FrameWorks Institute (www.frameworks.org) has resources to identify and reduce ageist messaging. Specifically, creators of communication products should attend to terms used to describe older and younger persons. For example, some organizations use "older adult" or "older person" instead of "old person," "the elderly," or "senior citizen," as many U.S. populations of older adults find these to be derogatory. The FrameWorks Institute also offers reframing resources related to adolescents and older adults.

Products should reflect the population represented by the evaluation data. Readers may recall a picture of one older, frail, White woman depicted in countless ads and presentations when stock images were even more homogenous than they are now. It is challenging to locate stock photos or vector images of older adults with diverse backgrounds, abilities, and interests. Intergenerational images available through stock image collections typically depict younger and older persons with similar characteristics, likely intended to depict families. If stock images do not sufficiently represent an intergenerational program, a professional designer should know how to access and edit images to represent participant groups.

Finally, before sending products to press or posting them to socials, they should be reviewed with partners to check how well they represent their experiences. This builds confidence and generates interest in the products. It is particularly powerful because youth and older adult voices are commonly dismissed; thus, having stakeholders review materials serves a dual purpose of verifying accuracy and empowering partners. Engaging in this process may evoke the feeling of "too many chefs in the kitchen." Partners should present findings and communication products, receive feedback respectfully without promising to respond to every critique, and identify areas where stakeholders can expect to see updates in final products. An advisory group with representatives from the different stakeholder groups may also serve in this review for a streamlined process.

Communicating evaluation outcomes, including strengths, weaknesses, and growth areas, demonstrates transparency, pride in the program, and respect for partners. It can build commitment to the program as partners look for themselves in the findings and think about how they can support continued growth.

A Call to Action

As the number, diversity, and reach of intergenerational programs grow, program evaluations should respond in kind. This does not require reinvention of the wheel, and resources exist to support program evaluation efforts. Four steps entail a call to action for intergenerational program practitioners and evaluators.

First, represent the experiences of different partners. This might include a more expansive assessment that includes staff and family members. Program goals for these groups will differ from those of early intergenerational programs, and evaluated outcomes should align with these program goals. Beyond the instruments listed in the Intergenerational Program Evaluation Toolkit (IPET), reliable, valid measures exist that can represent intended outcomes, such as an evaluation of the effects of implementing the REPRINTS intergenerational health promotion program on neighborhood trust.[55] (See *Handbook* chapter 22.) In other instances, representing diverse participants may involve inclusion of persons who have difficulty responding to standard assessments, perhaps due to language differences, cognitive abilities, or developmental stage (i.e., babies and toddlers). Janke and colleagues used observational measures such as the Menorah Park Engagement Scale to evaluate intergenerational program participation impacts on behaviors and quality of life of older adults with dementia.[56] In additional to quantitative indicators, qualitative field notes, journals, interviews, and documentation enable representation of varied stakeholder groups.

Second, collecting contextual information along with outcome assessments helps evaluators make sense of their findings. Context may be represented by different types of data, including demographic indicators, output data, descriptive indicators, and qualitative information. Evaluators may find that outcomes differ for persons with different backgrounds or experiences or among those with different levels of intergenerational program experience.[57] Qualitative notes or interviews can highlight themes in how programming supports progress toward goals. For example, evaluators may use focus group interviews to understand that a co-mentoring program better supported quantitative indicators of program goals when content was tailored to participants' cultural beliefs. Contextual information adds depth to program evaluation comprehension.

Third, utilize available reliable, valid measures to demonstrate progress toward program goals. These might be in a resource like the IPET, and they might come from other disciplines using intervention methods that are not intergenerational. With growing awareness of the link between social connections and health raised by the U.S. Surgeon General and national science associations, health indicators should figure more prominently in intergenerational program evaluations, such as the recent work by Leedahl and colleagues.[58] Using established measures gives consumers confidence in evaluation findings and a common language to talk about them.

Finally, evaluation results should be shared with partners in an accessible manner. These extend beyond funders and advisory board members to include staff, participants and families, and even other groups exploring intergenerational programming options. One of the top challenges described by intergenerational practitioners is locating resources to support program development.[59] Through traditional and emerging outlets, accessible, relatable reports of evaluation findings can be a resource for local and global audiences.

With these practices in play, the intergenerational field can benefit from enhanced evaluation methods integrated into program operations, supported by organizational and grant budgets, and disseminated through scientific, professional, and community outlets. As intergenerational responses to identified needs and resources grow more diverse, they should be represented in the evaluation literature.

Notes

1. Shannon E. Jarrott, "Where Have We Been and Where Are We Going? Content Analysis of Evaluation Research of Intergenerational Programs," *Journal of Intergenerational Relationships* 9, no. 1 (2011): 37–52, https://doi.org/10.1080/15350770.2011.544594.
2. W. S. Rybak et al., "A Foster Grandparent Program," *Psychiatric Services* 19, no. 2 (1968): 47, https://doi.org/10.1176/ps.19.2.47.
3. Jarrott, "Where Have We Been?"
4. Sally Newman et al., "Elder-Child Interaction Analysis." *Child & Youth Services* 20, no. 1–2 (1999): 129–45. https://doi.org/10.1300/j024v20n01_10.
5. Kathy Lee et al., "Documented Outcomes for Older Adults in Intergenerational Programming: A Scoping Review," *Journal of Intergenerational Relationships* 18, no. 2 (2019): 113–38, https://doi.org/10.1080/15350770.2019.1673276.
6. Jarrott, "Where Have We Been?"
7. Sally Newman, *Intergenerational Programs Past, Present and Future* (Washington, DC: Taylor and Francis, 1997).
8. John P. Kretzman and John McKnight, *Building Communities from the Inside Out: A Path toward Finding and Mobilizing a Community's Assets* (Chicago: The Asset-Based Community Development Institute, 1993).
9. Lella Gandini, "Foundations of the Reggio Emilia Approach," in *First 515. Steps toward Teaching the Reggio Way*, ed. J. Hendrick (Upper Saddle River, NJ: Merrill, 1997), 14–25; Paul B. Baltes, "Theoretical Propositions of Life-Span Developmental Psychology: On the Dynamics between Growth and Decline," *Developmental Psychology* 23, no. 5 (1987): 611–26. https://doi.org/10.1037/0012-1649.23.5.611.
10. Sheri Steinig, "Under One Roof: A Guide to Starting and Strengthening Intergenerational Shared Sites," Generations United, accessed October 9, 2023, https://www.gu.org/resources/under-one-roof-a-guide-to-starting-and-strengthening-intergenerational-shared-sites/.
11. Sharon Blake, "Pitt's 'Generations Together' Names New Director," University of Pittsburg, July 2, 2001. https://www.news.pitt.edu/news/pitts-generations-together-names-new-director.
12. Lee et al., "Documented Outcomes for Older Adults."

13. Lee et al., "Documented Outcomes for Older Adults."
14. Liat Ayalon and Senjooti Roy, "Measurement Development and Validation to Capture Perceptions of Younger People's Climate Action: An Opportunity for Intergenerational Collaboration and Dialogue," *Journal of Intergenerational Relationships* 22, no. 2 (2023): 1–15, https://doi.org/10.1080/15350770.2023.2205846.
15. Jarrott, "Where Have We Been?"; Shannon E. Jarrott et al., "Program Practices Predict Intergenerational Interaction among Children and Adults," *Gerontologist* 62, no. 3 (2021): 385–96, https://doi.org/10.1093/geront/gnab161; Alant Erna et al., "Developing Empathetic Skills among Teachers and Learners in High Schools in Tshwane: An Inter-Generational Approach Involving People with Dementia," *Sabinet African Journals* 33, no. 3 (2015): 141–58, https://hdl.handle.net/10520/EJC178494; Tara L. Gruenewald et al., "The Baltimore Experience Corps Trial: Enhancing Generativity via Intergenerational Activity Engagement in Later Life," *Journals of Gerontology Series B: Psychological Sciences and Social Sciences* 71, no. 4 (2015): 661–70, https://doi.org/10.1093/geronb/gbv005.
16. Neda Norouzi et al., "Designing Intergenerational Spaces: What to Learn from Children," *HERD: Health Environments Research & Design Journal* 16, no. 2 (2022): 174–88, https://doi.org/10.1177/19375867221138929.
17. Jarrott, "Where Have We Been?"
18. Raven Weaver et al., "Using Contact Theory to Assess Staff Perspectives on Training Initiatives of an Intergenerational Programming Intervention," *Gerontologist* 59, no. 4 (2019): 270–77, https://doi.org/10.1093/geront/gnx194; Shannon E. Jarrott and Kelly Bruno, "Shared Site Intergenerational Programs: A Case Study," *Journal of Applied Gerontology* 26, no. 3 (2007): 239–57, https://doi.org/10.1177/0733464807300225.
19. Weaver et al., "Using Contact Theory to Assess Staff Perspectives."
20. Weaver et al. "Using Contact Theory to Assess Staff Perspectives."
21. Carol Seefeldt, "The Effects of Preschoolers' Visits to a Nursing Home," *Gerontologist* 27, no. 2 (1987): 228–32, https://doi.org/10.1093/geront/27.2.228; Molly Middlecamp and Dana Gross, "Intergenerational Daycare and Preschoolers' Attitudes about Aging," *Educational Gerontology* 28, no. 4 (2002): 271–88, https://doi.org/10.1080/036012702753590398.
22. Shannon E. Jarrott et al. "Implementation of Evidence-Based Practices in Intergenerational Programming: A Scoping Review," *Research on Aging* 43, no. 7–8 (2021): 283–93, https://doi.org/10.1177/01640275211996191.
23. Shannon E. Jarrott, "Evidence-Based and Promising Practices Promote Successful Intergenerational Service Delivery," Commit to Connect, 2022, https://committoconnect.org/wp-content/uploads/2022/06/ACL-Literature-Review-summary-only-062322-JVL-MCH-SJ.pdf.
24. Jarrott et al., "Program Practices Predict Intergenerational Interaction."
25. Lee et al., "Documented Outcomes for Older Adults"; Anita De Bellis et al., "Intergenerational Activities Involving Adolescents and Residents of Aged Care Facilities: A Scoping Review," *Journal of Intergenerational Relationships* 21, no. 3 (2023): 380–401, https://doi.org/10.1080/15350770.2022.2073311.
26. Thomas F. Pettigrew, "Intergroup Contact Theory," *Annual Review of Psychology* 49 (1998): 65–85, https://doi.org/10.1146/annurev.psych.49.1.65.
27. Valerie S. Kuehne and Julie Melville, "The State of Our Art: A Review of Theories Used in Intergenerational Program Research (2003–2014) and Ways Forward," *Journal of Intergenerational Relationships* 12, no. 4 (2014): 317–46, https://doi.org/10.1080/15350770.2014.958969.
28. Weaver et al., "Using Contact Theory to Assess Staff Perspectives."
29. B. A. Israel et al., "Critical Issues in Developing and Following Community-Based Participatory Research Principles," In *Community-based Participatory Research for Health*, ed. M. Minkler and N. Wallerstein (New York: Jossey-Bass, 2013), 56–73.
30. Shannon E. Jarrott et al., "Developing Intergenerational Interventions to Address Food Insecurity among Pre-School Children: A Community-Based Participatory Approach," *Journal of Hunger & Environmental Nutrition* 16, no. 2 (2019): 196–212, https://doi.org/10.1080/19320248.2019.1640827.
31. Nancy Z. Henkin and Taryn Patterson, "Intergenerational Programming in Senior Housing: From Promise to Practice," Generations United, 2017, https://www.gu.org/resources/intergenerational-programming-in-senior-housing-from-promise-to-practice/.
32. Jarrott, "Where Have We Been?"
33. De Bellis et al., "Intergenerational Activities Involving Adolescents and Residents."

34. Ann S. Epstein and Christine Boisvert, "Let's Do Something Together," *Journal of Intergenerational Relationships* 4, no. 3 (2006): 87–109, https://doi.org/10.1300/j194v04n03_07.
35. Seefeldt, "The Effects of Preschoolers' Visits to a Nursing Home."
36. Elia E. Femia et al., "Intergenerational Preschool Experiences and the Young Child: Potential Benefits to Development," *Early Childhood Research Quarterly* 23, no. 2 (2008): 272–87, https://doi.org/10.1016/j.ecresq.2007.05.001; Sienna Caspar et al., "Intergenerational Programs: Breaking down Ageist Barriers and Improving Youth Experiences," *Therapeutic Recreation Journal* 53, no. 2 (2019): 149–64, https://doi.org/10.18666/trj-2019-v53-i2-9126.
37. Ronald H. Aday et al., "Changing Children's Attitudes towards the Elderly: The Longitudinal Effects of an Intergenerational Partners Program," *Journal of Research in Childhood Education* 10, no. 2 (1996): 143–51, https://doi.org/10.1080/02568549609594897.
38. Lisa A. Juckett, Shannon E. Jarrott, and Alicia C. Bunger, "Implementing Intergenerational Best Practices in Community-Based Settings: A Preliminary Study," *Health Promotion Practice* 23, no. 3 (2021): 473–81, https://doi.org/10.1177/1524839921994072.
39. Pettigrew, "Intergroup Contact Theory."
40. Jarrott, "Where Have We Been?"
41. Daniel W. Russell, "UCLA Loneliness Scale (Version 3): Reliability, Validity, and Factor Structure," *Journal of Personality Assessment* 66, no. 1 (1996): 20–40, https://doi.org/10.1207/s15327752jpa6601.
42. De Bellis et al., "Intergenerational Activities Involving Adolescents and Residents."
43. Christina Gigliotti, "An Intergenerational Summer Program Involving Persons with Dementia and Preschool Children," *Educational Gerontology* 31, no. 6 (2005): 425–41, https://doi.org/10.1080/03601270590928161.
44. Shannon E. Jarrott et al., "Where Do We Stand? Testing the Foundation of a Shared Site Intergenerational Program," *Journal of Intergenerational Relationships* 4, no. 2 (2006): 73–92, https://doi.org/10.1300/j194v04n02_06.
45. Jarrott, "Where Have We Been?"; Lee et al., "Documented Outcomes for Older Adults"; De Bellis et al., "Intergenerational Activities Involving Adolescents and Residents."
46. Shannon E. Jarrott, "Intergenerational Evaluation Toolkit," Generations United, 2019, https://www.gu.org/resources/intergenerational-evaluation-toolkit/.
47. Jarrott, "Intergenerational Evaluation Toolkit."
48. Shannon E. Jarrott et al., "Increasing the Power of Intergenerational Programs: Advancing an Evaluation Tool," *Journal of Applied Gerontology* 41, no. 3 (2021): 763–68, https://doi.org/10.1177/07334648211015459.
49. Jarrott et al. "Program Practices Predict Intergenerational Interaction."
50. Jarrott, "Intergenerational Evaluation Toolkit."
51. Jarrott, "Intergenerational Evaluation Toolkit."
52. Israel et al., "Critical Issues in Developing and Following Community-Based Participatory Research Principles."
53. Shelbie G. Turner et al., "Intergenerational Programming Increases Solid Food Consumption for Adult Day Center Attendees," *Journal of Applied Gerontology* 42, no. 2 (2022): 160–69, https://doi.org/10.1177/07334648221134179.
54. Yung Soo Lee et al., "The Effect of the Experience Corps® Program on Student Reading Outcomes," *Education and Urban Society* 44, no. 1 (2010): 97–118, https://doi.org/10.1177/0013124510381262.
55. Yoh Murayama et al., "The Impact of Intergenerational Programs on Social Capital in Japan: A Randomized Population-Based Cross-Sectional Study," *BMC Public Health* 19, no. 1 (2019): 156, https://doi.org/10.1186/s12889-019-6480-3.
56. Megan C. Janke et al., "Associations between Engagement Types, Outcome Behaviors, and Quality of Life for Adults with Dementia Participating in Intergenerational Programs," *Therapeutic Recreation Journal* 53, no. 2 (2019): 132–48, https://doi.org/10.18666/trj-2019-v53-i2-9647.
57. Gruenewald et al., "The Baltimore Experience Corps Trial."
58. "Advisory on the Healing Effects of Social Connection and Community. Our Epidemic of Loneliness and Social Isolation," U.S. Surgeon General, 2023, https://www.hhs.gov/sites/default/files/surgeon-general-social-connection-advisory.pdf; "Social Isolation and Loneliness in Older Adults: Opportunities for the Health Care System," National Academies of Sciences, Engineering, and Medicine (Washington, DC: The National Academies Press, 2020), https://doi.org/10.17226/25663; Skye N. Leedahl et al.,

"Using a Quasi-Experimental Study to Examine Program Participation and Outcomes for Older Adult Intergenerational Technology Program Participants," *Journal of Intergenerational Relationships* 22, no. 2 (2023): 1–23, https://doi.org/10.1080/15350770.2023.2209556.

59. Shannon E. Jarrott and Kathy Lee, "Shared Site Intergenerational Programs: A National Profile," *Journal of Aging & Social Policy* 35, no. 3 (2022): 393–410, https://doi.org/10.1080/08959420.2021.2024410.

Bibliography

Aday, Ronald H., Cyndee R. Sims, Wini McDuffie, and Emilie Evans. *Journal of Research in Childhood Education* 10, no. 2 (1996): 143–51. https://doi.org/10.1080/02568549609594897.

Ayalon, Liat, and Senjooti Roy. "Measurement Development and Validation to Capture Perceptions of Younger People's Climate Action: An Opportunity for Intergenerational Collaboration and Dialogue." *Journal of Intergenerational Relationships* 22, no. 2 (2023): 1–15. https://doi.org/10.1080/15350770.2023.2205846.

Baltes, Paul B. "Theoretical Propositions of Life-Span Developmental Psychology: On the Dynamics between Growth and Decline." *Developmental Psychology* 23, no. 5 (1987): 611–26. https://doi.org/10.1037/0012-1649.23.5.611.

Blake, Sharon. "Pitt's 'Generations Together' Names New Director." University of Pittsburg. July 2, 2001. https://www.news.pitt.edu/news/pitts-generations-together-names-new-director.

Caspar, Sienna, Erin Davis, Devan M. J. McNeill, and P. Kellett. "Intergenerational Programs: Breaking down Ageist Barriers and Improving Youth Experiences." *Therapeutic Recreation Journal* 53, no. 2 (2019): 149–64. https://doi.org/10.18666/trj-2019-v53-i2-9126.

De Bellis, Anita, Carolyn Gregoric, and Julian Grant. "Intergenerational Activities Involving Adolescents and Residents of Aged Care Facilities: A Scoping Review." *Journal of Intergenerational Relationships* 21, no. 3 (2023): 380–401. https://doi.org/10.1080/15350770.2022.2073311.

Epstein, Ann S., and Christine Boisvert. "Let's Do Something Together." *Journal of Intergenerational Relationships* 4, no. 3 (2006): 87–109. https://doi.org/10.1300/j194v04n03_07.

Erna, Alant, Stephanie Geyer, and Michael Verdr. "Developing Empathetic Skills among Teachers and Learners in High Schools in Tshwane: An Inter-Generational Approach Involving People with Dementia." *Sabinet African Journals* 33, no. 3 (2015). https://hdl.handle.net/10520/EJC178494.

Femia, Elia E., Steven H. Zarit, Clancy Blair, and Shannon E. Jarrott. "Intergenerational Preschool Experiences and the Young Child: Potential Benefits to Development." *Early Childhood Research Quarterly* 23, no. 2 (2008): 272–87. https://doi.org/10.1016/j.ecresq.2007.05.001.

Gigliotti, Christina, Matt Morris, Sara Smock, Shannon E. Jarrott, and Bonnie Graham. "An Intergenerational Summer Program Involving Persons with Dementia and Preschool Children." *Educational Gerontology* 31, no. 6 (2005): 425–41. https://doi.org/10.1080/03601270590928161.

Gruenewald, Tara L., Elizabeth K. Tanner, Linda P. Fried, Michelle C. Carlson, Qian-Li Xue, Jeanine M. Parisi, et al. "The Baltimore Experience Corps Trial: Enhancing Generativity via Intergenerational Activity Engagement in Later Life." *Journals of Gerontology Series B: Psychological Sciences and Social Sciences* 71, no. 4 (2015): 661–70. https://doi.org/10.1093/geronb/gbv005.

Hendrick, Joanne, and L. Gandini. "Foundations of the Reggio Emilia Approach." In *First Steps toward Teaching the Reggio Way*. Edited by J. Hedrick, 14–25. Upper Saddle River, NJ: Merrill, 1997.

Henkin, Nancy Z., and Taryn Patterson. "Intergenerational Programming in Senior Housing: From Promise to Practice." Generations United. 2017. https://www.gu.org/resources/intergenerational-programming-in-senior-housing-from-promise-to-practice/.

Israel, B. A., A. J. Schulz, E. A. Parker, A. B. Becker, A. Allen, and J. R. Guzman. "Critical Issues in Developing and Following Community-Based Participatory Research Principles." In *Community-based Participatory Research for Health*. Edited by M. Minkler and N. Wallerstein, 56–73. New York: Jossey-Bass, 2013.

Janke, Megan C., I'Yanna Purnell, Clifton Watts, and Kindal Shores. "Associations between Engagement Types, Outcome Behaviors, and Quality of Life for Adults with Dementia Participating in Intergenerational Programs." *Therapeutic Recreation Journal* 53, no. 2 (2019): 132–48. https://doi.org/10.18666/trj-2019-v53-i2-9647.

Jarrott, Shannon E. "Where Have We Been and Where Are We Going? Content Analysis of Evaluation Research of Intergenerational Programs." *Journal of Intergenerational Relationships* 9, no. 1 (2011): 37–52. https://doi.org/10.1080/15350770.2011.544594.

Jarrott, Shannon E. "Intergenerational Evaluation Toolkit." Generations United. 2019. https://www.gu.org/resources/intergenerational-evaluation-toolkit/.

Jarrott, Shannon E. "Evidence-Based and Promising Practices Promote Successful Intergenerational Service Delivery." Commit to Connect. 2022. https://committoconnect.org/wp-content/uploads/2022/06/ACL-Literature-Review-summary-only-062322-JVL-MCH-SJ.pdf.

Jarrott, Shannon E., Qiuchang Cao, Holly I. Dabelko-Schoeny, and Michelle L. Kaiser. "Developing Intergenerational Interventions to Address Food Insecurity among Pre-School Children: A Community-Based Participatory Approach." *Journal of Hunger & Environmental Nutrition* 16, no. 2 (2019): 196–212. https://doi.org/10.1080/19320248.2019.1640827.

Jarrott, Shannon E., Rachel M. Scrivano, Cherrie Park, and Angela N. Mendoza. "Implementation of Evidence-Based Practices in Intergenerational Programming: A Scoping Review." *Research on Aging* 43, no. 7–8 (2021): 283–93. https://doi.org/10.1177/0164027521996191.

Jarrott, Shannon E., Shelbie G. Turner, Jill Juris, Rachel M. Scrivano, and Rachel H. Weaver. "Program Practices Predict Intergenerational Interaction among Children and Adults." *Gerontologist* 62, no. 3 (2021): 385–96. https://doi.org/10.1093/geront/gnab161.

Jarrott, Shannon E., Shelbie G. Turner, Jill J. Naar, Lisa M. Juckett, and Rachel M. Scrivano. "Increasing the Power of Intergenerational Programs: Advancing an Evaluation Tool." *Journal of Applied Gerontology* 41, no. 3 (2021): 763–68. https://doi.org/10.1177/07334648211015459.

Jarrott, Shannon E., and Kelly Bruno. "Shared Site Intergenerational Programs: A Case Study." *Journal of Applied Gerontology* 26, no. 3 (2007): 239–57. https://doi.org/10.1177/0733464807300225.

Jarrott, Shannon E., Christina M. Gigliotti, and Sara A. Smock. "Where Do We Stand? Testing the Foundation of a Shared Site Intergenerational Program." *Journal of Intergenerational Relationships* 4, no. 2 (2006): 73–92. https://doi.org/10.1300/j194v04n02_06.

Jarrott, Shannon E., and Kathy Lee. "Shared Site Intergenerational Programs: A National Profile." *Journal of Aging & Social Policy* 35, no. 3 (2022): 393–410. https://doi.org/10.1080/08959420.2021.2024410.

Juckett, Lisa A., Shannon E. Jarrott, and Alicia C. Bunger. "Implementing Intergenerational Best Practices in Community-Based Settings: A Preliminary Study." *Health Promotion Practice* 23, no. 3 (2021): 473–81. https://doi.org/10.1177/1524839921994072.

Kretzman, John P., and John McKnight. *Building Communities from the Inside Out: A Path toward Finding and Mobilizing a Community's Assets*. Chicago: The Asset-Based Community Development Institute, 1993.

Kuehne, Valerie S., and Julie Melville. "The State of Our Art: A Review of Theories Used in Intergenerational Program Research (2003–2014) and Ways Forward." *Journal of Intergenerational Relationships* 12, no. 4 (2014): 317–46. https://doi.org/10.1080/15350770.2014.958969.

Lee, Kathy, Shannon E. Jarrott, and Lisa A. Juckett. "Documented Outcomes for Older Adults in Intergenerational Programming: A Scoping Review." *Journal of Intergenerational Relationships* 18, no. 2 (2019): 113–38. https://doi.org/10.1080/15350770.2019.1673276.

Lee, Yung Soo, Nancy Morrow-Howell, Melissa Johnson-Reid, and Stacey McCrary. "The Effect of the Experience Corps® Program on Student Reading Outcomes." *Education and Urban Society* 44, no. 1 (2010): 97–118. https://doi.org/10.1177/0013124510381262.

Leedahl, Skye N., Melanie Brasher, Alexandria Capolino, and Erica Estus. "Using a Quasi-Experimental Study to Examine Program Participation and Outcomes for Older Adult Intergenerational Technology Program Participants." *Journal of Intergenerational Relationships* 22, no. 2 (2023): 1–23. https://doi.org/10.1080/15350770.2023.2209556.

Middlecamp, Molly, and Dana Gross. "Intergenerational Daycare and Preschoolers' Attitudes about Aging." *Educational Gerontology* 28, no. 4 (2002): 271–88. https://doi.org/10.1080/036012702753590398.

Murayama, Yoh, Hiroshi Murayama, Masami Hasebe, Jun Yamaguchi, and Yoshinori Fujiwara. "The Impact of Intergenerational Programs on Social Capital in Japan: A Randomized Population-Based Cross-Sectional Study." *BMC Public Health* 19, no. 1 (2019): 156. https://doi.org/10.1186/s12889-019-6480-3.

National Academies of Sciences, Engineering, and Medicine. *Social Isolation and Loneliness in Older Adults*. Washington, DC: The National Academies Press, 2020. https://doi.org/10.17226/25663.

Newman, Sally. *Intergenerational Programs Past, Present and Future*. Washington, DC: Taylor and Francis, 1997.

Newman, Sally, Gregory A. Morris, and Heidi Streetman. "Elder-Child Interaction Analysis." *Child & Youth Services* 20, no. 1–2 (1999): 129–45. https://doi.org/10.1300/j024v20n01_10.

Norouzi, Neda, Jou-Chen Chen, Shannon E. Jarrott, and Afrooz Satari. "Designing Intergenerational Spaces: What to Learn from Children." *HERD: Health Environments Research & Design Journal* 16, no. 2 (2022): 174–88. https://doi.org/10.1177/19375867221138929.

Pettigrew, Thomas F. "Intergroup Contact Theory." *Annual Review of Psychology* 49 (1998): 65–85. https://doi.org/10.1146/annurev.psych.49.1.65.

Russell, Daniel W. "UCLA Loneliness Scale (Version 3): Reliability, Validity, and Factor Structure." *Journal of Personality Assessment* 66, no. 1 (1996): 20–40. https://doi.org/10.1207/s15327752jpa6601_

Rybak, W. S., J. M. Sadnavitch, and B. J. Mason. "A Foster Grandparent Program." *Psychiatric Services* 19, no. 2 (1968): 47–47. https://doi.org/10.1176/ps.19.2.47.

Seefeldt, Carol. "The Effects of Preschoolers' Visits to a Nursing Home." *Gerontologist* 27, no. 2 (1987): 228–32. https://doi.org/10.1093/geront/27.2.228.

Steinig, Sheri. "Under One Roof: A Guide to Starting and Strengthening Intergenerational Shared Sites." Generations United. Accessed October 9, 2023. https://www.gu.org/resources/under-one-roof-a-guide-to-starting-and-strengthening-intergenerational-shared-sites/.

Turner, Shelbie G., Shannon E. Jarrott, and Benjamin Katz. "Intergenerational Programming Increases Solid Food Consumption for Adult Day Center Attendees." *Journal of Applied Gerontology* 42, no. 2 (2022): 160–69. https://doi.org/10.1177/07334648221134179.

U. S. Surgeon General. "Advisory on the Healing Effects of Social Connection and Community. Our Epidemic of Loneliness and Isolation." 2023. https://www.hhs.gov/sites/default/files/surgeon-general-social-connection-advisory.pdf.

Wallerstein, Nina, Bonnie Duran, John G. Oetzel, and Meredith Minkler, eds. "Critical Issues in Developing and Following Community-Based Participatory Research Principles." In *Community-Based Participatory Research for Health*, 56–73. San Francisco: Jossey-Bass, 2018.

Weaver, Raven H., Jill J. Naar, and Shannon E. Jarrott. "Using Contact Theory to Assess Staff Perspectives on Training Initiatives of an Intergenerational Programming Intervention." *Gerontologist* 59, no. 4 (2019): 270–77. https://doi.org/10.1093/geront/gnx194.

CHAPTER 30

The Long View—Building Intergenerational Connections, Lessons Learned

Nancy Henkin *and* Matthew S. Kaplan

> **Abstract**
>
> This chapter delves into the evolution, challenges, and opportunities surrounding intergenerational programs, policies, and practices over the past fifty years. It reflects the views of the authors and eleven intergenerational thought leaders and draws upon research in the field. The chapter provides a historical perspective on intergenerational practice, policy, and research, discusses lessons learned across national borders, and identifies barriers to growth. It balances optimism with a realistic assessment of what it will take to more deeply embed an intergenerational lens into how we think, work, and learn. Acknowledging that a multilevel approach is needed to realize the full promise of intergenerational work, the authors highlight concrete strategies for changing mindsets, integrating an intergenerational lens into systems, and creating social structures that reflect the opportunities presented by an age-diverse society.
>
> **Key Words:** intergenerational leaders, intergenerational lens, intergenerational interdependence, intergenerational community-building, shared sites

When you know where you came from—you know where you are going.

—*Navajo proverb*

Introduction

Over the past fifty years, there has been a growing awareness of the value of intergenerational programs, policies, and practices as strategies for enhancing the quality of life for individuals of all ages and addressing the multitude of challenges we face in communities worldwide. What have we learned over this period? How do we move forward so this concept becomes "normalized," and *generational interdependence* becomes a core cultural value?

This chapter reflects the views of the authors and eleven intergenerational thought leaders (see appendix A) and draws upon research in the field. It focuses on the evolution of intergenerational work over time, challenges we continue to face, strategies for moving forward, and opportunities for deepening and broadening this work. There is now a strong foundation for this work, but much more needs to be done to ensure that thinking and acting "intergenerationally" become an integral part of how we live, work, and solve critical social issues. As we emerge from the COVID pandemic and face issues such as social isolation; political polarization; racial, ethnic, and income divides; regional wars; and climate change, intergenerational collaboration and connection become more important than ever.

Driving Forces

The intergenerational thought leaders interviewed for this chapter highlighted several trends that help explain the growth of intergenerational programs, practices, and policies over the past fifty years. Demographic changes (e.g., the "longevity revolution," declining birth rates), age-segregation and ageism, and the growing epidemic of social isolation and loneliness were cited as major forces driving increased interest and innovation aimed at promoting and deepening intergenerational engagement in diverse contexts.

Demographic Changes

Global projections suggest an expansion of the aging population globally from 10 percent in 2022 to 16 percent in 2050, with the sixty-five + population being almost equal to the population of youth under twelve years of age.[1] The greatest surge is expected among those eighty-five to ninety-nine in developed countries. We live in the most age-diverse society in history, with up to five generations living side by side. In the United States, there is an almost equal number of people under twenty-five years (23 percent) and over sixty years (23 percent).[2] The population pyramid is now more of a rectangle. There is also a growing "racial generational" gap between a predominantly older White population and a growing number of children of color, bringing significant challenges as well as opportunities.[3]

Medical and technological advances require us to rethink what different generations will need at different stages of life. The Stanford Center on Longevity[4] suggests that we shift from a deficit mindset to focusing on the contributions older adults can make to society. It also highlights the need for investment in health and education at every stage of life, the importance of work flexibility, and the impact of the physical environment on well-being across the life course.

Age Segregation and Ageism

Despite this generational diversity, we tend to live and work in age silos. Schools, workplaces, age-segregated housing, and age-segmented social structures reinforce ageist attitudes by restricting opportunities for forming meaningful cross-age relationships. When there is limited contact between different groups of people, in this case, based on age, the ground is fertile for stereotypical thinking and discrimination based on age differences to grow. "Ageism refers to stereotypes (how we think), prejudice (how we feel), and discrimination (how we act) directed towards people based on their age. It can be institutional, interpersonal, or self-directed."[5]

Ageism has been called the last socially acceptable prejudice.[6] It is a multifaceted prejudice that feeds negative attitudes and expectations that older age necessarily comes with increased incompetence, cognitive problems, and reduced physical activity.[7] Conversely, many youth are also on the receiving end of negative age-based stereotypes. We often hear about young people portrayed as potential "troublemakers" and underperformers in the workplace, presumably due to low motivation, a sense of entitlement, and a poor work ethic.

Social Isolation and Loneliness

Beyond demographic changes and efforts to counter age-based stereotypes, those interviewed for this chapter emphasized growing concerns about the detrimental effects of social isolation and loneliness, now considered a major public health problem in many countries. The recent pandemic highlighted the need to promote opportunities for social connectedness. Although intergenerational practitioners and advocates have often been at the forefront of establishing neighborhood-based friendly visiting, shopping assistance, book clubs, exercise groups, and other cross-age initiatives, many had to pivot toward using high-tech strategies—such as online video calls (via Skype, Face Time, Zoom meetings)—for keeping people in touch and engaged with one another during times of physical distancing.

Looking Back—A Fifty-Year Perspective

In 2009, the Beth Johnson Foundation created the following definition of intergenerational work: "To bring people together in purposeful, mutually beneficial activities which promote greater understanding and respect between generations and contribute to building more cohesive communities. They are inclusive, building on the positive resources the young and old have to offer each other and those around them."[8]

Although these goals are still relevant, the focus and form of intergenerational work have shifted in several important, though often nuanced ways:

- From placing primary emphasis on creating short-term, service-oriented activities with prescribed roles to developing more sustained and integrated interventions that are conducive to establishing meaningful relationships and strengthening communities
- From focusing on bringing generations together as an end in itself to using an intergenerational lens to address critical community concerns
- From targeting the "bookend generations" to a more expansive lifespan perspective that emphasizes the importance of intergenerational connections throughout the entire life course

- From the aging field driving intergenerational work to a more multidisciplinary, cross-sectoral balance of leaders and academics from multiple fields.

Although these shifts are evident across the globe, thought leaders agreed that there are some parallels as well as significant differences in the ways that intergenerational work evolved in the United States, Europe, Asia, and Australia.

Evolution of Intergenerational Practice in the United States

Rooted in the Foster Grandparent and RSVP (Retired Senior Volunteer Program) programs of the 1960s, formal intergenerational work began taking shape in the 1970s over concerns that geographic mobility and age-segregated institutions were depriving children of regular interaction with older adults. The Teaching and Learning Communities project in Ann Arbor, Michigan, highlighted the value of having older volunteers in classrooms, and the Teaching about Aging curriculum developed in Massachusetts provided tools for teachers to integrate aging issues into their classes. Several universities (e.g., Temple University and the University of Pittsburgh) created intergenerational centers that implemented and evaluated specific program models and trained practitioners nationwide.

In 1986, in response to concerns about generational equity and competition for resources, Generations United was created by the National Council on Aging, AARP, the Children's Defense Fund, and the Child Welfare League. Statewide intergenerational networks were developed soon after in California, Illinois, Kansas, Massachusetts, New Jersey, and New York to stimulate and support programs at the local level. Intergenerational programs were viewed as a way to strengthen a weakened social compact and address the unmet needs of children, youth, and older adults. Innovative service models were created in schools, community organizations, retirement communities, hospitals, and other community settings. Programs for youth focused on improving academic achievement and reducing school drop-out, teen pregnancy, and drug and alcohol abuse. In some models, older adult workers were employed to enhance child care programs and support children with special needs and their families. To meet the needs of older adults, programs recruited youth to provide support services for homebound elders, visit residents of long-term care facilities, teach English to older immigrants and refugees, and provide respite to caregivers of frail elders. Innovative arts programs engaged young people and older adults in activities designed to foster a mutual appreciation of local cultural heritage and increased understanding across ages. Most programs had a prescribed set of activities, time frames, and participants.

For much of the 1980s to early 2000s, the federal government played a major role in facilitating the growth of new intergenerational models. Funding from departments such as the Administration on Aging, the Administration for Children, Youth and Families, the Department of Education, the Department of Juvenile Justice, the Center for Substance

Abuse Prevention, and the Fund for the Improvement of Post-Secondary Education, was available to test out new program models designed to generate specific outcomes for young people and older adults. The creation of the Corporation for National and Community Service in 1993 served as a catalyst for intergenerational service learning in elementary and secondary schools and institutions of higher education. National initiatives such as Family Friends, Linking Lifetimes, SHINE, and Experience Corps demonstrated the efficacy of older adults and youth serving as resources for each other and their communities. During this period, specific competencies for intergenerational practitioners were identified, and intergenerational training institutes were offered nationwide.

As the number of programs grew, there was a significant expansion of the types and complexity of intergenerational work. Rather than focusing only on programs, there was increasing attention to the concept of *place*. Researchers started exploring how the built environment impacts intergenerational contact and relationship dynamics and vice versa. The idea of an *intergenerational intentional community* was initially put into practice in Hope Meadows, a purpose-built, community-wide initiative established in Rantoul, Illinois, in 1994 as a way to address the foster care crisis of the 1980s and 1990s. The Hope Meadows planned community offered rent-free housing to parents who could care for three or four children previously in the foster care system and rent-reduced housing for older adult volunteers who could provide mentoring, tutoring, and other support for the families.[9]

Another influential intergenerational community-building model was the Communities for All Ages framework that was developed by the Intergenerational Center at Temple University in 2002 and later implemented in twenty-three cities and towns across the United States. Utilizing an intergenerational and life span lens to community building, it brought together organizations representing diverse groups and residents of all ages to address critical community issues and strengthen intergenerational relationships.[10]

In recent years, the concept of *intergenerational contact zones* (ICZs) was introduced by intergenerational specialists based on four different continents (North America, Asia, Europe, and Africa) to describe places where different generations interact and build relationships. The ICZ conceptual framework "serves several functions, including as a conceptual tool (for studying complex, multi-generational community settings), programming tool (for broadening the range of intergenerational activity possibilities), and design tool (for generating innovative ideas for developing intergenerational meeting spaces)."[11]

The language used to describe intergenerational work has moved away from "program" only to phrases such as intergenerational community building or place-making, intergenerational design, and intergenerational engagement and using an intergenerational lens to add value to other approaches. There has also been increased focus on the relational aspects of intergenerational connections rather than just on the provision of services.

A Global Perspective

When examining intergenerational initiatives across national and cultural contexts, certain common themes emerge. One universal theme is how planned intergenerational connections tend to address common dimensions of human need: "In nations across the world, we recognize that the generations need to nurture and be nurtured, to teach and to be taught, to have a successful life review, and to learn from and about the past, to share cultural mores and to have a cultural identity, to communicate positive values, to have positive role models, to leave a legacy, and to be connected to a contiguous generation."[12]

We see how intergenerational initiatives across countries play an important role in transmitting cultural heritage—including values, cultural arts, knowledge (and ways of knowing), and language (and ways of communicating)—and in helping people of all ages to become more engaged and invested in community life.

Some of the intergenerational thought leaders that were interviewed noted similar trajectories across countries regarding how national attention to intergenerational work tends to begin with a focus on one or more high-profile programs and, over time, moves toward efforts to create organizational infrastructure to promote synergies between multiple frameworks of intergenerational practice. In many cases, we have seen how regional and national networks have played a major role as primary drivers for increases in the breadth and depth of intergenerational work. The first convening of the International Consortium of Intergenerational Programs in 1999 was an effort to facilitate the sharing and promotion of intergenerational practices as agents for global social change. Although that organization no longer exists, opportunities for global interchange between individual practitioners and researchers have expanded significantly over the years.

In the United Kingdom in 2001, the Beth Johnson Foundation spearheaded establishment of the UK Centre for Intergenerational Practice, which played a major role in securing government funding for intergenerational initiatives in forty locations. The Centre provided inspiration and support for intergenerational networks, conferences, and the development of curricular tools and materials. It served as one of the key drivers for establishing EMIL (European Map of Intergenerational Learning), which was launched in 2010 as a consortium of twenty-two partners from eighteen countries to facilitate the exchange of ideas, expertise, and effective practice. The Centre also planted the seeds and supported the growth of intergenerational innovation in other parts of the United Kingdom. For example, Generations Working Together (Scotland's intergenerational network; see *Handbook* chapter 18) has developed to the extent that it now receives funding through the National Lottery, Ministry of Education, Equality and Human Rights Commission, and several foundations to conduct local, national, and international training programs for students, intergenerational practitioners, and staff and administrators of community organizations and agencies and to develop curricular and program development materials. Linking Generations in Northern Ireland (see *Handbook* chapter 23) builds capacity within communities to deliver intergenerational approaches via their accredited training programs and localized networks. Although the Centre was not operational for some years due to changes in leadership, shifting government priorities, and lack of funding, it is being resurrected by the Beth Johnson Foundation in partnership with Apples and Honey Nightengale as the Centre for Intergenerational Practice, Research & Development (England).[13]

Spain has also been at the forefront of intergenerational research, theory, and practice. In 2018, the University of Granada and a social cooperative called Macrosad agreed to create the Macrosad Chair in Intergenerational Studies to boost the validation of intergenerational approaches in various community settings. Recently the region of Extremadura passed the first regional Intergenerational Plan, and efforts are underway in the Basque Country to build an intergenerational center that includes 100 residential places for older people and 40 rented apartments for young people.

Some of the intergenerational thought leaders who were interviewed alluded to a major distinction between how some Eastern and Western countries have embraced intergenerational connection ideologies over time. As confirmed and highlighted in the intergenerational literature from the late 1990s and early 2000s, in some countries in Asia, including Singapore, Japan, and China, there has been more of a tendency to focus on ways to strengthen intergenerational interdependencies and social cohesion in the family context, with the family unit being seen as the principal conduit in the intergenerational transmission of knowledge and values.[14]

However, if we look at the current mosaic of intergenerational initiatives in countries such as Singapore and Japan today (see *Handbook* chapters 20 and 22), although we will still see a major emphasis on the role of familial-based intergenerational relationships and supports, we also see a lot of growth in interventions and organizational infrastructure designed to strengthen and sustain *non*-familial intergenerational connections and relationships.

A broader intergenerational footprint has taken hold in Singapore. With the support of national ministries (e.g., Ministry of Family and Youth, Ministry of Health) and councils (e.g., Council for the Third Age and National Family Council), an intergenerational lens has been applied when shaping a wide range of programs, policies, and places of national significance. This includes creating multigenerational housing policies and models designed to promote physical activity and intergenerational interaction, age-integrated family service centers, support systems for family caregivers, and an array of senior volunteer- and service-oriented intergenerational programs.

In Japan, many intergenerational initiatives have been established in nonfamilial contexts yet have been framed as an extension of the traditional family ideal. For example, according to several accounts of life at Kotoen, an internationally known and respected Tokyo-based intergenerational shared site, unrelated children and older adults are referred to as "grandchildren" and "grandparents."[15] In a similar vein, an NHK-produced (1989) documentary on Kotoen was entitled *Mago Hachijunin no Daikazoku* (*Family with 80 Grandchildren*).

An important occurrence in the evolution of intergenerational work in Japan was the launching of the Japan Intergenerational Unity Association (JIUA) in 2004. JIUA played an important role in sustaining and strengthening intergenerational initiatives in Japan and establishing linkages with intergenerational initiatives in other countries.[16] What began as a small group of individuals in the social welfare, education, and health services sectors, grew to thirty-plus partnering organizations and agencies in Japan, including government ministries, local government agencies, research institutions, academic societies, and nonprofit organizations. JIUA was also instrumental in supporting various international exchanges, training programs, and conferences, thereby contributing to international exchanges of information and lessons learned across national borders. Complementary to the efforts and accomplishments of JIUA, an intergenerational studies-oriented organization emerged in 2010—the Japan Society for Intergenerational Studies (JSIS). Since 2011, JSIS leaders have published a journal, with occasional contributions from international scholars.

Australia is home to many intergenerational initiatives that have developed over the past twenty years. Programs that provided continuity for indigenous Aboriginal cultural practices for facilitating intergenerational bonding were highlighted in a report published by NYARS (Australia's National Youth Affairs Research Scheme). The authors noted how walking is viewed as a distinct intergenerational experience in communities where residents share Yiriman cultural and historical roots: "Walking is a means through which the young get exposed to education, hunt and collect food, meet other groups, travel to and carry out ceremonies, burn areas of land and carry out other land management practices, send messages and communicate, 'freshen up' paintings, collect and produce material culture such as tools and other implements, 'map' boundaries and collect intelligence and build knowledge."[17]

More recently in Australia, in an effort to address the growing social care needs of children and older adults, intergenerational shared sites became a major focal point for practice and research.[18] The popularity of the television series "Old People's Home for 4-Year-Olds" created nationwide interest in ways to connect generations. In 2021, the Australian Institute for Intergenerational Practice at Griffith University was created to help organizations create, implement, and evaluate high-quality intergenerational programs. It provides a platform for people to share their experiences, challenges, and successes. (See *Handbook* chapter 26.)

Lessons Learned

Over the past fifty years, we have learned a great deal about the development and evaluation of high-quality programs, theoretical frameworks that underlie intergenerational work, and the multiple pathways that can lead to meaningful intergenerational engagement. However, those interviewed for this chapter felt that we have not yet realized the full potential of intergenerational work. They acknowledged that some strategies that were used in the past may not be as effective today. The following are some learnings and challenges that must be addressed to move forward.

- Focusing primarily on intergenerational "programs" has not created sustainable institutional, structural, and cultural change. Although innovative program models have been created worldwide, many of these last only a few years, often ending when funding is unavailable or a passionate leader leaves the organization. More needs to be done to scale up successful programs and to connect to bigger systems.
- In many domains where interest in intergenerational work is considered and fostered, there is often a lack of clarity about what intergenerational work encompasses and how it can add value to efforts that address critical social and community concerns. Much intergenerational work is still seen as "nice" but not critical or urgent.
- Intergenerational work has not been as interdisciplinary and/or cross-sectoral as it needs to be. Although the diversity of practitioners and researchers has increased over time, age silos in academia, government, and philanthropy and among community-based organizations persist. A deeper commitment to intergenerational collaboration is needed to move policy and program efforts forward.
- More extensive and intensive use of theoretical frameworks and research to inform program and policy development are needed to enhance the quality and add legitimacy to intergenerational interventions.
- A lack of long-term funding has impeded the ability of intergenerational work to significantly expand. Funding streams are still age-segregated, and although there are some champions in the philanthropic sector in the United States (e.g., Eisner Foundation [see *Handbook* chapter 3], RRF, St. David's Foundation), many more are needed to change funding patterns. The declining amount of support from government agencies over the last decade has made it difficult to sustain successful program models.

Moving Forward—Closing the Gap between Practice and Promise

We are at a critical point in the evolution of intergenerational inquiry, practice, and policy. We have built a strong foundation for intergenerational programming, research, and policy, with concrete resource materials, training/certificate programs (e.g., Scotland, Spain, Australia), and strong organizations available to support the growth of this work. The number and diversity of practitioners and researchers interested in intergenerational work have increased and there has been a shift in popular culture about the value of cross-age relationships. Television shows (e.g., *Hacks* and *Only Murders in the Building*), top-selling joint albums by older and younger musicians (e.g., Tony Bennett and Lady Gaga), and movies (e.g., *A Man Called Otto, Mack and Rita, The Intern*) highlight the power of intergenerational relationships. We are even seeing an uptick in the use of the term "intergenerational" in the for-profit world in the form of commercials and marketing tools for all sorts of family- and community-oriented products and lifestyles.

The tide seems to be turning and there is growing momentum. However, the thought leaders who were interviewed were also quick to point out that barriers to growth still exist and that we need to take bold steps to ensure that the full promise of intergenerational work is realized.

"We need to tackle three problems—a failure of imagination, innovation, and investment."
M. Freedman

As we emerge from the devastating global pandemic that shuttered many shared sites and programs and isolated generations from each other in communities, we can *revitalize* and *reimagine* the nature and scope of intergenerational work. However, this will take a multi-level approach to changing mindsets and breaking down structural and institutional barriers that have limited our ability to think, work, and live intergenerationally.

Our panel of experts identified the following strategies that can help us move to the next stage of intergenerational work: 1) refining the message, 2) broadening engagement/strengthening collaboration, 3) understanding and deepening this work, and 4) reducing institutional and structural barriers. It is critical that we infuse an equity lens into all of these strategies to ensure that people of all ages and backgrounds can engage in and benefit from this work.

Refining the Message

As we move forward, a better understanding of the language we use to describe intergenerational work and how it is communicated is needed. Due to the wide range of intergenerational interventions, it is sometimes confusing what the "IT" is. Some thought leaders highlighted the importance of the INTER in intergenerational, suggesting that understanding the space "in-between" is critical to fostering meaningful cross-age relationships. Terms such as intergenerational lens, practice, perspective, engagement, exchange, opportunity, design, and community building have all emerged as practitioners, researchers, and policymakers explore ways to describe the work they are doing. Recently, the term "co-generational" has emerged to reflect generations working together with a common purpose to address a problem broader than those participating. (See *Handbook* chapter 4.) Needless to say, using language that reflects diverse cultural norms is essential.

Rather than promoting specific interventions, focusing on a clearly articulated shared vision (e.g., an age-integrated society) and a set of shared values that underlie our work may be more effective as we move forward. A consistent message that inspires different generations to engage in mutual learning, support, and problem-solving and emphasizes reciprocity, interdependence, inclusivity, respect, and relationships can help shift the cultural norms that limit intergenerational connection.

Messaging must be compelling and relevant to current realities. For much of the last twenty years, intergenerational work has been presented as an opportunity to engage in "service" and/or "volunteerism." Programs were presented in three categories—older people serving youth, young serving older adults, or youth and older people serving together. A recent article[19] suggests that a shift in language is taking place—from uni-directional service to an emphasis on bi-directional efforts that highlight words like reciprocity, engagement, and working together. Focusing on a unified message about the power of intergenerational relationships to reduce loneliness, combat ageism, and/or meet critical challenges is an inclusive way to promote this work.

> *"We need to find a language that focuses on meaningful relationships and building healthy, connected communities."* A Hatton-Yeo

As mentioned earlier, storytelling about intergenerational relationships has increased in popular media and hopefully will continue to do so. Little attention, however, has been paid to the use of social media (e.g., TikTok, Instagram) to help change the cultural narrative about intergenerational relationships. The "parasocial hypothesis"[20] suggests that attitudes toward a group can be shifted by showing images that portray what you want people to believe. Videos, in particular, have been shown to be highly effective. Creating and posting culturally diverse videos about different kinds of intergenerational relationships could be valuable in promoting this concept.

Broadening Engagement, Strengthening Collaboration

We must ask ourselves who is NOT at the table as we try to move the intergenerational concept forward. Although there has been growing interest by practitioners and researchers from fields outside of aging, it is critical that we expand the number and diversity of local and national partnerships, proactively reach out to individuals of diverse ages and backgrounds, and involve potential funders and policymakers in the early development of intergenerational collaborative efforts.

PARTNERSHIPS

Broadening the engagement of organizations with intersecting interests and goals is an important strategy for widening intergenerational work. In the United States, more active investment by government agencies such as the Environmental Protection Agency, Housing and Urban Development, National Endowment for the Arts, National Endowment for the Humanities, and National Science Foundation was suggested as a way to scale up successful initiatives and stimulate the development of significant policies and practices. The lack of a unified *lifespan* agenda rather than an age-focused agenda has limited opportunities for significant intergenerational collaboration. On a local level, more efforts are needed to bring together funders, health and social service practitioners, grassroots leaders (particularly in communities of color), educators, media, and the business community to explore using an intergenerational lens for strengthening their community. The concept of "collective impact"—the "commitment from different sectors to a common agenda for solving a specific social problem"[21]—is valuable for sharing and coordinating resources. However, many thought leaders stressed that a shift in thinking about collaboration is needed to move from a sense of "zero-sum competition" to a belief in the power of collective action. There is a growing awareness of the importance of relational work when trying to change systems. This involves building relational trust, placing people with lived experience at the center of collective impact efforts, examining personal biases, and transforming power dynamics.[22]

> *"The United States is the great segregationalist. We slice communities into a million pieces and then organize them in institutions as a way not to get along. We need to shift the cultural norms from intergenerational conflict to intergenerational harmony." E. Gonzales*

NETWORKS

Intergenerational networks can be an effective approach for sharing lessons and influencing public policy. Networks can bring practitioners and advocates together to share information and learning and explore the potential for collective action. Coming together increases the likelihood of integrating an intergenerational lens into systems and influencing policy. It is a means for dialogue across interest groups and collaborative activity. In the United States, several new networking efforts are underway. In Portland, Oregon, a social impact network called *Generations Together* was created that has a shared vision about the promise of intergenerational work and is committed to equity. In Pennsylvania, the Pennsylvania Intergenerational Network was created in 2022 to:

- Establish a "clearinghouse" for sharing best practices
- Provide technical assistance on issues related to programming and evaluation
- Advocate for institutional practices and policies that support and enrich intergenerational relations
- Stimulate new program development
- Launch education campaigns to raise public awareness about the value of intergenerational connection and collaboration.

Intergenerational networks are also "vision enablers." For those already engaged in intergenerational work, a network can help them effect social, organizational, and political change on a more ambitious level than when operating alone.

OUTREACH TO NEW AUDIENCES

"We need to build grassroots leadership and create entry points for people to get involved." D. Schubert

Bringing more young people to the table is key to the growth of intergenerational work. In 2022, Encore.org (now CoGenerate) commissioned the University of Chicago to conduct a survey (1,549 respondents aged 18 to 94) that explored the views of older people and young adults toward co-generational work.[23] (See *Handbook* chapter 4.) Findings reflected a hunger for intergenerational connection, particularly among young people and people of color across the age spectrum. Although different generations articulated different priorities, mutual interests such as the environment, mental health, and education suggest opportunities for cross-generational alliances. Offering leadership training to community residents of all ages who can serve as generational bridge builders can be an effective first step.

Building leadership among younger people is important not only for current initiatives but also for succession planning. Many of those interviewed for this chapter expressed the need to find ways to intentionally nurture the interests and passions of a new generation of leaders who will continue to move this work forward. A good example of this is the Eisner Foundation's current focus on uplifting the next leaders in the intergenerational space by providing new Eisner Fellows with financial resources, networking opportunities, and mentoring from former Eisner Prize winners with extensive experience in the field. Co-generate also incentivizes new leaders through its *Co-Gen Challenge to Advance Economic Opportunity* program. Awardees receive funds to advance their work and participate in a six-month accelerator, providing expert and peer coaching in program development, expansion, storytelling, and fundraising.

Understanding and Deepening the Work
EXPANDING THEORETICAL FRAMEWORKS

Intergenerational work has been grounded primarily in child and adult development, life course, and intergroup contact theories. Thought leaders identified the need to look beyond these to understand the intersection between age, race/ethnicity, gender/sexual orientation, and other sources of identity, stressing the importance of breaking down age silos across identities. Examining Critical Race, Relational, Ambivalence, and Empowerment theories can deepen our understanding of successful practices and help inform policy. As noted by other researchers, "We also need a broader theoretical base for intergenerational practice that delves deeper into the relational aspects of our work and continues to explore the value and composition of a uniquely intergenerational theory."[24] Creating spaces for practitioners, researchers, and policymakers to explore the links between theory, practice, and policy is essential for the continued evolution of intergenerational work.

> *"There are age silos in academia and a lack of interdisciplinary research. We must explore other fields—philosophy, anthropology, relational sociology, and systems change to look for possible synergies."* M. Sanchez

STRENGTHENING EVALUATION AND RESEARCH

Further growth will depend in part on our ability to demonstrate the legitimacy of this work. Most evaluation studies focus on small, local programs over a short period of time. Thought leaders agree that we need more rigorous, longitudinal studies that examine the impact of an intervention on participating individuals, organizations, and communities. More focus should be on the nature and complexity of intergenerational interactions and the processes that facilitate or inhibit cross-age understanding and connection. What makes interventions work? What practices facilitate cross-generational exchanges that foster collective action? How does the intensity of program involvement impact health outcomes? What prevents people from engaging in intergenerational interaction? These are some of the questions raised by intergenerational thought leaders.

SCALING PROMISING PRACTICES

Although many interventions have been created, not all have been nurtured so they take hold and become part of the fabric of a community. Small innovative pilots can be building blocks for more expansive efforts and can demonstrate the value of drawing upon local assets and skills. However, there needs to be an intentional strategy to grow these efforts into larger-scale, sustainable efforts and educate practitioners about public policies, institutional practices, and funding systems to support and expand this work. Linking intergenerational engagement, design, learning, caregiving, and community-building efforts will encourage buy-in from multiple sectors and open opportunities for new collaboration.

Reducing Structural and Institutional Barriers

As our society becomes more generationally diverse, it is clear that we need new structures and social systems that reflect our current reality. Thought leaders note that a structural lag still exists between changing demographics and the opportunities for intergenerational engagement afforded to people at different stages of life. Rather than segmenting learning, work, and leisure into prescribed stages, all agree that we need systems that provide flexible opportunities and support to individuals as they move through the life course.

Reshaping the age-segregated institutions that are deeply ingrained in our society will require changes in policies, practices, and mindsets. Suggestions shared by thought leaders include:

- Changing regulations that impose barriers to intergenerational housing and creating policies that support new models (e.g., home sharing, retirement communities on college campuses, homes for multi-generational families).
- Encouraging the creation of shared sites and transforming multi-generational spaces (e.g., community centers, libraries, cultural institutions, parks) into intergenerationally enriched environments.
- Focusing on the interdependent nature of lifelong caregiving and infusing a lifespan approach into systems of care.
- Restructuring educational institutions to embrace the Breaking down age-segregated funding streams and creating public-private ventures that support innovation and long-term sustainability.
- potential of intergenerational connections for enriching learning and fostering active citizenship.
- Fostering cross-age collaboration and effective knowledge transfer practices in the workplace.
- Examining ways to promote income redistribution across generations (e.g., universal savings accounts where current generations can help younger generations save for housing, caregiving, and education)
- Infusing awareness of how age is a dimension of diversity and should be part of broader DEI initiatives.
- Developing a strategic public awareness campaign using popular and social media to promote the " normalization" of intergenerational connections.

Conclusion

The in-depth conversations with eleven intergenerational thought leaders reflected both optimism and a realistic assessment of what it will take to embed an intergenerational lens into the way we think, work, and learn. The good news is that we are not starting with a blank slate. We have learned important lessons over the past fifty years that will help us move to the next stage of evolution. Questions still persist, however.

- What are the most effective ways of promoting cultural change and societal norms that value intergenerational interdependence, reciprocity, equity, and collaboration?
- How do we create a long-term, coordinated strategy that links intergenerational practice, research, and policy and leads to systemic (or structural) change?
- How do we bring new people and partners to the table and infuse this collaborative mindset and approach into existing initiatives?
- How can we increase support from foundations, government agencies, and public-private ventures to scale promising practices?

Defining intergenerational work is still challenging. It may be helpful to look at it in multiple ways, all of which are needed to move forward.

A VISION: a world that values all ages and offers opportunities for intergenerational connection, learning, and collective action.

A LENS: a way of thinking and acting that emphasizes interdependence, relationships, reciprocity, and collective responsibility.

A FRAMEWORK: policy, practice, and research strategies that engage and benefit multiple generations.

The thought leaders interviewed agreed that the intergenerational field will continue to grow as the challenges we face become increasingly complex. However, it will take innovation, investment, and our collective will to create not only effective programs and practices in the short term but also the long-term structural, institutional, and attitudinal changes necessary to make intergenerational connections a *way of life*.

Notes

1. United Nations, Department of Economic and Social Affairs, Population Division, "World Population Prospects: Ten Key Messages," accessed December 5, 2023, https://www.un.org/development/desa/pd/sites/www.un.org.development.desa.pd/files/undesa_pd_2022_wpp_key-messages.pdf.
2. N. J. Pierce and A. Emmerson, "The Power and Promise of Intergenerational Collaboration Higher Education Institutions as Proving Ground," working paper (2023): 6, https://drive.google.com/file/d/1ZS_kINBV8xE8dtpaYokqw9PofRANNm-J/view.
3. N. Henkin and C. Brown, "Building Communities for All Ages: Lessons Learned from an Intergenerational Community-Building Initiative," *Journal of Community and Applied Psychology* 24 (2014): 63–68.
4. "The New Map of Life." Stanford Center on Longevity, accessed December 5, 2023, https://longevity.stanford.edu/the-new-map-of-life-report/#1637124315004-b149a6e6-23ec.
5. A. Gutterman, "On Ableism, Aging, and the Intersections between Them," *Generations Journal* special edition 2023. https://generations.asaging.org/ableism-ageism-and-intersections-between-them.
6. K. Weir, "Ageism Is One of the Last Socially Acceptable Prejudices," American Psychological Association, March 2023, https://www.apa.org/monitor/2023/03/cover-new-concept-of-aging.
7. A. Lytle and M. Apriceno, "Understanding Intergenerational Tension during the COVID-19 Pandemic: The Role of Ambivalent Ageism." *Journal of Intergenerational Relationships* 21, no. 4 (2022): 461–76.
8. Beth Johnson Foundation, *A Guide to Intergenerational Practice* (Stoke-on-Trent, England: Beth Johnson Foundation, 2009).
9. B. K. Eheart et al., "Intergenerational Programming for Foster-adoptive Families: Creating Community at Hope Meadows." *Journal of Intergenerational Relationships* 1, no. 1 (2003): 17–28.
10. C. Brown and N. Henkin, "Communities for All Ages: Reinforcing and Reimagining the Social Compact," in *The Global Age-Friendly Community Movement*, ed. Philip Stafford (New York: Berghahn Books, 2019): 139–68.
11. M. Kaplan et al. (eds.), *Intergenerational Contact Zones: Place-Based Strategies for Promoting Social Inclusion and Belonging* (New York: Routledge, 2020), 6.
12. A. Hatton-Yeo and T. Ohsako, *Intergenerational Programs: Public Policy and Research Implications: An International Perspective* (Hamburg, Germany: UNESCO Institute for Education, 2000), 10.
13. Center for Intergenerational Practice, Research, and Development (England). "Intergenerational Working," 2023, https://www.bjf.org.uk/working-with-others/intergenerational-working/.
14. L. L. Thang et al., "Intergenerational Programming in Asia: Converging Diversities toward a Common Goal," *Journal of Intergenerational Relationships* 1, no. 1 (2003): 49–69.
15. L. L. Thang, *Generations in Touch: Linking the Old and Young in a Tokyo Neighborhood* (Ithaca, NY: Cornell University Press, 2001).

16. A. Kusano, "Profile of the Japan Intergenerational Unity Association," *Journal of Intergenerational Relationships* 7, no. 1 (2009): 104–10.
17. J. Maccallum et al. "Community-Building through Intergenerational Exchange Programs," *Report to the National Youth Affairs Research Scheme* (Australian Government Department of Families, Community Services, and Indigenous Affairs, 2006), 115.
18. A. Fitzgerald et al., "A New Project Shows Combining Childcare and Aged Care Has Social and Economic Benefits," 2018, https://theconversation.com/a-new-project-shows-combining-childcare-and-aged-care-has-social-and-economic-benefits-99837.
19. N. J. Pierce and A. Emmerson, "The Power and Promise of Intergenerational Collaboration: Higher Education Institutions as Proving Ground," working paper, 2023, https://drive.google.com/file/d/1ZS_kINBV8xE8dtpaYokqw9PofRANNm-J/view.
20. N. Green et al., "From Anti-Aging to Anti-Ageist: Changing Attitudes through Social Media" (New York: New York University, The Center for Health and Aging Innovation, 2023), https://www.nyuchai.org/publications.
21. J. Kania and M. Kramer, "Collective Impact," *Stanford Social Innovation Review* (Winter 2011): 36, https://ssir.org/articles/entry/collective_impact.
22. K. Milligan et al., "The Relational Work of Systems Change," *Stanford Social Innovation Review*, January 18, 2022, https://doi.org/10.48558/MDBH-DA38.
23. M. Freedman and E. Nichols, "COGENERATION: Is America Ready to Unleash a Multigenerational Force for Good?" accessed December 12, 2023, https://cogenerate.org/research/cogeneratin/.
24. V. S. Kuehne and J. Melville, "The State of Our Art: A Review of Theories Used in Intergenerational Program Research (2003-2004) and Ways Forward," *Journal of Intergenerational Relationships* 12 (2014): 317–46.

Bibliography

Beth Johnson Foundation. *A Guide to Intergenerational Practice*. Stoke-on-Trent, England: Beth Johnson Foundation, 2009. https://www.bjf.org.uk/working-with-others/intergenerational-working.

Brown, C., and N. Henkin. "Communities for All Ages: Reinforcing and Reimagining the Social Compact." In *The Global Age-Friendly Community Movement*. Edited by Philip Stafford, 139–68. New York: Berghahn Books, 2019.

Center for Intergenerational Practice, Research, and Development (England). "Intergenerational Working." 2023. https://www.bjf.org.uk/working-with-others/intergenerational-working/.

Drury, L., D. Abrams, and H. J. Swift. "Intergenerational Contact During and Beyond COVID-19." *Journal of Social Issues* 78, no. 4 (2022): 860–82. https://doi.org/10.1111/josi.12551.

Duffy, B. *The Generation Myth*. New York: Basic Books, 2021.

Eheart, B. K., Power, M. B., and D. E. Hopping. "Intergenerational Programming for Foster-Adoptive Families: Creating Community at Hope Meadows." *Journal of Intergenerational Relationships* 1, no. 1 (2003): 17–28.

Fitzgerald, A., K. Radford, and L. Kirsnan. "A New Project Shows Combining Childcare and Aged Care Has Social and Economic Benefits." The Conversion, 2018. https://theconversation.com/a-new-project-shows-combining-childcare-and-aged-care-has-social-and-economic-benefits-99837.

Freedman, M., and E. Nichols. "COGENERATION: Is America Ready to Unleash a Multigenerational Force for Good?" Accessed December 12, 2023. https://cogenerate.org/research/cogeneration/.

Freedman, M., and T. Stamp. "Overcoming Age-Segregation." *Stanford Social Innovation Review* 2021: 1–6. https://ssir.org/articles/entry/overcoming_age_segregation.

Gerhardt, M., Josephine Nachemson-Ekwall, and Brandon Fogel. "Harnessing the Power of Age Diversity." *Harvard Business Review*, 2020. https://hbr.org/2022/03/harnessing-the-power-of-age-diversity.

Green, N., A. Merz, and E. Gonzales. "From Anti-Aging to Anti-Ageist: Changing Attitudes through Social Media." New York: New York University Center for Health and Aging Innovation, 2023. https://archive.nyu.edu/bitstream/2451/64383/5/Parasocial_040423_final.pdf.

Grullon-Virgil, D., and S. Barreto. "Beyond Passing the Torch: Recommendations on Leveraging Age Diversity to Build a Stronger Democracy Now." https://drive.google.com/file/d/1T9-r5axrnWB3GN9MBg52OHJcGzfThIuD/view.

Gutterman, A. "On Ableism, Aging, and the Intersections Between Them." *Generations Journal* special edition, 2023. https://generations.asaging.org/ableism-ageism-and-intersections-between-them.

Hatton-Yeo, A., and T. Ohsako. *Intergenerational Programs: Public Policy and Research Implications: An International Perspective*. Hamburg, Germany: UNESCO Institute for Education, 2000.

Henkin, N., and C. Brown. "Building Communities for All Ages: Lessons Learned from an Intergenerational Community-Building Initiative." *Journal of Community and Applied Psychology* 24 (2014): 63–68.

Kania, J., and M. Kramer. "Collective Impact." *Stanford Social Innovation Review*, Winter 2011: 36. https://ssir.org/articles/entry/collective_impact.

Kaplan, M., M. Sanchez, and J. Hoffman. *Intergenerational Pathways to a Sustainable Society*. New York: Springer, 2017.

Kaplan, M., and M. Sánchez. "Intergenerational Programs and Policies in Aging Societies." In *International Handbook on Aging and Public Policy*, edited by S. Harper and K. Hamblin, 367–383. Cheltenham, UK: Edward Elgar, 2014.

Kaplan, M., L. L. Thang, M. Sanchez, and J. Hoffman (eds.). *Intergenerational Contact Zones: Place-Based Strategies for Promoting Social Inclusion and Belonging*. New York: Routledge, 2020.

Kuehne V. S., and J. Melville. "The State of Our Art: A Review of Theories Used in Intergenerational Program Research (2003-2004) and Ways Forward." *Journal of Intergenerational* Relationships 12 (2014): 317–46.

Kusano, A. "Profile of the Japan Intergenerational Unity Association." *Journal of Intergenerational Relationships* 7, no. 1 (2009): 104–10.

Luscher, K. "Ambivalence: A Sensitizing Construct for the Study and Practice of Intergenerational Relationships." *Journal of Intergenerational Relationships* 9, no. 2 (2011): 191–206.

Lytle, A., and M. Apriceno. "Understanding Intergenerational Tension during the COVID-19 Pandemic: The Role of Ambivalent Ageism." *Journal of Intergenerational Relationships* 21, no. 4 (2022): 461–76.

Maccallum, J., D. Palmer, P. Wright, W. Cumming-Potvin, and J. Northcote. "Community-Building through Intergenerational Exchange Programs." In *Report to the National Youth Affairs Research Scheme*. Australian Government Department of Families, Community Services, and Indigenous Affairs, 2006.

Mehta, K. K., and L. L. Thang. "Interdependence in Asian Families: The Singapore Case." Paper presented at the International Consortium for Intergenerational Programs, 2004, Victoria, BC, Canada.

Milligan, Katherine, Juanita Zerda, and John Kania. "The Relational Work of Systems Change." *Stanford Social Innovation Review*, January 18, 2022. https://doi.org/10.48558/MDBH-DA38.

Murray, S. "The Power of Connecting Generations." Accessed December 18, 2023. https://cogenerate.org/wp-content/uploads/2022/09/thepowerofcogenerating.pdf.

Newman, Sally, C. Ward, T. Smith, J. Wilson, and J. McCrea. *Intergenerational Programs: Past, Present, and Future*. Washington, DC: Taylor and Francis, 1997.

Pierce, N. J., and A. Emmerson. "The Power and Promise of Intergenerational Collaboration: Higher Education Institutions as Proving Ground." Working paper, 2023. https://drive.google.com/file/d/1ZS_kINBV8xE8dtpaYokqw9PofRANNm-J/view.

Sneed, R. S., and A. C. Y. Chan. "The Implications of Intergenerational Relationships for Minority Aging: A Review of Recent Literature." *Current Epidemiology Reports* 10, no. 1 (2023): 44–50. https://doi.org/10.1007/s40471-023-00319-x.

Stafford, Phillip. *The Global Age-Friendly Community Movement*. New York: Berghahn Books, 2019.

Stanford Center on Longevity. "The New Map of Life." Accessed December 5, 2023. https://longevity.stanford.edu/the-new-map-of-life-report/.

Thang, L. *Generations in Touch: Linking the Old and Young in a Tokyo Neighborhood*. Ithaca, NY: Cornell University Press, 2001.

Thang, L. L., M. Kaplan, and N. Henkin. "Intergenerational Programming in Asia: Converging Diversities toward a Common Goal." *Journal of Intergenerational Relationships* 1, no. 1 (2003): 49–69.

Trinh, D. "Reversing the Systemic Tide to Truly Lift All Boats." *Generations Journal*, special edition, 2023: 1–20. https://generations.asaging.org/reversing-systemic-tide-truly-lift-all-boats.

United Nations, Department of Economic and Social Affairs, Population Division. "World Population Prospects 2022: Ten Key Messages." July 2022. https://www.un.org/development/desa/pd/sites/www.un.org.development.desa.pd/files/undesa_pd_2022_wpp_key-messages.pdf.

Weir, K. "Ageism Is One of the Last Socially Acceptable Prejudices." American Psychological Association. March 2023. https://www.apa.org/monitor/2023/03/cover-new-concept-of-aging.

Appendix A Intergenerational Thought Leaders

Donna Butts, executive director, Generations United
Alison Clyde, chief executive officer, Generations Working Together (Scotland)
Anneke Fitzgerald, Ph.D., emeritus professor, Griffith University and director, Australian Institute of Intergenerational Practice
Marc Freedman, founder and Co-CEO, Co-Generate
Ernest Gonzales, PhD, professor of social work and director of The Center for Health and Aging Innovation, New York University.
Alan Hatton-Yeo, MBE, Alan Hatton-Yeo, former CEO of Beth Johnson Foundation, consultant
Shannon Jarrott, PhD, professor of social work, Ohio State University
Atsuko Kusano, PhD, professor emeritus, Shiraume Gakuen University, Tokyo, Japan
Mariano Sánchez, PhD, professor of sociology, University of Granada, and head of the Macrosad Chair in Intergenerational Studies
Derenda Schubert, PhD, executive director, Bridge Meadows
Leng Leng Thang, PhD, associate professor of Japanese studies, National University of Singapore

INDEX

For the benefit of digital users, indexed terms that span two pages (e.g., 52–53) may, on occasion, appear on only one of those pages.

A

AARP, 3–4, 24, 44, 196–97, 258, 337, 471
   Andrus Award for Community Service, 138
   Experience Corps, 3–4, 64, 173, 334, 458–59, 471–72
   Fraud Watch Network, 258
abuse, 29, 428–29, 431
Academy for Gerontology in Higher Education, 254
access, accessibility, 28, 43, 78–79, 238–39, 268, 292, 433–34, 452–53, 462
   to education, 40, 41, 83, 131, 132, 135, 154, 174, 225–26, 228–29, 292, 344–45
   to health care, 24, 43, 83, 222
   to internet, 3, 83, 210, 240–42, 283–84, 350–51
activism, 4, 32–33, 45, 185–86, 207, 258
adaptation, adaptability, 180, 184, 450
Aday, Ronald H., 455
advocacy, 23–24, 29–30, 45–46, 84, 120, 125, 131, 196–97, 226, 228–29, 353–54, 359–60, 375–76, 382
after-school programs, 3–4, 166–67, 170, 171, 299, 300–1
age, aging, 8–9, 38, 69, 166, 196–98, 235–36, 275, 296, 426–29, 431, 434–38
   active, 299, 302, 303, 312, 318–19, 353
   education and, 83–85, 86, 88, 221, 251
   health and, 212–13, 224, 227

population, 13, 15, 38, 47, 52, 68–70, 77, 83, 136, 197–98, 201, 221–22, 228–29, 236, 266, 296, 312, 327, 329–30, 334, 378, 469
   views on, 8, 44, 172, 223–24, 235, 243, 244, 249, 253–54, 256, 258, 297–98, 302, 312, 318–19, 327–28, 344, 382, 402, 433, 456
   workforce and, 44, 69, 77, 107–8, 136, 378
   See also ageism
aged care, 393, 394–95, 399–400, 456. *See also* eldercare
Age Discrimination in Employment Act, 196–97, 434
age-friendly movement, 7–8, 351–54, 359–60
Age-Friendly University (AFU) initiative, 8, 10–11, 13, 83–84, 85–86, 90, 91, 221, 228–29, 254, 257–58, 271
ageism, 3, 6, 8–9, 10, 14, 15–17, 27, 38–39, 46, 62, 84, 174, 196–97, 200–1, 221, 229, 235, 236, 238, 239–40, 244, 249, 251, 253–54, 258, 275, 276–77, 290, 291, 296, 346, 348, 364, 365, 369, 372, 373–74, 375, 376, 382, 393, 428, 431, 433, 460, 469–70
Age Platform Europe, 353
Aging Service Access Points, 240–42
Akron Art Museum, 185–86
Albert, David, 209
Alboher, Marci, 100

Alicke, Mark D., 379–81
Allport, Gordon W., 381
Alzheimer's. *See* cognitive health; dementia
American Academy of Child and Adolescent Psychiatry, 171
American Academy of Pediatrics, 171
American Association of Colleges and University, 253
American Planning Association, 28
American Rescue Plan Act, 168
American Society on Aging, 8–9
   Lifetime Education and Renewal Network (LEARN), 6–7
AmeriCorps, 3–4, 6–7, 24, 63, 158, 164–65, 167, 170, 175, 471–72
   Foster Grandparent Program, 3–4, 12, 27, 164–70, 173, 174, 449–50, 471
   National Civilian Community Corps (NCCC), 3–4, 164
   Retired and Senior Volunteer Program (RSVP), 27, 158, 164–65, 170, 471
   Senior Companion Program, 164–65, 169, 170
   Seniors, 3–4, 27, 159, 164–65, 167, 168, 169, 170, 173, 175
   VISTA, 3–4, 164
   Volunteering and Civic Life in America, 173
AmeriSpeak Panel, 10, 54
Ampact, 63
ancestors, ancestorhood, 207, 215, 329
Andreoletti, Carrie, 253–54

Angel, Jacqueline L., 198
Anishanaabe Seven Generations tradition, 363
Anthropocene, 205. *See also* climate change
anxiety. *See* mental health
Apples and Honey Nightingale, 274, 358, 473–74
Ards Borough Council, 346
Arizona State University, 83, 221
Art Resistance through Change (ART-C), 185–86
assets, asset-based framework, 8, 15, 17, 69, 74–75, 77, 133, 183, 185, 344, 348–49, 450
assisted living facilities, 14, 249–50, 251, 255–56, 304
Atchison, Brenda, 63–64
Atlantic Philanthropies, 15, 345, 346, 349, 356
Australia, 16, 399–405
  Belonging, Being and Becoming: Early Years Learning Framework, 399
  Creating Intergenerational Connections through Digital Storytelling, 399, 402–3
  Institute for Intergenerational Practice, 25
  Intergenerational Care Project, 399–402
  National Youth Affairs Research Scheme (NYARS), 475
authority figure, 86, 452, 456
awareness, 3, 6, 14, 26, 84, 90, 119, 133, 229, 266, 270–72, 273–74, 286, 301, 302, 307, 329–30, 353–54, 359, 363, 376, 381, 404, 433, 479, 482
Awareness@Work, 206, 209–10
Ayalon, Liat, 32–33, 451
Ayer Rajah Day Care Centre, 300

B
Baltes, Paul B., 450
Barreto, Sydelle, 121, 124, 125
Basque Country (Spain), 15, 313, 317–20
Beach, David, 187
Belfast City Council, 346, 353. *See also* Northern Ireland
belonging, 28, 29, 61, 123–24, 171, 172, 234, 288–89, 334, 373

Bernstein, Lewis, 63
Beth Johnson Foundation (BJF), 7, 15, 25, 270–71, 344–46, 347, 353, 356–58, 470, 473–74
  Centre for Intergenerational Practice, 356
bias, 6, 16, 109, 183, 184, 235, 271, 369, 381, 394, 418–19, 433–34, 437, 478–79. *See also* ageism
Biden, Joseph, 168, 170
Big & Mini, 62
Big Brothers Big Sisters, 64
Biggs, Simon, 70–71
Bisno, Elizabeth, 208, 209
Black History Month, 186
BMe Community, 74–75
BMK Consulting, 354
Bohm, David, 208
Bolton Clarke Retirement Villages, 402
bonding, 14–15, 296–98, 300, 301, 302, 303, 304, 306–7
Bonerath, Ethan, 206–8
Booth, Ruby Belle, 125
Boston:
  Age-Friendly Action Plan, 237–38, 239
  Housing Authority, 240–42
Boys & Girls Clubs, 3–4
Brandeis University, Center for Youth and Communities, 143
Brewer, Joe, 187
Bridge Meadows, 5, 43
Bridges Together, 6–7
Bronfenbrenner, Urie, 280
Brooks, David, 125
Bruner, Jerome, 279, 280
Buck, Carrie, 64
Buddy System, 7
building light-ups, 271–72, 359
Burgunder, Ann, 226–27

C
Cabrera, Angel and Elizabeth F., 383
Calouste Gulbenkian Foundation, 346
Canada, 15–16, 25–26, 363–76
  Cancity Employee Resource Programs, 372–74
  Centre for Addiction and Mental Health, 205
  Centre for Social Innovation (CSI), 371

  Charter of Rights and Freedoms, 365
  Community Animator Program (CAP), 371–72
  Free Agents, 369–71
  Greater Toronto Bioregional Learning Center, 207
  labor market in, 368
  Natural Resources Canada, 369
  Organisation for Economic Co-operation and Development, 364, 368
capacity building, 266, 350, 354, 356, 473–74
care, caregiving, 1–2, 3, 23–24, 28, 30, 39–40, 59–60, 120, 196, 201, 227, 296, 482
  family and, 28–29, 32, 43, 198, 199–200, 227, 228, 297–98, 328, 429, 430–31
  policy and, 29–30
  prevention and, 328–29
  social, 268–69, 272, 273, 281, 282, 356, 359–60, 475
career development and support, 11, 43, 83, 90, 98, 99, 100–2, 104–5, 106, 108, 110, 111–12, 132, 143, 227–28, 229, 249, 258, 365–67, 369–71, 430
Cares Family, 270–71
Caring Across Generations, 3
Case Western Reserve University, 187
Center for Substance Abuse Prevention, 471–72
Centers for Disease Control (CDC), 171–72, 173, 431
Central Connecticut State University, 249
  Working Together: Intergenerational Student/Senior Exchange, 14
Cervantes, Lucius, 146
Challenge Factory, 368, 369, 374
  Broken Talent Escalator model, 15–16, 365–67, 369–70, 376
  InterGen Lab, 375–76
Changing the Narrative (Colorado), 433
Child Abuse Protection and Treatment Act, 29
childcare, 39, 102, 164–65, 173, 182, 297–98, 300, 303, 304, 337, 339, 340, 356–58, 363, 394–95, 399, 458–59, 471

488 | INDEX

Children's Defense Fund, 24, 471
Children's Hospital Association, 171
Child Welfare League, 24, 471
China, 474
chronology, chronological essentialism, 434–38
Cigna Group, 234
Circle of Chairs, 4
circle of change revisited (COCR), 394, 395–405, 406
CIRKEL, 11, 98, 99–102, 113–14
    funding model, 105
    membership model, 100–1, 104–5
    onboarding process, 101–2
    outcomes, 106
    partnerships, 112–13
    quantifying success, 107–12
    scaling, 107, 112
    structure, 102–3
citizenship, 348, 437, 482
City Year, 170–71
civic engagement, 7–8, 10, 39, 45–46, 121, 124, 150, 163–64, 237–38, 297–98, 300, 348
Clark, Robert, 77
class, classism, 429, 430, 433, 468–69, 482
climate change, 32–33, 36, 45, 59, 122, 124, 205–6, 364, 468–69
    dialogue and, 206–10, 215–17
    health and, 211–13
    transdisciplinarity and, 214–15
Climate Dialogue Group (CDG), 206, 208, 209
Clinton, Bill, 164
coaching, 123, 136, 170–71, 189, 480
coalitions, 3–4, 24–25, 53
Coast Salish people, 372–73
cocreating, 118, 120, 121–22
CoGenerate, 3–4, 7, 10, 52, 53, 100, 107, 135, 163, 258, 480
    Challenge to Advance Academic Opportunity, 480
    Innovation Fellowships, 61–62, 112
cogeneration, 10, 52–60, 61–62, 64–65
    climate change and, 64
    education and, 62–64
    mental health and, 62, 64
    obstacles to, 60–61, 64–65
cognitive health, 13, 38, 39, 40, 70–71, 84–85, 89–90, 151, 152, 179, 181, 213–14, 226–28, 229, 256, 331, 332, 334, 339, 425, 451, 461, 470
    social isolation and, 169, 172–73, 234, 237, 239–40, 450
cohesion, 37, 38–39, 43, 46–47, 65, 84, 224–25, 226, 296, 297, 301, 312–13, 317, 319, 347, 348–49, 393
Coleman, Shawonna, 63
collaboration, 10, 11, 13, 24–25, 70–71, 76–77, 84, 110, 113, 121, 180, 205–6, 207, 214, 216–17, 235, 249, 258, 268, 274, 275, 304, 313, 328–29, 333, 339, 372, 382–83, 393, 395–96, 397–400, 402, 405, 468–69
    cross-disciplinary, 393–94, 395–97, 405–6
collective action, 45–46, 70, 71, 74, 76–77, 479, 483
collectivism, 72–73, 198, 210, 215–16, 397, 417–18
colocation sites, 300, 303, 304, 399
communication, 7–8, 60, 63, 206, 207, 208, 210, 299, 302, 393, 394, 395, 397–99, 405, 477. *See also* dialogue
Communities for All Ages, 349, 472
Communities in Schools, 170–71
community, community building, 3, 5, 7, 27, 28, 30, 37, 39, 41, 43, 45–46, 69–77, 80, 83, 84, 163–64, 169, 172–73, 180–81, 215, 234–35, 236, 237–40, 243, 245–46, 252–53, 254–56, 258, 267, 268–69, 275, 276–77, 280, 281–82, 283, 284–85, 287, 288–89, 290, 291–92, 296, 297–98, 301, 302, 305–6, 315, 319–20, 328–30, 331, 333, 334, 339, 347, 348, 350–51, 371, 372, 450, 470–71, 472, 477, 481
community of practice, 280–82, 285, 292, 354–55
comparison, social, 378–81, 382–86
confidence, 126, 131, 146, 148–49, 152–53, 155–56, 158–59, 165–66, 213, 229, 273–74, 275, 276, 349–50, 351, 404, 460–61
conflict, conflict resolution, 6, 70–71, 80, 208, 297, 330, 348–49, 365, 393, 394, 395, 405
connection, connectedness, 28, 33, 38, 47, 62, 72, 73–74, 84–85, 88, 89–90, 106, 123, 126, 174–75, 205, 209, 243–44, 249, 253, 277, 280, 287–88, 298, 331, 334, 348, 350–51, 382, 384, 393, 404–5, 425–26, 427, 428–34, 435–38, 468–69, 483
    in education, 145–46, 151, 171, 173, 174, 182, 183–84, 185–86
    health and, 46, 62, 84–85, 151, 171–72, 234, 237, 243, 268–69, 299, 456, 462, 470
    intercultural, 196, 198–99
    technology and, 151, 182, 183–84, 209, 234, 252, 269–70, 299, 470
    in workforce, 99, 101, 108, 110, 365–66, 373
Conservation Corps, 3–4
contact, contact theory, 27, 84–85, 86, 90, 312, 330, 379–80, 381–82, 384–85, 452, 456
contact zone, 296–97, 298, 300–1, 303, 304, 305–6, 307, 472
conversation. *See* dialogue
cooperation, 7, 26, 84, 86, 88
CorimAZ (Mexico), 271
Corporation for National and Community Service. *See* AmeriCorps
COVID-19 pandemic, 1–2, 12, 28–29, 32, 40, 46, 60, 75, 107–8, 113, 114, 132, 137–38, 148, 149, 150–52, 156, 159, 164, 165, 168, 170, 171, 180, 182, 183, 184–85, 199–200, 225, 237, 240, 244, 252, 267, 268–70, 285, 287, 290, 303, 305, 312, 314, 329, 340, 402–3, 468–69, 470
creativity, 3–4, 40, 86, 89–90, 122, 123, 124–25, 180, 181, 187–88, 206–7, 215–16, 235, 251, 269–70, 271–72, 290, 371, 428–29, 430, 431
Curnan, Susan, 143

D

decision-making, 87b, 272, 348–49, 394–95, 397, 402, 405, 437, 452–53

deficit model, 8, 17, 183, 344, 450, 469. *See also* assets, asset-based framework
dementia, 40, 89–90, 169, 172, 173, 179, 213–14, 226–28, 234, 268–69, 331, 332, 334, 339, 450, 461. *See also* cognitive health
demographic shifts, 1–2, 3, 6–7, 12–13, 30, 31, 47, 73–74, 83, 197–98, 236, 286, 297, 312, 317, 319, 327, 329–30, 340, 364, 426–27, 469. *See also* longevity; population *under* age, aging
depression. *See* mental health
Depth of Engagement Continuum Scale, 299–300
development, 43, 71–74, 268–69, 272, 374, 418–19
  bioregional, 206, 207, 214–15
  learning and, 168, 171, 174, 213, 229, 280, 289–90, 291
dialogue, 83, 118, 120–21, 187, 205–8, 209, 210, 215–16, 228–29, 249–51, 252–53, 258, 286, 372, 394, 395–96, 397–405, 406
  Bohm-inspired, 206, 208–10
  diversity and, 209–10, 216–17
Dickson, Doug, 124
di Costanzo, Diane, 99
digital divide, 240–42
disability, 29–30, 39, 165, 169, 179, 328, 337, 373, 429–30
discrimination, 16–17, 45–46, 174, 365, 429, 430, 432, 433, 437. *See also* ageism
diversity, 1–2, 10, 15–16, 31, 61–62, 65, 69–74, 77–79, 80, 83, 84, 90–91, 98, 131, 134, 163, 182, 184, 189, 195–96, 197–201, 221, 223, 227, 234, 238, 258, 284, 285, 288, 291, 302, 319, 364, 366–67, 368, 372, 373, 374, 375, 378–86, 393, 395–96, 399, 426–27, 430, 431, 433–34, 437–38, 482. *See also* equity; inclusion
DOROT, 4
DreamCatchers, 4
Driveways, 61
Dublin City University, 83, 254
Duffy, Bobby, 9

E

early childhood education and care (ECEC), 280, 281–82, 283–84, 287, 288–90, 291, 301
Economy League, #WellCityChallenge, 62
education, 1–2, 3, 69, 83, 118–19, 164, 235, 270, 283, 364, 394, 405
  academic success, 3–4, 124, 131, 141, 142–43, 148, 155–56, 158–59, 167, 168, 170–71, 179–80, 181, 183, 187, 315, 336, 351, 471
  access to, 40, 41, 83, 131, 132, 135, 154, 174, 225–26, 228–29, 292, 344–45
  climate change and, 187, 214–15
  cogenerational work and, 62–64
  community and, 186, 238–40, 284, 315
  connectedness and, 171, 174, 183–84
  disability and, 179
  diversity, equity, and inclusion in, 6, 8, 10–11, 41–42, 83–84, 85–86, 90–91, 121, 131, 135, 136, 171, 182, 189, 221, 223, 224–25, 227, 228–29, 254, 257, 284, 296, 315, 319, 344–45, 431–32, 482
  intergenerational connections in, 40–42, 86–90, 171, 174, 179–81, 183–84, 268–69, 272, 275, 276, 304, 312–20
  mental health and, 184–85, 188–89
  poverty and, 38, 131, 136, 137, 155, 213
  racial justice and, 182–83, 186
  relationship building and, 181, 185–86, 188, 189, 318–19, 351
  teacher shortage, 184–85
  technology and, 182, 183–84
  volunteering and, 164–67, 168, 169–70, 174, 226–28, 249–50, 254–55, 257, 298–99, 334–37, 344
  See also learning; mentoring; tutoring
Education Scotland, 275
Eisner Foundation, 10, 27–28, 36–37, 40, 43, 214, 224, 480
Eldera, 4

eldercare, 280, 292, 297–98, 300, 304, 337
elderhood, 71–72, 78–79, 215
Elder Justice Act, 29
elder rights, 207
empathy, 4, 39, 62, 63, 79, 87*b*, 88, 89–90, 108, 174, 385, 393
empowerment, 5, 39, 63, 276–77, 291, 307, 340, 480–81
Encore.org. *See* CoGenerate
EnCorps, 131, 132, 135–37, 142–43
  beneficiaries, 132
  competencies, 132–33
  measuring impact, 141
  profiles, 137–38
  retention rate, 133
  staff and board of directors, 134–35
  STEM Mentors Program, 143
  STEM Teachers Program, 131, 132, 133, 135, 137, 138
  STEMx Tutors Program, 131, 132, 133, 135, 137–42, 143
England, Inspiring Communities Programme, 345. *See also* United Kingdom
environment, 1–2, 3, 31, 32–33, 53, 59, 118–19, 123, 164, 180, 187, 205, 207–8, 211–12, 250–51, 372, 451, 480. *See also* climate change
Equatorial Voices Network (EVN), 206, 209
equity, 1–2, 30, 70, 74, 77–78, 90, 118, 119, 121, 124, 131, 133, 134–35, 171, 174, 182, 184, 189, 205, 214, 224–25, 242, 268, 346, 366–67, 373, 375, 399, 432, 433, 471, 477, 479–80, 482. *See also* diversity; inclusion
ethnicity, 54–55, 90, 195–201
European Union, 353
  Certificate of Intergenerational Learning, 356
  Day of Intergenerational Solidarity, 346, 353
  Erasmus+ Programme–Adult Education (KA2), 281, 356–58
  Grundtvig–Lifelong Learning Programme, 281
  Mainstreaming Intergenerational Solidarity (MATES), 347

490 INDEX

Map of Intergenerational Learning (EMIL), 346, 473–74
Qualifications Framework, 282
Year of Active Ageing and Intergenerational Solidarity, 346, 353
exercise, 300, 328, 332, 338, 470
Exeter University, 274–75
Experience Corps. *See under* AARP

F

Fairhill Center for Aging, 179
FaithActs, 306
Faith Lutheran College, 402
FallCreek, Stephanie, 179
family, 6, 30, 244
    bonding and, 296–98, 301, 302, 303
    care and, 297–98, 301, 328
    changes in, 290, 291, 312, 327
    grandfamilies, 29, 32
    institution of, 297
    state and, 312
Family Friends, 471–72
Farah, Kimberly S., 86
Farmer, Jared, 5
Fasbender, Ulrike, 379, 380–81
Federal Communications Commission (FCC), Affordable Connectivity Program, 240–42
Festinger, Leon, 379–80
Fitzpatrick, Anne, 280, 281
Fleet, Alexa and Brooks, 113–14
flexibility, 87b, 110, 140–41, 142, 147, 180, 210, 251, 280–81, 282–84, 469
Floyd, George, 182, 373
food insecurity, 3, 36, 88, 164, 212
foster care, 3–4, 5, 29, 36, 43
fourth turning framework, 71–74
Fraboni Scale of Ageism, 253–54
frailty prevention, 328–29, 330, 334
FrameWorks Institute, 460
Freedman, Marc, 120–21, 124–25
Freunde alter Menchen, Generation Nachbarschaft program, 245
Friedman, Marc, 135
friendship, 61, 63, 64, 87b, 88, 89, 110, 113–14, 123–24, 237, 239–40, 244, 288–89, 432

Fujiwara, Yoshinori, 330
Fuller-Thomson, Esme, 198
Fund for the Improvement of Post-Secondary Education, 471–72
funding. *See under* programs
future, 23–24, 32, 45, 46, 53, 54, 73–74, 84–85, 118–19, 120, 121, 123, 124, 125–26, 136, 143, 201, 205–6, 207, 209–10, 212–13, 214, 215–17, 223, 363, 375–76

G

GAIA (Global Activation of Intention and Action), 214
Gaithersburg Beloved Initiative, 31
gardens, gardening, 207–8, 211, 212, 213, 359
gender, 428, 429
    cogeneration and, 62
    community movements and, 75
    equity and, 121, 373
    leadership and, 79
    loneliness and, 39
    race and, 75
    STEM education and, 131
    volunteering and, 157, 337
    women in workforce, 312
Generation Connect, 4
generations, 8–9, 70–77
    archetypes, 71–74
    cogeneration and, 53, 54–61
    ethnic and racial diversity in, 197–201
    fourth turning framework, 71–74
    generational thinking, 411–12, 413–21
    generation gap, 6, 239–40, 312–13, 317, 327–28, 364
    power dynamics of, 121
    relationships between, 40, 70, 119–20, 125, 195–99, 312–13, 318–19, 329, 334, 348
Generations Over Dinner, 4
Generation Squeeze, 375
Generations Together, 6, 450, 479
Generations United, 3, 6–7, 9–10, 24–25, 26, 27–30, 31, 43, 108, 450, 471

Generations Working Together (GWT), 14, 25, 266–77, 345, 351, 356, 358, 473–74
    "A Connected Scotland: Recovering Our Connections 2023–2026," 268–69
    Creating Intergenerational Communities, 274
    Excellence Award program, 270, 274
Generation Uplift, 63
Generation Xchange, 41
generativity, 14, 62, 123, 143, 154, 249, 253–54, 258, 330, 339
George, Daniel, 211, 213–14
Georgia Reading and Math Corps, 63
Gerhardt, Megan, 271
Gerontological Society of America (GSA), 8, 228
    Age-Inclusivity Domains of Higher Education (AIDHE), 254
    Age Inclusivity in Higher Education Workgroup, 254
    Learning, Research, and Community Engagement Interest Group, 6–7
gerontology, 3, 8–9, 14, 38–39, 40, 222–23, 227–28, 249
Gerpott, Fabiola H., 379, 380–81
Global Intergenerational Week (GIW), 25, 270–72, 358–59
globalization, 364
Goldstone, Jack A., 73–74
government, governance. *See* policy
grandparents, 6, 29, 32, 198, 286, 291, 296, 297, 298, 301, 303, 359, 430. *See also* Foster Grandparent Program *under* AmeriCorps
Grantmakers in Aging, 126
Gray Panthers, 5, 258
Greece, 356–58
Greene, Ward, 118, 126
Griffith University, Australian Institute for Intergenerational Practice, 475
growth mindset, 133, 140, 174
Grullon-Virgil, Dairanys, 121, 124, 125
gun violence, 63, 88, 169–70
Gurung, Prabal, 100

H

Haberman, Martin, 132
Hardison, Bethann, 100
Harris, Kamala, 170
Harvard University, 41
   Study of Adult Development, 7, 46
health and well-being, 1–2, 3–4, 7, 29, 32, 38, 39–40, 45, 47, 62, 83, 164, 184–85, 199–200, 205, 211–12, 221, 222, 229, 235, 268–69, 272, 318–19, 346, 363, 375, 402, 403, 434–36, 437–38, 469
   climate change and, 205, 207, 208, 212–13
   connection and, 28, 38, 40, 42, 43, 84–85, 168–69, 172, 196, 234, 237, 239–40, 277, 296, 306, 425, 429–30, 462
   disparities in, 200–1, 329–30
   housing and, 225
   shared sites and, 27–28, 39
   volunteering and, 40, 41, 123–24, 150, 151, 152–54, 168–69, 172–73, 181, 213–14, 227, 330, 336–37
   See also cognitive health; mental health
health care, 3, 7–8, 59–60, 69, 211–12, 393, 394–95, 397–98
   access to, 24, 43
   ageism in, 235
heart disease, 169, 172, 234
Heath, Roderick, 63
Hellenic Open University, 282–83
Henkin, Nancy, 349, 353, 453
Herbst, Abbie, 63–64
Hey Auntie!, 62
Hively, Janet M., 7
Homeless Intervention Services, 64
homelessness, 36, 42–43, 59–60, 63, 224–25
HomeShare OC, 64
home-sharing, 6, 42–43
Hope Meadows, 472
housing, 1–2, 3, 7–8, 10, 69, 237–38, 375
   affordable, 13, 63–64, 224–25, 226, 234, 238, 239, 240, 303
   age segregation in, 6, 431–32
   cogenerational work and, 59–60, 63–64
   cost of, 31, 42
   disparities in, 199–201, 375–76
   environmental impact of, 32
   family and, 297–98
   housing insecurity, 64, 224–26, 229
   intergenerational interventions in, 42–43, 224–26, 268–69, 277, 327, 482
   multigenerational, 5, 7, 8, 13, 28–29, 43, 52, 98, 296, 327
   poverty and, 38
Howard, Jessica L., 253–54
Howe, Neil, 71
Huang, Lingli, 297
Hunter, Ciel, 98

I

identity, 3, 84, 189, 289–90, 373, 374, 379–80, 381, 382, 383, 385, 480–81
immigration, 30, 31, 88, 197–201, 312, 319
Immordino-Yang, Mary Helen, 62
impact. *See under* programs
inclusion, 1–2, 7–8, 79, 83–84, 85–86, 90–91, 206, 221, 223, 228–29, 237–38, 254, 257, 272, 282, 285, 286, 291–92, 302, 312–13, 315, 319, 347, 348–49, 351–53, 372, 374, 395–96, 397, 398–99, 433–34
independence, 23–24, 124, 173, 296, 403, 430
indigenization, 214
indigenous people, 73, 207, 363, 372–73
individualism, 71, 72–73, 196–97
Interaction Design Foundation, 102
interdependence, 9–10, 29–30, 43, 299–300, 301, 344–45, 365, 468–69
Intergenerational Evaluation Toolkit, 457, 458
Intergenerational Program Evaluation Tool (IPET), 457–58, 461, 462
Intergenerational Schools, 179–89, 213–15
   African-American Read-In, 186
   Black History Expo, 186
   Intergenerational Visits program, 180, 182
   Learning Partner program, 180, 182, 183–84, 185, 188, 213
   Math Learning Partner program, 188
Intergenerational Specialist Certificate, 450
intergenerativity, 216–17
International Certificate in Intergenerational Practice, 268, 356
International Child Development Initiatives, 281
International Consortium for Intergenerational Programmes (ICIP), 6, 25, 302, 344, 345, 473
internet access, 3, 83, 210, 240–42, 283–84, 350–51
intersectionality, 271, 373–74, 433
Ireland, 288–90, 291–92, 353, 356–58
Irish Senior Citizens Parliament, 271
isolation, 3, 7, 13, 27–28, 31, 32, 38, 40, 46, 62, 122, 150, 163, 168–69, 172, 183–84, 196, 224–25, 234–35, 236, 237, 239–40, 242, 243, 245–46, 268–70, 271, 275, 276–77, 286–87, 290, 296, 317, 350–51, 425, 468–69, 470. *See also* loneliness; mental health
Italy, 356–58

J

Janke, Megan C., 461
Japan, 15, 327–40, 474, 475
   Community Comprehensive Support Center (CCSC), 333
   Comprehensive Support Project for Care Prevention and Daily Life Support, 329
   Edogawa Smile Community Activity, 339
   Intergenerational Unity Association (JIUA), 25, 475
   Kotoen, 337–40, 474–75
   Ministry of Health, Labour, and Welfare, 328
   REPRINTS, 334–37, 461
   Respect for the Aged Day, 329
   Shibasaki Irodori Station, 331–34
   Social Welfare Council, 333

Society for Intergenerational Studies (JSIS), 475
Study Group on Promotion Strategies for General Care Prevention Projects, 328–29
Sumo Festival, 338
Japp, Charlotte, 98–99, 100, 112
Japp, Michael, 98–99
Jarrott, Shannon, 86–87, 88, 89, 91, 256–57, 451
Jetson, Raymond A., 79
Johfre, Sasha, 163
Johns Hopkins University, Everyone Graduates Center, 170–71
Journal of Intergenerational Relationships, 2, 6, 25
Juniper Consulting NI, 351
justice, social, 4, 133, 134, 185–86, 258, 346

K
kampong (village), 14–15, 297–98, 299–300, 305–6. *See also* Singapore
Karasik, Rona, 256
Katz, Elly, 62
Katzenbach, Jon, 124–25
Kenney, Nicole, 62
Keynes, John Maynard, 136
King, Eden, 9
King, Martin Luther, Jr., 186
knowledge, knowledge exchange, 23–24, 57–59, 69, 70–71, 75–76, 77, 79, 84–85, 101–2, 133, 134–35, 136, 163, 223–24, 244, 266, 268–69, 273–74, 275–76, 280, 281–82, 291, 292, 313, 315, 318–19, 366, 372, 378–86, 394–95, 451, 473
Koreatown (Los Angeles), 4
Kretzman, John P., 450
Kuhn, Maggie, 5
Kwakwaka'wakw people, 372–73

L
LaMarche, Gara, 4
language, 238–40, 274–75, 283–84, 298–99, 302, 304
Lansing, Sherry, 135
Lasell University, Lasell Village, 10–11, 42, 85–86, 88, 89–91
  Campus Conversations, 90
  Intergenerational Symposium, 88

Intergenerational Women's History Month Celebration, 88
Speakers Series, 88
Talk of Ages program, 86, 88, 90, 237, 251
leadership, 4, 10, 70, 75–76, 77, 98, 119–20, 124, 126, 132, 134, 188, 339, 356, 394, 405, 480
  behavioral model, 78
  characteristics model (Trait Era), 77–78
  coleadership model, 78–80
  shared, 395–96, 397
  transformational theory of, 78
learning, 57, 59, 84–85, 86, 89, 90, 109, 110, 135–37, 138–39, 179–81, 184, 228–29, 280–85, 286–92, 302, 304, 351, 399, 405
  active, 284
  community and, 284–85, 290, 291–92
  diversity and, 284, 288, 291
  experiential, 110, 253, 280–81, 286–88
  lifelong, 133, 184, 189, 283, 290, 302, 313, 317, 329, 334, 399
  online, 281–86
  practice-based, 356
  relationships and, 179, 184, 185–86, 188, 189, 213–14, 215
  social-emotional, 149, 188–89
  two-way, 8, 15, 84–85, 86, 140, 143, 180, 272, 300, 312–13, 317, 318–19, 382–83, 393
  See also education
Lee, Michelle, 100
Lee, Opal, 186
Leedahl, Skye N., 462
Levy, Sheri R., 84
LFT Trust, 356
LGBTQ+ people, 45–46, 252–53, 373, 430
Liederman, David, 24
life expectancy. *See* longevity
lifespan approach, 7, 29–30, 79, 84–85, 88, 110, 251, 450, 470, 472, 478–79, 482
Linking Lifetimes, 471–72
listening. *See* dialogue
literacy, 3–4, 145–46, 147–48, 154–56, 168, 173, 179–80, 213, 335, 336, 393

"big 5 skills," 147, 158–59
digital, 109, 240–42
Science of Reading, 149
Literations (Massachusetts), 3–4
Little Brothers–Friends of the Elderly, 13, 45–46, 233–35, 237–38, 242–44, 245–46
  CitySites program, 235, 238–42, 243–44, 245–46
  Digital Dividends, 240–42, 245–46
  "friendly calls" program, 244
  Friendly Visiting program, 237
living communities, 41–42, 103–4
Lloyds TSB Foundation for England and Wales, 345
loneliness, 3, 28, 31, 32, 39, 40, 53, 62, 64, 79, 125–26, 168–69, 172, 173, 196, 205, 212, 234–35, 236, 237, 239–40, 242, 243–44, 245–46, 268–70, 271, 275, 276–77, 291, 299, 318–19, 450, 469, 470. *See also* isolation; mental health
longevity, 43–44, 73–74, 83, 84, 88, 119, 123–24, 197–98, 200–1, 221–22, 229, 235–36, 296, 312, 372, 427, 469
long-term care facilities, 213–14, 328, 329, 333
Loyola Generativity Scale, 253–54

M
MacCraith, Brian, 221
MacDougall, Eileen, 173
Mann, Marylen, 146
Mannheim, Karl, 70–71, 73–74, 420
Maplecroft, Climate Change Vulnerability Index, 209
Marcus, Noelle, 63–64
marginalization, 42, 74–75, 373–74
Marquiset, Armand, 237
Maryville University, 154–55, 157
massive online open course (MOOC), 280–83, 284, 285
May Department Stores Company Foundation, 146
May, Margie, 146
McKibben, Bill, 45
McKnight, John, 450
Mead, Margaret, 318–19
measures. *See under* programs

INDEX | 493

Medicaid and Medicare, 38, 196–97, 201
Menand, Louis, 9
Menorah Park Engagement Scale, 461
mental health, 3–4, 29, 38–39, 43, 53, 59, 62, 64, 77–78, 84–85, 124, 125–26, 152, 169, 172, 184–85, 188–89, 196, 205, 207, 208, 210, 223–24, 330, 373, 429–30, 450, 451, 457, 480
  connection and, 46, 53, 62, 105, 171–72, 173, 207, 234, 318–19, 330, 429–30
  race and, 62, 64
  volunteering and, 40, 168–69, 172–73
MENTOR, 170–71
mentoring, 4, 11, 12, 40–41, 44, 45–46, 63, 64, 87*b*, 90, 99, 100–1, 104–5, 107, 111–12, 113, 121, 122, 136, 143, 145–46, 147, 149, 157, 158, 159, 165, 166–67, 168, 170–71, 173, 213, 225–26, 298, 300–1, 366, 369–70, 372. *See also* tutoring; volunteering
Merchant, Aditi, 62
Meredith Group, 99
MetroHealth Medical Center, 183
MetroMorphosis, 10, 74–75
  collective action networks, 76–77
  My Brother's Keeper Initiative, 75
  organizational structure, 77, 78–80
  Urban Congress on African-American Males (UC), 75
  Urban Elders Council, 75
  Urban Leadership Development Initiative, 75–76
  Youth Advisory Council, 75
Mexico, 271, 272
Micoli, Thea, 226–27
Milken Institute, Center for the Future of Aging, 107
Minkler, Meredith, 198
Mochan, Carol, 269
Montepare, Joann M., 86
More Perfect, 3–4
Morgan, Garret, 186
Morhardt, Darby, 226–27

Morrow-Howell, Nancy, 150
Morton, Peggy, 226–27
Moss, Peter, 288
Murthy, Vivek, 125–26, 168–69

N
Nardini, Gia, 72
Nash, Bernard E., 165, 166
nation, 267–68, 277
  majority-minority, 195–96, 197–98, 200–1
National Academies of Sciences, Engineering, and Medicine, 8–9
National and Community Service Act, 164
National Assessment of Educational Progress, 131
National Bureau of Economic Research, 77
National College Attainment Network, 170–71
National Council on Aging, 24, 471
National Issues Forum, 124
National Library of Medicine, 172
National Mentoring Resource Center, 147, 159
National Partnership for Student Success (NPSS), 12, 170–74
  Engaging Older Adults in Student Success Learning Community, 174
  Support Hub, 170–71, 174
National Student Support Accelerator and Accelerate, 170–71
Navajo Area Agency on Aging, 167–68
Nesterly, 42–43, 63–64
Netherlands, 356–58
networks, network building, 11, 76–77, 99–100, 101, 111–12, 154, 238–39, 245, 257, 268–69, 273–74, 276, 318–20, 344, 351, 353–55, 369–70, 371, 372, 373–74, 432, 473–74, 479–80
neurosequential model, 399
Newcastle University, National Institute on Ageing (NICA), 107–11
Newman, Sally, 6, 344, 450
New York Foundation for Senior Citizens (NYFSC), 13, 225

New York University:
  Alzheimer's Disease and Related Dementias Family Support Program Buddy Program, 40, 226–29
  Center for Health and Aging Innovation (CHAI), 13, 42–43, 224–26, 228–29
  Intergenerational Home Sharing Program, 224–26, 228–29
Norouzi, Neda, 451
Northeastern University, Public Evaluation Lab (NU-PEL), 242
Northern Ireland, 15, 271–72
  Age Concern, 345, 346
  Building Safer, Shared, and Confident Communities Strategy, 349–50
  Care Home ECHO group, 359–60
  Collaborating Towards an Age-Friendly NI, 353
  Commissioners for Older and Younger People, 359
  Department for Communities Active Ageing Strategy, 351–53
  Department of Education, 356
  Department of Justice (DOJ), 349–50
  Digital Age Project, 350–51
  EngAge Together Project, 353–54
  Intergenerational Safer Communities project, 350
  Intergenerational Steering Group, 346, 356
  Linking Generations Northern Ireland (LGNI) program, 270–71, 274, 345, 346–50, 351–60, 473–74
  Police Service of, 350
  Policing and Community Safety Partnerships (PCSPs), 349–50
  Policy Action Group on Loneliness, 359–60
  Public Health Agency, 351–54
  Reaching Out: Connecting Older People program, 350–51
  Soil Association, 359
  Troubles, 348–49

Twinkl Northern Ireland, 359
Workers Educational Authority, 350–51
See also United Kingdom
Northwestern University, Mezulum Center for Cognitive Neurology and Alzheimer's Disease, 226–27
nursing homes, 303, 337, 339, 340, 450, 454

O

Oasis Institute, 146
  Intergenerational Tutoring program, 64, 145–60, 173
OCER (Ohio Collaborative for Educating Remotely), 182, 183
Ohio City Farm, 181
Ohio Community Schools of Quality, 187
Oki, Chieko, 331, 332–33, 334
Older Americans Act, 196–97
Older People's Strategic Action Forum, 268–69
On Being Project, 3–4
ONEgenerational, 39
Ontario Student Drug Use and Health Survey, 205
openness, 106, 140, 209, 270, 288, 291, 370, 372, 395–96, 397, 433–34
opioid crisis, 32, 164
Orr, David, 187
Osher Lifelong Learning Institute, 223
Ossofsky, Jack, 24
outcomes. *See under* programs
ownership, 112–13, 133, 276–77, 304, 397

P

Papa, 4
partnerships, 7, 74, 76–77, 79, 85, 112–13, 146, 171, 180, 187–88, 212, 213, 238–39, 254–55, 257–58, 266, 268, 269, 272–73, 275, 276–77, 284, 356–60, 382–83, 399, 478–79
  evaluation-practice, 451, 452–56, 459–61
  public-private, 167, 170
Pass It On Network, 207
Patterson, Taryn, 453
PEACE (Positive education about aging and contact experiences) model, 84
Peace Corps, 3–4
Pennsylvania Intergenerational Network, 479–80
perspective taking, 384–85
Petits Frères des Pauvres (PFP), 237, 245–46
  International Federation of, 244–45
  Service Civique, 244
Pickering College, Global Leadership Program, 206–7
place, place-making, 296, 472
policy, 23–24, 29–30, 196–97, 226, 228–29, 236, 267, 268–69, 270, 271–72, 276, 282, 283, 297, 301, 327–29, 344–45, 353–54, 358–60, 363, 374–75, 433–34, 474, 476–77, 478–82, 483
Poo, Ai-jen, 3
population aging. *See under* age, aging
postal pals (pen pals), 149, 150, 151–52, 156
poverty, 23–24, 38, 131, 136, 137, 155, 164–65, 166–67, 213, 224–25, 346
Prescription Produce, 212
Presencing Institute, InterHub, 214
problem solving, 118, 123, 124–25, 188, 394–95, 397, 402
productivity, 37, 38, 77, 201, 208, 365, 375–76, 427–28, 430, 431
professional development, 63, 89, 98, 99, 104–5, 109, 111–12, 136–37, 138, 141, 142–43, 189, 281–82, 365–66, 367, 369, 370, 378–79, 395, 405
Program for International Student Assessment, 131
programs, 1–8, 26–27, 299–300
  access to, 238
  benefits of, 38–42
  best practices, 319–20
  challenges of, 102–7, 254–57, 267, 274–75, 276–77, 307, 330, 334, 337, 340, 402–3, 405
  cocreating, 118, 120, 121–22
  communicating on, 16, 17, 90, 180, 267–70, 273, 358, 451, 452–53, 460–61
  designing, 149–50, 180–81, 276
  evaluating, 237–38, 242–44, 245–46, 253–54, 256–57, 400–2, 404–5, 449–62, 481
  funding, 105, 276–77, 344–45, 353–54, 355–56, 359, 452, 476
  impact, 3–4, 29, 30, 37, 40, 64, 65, 74, 76, 84–85, 89, 91, 106–7, 110, 113, 133, 136, 137, 140–41, 143, 159, 167, 168–70, 174–75, 207, 227–28, 253–54, 256–57, 267, 270, 271–72, 274, 275, 276, 302, 304, 313, 315–17, 330, 333–34, 336–37, 339–40, 344–45, 346, 351–53, 365, 368, 376, 405, 451, 452, 453–54, 458–59, 461
  measures, 47, 119, 141, 213, 242–43, 253–54, 274, 297, 330, 370–72, 373, 374–75, 450–51, 452, 456, 457–58, 461, 462
  outcomes, 3, 29, 38, 40, 41, 42, 43–44, 76, 84–85, 91, 105, 106, 121, 124, 150, 167, 168–70, 208, 213–14, 223–24, 237, 239–40, 242, 253–54, 256–57, 258, 282, 330, 348–49, 354, 363, 372, 394, 395–96, 397–403, 404–5, 406, 413–14, 430, 451–52, 453–54, 456–57, 458–59, 460–61
  purpose and, 8, 26–27, 47, 53, 62, 108, 109–10, 122, 123–24, 146, 149, 158–59, 165, 172, 174, 347, 425, 453–54, 470, 477
  quality, quality indicators, 26–27, 148–49, 253–54, 274–75, 277, 282, 285, 288–89, 298–99, 358, 363, 368, 374–75, 382, 395, 403, 458, 461, 476
  recruitment and, 187, 188, 257, 403–4
  research on, 6, 86–90, 91, 107–12, 175, 256–57, 274–75, 280, 288–90, 292, 313–20, 330, 336–37, 346–47, 348, 353–54, 476, 481
  scaling, 106–7, 112, 166–67, 170, 174–75, 214–15, 226, 228, 250, 337, 370–71, 476, 481

INDEX | 495

programs (cont.)
  sustainability of, 239–40, 249–50, 276–77, 285, 304, 307, 330, 340, 358, 374, 476
  training, 4, 89, 98, 108, 109, 187, 268, 275, 276, 280–82, 330, 335, 336, 353–54, 356, 394, 404, 405
  value and, 8, 26–27, 37, 44, 57, 73–76, 84, 90, 104–5, 121, 123–24, 136, 137, 158, 159, 163–64, 179–80, 187, 195–96, 206, 213–14, 216–17, 225, 227, 236, 244, 255, 258, 268–69, 270–72, 274–75, 276, 288–90, 312, 346, 348–49, 350–51, 364, 365, 374–75, 383, 393, 394, 395–96, 405, 411–12, 451, 453–54, 455, 459–60, 468, 471, 472, 476–77, 479, 481, 482, 483
public health, 164, 168–69, 172, 234, 237, 470

Q
quality of life, 8, 29–30, 47, 118, 120, 122, 179, 181, 213–14, 235, 239–40, 243, 468
Queen's University Belfast, Ark Ageing Programme, 353

R
race, 90, 428, 429
  cogeneration and, 53, 54–55, 56–57, 59–60, 62, 64
  community and, 74–75, 77, 234
  critical race theory, 480–81
  demographic changes and, 31, 197–98
  in education, 186
  equity and, 30, 74, 121, 373
  gender and, 75
  generational gap and, 469
  interracial relationships, 195–201
  justice and, 59–60, 182
  leadership and, 79
  loneliness and, 234
  multigenerational households and, 29
  national service and, 166
  in public policy, 30
  social comparison and, 384–85
  STEM education and, 131
racism, 3, 30, 433, 468–69
Reading Partners, 64

regenerative farming, 206, 207, 214–15
Reggio Emilia child development model, 450
Reinert method, 314
Re:Source Cleveland (Refugee Response), 181
respect, 3, 7–8, 209, 226, 237–38, 270, 347, 348–49, 394, 399, 403
Ritter, Beth, 77
Rocchio, Daniel J., 154–55
role models, 131, 158, 189, 366, 473
Roodin, Paul, 256
RRF Foundation for Aging, 150, 152
Rudolph, Cort W., 8–9
Rybak, W. S., 449–50

S
safety, safe spaces, 171, 346, 349–50, 373, 374
SAGE (Senior Advocates for Generational Equity), 118–23, 124, 125, 126, 174
  Babies Club, 119
  Legacy Fellowship program, 119–20
  Service Across Generations, 122
  Young Leaders Advisory Board (LAB), 121, 122
Sages & Seekers, 46, 62
Sánchez, Mariano, 277
Sankofa, 73–74, 75–76
Scharmer, Otto, 214
Schwarz, Roberta, 123
Scotland, 266, 267–77, 351, 358, 473–74
  Centre for Intergenerational Practice, 345
  Fife Local Authority, 275
  Older People's Assembly, 268–69
  Play Scotland, 275
  ROAR do Digital, 269–70
  Strategy for an Ageing Population, 345
  See also Generations Working Together (GWT)
Seefeldt, Carol, 454
Seeman, Teresa, 41
segregation, age, 1–2, 6, 10, 16–17, 27–28, 31, 41–42, 53, 61, 64–65, 195–201, 290, 296, 300, 303, 430, 431–32, 433, 469–70, 481–82

self-esteem, 38, 146, 148–49, 158–59, 229, 298–99, 313, 315, 317, 318–19, 339, 429–30
service learning, 3–4, 24, 40, 63, 163–75, 226–28, 239, 249–50, 254–55, 257, 298–99. *See also* volunteering
sexism, 433
shared sites, 27–28, 39, 271, 275, 300, 303–4, 305–6, 307, 312–13, 482
Sharp, Melanie, 384–85
SHINE, 471–72
Shorter, Trabian, 74–75
Singapore, 296–97, 298–307, 474
  Action Plan for Successful Aging, 297–98, 303
  Association of Early Childhood Educators, 301
  Center of Excellence for Senior Volunteerism, 299
  Council for the Third Age (C3A), 302, 474
  Family Matters!, 301, 302
  G-Connect: Strengthening the Intergenerational Bond, 301, 302
  Golden Opportunities Fund (GO! Fund), 302
  Grandparent of the Year Award, 301
  Grandparents' Day, 301
  Health Day Centre for Seniors, 304
  HV Little Library, 305
  Intergenerational Bonding Awards, 302
  Inter-Ministerial Committee, 297, 301
  Joo Chiat Social Club, 304
  Kampung Admiralty, 303
  Maintenance of Parents Act, 297
  Methodist Girls School, 304
  Ministry of Education, 298–99
  Ministry of Family and Youth, 474
  Ministry of Social and Family Development (Ministry of Community Development), 301
  My First Skool, 304
  National Family Council, 474
  National Family Week, 301

National Library Board, 302–3
National Trade Union Congress, 304
People's Association, 303
Retired Senior Volunteer Program (RSVP), 299, 300–1
St. John's–St. Margaret's Village, 303
Values in Action (Community Involvement Program), 298–99
Slovenia, 356–58
Smith, Douglas, 124–25
social media, 99, 354, 358, 478, 482
Social Security, 77, 196–97, 201
solastalgia, 205
solidarity, 84, 302, 303, 313, 318–19, 353
Southeast Asian Community Alliance (SEACA), 45
South Eastern Health and Social Care Trust, 346
Spain, 356–58. *See also* Basque Country
sports, 268–69, 332, 338
Stanford Social Innovation Review (SSRI), 2
Stanford University, 41
　Center on Longevity, 6, 107, 469
　New Map of Life Program, 6
Statistics Canada, Quality of Life Framework, 363, 374–75
status, 428, 429, 431
STEAM (science, technology, engineering, arts, math), 157
STEM (science, technology, engineering, math), 131, 132, 133, 135, 137–38, 142–43
stereotypes, 8–9, 10, 15, 16–17, 27, 46, 64–65, 84–85, 108, 139, 141, 163, 174, 223, 227, 235, 249, 252, 253–54, 270, 271, 276–77, 312, 313, 344, 348, 365, 393, 394, 429, 432, 433
stereotype threat, 86
stigma, 226, 227, 239–40
St. Joseph's Home, 303
STL Village, 223
St Monica Trust, 270–71
Strauss, William, 71
substance abuse, 3, 32, 205
Sugi, Keiko, 338, 339–40
suicide. *See* mental health

Suls, Jerry, 384–85
Sun, Peter C., 150, 198
sustainability, 77, 239–40, 280, 282, 285, 291–92, 300, 304, 307, 330, 340, 358, 374, 375
SWAN 3G, 4, 63
Swinburne University, 402

T

Tampines 3-in-1 Family Center, 300
Teaching about Aging, 471
Teaching and Learning Communities (Ann Arbor, Michigan), 471
technology, 1–2, 87*b*, 90, 99, 244
　access and use, 3
　connectedness and, 252, 269–70, 299, 350–51
　digital, 4, 7–8, 11, 182, 183–84, 354, 358
　disparities, 240–42
　learning and, 285
　scaling impact and, 107
Temple University, 471
　Intergenerational Center, 349, 472
textual analysis, 314–17
Thang, Leng Leng, 337
Theory U learning model, 214
ThirdAct, 45
350.org, 45
TimeSlips, 89–90
Tippett, Krista, 3–4
Title 45-Public Welfare, 167
Together Old and Young (TOY), 280–85, 286–92
　Practitioners Learning and Upscaling Skills (TOY-PLUS), 281–85, 286–92, 356–58
Tokyo Metropolitan Institute for Geriatrics and Gerontology (TMIG), 329–30
　Social Participation and Health Promotion Team, 334
　See also Japan
toolkits, 26, 226, 275, 353, 457, 458
Torres-Gil, Fernando, 198
training. *See under* programs
transactional theory, 78
transdisciplinarity, 214–15
Triangle Community Center, 252

trust, 47, 76–77, 106, 112–13, 122, 205, 372, 373–74, 394, 397, 403, 461, 478–79
Turner, Shelbie G., 458–59
tutoring, 11–12, 39, 40–41, 63, 64, 132, 137–38, 139–42, 143, 145–60, 165, 166–67, 168, 170–71, 173

U

United Kingdom, 344–46, 356–58
　Age-Friendly Cities Network, 353
　Centre for Intergenerational Practice (CIP), 344–45, 473–74
　Equality and Human Rights Commission, 473–74
　Ministry of Education, 473–74
　National Health Action Zone Innovation Grants, 344
　See also Northern Ireland; Scotland; Wales
United Nations, 236
United States:
　Administration for Children, Youth and Families, 471–72
　Administration on Aging, 164–65, 471–72
　Bureau of Labor Statistics, 69
　Census Bureau, 236
　Current Population Survey, 54–55
　Department of Education, 170, 471–72
　Department of Health and Human Services, 168
　Department of Housing and Urban Development, 478–79
　Department of Juvenile Justice, 471–72
　Environmental Protection Agency, 478–79
　National Endowment for the Arts, 478–79
　National Endowment for the Humanities, 478–79
　National Science Foundation, 478–79
university-based retirement community (UBRCs), 85–86
University of Chicago, 480
　NORC, 10, 53–54, 64

University of Massachusetts Boston, Aging in Boston Report, 237–38
University of Michigan, Health and Retirement Study (HRS), 152
University of Notre Dame, 41
University of Oregon, 41
University of Pittsburgh, 471
    Intergenerational Specialist Award, 356
University of Strathclyde, 83
usefulness, 165–66, 169–70, 317, 318–19, 429–30

V

Vaillant, George, 120
values, 6, 7, 73–74, 78–79, 100–1, 134, 196–97, 199–200, 236, 272, 280, 283, 286, 287–88, 289, 291–92, 297, 298, 299–300, 304, 312, 313, 315, 319, 339–40, 364, 372, 429, 431, 433, 473, 474, 478
Vancity Credit Union (British Columbia), 372–73
veterans, 164
visibility, 287, 289
volunteering, 3–4, 6, 32–33, 38, 40–41, 46, 64, 120, 121, 122–23, 124, 146, 150, 158–59, 163–75, 213, 273–74, 276, 299, 302, 329, 333, 334–37, 344
    health and, 40, 41, 123–24, 150, 151, 152–54, 168–69, 172–73, 181, 213–14, 227, 330, 336–37
    recruitment, 156–57, 159, 171, 174, 185, 188
    retention, 150, 156
    virtual, 149, 150, 152, 165

W

Wagner, Lindsay Peoples, 100
Wales, 271–72, 363
    Bridging the Generations (Wales), 270–71
    National Intergenerational Strategy, 345
    National Strategy for Older People, 345
    See also United Kingdom
Washington University in St. Louis: Beyond Boundaries, 221–22
When I'm 64, 13, 221–24, 228–29
Weaver, Andrea, 6–7, 451
Whitehouse, Catherine and Peter, 179, 187, 205–6, 207, 212–15
White House Conference on Aging, 164–65
Williams, Gillian, 209, 214–15
Williams, Terry Tempest, 125
wisdom, 79, 214, 272, 287–88, 291, 397
WISE (Working Together: Intergenerational Student/senior Exchange), 249–58
Wood, Monica, 5–6
work, 3, 4, 43–45, 237–38, 244, 258, 363, 364–76, 435
    ageism in, 109, 235, 296, 364, 365, 369, 372, 375, 376, 382, 433
    changes to, 1–2, 69–70, 77–78, 378
    collaboration in, 110
    dialogue in, 209
    diversity, equity, and inclusion in, 8, 10, 98, 302, 344–45, 364, 366–67, 368, 372, 373, 374, 375, 378–86, 430, 431, 433–34, 482
    knowledge exchange in, 378–86
    multigenerational, 8–9, 52, 77, 78–80, 83, 99, 101, 113, 138, 271, 275, 299, 430
    women in, 312
World Health Organization (WHO), 27, 236, 254, 330, 351–53, 431
    Age-Friendly Cities and Communities, 7–8
World Population Aging Report, 236

Y

Yosso, Tara J., 74–75
Youth Coordinating Board (Minneapolis), 7
Yung, Jun, 100

Z

Zell, Ethan, 379–81
Zhan, Shaohua, 297